Memory Performance and Competencies

Issues in Growth and Development

Memory Performance and Competencies

Issues in Growth and Development

Edited by

Franz E. Weinert
Max Planck Institute for Psychological Research, Munich

Wolfgang Schneider
University of Würzburg

LEA LAWRENCE ERLBAUM ASSOCIATES, PUBLISHERS
1995 Mahwah, New Jersey   Hove, UK

Lawrence Erlbaum Associates, Inc., Publishers
10 Industrial Avenue
Mahwah, New Jersey 07430

Library of Congress Cataloging-in-Publication Data

Memory Performance and Competencies: Issues in Growth and
   Development / edited by Franz E. Weinert, Wolfgang Schneider.
         p.   cm.
   Papers originally presented at the International Conference on
Memory Development: State-of-the-Art and Future Directions, held at
Ringberg Castle, June 9–12, 1993.
   Includes bibliographical references and index.
   ISBN 0-8058-1645-3
   1. Memory—Congresses. I. Weinert, Franz E., 1930–
II. Schneider, Wolfgang, 1950–   . III. International Conference on
Memory Development: State-of-the-Art and Future Directions (1993 :
Ringberg Castle)
BF375.R47 1995
153.1′2—dc20   94-23761
                                                             CIP

Books published by Lawrence Erlbaum Associates are printed on acid-free paper,
and their bindings are chosen for strength and durability.

Printed in the United States of America
10 9 8 7 6 5 4 3 2 1

Contents

II MEMORY STRATEGIES AND METAMEMORY COMPETENCIES AS DETERMINANTS OF MEMORY DEVELOPMENT

III INTRA- AND INTERINDIVIDUAL DIFFERENCES IN MEMORY DEVELOPMENT

Preface

This book contains the contributions to the International Conference on Memory Development: State-of-the-Art and Future Directions, which took place June 9–12, 1993, at Ringberg Castle on the Tegernsee Lake in the Bavarian Alps.

We would like to thank all those who contributed their results to the conference and to this publication. First of all, we thank all the conference participants, who not only presented interesting papers but also ensured timely publication of this volume with their lively discussions held during the meeting, their reciprocal peer review of the papers, and their rapid preparation of the chapters in their final form. We are grateful to the English and U.S. participants who took on the difficult task of editing those chapters written by the German contributors.

We also wish to thank Mariele Kremling, Heidi Schulze, and Angelika Weber for their help in making all the arrangements before and during the conference.

Finally, we thank the Max Planck Society for the Advancement of Sciences for financial support, and the service personnel at the Ringberg Castle for the hospitable atmosphere in which the conference took place.

We hope that readers of this volume will gain a sense of the richness of the papers presented at the conference, the engaging scientific discussions, and the amicable cooperation.

—*Franz E. Weinert*
—*Wolfgang Schneider*

Introduction

Franz E. Weinert
Max Planck Institute for Psychological Research, Munich

Wolfgang Schneider
University of Würzburg

Historic analyses of the progress made in knowledge, the fate of research paradigms, and the temporary significance of certain issues in a scientific discipline frequently reveal a cyclic course. Expressed metaphorically, one could even speak of developmental regularities: from the blossoming childhood of a research program via its dynamic periods of youth and young adulthood to the increasing rigidity of old age. The past three decades of psychological research on the development of memory resemble this periodicity to some degree. Has this field of research reached the stage of old age by now or can one hope that it will not perish but awaken to a new cycle of life in the near future?

Looking back two decades, one can discern many studies concerning the development of memory in young children and a few studies about aging adults that were all theoretically very stimulating and exerted a large influence both on research on cognitive development and on the psychology of memory in general. Particularly striking in such a retrospective survey is the great variety of new and fresh approaches, hypotheses, models, and research instruments.

At a European conference in 1977 centered on a state-of-the-art review of the development of memory in childhood, no less than five competing explanatory hypotheses were reported, each of which possessed great power in directing research and stimulated many empirical studies (Weinert, 1979). These were:

1. *The intelligence hypothesis*, the theoretical assumption proposed by Piaget and Inhelder (1973) "that the development of memory with age is the history of gradual organizations closely dependent on the structuring activities of the

intelligence, though regulated by a special mechanism, namely, the structuring of the past or of past experiences" (p. 380).

2. *The capacity hypothesis*, the theoretical assumption that the age-correlated increase of memory performance in childhood is a function of maturational growth processes of the working memory capacity.

3. *The strategy hypothesis*, the theoretical assumption that the improvements of memory performance in childhood are strongly related to the acquisition and automatization of an increasing amount of appropriate learning and recall strategies.

4. *The metamemory hypothesis*, the theoretical assumption that not only the (individual) availability of memory strategies is decisive for the quantity and quality of memory performance. Instead, the crucial factor is the accessibility of knowledge about appropriate and effective strategies in a given situation. Thus, the development of metamemory seems to be the most important variable.

5. *The knowledge hypothesis*, the theoretical assumption that changes and differences in memory performance depend on the quantity and quality of domain-specific knowledge and—as a consequence—that memory development is determined by the increase of general world knowledge and the acquisition of content-specific knowledge in many domains.

Discussions held in the 1970s revolved around the question of whether these hypotheses represent alternative theoretical approaches to memory development, or whether the hypothesized constructs and/or variables can be used as components in more comprehensive models of memory development. It has been speculated that this second option might have played an important role in developmental memory research during the 1980s. And, indeed, these five hypotheses and some combinations of them did in fact dominate most research activities concerning memory development in the last 20 years or so.

When analyzing the contents of well-known textbooks (e.g., Kail, 1979, 1984, 1990; Schneider & Pressley, 1989), readers (e.g., Brainerd & Pressley, 1985; Kail & Hagen, 1977; Pressley & Brainerd, 1985), and published conference reports (Chi, 1983; Flavell, 1971; Ornstein, 1978; Schneider & Weinert, 1989, 1990; Weinert, 1979; Weinert & Kluwe, 1987; Weinert & Perlmutter, 1988), one gains the impression that a continuity of research regarding the influence of memory strategies, metacognitive competencies, and domain-specific as well as domain-general knowledge on the development of memory performance existed in the course of the last decades. Yet recently, it was not the investigation of these isolated developmental factors that occupied the center of attention but rather the reciprocal relations between the different components of declarative and procedural knowledge as determinants of age-related changes in the acquisition, storage, and recall of different classes of information. Continuity and progress could also be documented largely independently from this mainstream in research concerning the development of short-term memory (i.e., in the elaboration of working memory models) that was conceptualized as a decreasing limitation of memory performance over the course of child development.

The intelligence hypothesis of memory development that Piaget and Inhelder (1973) introduced into psychology has changed greatly over the course of time. The focus of theoretical thinking has increasingly shifted to the interplay between the development of cognitive resources in general and the functions of memory in particular. This statement should not, however, be given too much weight because Trabasso's (1983) prediction, made in his 10-year outlook on a conference in 1981 and which he considered unlikely but possible, has by no means occurred thus far: "Memory may . . . have lost its separate status as a psychological faculty and become a part of human cognition" (p. 122). Rather, his contrary expectation about the scientific fate of the question "How does memory develop?" has come to pass: "A safe prediction is that the main question and its component interpretation will continue to guide and dominate research on memory development" (p. 116)—and this during the years between 1981 and 1991!

And, indeed, after more than 20 years of research on memory development, we can recognize an astonishing continuity in themes, topics, and theories during the 1970s and 1980s. But what is the "real" scientific progress derived from all these activities and efforts substantiated in hundreds or maybe even thousands of relevant studies, papers, articles, and chapters in the field of memory development?

• There has been a huge number of small pieces of empirical evidence regarding developmental changes and individual differences in many memory phenomena.

• Many specific descriptive models about the interrelationships between the acquisition, the availability, and/or the accessibility of content-specific knowledge, general strategies, and metacognitive skills on the one hand, and changes or differences in memory performance on the other hand are now available.

• There have been some highly sophisticated theoretical discussions about the structural frames, the processes, and some hypothesized mechanisms of memory development.

But the assessment of significant progress in research on memory development is not the whole story. In the 1960s and 1970s, memory research was the forerunner in the scientific work on cognitive development. Many stimulating ideas, concepts, and models came from this domain and made a lasting impact on other fields of research on cognition and especially on cognitive development.

In contrast, it seems difficult to find new key concepts in research on memory development published within the last few years that are not derived from other fields of cognitive (developmental) research. This current lack of new and fresh ideas in the field has very often been compensated for by increasingly specialized investigations into existing concepts and hypotheses, and by the substitution for the classical laboratory tasks by everyday memory demands. Unsatisfactory results from many studies of cognitive determinants, processes, and mechanisms of memory functioning in childhood placed the hope of some researchers in the explanatory power of motivational and social context variables. Although there is no doubt that these are all very important questions, it is questionable whether such research activities can really contribute to a significant answer to John Flavell's (1971) old question: "What is memory development the development of?" (p. 272).

Nevertheless, critical symptoms in the research output on memory development in the last couple of years may provide a good opportunity to discuss anew the main approaches toward studying memory development, to evaluate the longlasting progress of theoretical thinking in the field, and to identify some fruitful new directions, concepts, and theories for future research.

And indeed, several indicators for the start of a new dynamic cycle in memory development research can presently be discerned. If the stimulating information-processing view on memory functioning was the generator of new ideas 30 years ago, then the current breakup of the encrusted developmental psychology of memory that can be identified in many places strikes a hopeful note. The main line of inquiry no longer concentrates on the empirical description (and speculative explanation) of universal changes in memory performance and memory processes, but rather on how the cognitive system does or does not change under certain situational conditions over the life-span and on what consequences this has for the different functions of memory. Several tendencies play a role at this point:

• The belief that one can interpret the average differences in performance between several age groups of children as a valid indicator of universal and individual developmental processes of cognitive competencies is gradually diminishing (Weinert & Schneider, 1993). This means that more individual variability in the performance, in the task-related cognitive processes, and in the determinants of these processes was found than had been expected. "The general lesson seems to be that explicitly recognizing the great variability of infants' and young children's thinking, and attempting to explain how it is generated and constrained will advance our understanding of the central mystery about cognitive development—how change occurs" (Siegler, 1994, p. 5).

• The fusion of studies on memory development with research on cognitive phenomena in general that Trabasso (1983) expected would occur does not ensue from giving up the memory concept but rather by changing the theoretical conception which holds that in dealing with memory one is dealing with a more or less separable human faculty. For the time being, the research interest is concentrated both on the interdependence of different cognitive processes in understanding learning or memory tasks and on the development of the relevant cognitive resources employed (Brainerd & Reyna, 1993; Howe, Rabinowitz, & Grant, 1993).

• Developmental psychology theorists are seeking out and finding increasingly closer associations to hypotheses and findings of neuropsychological research. This applies to studies concerning cognitive development in general (Fischer & Rose, 1994; Magnusson, in press) and to the genesis of memory competencies in particular (Meltzoff, 1990).

• Childhood is no longer the exclusively or dominantly preferred age period for studying the development of human memory. An increasing number of investigations use a life-span perspective or at least undertake systematic comparisons between the performance of young children and that of older adults. Many experiments harboring ambitious theoretical expectations about cognitive development over the life-span have clearly failed. Efforts to transfer the Ribotian law (first in–last out) to cognitive development (Bäckman, 1987) have not been successful. This is also true, for example, in the case of the development of action memory, a prominent candidate for a cognitive function assumed to remain unchanged from early childhood until advanced age (Knopf, in press).

Of greater importance in this research approach is the consideration of new possibilities for gathering knowledge, including not only the investigation of old and young adults, adolescents, and children, but also the memory performance of young infants (for infant memory research see, e.g., Rovee-Collier, 1990). In this way, the question of how different phenomena and functions of memory develop over the course of the life-span can be answered. For example, can differences in development be uncovered between recognition and recall (Perlmutter & Lange, 1978), between short-term and long-term memory (Howe & Brainerd, 1989), and between implicit and explicit memory (Graf, 1990)? Which developmental processes can be observed among such diverging memory functions, and how can the stability or variability of performance across the life-span be explained? The systematic investigation of memory development at an advanced age is of special importance at this juncture, not only because particular aging phenomena can be studied but because such study provides fundamental insights into the cognitive conditions and mechanisms of memory performance. Good examples are papers concerning working memory in childhood (de Ribaupierre & Hitch, 1994) and in advanced adulthood (Salthouse & Babcock, 1991).

• There has been a longstanding demand for complementing laboratory-based memory research with studies conducted under everyday conditions in different cultural and environmental contexts. This also involves, but not exclusively, the improved determination of social and motivational influences on memory performance and development. The question of how the results of laboratory research can be applied to the development of memory in schools, in professional training, or to the design of training programs does not lie at the heart of many studies; instead, the focus is directed toward the fundamental theoretical interest in the situative and contextual variability of memory processes and their development.

This list contains only a few current tendencies and trends of developmental research in memory. Many other facets of changes could be added. Many of these changes raise hope for future research. This was the main reason for conducting a conference at Schloß Ringberg at the Tegernsee Lake in the Bavarian Alps in June 1993. This meeting was the fifth in a series of conferences covering the years 1977 (Weinert, 1979), 1980 (Weinert & Kluwe, 1987), 1984 (Weinert & Perlmutter, 1988), 1989 (Schneider & Weinert, 1990), and 1993 (documented in this volume).

A main goal of the last conference was to discuss various recent trends in research on memory development in order to come up with fruitful suggestions for future directions of developmental research in memory. This book contains the results of this effort.

REFERENCES

Bäckman, L. (1987). Applications of Ribot's law to life-span cognitive development. In G. L. Maddox & E. W. Busse (Eds.), *Aging: The universal human experience* (pp. 403–410). New York: Springer-Verlag.

Brainerd, C. J., & Pressley, M. (1985). *Basic processes in memory development—Progress in cognitive development research*. New York: Springer-Verlag.

Brainerd, C. J., & Reyna, V. F. (1993). Memory independence and memory interference in cognitive development. *Psychological Review, 100*, 42–67.

Chi, M. T. H. (1983). *Trends in memory development research* (Vol. 9). Basel: Karger.

de Ribaupierre, A., & Hitch, G. J. (Eds.). (1994). The development of working memory. *International Journal of Behavioral Development, 17*, 1–200.

Fischer, K. W., & Rose, S. P. (1994). Dynamic development of coordination of components in brain and behavior. In G. Dawson & K. W. Fischer (Eds.), *Human behavior and the developing brain* (pp. 3–66). New York: Guilford.

Flavell, J. H. (1971). What is memory development the development of? *Human Development, 14*, 227–235.

Graf, P. (1990). Life-span changes in implicit and explicit memory. *Bulletin of the Psychonomic Society, 28*, 353–358.

Howe, M. L., & Brainerd, C. J. (1989). Development of children's long-term retention. *Developmental Review, 9*, 301–340.

Howe, M. L., Rabinowitz, F. M., & Grant, M. J. (1993). On measuring (in)dependence of cognitive processes. *Psychological Review, 100*, 737–747.

Kail, R. V. (1979). *The development of memory in children*. New York: Freeman.

Kail, R. V. (1984). *The development of memory in children* (2nd ed.). New York: Freeman.

Kail, R. V. (1990). *The development of memory in children* (3rd ed.). New York: Freeman.

Kail, R. V., & Hagen, J. W. (1977). *Perspectives on the development of memory and cognition*. Hillsdale, NJ: Lawrence Erlbaum Associates.

Knopf, M. (in press). *Gedächtnis für Handlungen* [Memory for action]. Göttingen: Hogrefe.

Magnusson, D. (Ed.). (in press). *Individual development over the lifespan: Biological and psychological perspectives*. New York: Cambridge University Press.

Meltzoff, A. N. (1990). Towards a developmental cognitive science: The implications of cross-modal matching and imitation for the development of representation and memory in infancy. In A. Diamond (Ed.), *The development and neural bases of higher cognitive functions. Annals of the New York Academy of Sciences*, 608, 517–542.

Ornstein, P. A. (1978). *Memory development in children*. Hillsdale, NJ: Lawrence Erlbaum Associates.

Perlmutter, M., & Lange, G. (1978). A developmental analysis of recall-recognition distinctions. In P. A. Ornstein (Ed.), *Memory development in children* (pp. 243–258). Hillsdale, NJ: Lawrence Erlbaum Associates.

Piaget, J., & Inhelder, B. (1973). *Memory and intelligence*. New York: Basic Books.

Pressley, M., & Brainerd, C. J. (1985). *Cognitive learning and memory in children—Progress in cognitive development research*. New York: Springer-Verlag.

Rovee-Collier, C. (1990). The "memory system" of prelinguistic infants. In A. Diamond (Ed.), *The development and neural bases of higher cognitive functions. Annals of the New York Academy of Sciences*, 608, 517–542.

Salthouse, T. A., & Babcock, R. L. (1991). Decomposing adult age differences in working memory. *Developmental Psychology*, 27, 763–776.

Schneider, W., & Pressley, M. (1989). *Memory development between 2 and 20*. New York: Springer-Verlag.

Schneider, W., & Weinert, F. E. (1989). Universal trends and individual differences in memory development. In A. de Ribaupierre (Ed.), *Transition mechanisms in child development: The longitudinal perspective*. Cambridge: Cambridge University Press.

Schneider, W., & Weinert, F. E. (Eds.). (1990). *Interactions among aptitudes, strategies, and knowledge in cognitive performance*. New York: Springer-Verlag.

Siegler, R. S. (1994). Cognitive variability: A key to understanding cognitive development. *Current Directions in Psychological Science*, 3, 1–5.

Trabasso, T. (1983). Discussion: What is memory development to be the development of? *Contributions to Human Development*, 9, 116–122.

Weinert, F. E. (1979). Entwicklungsabhängigkeit des Lernens und des Gedächtnisses [Development of learning and memory]. In L. Montada (Ed.), *Brennpunkte der Entwicklungspsychologie* (pp. 61–76). Stuttgart: Kohlhammer.

Weinert, F. E., & Kluwe, R. H. (1987). *Metacognition, motivation, and understanding*. Hillsdale, NJ: Lawrence Erlbaum Associates.

Weinert, F. E., & Perlmutter, M. (1988). *Memory development: Universal changes and individual differences*. Hillsdale, NJ: Lawrence Erlbaum Associates.

Weinert, F. E., & Schneider, W. (1993). Cognitive, social and emotional development. In D. Magnusson & P. Casaer (Eds.), *Longitudinal research on individual development: Present status and future perspectives* (pp. 75–94). Cambridge: Cambridge University Press.

Part I

WORKING MEMORY
AND PROCESSING CAPACITY
AS DETERMINANTS
OF MEMORY DEVELOPMENT

Chapter 1

Working Memory: What Develops?

Graham J. Hitch
University of Lancaster

John N. Towse
University of London

Working memory is the dynamic part of the memory system that is responsible for maintaining temporary information during mental operations. It has a limited capacity that constrains the performance of cognitive skills such as reading and arithmetic, reasoning and problem solving (Baddeley, 1986; Baddeley & Hitch, 1974). The development of working memory is therefore of interest not only from the point of view of how memory develops, but also in the wider context of the development of cognitive skills (see, e.g., Case, 1985). The present discussion focuses on the role of processing speed in the development of working memory, an issue that is currently attracting considerable theoretical interest. Kail's chapter (chap. 4) in the present volume shares the same theme, and it features also in the chapters by Case (chap. 2) and by Salthouse (chap. 6).

Two different types of task are used to study the development of working memory. One is the standard short-term memory task, which involves recalling a list of items either immediately after a single presentation or, at most, a few seconds' delay. *Memory span* is the most widely known measure of short-term memory performance and is the longest list that can be recalled correctly on 50% of trials on immediate test. Memory span is only a few items in young children, and is typically between five and nine items, even in adults (Dempster, 1981). However, memory span may fail to reflect the dynamic aspect of working memory, because it does not involve transforming temporary information. Daneman and Carpenter (1980) found that memory span was a much poorer predictor of reading ability in adult subjects than a more complex *reading span* task, which assesses how many words can be remembered at the same time as reading sentences. Subsequently, a number of complex span tasks that combine processing with temporary storage have been devised. For example, *operation span* assesses the capacity for storing previous calculation results while performing further mathematical operations (Turner & Engle, 1989; see also Salthouse, this volume). In a pioneering developmental study, Case, Kurland, and Goldberg (1982) required children to count the number of items in a visual array while keeping track of the totals of previously counted arrays. By varying the number of arrays presented, Case et al. were able to obtain a measure of *counting span*, the maximum number of totals that could be remembered at the same time as counting a further array. Counting span was small in young children and increased steadily during development.

Adult performance on complex tasks like reading span and operation span is widely interpreted as reflecting a trade-off between limited resources for mental operations and information storage in a central workspace (Engle, Cantor, & Carullo, 1992; Just & Carpenter, 1992; King & Just, 1991). For example, King and Just (1991) found that maintaining a memory load impaired subjects' reading comprehension, the degree of impairment being related to their reading span. Children's performance has also been interpreted in terms of resource trade-off, and Case et al. (1982) offered such an account for standard memory span, as well as their novel counting span. Whether or not it is appropriate to conceptualize children's performance in this way is the central concern of the present chapter.

THE DEVELOPMENT OF WORKING MEMORY

A prevalent theme coming out of research using standard short-term memory tasks is that there are important qualitative changes as children develop. For example, there is much evidence that the strategy of active rehearsal develops some time after age 7 or thereabouts (see Kail, 1990). In a particularly well-known study, Flavell, Beach, and Chinsky (1966) asked children between the ages of 5 and 11 to remember a set of pictures over a short retention interval. Older children showed signs of lip movements during the interval, suggesting that they were subvocally rehearsing, but such activity was rarely observed in the youngest children. Rehearsal is the most intensively studied aspect of the development of short-term memory, but other types of strategy and factors such as storage capacity, long-term memory, and metacognitive knowledge have also been discussed extensively (see Kail, 1990, for an overview).

Our knowledge of developmental changes in dynamic tasks is largely restricted to Case's work. In sharp contrast to the multiplicity of factors that were invoked to explain age differences in standard short-term memory tasks, Case et al. (1982) proposed that changes in information processing speed, or *operational efficiency* influence the growth of counting span via their influence on the trade-off between resources for processing and storage. Case et al. also extended this account to explain the growth of standard memory span.

SPEED OF PROCESSING AND TOTAL PROCESSING SPACE

Case et al. (1982) made the interesting discovery that developmental changes in short-term memory span and counting span were systematically related to changes in the speed of information processing. Thus, the increase in short-term memory span for auditorily presented words between ages 3 and 6 was closely paralleled by the increase in the rate at which the words could be processed, as measured by the time taken to identify them perceptually (Fig. 1.1). Similarly, counting span increased continuously from age 6 to 12, according to a linear relationship with the time taken to perform the counting operations (see Fig. 1.2).

According to Case et al. (1982), the relationship between span and processing speed reflects a trade-off between operations and storage within the limited resources of a central, *total processing space*. They argued that as development proceeds, operations become faster but the total processing space remains constant. As operations become faster, they become more efficient, and so take up less of the total processing space, leaving more available for information storage. Hence, span increases in proportion to the reduction in processing speed. As a test of such an interpretation, Case et al. measured adult subjects' speed of processing and memory span for unfamiliar items. With these items, their speed

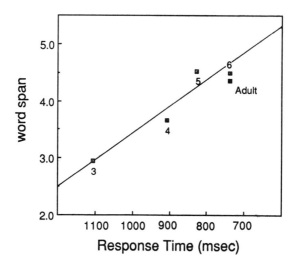

FIG. 1.1. Relationship between word span and speed of word identification at different ages (numbers by data points correspond to ages). Replotted from data in Case et al. (1982).

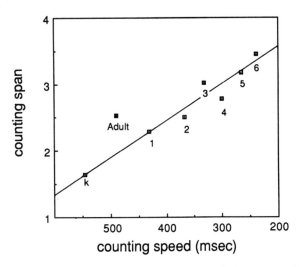

FIG. 1.2. Relationship between counting span and speed of counting at different ages (numbers by data points correspond to grade levels, k = kindergarten). Replotted from data in Case et al. (1982).

of processing was slowed to the level of 6-year-olds given familiar items. The interesting result was that adults' and 6-year-olds' short-term memory spans for these materials were also the same. Similarly, when adults were required to use an unfamiliar method of counting that made them slow and inefficient, their counting spans were reduced in proportion to the reduction in their speed of processing (see Figs. 1.1 and 1.2).

The notion of trade-off is central to Case's (1985) broader theory of general cognitive development in which he argued that, as operational efficiency increases, more temporary information can be stored in the workspace while carrying out mental operations, with the result that more complex cognitive tasks can be accomplished. The use of counting span as a valid measure of central resources is a key feature of this approach (see, e.g., Case, chap. 2, this volume).

The idea that there is a trade-off between resources for mental operations and information storage in working memory is a strong claim about the nature of working memory, one that we noted is not uncommon (see, e.g., Engle et al., 1992; Just & Carpenter, 1992). However, the idea of a limited pool of central resources was subjected to serious criticisms (Allport, 1980; Daneman & Tardiff, 1987; Halford, 1993). And although Baddeley and Hitch (1974; see also Hitch & Baddeley, 1976) assumed a simple trade-off between storage and processing in their original conceptualization of the central workspace, subsequent developments of their model adopted a more complex interpretation (Baddeley, 1986). Given such uncertainty about the central workspace, and the possibility that children may differ from adults in this respect, we critically re-examined the evidence that the development of working memory involves resource trade-off in a central workspace. We begin by examining a different account of the resources contributing to memory span.

SPEED OF ARTICULATION
AND THE ARTICULATORY LOOP

Case et al.'s model emphasized a unitary view of working memory resources that can be contrasted with multiple component models, such as that of Baddeley and Hitch (1974). According to Baddeley and Hitch (see also Baddeley, 1983), working memory contains a central executive workspace that is similar but not identical to Case's notion of total processing space. However, the central executive is backed up by two temporary, modality-specific stores: one for phonologically coded information known as the *articulatory loop*, and the other for visuo-spatial information, known as the *visuo-spatial scratchpad* (see Fig. 1.3). The executive controls the use of these peripheral subsystems. For example, in the case of verbal materials, the executive initiates subvocal rehearsal in the articulatory loop. Evidence that working memory can be decomposed into separate subsystems comes from a wide range of studies of normal adults and patients with specific neuropsychological impairments, and was summarized by Baddeley (1986). Although Case (1985) acknowledged that operations in different modalities have different properties, his theory remained focused on the dynamics of the central processor, and made no direct reference to specific subsystems.

A fundamental claim of the Baddeley and Hitch (1974) model was that short-term memory span for verbal information reflects a major contribution from the articulatory loop in addition to the central executive. Phonological memory traces stored in the articulatory loop are subject to a rapid decay process

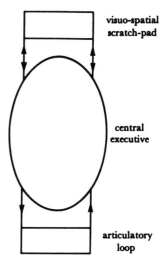

FIG. 1.3. Simplified representation of the working memory model (from Baddeley, 1983).

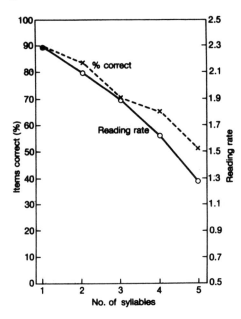

FIG. 1.4. Relationship between oral reading rate and recall for words of different lengths (Baddeley et al., 1975).

that can be offset by refreshing them using subvocal rehearsal. Because rehearsal is a serial process, slower rehearsal will mean that fewer traces can be kept refreshed within the time limit set by trace decay. In support of this account, Baddeley, Thomson, and Buchanan (1975) found that adult subjects could remember fewer long words than short words. There was a close relationship between how many words could be recalled and how fast they could be read aloud (see Fig. 1.4), such that when recall was plotted as a function of reading rate, the data fit a straight line. In addition, fast readers tended to remember more than slow readers, as one would expect if they rehearse more rapidly. Further support for the articulatory loop model comes from a mass of evidence on the effects on normal adult performance of suppressing articulation, making items phonemically similar and being exposed to irrelevant speech, as well as data on neuropsychological deficits of short-term memory (see Baddeley, 1986, for a summary). For example, articulatory suppression, a technique in which subjects are required to repeat a redundant word (e.g., the, the, the . . .), removes the influence of word length on short-term memory performance (Baddeley, Lewis, & Vallar, 1984; Baddeley et al., 1975). It seems reasonable to assume that articulatory suppression has this effect because it disrupts subvocal rehearsal.

Although the Baddeley and Hitch model was initially proposed as an account of working memory in adults, studies of children showed the same relationship between number of words recalled and the rate at which they can be articulated. In the first demonstration, Nicolson (1981) reported data on short-term memory for visually presented words of different lengths and the rate at which the words could be read aloud in children 8 years old and older. The results revealed that

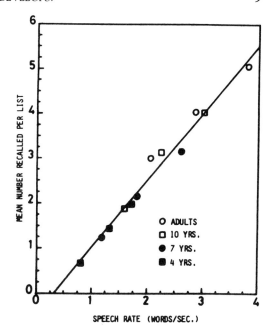

FIG. 1.5. Relationship between speech rate and recall at different ages (points within age groups correspond to words of different length). Data from Hulme et al. (1984).

age differences in recall were linearly related to developmental differences in speed of articulation. Similar results have been described by other investigators, despite minor variations in the methods used, indicating that this is a robust finding (Hitch & Halliday, 1983; Hulme, Thomson, Muir, & Lawrence, 1984). Figure 1.5 illustrates data from the Hulme et al. (1984) study. In terms of the articulatory loop, these data indicate that there is a constant rate of decay of phonological information across both materials and age groups. Hitch and Halliday suggested that the developmental improvement in short-term recall can be accounted for in terms of the speeding up of subvocal rehearsal. However, it is important to note that the data are correlational and so do not establish a causal link. Neither do they rule out the possibility that other factors contribute to developmental change.

RESOURCE TRADE-OFF VERSUS TRACE DECAY

The empirical relationship between short-term memory performance and rate of articulation during development is evidently similar to the relationship with speed of operations reported by Case et al. (1982). Indeed, such a convergence is only to be expected given that the speeds of a wide range of psychological processes undergo a similar pattern of developmental improvement (Kail, 1991). However, the theoretical interpretations offered by the total processing space and articulatory loop accounts differ markedly. One emphasizes a trade-off of resources within a central workspace, whereas the other is concerned with re-hearsal and trace decay within a phonological storage system. The key empirical issue, therefore, is whether or not there is a specific relationship between memory performance and articulation rate that is separate from the relationship between memory performance and measures of general operational efficiency. Dempster (1981) identified this issue in a major review of the development of short-term memory and challenged the need to invoke the articulatory loop to account for the word length effect. He suggested that word length might influence operational efficiency, as measured by the speed of perceptually identifying long and short words. If this were the case, the word length effect could be reinterpreted in terms of the more general mechanisms of resource trade-off using Case et al.'s (1982) model. On such an account, the processes of perceiving longer words take up more total processing capacity, leaving less available for storing them.

In the next section, we describe two experiments designed to compare the peripheral (articulatory loop) and central (total processing space) accounts of the word length effect and the development of verbal short-term memory. If the word length effect can be related to general operational efficiency rather than subvocal articulation *per se*, this would argue against the need for a separate articulatory loop account.

Short-Term Memory Span

In an experiment designed to investigate Dempster's suggestion directly, Hitch, Halliday, and Littler (1989) examined short-term memory span for visually presented words of different spoken durations (but matched for frequency of occurrence). The subjects were 8- and 11-year-old children. For words of each length, separate measures were made of the time taken to perceptually identify the items and to articulate them. Figure 1.6 shows the plots of mean span against articulation rate and perceptual identification time. It is clear that articulation rate is the better predictor of memory span, because a single linear relationship neatly accounts for changes with both age and word length. Perceptual identification time failed to provide an adequate account of differences in span associated with word length. In a further part of the experiment, memory span was assessed while children engaged in articulatory suppression. The effect of suppression was markedly to reduce the word length effect, consistent with the assumption that the word length effect is mediated by subvocal rehearsal in the articulatory loop (see Table 1.1a). However, suppression did not abolish age differences, indicating that developmental change in span is not entirely attributable to faster rehearsal in the articulatory loop.

Despite these clear results, it is appropriate to be cautious in generalizing from the Hitch et al. (1989) study, because Case et al.'s (1982) evidence implicating perceptual identification time was obtained using children between 3 and 6 years of age and auditory stimuli. Hitch et al.'s children were 8 years old or over and stimuli were presented visually. Age might be particularly important given evi-

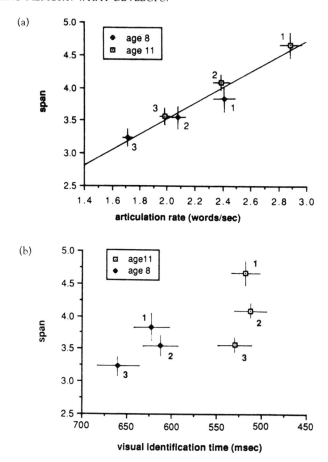

FIG. 1.6. Memory span for visually presented words as a function of (a) articulation rate and (b) identification time (numerals by data points denote word length in number of syllables). Data from Hitch et al. (1989).

dence that younger children use verbal rehearsal less than older children (Kail, 1990). Accordingly, Hitch, Halliday, and Littler (1993) carried out a further study in which auditory memory spans, articulation rates, and perceptual identification times were assessed at ages 5, 8, and 11 for words of different lengths. The results once again showed that a single straight line described the variation of span with articulation rate and there was no equivalent relationship between span and perceptual identification time (see Fig. 1.7). Furthermore, span was lower and the word length effect was markedly reduced when 8- and 11-year-olds were assessed under articulatory suppression. However, suppression did not abolish age differences in span (see Table 1.1b). Thus, results obtained with auditorily presented lists and younger children confirmed all the major features of the Hitch et al. (1989) investigation.

TABLE 1.1
Mean Memory Span Word Lists as a Function of
Age, Word Length, and Articulatory Suppression

| | Visual presentation | | | | | |
| | Control | | | Suppression | | |
Age group	1-syll	2-syll	3-syll	1-syll	2-syll	3-syll
8	3.83	3.55	3.24	2.45	2.25	2.12
11	4.67	4.09	3.57	2.78	3.00	2.70
	Auditory presentation					
5	3.94	3.48	3.26		not measured	
8	4.57	4.07	3.67	3.26	3.15	2.87
11	5.01	4.41	3.98	3.63	3.42	3.37

Note. Visual presentation data from Hitch et al. (1989); auditory presentation data from Hitch et al. (1993).

Taken together, these two studies make a strong case that the word length effect in children's short-term memory is unlikely to reflect a trade-off between storage and processing operations in a general-purpose workspace. To uphold such an explanation, one would have to find convincing arguments why articulatory suppression should selectively reduce the influence of word length on span, and why articulation rate should be a better measure of operational efficiency than perceptual identification time. The articulatory loop model readily explains both of these findings by assuming that span involves a speech-specific subsystem of working memory in which stored information is subject to decay. Notice, however, that it is not possible to construct an adequate account of the word length effect in children solely in terms of the rehearsal of decaying phonological traces. Instead, there are grounds for preferring a more complex explanation that stresses the importance of the rate of translating between phonological traces and articulatory output in addition to rehearsal (Gathercole & Hitch, 1993). This additional complication is needed to account for the presence of word length effects in recall of spoken word lists in children who are clearly too young to have acquired rehearsal strategies.

A further feature of the two studies described is that the suppression data isolate a second component of short-term memory span besides the articulatory loop. Given that age differences in span survive articulatory suppression, it is clear that there is developmental change in this second component. Kail's chapter (chap. 4, this volume; see also Kail, 1992) describes results that are consistent with a two component account. He reports a correlational study of individual differences in span in children of different ages. Path analysis revealed two independent links between age and memory span. One was a direct path between age and span. The other was an indirect path involving global information processing speed and

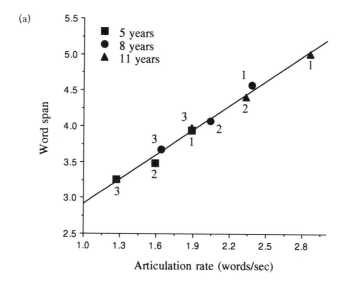

(a)

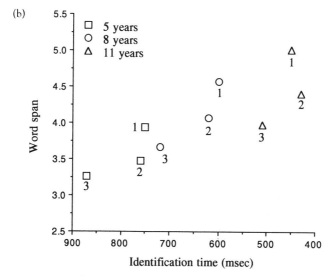

(b)

FIG. 1.7. Memory span for orally presented words as a function of (a) articulation rate and (b) identification time (numerals by data points denote word length in number of syllables). Data from Hitch et al. (1993).

13

articulation rate in which global speed accounted for little variance that was not already explained by articulation rate. Hitch et al. (1989, 1993) suggested that the second component of span might reflect a general workspace along the lines envisaged by Case et al. (1982). However, Kail's analysis did not encourage this type of interpretation, given that in his study, the second component was independent of processing speed. Another possibility is that performance on short-term memory tasks includes a contribution from long-term memory (Hebb, 1961). It may be the long-term memory component that undergoes developmental change (Chi, 1981). Hulme, Maugham, and Brown (1991) succeeded in neatly separating out the short- and long-term components of immediate recall by comparing memory for words with pronounceable nonwords of different spoken durations. Pronounceable nonwords differ from words in having no existing representation in long-term memory. Hulme et al. found a length effect for both types of material and an advantage of words relative to nonwords that was independent of length (see Fig. 1.8). This is clear evidence for a long-term memory component of span that is independent of the short-term phonological store.

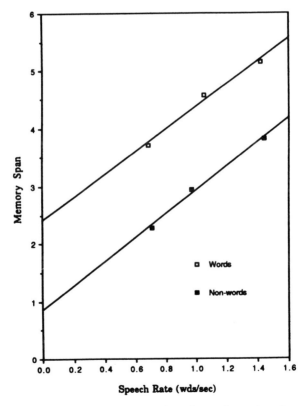

FIG. 1.8. Memory span as a function of speech rate for words and nonwords containing different numbers of syllables. Data from Hulme et al. (1991).

Thus, to sum up the argument so far, there is compelling evidence that the word length effect in memory span reflects decay in a speech-specific store rather than a limit on central workspace capacity. Developmental change in memory span involves changes associated with the articulatory loop, but there is also a second, independent factor. The nature of this second factor is unresolved. It may involve changes in general-purpose workspace capacity, or long-term memory, or both. In any event, it is evident that the role of general information processing speed and the central workspace in short-term memory span has less explanatory importance than was assumed in the account proposed by Case et al. (1982).

Counting Span

In line with the introductory discussion, a more promising source of evidence for central workspace capacity limitations in development may be in tasks like counting span that explicitly combine temporary information storage with concurrent information processing. However, little is known about children's performance on such tasks. In order to further explore resource trade-off in children, we carried out a critical examination of counting span (Towse & Hitch, 1995).

We began by noting that the evidence for a trade-off between processing and storage in Case et al.'s (1982) study of counting span could be given a different interpretation. Their two key findings were the correlation between counting span and counting speed across age, and the reduction in counting span when adults were required to use an unpracticed and, therefore, slow method of counting. Recall that Case et al. explained these results by assuming that when counting is slower it is more demanding, and so leaves less of the workspace available for storage. However, because the demands of counting are equated with how long it takes, the relationship between counting span and counting speed can be reinterpreted in terms of trace decay. Thus, the greater the time taken in counting each array, the longer the totals of previous arrays will have to be held in store and the greater the forgetting. Although Case et al. were careful not to reject decay, they were explicit that they did not favor such an interpretation. The possibility that decay may be important in counting span is indirectly supported by evidence for the involvement of the articulatory loop in counting tasks in children and adults (Hitch, Cundick, Haughey, Pugh, & Wright, 1987; Logie & Baddeley, 1987).

In order to distinguish between decay and resource-sharing accounts of counting span, it is necessary to manipulate the difficulty of counting operations independently of the time taken up in counting. To achieve this, we varied the type of visual array children were required to count. In one version, they were asked to count blue squares in an array containing blue squares and orange triangles (see Fig. 1.9a). Thus, targets could be easily differentiated from distractors by the visual feature of color. In another version, children counted blue

a)

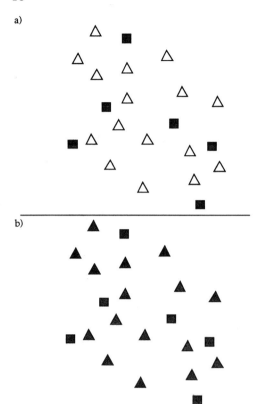

b)

FIG. 1.9. Types of visual array used by Towse and Hitch (in press). Shaded stimuli were colored blue, unshaded stimuli were colored orange.

squares among blue triangles (see Fig. 1.9b). Here, targets were differentiated from distractors by a conjunction of line orientation features. Research on visual attention has shown that searching for targets defined by individual features is much less effortful than searching for targets defined by conjunctions of features (Treisman & Gelade, 1980). According to Treisman's feature integration theory, targets defined by single features can be detected without fully identifying distractors, whereas the detection of targets defined by feature conjunctions involves the much slower process of serially scanning all the items in the array. An initial experiment established that the displays in Fig. 1.9 led to this dichotomy of detection performance. We refer to them here as *feature* (*fast*) and *conjunction* (*slow*) arrays to indicate both the type and duration of processing.

In the main experiment, we investigated counting span for feature (fast) and conjunction (slow) arrays in children of 6, 7, 8, and 11 years of age. Both trade-off and decay predict that counting span will be lower for conjunction (slow) than feature (fast) arrays. According to the trade-off hypothesis, this is because of the difference in processing load, whereas according to decay, it is due to the difference in processing time. However, we also included a third *feature* (*slow*) condition in which the average number of targets in feature arrays was increased so that they took as long to count as conjunction (slow) arrays. If decay is the limiting factor, counting spans for feature (slow) and conjunction (slow) arrays should be the same because of the temporal matching. However, if resource trade-off is critical, the lower processing demand of counting feature (slow) relative to conjunction (slow) arrays should result in a higher counting span.

The results of the study were clear. Analysis of counting errors confirmed that feature arrays were easier to count than conjunction arrays, even when they contained more targets. Figure 1.10a illustrates the data on counting speed. As expected, feature (fast) arrays took less time to count than conjunction (slow) arrays. Furthermore, the increased number of targets in feature (slow) arrays resulted in counting times that were fairly well-matched with those for conjunction (slow) arrays. These results held for all age groups, the main effect of age being a general decrease in the times taken to count.

Counting spans were determined using the procedure of Case et al. (1982) with some minor modifications. The results are illustrated in Fig. 1.10b. As expected, span increased with age. Differences among conditions followed a similar pattern in each age group. Counting spans were lower for conjunction (slow) than feature (fast) arrays, in accordance with both hypotheses. However, spans for feature (slow) arrays were the same as spans for conjunction (slow) arrays. Thus, the time taken to count the arrays was more important for counting span than the attentional demands of the counting operations. This result is consistent with the trace decay hypothesis and argues against the notion that counting span reflects a trade-off between resources for counting and storage. It suggests a simple alternative to Case's account of the developmental improvement in counting span, namely that older children's faster processing enables them to store more count totals in the articulatory loop within the time limit set by the rate of decay of stored information. However, the experiment was not designed to show whether or not children store count totals in the articulatory loop, and further studies are needed to establish whether or not this is the case. A detailed analysis of the data indicated that the rate of decay was somewhat slower than is normally found in simple memory span tasks (see Towse & Hitch, 1995).

The interpretation of our findings that we currently prefer is that children perform the counting span task by serially switching the resources of working memory between array counting and maintaining stored information, rather than simultaneously sharing such resources between these two competing demands. In this view, the record of previous totals is passively stored and is not actively maintained during the counting of each array. Children may be constrained to use this strategy because time-sharing would overload the resources of their working memories. Guttentag (1984; see also Guttentag, 1989) studied the development of time-sharing by having children between 7 and 11 years of age perform a secondary finger tapping task at the same time as a short-term memory task requiring overt cumulative rehearsal. The dual-task decrement was bigger for the younger children, consistent with higher resource demands of time-shar-

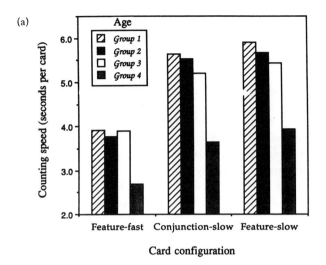

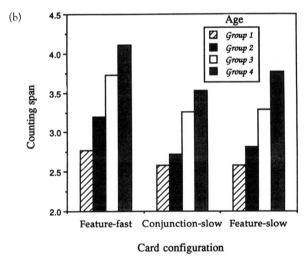

FIG. 1.10. (a) Counting speed and (b) counting span for different types of visual array. Data from Towse and Hitch (in press).

ing. More generally, it may be that for any task that involves working memory but does not by its nature enforce time-sharing, young children will opt instead for serial resource-allocation strategies.

To sum up, the Towse and Hitch (1995) results pose several problems for the claim that the allocation of working memory resources involves a simple trade-off between processing and storage that steadily shifts throughout development. At the most general level, they show that the time has come to tighten our understanding of the differences and similarities between different working memory tasks and to identify more precisely the conditions under which re-source-sharing does occur. More specifically, the Towse and Hitch results suggest that counting span does not involve the central executive in the same way in children as in adults. A more parsimonious interpretation is that children's performance in both counting span and short-term memory span is limited by the articulatory loop, such that their slower processing makes them more vul-nerable to the effects of trace decay in this peripheral store. The evidence that simple memory span and complex tasks like reading span tap different resources in adulthood (Daneman & Carpenter, 1980) suggests that as development pro-ceeds, complex verbal tasks become less dependent on the articulatory loop, and more dependent on the capacity for sharing workspace resources. This is plausible if one assumes a decline in the resource demands of time-sharing (see Guttentag, 1984). It is interesting to note that Salthouse (chap. 6, this vol-ume) attributes the eventual decline in memory performance in old age to the combined effects of slower processing and a constant rate of forgetting, on similar lines to the decay/rehearsal hypothesis advanced here to account for early developmental improvements. If true, this might indicate that decay be-comes a limiting factor in working memory tasks when processing speed is es-pecially slow.

WHAT DEVELOPS?

To return to the general question of how working memory develops in children, the evidence points to a number of conclusions. First, the speed at which infor-mation can be processed is clearly an important factor (Kail, 1991). Both short-term memory span and counting span show a remarkably similar pattern of continuous developmental growth that is evidently related to improvements in speed of processing (Case et al., 1982). The data showing that artificially slowing down speed of processing in adults reduces their spans is particularly striking. However, the interpretation of these speed relationships in terms of resource trade-off in a central workspace remains at issue. The effects of word length on short-term memory span, and the results of separating out processing time from processing difficulty in counting span, are consistent with the alternative hy-pothesis that processing speed is important because it allows less time for traces to decay in the phonological subsystem of working memory. However, because developmental differences in short-term memory span are not abolished by ar-ticulatory suppression, it is clear that changes in the phonological loop can explain only part of the developmental growth. Thus, the possibility of a further contribution from the central workspace remains. However, there are some prob-lems for this view. First, it is not clear that the nonphonological component of short-term memory span is related to processing speed (Kail, chap. 4, this vol-ume). Second, it is worth more systematically exploring the extent to which other factors, such as changes in long-term memory, contribute to developmental improvements in performing working memory tasks.

In summary, although the notion of resource trade-off in a central workspace offers an elegantly simple theoretical account of the development of working memory, some features of children's performance are more readily explained in terms of the consequences of processing speed for trace decay. A more adequate account will include the role of the phonological loop, and possibly the influence of long-term memory on working memory.

ACKNOWLEDGMENTS

We are grateful to the Medical Research Council and to the Economic and Social Research Council for supporting the research described here, some of which formed part of a doctoral thesis by the second author at the University of Manchester. We also wish to acknowledge, with many thanks, Robbie Case for his helpful and insightful comments on the original chapter.

REFERENCES

Allport, D. A. (1980). Attention and performance. In G. Claxton (Ed.), *Cognitive psychology: New directions* (pp. 154–196). London: Routledge & Kegan Paul.

Baddeley, A. D. (1983). Working memory. *Philosophical Transactions of the Royal Society, B302,* 311–324.

Baddeley, A. D. (1986). *Working memory.* Oxford: Clarendon.

Baddeley, A. D., & Hitch, G. J. (1974). Working memory. In G. Bower (Ed.), *The psychology of learning and motivation: Advances in research and theory* (Vol. 8, pp. 47–90). New York: Academic Press.

Baddeley, A. D., Lewis, V. J., & Vallar, G. (1984). Exploring the articulatory loop. *Quarterly Journal of Experimental Psychology, 36,* 233–252.

Baddeley, A. D., Thomson, N., & Buchanan, M. (1975). Word length and the structure of short-term memory. *Journal of Verbal Learning and Verbal Behavior, 14,* 575–589.

Case, R. (1985). *Intellectual development: Birth to adulthood.* New York: Academic Press.

Case, R., Kurland, D. M., & Goldberg, J. (1982). Operational efficiency and the growth of short term memory span. *Journal of Experimental Child Psychology, 33,* 386–404.

Chi, M. T. H. (1981). Knowledge development and memory performance. In M. P. Friedman, J. P. Das, & N. O'Connor (Eds.), *Intelligence and Learning.* New York: Plenum.

Daneman, M., & Carpenter, P. A. (1980). Individual differences in working memory and reading. *Journal of Verbal Learning and Verbal Behavior, 19,* 450–466.

Daneman, M., & Tardif, T. (1987). Working memory and reading skill reexamined. In M. Coltheart (Ed.), *Attention and performance: Vol. 12. The psychology of reading* (pp. 491–508). Hillsdale, NJ: Lawrence Erlbaum Associates.

Dempster, F. N. (1981). Memory span: Sources of individual and developmental differences. *Psychological Bulletin, 89,* 63–100.

Engle, R. W., Cantor, J., & Carullo, J. J. (1992). Individual differences in working memory and comprehension: A test of four hypotheses. *Journal of Experimental Psychology: Learning Memory and Cognition, 18,* 972–992.

Flavell, J. H., Beach, D. R., & Chinsky, J. M. (1966). Spontaneous verbal rehearsal in a memory task as a function of age. *Child Development, 37,* 283–299.

Gathercole, S. E., & Hitch, G. J. (1993). Developmental changes in short-term memory: A revised working memory perspective. In A. Collins, S. E. Gathercole, M. A. Conway, & P. E. Morris (Eds.), *Theories of memory* (pp. 189–209). Hillsdale, NJ: Lawrence Erlbaum Associates.

Guttentag, R. E. (1984). The mental effort requirement of cumulative rehearsal: A developmental study. *Journal of Experimental Child Psychology, 37,* 92–106.

Guttentag, R. E. (1989). Age differences in dual task performance: Procedures, assumptions, and results. *Developmental Review, 9,* 146–170.

Halford, G. S. (1993). *Children's understanding: The development of mental models.* Hillsdale, NJ: Lawrence Erlbaum Associates.

Hebb, D. O. (1961). Distinctive features of learning in the higher animal. In J. F. Delafresnaye (Ed.), *Brain mechanisms and learning.* London: Blackwell.

Hitch, G. J., & Baddeley, A. D. (1976). Verbal reasoning and working memory. *Quarterly Journal of Experimental Psychology, 28,* 603–621.

Hitch, G. J., Cundick, J., Haughey, M., Pugh, R., & Wright, H. (1987). Aspects of counting in children's arithmetic. In J. A. Sloboda & D. Rogers (Eds.), *Cognitive processes in mathematics* (pp. 26–41). Oxford: Clarendon Press.

Hitch, G. J., & Halliday, M. S. (1983). Working memory in children. *Philosophical Transactions of the Royal Society, B302,* 324–340.

Hitch, G. J., Halliday, M. S., & Littler, J. E. (1989). Item identification time and rehearsal rate as predictors of memory span in children. *Quarterly Journal of Experimental Psychology, 41A,* 321–337.

Hitch, G. J., Halliday, M. S., & Littler, J. E. (1993). Development of memory span for spoken words: The role of rehearsal and item identification processes. *British Journal of Developmental Psychology, 11,* 159–169.

Hulme, C., Thompson, N., Muir, C., & Lawrence, A. (1984). Speech rate and the development of short-term memory span. *Journal of Experimental Child Psychology, 38,* 241–253.

Hulme, C., Maugham, S., & Brown, G. D. A. (1991). Memory for familiar and unfamiliar words: Evidence for a long-term memory contribution to short-term memory span. *Journal of Memory and Language, 30,* 685–701.

Just, M. A., & Carpenter, P. A. (1992). A capacity theory of comprehension: Individual differences in working memory. *Psychological Review, 99,* 122–149.

Kail, R. (1990). *The development of memory in children* (3rd ed.). New York: Freeman.

Kail, R. (1991). Developmental change in speed of processing during childhood and adolescence. *Psychological Bulletin, 109,* 490–501.

Kail, R. (1992). Processing speed, speech rate and memory. *Developmental Psychology, 28,* 899–904.

King, J., & Just, M. A. (1991). Individual differences in syntactic processing: The role of working memory. *Journal of Memory and Language, 30,* 580–602.

Logie, R. H., & Baddeley, A. D. (1987). Cognitive processes in counting. *Journal of Experimental Psychology: Learning, Memory & Cognition, 13,* 310–326.

Nicolson, R. (1981). The relationship between memory span and processing speed. In M. P. Friedman, J. P. Das, & N. O'Connor (Eds.), *Intelligence and learning* (pp. 179–183). New York: Plenum.

Towse, J. N., & Hitch, G. J. (1995). The relationship between task demand and storage space in working memory. *Quarterly Journal of Experimental Psychology, 48A,* 108–124.

Treisman, A., & Gelade, G. (1980). A feature integration theory of attention. *Cognitive Psychology, 12,* 97–136.

Turner, M. L., & Engle, R. W. (1989). Is working memory capacity task dependent? *Journal of Memory and Language, 28,* 127–154.

Chapter 2

Capacity-Based Explanations of Working Memory Growth: A Brief History and Reevaluation

Robbie Case
University of Toronto

EARLY STUDIES OF WORKING MEMORY GROWTH IN THE NEO-PIAGETIAN TRADITION

In 1970, Pascual-Leone published a seminal paper in which he made a number of important suggestions. One was that progress through Piaget's stages of cognitive development could be explained by the growth of a quantitative parameter, which he labeled *Mental (M)-power*, or central computing space—what today would be referred to as *working memory*. Another was that M-Power grew from $a + 1$ to $a + 7$ units between the ages of 4 and 16, under the control of epigenetic (as opposed to specific experiential) factors.[1]

Early studies designed to test Pascual-Leone's model used a number of newly constructed tasks. These were much like tests of short-term memory, except that some cognitive work was required, that is, some transformation rather than simple recognition and reproduction of input. One of the best known of these tasks was the Compound Stimulus Visual Information Test (CSVI). Before the test was administered, children were taught a number of hand gestures to make in response to a number of discrete visual cues. Several of these cues were then embedded in a single compound stimulus, which was presented for 5 seconds. The children's task was to pretend they were spies, to scan the compound stimulus carefully, and to signal the secret message that each stimulus contained, using the gestural code they had just mastered.

---

[1] In Pascual-Leone's original notation, the symbol a stood for schemes representing the instructions and general task situation. In later work he changed a to e, with the new symbol e representing the space required for the task "executive."

Because the children never knew how many cues would be present in the compound stimulus from one trial to the next, their ability to attend to and signal the full set of stimuli was limited by the size of their working memory. Pascual-Leone developed a detailed model for predicting the distribution of children's responses to the compound stimulus, on the assumption that the values of working memory for different age groups were those specified by his theory. As shown in Fig. 2.1, the data fit the predictions well. Later work showed that the predictions still held under different simplifying assumptions (Case & Serlin, 1979).

The CSVI was just one of a family of measures designed to test Pascual-Leone's model. Another such measure was the Digit Placement Test (Case, 1972). On this test the stimuli were numbers rather than shapes, and the required transformation was numerical ordering. Children were seated in front of an apparatus on which a row of small doors was mounted. On each trial, the doors were opened from left to right for 2 seconds each, thus revealing a series of numerals in ascending order of magnitude (e.g., 2, 6, 11). As each number was presented, subjects had to label it. After the last numeral in the initial series had disappeared, a final numeral appeared for 2 seconds at the extreme right of the display panel

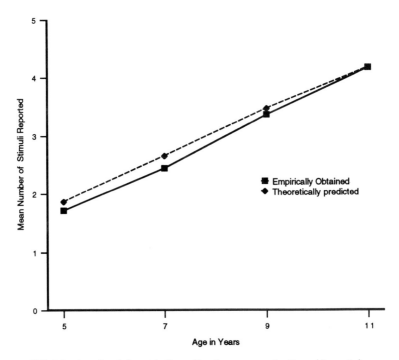

FIG. 2.1. Actual and theoretically predicted mean scores for Pascual-Leone's first test of M-power: the Compound Stimulus Visual Information test or CSVI (Pascual-Leone, 1970).

(e.g., 8). As soon as this number disappeared, the subjects' task was to indicate, by placement of a token, where this final number belonged with regard to the initial series (in this example, between 6 and 11).

The Digit Placement Task (DPT) was presented to children who were 6.5, 8.5, and 10.5 years of age, respectively. As was expected, children in all three groups found the task easy, as long as the original series was short. However, as the series length increased, their performance declined quite sharply. The working memory span of an age group was defined as the largest set of numbers (including the final number) for which the group could consistently succeed on the DPT across a block of five trials. The question of interest was whether or not there would be any relationship between the working memory span of an age group as defined in this fashion, and their working memory span as indexed by the CSVI. As is indicated in Fig. 2.2, the two sets of values agreed quite closely. Indeed, once adjustments were made for guessing, mean scores on the two tasks were virtually identical (Case, 1972). On the basis of these data, and others like them (e.g., Parkinson, 1976), it was concluded that Pascual-Leone's model held great promise.

WORKING MEMORY GROWTH AND THE DEVELOPMENT OF EXECUTIVE STRATEGIES

While Pascual-Leone and his colleagues were exploring the change in children's working memory during this age range, other investigators were studying a change that takes place in their repertoire of *executive strategies*. The theoretical inspiration for this work came from the emerging discipline of cognitive science, which highlighted the importance of executive processes in tasks involving problem solving and/or controlled attention (Atkinson & Shiffrin, 1968; Miller, Gallanter, & Pribram, 1960; Newell, Shaw, & Simon, 1958). Just prior to the stage of concrete operations, strategies such as systematic search and subvocal rehearsal emerge for the first time. They then show a systematic development throughout this period (Bruner, Olver, & Greenfield, 1967; Flavell, Beach, & Chinsky, 1966; Olson, 1967). One question these data raised was whether the change in children's executive strategies might explain the changes that are observed in their logical reasoning during the same time period (Olson, 1967). Another question was whether these changes might also explain the increase in children's working memory (Belmont & Butterfield, 1971; Case, 1970, 1974a).

In an early attempt to answer this latter question, I conducted a study in which children were presented with the DPT under three conditions (Case, 1970, 1974a). In the first condition, a memory-saving strategy for opening the doors was modeled and children were invited to use it. The strategy was to open the door concealing the final number first, and then open the other doors in the standard order. This strategy reduces the load on working memory. Subjects who use it know the number to be placed before they see the series; thus, they can simply work their

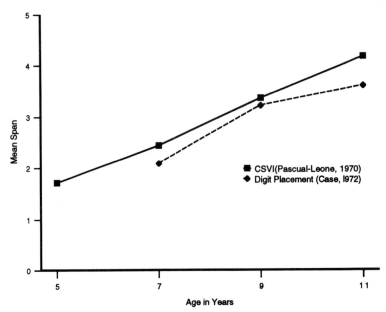

FIG. 2.2. Mean scores from the Digit Placement Task (Case, 1972) compared to mean score data from CSVI (Pascual-Leone, 1970).

way up the series to the point where the number to be placed is bigger than the number in the series they have just viewed, but smaller than the number that they are currently viewing. This means they need never pay attention to more than three numbers at once, no matter how long the series becomes.

In the strategy-modeling condition, the advantages of this viewing method were explained to children, and they were asked to try it out for themselves to see how well it worked. In a second condition, children were given the opportunity to discover the strategy, but were not taught it. They were simply told that they could open the doors in any order they wished, and that certain orders were easier than others. Before the testing began, they were given a number of practice trials to select an order they favored. Finally, in a third condition, the doors were opened by the experimenter in the standard (left to right) order.

As was expected, most of the children who used the last-number-first strategy were able to succeed on series of any length, whereas those who used other strategies showed a sharp drop in performance as the series length increased. Further, the proportion of children using the last-first strategy was high in the modeling condition, moderate in the neutral condition, and zero in the experimenter controlled condition. Figure 2.3 shows the number of children in each condition whose mean scores exceeded the M values specified by Pascual-Leone's model.

Several conclusions were drawn from these data. One was that children's ability to use efficient executive strategies increases sharply between 6 and 10 years of age. A second was that children's performance can dramatically improve

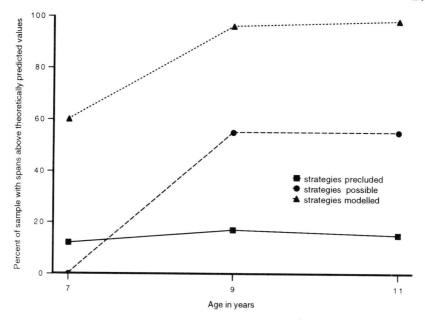

FIG. 2.3. Percentage of subjects receiving working memory scores higher than Pascual-Leone's M-estimates on the DPT, under three conditions: strategy modeled (Case, 1976); strategy not modeled but possible (Case, 1974a), and strategy actively precluded (Case, 1972).

once such strategies are mastered. A third was that Pascual-Leone's model can only be used to make quantitative predictions for any task once the strategy that children are using has been specified (Case, 1974a). With these conclusions in mind, three lines of further work were initiated. One was devoted to specifying the strategies children in this age characteristically deploy, across a range of problem-solving and/or school learning situations (Case, 1974b, 1975, 1979). A second was devoted to teaching children strategies that are more efficient than their natural ones, and evaluating the extent to which this improves their performance (Case, 1975, 1978a). A third was devoted to devising new measures of working memory, ones in which the strategies that children employ can be more carefully evaluated and controlled (Case, Kurland, & Daneman, 1979).

COVERT VERBAL REHEARSAL AND THE GROWTH OF WORKING MEMORY

It is the third line of work that is most relevant to the topic of the present chapter. This work was strongly influenced by the writings of Chi (1975, 1976) and Dempster (1977), as well as by the experiment on strategy use just described. Chi and Dempster argued that existing controls for chunking and covert rehearsal on tests of working memory were inadequate, and that the apparent growth in span that these measures reveal might actually be due to subtle strategic and/or organizational factors. In order to address their concern, we designed a number of "second generation" working memory measures in which greater control could be exercised over these factors (Case, Kurland, & Daneman, 1979).

The Counting Span (CS) task was the most widely used of these new measures. In this test children were required to count a series of dots, each of which was arrayed on its own separate card. Working memory was measured by recording the maximum number of dot totals recalled in the correct order. To rule out the possibility of chunking, number sequences in which some higher order pattern appeared to be present were eliminated (e.g., 2, 4, 6). To prevent covert rehearsal, further controls were introduced. (a) Children were asked to count each array of dots out loud. This introduced interpolated verbal activity between presentation of each successive item—a manipulation long known to suppress covert rehearsal (see Hitch & Towse, this volume). (b) All trials where subjects pause after an array was presented were eliminated, because covert rehearsal might be possible during the pause. (c) Subjects were asked not to rehearse before the test was presented, and were reinterviewed afterwards to see if they had complied; the protocols of any subject who reported rehearsing were eliminated before the mean spans for any age group were computed.

In spite of these elaborate precautions, the norms on these working memory tests were the same as those on the first generation measures, such as the CSVI and the DPT. The data are illustrated in Fig. 2.4. Note that these data are

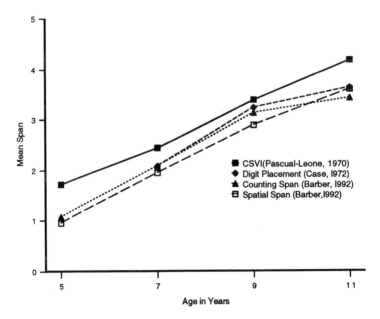

FIG. 2.4. Comparison of data from first generation measures of working memory (CSVI, DPT), and second generation measures (Counting Span, Spatial Span).

different from those for short-term memory measures during the same age range. When similar controls are introduced in these other measures, the growth of span is sharply attenuated (Dempster, 1977, 1978). Note further that children's working memory for numbers and shapes are close in magnitude. The data for tests of short-term memory show a different pattern in this regard also. Short-term memory tests using verbal items yield higher means than those using nonverbal items, presumably due to the fact that covert rehearsal is easier for verbal than for nonverbal material (Case, 1978b).

These two sets of data suggest that the controls we introduced in our second generation measures were successful, and that the measures tap the true structural limits of children's working memory system, not just the apparent limits that can be achieved with the aid of chunking or verbal rehearsal. Using the terms employed by Baddeley and Hitch (1974), we may say that our measures tap the *core capacity* of children's working memory, not just the size of the *verbal rehearsal loop*.

SPEED OF PROCESSING AND THE GROWTH OF WORKING MEMORY

As our work on the growth of this core capacity proceeded, we became interested in a factor that had not yet received much attention in the working memory literature: the efficiency with which basic mental operations can be executed. As mentioned in the Introduction, all tests of working memory are designed so that some sort of stimulus transformation is necessary. Although children are given the opportunity to practice these operations extensively prior to testing, the components of these operations (e.g., recognizing a familiar shape, deciding which of two numbers is larger, finding the next object to be touched in a visual array) are ones with which children of different ages are differentially familiar. It therefore follows that this differential familiarity—and the differential cognitive efficiency to which it leads—might be the source of some (or all) of the advantage older children enjoy on such tasks.

The CS test provided a convenient context in which to evaluate this possibility. To measure the efficiency of children's counting independently of their counting span, we asked them to count several arrays of dots as fast as they could, in a context where they did not have to remember any of the array totals. We then recorded their average speed of counting per dot, and treated this as an index of counting efficiency. Performance on this new test showed a strong linear correlation with performance on the Counting Span test (Case, Kurland, & Daneman, 1979; Case, Kurland, & Goldberg, 1982). Moreover, when adults' counting speed was equated with that of young children (by requiring the adults to count in a newly learned language), there was no significant difference between the two groups in their measured counting span. These data are illustrated in Fig. 2.5.

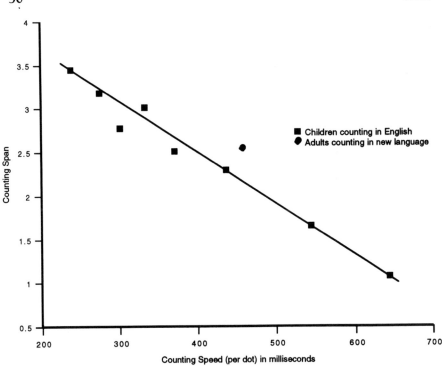

FIG. 2.5. Results from the studies on counting speed and counting span (data from Case, Kurland, & Daneman, 1979; Crammond, 1992).

The data in Fig. 2.5 indicate a clear developmental trade-off between the time it takes to execute an operation and the number of operational products that can be stored. However, they do not indicate why the speed of children's processing increases in the first place. One possible explanation is the one just mentioned: that older children have more highly practiced basic operations. A second possibility is that older children have more efficient neurological systems.

In an attempt to decide between these two explanations, Kurland (1978) conducted an extensive training study. Children were given 20 minutes of counting practice, morning and afternoon, for a 3-month period, and their counting speed and span was examined. Although the trained children did appear to show a modest initial gain in speed and span over the controls, their performance soon asymptoted. Moreover, the level at which this asymptoting took place was predicted by Pascual-Leone's model. The conclusion that Kurland drew, then, was that not that the normal increase in working memory span takes place by practice and automatization. Rather, it was that practice and automatization constitute necessary but insufficient conditions for working memory growth to take place. In addition, some sort of maturational change must take place (Kurland, 1978; reported in Case, 1985).

MATURATIONAL CONSTRAINTS ON THE GROWTH OF PROCESSING SPEED

Unfortunately, the maturational explanation is difficult to test directly. If no experiential factor can be documented to be at work, one can always suggest that maturation or capacity growth must be the cause of whatever developmental increase one has observed. However, one can never be certain that one has looked at the right set of experiential factors. This being the case, it is worth asking what maturational variable might be involved, so that one can examine its effect directly.

One possible maturational variable might be *mylenization*. As children grow older, there is a gradual change in the size of the myelin sheaths that surround the long distance axons connecting different neural groups in the cortex. Mylenization is known to have two effects: First, it increases the speed of linear transmission from one cell to the next. Second, it acts as an electric insulator, thus decreasing lateral transmission and interference (Taskaki, 1953). Here, then, is a variable that could explain the maturational growth in speed and in span. It might even explain the age at which new operations first emerge in development. Myelin build up is known to take place in waves that start and terminate at different ages in different cortical systems (Yakovlev & Lecours, 1969). The initial mylenization of a cortical system might influence the youngest age at which a new operation could be assembled, in response to instruction. Continued mylenization of the same system might then affect the asymptotal rate of operating in response to massive practice, and the number of operational products that can be stored without being overcome by interference (Case, 1985). Unfortunately, the width of myelin sheaths is not easy to measure in a nonintrusive fashion.

MODELING THE DEVELOPMENTAL RELATIONSHIP BETWEEN SPAN AND PROCESSING SPEED

The maturational question was not the only one raised by the data in Fig. 2.5. Another question was how to explain the observed speed–span relationship. Two possibilities suggested themselves. The first drew on Hebb's (1949) notion of a *reverbatory loop*. According to this explanation, children with faster operating times can "get back" to an original trace more rapidly to "refresh" it before it decays (Baddeley & Hitch, 1974). A second explanation drew on the notion that *spreading activation* can produce interference, especially when the items to be remembered are similar. According to this latter explanation, children with faster operating times have cognitive and/or neurological operations that are more "dedicated": that is, that can be activated with less search and/or spread of lateral activation. These operations interfere less with storage; thus, more items can be remembered (Case, Kurland, & Goldberg, 1982).

In an early consideration of those two possibilities (Case, 1970), the explanation I favored was the first one. At the time we first published the data, however, I expressed a preference for the latter explanation, on the basis of some preliminary data we had gathered in the meantime. In a recent series of studies, Hitch and Towse (chapter 1, this volume) present new data that they believe bear on this question. Most of the data are from tests of short-term memory rather than working memory. Thus, it is difficult to generalize their findings to measures such as those we have used. Still, their suggestion is that decay time may be playing a vital role as well. If they are right, both factors—decreased reactivation time and decreased interference—may be of developmental significance.[2]

Whichever factor turns out to be more important, we must still find a way to understand how maturation might exert an impact on it. In this regard, the myelinzation plus practice model offers an advantage, because it suggests a way in which *both* the factors could be impacted. As a function of changes in the speed of long distance transmission, children might be able to return to any given trace more rapidly. In addition, as a function of decreases in lateral activation, children might be able to activate any single trace more easily, that is, with less interference. The net result would be that rehearsal time and interference would both be impacted by the same underlying maturational change.

A COUNTER INTERPRETATION INVOLVING GENERAL CONCEPTUAL STRUCTURES

As Chi (1976, 1981) has pointed out, the mylenization plus practice model is not the only one that can account for the speed–span relationship. Children's improved counting speed could be the result, not of maturation or practice, but of acquiring a richer conceptual structure for representing numbers. In turn, a richer conceptual structure for numbers could result from experience in thinking about and using numbers, both inside school and out. As a result of this experience, children's networks for representing numbers might become more differentiated and integrated. Because of the richer network of connections that such networks now entail, children might be able to access any individual item in a given network more rapidly. They might also be able to store items with less interference. By the same general mechanisms as mentioned previously, then, their working memory span might increase with development. Their strategies for using numbers might also change, because they would understand the underlying nature of numbers more deeply.

---

[2]One might conceivably go further, and interpret the Hitch and Towse data as ruling out the interference explanation completely. It seems to me, however, that this conclusion would be premature. For one thing, their data are from short-term memory measures rather than working memory measures, and the significance of interference relative to time is naturally decreased under such conditions. For another thing, the manipulation that Hitch and Towse use to disentangle time from interference may still leave the two variables confounded.

Chi's counterinterpretation seemed interesting to us for several reasons: First, it seemed theoretically plausible. Second, it seemed more parsimonious than our explanation because it suggested that changes in speed, changes in span, and changes in children's cognitive strategies might all result from changes in a single underlying variable, namely, the complexity of children's conceptual structures. Finally, it reversed the direction of causality we had suggested. Rather than changes in speed potentiating a change in children's span, and this change potentiating a further change in the sophistication of children's conceptual understanding, Chi's proposal was that children's conceptual structures change first, and this change potentiates a change in their strategies, span, and speed of processing.

MAPPING THE CHANGE IN CHILDREN'S CENTRAL CONCEPTUAL STRUCTURES DURING MIDDLE CHILDHOOD

Although plausible, parsimonious, and important, Chi's hypothesis was difficult to test experimentally. One reason was that it was difficult to specify the contents of children's conceptual networks in detail. Another reason was that, even if one could have specified these structures, there was no known means of accelerating the acquisition of such networks in order to see if growth of counting speed and span would be impacted. The net result was that no direct test of Chi's hypothesis was conducted for about a decade.

During the early 1980s, like many other investigators, we turned our attention from the study of working memory capacity and executive strategies to the study of conceptual structures. The tasks we studied included the Balance Beam (Siegler, 1986), Money Knowledge and Time Telling (Griffin, Case, & Sandieson, 1992), The Birthday Party Task (Marini, 1992), Piaget's Shadows Task (Marini, 1992), Musical Sight Reading (Capodilupo, 1992) and Distributive Justice (Marini, 1992). Remarkably, the same pattern of conceptual change was evident on all of these measures. On each task, the question that children were asked was simple (e.g., "Which side of the balance will go down?" "Which of these two piles of money is worth more?" "Which of these two clocks shows an earlier time?" "Which of these two shadows is the tallest?"). Four-year-olds could only answer the question, however, when the perceptual array provided a clear visual cue to quantity. When there was no clear visual cue to quantity, and two or more arrays had to be quantified to arrive at the solution, none of the tasks were passed until the age of 6.

Over the past several years, we have developed a model that we believe accounts for this general pattern of change (Case, 1992a; Case & Griffin, 1990; Case & Sandieson, 1987). Our hypothesis is that children's central conceptual structures for number are different at different ages and change in much the same fashion as Chi (1983) suggested. Four-year-olds have enumeration and

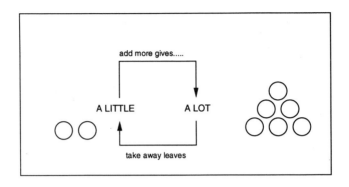

A: Add/ Take Away Schema   (Starkey, 1992)

add more gives.....

A LITTLE   A LOT

take away leaves

B: Count Schema   (Gelman, 1988)

Say "one" next "two" next "three" next "four"

Begin as you   End

Touch next   next   next

last word = answer to question, "How many things are in this group?"

FIG. 2.6. Hypothesized cognitive structures underlying 4-year-olds' numerical understanding (from Case, 1992a).

quantification schemata that are relatively primitive and separate from each other. It is as though they were in separate files in a database (see Fig. 2.6). Six-year-olds have more elaborate and differentiated schemata to represent enumeration and quantification. Of even greater importance, they have integrated these two schemata into a superordinate schema (see Fig. 2.7). It is the presence of this superordinate schema that makes them realize that counting is relevant to all the tasks mentioned previously, and that guides their efforts to use it.

We have now completed a variety of tests of the conceptual model implied by Fig. 2.7. The tests used a variety of techniques, including creation of new tasks and prediction of new developmental norms, factor analysis of new tests batteries (Case, Okamoto, Henderson, & McKeough, 1993), computer simula-

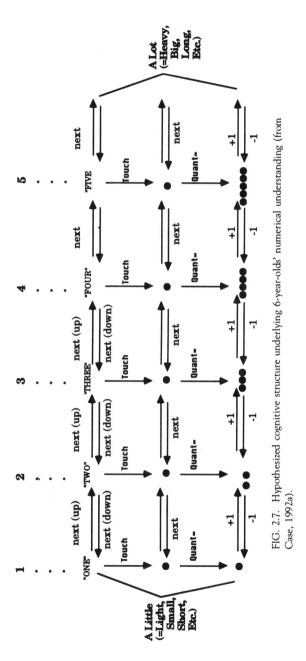

FIG. 2.7. Hypothesized cognitive structure underlying 6-year-olds' numerical understanding (from Case, 1992a).

tion of the hypothesized structure and extension to new problems (Okamoto, 1992), and training studies that focus on a teaching a subset of the total conceptual network (Griffin, Case, & Capodilupo, in press). For the purpose of the present discussion, it is the training studies that are most important.

TRAINING THE CENTRAL CONCEPTUAL STRUCTURE FOR NUMBER

Let us suppose for a moment that the model in Fig. 2.7 is correct, and that the structure is taught to children who are 5 or 6 years old, but who have not yet spontaneously acquired the structure. What should be the result? If our hypothesis is correct, the subjects should stop using 4-year-old strategies and start using 6-year-old strategies on all of the tasks mentioned.

In order to test this hypothesis, Griffin and I developed a kindergarten curriculum to teach the specific set of nodes and relations depicted. The curriculum used a series of 30 interactive games that provide hands-on opportunities for children to construct and consolidate the understandings depicted in each of the nodes and relations within the structure (Griffin, Case, & Siegler, 1994).

None of the games included a balance beam, or any of the other props that were used in our original measures. However, after they had completed the program, children started behaving like 6-year-olds on the full range of these tasks (Balance Beam, Money, Time, Distributive Justice, Musical Sight Reading, etc.). Controls who were exposed to a variety of conditions (no training, training in a different structure, training in a different set of component structures) showed no such improvement. We therefore concluded that 5- and 6-year-olds could be enabled to acquire the age-typical number structure, under conditions where they had not done so spontaneously (Case & Sandieson, 1992; Griffin, Case, & Capodilupo, in press; Griffin, Case, & Siegler, 1994).

EFFECTS OF CONCEPTUAL TRAINING ON THE GROWTH OF WORKING MEMORY

Once this had been demonstrated, it became possible to test Chi's hypothesis. The question was what would happen to children's counting speed and span as a result of the instructional manipulation. In one of our training studies, Griffin (1994) directly addressed this question, by administering these two tests before and after training. At the time of the pretest, there was a strong correlation between performance on the CS test and performance on tests of children's numerical understanding, as both Chi's model and ours would predict. The telling results were those obtained on the posttest. Compared to controls, treatment subjects showed the usual superiority on our conceptual tests, but no superiority on the Counting Speed and Counting Span tests.

On the basis of children's performance on the conceptual transfer tasks, we concluded that children's conceptual networks for representing number had been impacted by the training as in earlier studies. Because there was no concomitant improvement in speed or span, however, we concluded that Chi's hypothesis must be rejected. Although the acquisition of a richer conceptual network for representing numbers may increase speed and span up to a point, there is a maturational ceiling beyond which this manipulation has little or no effect.

MATURATIONAL INFLUENCES ON SPEED AND SPAN REVISITED

As mentioned previously, a problem with the maturational hypothesis is that it tends to be involved only by default, once experiential variables are shown to have no effect. This puts the position in a tenuous position with regard to its underlying logic. In the two cases that have been considered so far (simple practice and conceptual learning), experience has not been shown to have an impact on children's speed or span, once an age-typical level of functioning has been reached. However, it is always possible that some other experience may be found in the future that does exert an impact. The mere absence of any effect due to known experiential factors can thus not be taken as proof that maturation is playing an important role in producing the age-related changes in performance that are observed. In a recent meta-analysis, Kail (1991, 1992, chapter 4, this volume) has examined the pattern of speed changes that take place in children's development across a wide variety of tasks and has shown that it is not consistent with any explanation that involves specific experience. This considerably strengthens the maturational argument. Still, the issue is unlikely to be laid to rest until the relevant maturational changes can be specified and directly investigated. Before concluding, I review recent evidence that may bring us one step closer to this goal.

In a recent series of studies, Thatcher and his colleagues (Thatcher, 1992; Thatcher, Walker, & Guidice, 1987) examined the extent to which electrical activity in different parts of the cortex is synchronized. The measure that Thatcher used to assess synchrony was EEG coherence, that is, the extent to which the EEG waves that are generated in different parts of the cortex are in phase with each other. One of the most important of Thatcher's findings was that EEG coherence between the frontal and posterior lobes increases with development at a rate similar to that at which change takes place on Kail's reaction time measures. There also appear to be smaller waves of growth that have the same shape as those obtained on our working memory measures (see Fig. 2.8). Thus, it may well be that the variable Thatcher examined provides a window on the general increase in processing time that takes place with age,

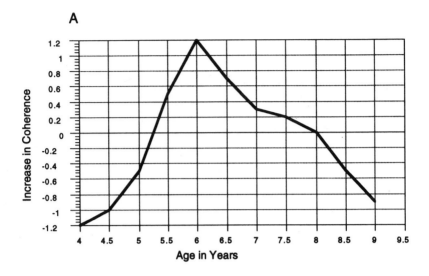

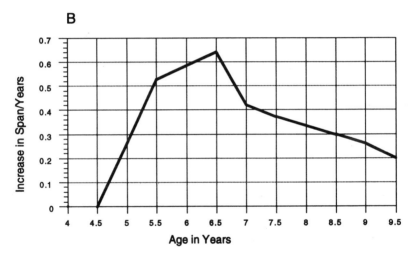

FIG. 2.8.   Rate of growth of EEG coherence between frontal and posterior lobes during middle childhood, and rate of growth of working memory (counting span and spatial span) during the same age range (from Case, 1992b).

and the more particular changes in working memory that are related to them. This latter conclusion gains strength in light of other recent work that shows (a) that the frontal lobes play an important role in mediating working memory, both in humans and in other primates (Goldman-Rakic, 1989a, 1989b; Stuss & Benson, 1986), and (b) that frontal EEG activity directly correlates with working memory performance (Menna, 1989; Pascual-Léone, Hamstra, Benson, Khan, & England, 1990).

Thatcher interprets the increase in EEG coherence across frontal and posterior sites as indicating that the frontal lobes are acquiring a greater degree of executive control over posterior lobe activity, due to an increase in the speed of long distance conduction between the two regions. Although he acknowledges that myelin might possibly play a role in this process, he interprets the effect in his own data as being primarily due to the presence of increased dendritic connections in the long distance fibres connecting the frontal and posterior lobes. In turn, he sees the increase in these connections as occurring due to waves of dendritic branching and pruning, of the same sort that is known to occur in early ontogenesis (Greenough, Black, & Wallace, 1987).

One final aspect of Thatcher's data is relevant. There is a decrease in EEG coherence between adjacent areas in the posterior and frontal cortexes that precisely parallels the increase in long distance coherence. Thatcher's interpretation of this latter change is that it indicates the presence of short distance synaptic connections that are formed during the same waves of synaptic growth, which are inhibitory rather than excitatory in nature. The result is a greater potential differentiation within lobes that closely parallels the greater potential for integration across them.

Thatcher's model has a number of advantages. Like the mylenization plus practice model, it specifies a set of maturational changes that could affect both the speed of trace reactivation in a reverbatory loop, and the difficulty of sustaining any single trace in an active state due to interference. It therefore offers an explanation for the developmental changes that take place in both factors. In addition, like Chi's model, Thatcher's model suggests how these same changes might increase children's potential for forming conceptual structures in which more schemes are integrated and the schemes themselves become more differentiated, namely that the cortex itself is becoming more integrated and differentiated. One can thus see how changes in children's conceptual structures and strategic utilization might be dependent on the same underlying set of maturational changes as are changes in their speed and span.

SUMMARY AND CONCLUSION

The present chapter provides a brief summary of the work conducted over the past 25 years to explore the capacity theory of working memory growth. This work was stimulated by two hypotheses advanced by Pascual-Leone (1970), namely, that working memory growth plays an important role in influencing children's cognitive development, and that this growth is controlled by epigenetic (as opposed to specific experiential) factors. Early critiques of these proposals suggested that changes in children's executive strategies might be responsible for much of the growth that was observed in each area. Strategy change was shown to be an important developmental variable. However, there was a residual growth in quantitative capacity that could not be accounted for by strategic change, and that appeared to be a prerequisite for strategic change to occur in the first place. Because this growth was of precisely the magnitude suggested by Pascual-Leone, additional credibility was given to his model, and additional attention focused on it.

The next concern that was raised, as the new measures designed by Pascual-Leone and myself were scrutinized, was whether or not the observed increase on these measures might be due to changes in chunking or covert rehearsal. Investigations designed to control these factors still showed a strong increase in quantitative capacity with development. Thus, we concluded that these variables did not play a major role on our measures, and that what we were measuring was the growth of some core capacity. Our attention next shifted to the question of how this improvement in core capacity might be produced. Here, the most productive line of inquiry appeared to be one that focused on operational efficiency, and/or speed of processing. This variable correlated with increases in span. Moreover, when different developmental groups were equated on this factor—by teaching adults new operations that they performed as slowly and inefficiently as children—cross-age differences in span disappeared (Case, Kurland, & Daneman, 1979; Case, Kurland, & Goldberg, 1982).

The next question was whether speed changes were exclusively under the control of specific experiential factors such as practice and conceptual learning, or whether they were also influenced by epigenetic (i.e., maturational and general experiential) factors. The practice study conducted by Kurland (1978) and the conceptual training study conducted by Griffin (1994) tended to support the latter possibility. Griffin's data seem particularly compelling: Although experience can produce massive change in children's conceptual understanding, and through this, produce a change in their executive strategies, the same experience appears to produce negligible changes in speed or span once a certain age-typical level of responding has been reached. At least by default, then, one may conclude that some sort of maturational influence must be operative. This conclusion gains strength in light of Kail's (1991) meta-analysis of reaction time studies, suggesting that the changes taking place with age must be controlled by a general rather than any specific experiential factor.

Exactly what maturational change might underlie such changes in speed of processing is not yet completely clear. One early account cited myelinization as a possible factor, because myelinization might be expected to produce concurrent changes in both linear conductance and lateral spread. A more recent hypothesis—one with the same general features—is that the relevant variable may be the extent to which long distance transmission across frontal and posterior lobes becomes more rapid, while activation spread within these lobes is reduced. These changes could in turn be controlled by waves of dendritic branching and pruning in which both maturation and experience play a critical role.

The conceptual progression summarized in this chapter has had a dialectical character, with critiques of Pascual-Leone's original model leading to new studies, which led to refinements of the model, which led to further critiques, and so on. Given that this sort of progression has taken place in the past, it is both likely and desirable that it will continue to take place in the future. In this regard, the data and criticisms by Hitch and Towse (chapter 1, this volume) are important. As indicated, I do not agree with all the conclusions these authors draw from their studies. However, I do think that their data provide a welcome challenge. As I see it, the challenge is one of building a more refined model, one in which the maturational and experiential mechanisms underlying changes in operational speed are explicated in greater detail, as is the way in which these changes impact on the three variables discussed in the present chapter: children's working memory span, their conceptual structures, and their cognitive strategies.

ACKNOWLEDGMENTS

Preparation of this chapter was facilitated by a grant from the J. S. McDonnell Foundation, whose assistance is gratefully acknowledged. Thanks are also extended to Sharon Griffin and Graham Hitch for their comments on an earlier draft of the chapter.

REFERENCES

Atkinson, R. C., & Shiffrin, R. M. (1968). Human Memory: A proposed system and its control processes. In K. W. Spence & J. T. Spence (Eds.), The psychology of learning and motivation (pp. 89–195). New York: Academic Press.

Baddeley, A. D., & Hitch, G. J. (1974). Working memory. In G. Bower (Ed.), The psychology of learning and motivation: Advances in research and theory (Vol. 8, pp. 47–90). New York: Academic Press.

Belmont, J. M., & Butterfield, E. C. (1971). What the development of short term memory is. Human Development, 14, 236–248.

Bruner, J. S., Olver, R. R., & Greenfield, P. M. (1967). Studies in cognitive growth. New York: Wiley.

Capodilupo, A. M. (1992). A neo-structural analysis of children's response to instruction in the sight-reading of musical notation. In R. Case (Ed.), The mind's staircase (pp. 99–115). Hillsdale, NJ: Lawrence Erlbaum Associates.

Case, R. (1970). Information processing, social class, and instruction: A developmental investigation. Unpublished doctoral dissertation. University of Toronto, Ontario.

Case, R. (1972). Validation of a neo-Piagetian capacity construct. Journal of Experimental Child Psychology, 14, 287–302.

Case, R. (1974a). Mental strategies, mental capacity, and instruction: A neo-Piagetian investigation. Journal of Experimental Child Psychology, 18, 382–397.

Case, R. (1974b). Structures and structures: Some functional limitations on the course of cognitive growth. Cognitive Psychology, 18, 544–573.

Case, R. (1975). Gearing the demands of instruction to the developmental capacities of the learner. Review of Educational Research, 45, 59–87.

Case, R. (1976). Social class differences in intellectual development: A neo-Piagetian investigation. Canadian Journal of Behavioral Science, 7, 78–95.

Case, R. (1978a). A developmentally based theory and technology of instruction. *Review of Educational Research, 48,* 439–463.

Case, R. (1978b). *Intellectual and linguistic development in the preschool years.* Final report submitted to the Canada Council.

Case, R. (1979). Piaget and beyond: Toward a developmentally based theory and technology of instruction. In R. Glaser (Ed.), *Advances in instructional psychology* (Vol. 1, pp. 167–228). Hillsdale, NJ: Lawrence Erlbaum Associates.

Case, R. (1985). *Intellectual development: Birth to adulthood.* New York: Academic Press.

Case, R. (1992a). *The mind's staircase.* Hillsdale, NJ: Lawrence Erlbaum Associates.

Case, R. (1992b). The role of the frontal lobes in the regulation of cognitive development. *Brain and Cognition, 20,* 51–73.

Case, R., & Griffin, S. (1990). Child cognitive development: The role of central conceptual structures in the development of scientific and social thought. In C. A. Hauert (Ed.), *Advances in psychology: Developmental psychology* (pp. 193–230). Amsterdam: North-Holland (Elsevier).

Case, R., Kurland, M., & Daneman, M. (1979, April). *Operational efficiency and the growth of working memory.* Paper presented at the biennial meeting of the Society for Research in Child Development, San Francisco, CA.

Case, R., Kurland, D. M., & Goldberg, J. (1982). Operational efficiency and the growth of short term memory. *Journal of Experimental Child Psychology, 33,* 386–404.

Case, R., Okamoto, Y., Henderson, B., & McKeough, A. (1993). Individual variability and consistency in cognitive development: New evidence for the existence of central conceptual structures. In R. Case & W. Edelstein (Eds.), *The new structuralism in cognitive development* (pp. 91–100). Basel, Switzerland: Karger.

Case, R., & Sandieson, R. (1987, April). *General developmental constraints on the acquisition of special procedures (and vice versa).* Paper presented at the annual meeting of the American Educational Research Association, Baltimore, MD.

Case, R., & Sandieson, R. (1992). Testing for the presence of a central quantitative structure: Use of the transfer paradigm. In R. Case (Ed.), *The mind's staircase* (pp. 117–132). Hillsdale, NJ: Lawrence Erlbaum Associates.

Case, R., & Serlin, R. (1979). A new model for predicting performance on Pascual-Leone's test of M-space. *Cognitive Psychology, 11,* 308–326.

Case, R., & Sowder, J. T. (1990). The development of computational estimation: A neo-Piagetian analysis. *Cognition and Instruction, 7,* 79–104.

Chi, M. T. H. (1975). *The development of short-term memory capacity.* Unpublished doctoral dissertation. Carnegie-Mellon University, Pittsburgh, PA.

Chi, M. T. H. (1976). Short term memory limitations in children: Capacity or processing deficits? *Memory and Cognition, 23,* 266–281.

Chi, M. T. H. (1981). Knowledge development and memory performance. In M. Friedman, J. P. Das, & N. O'Connor (Eds.), *Intelligence and learning.* New York: Plenum.

Chi, M. T. H. (1983). Children's lack of access and knowledge reorganization: An example from the concept of animism. In M. Perlmutter & F. E. Weinert (Eds.), *Memory development: Universal changes and individual differences* (pp. 169–194). Hillsdale, NJ: Lawrence Erlbaum Associates.

Crammond, J. (1992). Analyzing the basic cognitive developmental processes of children with specific types of learning disability. In R. Case (Ed.), *The mind's staircase* (pp. 285–302). Hillsdale, NJ: Lawrence Erlbaum Associates.

Dempster, F. N. (1977). *Short term storage space and chunking: A developmental study.* Unpublished doctoral dissertation. University of California, Berkeley.

Dempster, F. N. (1978). Memory span and short term memory: A developmental study. *Journal of Experimental Child Psychology, 26,* 419–431.

Flavell, J. H., Beach, D. R., & Chinsky, J. M. (1966). Spontaneous verbal rehearsal in a memory task as a function of age. *Child Development, 37,* 283–299.

Gelman, R. (1978). Counting in the preschooler: What does and does not develop. In R. S. Siegler (Ed.), *Children's thinking: What develops?* (pp. 213–242). Hillsdale, NJ: Lawrence Erlbaum Associates.

Goldman-Rakic, P. (1989a). *Cellular and circuit basis of working memory in prefrontal cortex of non human primates.* Paper prepared for *The prefrontal cortex.* Amsterdam: Netherlands Institute for Brain Research.

Goldman-Rakic, P. (1989b, June). *Working memory and the frontal lobes.* Paper presented at the Toronto General Hospital.

Greenough, W. T., Black, J. E., & Wallace, C. S. (1987). Experience and brain development. *Child Development, 58,* 539–559.

Griffin, S. A. (1994, June). *Working memory capacity and the acquisition of mathematical knowledge: Implications for learning and development.* Paper presented at the biennial meeting of the International Society for the Study of Behavioral Development, Amsterdam.

Griffin, S. A., Case, R., & Capodilupo, A. (in press). Teaching for understanding: The importance of central conceptual structures in the elementary mathematics curriculum. In A. McKeough & J. Lupert (Eds.), *Teaching for transfer.* Hillsdale, NJ: Lawrence Erlbaum Associates.

Griffin, S. A., Case, R., & Sandieson, R. (1992). Synchrony and asynchrony in the acquisition of children's everyday mathematical knowledge. In R. Case (Ed.), *The mind's staircase* (pp. 75–97). Hillsdale, NJ: Lawrence Erlbaum Associates.

Griffin, S. A., Case, R., & Siegler, R. S. (1994). Rightstart: Providing the central conceptual prerequisites for first formal learning of arithmetic to students at risk for school failure. In K. McGilly (Ed.), *Classroom lessons: Integrating cognitive theory & classroom practice* (pp. 25–50). Cambridge: MIT Press/Bradford Books.

Hebb, D. O. (1949). *The organization of behavior.* New York: Wiley.

Kail, R. (1991). Developmental change in speed of processing during childhood. *Psychological Bulletin, 109,* 490–501.

Kail, R. (1992). Processing speed, speech rate, and memory. *Developmental Psychology, 28,* 899–904.

Kurland, D. M. (1978). *The effect of massive practice on children's operational efficiency and memory span.* Unpublished doctoral dissertation. University of Toronto, Ontario.

Marini, Z. (1992). Synchrony and asynchrony in the development of children's scientific reasoning. In R. Case (Ed.), *The mind's staircase* (pp. 55–73). Hillsdale, NJ: Lawrence Erlbaum Associates.

Menna, R. (1989). *Electrophysiological traits correlates of memory in a group of 15-year-olds.* Unpublished master's thesis. University of Toronto, Ontario.

Miller, G. A., Gallanter, E., & Pribram, K. H. (1960). *Plans and the structure of behaviour.* New York: Holt, Rinehart & Winston.

Newell, A. P., Shaw, J. C., & Simon, H. A. (1958). Elements of a theory of human problem solving. *Psychological Review, 65,* 151–166.

Okamoto, Y. (1992, April). The role of central conceptual structures in children's arithmetic word-problem solving. Paper presented at the annual meeting of the American Educational Research Association, San Francisco, CA.

Olson, D. R. (1967). On conceptual strategies. In J. S. Bruner, R. R. Olver, & P. M. Greenfield (Eds.), *Studies in cognitive growth* (pp. 135–153). New York: Wiley.

Parkinson, G. M. (1976). *The limits of learning.* Unpublished doctoral dissertation. York University, England.

Pascual-Leone, J. (1970). A mathematical model for the transition rule in Piaget's developmental stages. *Acta Psychologica, 32,* 301–345.

Pascual-Leone, J., Hamstra, N., Benson, N., Khan, I., & England, R. (1990). *The P300 event-related potential and mental capacity.* Proceedings of the Fourth International Symposium on Evoked Potential, Toronto, Ontario.

Siegler, R. S. (1976). Three aspects of cognitive development. *Cognitive Psychology, 4,* 481–520.

Starkey, P. (1992). The early development of numerical reasoning. *Cognition, 43,* 93–126.

Stuss, D. T., & Benson, D. F. (1986). *The frontal lobes.* New York: Oxford University Press.

Taskaki, I. (1953). *Nervous transmission.* Springfield, IL: Thomas.

Thatcher, R. W. (1992). Cyclical cortical reorganization during early childhood. *Brain and Cognition, 20,* 24–50.

Thatcher, R. W., Walker, R. A., & Guidice, S. (1987). Human cerebral hemispheres develop at different rates and ages. *Science, 236,* 1110–1113.

Yakovlev, P. I., & Lecours, A. R. (1969). The myelenogenetic cycles of regional maturation of the brain. In A. Minkowski (Ed.), *Regional development of the brain in early life.* Oxford, England: Blackwell.

Chapter 3

Development of Attentional Capacity in Childhood: A Longitudinal Study

Anik de Ribaupierre
Christine Bailleux
University of Geneva

Neo-Piagetian models share a number of common postulates (for a review see Case, 1992a), three of which are particularly important for our purpose. First, general stages should be defined in terms of an upper limit at which children of a given age or cognitive level can function. This allows for generality across domains and for considerable variation across situations and subjects. Indeed, the postulate of a general ceiling in performance is entirely compatible with the large situational and individual variability that has been repeatedly reported in the developmental literature.

Second, following the pioneering work of McLaughlin (1963) and Pascual-Leone (1970), a number of neo-Piagetians consider that attentional capacity or working memory plays a strong, if not causal, role in determining this upper limit (e.g., Case, 1974, 1985; Chapman, 1987; Halford, 1987, 1993; Fischer, 1980; Pascual-Leone, 1987, 1989). It should be noted from the start that neo-Piagetian models are of course not all alike, nor do they all explicitly address working memory (e.g., Case, 1987, 1992a, 1992b; Dasen & de Ribaupierre, 1987). Even with respect to working memory, different constructs have been used, such as working memory, attentional capacity, M space, M power, mental attention, and processing space. For the sake of simplicity, we consider, in this chapter, these constructs equivalent, in the sense that they all refer to a limited capacity for storage and manipulation of mental information for use in cognitive tasks.[1] Growth in attentional capacity, probably due to maturational change, is viewed as one of the causal factors of cognitive development.

---

[1]This general definition is also close to the one commonly adopted in studies on working memory in adults. We argued elsewhere (de Ribaupierre & Bailleux, 1994) that neo-Piagetian models and Baddeley's model are complementary rather than antagonistic.

Third, most neo-Piagetians recognize the importance of situational variability (whether in a narrow sense, referring to experimental situations, or relative to general environmental context), as well as that of individual differences. As a consequence, development is no longer viewed from a unidimensional perspective, but is multidetermined (see, for instance, Fischer & Silvern, 1985; de Ribaupierre, 1993; de Ribaupierre, Neirynck, & Spira, 1989; de Ribaupierre, Rieben, & Lautrey, 1991; Rieben, de Ribaupierre, & Lautrey, 1990). In such a multidimensional framework, attentional capacity is only one factor of development among others; that is, it is considered necessary, but not sufficient. This has allowed a number of researchers to posit a relation of implication between attentional capacity and performances in cognitive tasks (e.g., Case, 1985; Chapman, 1990; Chapman & Lindenberger, 1989; de Ribaupierre & Pascual-Leone, 1979). The development of attentional capacity is probably responsible for the universal aspects of development, whereas other factors, such as past experience or differential variables, account for the diversity of behaviors within a given general stage. This is the reason why task analysis has taken a great importance in many neo-Piagetian approaches (e.g., Case, 1992a; de Ribaupierre & Pascual-Leone, 1979, 1984). Not all developmental tasks, nor even all short-term memory tasks, provide good estimates of attentional capacity; experimental paradigms have to be developed that ensure that attentional capacity is not confounded with other factors. In particular, tasks of attentional capacity should not allow chunking, nor the use of facilitating strategies that would lower the complexity of the task. They should be simple enough to ensure that performances do not vary across subjects because of individual differences in other factors, such as knowledge base or previous experience; they should, however, require mental effort. Thus perceptual information should not be too salient, or else the complexity of the task would again be lowered.

Pascual-Leone and Case provided suggestions relative not only to the role played by working memory in development, but also to the functioning and the development of attentional capacity. In particular, they proposed that attentional capacity develops in stages, supposed to last for approximately 2 years. Pascual-Leone suggested the existence of an underlying operator, the M-*operator*, which serves to activate task-relevant schemes not directly activated by the input or by other operators. M-power corresponds to the maximum number of units or schemes that can be activated in a single operation. The limits in M-power increase maturationally with age, growing from 1 at age 3 to 7 at age 15. Growth in M-power is assumed to be continuous; however, enough M-power has to accumulate before a supplementary scheme can be activated. This is supposed to require 2 years.[2] These assumptions were validated in a number of empirical

---

[2]M–stages are supposed to be shorter during the sensorimotor period, because each scheme requires less M-power to be activated (Pascual-Leone & Johnson, 1991).

studies, most of which were cross-sectional, using different samples and different tasks (e.g., Pascual-Leone, 1970, 1987). Although we do not go into detail here, Pascual-Leone defined a number of other underlying operators; cognitive development in general—that is, the increase with age in performances in cognitive tasks—results from the combined influence of these different operators, and not only from the influence of the M-operator.

Case (e.g., 1985) used the term *executive processing space* to refer to a construct similar to Pascual-Leone's M-power. Processing space is further divided into *operating space*, which is devoted to the activation of ongoing operations, and *short term storage space* (STSS), which serves for the maintenance and/or retrieval of recently activated units. Case developed a number of STSS tasks corresponding to the different qualitative stages distinguished in the general developmental model. A number of studies, again most of which were cross-sectional, showed that the increase in STSS is approximately one unit every 2 years.

The main objective of our study was to determine, using a longitudinal design, whether or not the developmental stages postulated by Pascual-Leone and Case could be observed at an intraindividual level. Indeed, all empirical validations relied only on cross-sectional studies, or on short longitudinal studies, although it is mandatory that developmental change be also studied longitudinally over long periods (see Hoppe-Graff, 1989; Schneider & Weinert, 1989).

The purpose of this chapter is, therefore, to report on a recently completed cohort sequential study (i.e., a study using both a longitudinal and a cross-sectional design) on the development of attentional capacity. Four groups of children, ages 5, 6, 8, and 10 at the onset of the study, were examined once a year, over 5 years. Each year, four attentional capacity tasks were used, three of which were used throughout the project (two versions of the Mr. Peanut task and the CSVI task), whereas the fourth task varied across years.

A general overview of the study and of the experimental procedures is presented. Then, three types of questions are addressed: First, do the various attentional capacity tasks used in the project measure the same processes? Second, what is the extent and the form of developmental change observed over the 5 years? Longitudinal results are described for each of the three tasks used repeatedly and the results of latent growth curve analyses conducted on the mean performances of the whole sample are reported. These analyses show the importance of situational changes, as well as the difficulty in disentangling development from learning. Third, are there individual differences in developmental change? Individual empirical growth curves are presented to illustrate interindividual differences. Hierarchical linear modeling (HLM) analyses were used to assess whether or not developmental change in each of the three tasks was subject to large individual variability and varied as a function of other variables.

METHOD

Subjects

The initial sample consisted of 4 age groups composed of 30 children each, ages 5, 6, 8, and 10 at the onset of the study. Children were examined within 2 months of their birthday each year; the interval between each assessment was 1 year (± 1 month). The attrition rate over the 5 years was 15% (N = 18). The number of subjects per task varied slightly, because all of the tasks could not always be administered to all of the subjects.

Tasks

Three types of tasks were used over the 5 years: attentional capacity tasks, Piagetian tasks, and control or miscellaneous tasks, such as Raven's Progressive Matrices, the Children's Embedded Figures Test, and a task of articulatory speed. Only the attentional capacity tasks are described here.

Compound Stimuli Visual Information Task (CSVI). Developed by Pascual-Leone (e.g., 1970), this task was used each year. It was computerized on Year 2. It consists of three phases:

1. An introduction, during which subjects are shown simple visual stimuli or instances (presented as coded messages) projected onto a screen, to which they learn to associate a simple response. Responses are given by pressing on a nine-key keyboard. For instance, each time children are shown a square figure (other shapes in the test are triangles, circles and crosses and do not constitute messages), they have to press a specific button (e.g., a round, white button); each time a figure is red, they have to press another button (e.g., a diamond-shaped yellow button), and so on. There were nine such pairs (seven for the younger subjects). Simple stimuli, each of which was paired with a different button on the keyboard, were: square, big, red, circle in the middle of the figure, cross in the middle of the figure, dotted outline, frame around the figure, and underlined, purple background. The last two stimuli were used only in the nine-stimuli version.

2. A learning phase, during which subjects are presented with a single message at a time and have to overlearn the association stimulus–response. The criterion was 60 consecutive correct items, allowing for three errors.

3. A testing phase, in which the simple stimuli are nested in a composite stimulus, the task being to respond to all the instances that can be remembered. For instance, subjects saw a red, big square with a cross in the middle and had to press four different keys; or they saw a green small triangle with a circle in the middle, on a purple background. In the latter case, they only had to press

two keys, since the particular values of the color, size, and shape variables were not messages. Item complexity was defined on the basis of the number of instances embedded in the complex one (from two to eight for the most difficult version). Items were presented in random order.

Children were instructed to respond to all the messages they saw, and to indicate when they had finished responding, by pressing on an end-button located beside the keyboard.

The task was used as a memory task: The complex stimulus was presented for a limited amount of time, and children could only respond once the stimulus had disappeared from the screen. Response time was free.

The general experimental procedure remained similar over the 5 years. In particular, the same nine instances were used throughout. However, several changes were introduced over the years, some of which induced important differences in the performances. Notable changes were the following: (a) Each year, the position of the specific buttons was changed, although the general layout of the keyboard remained identical; the specific associations between instances and buttons were also changed each year. (b) Exposure time was modified: it was 5 seconds for Years 1–3, and 110 milliseconds on Years 4 and 5. In the tachistoscopic presentation, the stimulus was followed by a mask. This important modification was introduced because the task had to be made more difficult: Ceiling effects had shown in the older age group. Pascual-Leone and collaborators had already used a tachistoscopic presentation. (c) The number of items changed on Year 5. For the first 4 years, the task consisted of 12 items per class; there were 84 items for the more difficult version (Class 2 to 8) and 60 items for the easier one (Class 2 to 6). Until Class 6, items were strictly identical in the two versions and only their order changed; that is, the two supplementary instances incorporated in the more difficult version (i.e., underline and purple background) were used in Class 7 and 8 only. On Year 5, the task was reduced to six items per class (Class 2 to 8 for a total of 42 items, administered to all subjects); on this occasion, new items were constructed and the nine instances were distributed across all classes.

Mr. Peanut Tasks (Peanut–P, Peanut–C). Two versions of this task were used each year. They were adapted from the one-version Cucumber task developed by Case (1985), in turn adapted from the Cucui task (Pascual-Leone, personal communication, July, 1987).

This is a short-term memory task. Children were presented with a clown figure with colored dots painted on different body parts (eyes, ears, arms, legs, antennas, cheeks, mouth, and nose). The picture was then removed and replaced with a blank figure on which children had to place colored chips on the parts that were painted in the previous picture.

Two versions were constructed: a purple version (Peanut–P), in which all colored dots and all chips were of the same color, and a colored version (Peanut–C), in which children had to remember both the location and the color of the dots. Item complexity, defined by the number of colored dots in the picture, varied from one to six for the most difficult version. Five items per class were used; items were presented in a random order. Exposure time was 1 second per colored dot (e.g., 5 seconds for a Class 5 item).

A number of methodological precautions were taken to minimize the use of facilitating strategies. Colored dots were never placed on symmetrical parts (e.g., on the two eyes), and, as far as possible, figural patterns were avoided (e.g., a straight line across the figure). Seven colors were used so that all colors were never used in a single item; identical positions were not repeated on consecutive items.

Two changes were introduced during the study, both on Year 4. The clown figure was modified (a basket was added on each arm), so as to add two possible locations. As a consequence, new items were constructed. A more important change, which proved to have a significant effect on performances, consisted in computerizing the task. The clown figure was presented on a computer screen and children had to place the colored dots on the blank figure by using a computer mouse.

Figural Intersections Task (FIT). This task was developed by Pascual-Leone (Pascual-Leone & Baillargeon, 1994; Pascual-Leone & Ijaz, 1989) and was used on Years 1 and 3.

This test is composed of geometrical figures. A number of simple geometrical figures is presented separately on the right-hand side of the page and embedded in a composite on the left-hand side. For every item, children were asked to place a dot inside each figure on the right-hand side, and then a single dot on the compound figure on the left side, at the intersection of all of the relevant figures (the relevant figures being those found on the right side).

Classes of complexity, defined on the basis of the number of relevant figures, varied from two to eight for the most difficult version (five items per class); items were presented in random order.

The same version of the task was used on the 2 years in which it was administered; however, figures underwent a 45° clockwise rotation (Pascual-Leone, personal communication, July, 1989).

Counting Span (CS). This task was developed by Case (1985; Case, Kurland, & Goldberg, 1982) and was used on Year 2. Children were presented with a series of cards, each containing green and yellow dots. They were instructed to count the green dots and retain that total while counting the number of green dots on subsequent cards, the preceding ones being removed. At the end of each series, subjects had to report the totals.

Digits to be recalled never exceeded nine; series following the natural order of numbers were avoided. Item complexity, defined by the number of sets to count, or totals to report, ranged from one to six in the most difficult version (three items per class); items were presented in random order.

Listening Span (LS). Adapted from the Reading Span task (Daneman & Carpenter, 1980), LS was used on Year 4. Subjects listened to a sequence of sentences, were required to process each sentence and decide whether or not it was semantically correct, while retaining the last word. At the end of the series, they had to report all the final words. Sentences were presented by means of a tape recorder; the interval between sentences was fixed and long enough for children to respond. The tape recorder was stopped for recall and the children's responses were manually recorded. The number of correct and false sentences and the length of the last words were controlled across classes of complexity. Sentences were all approximately the same length (from six to eight words).

Classes of complexity, defined by the number of sentences, or final words to retain, varied from two to seven (three items per class). Items were presented in increasing order of complexity, and testing was terminated when children failed all items of a class.

Reading Span (RS). This task was used on Year 5. It was in all points comparable to the Listening task, except that now children had to read sentences on a computer screen and answer yes–no for each sentence by pressing a key on the computer keyboard; as soon as the response was given, the next sentence appeared. The end of an item was signaled on the screen and children had to orally recall all of the last words. The computerization of the task allowed the recording of response times. A preliminary phase was added in which 18 sentences were presented without memory load: Children had only to decide whether the sentence was correct or false. This was meant to measure a base processing time, to be compared with the response time necessary to process the sentence and rehearse the last word.

Scoring

For all tasks, several scores were computed based either on passed–failed items, or on response values per item (e.g., how many correct responses in a Class 5 item). Several finer scores were also established, as well as response times whenever possible. For reasons of space, results reported in this chapter are based on passed–failed items only. The task score was the sum of correct items divided by the number of items per class; it is thus comparable to a traditional span score. When no Class 1 items were given (like in CSVI), a one-point credit was given, which may favor the youngest children.

Procedure

Children were individually examined each year in their schools with the tasks described. Recall that a number of other tasks were also administered, of which only the Children's Embedded Figures Test (CEFT; Witkin, Oltman, Raskin, & Karp, 1971) given on Years 1 and 3, and the Raven's Progressive matrices given on Year 2 are of interest here. Testing required three to five 45-minute annual testing sessions, grouped over 2 to 3 weeks. Different versions of the tasks were administered to the different age groups, in an attempt to ensure that the difficulty of the task was adapted to the children's level.

RESULTS

Given the considerable amount of data collected in this research, it is impossible to report in detail results on all the attentional capacity tasks. As mentioned in the introduction, presentation is made according to three questions:

1. Is there a relation between the attentional capacity tasks that were used? Analyses here are cross-sectional, but we also ask whether or not between-task relationships were stable across the 5 years.
2. What was the developmental change observed over the 5 years? This question concerns only the two Peanut tasks and the CSVI task, each of which is examined separately.
3. What is the extent of interindividual and intergroup variability in developmental change? This question is explored by looking at empirical individual growth curves, and by means of hierarchical linear modeling.

Relationships Between the Attentional Capacity Tasks: Cross-Sectional Analyses

As mentioned, four attentional capacity tasks were used each year. In order to evaluate whether these tasks covary, confirmatory factor analyses using LISREL were conducted. Given the size of the sample, analyses had to be performed on the four age groups together.[3] If all the tasks tap the same underlying processes, they should all load on the same factor. Therefore, a single-factor model was tested each year. Table 3.1 presents the parameter estimates for each year, and the χ^2 values obtained. The single-factor model proved satisfactory each year, except for Year 5 ($\chi^2(2, N = 82) = 7.2, p = .03$). The parameter estimates varied for the different tasks and were generally higher for the Peanut tasks and for CSVI—except on Year 5, as concerns the latter task—than for the other tasks.

Results show that all tasks tend to measure the same process, as would be expected if they indeed measure attentional capacity. However, the factor may

---

[3]For reasons of simplification, results reported in this chapter are based on longitudinal subjects only; that is, on the subjects who were present each year. The present confirmatory factor analyses were performed on the subjects who not only were present each year in the project but also were administered all the tasks. Because of the further reduction in the size of the sample ($N = 82$), cross-sectional analyses were also conducted on all the subjects available on any given year (N ranged from 95–110). Results were equivalent.

TABLE 3.1

Cross-Sectional Confirmatory Factor Analyses for the 1-Factor Model:
Parameter Estimates (Standardized Solutions)

	Year 1		Year 2		Year 3		Year 4		Year 5	
	λx	$\Theta\delta$	λx	$\Theta\delta$	λx	$\Theta\delta$	λx	$\Theta\delta$	λx	$\Theta\delta$
Peanut–Purple	.88	.23	.95	.09	.94	.12	.90	.19	.93	.13
Peanut–Colored	.89	.21	.90	.20	.86	.26	.91	.18	.80	.36
CSVI	.90	.18	.84	.30	.83	.31	.78	.39	.69	.52
FIT	.74	.45	—	—	.81	.34	—	—	—	—
Counting span	—	—	.82	.33	—	—	—	—	—	—
Listening span	—	—	—	—	—	—	.67	.55	—	—
Reading span	—	—	—	—	—	—	—	—	.55	.70
$\chi^2_{df = 2}$	1.85		4.33		5.34		2.82		7.20	
p	.40		.12		.07		.24		.03	

merely reflect a general developmental factor, so much more so because all age groups had to be analyzed together. Therefore, two additional analyses were performed.

First, other developmental variables used in the project on Years 1–3 were included: CEFT on Years 1 and 3, and Progressive Matrices (PM) on Year 2. With these additional variables, single-factor models were insignificant: $\chi^2(2, N = 82) = 10.01$, $p = .08$, $\chi^2(5, N = 82) = 10.34$, $p = .066$ and $\chi^2(5, N = 82) = 13.46$, $p = .02$ for Years 1 to 3, respectively. The difference between these models and those defined on the basis of the four attentional capacity tasks only was significant for Years 1 and 3, and significant for Year 2.

Second, *age* was defined as a second-order latent variable (a ξ variable, totally equated with the observed value of age via a fixed-option), to test whether or not the single-factor models merely reflect the influence of age. Results turned out not to be significantly different from the single-factor solutions obtained with the four attentional capacity tasks alone, provided the parameter γ_{11} linking age to attentional capacity (the latent variable η) was left free to vary. Although the estimates of γ_{11} were high (ranging from .76 to .91), the model proved inadequate as soon as this parameter was fixed to 1. It can thus be safely concluded that, although age accounts for a good part of the covariance between the four attentional capacity tasks, some of the between-task common variance is not related to age (see also Kliegl & Mayr, 1992, for the use of a similar method).

Because the same factorial structure proved adequate each year, it seemed interesting to test its stability across assessments. One can ask whether or not the latent variable takes the same meaning each year and is stable across years, especially because there was variation in the battery of tasks used each year. Obviously, these two aspects (meaning and stability) are different, but cannot be disentangled at present. Figure 3.1 reports the two simplex models that were

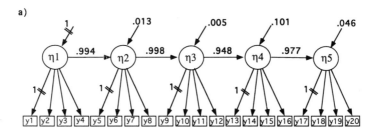

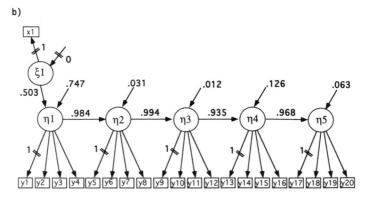

FIG. 3.1. Models used to test the stability in the covariance structure over the 5 years. Panel a: latent variable defined on the attentional capacity tasks only. Panel b: effect of age. The observed variables y1–y4 stand for the observed variables on Year 1, y5–y8 for Year 2, y9–y12 for Year 3, y13–y16 for Year 4, and y17–y20 for Year 5. The sign \ \ means that this parameter was fixed.

used: one dealing with the attentional capacity tasks only (Fig. 3.1a), and in which age was entered as a second-order variable (Fig. 3.1b). Both models provided satisfactory solutions, and did not differ significantly from each other: $\chi^2(166, N = 82) = 26.40$ and $\chi^2(185, N = 82) = 52.86$, respectively. This means that the between-task relationship remained stable over the 5 years, and that age accounted for a good part of it. Two remarks are in order, however. First, the estimate of γ_{11}, linking age to the latent variable defined on Year 1, is .55; once again, this means that age does not explain all the covariance between the attentional capacity tasks. Second, in these two models, the λ values that link the observed variables to the latent variables η are much lower than those obtained in the cross-sectional analyses. They ranged from .44 to .60. This probably points to unreliability in our measures.

In summary, the results are convergent with the hypothesis that the different attentional capacity tasks address the same basic underlying process. They also point to a relatively high stability in the covariance structure, most of which can probably be accounted for by age. Given the size of each cohort, it is, however, not possible to test stability, controlling for age. Nevertheless, inter-individual variability seemed to be the rule. This point is addressed again in a later section.

Extent and Form of Developmental Change

The analyses reported in the preceding section concerned the between-task relationships and their stability over the 5 years. They did not give any information relative to the level of performances. Figure 3.2 presents the group means over the 5 years by cohort and by task, for each of the three tasks used throughout the project.

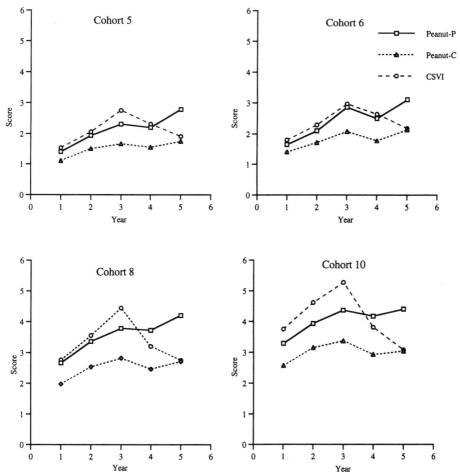

FIG. 3.2. Mean number of passed items (span score) by year, task, and cohort.

Three points are worth stressing in view of these curves. First, cross-sectional age effects (i.e., developmental differences) were observed each year. Main effects of age were systematically obtained in analyses of variance conducted on the cross-sectional results. Contrast analyses showed that the performances of Cohorts 5 and 6 were systematically lower than Cohort 8, in turn lower than Cohort 10. The difference between Cohorts 5 and 6 was much smaller, and was often nonsignificant.

Second, retest effects were observed over the first 3 years. Keeping chronological age constant, performances were higher for children having had more encounters with the tasks. For instance, Cohort 5 had higher scores on Years 2 and 3 than Cohort 6 on Years 1 and 2 (both cohorts being then ages 6 and 7). Likewise, Cohort 6 had higher scores on Year 3 when it was age 8, than Cohort 8 on Year 1. Retest effects were stronger for the CSVI task than for the Peanut tasks, and for Peanut–P than for Peanut–C. Retest effects also showed in an independent, parallel study in which 6-, 8-, and 10-year-olds were examined twice with the CSVI and the Peanut tasks over an interval of 1 month (de Ribaupierre & Spira, 1991; Spira & Keizer, 1991). They are probably due to the intervention of more elaborate encoding and processing strategies resulting in larger chunks, which children can develop when they know the task better and may be due to other processes (learning factors, executive schemes) than attentional capacity (see also de Ribaupierre & Bailleux, 1993). The developmental curves observed over the first 3 years thus clearly point to the difficulty of dissociating learning and developmental changes.

Third, on Year 4, performances dropped drastically on all three tasks as a result of the important changes introduced in the experimental procedures. Recall that there was a change in the mode of response in the Peanut tasks due to their computerization, and in the time of exposure in the CSVI task. That these changes would have an effect on the level of performance was to be expected, particularly as regards the CSVI task: A drastic reduction in time of presentation certainly modifies the number of simple stimuli that can be attended, and perhaps even the type of processes used at encoding. With respect to the Peanut tasks, our current hypothesis is that responding by means of a computer mouse not only represents an additional attentional load, but also constitutes a concurrent spatial task interfering with the rehearsal and retrieval of positions. This result was used elsewhere to illustrate the complementarity of Baddeley's model and neo-Piagetian models of working memory (see de Ribaupierre & Bailleux, 1992, 1994). In the line of Baddeley's model (e.g., Baddeley, 1986), the Peanut task and the monitoring of the mouse are both likely to draw upon the resources of the same slave system (the VSSP system); therefore, one can expect an effect of interference. In terms of Pascual-Leone's model, monitoring the mouse requires good executive schemes. In addition, there might be an incompatibility between the displacement of the mouse on the table and the displacement of the dot on the screen, particularly with respect to the up-and-down movement (on a horizontal versus a vertical plane).

This probably transforms the monitoring of the mouse in a misleading task, which requires the intervention of the I-operator, independent from the M-operator. It may even necessitate additional activation by M.

Performances increased again on Year 5 for the Peanut tasks, showing renewed developmental progression, possibly confounded with retest effects. In contrast, performances decreased again significantly on the CSVI task. Our explanation is that the construction of new items and the redistribution of all instances across classes that ensued, further prevented the use of chunking strategies.

Latent growth curve analyses were used to estimate the developmental trends obtained in each task over the 5 years (e.g., McArdle & Epstein, 1987; Rudinger, Andres, & Rietz, 1991). The variables y correspond to the observed variables of each successive year. Three latent variables were introduced: $\eta1$ for the means, related both to the observed variables and to the observed means (the variable x to which $\eta1$ is equated through a fixed-options corresponds to the observed means), $\eta2$ for the variances, and $\eta3$ for the increase in means on Years 2 to 5. The addition of $\eta1$, $\eta2$, and $\eta3$ parameters for each year, respectively, should allow the reconstruction of the observed scores. Figure 3.3 presents, as an ex-

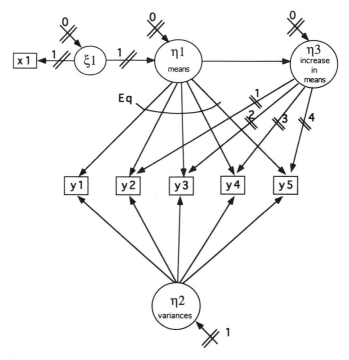

FIG. 3.3. Latent growth curve model used to test a linear increase in the means. y1 to y5 stand for the observed variable on each of the 5 years. The sign \ \ means that the parameter was fixed. Eq means that these five parameters were equalized, but left free to vary.

ample, the model used to test a linear increase. The parameter estimates obtained for each task and for each model are reported in Table 3.2. Because the goal of these analyses was to estimate the increase in means over the years, the parameters linking the y variables to $\eta 1$ were set equal across the 5 years. We had no specific hypothesis relative to the change in variances; therefore, the parameters of $\eta 2$ were left free. With respect to the change in means (parameters of $\eta 3$), several models were contrasted.

The free model, in which all parameters were left free to vary, helped us to estimate the developmental trends. A linear model was also tested, although it was already obvious from the empirical curves that it would not fit. A linear trend would be expected if learning and development are confounded, provided there is no major change in the situations.

A third model was tested, labeled post hoc model because it was defined on the basis of the empirical curves. For Peanut–P, it was assumed that the increase was linear from Year 1 to Year 3 (coefficients of 0, 1, and 2 on $\eta 3$ respectively), as well as from Year 4 to Year 5 (coefficients of 1.5 and 2.5), the latter increase being of the same magnitude as that observed during the first 3 years. This amounts to saying that performances on Year 4 were exactly midway between Year 2 and Year 3, whereas performances on Year 5 were higher than on Year 3. For Peanut–C, the increase was considered greater from Year 1 to Year 2 than from Year 2 to Year 3 (coefficients of 1 and 1.5 on $\eta 3$, respectively). Performances on Year 4 were considered identical to Year 2, and performances on Year 5 identical to Year 3; again, the increase from Year 4 to Year 5 was considered equivalent to the increase from Year 2 to Year 3. Thus, when considering level on previous years as the criterion, the increase from Year 1 to Year 3 was steeper and more linear for Peanut–P than for Peanut–C. The interference created by the monitoring of the mouse was assumed to be stronger in Peanut–C than in Peanut–P. With respect to the CSVI task, a linear increase was modeled for the first 3 years (coefficients of 1 and 2 on $\eta 3$); on Year 4, performances were halfway between Year 1 and Year 2, whereas they regressed to their initial level on Year 5 (coefficients of 0 for Years 1 and 5). Thus, with reference to the levels observed on the first year, the slope of the developmental change was assumed to be similar in CSVI and in Peanut–P, whereas it was less steep in Peanut–C. The regression was largest in CSVI and smallest in Peanut–P.

A staged model, more in accord with the neo-Piagetian hypothesis of stages lasting 2 years, was also tested. According to Pascual-Leone's model of the development of M–operator, the performances of the 6-, 8-, and 10-year-old cohorts should increase from Year 1 to Year 2 and from Year 3 to Year 4, and should remain stable in Years 3 and 5; in contrast, the performances of 5-year-olds should be equivalent on Years 1 and 2, and on Years 3 and 4. Therefore, only the 6-, 8-, and 10-year-olds were analyzed together. The increase in means for Years 2 and 3 and for Years 4 and 5 were equalized, and the amount of change was left free to be estimated. Note that a strong stage hypothesis, such as was

TABLE 3.2

Parameters Estimates for the Three Models Used in the Latent Growth Curve Analyses (Standardized Solution)

	Free Model			Linear Model				Post Hoc Model				Staged Model (6–10 only)			
	η1	η2	η3	η1	η2	η3	coef[a]	η1	η2	η3	coef[a]	η1	η2	η3	coef[a]
Peanut–P (N = 100)															
y1	2.21	.80	.00	2.37	.80	.00	1	2.21	.80	.00	1	2.88	.80	.00	
y2	2.21	.92	.58	2.37	.91	.31	2	2.21	.92	.55	2	2.88	1.05	.91	eq1[b]
y3	2.21	.86	1.09	2.37	.84	.61	3	2.21	.86	1.09	1.5	2.88	.64	.91	eq1
y4	2.21	.92	.91	2.37	.91	.91	4	2.21	.92	.82	2.5	2.88	.96	1.12	eq2
y5	2.21	.84	1.37	2.37	.85	1.22		2.21	.84	1.36		2.88	.75	1.12	eq2
		$\chi^2_{(df=5)} = 11.67$ $p = .040$			$\chi^2_{(df=8)} = 86.15$ $p < .001$				$c^2_{(df=8)} = 14.94$ $p = .06$				$\chi^2_{(df=7)} = 77.38$ $p < .001$		
Peanut–C (N = 100)															
y1	1.73	.62	.00	1.54	.63	.00	1	1.70	.62	.00	1	1.95	.57	.00	
y2	1.73	.73	.47	1.54	.90	.14	2	1.70	.73	.47	1.5	1.95	.66	.64	eq1
y3	1.73	.79	.73	1.54	1.00	.27	3	1.70	.79	.70	1	1.95	.69	.64	eq1
y4	1.73	.62	.43	1.54	.65	.41	4	1.70	.62	.47	1.5	1.95	.56	.51	eq2
y5	1.73	.62	.68	1.54	.70	.55		1.70	.62	.70		1.95	.57	.51	eq2
		$\chi^2_{(df=5)} = 11.67$ $p = .04$			$\chi^2_{(df=8)} = 88.66$ $p < .001$				$\chi^2_{(df=8)} = 13.36$ $p = .100$				$\chi^2_{(df=7)} = 37.63$ $p < .001$		
CSVI (N = 89)															
y1	2.5	.98	.00	1.39	1.47	.00	1	2.62	.98	.00	1	2.32	1.07	.00	
y2	2.5	1.18	.69	1.39	1.99	.20	2	2.62	1.19	.73	2	2.32	1.09	.96	eq1
y3	2.5	1.24	1.42	1.39	2.45	.41	3	2.62	1.25	1.45	.5	2.32	1.48	.96	eq1
y4	2.5	.70	.51	1.39	1.23	.61	4	2.62	.69	.36		2.32	.82	.41	eq2
y5	2.5	.56	.00	1.39	.58	.81		2.62	.56	.00		2.32	.44	.41	eq2
		$\chi^2_{(df=5)} = 22.31$ $p < .001$			$\chi^2_{(df=8)} = 155.91$ $p < .001$				$c^2_{(df=8)} = 28.83$ $p < .001$				$\chi^2_{(df=7)} = 86.24$ $p < .001$		

Note. y1 to y5 stand for observed variables on Years 1 to 5. Latent variables η1, η2, and η3 stand for the means (set equal), the variances (left free), and the increase in means (left free in free model and set to fixed values in the other models), respectively.

[a]The coefficients correspond to the values of the fixed parameters; for instance, the coefficient 2 for Year 3 in the linear model means that the model assumes that increase from Year 2 to Year 3 is twice the increase from Year 1 to Year 2.

[b]These parameters were left free, but equalized for Years 2 and 3, and Years 4 and 5, respectively.

tested in Model 4, can only hold if the task does not undergo changes and, more importantly, if attentional capacity is singled out. As soon as learning effects come into play (e.g., during the first 3 years), a linear change is more likely. Therefore, we did not expect the staged model to present a good fit.

The free model should provide the most adequate solution; this is trivial, because it consists in merely reconstructing a 1-factor confirmatory model while decomposing means and variances. The second best model should be the post hoc model. Once again, this is trivial because it was modeled after the empirical curves; nevertheless, it allowed us to assess the extent of developmental change. Finally, we assumed that the staged model should provide a better fit than the linear one. A direct comparison of the staged model with the other models is difficult on the basis of the values provided in Table 3.2, because the size of the sample is not the same. Nevertheless, a global comparison in terms of fit is possible; further, the first three models were also run on the reduced 6–10-year-old sample and results were similar. Results (see Table 3.2) show that the hypothesized order holds for the three tasks. The post hoc models are satisfactory, and equivalent or even better when considering the level of significance, than is the free model, despite stricter constraints. Of course, the post hoc model was also significantly better than the linear model. The staged model did not provide a good fit; however, it generally led to lower χ^2 values than the linear model, except for the Peanut–P task.

In summary, one can conclude that the developmental trends in these three tasks do not support a strong stage hypothesis, but are more likely to reflect a combination of developmental and learning effects. In addition, they are sensitive to changes in situations. A last methodological remark is in order: These analyses were run on an insensitive score—the number of passed items. As a replication, they should also be performed on the number of correct responses, retaining more information than the average number of passed items. In both cases, it may be preferable to attempt to estimate a latent ability using the techniques of item response theory. This is planned as a further step in the study.

Are There Individual Differences in Developmental Change?

The analyses reported in the preceding section were conducted on the whole sample. This proved necessary because of the requirements that LISREL sets on the number of subjects. It is nevertheless interesting to determine whether there is interindividual variability not only in performances, but in developmental change. On simple visual inspection, this seems to be the case. Figure 3.4 presents a sample of the empirical, individual growth curves observed in the different age groups. Not only is progression more or less steep across children, but the direction of the change also varies: Although the mean level of performance regressed on Year 4, some children did progress from Year 3 to Year 4. Likewise, some children did not progress, but even regressed, from Year 1 to Year 2 or from Year 2 to Year 3.

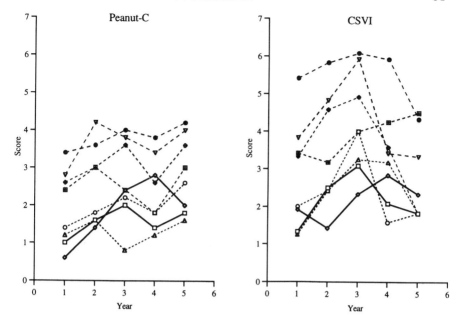

FIG. 3.4. Sample of individual curves (two children per cohort) on two attentional capacity tasks. The plain line stands for Cohort 5 children, the dotted line for Cohort 6, the broken line for Cohort 8, and the dashed–dotted line for Cohort 10.

In order to estimate the importance and reliability of this interindividual variability, we used Hierarchical Linear Modeling (HLM; Bryk & Raudenbush, 1987, 1992; Willett, 1994), based on regression analysis. This technique allows one to dissociate within- and person-variables and to assess the effect of the between-person (Level 2) variables on the within-subject (Level 1) ones.

In the present case, the Level 1 variables were the number of passed items (means) and the slope over the 5 years. In view of the results reported in the last section, it seemed meaningless to compute individual, linear regression lines over the 5 years.[4] Therefore, we decided to break up the growth trajectories into two components: the trajectory from Year 1 to Year 3, and the trajectory from Year 3 to Year 5. In the second case, the empirical curve was not linear either, except for CSVI. Nevertheless, we thought it important to retain at least three points of measurement. Applying a linear model to the second portion of the curve has as a probable result to flatten the curves and to lower the reliability of the parameter estimates.

As a second step, we asked whether the slopes of the developmental curves vary as a function of age (cohort), field-dependence–independence (FDI), gender,

---

[4]Although, theoretically, HLM allows one to model quadratic or even cubic growth curves, we could not figure out how to do it in the version of the program we have.

or socioeconomic status (SES). Preliminary analyses showed that gender and SES had no effect, either on the intercept or on the slope in any of the three tasks. Therefore, only Age and FDI were retained. With respect to the latter variable, recall that the CEFT was administered twice. To control for the effect of age, z scores were computed by age and averaged over the two administrations. We also decided to enter the progression observed from Year 1 to Year 3 (the difference between Years 1 and 3) as a Level 2 variable for the second component of the curve. That is, we asked whether the change taking place during the first 3 years accounts for the intercept and/or the slope of the change observed in the last 3 years. As mentioned with respect to retest effects, a strong progression may be indicative of the fact that subjects use facilitating strategies. Because strategies were harder to apply in the modified tasks, subjects using them in the first 3 years should be penalized more by the changes introduced in the tasks than subjects who progressed less to start with. Therefore, we expected that the subjects who progressed most during the first 3 years were also those who regressed most on Year 4 for the three tasks, and on Year 5 for CSVI. For reasons that cannot be developed here, it was hypothesized that such developmental patterns of a stronger progression over the first 3 years coupled with a stronger regression on Year 4 were more likely to be found in older children and in field-independent children.

Six analyses were conducted, two series per task, on the longitudinal subjects who received the three tasks ($N = 87$). Table 3.3 presents, as an example, the results obtained for the models used on the second part of the curve (Year 3 to Year 5) in the CSVI. They are commented upon in some detail because of the novelty of this type of technique (see also Alsaker, 1992; Bryk & Raudenbush, 1992; Schneider, 1993). The first panel of Table 3.3 reports the results of an unconditional model, that is, a model in which no Level 2 variable was introduced, interpreted as an ANOVA with fixed and random effects. The estimated mean intercept (initial status) and the mean growth rate were 5.97 with a standard error of .29[5] and −.71, respectively. This indicates that the regression was approximately .7 item per year. The significant t ratios show that both parameters are necessary to account for the mean growth trajectory. The estimates for the variances of the individual parameters (random effects) are 5.21 and .14, respectively; both are significant, meaning that there was large interindividual variability. The reliabilities of the growth parameters that the estimation of the unconditional model also allowed us to investigate were .70 and .50; although not high, they indicate there is true individual variability.

All three predictors introduced in the Level 2 model (second panel in Table 3.3) related significantly to the initial status or intercept. This is rather trivial

---

[5]The outcome variable was not centered; therefore, the intercept corresponds to an estimate for Year 2. Because scores decreased from Year 3 to Year 5, the estimate for Year 2 is higher than the estimate for Year 3, and therefore much higher than the actual Year 2 score.

TABLE 3.3
Linear Model of Growth in CSVI, Year 3 to Year 5

(a) Unconditional Model (Level 1 Model)

Fixed Effect	Coefficient	se	t Ratio
Initial status	5.97	.29	20.41**
Growth rate	−.71	.06	−12.69**

Random Effect	Variance Component	df	χ^2
Initial status	5.21	86	286.30**
Growth rate	.14	86	173.53**

Reliability of OLS Regression Coefficient Estimate

Initial status	.70
Growth rate	.50

(b) Effects of Age, CEFT, and P3 − P1 (Level 2 model)

Fixed Effect	Coefficient	se	t Ratio
Model for initial status			
Base	−1.90	1.10	−1.73
Age	.76	.09	8.95**
CEFT	.43	.20	2.20*
Diff P3 − P1	1.93	.22	8.97**
Model for growth rate			
Base	.50	.27	1.88
Age	−.11	.02	−5.25**
CEFT	−.07	.05	−1.47
Diff P3 − P1	−.38	.05	−7.28**

(c) Variance Explained in Initial Status and Growth Rate as a Result of Age, CEFT, and P3 − P1

Model	Initial Status	Growth Rate
Unconditional	5.21**	.14**
Conditional on Age and CEFT	.06	.003
Proportion of variance explained	98%	97%

*$p < .05$. **$p < .01$.

inasmuch as Age and the progression from Year 1 to Year 3 are concerned: Older children, field-independent children as well as children who had progressed more obtained higher scores on Year 3. Results show that Age and Progression, but not FDI, also related significantly to the rate of growth. The negative value indicates that, consistent with our hypothesis, the children who regressed more were those who progressed more on the first 3 years; they were also older. Finally, the estimated residual variances for both models (third panel) can be compared; the residual variances in the Level 2 model were .06 and .003, respectively. When combined, the three predictors accounted for a high reduction of the initial variance (98% and 97% for initial status and rate of growth, respectively).

These results are summarized in Table 3.4, together with the five other analyses. The estimates of reliability tended to be low in the other tasks. This supports our intent to conduct future analyses on estimates of latent ability rather than on observed scores. For the time being, results should be taken with some reservations. The unconditional models showed that, in all analyses, children varied significantly in initial status, which is not surprising; however, despite the impression left by the visual inspection of individual curves, individual differences in growth rates were less striking. They were significant for CSVI, as already discussed, and for the second part of Peanut-C, but not for Peanut-P. This may be due to the fact that the change from Year 3 to Year 5 was not linear. Again not surprisingly, Age was a significant predictor of initial status; however, Age did not predict growth rate, except for CSVI. For this latter task, older children tended to progress more from Year 1 to Year 3, and, as mentioned, to regress more from Year 3 to Year 5. Contrary to our hypothesis, the effects of FDI were not strong; they showed only for Year 1 in Peanut-P and for Year 3 in CSVI, and did not account for the rate of change. Finally, as expected, the rate of progression from Year 1 to Year 3 had a strong impact not only on the initial status, but also on the rate of change from Year 3 to Year 5. In all three tasks, the children who showed the stronger progression during the first 3 years regressed more from Year 3 on.

CONCLUSION

The objective of this chapter is to give a general overview of the results obtained in administering a number of attentional capacity tasks each year, on 5 consecutive years, to children ages 5 to 10 at the onset of the study. Three series of questions were asked, concerning the between-task relationships and their stability, the developmental change observed, and the extent of individual differences. Confirmatory factor analyses showed that, despite changes in the tasks, they all seemed to address the same underlying processes because a single factor was sufficient to account for their covariance; furthermore, the covariance structure proved stable across years. Of course, the age differences within the sample account for a good part of the variance, whether cross-sectionally or longitudinally. Nevertheless, the single factor attested by the confirmatory factor analyses did not merely reflect a general, theoretically undefined developmental factor. When other developmental tasks such as CEFT or the Raven's Progressive Matrices were taken into consideration, a two-factor solution proved more adequate. This shows that, congruent with neo-Piagetian hypotheses, attentional capacity

TABLE 3.4

Growth Rate in the Three Attentional Capacity Tasks: Summary of the HLM Analyses

	Peanut–P		Peanut–C		CSVI	
	Years 1–3	Years 3–5	Years 1–3	Years 3–5	Years 1–3	Years 3–5
Interindividual differences in (unconditional model):						
Initial status	Yes**	Yes*	Yes**	Yes**	Yes**	Yes**
Growth rate	No	No	No	Yes*	Yes**	Yes**
t ratios for the effect of:						
Age on initial status	9.23**	6.61**	8.28**	5.28**	9.56**	9.95**
Age on growth rate	.44	–1.70	1.23	–1.48	2.14*	–5.25**
CEFT on initial status	2.02	–.47	–.26	–.85	1.56	2.20*
CEFT on growth rate	–.28	1.76	2.09*	1.85	1.23	–1.47
(P3 – P1) on initial status	—	5.47**	—	6.76**	—	8.97**
(P3 – P1) on growth rate	—	–5.09**	—	–5.70**	—	–7.28**
Reduction in variance brought by Level 2 variables and level of significance of remaining variance:						
In initial status	85%*	94%	96%	98%	82%*	98%
In growth rate	0%	0%	0%	93%	17%**	97%

Note. (P3 – P1) stands for the difference between Year 3 and Year 1.
*p < .05. **p < .01.

tasks constitute good developmental tasks. Results are also in accord with other studies that showed, in adults, the existence of a general memory factor (e.g., Kyllonen & Christal, 1990).

This does not mean that interindividual differences are not important. On the contrary, HLM analyses showed that individual variability is important, not only in initial status, but also in the developmental growth curves. In the latter case, individual differences were not always significant, but this may have been due to a relative lack of reliability of our measures. Combining the results of the longitudinal structural equations model and of the HLM analyses, it can be concluded that age accounts for a good part of the variance, but is not sufficient. The number of variables that could serve as predictors of individual differences was limited in the study; it is therefore difficult to explore further sources. Neither gender nor socioeconomic status, traditionally used when raising the issue of interindividual differences, had any effect.

The initial objective of the study was to test the neo-Piagetian hypothesis that there are developmental stages of a 2-year duration. Results did not support this hypothesis; in particular the latent growth curve analyses showed that a staged model provided a poor fit, even when tested on only the 6–10-year-olds, who should have progressed in a similar manner. However, it is only fair to the neo-Piagetian models to say that the experimental procedure adopted in the present study does not provide a clear test. There are at least two reasons for that, namely learning effects and the situational changes introduced after 3 years. The repeated administration of the tasks induced evident practice effects, already apparent on the second year; incidentally, this is one of the reasons why modifications were made, because there was a risk of ceiling effects after Year 3. Pascual-Leone (e.g., Pascual-Leone & Goodman, 1979) warned that step functions cannot be observed when learning effects are combined with strictly developmental change. Indeed, his theory postulates that the first (odd) year of a stage corresponds to an increase in M-power, whereas the second (even) year consists in a consolidation made possible by the greater importance taken by a learning operator. In particular, subjects are then better able to assemble better, more efficient executive schemes. Thus, the combination of M–power and learning leads to a hypothesis of the linear developmental curve observed in the first 3 years of our study. Attentional capacity tasks should not be used more than once if they are to provide a good measure of M-capacity. In a longitudinal study, different, equivalent tasks should be used. However, truly equivalent tasks are scarce, as is well demonstrated in the literature. This makes an assessment of developmental change extremely difficult, when the objective of the study is to assess the extent and form of intraindividual developmental change, and not only the stability of individual differences.

The importance of situational variability was also clearly shown in the present project: The modifications introduced in the tasks caused important inflexion points in the growth curves. They did not only counteract the effects of learning by preventing the subjects to continue using the facilitating strategies elaborated over the previous years, but probably raised the intrinsic difficulty level of the tasks. Three modifications proved disruptive: the reduction in exposure time and the construction of new items in the CSVI task, and the computerization of the Peanut tasks. Although explanations can be found within the framework of neo-Piagetian theories, they are mainly post hoc, particularly as regards the Peanut tasks. Each of the three effects requires a different explanation. Obviously, the easiest one to account for is the regression caused by a tachistoscopic presentation in the CSVI task; this effect was predictable within Pascual-Leone's theory. In this case, we deliberately resorted to this mode of presentation to limit the ceiling effects that were appearing in the oldest cohort. Yet, it complicates the comparison of levels of performances across years, although the theoretical type of scoring (k estimates) proposed by Pascual-Leone (1970) allows us to bridge the two types of tasks. The further regression brought about on Year 5 by the reduction in the number of items in the CSVI task was less predictable. It is not due to a mere reduction in the length of the task, but probably to the fact that the construction of new items led to a redistribution of all instances across classes. This modification is likely to have further prevented chunking strategies that subjects might still use despite the brief presentation time. Learning effects may no longer be effective on Year 5, which in turn could explain why results for this year are different in the confirmatory factor analyses. As support for this hypothesis, it is only for Year 5 and for Year 1 that the theoretical scores predicted by Pascual-Leone in terms of k estimates on the basis of age found empirical support; for the 3 other years, they were too high.

Finally, the importance of the change caused by the computerization of the Peanut tasks was the least predictable. Again, it is probably not the computerization that was responsible for the regression in performance, but rather the change in the response mode. In the manual version, children had to place chips on a sheet of paper by a simple motor movement. In the computerized task, they had to use a computer mouse. Of course, some children probably lacked practice. However, monitoring a mouse requires processing resources that are no longer available for handling the Peanut task. An explanation was previously offered that drew on Pascual-Leone's model and on Baddeley's model. A series of experimentations is currently in progress to investigate this hypothesis further and more systematically.

ACKNOWLEDGMENTS

This research was supported by grants from the Fonds National Suisse de la Recherche Scientifique (grants 1.437–0.86 and 11.27671.89). We thank Professors J. Pascual-Leone and R. Case for permission and advice in using their tasks, and R. Kail for useful comments on a first version of this chapter. We would also like to thank Professor G. Rudinger for his help in conducting confirmatory factor analyses and latent growth curve analyses both in Geneva and in Bonn where he agreed to host C. Bailleux while she was holding an ESF fellowship. We are grateful to Sylvain Dionnet, Ineke Keizer, Thierry Lecerf, Santino Livoti, Caroline Moutia, Francisco Pons, Ana Sancho, Anne Spira, and Laurence Thomas who were actively involved in the collection and analysis of the data. Finally, we also want to thank the children who willingly participated in the study, despite its length and, at times, repetitive aspects.

REFERENCES

Alsaker, F. (1992). Modeling quantitative developmental change. In J. B. Asendorpf & J. Valsiner (Eds.), *Stability and change in development* (pp. 88–109). Newbury Park: Sage.

Baddeley, A. D. (1986). *Working memory*. Oxford, England: Oxford University Press.

Bryk, A. S., & Raudenbush, S. W. (1987). Application of hierarchical linear models to assessing change. *Psychological Bulletin, 101*, 147–158.

Bryk, A. S., & Raudenbush, S. W. (1992). *Hierarchical linear models: Applications and data analysis methods*. Newbury Park: Sage.

Case, R. (1974). Structures and strictures: Some functional limitations on the course of cognitive growth. *Cognitive Psychology, 6*, 544–573.

Case, R. (1985). *Intellectual development. Birth to adulthood*. New York: Academic Press.

Case, R. (1987). Neo-Piagetian theory: Retrospect and prospect. *International Journal of Psychology, 22*, 773–791.

Case, R. (1992a). Neo-Piagetian theories of child development. In R. J. Sternberg & C. A. Berg (Eds.), *Intellectual development* (pp. 161–196). Cambridge, England: Cambridge University Press.

Case, R. (1992b). Neo-Piagetian theories of intellectual development. In H. Beilin & P. B. Pufall (Eds.), *Piaget's theory: Prospects and possibilities* (pp. 61–104). Hillsdale, NJ: Lawrence Erlbaum Associates.

Case, R., Kurland, D. M., & Goldberg, J. (1982). Operational efficiency and the growth of short-term memory span. *Journal of Experimental Child Psychology, 33*, 386–404.

Chapman, M. (1987). Piaget, attentional capacity and the functional implications of formal structure. In H. W. Reese (Ed.), *Advances in child development and behavior* (Vol. 20, pp. 289–334). Orlando, FL: Academic Press.

Chapman, M. (1990). Cognitive development and the growth of capacity: Issues in neo-Piagetian theory. In J. T. Enns (Ed.), *The development of attention: Research and theory* (pp. 263–287). Amsterdam: North Holland.

Chapman, M., & Lindenberger, U. (1989). Concrete operations and attentional capacity. *Journal of Experimental Child Psychology, 47*, 236–258.

Daneman, M., & Carpenter, P. A. (1980). Individual differences in working memory and reading. *Journal of Verbal Learning and Verbal Behavior, 19*, 450–466.

Dasen, P. R., & de Ribaupierre, A. (1987). Neo-Piagetian theories: Cross-cultural and differential perspectives. *International Journal of Psychology, 22*, 793–832.

Fischer, K. W. (1980). A theory of cognitive development: The control and construction of hierarchies of skills. *Psychological Review, 87*, 477–531.

Fischer, K. W., & Silvern, L. (1985). Stages and individual differences in cognitive development. *Annual Review of Psychology, 36*, 613–648.

Halford, G. S. (1987). A structure-mapping approach to cognitive development. *International Journal of Psychology, 22*, 609–642.

Halford, G. S. (1993). *Children's understanding: The development of mental models*. Hillsdale, NJ: Lawrence Erlbaum Associates.

Hoppe-Graff, S. (1989). The study of transitions in development: Potentialities of the longitudinal approach. In A. de Ribaupierre (Ed.), Transition mechanisms in child development: The longitudinal perspective (pp. 1–30). New York: Cambridge University Press.

Kliegl, R., & Mayr, U. (1992). Commentary. Human Development, 35, 343–349.

Kyllonen, P., & Christal, R. E. (1990). Reasoning ability is (little more than) working-memory capacity?! Intelligence, 14, 389–433.

McArdle, J. J., & Epstein, D. (1987). Latent growth curves within developmental structural equations models. Child Development, 58, 110–133.

McLaughlin, G. H. (1963). Psycho-logic: A possible alternative to Piaget's formulation. British Journal of Educational Psychology, 33, 61–67.

Pascual-Leone, J. (1970). A mathematical model for the transition rule in Piaget's developmental stages. Acta Psychologica, 32, 301–345.

Pascual-Leone, J. (1987). Organismic processes for neo-Piagetian theories: A dialectical causal account of cognitive development. International Journal of Psychology, 22, 531–570.

Pascual-Leone, J. (1989). An organismic process model of Witkin's field-dependence–independence. In T. Globerson & T. Zelniker (Eds.), Cognitive style and cognitive development (pp. 36–70). Norwood, NJ: Ablex.

Pascual-Leone, J., & Baillargeon, R. (1994). Developmental measurement of mental attention. International Journal of Behavioral Development, 17, 161–200.

Pascual-Leone, J., & Goodman, D. R. (1979). Intelligence and experience: A neo-Piagetian approach. Instructional Science, 8, 301–367.

Pascual-Leone, J., & Ijaz, I. (1989). Mental capacity testing as a form of intellectual–developmental assessment. In R. J. Samuda, S. L. Kong, J. Cummins, J. Pascual-Leone, & J. Lewis (Eds.), Assessment and placement of minority students (pp. 143–171). Toronto: C. J. Hogrefe.

Pascual-Leone, J., & Johnson, J. (1991). The psychological unit and its role in task analysis: A reinterpretation of object permanence. In M. Chandler & M. Chapman (Eds.), Criteria for competence (pp. 153–187). Hillsdale, NJ: Lawrence Erlbaum Associates.

de Ribaupierre, A. (1993). Structural invariants and individual differences: On the difficulty of dissociating developmental and differential processes. In R. Case & W. Edelstein (Eds.), The new structuralism in cognitive development: Theory and research on individual pathways (Contributions to Human Development) (pp. 11–32). Basel, Switzerland: Karger.

de Ribaupierre, A., & Bailleux, C. (1992, September). Developmental change in a spatial task of attentional capacity: A comparison of two modes of response. Paper presented at the 5th European Developmental Conference, Seville, Spain.

de Ribaupierre, A., & Bailleux, C. (1993, August). Inter- and intra-individual variability in two neo-Piagetian working memory tasks. Paper presented at the 6th European Developmental Conference, Bonn, Germany.

de Ribaupierre, A., & Bailleux, C. (1994). Developmental change in a spatial task of attentional capacity: An essay toward an integration of two models of working memory. International Journal of Behavioral Development, 17, 5–35.

de Ribaupierre, A., Neirynck, I., & Spira, A. (1989). Interactions between basic capacity and strategies in children's memory: Construction of a developmental paradigm. Cahiers de Psychologie Cognitive, 9, 471–504.

de Ribaupierre, A., & Pascual-Leone, J. (1979). Formal operations and M-Power: A neo-Piagetian investigation. In D. Kuhn (Ed.), Intellectual development beyond childhood (New Directions in Child Development) (pp. 1–43). San Francisco: Jossey-Bass.

de Ribaupierre, A., & Pascual-Leone, J. (1984). Pour une intégration des méthodes en psychologie: Approches expérimentale, psycho-génétique et différentielle [For an integration of methods in psychology: Experimental, developmental, and differential approaches]. L'Année Psychologique, 84, 227–250.

de Ribaupierre, A., Rieben, L., & Lautrey, J. (1991). Developmental change and individual differences. A longitudinal study using Piagetian tasks. *Genetic, Social, and General Psychology Monographs, 117*, 285–311.

de Ribaupierre, A., & Spira, A. (1991, March). *Attentional capacity and cognitive development from 5 to 14: Overall presentation and some methodological problems.* Paper presented at the European Science Foundation Conference on Longitudinal Research: Challenges for the Future, Budapest, Hungary.

Rieben, L., de Ribaupierre, A., & Lautrey, J. (1990). Structural invariants and individual modes of processing: On the necessity of a minimally structuralist approach of development for education. *Archives de Psychologie, 58*, 29–53.

Rudinger, G., Andres, J., & Rietz, C. (1991). Structural equation models for studying intellectual development. In D. Magnusson, L. R. Bergman, G. Rudinger, & B. Törestad (Eds.), *Problems and methods in longitudinal research: Stability and change* (pp. 274–307). Cambridge, England: Cambridge University Press.

Schneider, W. (1993). The longitudinal study of motor development: Methodological issues. In A. F. Kalverboer, B. Hopkins, & R. Geuze (Eds), *Motor development in early and later childhood: Longitudinal approaches* (pp. 317–342). Cambridge, England: Cambridge University Press.

Schneider, W., & Weinert, F. E. (1989). Universal trends and individual differences in memory development. In A. de Ribaupierre (Ed.), *Transition mechanisms in child development. The longitudinal perspective* (pp. 68–106). New York: Cambridge University Press.

Spira, A., & Keizer, I. (1991, July). *Developmental changes versus retest effects in a working memory task.* Paper presented at the 11th meeting of the International Society for the Study of Behavioral Development, Minneapolis, MN.

Willett, J. B. (1994). Measurement of change. In T. Husèn & T. N. Postlewaite (Eds.), *The international encyclopedia of education* (Vol. 2, pp. 671–678). Oxford, England: Pergamon.

Witkin, H. A., Oltman, P. K., Raskin, E., & Karp, S. A. (1971). *Manual for Embedded Figures test.* Palo Alto, CA: Consulting Psychologists Press.

Chapter 4

Processing Speed, Memory, and Cognition

Robert Kail
Purdue University

A few hundred years before the beginning of modern psychology, Shakespeare claimed, "Wisely and slow: they stumble that run fast." More than a half-century ago, Gandhi noted, "There is more to life than increasing its speed." And, among contemporary psychologists, Sternberg (1984) observed that "to be quick is not always to be smart" (p. 282). Although the nuances of their remarks differ, each member of this esteemed trio of human observers is pointing to the liabilities of doing things rapidly. Much the same view is traditionally popular among developmental psychologists. At best, the speed with which children or adolescents respond is viewed as an incidental aspect of their behavior. At worst, rapid responding is thought to reflect immaturity and is contrasted with a more desirable reflective cognitive style.

My objective in this chapter is to demonstrate that the prevailing views are incorrect. I intend to show that speed of processing systematically changes as children develop and that these age-related changes in processing speed are beneficial in the sense that they facilitate performance in a number of domains. The chapter has two parts. The first provides a sketch of research concerning the nature of age-related change in processing speed. The second presents evidence suggesting that this increased speed of processing may be a key element of general improved performance in cognitive development.

THE NATURE OF AGE-RELATED CHANGE IN SPEED OF MENTAL PROCESSES

My research on the nature of age-related change in speed of mental processes followed three paths, each of which led me to believe that there are important general components to mental development. Specifically, I believe that a global mechanism limits the speed with which children and adolescents process information. The mechanism is not specific to particular tasks or domains but is, instead, a fundamental characteristic of the developing information-processing system.

The first systematic evidence implicating a global mechanism came from studies of developmental functions. The rationale behind these studies was that if speeds of different processes are limited by a common, global mechanism, then the same pattern of developmental change in processing speed is expected for these processes. This is the case because all processes would reflect change in the underlying global limiting mechanism. In contrast, if speeds of different processes reflect the acquisition of distinct task-specific skills, speeds of different processes would not necessarily change at the same rate. Of course, domain-specific skills could develop at the same rate, thereby producing a common developmental function, but this must be the exception rather than the rule for domain-specific mechanisms to have much heuristic value.

In fact, consistent with the view that some global mechanism is responsible for age differences in speed of processing, performance on many speeded tasks yields the same pattern of development: Processing time decreases steadily in middle childhood and continues to do so in late childhood and early adolescence, but much more slowly. For example, Fig. 4.1 illustrates developmental change in speeds of several cognitive processes. In each case, change is well described by an exponential function in which the parameter that controls rate of development is constant across the five processes. A common rate of exponential change across processes is consistent with the notion of a global mechanism but is not readily reconciled with the view that domain-specific factors are primarily responsible.

A second line of evidence is based on the method of statistical control (Kail & Salthouse, 1994). If two measures reflect a common age-related mechanism, then statistical control of the variance in one of the measures should greatly reduce the age-related variance in the other. According to this logic, if a global mechanism is responsible for age-related change in processing speed, then statistical control of one measure of processing speed should substantially reduce age effects in other measures. If, instead, each speeded process changes with age at a unique rate, then statistical control of one speeded measure should have a relatively small impact on the magnitude of age-related variance on other measures. In fact, Table 4.1 shows that age-related differences in speeds of various mental processes are typically attenuated by approximately 70% to 90% when the variance associated with speeded performance on the WISC Coding Task is eliminated. This result is readily reconciled with the notion of a substantial general component to the development of processing speed, but not with the view of domain-specific developmental change. At the same time, it is important to note that most of the residual r^2s are significantly greater than 0, meaning that the hypothesized general component does not account for all of the age-related variance in speed of processing; task-specific components are surely important, too.

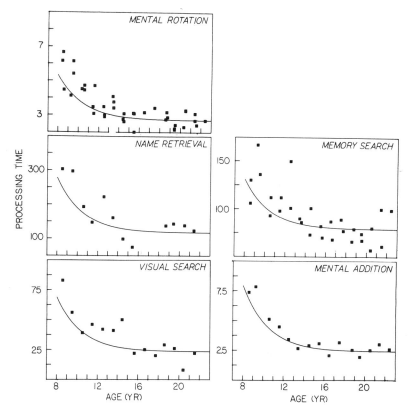

FIG. 4.1. Mean rate of processing for five different processes, as a function of age. Also shown are the best-fitting exponential functions. From Kail (1988). Copyright © 1988 by Academic Press. Reprinted with permission.

A third line of evidence is based on logic borrowed from studies of cognitive aging. Assume that adults' response time (RT_a) on a task involves several processes

$$RT_a = f + g + h + \ldots \tag{1}$$

where f is the time to execute process F, g is the time for process G, and so on. If children at age j execute each process more slowly, by the same factor, m_j, then the corresponding equation for children would be

$$RT_j = m_j f + m_j g + m_j h \ldots = m_j(f + g + h \ldots) \tag{2}$$

Rewriting Equation 2 to express children's RTs as a function of adults' RTs yields

$$RT_j = m_j RT_a \tag{3}$$

TABLE 4.1
R^2 Associated With Age in the Prediction of Task Performance
Before and After Statistical Control of Times on the WISC–R Coding Task

Task	R^2 for Age Alone	R^2 for Age after Coding	% Attenuation
Simple RT	.407	.089	78.1
Tapping	.309	.072	76.7
Pegboard	.398	.096	75.9
Name retrieval	.035	.015	57.1
Analogical reasoning	.293	.039	86.7
Matrix reasoning	.274	.018	93.4

Note. Adapted from Kail & Salthouse (1994).

Key predictions derived from Equation 3 are that children's RTs increase linearly as a function of adults' RTs from the corresponding experimental conditions and that the slope of this function, which estimates m_j, is greater than 1.

The predicted linear increase in children's RTs has been consistently found and the value of m_j declines exponentially with age to an asymptotic value of 1. Some of the initial evidence of this sort, shown in Fig. 4.2, came from a meta-analysis of studies of speeded performance that included nearly 2,000 pairs of RTs for 4- to 14-year-olds (Kail, 1991b). At each age, children's RTs increased linearly as a function of adults' RTs; the correlation between children's and adults' RTs was never less than .95. Furthermore, the slope of the linear function—which estimates m, the factor by which children respond more slowly than adults—changed substantially in early and middle childhood, but more slowly thereafter, a pattern that was well described by an exponential function (Kail, 1991b).

Equation 3 is also able to account for three other important phenomena associated with speeded processing, that is, practice, the speed–accuracy tradeoff, and variability in RTs. First, consider practice. Children, like adults, respond more rapidly with practice. These improvements are often attributed to more efficient processing, where efficiency means that fewer steps are required for task performance (Anderson, 1987). For example, if performance prior to practice involves the component times f, g, and h of Equation 1, performance after practice might be represented by k, the time to execute the single process that is now responsible for task performance. If the impact of practice is qualitatively the same for children and adults, then children's RTs should be given by the product of m and k. Thus, a single function should relate youth's and adults' RTs prior to and after practice. In fact, in studies of the impact of practice on performance on mental rotation tasks, a single function typically describes performance before and after practice (see Fig. 4.3a).

A similar prediction can be made for another common phenomenon, the trade-off between speed and accuracy. Children and adults can regulate their

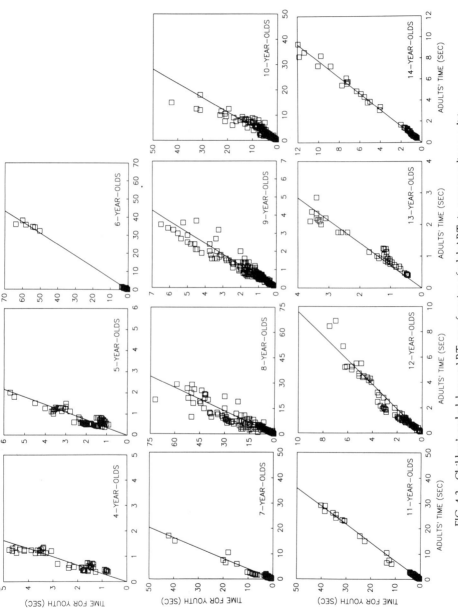

FIG. 4.2. Children's and adolescents' RTs as a function of adults' RTs in corresponding conditions. Also shown is the linear equation corresponding to Equation 3. From Kail (1991b). Copyright © 1991 by American Psychological Association. Reprinted with permission.

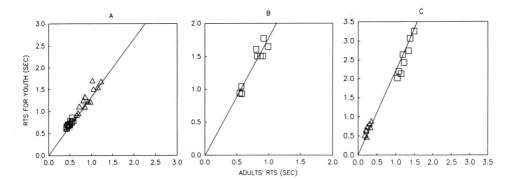

FIG. 4.3. Each panel depicts children's RTs as a function of adults' RTs in corresponding conditions, as well as the linear equation that corresponds to Equation 3. Panel a depicts the results of a study of mental rotation training in 13-year-olds and adults (Kail & Park, 1990); the triangles depict performance prior to practice and the squares, performance after practice. Panel b depicts the results of an unpublished study with 10-year-olds and adults on the impact of speed and accuracy instructions on speed of visual search. The squares closer to the origin represent means for conditions emphasizing speed; those further from the origin, conditions emphasizing accuracy. Panel c depicts the results of an unpublished study with 10-year-olds and adults of variability in mental-addition performance. The triangles depict children's standard deviations as a function of adults' standard deviations for six different sums; the squares, children's means as a function of adults' means.

response speed, emphasizing speed at the cost of accuracy or emphasizing accuracy at the cost of speed (e.g., Kail, 1985). The impact of these differing emphases on response time can be incorporated in Equations 1–3 by assuming that instructions simply introduce additional constants to both children's and adult's RTs. Emphasizing accuracy might increase RTs by a factor of 1.2 over RTs in a neutral condition. Emphasizing speed might decrease RTs by a factor of .8 relative to RTs in a neutral condition. If these constants are approximately the same for children and adults, the result is that across various speed and accuracy conditions, children's RTs should be greater than adults' RTs by the familiar m constant.

Figure 4.3b shows that these predictions were born out in a study in which 10-year-olds and adults performed a visual search task under instructions that emphasized speed, accuracy, or both speed and accuracy. RTs closer to the origin are from conditions that emphasized speed; those further away, from conditions that emphasized accuracy. A single linear function captures the increase in children's RTs as a function of adults' RTs across the three conditions. Thus, for different trade-offs between speed and accuracy, as was the case for the impact of training, Equation 3 adequately characterizes children's RTs.

The last phenomenon to be considered is the age-related decrease in variability of RTs that typically accompanies the age-related decrease in mean RTs. Typically, children's RTs are more variable than adults'. That is, the variability of raw RTs about an individual child's mean RT tends to be greater than the variability of an individual adult's RTs about his or her mean RT (Kerr, Davidson, Nelson, & Haley, 1982).

Equation 3 can readily account for this phenomenon. For any given condition, the standard deviation of a child's RTs should simply be the adult's standard deviation multiplied by the m constant. This is the case because all of the child's raw RTs will be multiplied by the constant m. Consequently, the child's standard deviation will simply be m times the adult standard deviation, reflecting the familiar fact that when all scores in a distribution are multiplied by a constant, the new standard deviation is simply the product of the original standard deviation and the constant. The implication is that means and standard deviations for children's and adults' RTs should be linked by a common function, with slope m. Figure 4.3c shows that this was the case in a study of mental addition by 10-year-olds and adults. The open squares, in the upper-right corner of the graph, show the now familiar increase in children's mean RTs as a function of adults' mean RTs. The novel result is in the lower-left corner, showing that children's standard deviations increase linearly as a function of adults' standard deviations in the same condition. And, as predicted, the data for means and standard deviations fall along a common function, with slope m.

In summary, three lines of evidence were described. First, speeds of different processes develop at a common exponential rate. Second, age-related variance in speeded measures is virtually eliminated through statistical control of other measures of processing speed. Third, children's RTs are often a simple multiple of adults' RTs in those same tasks or conditions, across a wide range of tasks and conditions. These findings appear to converge on the single conclusion that some sort of global mechanism limits the speed with which children process information. This mechanism changes exponentially with age and is manifest in children's performance on most speeded tasks.

Given this conclusion, three topics loom large on the research horizon. One is the nature of the global mechanism. Our initial hunch was that processing resources would be an ideal candidate for the proposed global mechanism. Generally, when greater processing resources can be allocated to performance, speed increases. Consequently, an age-related increase in the amount of processing resources could produce age-related increases in processing speed. However, this explanation rapidly ran aground. We performed dual-task experiments in which subjects performed a task alone as well as concurrently with another task. If both tasks required limited processing resources, then concurrent performance of the task should have been inferior to performance without the concurrent task, particularly so for children, whose resources are presumed to be more limited. However, the predicted pattern of interference did not emerge (Kail, 1991a).

In subsequent experimentation, we examined another possible candidate for the global model, loss of information in successive processing steps. This work was based on a model devised by Myerson and his colleagues (Myerson, Hale, Wagstaff, Poon, & Smith, 1990) to explain cognitive slowing that is associated with aging. In this model, information is lost at each step of processing—more rapidly by older adults—meaning that a processing step must wait longer for sufficient information to accrue to begin processing. These delays become progressively longer at successive steps of processing and the relative length is greater for older adults because they lose more information. This model predicts that young and older adults' RTs should be linked by a power function, which is typically the case (e.g., Myerson et al., 1990).

Applied to age-related change in processing speed during childhood and adolescence, the amount of information that is lost at each processing step would presumably decline with development in childhood and adolescence. The problem here is that the evidence indicates that the relation between children's and adults' RTs is linear, not a power function as predicted by the information-loss model (Kail, 1993).

Nevertheless, the information-loss model is useful in suggesting other possible sources of children's slower processing. In this model, RTs are derived from the following equation:

$$RT = \sum_{k=0}^{n=1} D/[I\,(1 - p)^k] \tag{4}$$

In this equation, D is the duration of a processing step when no information has been lost, I is the proportion of information that is encoded initially, p is the proportion of information that is lost during a processing step, and k denotes the number of processing steps. If children lose more information per step than young adults—that is, the p parameter is greater for children than for adults—then RTs for children would increase nonlinearly as a function of adults' RTs. The fact that the increase in children's RTs is linear implies that p, the loss rate, is the same for children and adults. However, age differences in either of the remaining parameters, D or I, yield a linear increase in children's RTs as a function of adults' RTs. If the D parameter were larger for children than for adults, this would mean that children execute processes more slowly than adults when no information has been lost. If the I parameter were less for children, this would mean that children encode less task-relevant information. Thus, the m constant described earlier could reflect either the ratio of the times taken by children and adults to execute a processing step when no information has been lost, or the ratio of the proportion of information encoded by adults and children.

Possible differences in the D parameter are not particularly enlightening: Here, age differences in overall RT are attributed to differences in times for individual processing steps, without any reasons as to why times for these steps should change with age. However, attributing age differences to the I parameter has more heuristic value because it links the present work to an extensive literature on age differences in encoding. That is, compared to adults, children often encode information less extensively, with the result that their performance is poorer than adults on a range of tasks (Siegler, 1989). Thus, age-related differences in the scope of encoding may account for a variety of developmental changes on speeded and nonspeeded tasks.

A second issue concerns domain-specific influences on speed of processing. Historically, global developmental mechanisms were pitted against domain-specific influences. For example, Piaget's explanations of children's performance in terms of global mechanisms were contrasted with information-processing accounts that included a number of task-specific processes. Of course, positing a global limiting mechanism does not preclude task- and domain-specific influences, any more than a general factor in intelligence precludes specific abilities. One of the current challenges for cognitive development research is to understand the connections between these global and domain-specific influences.

The third issue concerns the impact of these changes in speed of processing on cognitive development generally, an issue that is the focus of the remainder of this chapter.

IMPACT OF PROCESSING SPEED ON COGNITIVE DEVELOPMENT

When colleagues of Piagetian bent see results like those presented here, they often smile patronizingly and remind me that such exclusive emphasis on quantitative change is hardly the mark of a true developmentalist. Contextualist friends chide me, saying that pushing buttons in response to computer-presented stimuli is not chic in the current zeitgeist. My response to these criticisms—only partly facetious—is that life is one big speeded task. It is a basic fact of mental life that much cognitive processing is temporally limited; processing must occur in a finite window of time or it fails. Put another way, speed of processing may be critical whenever rate of stimulation or pacing of responses is externally controlled, or, more generally, whenever a number of activities must be completed in a fixed period. In these instances, slow processing speed may result in reduced performance because children or adolescents cannot complete the necessary components of task performance in the time allotted. Thus, I would claim that although the impact of limited processing speed is particularly salient in performance on speeded tasks, it is definitely not limited to those tasks.

Two examples illustrate the sort of influence suggested here. First, consider a rote-rehearsal strategy, in which items in a list are rehearsed in alternation with the encoding of new items. If children execute the components of rote rehearsal—that is, encoding and repetitive naming—less rapidly than adults, then children would complete fewer rehearsals in a fixed period of time and would probably recall less as a consequence. Second, consider the impact of word decoding speed on reading comprehension. If children decode words less rapidly than adults, then representations of previously decoded words may be lost from working memory before children can link these representations to generate meaning for a phrase or sentence.

In these examples, children's slower processing leads to poorer performance in situations that lack an obvious speeded component. In fact, neither example is hypothetical. Age-related change in speed of articulation accounts for a substantial portion of the variance in age-related change in memory span (Hitch, Halliday, & Littler, 1989; Nicolson, 1981). Similarly, speed of word decoding is often related, substantially, to measures of comprehension. Wolf and colleagues (Wolf, Bally, & Morris, 1986), for example, reported a correlation of −.54 between the speed with which 7- and 8-year-olds read individual words and scores on a standardized test of reading comprehension.

In these examples, quality of performance—memory span or reading comprehension—was related to the speed with which children could execute specific processes—articulation rate or word decoding. A more general view, however, is that speeds of these specific processes are limited by the global mechanism that was implicated in studies of age-related change in processing speed. That is, speeds of articulation and word recognition would be limited, in part, by this global mechanism. Increased processing speed with age would yield more rapid articulation and word decoding articulation, which, in turn, would yield more accurate retention and superior comprehension.

These examples lead to a general framework that is illustrated in Fig. 4.4. The essential idea is that processing speed becomes more rapid with age, reflecting

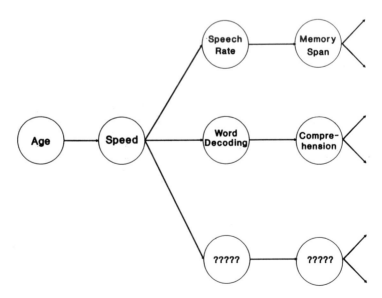

FIG. 4.4. A framework suggesting possible links between age-related change in processing speed and cognitive development generally.

changing limits of the global mechanism, meaning that processes responsible for performance on a particular task are executed more rapidly, resulting in superior performance. Recently, my colleagues and I attempted to flesh out this general framework, using the two domains illustrated in my examples, memory and reading comprehension. The initial work was done with memory, largely because the work by Hitch et al. (1989) provided such a natural and obvious point of departure. Recall that Hitch and his colleagues showed that age-related change in memory span is linked specifically to age-related increases in articulation rate, which reflect the rate with which information is refreshed in the articulatory rehearsal loop of working memory. A more general view would be that articulation rate is a reflection of general developmental change in processing speed. That is, increased processing speed would yield more rapid articulation, which, in turn, would yield more accurate retention. These relations are depicted in Fig. 4.5. In this framework, the effects of age on memory might be mediated entirely by a path that runs from age to processing speed to articulation rate to memory. However, other paths are also possible. Age might have direct effects on rate of articulation, perhaps reflecting an age-related increase in the familiarity of information to be remembered. Moreover, processing speed might have direct effects on memory in addition to those mediated by articulation rate. Age-related change in processing speed might also lead to more rapid initial encoding of stimuli, independent of the rate with which they are subsequently rehearsed. Finally, if global and specific processing speeds cannot account for all of the age-related variation in memory span, then age would be linked directly to span.

We evaluated this framework in several experiments (e.g., Kail, 1992). In the two most recent studies, Park and I (Kail & Park, 1994) tested 288 7- to 14-

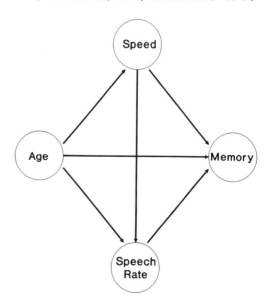

FIG. 4.5. A framework linking age, speed, articulation rate, and memory span that was evaluated in studies by Kail and Park (1994). Copyright © 1994 by Academic Press. Reprinted with permission.

year-olds and adults living in the United States, as well as 84 7- to 14-year-olds and adults living in Korea. All were tested with a set of tasks assessing the three primary constructs depicted in Fig. 4.5. For processing speed, subjects completed the Identical Pictures and Number Comparisons tasks, two measures of perceptual speed (French, Ekstrom, & Price, 1963); for rate of articulation, we measured the time to repeat sets of three letters or three digits aloud; finally, we assessed digit and letter spans in the standard way. From performance on these tasks, composite scores were created for each theoretical construct. For example, the speed composite was derived from performance on the Identical Pictures and Number Comparisons tasks. In both samples, age was positively correlated with memory span but negatively correlated with processing time and articulation time. These composite scores were then used to estimate coefficients for the paths linking the various constructs.

Results from both samples are shown in Table 4.2. As expected, the link between memory and speech rate was significant. Processing speed is linked significantly to speech rate but not to memory. This indicates that the impact of processing speed on memory is mediated entirely by increases in rate of articulation. However, also notice that the link between age and memory remains significant in both samples. This link means that other age-related variables not included in the general framework play a mediating role in the age-memory span relation (cf. Henry & Millar, 1991).[1]

Although this work establishes a specific link between processing speed and memory span, the influence of processing speed on memory need not be limited to memory span. On the contrary, processing speed may also be linked to other components of memory. For example, the model of working memory that includes the articulatory loop used to store phonological information also includes a visual-spatial sketchpad, ". . . a system especially well adapted to the temporary storage of spatial information, much as a pad of paper might be used by someone trying . . . to work out a geometric puzzle" (Baddeley, 1986, p. 109). As with the articulatory loop, information is lost rapidly from the visual–spatial sketchpad. However, loss can be avoided if the image is regenerated using visual rehearsal. Presumably, just as the speed with which information is articulated in the phonological loop predicts verbal span, the speed with which images are regenerated in the visual–spatial sketchpad might predict visual-spatial span.

Our second effort to place processing speed in a broad cognitive context involved reading. Several investigators reported that the speed with which children name familiar objects is correlated with measures of decoding skills. Wolf et al. (1986), for example, reported a correlation of .66 between the speed with

---

[1]The only difference between the samples was the presence of a significant relation between age and speech rate in the Korean sample but not in the U.S. sample. This could reflect phenomena specific to spoken Korean, but it also may represent a Type II error, as this link was significant in a previous study with a U.S. sample (Kail, 1992).

TABLE 4.2
Coefficients for Paths in Figure 4.5

Path	Coefficient	
	U.S. Sample	Korean Sample
Age → speed	−.77**	−.76**
Age → speech rate	.07	−.37**
Age → memory	.21*	.46**
Speed → speech rate	.50**	.31*
Speed → memory	.09	.19
Speech rate → memory	−.35**	−.33**

Note. From Kail and Park (1994).
*p < .05 **p < .01

which kindergarten children named familiar letters and digits and their perform-ance on a word recognition task in Grade 2. Word recognition was measured by the speed with which children read lists of words and pseudowords, but the same relation obtains when word recognition is assessed with untimed tasks. Relevant evidence comes from work by Spring and Davis (1988) with children in grades 4–10. With age controlled, digit naming speed correlated .50 with scores on the Word Recognition Subtest task of the PIAT (in which children point to a picture that denotes a word spoken by the experimenter). That is, children who named digits more rapidly typically recognized more words than did children who named digits slowly. In addition, although there was a corre-lation of .23 between digit naming speed and scores on the Reading Compre-hension Subtest of the PIAT, this correlation was attributable entirely to the variance that these measures shared with word-recognition scores. That is, the correlation between naming speed and comprehension approximated zero with word recognition partialed out. In summary, rapid naming of digits predicted word recognition, which predicted comprehension.

Spring and Davis (1988), like others before them (e.g., Wolf et al., 1986) believed that ". . . continuous digit naming speed is an index of the automaticity with which letter codes are accessed in memory, and that automatization of this process is a prerequisite for the accurate performance of certain other higher level reading processes . . ." (p. 330). Thus, their interpretation of these results was that children who access letter codes automatically are more likely to rec-ognize words, and these same children better understand what they read.

A somewhat different view, based on the conceptual framework developed here, is that performance on tasks involving rapid naming of familiar stimuli such as digits and letters is under the influence of the global mechanism that limits performance on all speeded tasks. That is, access to letter codes becomes more rapid with age because of age-related change in this global mechanism, not only because recognition of individual characters is now automatic.

Figure 4.6 can be used to illustrate the contrasts between these two views. In both views, rapid naming should predict word recognition, which should predict comprehension. The views differ in the antecedents of rapid naming. According to the view developed throughout this chapter, measures of global processing speed should predict rapid naming; that is, more rapid naming is simply one more manifestation of age-related change in processing speed. In contrast, if rapid naming reflects automatic access to characters, measures of global processing speed need not predict naming speed because automaticity is based on an individual's experience, not his or her age. That is, although there is hardly consensus concerning the exact nature of automatic processing, there is agreement that such processing depends upon experience, practice, or training in specific domains (Logan, 1988). Consequently, frequency of exposure to printed matter should predict speed of naming letters and digits but age or global processing speed should not.

Links between these constructs were examined in a study by Kail and Hall (1994) in which 144 8- to 13-year-olds were tested. All were administered the Reading Recognition and Comprehension Subtests from the PIAT. In the former, children read individual words aloud; in the latter, they read a sentence silently, then select the picture that depicts the meaning of the sentence. In addition, we administered three of the naming tasks that had been used in earlier studies:

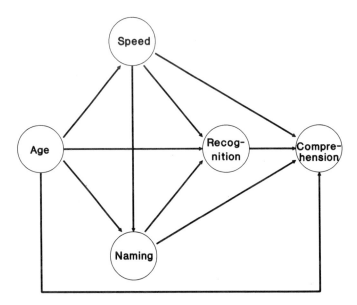

FIG. 4.6. A proposed model of possible causal connections between age, global speed of processing, naming time, reading recognition, and reading comprehension that was evaluated by Kail & Hall (1994). Copyright © 1994 by American Psychological Association. Reprinted with permission.

TABLE 4.3
Coefficients for Paths in Figure 4.6

Path	Coefficient
Age → speed	−.70**
Age → naming time	.02
Age → recognition	.46**
Age → comprehension	.09
Speed → naming time	.77**
Speed → recognition	−.10
Speed → comprehension	.04
Naming → recognition	−.33**
Naming → comprehension	−.07
Recognition → comprehension	.77**

Note. From Kail and Hall (1994).
**$p < .01$

naming digits, letters, and colors. In each case, we measured the amount of time that it took children to name 50 exemplars of the stimuli that were printed on a page. In addition, we administered three measures of perceptual speed: the Visual Matching and Cross-Out Tasks from the Revised Woodcock-Johnson Tests of Cognitive Ability as well as the Coding task from the WISC-R. For the naming and processing speed tasks, composite measures were created, using the procedures that I previously described. As expected, age was positively correlated with scores on the two PIAT reading tests but was correlated negatively with the speed and naming subtasks. More interesting were the results of the path analysis, shown in Table 4.3. Five of the path coefficients were significant. Three replicate previous findings. The link between age and processing time replicates the findings of the memory studies that I just described. In addition, naming times predicted reading recognition, which predicted comprehension, but naming time did not predict comprehension, a pattern that replicates the findings of Spring and Davis (1988).

More important for the issue that motivated the study, naming times were predicted by processing speed times, as would be predicted by the view that naming times are limited by the global mechanism. However, naming times were not predicted by age, as would be expected if naming times reflected age-related reading experience that results in automatic access to codes for familiar stimuli. Finally, the link between age and recognition was significant, indicating that some reliable age-related variation in recognition that was not captured by either processing time or naming time. Thus, with one minor exception, the present results can be summarized quite succinctly: Age leads to more rapid processing speed, which, in turn, leads to more rapid naming, higher reading recognition scores, and higher reading comprehension scores. The exception is the path between age and reading recognition.

CONCLUDING REMARKS

Each of the two parts of this chapter leads to a simple and straightforward conclusion. The research described in the first part of this chapter points to a common, nonspecific component in age-related change in the speed with which people process information. The research described in the second part of the chapter illustrates that the impact of processing speed is not limited to RT tasks or to other settings in which people are encouraged to respond rapidly. Instead, its influence was demonstrated on memory and reading comprehension, in each case mediated by other variables.

Given these findings, it seems reasonable to propose that processing speed may be one of several plausible successors to traditional developmental mechanisms such as differentiation, assimilation, and accommodation, which are notoriously difficult to operationalize. Processing speed seems to be a plausible candidate, because its course of development is quite systematic and its impact is pervasive. Furthermore, it can be linked naturally to another developmental mechanism that figured prominently in modern neo-Piagetian theories (e.g., Case, 1985): working memory (or short-term storage space). As shown in Fig. 4.7, age-related change in speed of processing may result directly in developmental change because processes are executed more rapidly; it may also influence change indirectly by improving the functioning of other developmental mechanisms.

This framework, in which processing speed and working memory are key mechanisms of change, has several attractive features. First, with speed and memory at the core, it can help to explain a wide range of cognitive developmental change. Second, the framework can be easily elaborated to incorporate

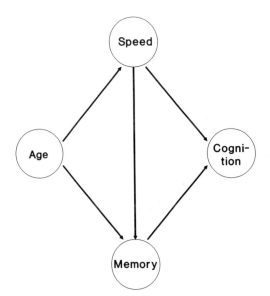

FIG. 4.7. A general framework in which processing speed and working memory are key and complementary growth mechanisms.

additional mediating variables that turn out to be crucial in particular domains. Third, the framework is also useful in understanding cognitive aging (Salthouse, 1992) and thus provides the basis for life-span developmental analyses.

My enthusiasm for this general approach is based largely on its potential rather than its documented successes. But even if the framework should prove to be wrong, we will have gained much by focusing our efforts on broader developmental issues concerning general connections between age, memory, speed of processing, and cognitive change in an assortment of domains.

ACKNOWLEDGMENTS

The research described here was supported by Grant No. 19447 from the National Institute of Child Health and Human Development. I am grateful to Anik de Ribaupierre for her comments on a previous draft of this chapter.

REFERENCES

Anderson, J. R. (1987). Skill acquisition: Compilation of weak-method problem solutions. *Psychological Review, 94*, 192–210.

Baddeley, A. (1986). *Working Memory.* Oxford, England: Clarendon.

French, J. W., Ekstrom, R. B., & Price, L. A. (1963). *Kit of reference tests for cognitive factors.* Princeton, NJ: Educational Testing Service.

Case, R. (1985). *Intellectual development.* Orlando, FL: Academic Press.

Henry, L. A., & Millar, S. (1991). Memory span increase with age: A test of two hypotheses. *Journal of Experimental Child Psychology, 51*, 459–484.

Hitch, G. J., Halliday, M. S., & Littler, J. E. (1989). Item identification and rehearsal rate as predictors of memory span in children. *Quarterly Journal of Experimental Psychology, 41A*, 321–337.

Kail, R. (1985). Development of mental rotation: A speed-accuracy study. *Journal of Experimental Child Psychology, 40*, 181–192.

Kail, R. (1988). Developmental functions for speeds of cognitive processes. *Journal of Experimental Child Psychology, 45*, 339–364.

Kail, R. (1991a). Controlled and automatic processing during mental rotation. *Journal of Experimental Child Psychology, 51*, 337–347.

Kail, R. (1991b). Developmental change in speed of processing during childhood and adolescence. *Psychological Bulletin, 109*, 490–501.

Kail, R. (1992). Processing speed, speech rate, and memory. *Developmental Psychology, 28*, 899–904.

Kail, R. (1993). Processing time changes globally at an exponential rate during childhood and adolescence. *Journal of Experimental Child Psychology, 56*, 254–265.

Kail, R., & Hall, L. K. (1994). Processing speed, naming speed, and reading. *Developmental Psychology, 30*, 949–954.

Kail, R., & Park, Y. (1990). Impact of practice on speed of mental rotation. *Journal of Experimental Child Psychology, 49*, 227–244.

Kail, R., & Park, Y. (1994). Processing time, articulation time, and memory span. *Journal of Experimental Child Psychology, 57*, 281–291.

Kail, R., & Salthouse, T. A. (1994). Processing speed as a mental capacity. *Acta Psychologica, 86*, 199–225.

Kerr, B., Davidson, J., Nelson, J., & Haley, S. (1982). Stimulus and response contributions to the children's reaction-time repetition effect. *Journal of Experimental Child Psychology, 34*, 526–541.

Logan, G. D. (1988). Toward an instance theory of automatization. *Psychological Review, 95*, 492–527.

Myerson, J., Hale, S., Wagstaff, D., Poon, L. W., & Smith, G. A. (1990). The information loss model: A mathematical theory of age-related cognitive slowing. *Psychological Review, 97*, 475–487.

Nicolson, R. (1981). The relationship between memory span and processing speed. In M. P. Friedman, J. P. Das, & N. O'Connor (Eds.), *Intelligence and learning* (pp. 179–183). New York: Plenum.

Salthouse, T. A. (1992). *Mechanisms of age-cognition relations in adulthood.* Hillsdale, NJ: Lawrence Erlbaum Associates.

Siegler, R. S. (1989). Mechanisms of cognitive development. *Annual Review of Psychology, 40*, 353–379.

Spring, C., & Davis, J. M. (1988). Relations of digit naming speed with three components of reading. *Applied Psycholinguistics, 9*, 315–334.

Sternberg, R. J. (1984). Toward a triarchic theory of human intelligence. *The Behavioral and Brain Sciences, 7*, 269–315.

Wolf, M., Bally, H., & Morris, R. (1986). Automaticity, retrieval processes, and reading: A longitudinal study in average and impaired readers. *Child Development, 57*, 988–1000.

Chapter 5

From Presentation Time to Processing Time: A Psychophysics Approach to Episodic Memory

Reinhold Kliegl
Max Planck Institute for Human Development and Education, Berlin

Manipulations of presentation time have a long history in research on the development of memory, with a number of paradoxical results deriving from methodological shortcomings as well as from insufficient theoretical specifications. After a look at some of the problems in earlier research, a psychophysics approach to investigate episodic memory functions is presented in which criterion-referenced manipulation of presentation time is used to estimate the effects of experimental manipulations and the effects of individual differences. *Criterion-referenced presentation time* (CRPT), defined as the time required to score at an a priori specified level of accuracy, is interpreted as a preliminary indicator of internal processing time. CRPTs are shown to be valid predictors of traditional measures of memory accuracy. Moreover, an extension of this psychophysics approach yields estimates of complete condition-specific time-accuracy functions and of function-specific processing times (plus other parameters) for individual subjects. It is argued that both from a cognitive and a developmental perspective it is often advantageous to trade experimental equivalence in presentation times for functional equivalence in accuracy of performance; this applies not only to episodic memory processes.

THE MIXED MESSAGES OF PRESENTATION TIMES

Presentation time is an important variable in memory research because it limits the processing of information in working memory. The general expectation is that memory accuracy is monotonically related to presentation time, with longer presentation times leading to better performance. Consequently, manipulations of presentation time can be considered manipulations of general task difficulty: the shorter the presentation time, the more severe the limit on working memory, the worse the performance. Empirical results are generally consistent with this line of reasoning.

The notion that short presentation times imply high task difficulty led to specific expectations in developmental research: The more difficult a task, the larger age differences are expected to be; therefore, shorter presentation times should yield larger age differences than longer ones. For example, we initially thought of manipulations of presentation times as an instantiation of testing-the-limits, with especially large age differences predicted for short presentation times (Kliegl, Smith, & Baltes, 1989). This position was also consistent with the view by Craik and Rabinowitz (1984, 1985; Rabinowitz, 1989) and Bäckman (1986), that longer presentation times represent a higher degree of environmental support by reducing the demands on limited cognitive resources. Higher support is expected to decrease the negative effect of age on memory. A decrease in age differences with longer presentation times was also postulated by Burke and Light (1981) and Simon (1979).

In the field of cognitive aging, empirical support for this position was scant for episodic memory (for a recent review, see Craik & Jennings, 1992). The dominant result (aside from the usual main effect) was no Age × Time interaction (e.g., Kliegl et al., 1989), or interactions opposite to the expected pattern (i.e., age differences were larger for long presentation times; e.g., Craik & Rabinowitz, 1985; Thompson & Kliegl, 1991). Given these inconsistencies, the developmental implications of the relationship between presentation time and recall is in need of re-evaluation.

A THEORETICAL FRAMEWORK

The confusing state of affairs regarding the direction of effects of presentation time in age-comparative studies can be resolved in a model that assumes (a) a minimum amount of presentation time is required to initiate task-relevant memory processes, (b) beyond this threshold, presentation time is translated into constructing stable memory traces, and (c) after a certain maximum amount of presentation time there is little to be gained by having more presentation time available (Kliegl, Mayr, & Krampe, 1994). Figure 5.1 illustrates this conception assuming a negative exponential function for converting presentation time into memory strengths (recall probability) up to an asymptotic maximum strength.

The assumption that presentation time is converted into memory strength highlights the role of a time constant in these models that I call *processing time*. It is the reciprocal value of the slope (steepness) of the curves in Fig. 5.1. Traditionally, the slopes are interpreted as rates; rates are scaled in *unit per time*.

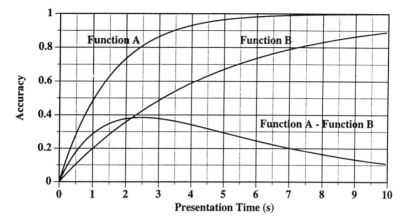

FIG. 5.1. Time-accuracy functions based on negatively accelerated exponential functions (Function A and Function B) and the corresponding vertical difference function.

Thus, the reciprocal value is a measure of *time per unit*; processing times were 1.5 sec and 4.5 sec for Functions A and B of Fig. 5.1, respectively. Thinking in terms of processing time instead of rates has two advantages. First, mental schemata imprinted on us by decades of response-latency research can be transferred: Large processing times are characteristic of more difficult tasks, less able groups, and early stages of practice. In Function B of Fig. 5.1, more processing time is needed to reduce the error probability by a constant proportion of the level of accuracy already attained than is the case for Function A. Second, a latent time measure of memory efficiency allows us to think about developmental differences in terms of cognitive slowing in adult development, or speed-up of information processing in child development. It represents an attempt to operationalize time as an external resource of cognitive processing that can be tracked with respect to general, domain-specific and process-specific effects of development (e.g., Kail, 1991; Salthouse, 1985). In other words, we define a metric for describing the efficiency of cognitive performance at different levels of generality.

The proposal to trace age-related memory differences to specific or general slowing of cognitive processing, to my knowledge, was first advanced in the context of models of short-term or working memory. Salthouse (1980) and Waugh and Barr (1980) postulated differences in rehearsal rate as the source of age differences (see also Baddeley, Thomson, & Buchanan, 1975; Balota & Duchek, 1988; Hasselhorn, 1988). Speech rate served as an indicator of rehearsal rate in these studies. Only recently was this idea generalized to episodic memory in terms of age differences in elaboration rate (cf. Kausler, 1991; Kliegl et al., 1989; Salthouse, 1985; Salthouse & Kail, 1983). This conceptual extension was made without much empirical support.

How might one explain the systematic relation between recall accuracy and presentation time? What are the theoretical mechanisms? In memory tasks conducted in our laboratory, subjects have to forge a mental image between two words, typically between a location cue such as church, museum, and so forth, and a concrete randomly selected noun such as tiger or car. If it takes young adults 1.5 sec and old adults 4.5 sec to establish such a relation, then, if both are given 9 sec, the young will have forged three times as many elaborations (six) than the old adults, who would only have had time for two; with identical presentation times, young adults' recall should be much better than that of old adults. Note that with this kind of reasoning we explain age differences in memory accuracy in terms of processing time: The less time one needs to generate an elaboration, the more of them can be generated in a fixed amount of time. The search for new elaborations probably becomes more difficult; it is hard not to think of the same elaborations again and again. Previously used thoughts or images may contribute negligibly, if at all, to the strength of the trace to be constructed. In this case, the relation between presentation time and accuracy will take the form of a negatively accelerated exponential function as shown in Fig. 5.1. The negative exponential function is compatible with the stochastic replacement model of learning; the assumption is that sampled images (elaborations) are put back into the memory store (e.g., Restle & Greeno, 1970). Therefore, the likelihood of resampling the same images or thoughts increases across time. Consequently, there will be diminishing returns of elaborative processing cycles as presentation time is extended.

In the context of developmental research, the model can account for an increase, a decrease, and the absence of age differences in correct recall across presentation time—independent of possible problems of statistical power or floor and ceiling effects. Figure 5.1 contains a function depicting the difference between Function A and Function B. Assume Function A and Function B represent performance of high ability (e.g., young) and low ability (e.g., old) adults. Whether we obtain an increase or a decrease of the age difference in accuracy by extending presentation time, or whether or not there is an interaction between age and presentation time depends on the times used. If we sample times from the segment left of the peak of the difference function we observe an increase, if we sample from the segment to the right the age difference decreases, and it will appear to be independent of presentation time if we use times with identical difference scores from the left and the right of the peak. If accuracy is determined by the stochastic sampling of images, these interactions (or their absence) would be spurious; they are the consequence of a difference in the processing time required for one elaborative cycle. Thus, what might look like a presentation-time specific age difference in terms of absolute accuracy differences between age groups could be the consequence of age-related slowing in sampling of images.

Although the model was described in terms of encoding operations, it does not fix the age difference in the encoding stage. For example, in Fig. 5.1, Function A could represent performance for a cued and Function B performance for a free recall format. The effect of this experimental manipulation would also be reflected in a difference of the fundamental processing-time parameter: More presentation time is required for the same level of accuracy to overcome the greater difficulty of free-recall compared to cued-recall retrieval. Moreover, sampling of ideas for the construction of images during encoding requires retrieval from memory. Thus, longer processing times associated with elaborative cycles may reflect a retrieval problem embedded in the encoding phase. Any experimental or organismic manipulation impeding performance in traditional experimental designs will increase the time demand for equal accuracy. In summary, the processing-time constant governing the translation of presentation time into accuracy (precisely, the proportional reduction of error probability) is not necessarily tied to a particular processing stage. As is shown in the course of this chapter, however, its determination promises to alleviate methodological problems that constrained the interpretation of developmental differences in the past.

METHODOLOGICAL PROBLEMS OF INFERRING PROCESSING TIMES FROM PRESENTATION TIMES

There have been few attempts to map developmental differences in episodic memory onto differences in such processing times. One reason may be that the traditional approach is to use presentation time as a proxy for processing time. In other words, manipulations of presentation time were interpreted as direct manipulations of processing time. This would be true only if the function mapping presentation time into processing time were strictly linear but, unfortunately, this is unlikely to be the case. There is still a lack of good empirical indicators of processing time for memory-related processes (Salthouse, 1985). The main point of the following argument is that there are problems inherent to the experimental designs involving manipulations of presentation time for the investigation of memory processes. After illustrating a few such problems with data from our own studies, we describe an alternative approach, consistent with the psychophysics tradition of experimental psychology.

Functional Limits of Processing: Floor and Ceiling Effects

Figure 5.2 (top panel) shows performance at the end of a 38-session mnemonic training study in which participants received extensive practice in the method-of-loci mnemonic (Baltes & Kliegl, 1992; Kliegl, Smith, & Baltes, 1989). As a final assessment, we presented 12 lists of 30 words with 12 different presentation times ranging from 20 sec down to 0.8 sec per word. The vertical line shows that the four slow lists and the eight fast lists were administered in two consecutive sessions. Obviously, there are three segments with respect to age differences: they are small for short, very large for medium, and large for long presentation times. There is restriction of variance for short presentation times for young and old adults, and possibly also for long presentation times for young adults only.

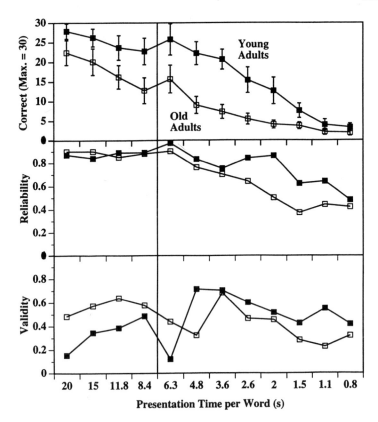

FIG. 5.2. Top panel: Correct serial recall of young and old adults for 12 lists of 30 words presented for the times listed on the x-axis. Error bars are 95%-confidence intervals. Middle panel: Reliability (Cronbach's alpha) for the twelve lists. Bottom panel: Correlation of correct serial recall with the logarithm of presentation times required for 50% correct recall.

The pattern of results is somewhat consistent with the theoretical curves of Fig. 5.1, but obvious floor and potential ceiling effects render it difficult to decide which presentation times could be included in the analysis of variance; in the Baltes and Kliegl (1992) article, data for the four shortest presentation times were excluded due to the analyses reported in the next section. In general, the pattern of results was counter to our original expectations of larger age differences for shorter presentation times. However, the data were consistent with the assumption that below a minimum amount of time, about less than three sec in this case, neither young nor old adults could execute the processes required for elaborative processing.

The results suggest an interpretation of presentation time as a *threshold time* for deploying the effective mnemonic strategy. If the available time is below a critical value, it cannot be used, and performance collapses. If the time is beyond the threshold, the mnemonic device can be used. It is difficult to determine from these data whether or not there are age differences in the efficiency with which presentation time is converted into accuracy. Depending on the difficulty of the memory task (e.g., manipulations of material, training, mnemonic instructions) or individual differences (e.g., age or expertise) one or more conditions are frequently too difficult for one, and other conditions too easy for other experimental or nonexperimental manipulations. Functional limits that give rise to such floor and ceiling effects are probably rarely identical across individuals— even within age-homogeneous groups. For example, in the 20 sec condition, 4 of 16 young but none of 19 old adults had perfect scores. Thus, interactions between presentation time and age group could be the consequence of, for example, the experimental curtailing of maximum performance for a larger proportion of young than old adults. Without the task ceiling, for example with longer word lists, we might have observed larger age differences for 20 sec than 15 sec per word.

Problems of Internal Consistency (Reliability)

Changes in the consistency of cognitive processing, perhaps even a shift from one mode of processing into a different one, might be indicated in systematic changes of internal consistency (reliability) of performance. If the 30 words of a memory list are considered as items of a scale, one can compute Cronbach's alpha as an indicator of internal consistency or reliability. This provides an index of whether or not performance over a group of items (words) reflects an ability to remember that is congruent with performance over other groups of items (words). The age differential effects of presentation time on internal consistency are illustrated in the middle panel of Fig. 5.2. Obviously, internal consistencies were high and similar for both groups up to presentation times of 3.6 sec. For the four short times, the drop was more rapid for old than young adults; values were similar again for the shortest time (0.8 sec) administered. We took some comfort from the age similarities in internal consistency for long presentation times; as values were smaller and less regular for pretraining scores, this was partially due to the extensive training participants received. Nevertheless, there were also age differences in internal consistencies for a segment of the presentation time spectrum (below 3.6 sec). Thus, it would be problematic to interpret the Age × Presentation Time interaction in terms of a global construct of internal processing time, assumed to determine all levels of functioning between chance and maximum performance. Rather, it may also be taken to indicate different types of processing. As a further complication, it is likely that such shifts in the cognitive algorithm occur at different presentation times for persons of different ages. Averaging data across subjects without concern for individual differences in such algorithmic breakpoints leads to group curves that represent a mixture of qualitative (cognitive algorithms) and quantitative (processing times) differences.

CRITERION-REFERENCED PRESENTATION TIMES

The following proposal, intended to overcome the difficulty in interpreting time-accuracy relations, originated in the design of the practice sessions of our memory experiments (e.g., Kliegl et al., 1989). We wanted to provide all participants with as beneficial a learning environment as possible. To this end, practice sessions were closely tailored to each individual's ability. In particular, we aimed at intermediate levels of difficulty for each individual (e.g., adjusted presentation times so that subjects maintained a 50% accuracy rate over lists), at which they would practice the skill. In this way, we hoped to avoid boredom due to lack of challenge and frustration due to performance demands beyond the reach of the current ability. The inequivalence in presentation times between participants is of minor concern because task demands focused on accuracy (they always tried to get 100% correct), rather than on the time required to achieve accuracy.

Criterion-referenced testing corresponds to the psychophysical method of limits in which the amount of stimulus energy (e.g., quanta of light) is varied contingent on stimulus identification to determine perceptual thresholds. In our application, presentation time assumes the role of stimulus energy. For example, when persons practiced the recall of word lists with a mnemonic technique, we decided on a performance criterion, for example, 15 out of 30 words. If, in a given list, a participant met this criterion, the presentation time was shortened in the following list. If he or she did not meet the criterion, more presentation time was available on the next list. As shown in Fig. 5.3 from Kliegl and

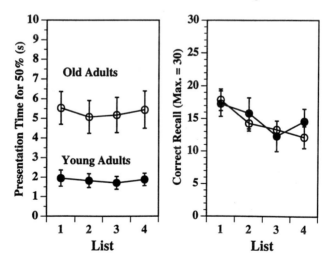

FIG. 5.3. Illustration of criterion-referenced testing across four lists of an experimental session. Age differences are reflected in the presentation times needed to maintain a 50% level of correct recall. Data are from Kliegl and Lindenberger (1993).

Lindenberger (1993), on average, old adults were allotted more presentation time per word than young adults, and there was no difference between age groups in recall accuracy, as expected.

Descriptive Statistics and Construct Validity

Can we consider the criterion-referenced presentation time (CRPT) as an alternative global measure of memory ability? We converted the CRPTs to proportional elaboration times by taking logarithms (and adding one to avoid negative values); the logarithmic transformation also brought the data in line with various distributional statistical assumptions (e.g., homogeneity of variance, homoscedasticity of regression residuals). Equal-accuracy elaboration times should be shorter for young than old adults. Table 5.1 summarizes age-comparative statistics from two experiments (i.e., Kliegl & Lindenberger, 1993; Thompson & Kliegl, 1991). The data of Experiment 1 were collected in Sessions 22 and 23 of the Baltes and Kliegl (1992) study previously mentioned. In both experiments, test–retest stabilities were high; there was no difference in recall accuracy. In previous research, we showed that mnemonic training leads to an almost complete separation of young and old adults' distributions of recall accuracy (Baltes & Kliegl, 1992; Kliegl et al., 1989). As shown in Fig. 5.4, elaboration times lead to a similar separation.

The next question was one of validity. As a construct validation, we asked whether or not equal-accuracy elaboration times predict traditional memory-accuracy scores that are based on the recall of lists administered under identical presentation-time conditions for all participants. The analyses of internal consistency (reliability) suggested that age groups were similar for times longer than 2.5 sec per word. The bottom panel of Fig. 5.2 displays the within-group correlations between correct recall (i.e., the scores summarized in the top panel) and elaboration times based on criterion-referenced testing (i.e., data shown in Fig. 5.4, Exp. 1). The higher the correlation, the more similar the rank orders. Such

TABLE 5.1
Statistical Characteristics of Elaboration Times

	CRPT (s)		Elaboration Time		Stability	Correct Recall	
	M	SD	M	SD	r	M	SD
Exp. 1							
Young	1.84	0.74	1.63	0.40	0.86	15.0	2.1
Old	5.31	1.64	2.62	0.30	0.83	14.4	1.2
Exp. 2							
Young	2.40	1.05	1.76	0.46	0.87	14.6	1.3
Old	7.73	3.30	3.93	0.50	0.89	14.5	0.7

Note. Exp. 1 = Kliegl and Lindenberger (1993, Exp. 1); Exp. 2 = Thompson and Kliegl (1991); CRPT = criterion-referenced presentation time (sec); elaboration time = ln (CRPT) + 1.

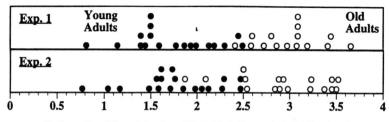

Elaboration Time (s) = Log (Crit.-Ref. Presentation Time) + 1

FIG. 5.4. Distributions of elaboration times (= logarithm of criterion-referenced presentation time + 1) for young and old adults; Exp 1: Kliegl and Lindenberger (1993; Exp. 1); Exp. 2: Thompson and Kliegl (1991; Exp. 1).

correlations are consistent with an underlying process similarity between serial recall with a fixed presentation time and processes required for maintaining 50% accuracy across lists of words.

The presentation-time profile is different between internal consistencies and validities. The major result was a reversal in the sign of age-related differences for the size of correlations associated with short and long presentation times. For short presentation times, elaboration time predicted young adults' correct recall better than that of old adults; this result was to be expected on the basis of the age differences in internal consistency (middle panel of Fig. 5.2). For long presentation times, elaboration time predicted old adults' correct recall better than that of young adults. In addition, old adults' correlations were largest for long presentation times.

As there was no age difference in internal consistency for presentation times of 3.6 sec and longer, a sufficiently general age-related shift in processing strategy must have been responsible for the divergence. One possibility is that, with long presentation times, young adults did not use all of the available presentation time to generate elaborations; perhaps they were content with two, three or four elaborations and stopped processing after that. In this case, presentation time is no longer a valid indicator of processing time as specified in the simple model depicted in Fig. 5.1. In contrast, longer times may have been a prerequisite for old adults to fully deploy the mnemonic strategy. Therefore, one conclusion from this analysis is that it is difficult to maintain the assumption of age-invariant cognitive processing across the presentation-time spectrum even after extensive training in the cognitive strategy to be used.

Criterion-referenced presentation times are valid indicators of the ability traditionally measured in terms of accuracy (coefficients were always significant) but, obviously, the degree of correspondence depended on the presentation time. For presentation times with similar values in internal consistency and validity for the two age groups, interindividual differences in accuracy should be predicted by elaboration time. Figure 5.5 illustrates this point for the regression of serial recall (averaged across presentation times ranging between 2.7 sec and 5 sec per

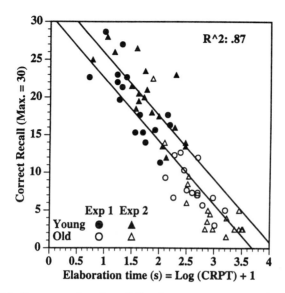

FIG. 5.5. Regression of serial recall (based on presentation times between 2.5 sec and 5 sec; see Fig. 5.1) on elaboration times. Exp. 1: Kliegl and Lindenberger (1993); Exp. 2: Thompson and Kliegl (1991).

word) on elaboration time for the participants of two experiments. CRPTs accounted for 87% of the variance in serial recall; within-group correlations were .72 for young and .81 for old adults. There was a remaining significant age difference in serial recall (reflected in the difference between the two regression lines), probably due to differences between the assessment format; this difference did not interact with CRPT. Finally, neither the main effect of experiment nor any interaction terms were significant. We interpret Fig. 5.5 as strong evidence for the proposition that CRPTs capture individual differences reflected in traditional memory accuracy scores.

Equal-Accuracy Young–Old Functions

There is an interesting twist to CRPTs. On the one hand, CRPTs indicate that older adults have a much worse memory than young adults. On the other hand, they indicate that old adults can have as accurate a memory as young adults if given enough time to generate the memory traces. This raises the question of compensation. Can older adults always compensate the decline in memory accuracy by taking more time to complete the task? The data presented suggest that this is the case when 15 of 30 words must be recalled. It is possible, however, that with higher accuracy demands, for example, if we determine the presentation time needed to recall 100% of the words, with different material, or memory tasks with high interference, this would no longer hold true. A task difference that cannot be compensated for with longer study time might lead to important aging-related constraints on cognitive processing. If old adults can compensate for the decline in memory accuracy with more presentation time, then the questions are whether or not age differences in CRPTs increase in a proportional fashion with the difficulty of the memory task, and whether or not this increase is comparable to the slowing observed in other domains of cognitive functioning. Both questions relate to the *correspondence assumption of cognitive aging* (Cerella, 1990); that is, the assumption that young and old adults (or young adults and children) do not differ in the kind and sequence of mental operations, but only in a general characteristic of the cognitive system (such as slowing or susceptibility to internal processing errors).

CRPTs are available from 4 experiments with a total of 10 different conditions. A simple graphical way to check the possibility that age differences increase with the difficulty of the experimental condition is to plot CRPTs of old adults against those of young adults of corresponding conditions (Brinley, 1965; see also Kail, this volume; Salthouse, this volume). In Fig. 5.6, the regression line represents young and old adults' time demands for equal accuracy. For example, the triangle in the lower left gives the time that was needed by both age groups when they had to recall 12 of 16 words (75% accuracy); the triangle in the upper right gives the

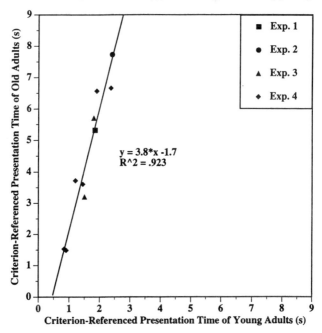

FIG. 5.6. Meta-analysis of age differences in criterion-referenced presentation times (equal-accuracy young–old function) based on four experiments (Kliegl & Lindenberger, 1993; Baltes & Kliegl, 1992, second training phase; Thompson & Kliegl, 1991; Kliegl, Mayr, & Krampe, 1994).

values for 16 out of 16 words (100% accuracy) in the same experiment. The slope of the regression of old on young adults' CRPTs was 3.8; the amount of variance explained by the linear regression was 87%. This highly systematic relation was obtained despite the fact that the experiments were quite different in their design. For example, they differed in the length of the lists, which ranged from 16 to 30 words. They also differed in the criterion; we used values between 50% and 100%. The common feature across all experiments was that they required the generation of memory traces on the basis of a mnemonic technique. Manipulations of the difficulty of the memory task affected young and old adults in a similar way when we look at proportionate age differences in CRPTs. Whatever manipulation increased the presentation time required by young adults by 1 sec, increased the presentation time required by old adults by an additional 3.8 sec.

The slope of 3.8 suggests that the effects of age on episodic memory are more than twice as large as one would expect from much of the other cognitive aging research, in particular from research based on tasks with response latencies as a dependent variable. When performances of old adults are plotted against those of young adults in a similar way, the slope of the best fitting linear function is about 1.5 to 1.8 (for a review, see Cerella, 1990). Thus, the determination of CRPTs reveals larger age differences in cognitive processing time for memory than do traditional measures of cognitive aging. There is a confound between type of task and method of assessment: Perhaps the steeper slope in episodic memory compared to search tasks is not the inherently greater complexity of the former, but is due to the format of assessment—that is, CRPTs instead of response times. Therefore, we determined the slope of search tasks also with CRPTs—the amount of presentation time required to achieve various levels of accuracy in searching for words and figural objects. The slope obtained for episodic memory tasks was significantly steeper than the slope based on CRPTs without demands on episodic memory, such as simple visual and word search tasks (Kliegl, Mayr, & Krampe, 1994; Mayr & Kliegl, 1993). Proportional models adequately describe the age difference; there is not much support for models postulating a power or quadratic function for the shape of the equal-accuracy young–old function (Cerella, 1990; Myerson, Hale, Wagstaff, Poon, & Smith, 1990).

TIME-ACCURACY FUNCTIONS

Determining More Than One CRPT

The determination of criterion-referenced presentation times we used to provide practice conditions of intermediate difficulty for each participant triggered a new line of research (Kliegl et al., 1994). Obviously, if we can determine the amount of time required to reach a specific level of accuracy, we should also be able to determine the amount of time required for any level of accuracy. Indeed, the data collected to determine CRPTs for three different accuracy criteria were sufficient to determine complete time-accuracy functions covering the entire range between chance and asymptotically perfect performance. Most importantly, as shown in Fig. 5.7a, condition-specific functions of this kind could be determined for individual subjects.

The graphs illustrate, for a word scanning and a memory task, how presentation time relates to performance accuracy in one young and one old adult. In word scanning, we measured the time demand for reading four words; in the

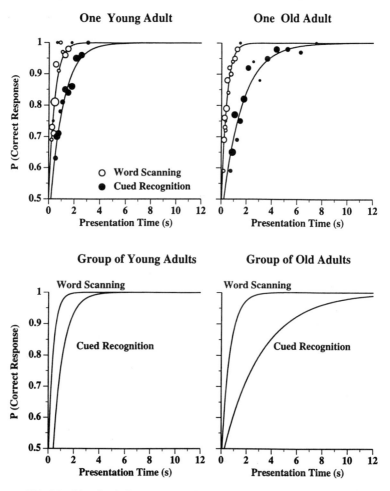

FIG. 5.7. (a) Individual time-accuracy functions for one young and one old adult in word scanning and cued recognition. (b) Corresponding functions for groups of young and old adults. Curves are based on the means of two parameters (x-intercept, slope) estimated for each person in each condition (Kliegl, Mayr, & Krampe, 1994).

memory task, we measured the time demand for reading and remembering a word pair. Procedural details about how one obtains enough information at the level of experimental conditions for individual subjects were described in Kliegl et al. (1994). Briefly, the adaptive determination of CRPTs selectively samples for each experimental condition and each subject the segment of the presentation-time dimension that corresponds to the specified accuracy criterion. By combining data for different criteria, scatterplots can be produced with mean accuracy as a function of presentation time. The size of the symbols in Fig. 5.7a codes the number of times the particular presentation time was sampled for this person. The number and sizes of these symbols differed across tasks and between persons because of the adaptive testing procedure. The continuous lines show the best fitting exponential functions for one subject. Group curves can be computed by averaging the free parameters (intercept and slope) for young and old adults (Fig. 5.7b).

The difficulty of interpreting interactions related to presentation time and experimental condition were already touched upon (see Fig. 5.1). Problems are exacerbated if, in addition, an organismic variable (such as age group) must be considered. Fortunately, if a specific functional relation between presentation time and accuracy is compatible with the data (e.g., if negative exponentials such as those shown in Figs. 5.1 and 5.7 yield acceptable goodness-of-fit statistics), the effect of age with respect to the implemented experimental manipulations can be addressed in a way that is compatible with the line of reasoning advanced thus far: If we plot old adults' time demands over those for young adults for corresponding levels of accuracy, we obtain a young–old function for each experimental condition that, for negative exponential time-accuracy functions, turns out to be linear (see Fig. 5.8a). Moreover, a repeated-measures analysis of variance of the logarithm of parameter estimates for slopes of the exponential functions (estimated for each subject in each condition) provides a test of whether or not the slopes of the young–old functions are significantly different from each other (Kliegl et al., 1994). The set of data displayed in Fig. 5.8 passed this test. Therefore, proportional age differences in CRPTs for word scanning are significantly smaller than those for episodic memory.

An alternative presentation of the data, plotting for equal accuracy time demands of the memory task over the time demand for word scanning, yields state traces for young and old adults (see Fig. 5.8b; Bamber, 1979; Kliegl et al., 1994). The significant difference between young–old functions implies a significant difference between state traces. The significant difference between state traces implies an interaction between age group and word scanning for predicting criterion-referenced presentation times in the complex memory task with criterion-referenced presentation times from the simple word scanning task. Thus, the approach implicitly provides a statistical test of the significance of unique age-related variance in the complex task—that is, of age-related variance that cannot be accounted for by interindividual differences in the simple task (see

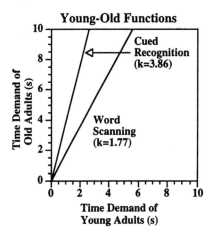

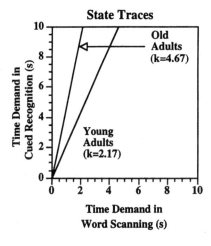

FIG. 5.8. Time demands for equal accuracy. (a) Time demand of old adults as a·function of time demand of young adults. (b) Time demand in complex task as a function of time demand in the simple task.

Salthouse, 1991, 1993, this volume). Frequently, in hierarchical regression analyses, only the incremental r^2 due to age is determined. Such an effect does not imply a difference in slope, but a difference in the intercept for the two age groups; within each age group the slopes relating the complex to the simple task could still be parallel. The difference in slopes reported here corresponds to a significant effect of the multiplicative interaction term of age and simple task, rather than the main effect of age by itself. Only the latter provides evidence for task-specific age-related slowing factors.

Relation of Single CRPT to Time-Accuracy Function

Depending on the complexity of the tasks examined, it may be time consuming to determine CRPTs for several levels of accuracy. What is the additional information gained from complete time-accuracy functions? The relation between

CRPTs (interpreted to yield estimates of processing time) and processing-time estimates based on the slope parameter of the time-accuracy function are as follows: CRPTs are indicators of elaboration times required to achieve a specified level of accuracy with all the interpretational qualifications mentioned earlier in the chapter. Thus, each point on the time-accuracy curve represents a specific CRPT. If we assume (a) that the negative exponential is the correct specification for all persons, young and old, and (b) that differences between persons are restricted to the fundamental processing time—that is, the slope of the function, then any single CRPT specifies the correct ranking of individuals for the entire functional range of performance on a task (see Fig. 5.9a).

Unfortunately, there are alternative possibilities. As illustrated in Fig. 5.9b, for example, group differences in the minimum amount of time required for the function to get better than chance performance, that is the x-intercept of the curve (parameter a), could also yield a ranking of individuals compatible with a single CRPT, although no difference was assumed for slope (parameter b) and asymptotic level of performance (parameter c). Similarly, differences in the asymptote (parameter c) could generate a ranking of individuals compatible with the ranking on a single CRPT (Fig. 5.9c). Thus, whereas in most cases a single CRPT will probably work well as a proxy of processing time, the complete function is necessary to correctly delineate the contributions of parameters other than processing time.

PERSPECTIVES AND FUTURE DIRECTIONS

An important goal of cognitive aging research—and of developmental research in general—is an operationalization of concepts such as cognitive potential and limits (Baltes, 1993) or processing capacities and resources (Salthouse, 1985, 1991). For the case of episodic memory, it was shown how a move from assessing experimental effects by manipulations of presentation time to assessing them via the determination of criterion-referenced presentation times can yield estimates of a general parameter of cognitive efficiency—that is, the processing time required for comparable reductions of error probability across experimental conditions and age groups. Also determining several CRPTs per experimental condition per person will lead to complete time-accuracy functions. These can be used to assess interactions between age and experimental condition in terms of proportional differences.

We applied this procedure in different contexts. In one recent study, the goal was to examine age differences in proactive interference with this paradigm. In the tradition of verbal learning, we contrasted time-accuracy functions for (A-B, A-C)- and (A-B, A-Br)-paradigm. Initial results indicate that the critical age difference appears to be in the asymptote of the functions. Old adults, even with generous allotments of presentation time and after much practice, appear to be

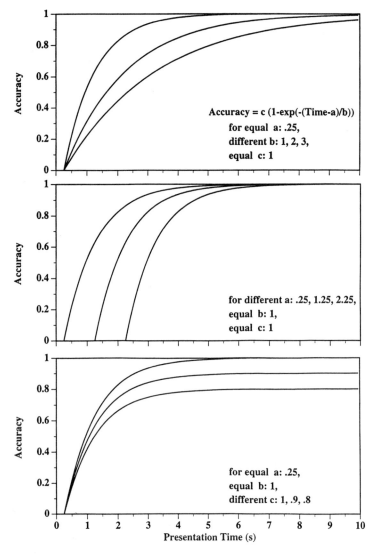

FIG. 5.9. Influence of three parameters of a negative exponential function on horizontal ordering of time-accuracy relations (a: intercept with x-axis; b: slope; c: asymptote).

unable to achieve maximum accuracy. There were no age differences in the ratios of processing time for the two episodic time-accuracy functions (Kliegl, Krampe, & Mayr, 1993).

The determination of time-accuracy functions is not limited to episodic memory processes. Indeed, focusing on the time demand to achieve various levels of accuracy can help bridge task domains that, in the past, were primarily separated by their choice of dependent measures. For example, in simple search tasks the typical measure is the reaction time, in complex reasoning (or episodic memory), accuracy is used more frequently. The determination of CRPTs and time-accuracy functions for representative tasks of both domains allowed us to isolate two proportional slowing factors for tasks characterized by the presence or absence of coordinative demands on working memory (Kliegl et al., 1994; Mayr & Kliegl, 1993). In a recent study, this approach was also used to contrast information-processing dynamics in children, young adults, and old adults. Children were less affected by coordinative demands than old adults (Mayr, Kliegl, & Krampe, 1993).

Time-accuracy functions are linked to models of information accumulation. For many tasks, the expectation is that this function takes a negatively accelerated course. The negative exponential is but one possibility; power, hyperbolic, and logistic functions are alternatives. With a high density of observations it may be possible to empirically rule out one or the other function (Kliegl et al., 1994). Such exclusion of functions constrains models of information integration. Moreover, there are task domains for which the time-accuracy relation may follow a very different course. For example, in ongoing research, we showed that both very short and very long time intervals render it more difficult to reproduce a specific rhythm (Krampe, Kliegl, & Mayr, 1993). The accuracy to reproduce a rhythmic sequence of strokes on the piano will be lower for very short time intervals because of biomechanical constraints; it will also be lower relative to an optimum for very long intervals due to an increase in cognitive coordination. Again, such time-accuracy functions vary according to experimental condition (e.g., isochrone rhythms vs. polyrhythms) and group characteristics (e.g., amateur vs. professional pianists). Thus, although the functions may initially appear to be largely descriptive in character—because they generate a vector of dependent variables—their inherent linkage to different assumptions about cognitive processing dynamics implies strong theoretical propositions.

Two limitations of the research carried out thus far relate to the specificity of the processing dynamics. First, we need to become more precise about the component processes generating such time-accuracy functions. Time-accuracy functions are basically cumulative probability functions; that is, for any random presentation time they tell us the probability that the cognitive process completed at a time less than or equal to this time. If we differentiate the cumulative probability function we obtain the probability density function that gives us the completion probability for any particular presentation time. Almost always, this probability density function is the result of summing process durations associated with two or more cognitive component processes—the total time is the result of a convolution of component times (e.g., McClelland, 1979; Townsend & Ashby, 1983). The determination of condition-specific time-accuracy functions at the individual level is bound to facilitate such deconvolutions of complex cognitive processes and the identification of process-specific developmental differences.

The second limitation concerns the assumption of homogeneity of processing within individuals across presentation times. The examples presented assume that the same type of cognitive processing occurs irrespective of whether performance is close to chance or close to perfect. This is unlikely to be true. At least for episodic memory tasks, there are shifts in retrieval strategies that depend on the overall level of available information. The negative exponential (or a continuous alternative function) is a preliminary platform from which shifts in cognitive strategy can be documented and examined in greater detail. The success of such microgenetic work will depend greatly on the observational density one is willing to realize for individuals. Ideally, we should trace the developmental course of shifts in cognitive strategies within individual time-accuracy functions, thus linking microgenetic processing dynamics with ontogenesis (see also Siegler, 1987, 1991, this volume).

In adopting the time-accuracy function approach, one sacrifices experimental equivalence in presentation times for functional equivalence in terms of performance accuracy. The problems one encounters when experimental equivalence is enforced were illustrated. Of course, functional equivalence incurs problems of comparability across groups and conditions. The tolerance of this inequivalence will depend on the coherence that the determination of processing times from time-accuracy functions brings to developmental and cognitive issues.

ACKNOWLEDGMENTS

Research reported in this chapter was carried out in the context of the projects Expertise and Cognitive Aging and Functional Limits in Cognitive Development. I gratefully acknowledge the contributions of Paul B. Baltes, Ralf Th. Krampe, Ulman Lindenberger, Ulrich Mayr, Jacqui Smith, and Laura A. Thompson. I also thank Michael Marsiske for helpful comments.

REFERENCES

Baddeley, A. D., Thomson, N., & Buchanan, M. (1975). Word length and the structure of short-term memory. *Journal of Verbal Learning and Verbal Behavior, 14*, 575–589.

Bäckman, L. (1986). Adult age differences in cross-modal recoding and mental tempo, and older adults' utilization of compensatory task conditions. *Experimental Aging Research, 12*, 135–140.

Balota, D. A., & Duchek, J. M. (1988). Age-related differences in lexical access, spreading activation, and simple pronunciation. *Psychology and Aging, 3*, 84–93.

Baltes, P. B. (1993). The aging mind: Potential and limits. *Gerontologist, 33*, 580–594.

Baltes, P. B., & Kliegl, R. (1992). Further testing of limits of cognitive plasticity: Negative age differences in a mnemonic skill are robust. *Developmental Psychology, 28*, 121–125.

Bamber, D. (1979). State-trace analysis: A method for testing simple theories of causation. *Journal of Mathematical Psychology, 19*, 137–181.

Brinley, J. (1965). Cognitive sets, speed, and accuracy of performance in the elderly. In A. T. Welford & J. E. Birren (Eds.), *Behavior, aging, and the nervous system* (pp. 114–149). Springfield, IL: Thomas.

Burke, D. M., & Light, L. L. (1981). Memory and aging. *Psychological Bulletin, 90*, 513–546.

Cerella, J. (1990). Aging and information processing rates in the elderly. In J. E. Birren & K. W. Schaie (Eds.), *Handbook of the psychology of aging* (3rd ed., pp. 201–221). New York: Academic Press.

Craik, F. I. M., & Jennings, J. M. (1992). Human memory. In F. I. M. Craik & T. A. Salthouse (Eds.), *The handbook of aging and cognition* (pp. 51–110). Hillsdale, NJ: Lawrence Erlbaum Associates.

Craik, F. I. M., & Rabinowitz, J. (1984). Age differences in the acquisition and use of verbal information: A tutorial review. In H. Bouma & D. G. Bouwhuis (Eds.), *Attention and performance X: Control of language processes* (pp. 471–499). Hillsdale, NJ: Lawrence Erlbaum Associates.

Craik, F. I. M., & Rabinowitz, J. (1985). The effect of presentation rate and encoding task on age-related memory deficits. *Journal of Gerontology, 40*, 309–315.

Hasselhorn, M. (1988). Wie and warum verändert sich die Gedächtnisspanne über die Lebensspanne? [How and when does memory span change across the life span?]. *Zeitschrift für Entwicklungspsychologie und Pädagogische Psychologie, 20*, 322–337.

Kail, R. (1991). Developmental change in speed of processing during childhood and adolescence. *Psychological Bulletin, 109*, 490–501.

Kausler, D. H. (1991). *Experimental psychology, cognition, and human aging* (2nd ed.). New York: Springer.

Kliegl, R., Krampe, R. T., & Mayr, U. (1993, April). *Der Nachweis proaktiver Interferenz mit Zeit-Genauigkeits-Funktionen* [Demonstration of proactive interference with time accuracy functions]. Paper presented at the 35th Tagung experimentell arbeitender Psychologen, Münster.

Kliegl, R., & Lindenberger, U. (1993). Modeling intrusions and correct recall in episodic memory: Adult age differences in encoding of list context. *Journal of Experimental Psychology: Learning, Memory, and Cognition, 19*, 617–637.

Kliegl, R., Mayr, U., & Krampe, R. T. (1994). Time-accuracy functions for determining process and person differences: An application to cognitive aging. *Cognitive Psychology, 26*, 134–164.

Kliegl, R., Smith, J., & Baltes, P. B. (1989). Testing-the-limits and the study of adult age differences in cognitive plasticity of a mnemonic skill. *Developmental Psychology, 25*, 247–256.

Krampe, R. T., Kliegl, R., & Mayr, U. (1993, November). *The fast and the slow of bimanual movement timing.* Poster presented at the Meetings of the Psychonomic Society, Washington, DC.

Mayr, U., & Kliegl, R. (1993). Sequential and coordinative complexity: Age-based processing limitations in figural transformations. *Journal of Experimental Psychology: Learning, Memory, and Cognition, 19*, 1297–1320.

Mayr, U., Kliegl, R., & Krampe, R. T. (1993, November). *Sequential and coordinative processing dynamics from childhood to old age.* Poster presented at the Meetings of the Psychonomic Society, Washington, DC.

McClelland, J. L. (1979). On the time relations of mental processes: An examination of systems of processes in cascade. *Psychological Review, 86*, 287–324.

Myerson, J., Hale, S., Wagstaff, D., Poon, L. W., & Smith, G. A. (1990). The information-loss model: A mathematical theory of age-related cognitive slowing. *Psychological Review, 97*, 475–487.

Rabinowitz, J. (1989). Age deficits under optimal study conditions. *Psychology and Aging, 4*, 259–268.

Restle, F., & Greeno, J. (1970). *Introduction to mathematical psychology.* Reading, MA: Addison-Wesley.

Salthouse, T. A. (1980). Age and memory: Strategies for localizing the loss. In L. W. Poon, J. L. Fozard, L. Cermak, D. Arenberg, & L. W. Thompson (Eds.), *New directions in memory and aging* (pp. 47–65). Hillsdale, NJ: Lawrence Erlbaum Associates.

Salthouse, T. A. (1985). *A theory of cognitive aging.* Amsterdam: North Holland Press.

Salthouse, T. A. (1991). *Theoretical perspectives on cognitive aging.* Hillsdale, NJ: Lawrence Erlbaum Associates.

Salthouse, T. A. (1993). Speed mediation of adult age differences in cognition. *Developmental Psychology, 29,* 722–738.

Salthouse, T. A., & Kail, R. (1983). Memory development throughout the lifespan: The role of processing rate. In P. B. Baltes & G. O. Brim (Eds.), *Life-span development and behavior, Vol. 5* (pp. 89–116). New York: Academic Press.

Siegler, R. S. (1987). The perils of averaging data over strategies: An example from children's addition. *Journal of Experimental Psychology: General, 116,* 250–264.

Siegler, R. S. (1991). The microgenetic method. *American Psychologist, 46,* 606–620.

Simon, E. (1979). Depth and elaboration of processing in relation to age. *Journal of Experimental Psychology: Human Learning and Memory, 5,* 115–124.

Thompson, L. A., & Kliegl, R. (1991). Adult age effects of plausibility on memory: The role of time constraints during encoding. *Journal of Experimental Psychology: Learning, Memory, and Cognition, 17,* 542–555.

Townsend, J. T., & Ashby, F. G. (1983). *The stochastic modeling of elementary psychological processes.* Cambridge, England: Cambridge University Press.

Waugh, N. C., & Barr, R. (1980). Memory and mental tempo. In L. W. Poon, J. L. Fozard, L. Cermak, D. Arenberg, & L. W. Thompson (Eds.), *New directions in memory and aging* (pp. 251–260). Hillsdale, NJ: Lawrence Erlbaum Associates.

Chapter 6

Processing Capacity and Its Role on the Relations Between Age and Memory

Timothy A. Salthouse
Georgia Institute of Technology

There are three goals of this chapter. The first is to discuss some of the assumptions inherent in the concept of processing capacity as it is applied to developmental phenomena. Because interpretations based on such constructs are difficult to evaluate, a second goal is to outline a scheme that can be used to classify and help understand the role of different methods of investigation in explanatory developmental research. The final goal is to briefly describe a program of research focused on one particular hypothesis. This hypothesis asserts that information-processing speed functions as a form of processing capacity that influences memory and other forms of cognitive functioning in the adult portion of the life span.

I am an outsider relative to most of the other contributors to this volume because my research focuses on changes in memory and other cognitive processes occurring across the adult portion of the life span, rather than those occurring from birth to maturity. Although the relevant phenomena take place over a much longer time, and there is no assurance that identical change mechanisms are operating, many of the same issues concerned with the description and explanation of cognitive change are important regardless of the segment of the life span under investigation. In particular, I believe that the classification scheme I discuss, and the importance of what I refer to as *Phase 2 research*, are equally applicable to childhood and adulthood.

PROCESSING CAPACITY

Adult age differences in memory are well documented, and memory problems are frequently mentioned behavioral characteristics associated with aging (Crook & Larrabee, 1990; Dixon & Hultsch, 1983; Hultsch, Hertzog, & Dixon, 1987). Although there is not yet any consensus regarding the causes of age-related memory declines in the adult years, several researchers suggested that the relation between age and memory (and between age and other cognitive functions) might be partially attributable to an age-related reduction in processing capacity or resources (e.g., Craik & Byrd, 1982; Hasher & Zacks, 1979; Salthouse, 1988a, 1988b). However, these speculations were controversial because the concept of *capacity* or *resources* was not explicitly defined, and the methods by which hypotheses based on processing capacity might be investigated were not specified.

The term *capacity* is particularly ambiguous because it has at least two distinct, relevant meanings. *Webster's Seventh New Collegiate Dictionary* (1972) contains the following two definitions: ". . . ability to hold, receive, store, or accommodate," and ". . . power to grasp and analyze ideas and cope with problems" (p. 123). The former definition has a connotation of basic processing efficiency, whereas the latter seems to refer to overall mental capability or competence. Speculations based on the second interpretation of capacity are unlikely to be meaningful because there is little value in attributing performance variations in a particular task to variations in an unspecified type of competence or capability. This usage may even be circular if the differences in capacity are inferred to exist on the basis of the same performance differences that capacity differences are used to explain (see Light & Burke, 1988; Salthouse, 1988a, 1988b).

For this reason, some variant of the first interpretation is usually intended when the term capacity is used in cognitive psychology. The fundamental assumption is that human cognition is limited by quantitative constraints on processing—or limitations of capacity—in addition to restrictions associated with the quantity, quality, or effective application of different types of knowledge (e.g., declarative and procedural). The relative importance of structural or capacity factors and knowledge factors will vary across tasks, but a basic premise of the processing capacity approach is that some individual differences in cognition are attributable to variations in parameters representing the efficiency of elementary processing.

Three characteristics of the processing capacity perspective should be noted. The first is that capacity limitations are assumed to be relevant to many different cognitive activities, and are not local, or restricted to a small number of tasks. In other words, the consequences of capacity limitations are postulated to be general rather than highly specific. However, processing capacity is not necessarily unitary because there is nothing inherent in this perspective that rules out the possibility of multiple capacities. Interpretations become more complicated when more than one capacity is postulated, but some degree of capacity independence or modularity is not inconsistent with the capacity perspective.

The second characteristic of the capacity perspective is that capacity limitations are assumed to be only one of several determinants of cognitive functioning, and should not be viewed as the exclusive source of all performance differences in any cognitive task. This perspective does not deny the existence of other factors contributing to developmental differences in memory or other cognitive functions, but maintains that capacity limitations could be an important influence on performance, in addition to any other influences that might be operating.

The third characteristic of the processing capacity perspective is that most theorists tend to think of processing capacity as an entity intermediate between neurophysiology and higher order cognition. For example, various characteristics of attention, such as its selectivity, divisibility, sustainability, or degree of inhibitory control have been discussed as possible candidates for the resources or capacity construct. In recent years, there has also been considerable interest in the efficiency or effectiveness of working memory as a fundamental processing resource or capacity. Another possibility, and one that I have been interested in for several years, is that processing speed may function as a basic type of capacity, perhaps in a manner analogous to how the clock rate of a computer serves as a crude index of the computer's power or capacity. Although the processing capacity construct could be interpreted in completely neurophysiological terms, an intermediate level of theorizing is generally preferred, because the linkage to cognitive performance is more plausible when the constructs are more similar to the phenomena to be explained.

Regardless of the manner in which it is conceptualized, speculations about the role of processing capacity need to be tested. That is, no matter how intriguing and potentially parsimonious the concept of processing capacity might be, interpretations based on this notion cannot be taken very seriously without convincing empirical evidence. The next section of the chapter is therefore devoted to a discussion of the different phases of research concerned with investigating the role of explanatory constructs, such as processing capacity, in cognitive development.

PROPOSED CLASSIFICATION OF DEVELOPMENTAL RESEARCH

Three phases of explanatory, as opposed to descriptive, developmental research can be distinguished. The phases are not mutually exclusive, nor necessarily sequential, because it is possible that research can address several phases simultaneously. Nevertheless, the phases appear to represent a logical, if not strictly chronological, progression.

Phase 1

The primary goal of Phase 1 research is to establish the existence of a relation between age and the relevant theoretical construct. Research in this phase often relies on a measure of performance from a specific task to provide an index of the construct. However, inferences about age relations in the construct can also be based on a contrast across experimental manipulations. In this case, a significant Age × Condition interaction would indicate that the critical construct, whose influence is presumed to vary across conditions, is particularly sensitive to age. Much of the aging and cognition research of the last 10 to 20 years was of one of these two types, in that the major purpose was to investigate relations between age and some hypothesized construct.

A list of some of the theoretical constructs that were investigated in this manner is presented in Fig. 6.1. However, the mere existence of such a large number of alternative or rival explanatory constructs constitutes a potential problem if there is no means of evaluating the importance of a particular construct on the relationship between age and memory. That is, even if reasonable arguments could be proposed regarding the influence of a specific factor on the relations between age and memory, empirical evidence is still needed to determine the contribution of that factor relative to other possible factors. Information of this type, and information about the relations of the factors to one another, can be provided from Phase 2 research.

Phase 2

Figure 6.2 illustrates that at least three relations are involved if a construct is hypothesized to contribute to the mediation of relations between age and memory. Because Phase 1 research is only concerned with the relation between age and the hypothesized mediating construct, it does not directly address the question of whether, and if so to what extent, that construct contributes to the age differences in memory. This issue can be examined in the second phase because a major purpose of Phase 2 is to determine the plausibility and importance of the relevant construct as a determinant, or mediator, of the relationship between age and memory.

Many variables and constructs are related to age, and it should not be assumed that because two variables are both related to age, one of those variables has a causal influence on the relations between age and the other variable. For example, grayness of hair or wrinkling of the skin are known to be associated with increased age, but neither of these variables may have any relation to performance on tests of memory or other cognitive functions. Only when the relationship of the hypothesized intervening variable to age and to a measure of memory are available, can one determine the role of the variable as a potential mediator of the influence of age on memory. (See Horn, 1982, for further discussion of this point, which Horn refers to as the "missing link issue.")

The number of potential mediators between age and memory is large, but it is unlikely that all of them operate in every situation. Moreover, even if several are operating simultaneously, they may not be equally important or powerful. Because one aspect of progress in science consists of discriminating relevant from

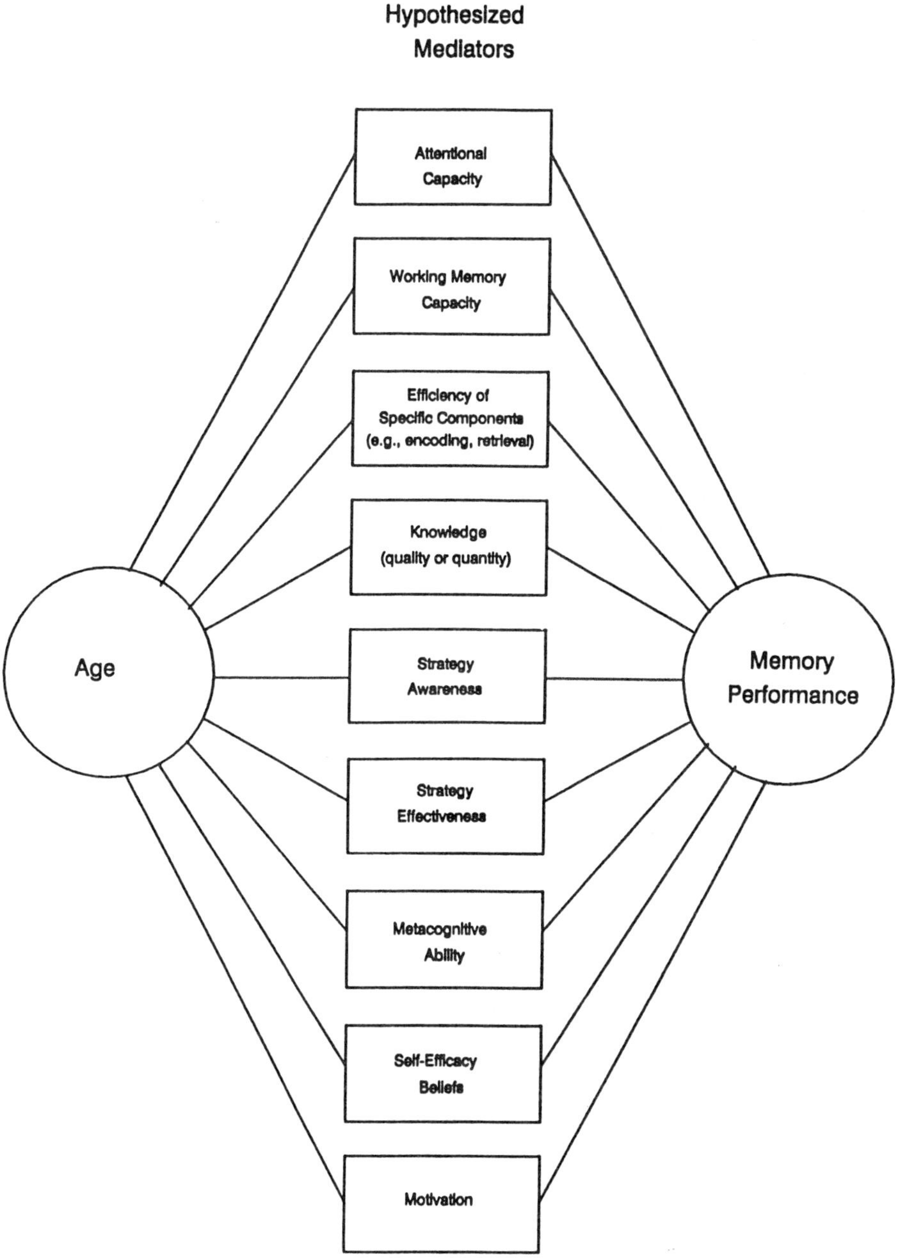

FIG. 6.1. Constructs hypothesized to contribute to relations between age and memory.

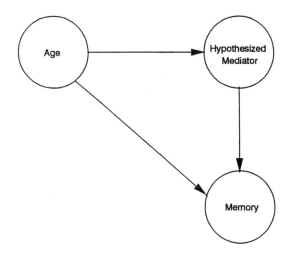

FIG. 6.2. Potential relations among age, memory, and a construct hypothesized to contribute to the mediation of the influence of age on memory.

irrelevant constructs, some means of eliminating extraneous or peripheral variables is necessary. A major purpose of Phase 2 research is to provide this type of information.

Another important function of Phase 2 research is to determine how various theoretical constructs are related to one another. Relations between constructs can be examined to verify that presumably distinct constructs are truly independent, and to determine whether or not the effects of one construct vary according to the level of other constructs. Among the specific issues that could be addressed in this manner are the empirical distinction between alternative conceptualizations of processing capacity (e.g., attention and working memory), and the relation between amount of processing capacity and aspects of higher order cognition, such as the usage of particular types of strategies.

Correlational data provide the primary source of information about the interrelations among variables in Phase 2 research. Because researchers who generally rely on experimental manipulations may not be very familiar with correlational procedures, two special requirements of this type of research should be noted. One requirement is that all relevant variables should be assessed in as reliable a fashion as possible because associations with other variables cannot be expected if the variables have little systematic variance. Reliability of a construct is enhanced by increasing the number of relevant observations, and by assessment with multiple measures (e.g., Rushton, Brainerd, & Pressley, 1983; Sullivan & Feldman, 1979). The use of multiple or converging operations also serves to increase the validity of measurement by minimizing influences extraneous to the theoretical construct, such as those associated with the particular methods, materials, or measures used in a given study.

A second requirement of correlational research is moderately large samples of research participants. This is necessary to increase the precision, in the sense of minimizing confidence intervals, of the estimated proportions of variance in each variable. That is, it is not simply statistical significance that is of primary interest in this type of research, but also the strength of the relevant relations, and sample sizes of 100 or more are often needed to obtain accurate estimates of strength of relationship.

Research with multiple measures and large samples is expensive and time-consuming, but it yields valuable information about the influence of specific theoretical constructs on the relations between age and memory. Although results from Phase 1 research are often interpreted as supporting the plausibility of a construct as a potential mediator of the relations between age and memory, Phase 2 research is required to establish that the construct actually does contribute to the influence of age on memory. Furthermore, because it is unlikely that any single factor would account for all of the age-related variance in a cognitive variable, it is desirable to use techniques that allow the relative importance of different factors or determinants to be evaluated. Such information can be derived from a variety of correlational procedures.

As an example, hierarchical regression analyses can be used to estimate the magnitude of the influence of the hypothesized construct on age-memory relations. That is, two separate regression equations can be constructed; one in which age is the only predictor of memory performance, and one in which age is entered in the equation after the construct hypothesized to function as a mediator. This latter equation indicates the unique age-related variance in the form of the increment in R^2 associated with age after the variance associated with the hypothesized mediating construct has been controlled, or removed by statistical means. The influence of the construct on the total age-related effects can then be determined by subtracting the unique age-related variance from the total age-related variance. This difference can be interpreted as an estimate of the contribution of the controlled variable to the relations between age and memory.

Other analytical techniques could obviously be used to evaluate the influence of a construct to age-memory relations. Regardless of the particular analytical method employed, however, a valuable outcome of Phase 2 research not provided in either Phase 1 or Phase 3, is information about the relative importance of the theoretical construct to the developmental phenomena of interest. If the hypothesized construct plays a major role in the relationship between age and memory, this influence should be demonstrable in the results of Phase 2 research. Furthermore, because the primary requirement of the analytical procedures is the availability of an index of the proposed mediating construct, the procedures are quite general and can be used with virtually any theoretical construct amenable to operationalization.

Correlational procedures can also be used to examine the relations among variables hypothesized to function as moderators or mediators of the relations between age and memory. For example, multiple regression analyses could reveal whether or not the effectiveness of a particular strategy varies according to the level of an index of some type of processing capacity. That is, a measure of strategy usage could serve as the criterion variable and an index of processing capacity could be entered as a control variable (to examine mediating influences), or as a cross-product interaction term with age (to examine moderating influences). Alternatively, patterns of relationships between indices of different conceptions of processing capacity could be examined with path analysis or latent construct structural modeling techniques.

Reservations are frequently expressed about inferences based on correlational data because correlations are equivocal with respect to causality. Correlations do not imply causation, and single-occasion correlational data are ambiguous about the direction of any causal influences that might be operating. Furthermore, many different structural models can usually be found to provide equivalent fits to a given set of data (e.g., MacCallum, Wegener, Uchino, & Fabrigar, 1993). Nevertheless, the presence or absence of a relation can be informative even if the direction of the relation cannot be determined from the available data. As an example, if one hypothesizes that age differences in memory are a function of differential strategy use, then a discovery that there was no significant relation between a measure of strategy use and memory performance would obviously be relevant to that hypothesis. Correlational data can therefore provide constraints on the types of hypotheses that might be viable, and in the process, yield information about the plausibility of specific hypotheses.

Phase 3

If the results of Phase 2 research indicate that the construct has plausibility as a potential mediator of the relations between age and memory, then the mechanisms responsible for the relevant relations need to be identified. In particular, attempts should be made to explain both the relation between age and the construct, and the relation between the construct and the measure of memory.

Correlational evidence from Phase 2 can indicate that the hypothesized relations exist and that the construct is likely to be involved in the influence of age on memory. However, correlational data are limited in the information they can provide regarding the processes or mechanisms responsible for those relations. Comparison of the strength of the relations with different combinations of variables can be informative, but other types of evidence are still desirable because of the ambiguity about causal direction inherent in most cross-sectional correlational research.

A wide variety of methods could be used to examine the mechanisms involved in the relations between age and the construct, and between the construct and memory. For example, experimental manipulations might be used to explore specific predictions, or various types of formal modeling could be used to establish the sufficiency of a particular mechanism for the construct–memory relation. Furthermore, certain types of neurophysiological evidence might be helpful in understanding the age–construct relation.

There is a sense in which Phase 3 research is a natural extension of Phase 1 research in that the focus in Phase 3 is explaining why the relations established in Phase 1 occur. However, an important difference between the two types of research is that the task of accounting for the relations is of much greater relevance when the evidence from Phase 2 research indicates that those relations are actually involved in the developmental phenomena of interest. That is, only when the results of Phase 2 are available can one have confidence that the theoretical construct really does contribute to the influence of age on memory.

PROCESSING SPEED AS A REFLECTION OF PROCESSING CAPACITY IN ADULTHOOD

In the remainder of this chapter, I briefly describe research in the three phases just outlined for a program of research designed to determine why increased age is associated with lower performance in various types of cognitive functioning. A more complete description of the research program is contained in Salthouse (1992b).

Phase 1

A project described in Salthouse (1993a) focused on the relations between age and performance on the Raven's Progressive Matrices Test. Many previous studies reported substantial age-related declines on this test, and these age relations were confirmed in my laboratory. For example, the correlation between age and the number of correct responses with the standard paper-and-pencil (Advanced) test was $-.57$ ($n = 221$) in Study 1. A computer administered version of the test in which subjects could take as long as they wanted to work on the problems was used in Study 1 of Salthouse (1994). The correlation between age and the percentage of correct answers in this study was $-.39$ ($n = 246$).

Because the solution of matrix problems seems to require working memory in order to detect the rules relating matrix elements to one another, it was hypothesized that working memory might function as a mediator of the relations between age and performance in the Raven's test. This hypothesis seemed plausible because previous research revealed substantial negative correlations between age and measures of working memory functioning. For example, two variants of the Daneman and Carpenter (1980) reading span task were used to measure working memory in my laboratory. In five separate studies, each involving over 200 adults from a wide range of ages, the correlations between age and measures of working memory derived from these tasks ranged from $-.39$ to $-.54$ (Salthouse, 1991; Salthouse & Babcock, 1991).

These two sets of results—significant relations between age and Raven's performance, and significant relations between age and measures of working memory—are examples of Phase 1 research. That is, although a mediational relation is hypothesized, the discovery that two variables are both related to age does not allow a conclusion that one variable mediates the age-related influences on the other variable. Evidence relevant to that hypothesis must come from Phase 2 research.

Phase 2

Subjects in the first study in the Salthouse (1993a) project performed the Raven's Progressive Matrices Test, and also two working memory tasks. In addition, each of these individuals reported the number of years of formal education completed and made an evaluation of his or her level of health. These latter two variables were included because health and education are often mentioned as possible mediators of age-cognition relations.

An initial analysis of the data from this study revealed that age was associated with a sizable proportion of variance in Raven's performance (i.e., R^2 of .322), but that the age-related variance that was independent of working memory was considerably smaller (i.e., increment in r^2 associated with age after control of working memory of .053). Because the age-related variance was reduced by over 83% when the measure of working memory was statistically controlled, these results suggest that working memory does indeed contribute to the relations between age and Raven's performance.

Figure 6.3 contains a path diagram representing the relations among the variables in this study. Three results should be noted. First, the hypothesized importance of working memory on the relations between age and Raven's performance is supported by the significant coefficients for the paths between age and working memory, and between working memory and Raven's performance. Second, there is no evidence that education contributes to the age differences in Raven's performance because there was no relation between age and education in this sample. And third, self-reported health status does not have a direct influence on performance in the Raven's Test. These latter two results suggest that education and health are probably not important mediators of the relations between age and Raven's performance.

Because of the evidence in this and other studies (e.g., Salthouse, 1992b) that working memory contributes to the relations between age and measures of cognitive functioning, additional studies were designed to attempt to understand the relations between age and working memory. Salthouse and Babcock (1991) hypothesized that working memory could be conceptualized in terms of three components: storage capacity, processing efficiency, and coordination effectiveness. Each hypothesized component was measured in two different tasks based on different versions of the working memory task. For example, the reading span

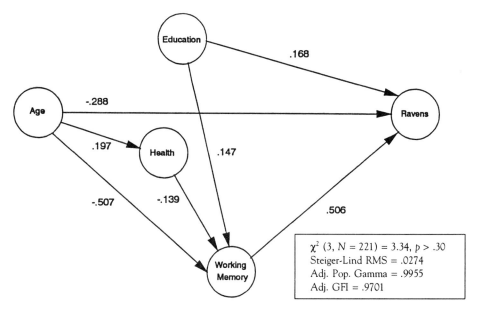

FIG. 6.3. Path diagram illustrating relations among Age, Raven's Progressive Matrices, and three possible mediators (data from Study 1, Salthouse, 1993a).

working memory task required the subject to remember the last word in each sentence while also answering a question about the sentence. The subject's span corresponded to the largest number of sentences for which both the processing (answering sentences) and storage (recalling words) requirements were satisfied on at least two of three trials. A measure of storage capacity was obtained by measuring the subject's word span, a measure of processing efficiency was obtained by measuring the speed with which sentence comprehension questions could be answered, and coordination effectiveness was measured by the speed with which two activities could be performed simultaneously.

A path diagram illustrating the relations among the variables in this study is presented in Fig. 6.4. Notice that the three hypothesized components were all moderately related to one another. However, there was no relation between the measure of coordination effectiveness and working memory functioning. At least as measured in this study, therefore, the coordination efffectiveness component does not appear to be an independent contributor to the age-related differences in working memory.

The fact that a path was needed between age and working memory indicates that there were influences of age on working memory independent of the hypothesized components. A second study was therefore designed to investigate the possibility that a more fundamental common factor might contribute to the relations between age and aspects of working memory. Study 2 in the Salthouse and Babcock (1991) project included measures of processing speed, as represented

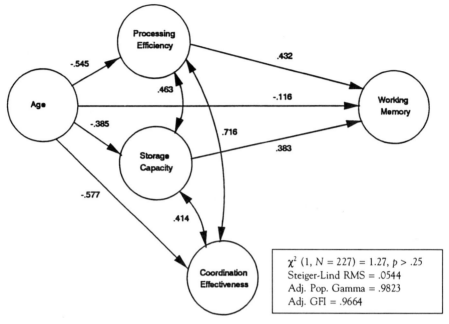

FIG. 6.4. Path diagram illustrating relations among Age, Working Memory, and three hypothesized components of working memory (data from Study 1, Salthouse & Babcock, 1991).

by the speed of making simple perceptual comparisons. Two measures of this construct were added, and the measures of coordination effectiveness dropped.

Relations among the variables in this study are illustrated in the path diagram in Fig. 6.5. The most important result to be noted is that there was no independent influence of age on either working memory, or on the hypothesized components of working memory. It therefore appears that all of the age-related effects on working memory in this particular sample can be accounted for in terms of the influence of processing speed. Other studies using different methods of assessing processing speed and working memory (e.g., Salthouse, 1992b; Salthouse & Coon, 1993; Salthouse & Kersten, 1993) confirmed the large influence of processing speed, although the attenuation of the age-related variance in working memory in these studies was smaller than that in the Salthouse and Babcock (1991) study.

Phase 3

The evidence summarized above is consistent with the hypothesis that processing speed functions as an important mediator of the relations between age and working memory, and probably also of the relations between age and other measures of cognition. The Phase 2 research served a valuable purpose of establishing the relevance of one hypothesized mediator of age-related influences on memory.

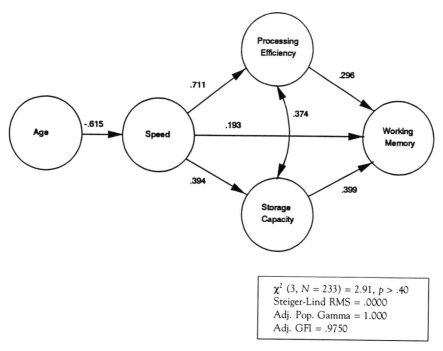

FIG. 6.5. Path diagram illustrating relations among Age, Working Memory, Perceptual Speed, and two hypothesized components of working memory (data from Study 2, Salthouse & Babcock, 1991).

Justification now exists for a focus on explaining why increased age is apparently associated with a slower rate of executing many processing operations, and how slower processing speed contributes to poorer performance in memory and other cognitive tasks.

It seems highly likely that neurophysiological processes are involved in the relations between age and speed. Changes could occur at the level of individual neurons, perhaps because of loss of myelination or a reduction in synaptic transmitters. The number of functional neural cells may also decrease with age, thereby requiring more circuitous pathways for communication. Although numerous plausible mechanisms could be postulated, it is not clear that the alternatives can be discriminated solely on the basis of behavioral measures. Neurophysiological research will therefore probably be required before a definitive conclusion can be reached regarding the processes responsible for relations between age and speed.

A key assumption in the interpretation of relations between speed and cognition is that nearly all cognitive processes require time for their completion, and during that time the information upon which they operate is degrading in either quality or availability. Effectiveness of the processing is greatest when it is more rapid and can be based on the largest amount of accurate information.

Moreover, if the processing is slow, then the amount of simultaneously available information may be reduced, thus impairing higher order cognitive processes dependent on the integration or abstraction of different types of information.

Evidence consistent with the preceding interpretation has accumulated from a variety of sources. For example, the duration of a number of different cognitive processes was found to be slower with increased age (Salthouse & Coon, 1993; Salthouse & Kersten, 1993). Other research found that processing speed has a direct influence on decision accuracy, and not just on study time or decision time (Salthouse, 1994). And finally, examination of different speed measures has revealed that the relations between speed and measures of cognitive functioning are greatest when the speed measures do not simply reflect sensory and motor processes, but also contain a cognitive component such as comparison or substitution (Salthouse, 1993b, 1994).

Neither the mechanisms responsible for the relations between age and speed, nor between speed and cognition, are fully understood at the current time. Nevertheless, the speculations described represent plausible, and most importantly, testable, hypotheses. Furthermore, because the evidence from Phase 2 research indicates that speed does contribute to the relations between age and cognition, one can have confidence that those hypotheses are both relevant and important.

CONCLUSION

I conclude with a brief summary of the major points I attempted to make. I began by describing reasons for the appeal of the notion of processing capacity as an explanatory construct in developmental research. However, because the meaningfulness of any construct is a function of the quality and quantity of relevant evidence, I then discussed three phases of research concerned with investigating the involvement of a hypothesized mediator such as processing capacity in developmental phenomena. Finally, I summarized some of my own research in each of the three proposed research phases focused on the hypothesis that speed or rate of processing functions as a type of processing capacity during adulthood. The processing speed interpretation is still at the speculative stage with respect to mechanisms, but the evidence relevant to the role of processing speed on adult age differences in memory, particularly in what I termed Phase 2 research, suggests that this construct should play a prominent role in any comprehensive explanation of memory development in adulthood.

REFERENCES

Craik, F. I. M., & Byrd, M. (1982). Aging and cognitive deficits: The role of attentional resources. In F. I. M. Craik & S. Trehub (Eds.), *Aging and cognitive processes* (pp. 191–211). New York: Plenum.

Crook, T. H., & Larrabee, G. J. (1990). A self-rating scale for evaluating memory in everyday life. *Psychology and Aging, 5,* 48–57.

Daneman, M., & Carpenter, P. A. (1980). Individual differences in working memory and reading. *Journal of Verbal Learning and Verbal Behavior, 19,* 450–466.

Dixon, R. A., & Hultsch, D. F. (1983). Metamemory and memory for text relationships in adulthood: A cross-validation study. *Journal of Gerontology, 38,* 689–694.

Hasher, L., & Zacks, R. T. (1979). Automatic and effortful processes in memory. *Journal of Experimental Psychology: General, 108,* 356–388.

Horn, J. L. (1982). The theory of fluid and crystallized intelligence in relation to concepts of cognitive psychology and aging in adulthood. In F. I. M. Craik & S. Trehub (Eds.), *Aging and cognitive processes* (pp. 237–278). New York: Plenum.

Hultsch, D. F., Hertzog, C., & Dixon, R. A. (1987). Age differences in metamemory: Resolving the inconsistencies. *Canadian Journal of Psychology, 41,* 193–208.

Light, L. L., & Burke, D. M. (1988). Patterns of language and memory in old age. In L. L. Light & D. M. Burke (Eds.), *Language, memory and aging* (pp. 244–271). New York: Cambridge University Press.

MacCallum, R. C., Wegener, D. T., Uchino, B. N., & Fabrigar, L. R. (1993). The problem of equivalent models in applications of covariance structure analysis. *Psychological Bulletin, 114,* 185–199.

Rushton, J. P., Brainerd, C. J., & Pressley, M. (1983). Behavioral development and construct validity: The principle of aggregation. *Psychological Bulletin, 94,* 18–38.

Salthouse, T. A. (1988a). Resource-reduction interpretations of cognitive aging. *Developmental Review, 8,* 238–272.

Salthouse, T. A. (1988b). The role of processing resources in cognitive aging. In M. L. Howe & C. J. Brainerd (Eds.), *Cognitive development in adulthood* (pp. 185–239). New York: Springer-Verlag.

Salthouse, T. A. (1991). Mediation of adult age differences in cognition by reductions in working memory and speed of processing. *Psychological Science, 2,* 179–183.

Salthouse, T. A. (1992a). Influence of processing speed on adult age differences in working memory. *Acta Psychologica, 79,* 155–170.

Salthouse, T. A. (1992b). *Mechanisms of age-cognition relations in adulthood.* Hillsdale, NJ: Lawrence Erlbaum Associates.

Salthouse, T. A. (1993a). Influence of working memory on adult age differences in matrix reasoning. *British Journal of Psychology, 84,* 171–199.

Salthouse, T. A. (1993b). Speed mediation of adult age differences in cognition. *Developmental Psychology, 29,* 722–738.

Salthouse, T. A. (1994). The nature of the influence of speed on adult age differences in cognition. *Developmental Psychology, 30,* 240–259.

Salthouse, T. A., & Babcock, R. L. (1991). Decomposing adult age differences in working memory. *Developmental Psychology, 27,* 763–776.

Salthouse, T. A., & Coon, V. E. (1993). Influence of task-specific processing speed on age differences in memory. *Journal of Gerontology: Psychological Sciences, 48,* P245–P255.

Salthouse, T. A., & Kersten, A. W. (1993). Decomposing adult age differences in symbol arithmetic. *Memory & Cognition, 21,* 699–710.

Sullivan, J. L., & Feldman, S. (1979). *Multiple indicators.* Beverly Hills, CA: Sage.

Webster's Seventh New Collegiate Dictionary (1972). Springfield, MA: Merriam.

Chapter 7

Memory for Action Events: Structure and Development in Adulthood

Monika Knopf
Max Planck Institute for Psychological Research, Munich

The development of memory abilities over the life span has been studied almost exclusively with verbal materials (Kausler, 1991; Salthouse, 1991). In typical studies on memory and aging, younger and older adults are required to learn and remember series of numbers, letters, words, or sometimes text material. Because of this focus on verbal material, it is still an open question whether the memory deficits found in older adults in such studies indicate generalized age-related memory deficits or whether they are limited to verbal material only.

There are some considerations that make it quite plausible that memory deficits in older individuals might be especially large in the verbal domain:

1. There is little correspondence between the verbal materials used in typical experimental tasks and the memory tasks that older individuals encounter in everyday learning experiences (Schaie, 1987). Thus, it is unlikely that older adults have well-developed routines or strategies for dealing with such verbal materials.

2. Verbal learning and memory are generally assessed with artificial tasks. Older individuals are less likely than younger ones to successfully solve such artificial tasks, because they have less cognitive flexibility in dealing with new task types (Schaie, 1983) and because they have motivational deficits (Perlmuter & Monty, 1989).

Dissatisfaction with an emphasis on verbal materials in traditional memory research has led to a new research paradigm that focuses on memory for material that is more relevant to everyday experiences—specifically, on memory for simple, everyday actions. This research paradigm was developed independently by Cohen (1981) and Engelkamp and Krumnacker (1980). The goal of research using this paradigm in developmental studies with older adults is to analyze how well older individuals can remember actions that they have performed. It is assumed that self-performed actions represent the everyday learning situations that older adults encounter. Remembering that one has done something (e.g., closed a window before leaving the house, fed the dog in the morning) are memory tasks that are claimed to tap the everyday learning contexts of older adults particularly well.

The first study with older subjects in this paradigm, by the Swedish researcher Bäckman (1984; Bäckman & Nilsson, 1984, 1985), did produce novel results. Older subjects were asked to perform series of everyday actions (e.g., lift the spoon, look in the mirror) named by an experimenter in a laboratory context, and were asked to encode these actions for later recall. This type of encoding has been labeled *subject-performed task* (SPT) (Cohen, 1981). Under SPT conditions, memory performance of older adults was equivalent to that of younger subjects. However, typical memory deficits appeared in the older adults for equivalent actions encoded verbally. Bäckman (1984) interpreted these results as support for the idea that learning by doing (SPT condition) produced a memory trace that was resistant to age-related deficits. Bäckman argued that the primary reason that the age deficits were eliminated was that enactive encoding engages information processing that simultaneously involves different modalities, thus producing an especially rich memory trace: Not only the verbal, but also the visual and motor systems are involved in learning by doing (see also Nyberg, Nilsson, & Bäckman, 1991). Moreover, Bäckman (1987) referred to Ribot's Law (1882) which claims that, whereas other information processing systems lose their efficiency with aging, the motor information processing system remains efficient until old age.

Because of its unusual results, Bäckman's study provided us with a point of departure for a series of studies on memory for self-performed actions in older adults. In what follows, these studies and the most important results are described.

THE DEVELOPMENT OF ACTION MEMORY IN ADULTHOOD

Study 1[1]

The goal of the first study was to replicate the results from Bäckman's study with a more detailed procedure. Bäckman (1984) used only highly familiar everyday actions as learning material. It is, however, well known in gerontological

---

[1]Studies 1 and 2 were published in more detail in Knopf and Neidhardt (1989).

research that familiarity itself can provide an important condition that facilitates learning in older adults even more than in younger subjects (Bäckman, 1989; Knopf, 1987; Salthouse, 1990). Thus, the extent to which the elimination of the usual Age effect in memory after encoding by acting was actually due to performance of actions and a better memory trace, rather than to familiarity, was unclear.

To assess the effects of familiarity, the materials used in the first experiment included highly familiar actions (e.g., *pour milk into the coffee*), unfamiliar (e.g., *throw a lasso*), or middle-level actions that were parallel to the highly familiar actions in their motor components, but that had less familiar content (e.g., *pour oil in the lamp* as an item parallel to *pour milk into the coffee*). The purpose of including these middle-level actions was to allow us to separate the effects of content familiarity and familiarity of motor components on memory performance.

The actions were presented to subjects in three blocks of 22 items each. Within each block, items were homogeneous with respect to familiarity. The subjects' task in each block was to perform each action and encode it for a later memory task. Action performance was symbolic—that is, subjects produced the action movements in the absence of any related object props, a procedure that was analogous to that used by Bäckman (1984). A fourth block of 22 highly familiar actions was presented to subjects with instructions to verbally encode them for a subsequent memory test. The purpose of this block was to assess learning and memory performance for actions encoded only verbally.

Norms for action familiarity were determined in an independent rating study with older and younger adults. Highly familiar actions were defined as those that are typical of everyday life activities and that were recently performed. Unfamiliar actions were defined as those that were seldomly or never performed in everyday activities and had not been performed recently. Only those actions that were rated consistently and that showed no age or sex differences were retained for the memory study.

Each subject in the memory study learned the items in each of the four blocks. The verbal encoding block was always presented first to prevent possible learning strategy transfer from the action performance conditions (e.g., mental imagination of action performance during verbal learning). The order of the three blocks of actions was counterbalanced. A free recall test was presented immediately after each item block. In this test, subjects were asked to remember each of the 22 items in that block in any order. After learning and recalling all four blocks, a second delayed free recall test was given. In this test, subjects were to remember all 88 items from the four blocks. The delayed test occurred about 1½ hours after the beginning of the study.

The study included 30 younger adults (age $M = 26.4$, $SD = 3.9$) and 30 normally aging older adults ($M = 67.2$, $SD = 6.9$). The educational and professional backgrounds of subjects in both age groups were similar and represented a mostly nonacademic population.

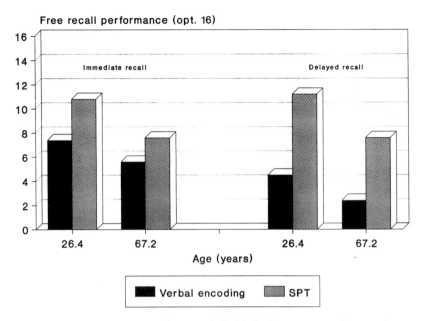

FIG. 7.1. Mean memory performance for highly familiar actions as a function of
type of encoding and retention interval.

The mean free recall performance for highly familiar actions is shown in Fig.
7.1 as a function of age, encoding type, and retention interval. This material is
the most similar to that used by Bäckman (1984). Because the first and last
. three items of each block were excluded from data analysis to control for primacy
and recency effects, the optimal performance score for each block was 16.

As expected, Fig. 7.1 shows an Age effect for the recall of verbally encoded
actions; the performance of older adults was worse than that of younger individuals. This result replicates Bäckman's (1984) findings. Surprisingly, however,
there was also an Age effect for enactively encoded actions, and this effect
occurred for both short and longer retention intervals. Thus, in our study, there
was an Age effect favoring younger subjects regardless of encoding type.

Figure 7.1 also shows that enactive encoding facilitated memory. Performed
actions were remembered significantly better than those that were encoded only
verbally. This performance-enhancing effect of learning by doing was also found
in several current nondevelopmental cognitive studies with younger adults (Cohen, 1985; Engelkamp, 1990; Helstrup, 1986, 1987) and is characterized in this
literature as an *enacting effect* in memory.

However, the Age effect also occurred after enactive encoding, and not just
for highly familiar actions, but also for actions with other levels of familiarity.
This is shown in Fig. 7.2 in which free recall for actions varying in familiarity
is portrayed as a function of age group and retention interval.

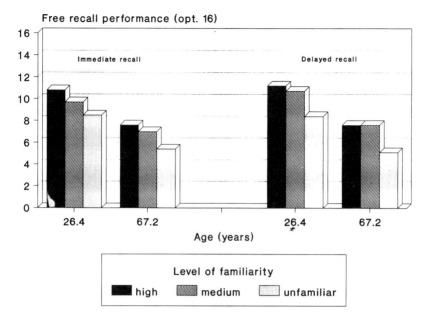

FIG. 7.2. Mean memory performance for subject-performed actions of different familiarity levels as a function of age and retention interval.

As shown, older subjects remembered SPTs more poorly than younger subjects, and this difference was maintained not only for highly familiar actions, as shown in the first figure, but also for actions with low or medium familiarity levels. Thus, the Age effect for memory for subject performed actions was independent of action familiarity, that is, it occurred at all levels of familiarity.

The familiarity-dependent differences in memory performance shown in Fig. 7.2 suggest that free recall varies as a function of material familiarity even after enactive encoding: The more familiar a produced action, the better it is remembered. Similar results suggesting a facilitatory effect of prior knowledge are also found in traditional studies on verbal learning.

In summary, the results of this first experiment show (a) an *Action effect*, that is, learning by doing is an effective learning method and memory performance is superior to that attained with parallel verbal materials; (b) a *Familiarity effect*, that is, similar to results from verbal learning studies, familiarity of actions is one determinant of free recall performance—familiar actions can be recalled better than unfamiliar ones. Thus, the Action effect does not eliminate the Familiarity effect; and (c) an *Age effect*, that is, all material, not just material encoded verbally, was recalled more poorly by older than by younger subjects. The Age effect occurred after enactive as well as verbal encoding. Thus, Bäckman's finding of no Age effect for learning by doing (at least for highly familiar actions) was not replicated.

Study 2

The purpose of the second study was to replicate the results from the first study. With the exception of the inclusion of a modified memory test, Study 2 was a repetition of Study 1.

The memory test was modified in Study 2 to more closely reproduce the procedure used by Bäckman (1984), who limited the time available for retrieval. Such a time limitation was not used in Study 1 because learning and remembering in older adults is inhibited by time constraints (Salthouse, 1991). However, the discrepant findings of no age group differences in Bäckman's studies and an Age effect in our Study 1 may have occurred because the younger adults in Bäckman's studies with time restrictions may not have been able to fully utilize their episodic memory under a time restriction condition, whereas they could in our Study 1 with an unlimited retrieval interval.

To test this idea, Study 2 included an additional memory measure after a limited time interval. To accomplish this, subjects were told that they had 3 minutes for recall in each immediate recall test, and 10 minutes in the delayed recall test. At the end of these recall times, subjects were asked to mark the recall protocol sheets. They were then instructed to continue to try to recall actions until they had noted all the items they could. This variation in the memory test procedure did not depress memory performance because recall performance after the unlimited retrieval intervals was similar for Studies 1 and 2.

The subjects in Study 2 included 30 younger adults (age M = 25.7, SD = 2.8) and 36 normally aging older adults (M = 63.4, SD = 3.1). The educational and professional backgrounds of both age groups were similar.

The results from Study 2 replicated the central results from Study 1. These findings are partly given in Fig. 7.3, depicting the free recall performance for highly familiar actions in the direct free recall test as a function of age, encoding type, and retrieval interval.

Figure 7.3 shows that older subjects' recall was poorer for both verbally encoded and enactively encoded material. This Age effect was apparent after the unlimited retrieval interval and limited recall time. The hypothesis that the discrepancy between Bäckman's findings and the results of our study was due to temporal limitations in the retrieval interval was not supported. A further attempt to explore the reasons for this discrepancy was undertaken in Study 3.

Study 3

In Study 3, the difficulty of the task was varied. The number of items to be learned was varied from short lists of 12 items to long lists of 36 items. This variation was included because Bäckman (1984) used short lists of 12 items and it is possible that the Age effect we found for enactive encoding might be eliminated only with easier tasks. Task difficulty and complexity of the materials can modify the extent of an Age effect (Salthouse, 1991).

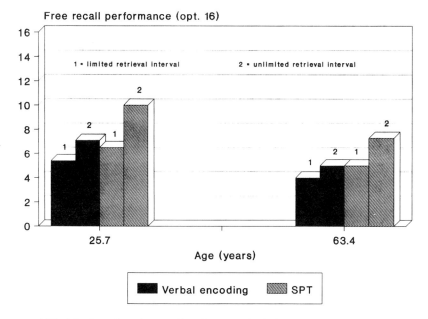

FIG. 7.3. Immediate free recall performance for highly familiar actions as a function of age, type of encoding, and retrieval interval.

The experimental procedure, the material to be learned, and the subject groups in Study 3 were essentially the same as those used in Studies 1 and 2.

The variation in task difficulty did not lead to different results from those already reported. Once again, enactive encoding led to better learning and memory performance; that is, there was an Action effect, and this effect was present for both levels of task difficulty. There was also a Familiarity effect demonstrating that recall performance varied as a function of action familiarity. And there was also an Age effect for verbally encoded and enactively encoded material, that is, the performance of older adults was worse than that of younger subjects. Although the percent of items recalled per block was higher for shorter lists than for longer, this task difficulty effect was similar across age groups, and thus did not eliminate the Age effect in recall performance.

Thus, task difficulty does not account for the failure to eliminate the Age effect we found in our earlier studies.

Study 4

Study 4 was another attempt to eliminate the Age effect in memory for subject-performed actions. In this study, the items were not performed symbolically, but were performed using those objects and props required to actually carry out each action. To do this, the objects typically used for the actions were made available

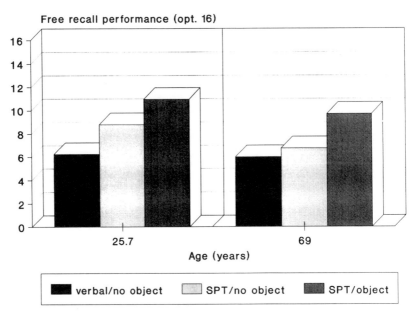

FIG. 7.4. Immediate free recall of actions as a function of type of encoding and age.

while encoding. Subjects used the appropriate objects for performing each action, and then put them into a container so that they were no longer available during recall. It was assumed that learning and memory performance, especially of older individuals, might improve with such enrichment in the acquisition phase.

The experimental procedure, the memory material, and the subjects in Study 4 were virtually identical to those in the previous studies.

Figure 7.4 shows the immediate free recall performance for highly familiar actions as a function of age group and encoding type.

The results from this study replicated the central results of the other studies: Enactive encoding led to better learning and memory performance than verbal encoding (Action effect) and older subjects showed poorer performance than younger subjects (Age effect). Providing objects during encoding improved performance over symbolic encoding, but because this improvement occurred similarly across both age groups, the Age effect was not eliminated. Similar findings were reported by Norris and West (1990).

Despite other variations in the learning materials (e.g., the use of novel actions to eliminate knowledge related interference processes in older subjects; see Knopf, 1991), and despite variations in the learning task (e.g., increasing encoding time), we were unable to eliminate the Age effect after encoding by acting. We thus conclude that older adults show the same memory deficits when encoding and recalling self-performed actions that they show when learning and remembering verbally encoded material or verbally encoded actions.

Kausler and Lichty (1988) came to a similar conclusion in a review of the literature. In addition, Kausler and Lichty showed that a similar Age effect in memory occurs, when more cognitive activities were used as memory material, in which the motor activity was manipulating paper and pencil (e.g., problem solving tasks, anagrams, perceptual motor tasks). A more optimistic view was provided in a recent review of literature by Norris and West (1990).

HOW ARE SUBJECT-PERFORMED ACTIONS LEARNED AND REMEMBERED?

The assumption in both Bäckman's (1984) beginning study and in cognitive psychological research (Engelkamp, 1990) is that motor information is essential for the memory performance improvement that occurs with enactive encoding. One may, alternatively, assume that nonmotoric action related components (e.g., preparation for performing the action, evaluation of action performance) are responsible for the occurrence of the Action effect. To test this alternative assumption, we conducted a series of studies with students as subjects in which various components involved in action performance were successively and systematically eliminated. For example, in one study subjects performed the actions to be remembered without seeing their own activities, so that visual information was not available. In another study, subjects did not plan the actions themselves, but rather imitated the actions of others, so that a planning phase was not present (Knopf, 1992).

The purpose of this subtractive method was to test the importance of single components of the SPTs for the occurrence of the Action effect. The Action effect occurred even under those conditions in which subjects did not actually perform the action motorically but simply planned the action and then delegated the production to someone else. Memory performance under this condition was as good as performance when subjects actually performed the action. We conclude from this that the information-processing activities crucial for the Action effect are not actually based on the processing of motor information, but occur when the performance of an action is planned. The Action effect is, from our perspective, an effect of memory traces laid down when preparing for performing an action. These traces apparently depend on the processing of conceptual information and not the processing of motor information. Motor information is thus not essential for the Action effect. The information processes studied when subjects learn and remember self-performed actions are similar to those processes studied in traditional developmental memory research, though the task is new. Thus the similarity between age-related deficits with verbal and enactive encoding of actions in older individuals is understandable.

How is it then possible to account for Bäckman's contradictory findings, specifically the better performance of older adults after encoding by acting? A

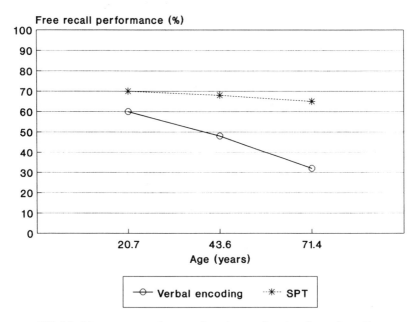

FIG. 7.5. Mean memory performance for actions as a function of type of encoding (data from Bäckman & Nilsson, 1984).

closer look at Bäckman's results (1984) shows that his surprising elimination of the Age effect was related to another result which was also atypical. This is shown in Fig. 7.5, which includes the data of the Bäckman Study (Bäckman & Nilsson, 1984).

Figure 7.5 shows that the elimination of the Age effect in memory for enactively encoded material found by Bäckman (1984) was accompanied by an elimination of the Action effect in younger subjects. The elimination of an Action effect in younger subjects is atypical, and contradicts a large number of findings from other nondevelopmental cognitive studies (Cohen, 1985; Engelkamp, 1990; Helstrup, 1986). This may have resulted from task difficulty differences or from possible population differences. The unexpected failure to find an Action effect on memory performance in younger adults is probably the primary reason for the equally unexpected elimination of the Age effect.

CONCLUSION

The most important results of our studies on learning and remembering subject-performed tasks in younger and older adults are summarized in four points:

1. The Age effect in memory is broader than traditionally assumed in the literature on memory and aging. The deficits older adults show when learning

and remembering SPTs are similar to those that have been demonstrated many times for verbal materials. Thus, the Age effect is not limited to verbal materials, but can also be found when self-performed actions have to be recalled by older individuals.

2. Although the Age effect in memory cannot be eliminated by enactive encoding, learning by doing does provide an effective method for the acquisition of memory material. Memory performance of both older and younger subjects improved significantly with enactive encoding compared to equivalent material encoded verbally.

3. Detailed analyses focused on identifying the critical information processing underlying enactive encoding showed that the processing of motor information while encoding is not crucial for the occurrence of the Action effect. The Action effect seems to arise from cognitions made in preparation for acting. The Action effect, therefore, is based on conceptual information processing.

4. The fact that all attempts to vary the memory material, the memory tasks, and the encoding procedures had similar, age-independent effects on memory performance suggests that age changes in memory are more quantitative than qualitative in nature.

REFERENCES

Bäckman, L. (1984). *Age differences in memory performance: Rules and exceptions.* Unpublished doctoral dissertation, University of Umea, Sweden.

Bäckman, L. (1987). Applications of Ribot's law to life-span cognitive development. In G. L. Maddox & E. W. Busse (Eds.), *Aging: The universal human experience* (pp. 403–410). New York: Springer.

Bäckman, L. (1989). Varieties of memory compensation by older adults in episodic remembering. In L. W. Poon, D. C. Rubin, & B. A. Wilson (Eds.), *Everyday cognition in adulthood and late life* (pp. 509–544). Cambridge, England: Cambridge University Press.

Bäckman, L., & Nilsson, L. G. (1984). Aging effects in free recall: An exception to the rule. *Human Learning, 3,* 53–69.

Bäckman, L., & Nilsson, L. G. (1985). Prerequisites for the lack of age differences in memory performance. *Experimental Aging Research, 11,* 67–73.

Cohen, R. L. (1981). On the generality of some memory laws. *Scandinavian Journal of Psychology, 22,* 267–282.

Cohen, R. L. (1985). On the generality of the laws of memory. In L. G. Nilsson & T. Archer (Eds.), *Perspectives on learning and memory* (pp. 247–277). Hillsdale, NJ: Lawrence Erlbaum Associates.

Engelkamp, J. (1990). *Das menschliche Gedächtnis* [Human memory]. Göttingen: Hogrefe.

Engelkamp, J., & Krumnacker, H. (1980). Imaginale und motorische Prozesse beim Behalten verbalen Materials [The role of imaginal and motor-encoding processes for verbal free recall]. *Zeitschrift für experimentelle und angewandte Psychologie, 12,* 511–533.

Helstrup, T. (1986). Separate memory laws for recall of performed acts? *Scandinavian Journal of Psychology, 27,* 1–29.

Helstrup, T. (1987). One, two, or three memories? A problem-solving approach to memory for performed acts. *Acta Psychologica, 66,* 37–68.

Kausler, D. H. (1991). *Experimental psychology, cognition, and human aging* (2nd ed.). New York: Springer.

Kausler, D. H., & Lichty, W. (1988). Memory for activities: Rehearsal-independence and aging. In M. L. Howe & C. J. Brainerd (Eds.), Cognitive development in adulthood (pp. 93–131). New York: Springer.

Knopf, M. (1987). Gedächtnis im Alter - Empirische Studien zur Entwicklung des verbalen Gedächtnisses bei älteren Menschen [Memory in the elderly—The development of verbal memory in later adulthood and old age]. Heidelberg: Springer.

Knopf, M. (1991). Having shaved a kiwi-fruit: Memory for unfamiliar subject-performed actions. Psychological Research, 53, 203–211.

Knopf, M. (1992). Gedächtnis für Handlungen - Funktionsweise und Entwicklung [Memory for action events—Functional and developmental aspects]. Habilitationsschrift an der Fakultät für Sozial- und Verhaltenswissenschaften der Ruprecht-Karls-Universität Heidelberg.

Knopf, M., & Neidhardt, E. (1989). Aging and memory for action events: The role of familiarity. Developmental Psychology, 25, 780–786.

Norris, M. P., & West, R. L. (1990). Adult age differences in activity memory: Cue and strategy utilization. In T. M. Hess (Ed.), Aging and cognition: Knowledge organization and utilization (pp. 1–31). Amsterdam: North-Holland.

Nyberg, L., Nilsson, L. G., & Bäckman, L. (1991). A component analysis of action events. Psychological Research, 53, 219–225.

Perlmuter, L. C., & Monty, R. A. (1989). Motivation and aging. In L. W. Poon, D. C. Rubin, & B. A. Wilson (Eds.), Everyday cognition in adulthood and late life (pp. 373–393). New York: Cambridge University Press.

Ribot, T. (1882). Diseases of memory. New York: Appleton-Century-Crofts.

Salthouse, T. A. (1990). Cognitive competence and expertise in aging. In J. E. Birren & K. W. Schaie (Eds.), Handbook of the psychology of aging (3rd ed., pp. 310–319). San Diego, CA: Academic Press.

Salthouse, T. A. (1991). Theoretical perspectives on cognitive aging. Hillsdale, NJ: Lawrence Erlbaum Associates.

Schaie, K. W. (1983). The Seattle Longitudinal Study: A 21-year exploration of psychometric intelligence in adulthood. In K. W. Schaie (Ed.), Longitudinal studies of adult psychological development (pp. 64–135). New York: Guilford.

Schaie, K. W. (1987). Application of psychometric intelligence to the prediction of everyday competence in the elderly. In C. Schooler & K. W. Schaie (Eds.), Cognitive functioning and social structure over the life course (pp. 50–58). New York: Ablex.

Part II

MEMORY STRATEGIES AND METAMEMORY COMPETENCIES AS DETERMINANTS OF MEMORY DEVELOPMENT

Beyond Production Deficiency and Utilization Inefficiency: Mechanisms of the Emergence of Strategic Categorization in Episodic Memory Tasks

Marcus Hasselhorn
Technical University of Dresden

In the late 1960s, Flavell (e.g., 1970) stimulated memory development research by focusing on children's information-processing activities (cf. Schneider & Pressley, 1989). The pioneering work of Flavell and his associates was concerned with the conscious and intentional memory activities now known as strategies. One of the most frequently studied mnemonic strategies is semantic grouping or categorical organization, an approach studied by Flavell in his early work. *Organizational strategies* are typically observed in recall studies when subjects are given a list of items that can be devided into semantic categories (e.g., several instances of *furniture*, *body parts*, and *vehicles* are used), with the items presented randomly. When subjects' recall of the items is related to the tendency to cluster according to the underlying semantic categories of the list, the inference has often been made that the learner used categorization strategically, either at encoding, retrieval, or both.

FAILURES OF CHILDREN'S USE OF ORGANIZATIONAL STRATEGIES: PRODUCTION DEFICIENCY AND UTILIZATION INEFFICIENCY EXPLANATIONS

In the early 1970s, there was a consistent pattern of results in studies of organization of recall: First, memory performance increased from early childhood through adolescence. Second, there was an increase in the extent of clustering on the basis of predetermined semantic relations during recall between age 2 and college level. And third, there were usually correlations between the amount recalled and the level of categorical organization, with the magnitude of the correlation increasing with increasing age of the individuals tested (cf. reviews by Lange, 1978; Moely, 1977; Ornstein & Corsale, 1979).

One of the first attempts to explain younger children's failure to cluster items on the basis of semantic relations was provided by Lange (1973, 1978). He proposed that elementary school children's clustering behavior varies with the strength of interitem associations. For example, Haynes and Kulhavy (1976, Exp. 1) contrasted recall clustering among 7-, 9-, and 12-year-olds for high- and low-associate items and found superior clustering for high-associates. Because associated items can automatically elicit one another at recall and additionally are likely to be recognized by the child as preorganized units, Lange (1978) concluded "that the recall organization we sometimes see in preschool and elementary school children has an exogenous basis and occurs through a series of involuntary actions that can operate at both the perceptual-encoding and retrieval phases of processing" (p. 107). In other words, children's knowledge of associations permits ready identification of associations when a list is first presented and facilitates retrieval of list items at testing.

Lange's position stimulated other researchers to elaborate this knowledge base account of children's processing of categorizable lists (Bjorklund, 1985, 1987). In the mid-1980s, Bjorklund argued that the developmental increase in children's free recall clustering is mediated by mechanisms representing unconscious and automatic side effects of age differences in semantic memory (i.e., older children have more and stronger associations permitting more certain automatic categorization at study and more automatic associatively based retrieval at testing). According to this view, spontaneous and deliberate (i.e., strategic) organization does not arise before adolescence.

For several years Bjorklund (1985, 1987) preferred to classify children's category organization behavior as *production deficient*, a term proposed by Flavell (1970) to describe a developmental stage in which children do not spontaneously use strategies they are able to use. Production deficiencies reflect lack of awareness of the strategic utility of categorical organization, a specific metamemory deficiency. Accordingly, production deficient children should lack understanding of the mnemonic significance of categorization. Because most 10-year-old children were found to have adequate metamnemonic knowledge about organizational strategies (Hasselhorn, 1990a, 1990b; Justice, 1986; Schneider, 1986), the production deficiency explanation of children's organizational failures seemed questionable.

In a recent paper Bjorklund, Coyle, and Gaultney (1992) introduced a new characterization of children's use of categorization in episodic memory tasks. Bjorklund and Harnishfeger (1987) observed that when children first use a strategy, they often do not reap memory benefits. Thus, the authors suggested a transitional phase in the development of organizational strategies they dubbed a *utilization deficiency* following a distinction offered by Miller (1990). The utilization deficient 9- or 10-year-old spontaneously generates categorical organizations, but either does not benefit, or experiences less benefit than shown by older children. Sometimes, there is even a decline in memory performance as a function of using the strategy.

Bjorklund et al. (1992) presented to 6-, 9-, and 13-year-olds five free-recall trials using different lists and different categories on each trial. Levels of recall and clustering increased with age. Although both 9- and 13-year-olds demonstrated the use of an organizational strategy, this led to increased performance for only the 13-year-olds. Thus, a utilization deficiency was shown for the 9-year-olds, interpreted by Bjorklund et al. to be a transitional phase in strategy development.

Although the demonstration of the spontaneous generation of categorical organization in recall tasks without related improvements in retention is empirically and theoretically interesting, I feel ill at ease with use of the term utilization deficiency to characterize this phenomenon. The phenomenon demonstrated by Bjorklund et al. (1992) might more fairly be termed *utilization inefficiency*, because the strategic behavior was produced spontaneously by the 9-year-olds (i.e., with no production deficiency) but was inefficient. In contrast, a utilization deficiency would occur if a subject intends to use an organizational strategy but does not have enough knowledge about the categorical relationships between list items to do so (see Reese, 1976, for a similar argument regarding the distinction between deficiencies and inefficiencies). A second reason for concern about the term utilization deficiency pertains to its theoretical status. Is it possible to go beyond the pure description of behavioral patterns to theoretical constructs that might explain the utilization deficiency?

PRODUCTION DEFICIENCY AND UTILIZATION INEFFICIENCY: DESCRIPTIVE OR EXPLANATORY TERMS?

As descriptive terms, production deficiency and utilization inefficiency characterize specific behavioral problems during learning and remembering without explicating the functional mechanisms surrounding the observed behavioral deficits. This is consistent with the neobehavioristic roots of these concepts. For example, Kendler (1972) used the S–r–s–R scheme of mediational theory to characterize production deficiencies. From her point of view, production deficiency "refers to a failure of the environmental event, S, to produce a hypothetical mediator, r, even though the mediator is in the repertoire of the subject" (p. 2).

From a developmental perspective, there is a serious problem with this approach. Although developmental sequences were formulated to characterize the growth of memory strategies, they are descriptive rather than explanatory. One well-known example of such a descriptive model is the five-level progression of mnemonic effectiveness provided by Ornstein, Baker-Ward, and Naus (1988):

1. At early points along this continuum, the young child does not utilize strategies in the context of deliberate memory tasks.

2. Somewhat later, in the preschool years, a child may behave strategically in some situations that require remembering, but the effects of these mnemonic efforts may not be realized in actual memory "dividends".

3. Further along the early elementary-school years, the child's mnemonic efforts may be somewhat effective, but the deployment of strategies may be in part determined by the salience of the stimulus materials.

4. Later still, strategies may be used in a variety of settings, with stimuli of varying degrees of saliency, and these strategies are effective.

5. Finally, strategy implementation becomes increasingly effective, reflecting the routinization and automatization that comes from both practice and the development of certain underlying information handling skills. (p. 38)

Apart from the allusion to certain underlying information processing skills, this model of memory strategy development is hard to discriminate from the mechanistic and environmentalistic theorizing of neobehaviorism, because no internal mechanisms are postulated to explain the child's progression from one level to the next. If a child fails to use a particular memory strategy spontaneously when the situation calls for it, or if he or she produces the strategy inefficiently, there are at least two classes of functional explanations: Either the necessary cognitive competencies are not well developed, or the contextual conditions do not elicit or permit the previously available competencies. It is impossible to know why strategies were not used or were not used efficiently from the failure to observe effective strategic processes on a memory task.

This general problem motivated Fischer (1980) to introduce the distinction between the *functional level* and the *optimal level* of skills that a person can construct and control. This basic distinction of skill theory took into account that the individual's behavior varies in quality across contexts and from moment to moment. Fischer stated that what shows true developmental level is the upper limit of a person's skill. Thus, developmental changes are best measured by attending to optimal levels of performance. I am convinced that focusing on optimal levels is the best way to overcome the environmentalistic heritage of neobehaviorism.

AN ALTERNATIVE VIEW ON THE DEVELOPMENT OF ORGANIZATIONAL STRATEGIES: THE STRATEGY EMERGENCE THEORY

During the last few years, I developed an alternative theory to the automatic knowledge activation accounts of children's categorical organization in memory tasks (see Hasselhorn, 1992b). This theory—the strategy emergence theory—

might also replace the descriptive production deficiency and utilization inefficiency accounts of children's suboptimal use of mnemonic strategies. The strategy emergence theory is an optimal level theory of the emergence of deliberate strategic categorization in late childhood. Its core idea is that between 8 and 10 years of age, most children acquire sufficient metamnemonic knowledge about organizational strategies so that they can use them effectively. As a consequence, 10-year-olds, in contrast to 8-year-olds, are able to make strategic use of their knowledge about the categorical structure of list items presented for study.

Theoretical Framework

An elaborated information-processing framework that integrates three successful models of current memory research was used as the theoretical background to explicate the strategy emergence theory: (a) Baddeley's (1986) working memory model as a powerful functional alternative to common generic resource views of human information-processing capacity; (b) the semantic network model of the representational properties of a subject's knowledge base, including the assumption of automatic spreading activation (cf. Anderson & Pirolli, 1984; Collins & Loftus, 1975; Rabinowitz & Chi, 1987); and (c) Tulving's (1982, 1983) synergistic ecphory model that postulates two kinds of processes involved in the retrieval of memory contents, namely *ecphory* and *conversion*.

Working Memory. Baddeley and Hitch (1974) introduced the concept of a working memory system to stress the functional role of short-term memory in performing complex cognitive tasks. The authors put great emphasis on the short-term functions of memory in the processing of information in everyday activities, such as the retention of information for short periods when reading so that ideas can be integrated. Perhaps the main difference between their working memory model and previous concepts of short-term memory is that working memory is a complex arrangement of systems rather than a unitary store. Baddeley (1986; Baddeley & Hitch, 1974) proposed a model of working memory in which a controlling attentional system supervises and coordinates a number of short-term storage slave systems, each specialized for a particular type of information: These include the speech-based articulatory or phonological loop and the visual–spatial sketchpad, assumed to be responsible for setting up and manipulating visual images. Because categorical organization, like most memory strategies addressed in the memory development literature, is a powerful tool for processing verbal materials, the phonological loop is the slave-system of interest in the present context.

The phonological loop is comprised of two components, a phonological store capable of holding speech-based information and an articulatory control process based on subvocal rehearsal. Memory traces within the phonological store are assumed to fade and become unretrievable after about 1.5 to 2 sec. The memory trace can, however, be refreshed by subvocal rehearsal processes. The limited functional capacity or the operational efficiency of the phonological loop is defined in terms of time, because the system capacity is determined in part by the speed of the subvocal rehearsal processes (i.e., the slower the vocalization the less that can be held in the phonological loop). Another important factor determining the functional capacity of working memory is the limit in resources of the central executive, assumed to control the manipulation and flow of information in the phonological loop.

Semantic Network. As can be seen in Fig. 8.1, working memory in the present framework is considered to be a functional system that works within and upon one's knowledge base. Analogous to Bjorklund's (1985, 1987) thinking, I conceptualize representation and activation of the knowledge base in terms of a semantic network (cf. Anderson & Pirolli, 1984; Collins & Loftus, 1975). Within this network, concepts are represented as nodes that are interconnected by associative links (for illustration of the network structure, the magnifying glass was marked in Fig. 8.1). The input of information (e.g., by the presentation of an item) activates related nodes in the associative network. Activation then spreads from those nodes to related nodes across the associative links. The amount and direction of this spreading activation depends on the strength of the associative links between concepts, with stronger associations leading to stronger activations.

Rabinowitz and Chi (1987), in particular, tried to make the spreading activation concept more precise. First, they claimed that when no nodes are active (i.e., in a quiet system, where no information has yet been presented), the activation level of all nodes is equivalent to their resting state. Upon presentation of an item, the activation level of the node representing that item rises from the resting state. The spread of activation, however, does not start until the activation level of the node exceeds a threshold point. Once exceeded, the spread of activation does not follow an all-or-none principle. Rather, the amount of activation depends not only on the strength of the associative link, but also on the level of activation of the node. The probability of one's being aware of the activation of a concept increases as the level of activation increases above the threshold value. Once a node starts to become active, there is always a tendency for that node to decay back to its resting state, unless it is reactivated. There are different kinds of links in the network (e.g., associative, thematic, categorical, etc.) whose activation may be promoted or hindered by control processes supervised by the central executive of the working memory. That is, the executive may point the activation to categorically associated nodes if the task the subject is doing demands categorical information.

The semantic network not only incorporates all pieces of declarative world knowledge, but also experience-based knowledge about one's own memory (i.e., metamemory). This part of the associative network is responsible for the optimal

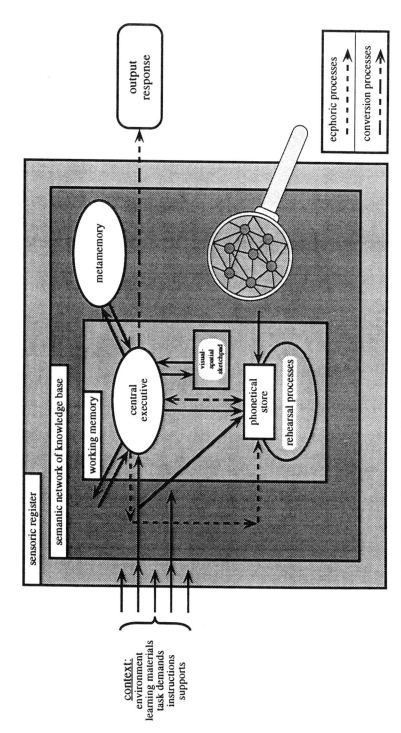

FIG. 8.1.   Theoretical framework of the information-processing system: Structures and mechanisms.

147

level quality of the control processes, which can be activated and regulated by the central executive. That is, it encodes information about where and when particular control processes are appropriate.

Synergistic Ecphory. According to Tulving (1983), information acquired during a learning episode, and thus represented in one's knowledge base, can be retrieved by *synergistic ecphory*. Synergistic ecphory includes two kinds of processes, called ecphory and conversion. Ecphoric processes are invoked by retrieval cues and are responsible for the activation of potentially relevant nodes in the knowledge base. The pieces of knowledge activated by ecphory are checked by conversion processes, which as a consequence, regulate the output behavior in a memory situation. The kind of actual conversion process is determined by the given retrieval demands. For instance, in a recall task requiring a detailed description of an event or its characteristics, the ecphoric information (i.e., the product of the ecphoric processes) that, for example, a red vehicle was among the relevant items, may be not sufficient to recall that a red bus (and not a fire truck) had been presented.

The three outlined models and concepts from recent memory research are the components of the integrated framework illustrated in Fig. 8.1, in which the specific developmental assumptions of the strategy emergence theory can be explicated.

Developmental Assumptions

Strategy emergence theory postulates the emergence of strategic knowledge activation between ages 8 and 10. The production of categorical organization in younger children is seen to be a byproduct of the spreading of activation within the semantic network, which is thought to occur automatically, without conscious control by the child. Similar explanations were provided by Bjorklund (1985, 1987) and by Rabinowitz and McAuley (1990). Of course, these authors suggested that this is the best explanation, at least up to the preadolescent years. In contrast, strategy emergence theory postulates that the automatic spreading activation account is a sufficient explanation of children's use of categorical organization only for younger children up to age 8 or 9.

Although nearly all structures and processes introduced in the outlined framework are affected by developmental changes during elementary school years, strategy emergence theory emphasizes the qualitative changes in the control processes involved in the encoding and retrieval of information. These qualitative changes in control processes are the result of the acquisition of specific metamemory concerning organizational strategies. As a consequence, when categorizable lists are presented for learning, the categorical information is processed deliberately as soon as the child detects that two or more items are from the same category.

Another implication of a sufficient or adequate metamemory at about 10 years of age is that the central executive activates categorically aligned ecphoric search processes during retrieval. Thus, the probability that categorically related nodes are activated, transferred into the phonological store, and then are held in readiness for conversion by subvocal rehearsal, increases dramatically. The result is a qualitative change in the use of categorical organization at about 10 years.

Four main predictions may be deduced from strategy emergence theory, suitable to test the outlined developmental assumptions:

1. Between ages 8 and 10, the percentage of children with an adequate metamemory regarding organizational strategies increases more rapidly than between adjacent age groups.
2. The percentage of children with strategic usage of categorization increases between 8 and 10, as well.
3. In contrast to younger children, there is a substantial positive relationship between task-specific metamemory and strategic categorization among 10-year-olds.
4. Ten-year-olds are able to utilize organizational strategies efficiently (i.e., their strategic use of categorization leads to higher levels of recall performance).

Empirical Evidence From Different Memory Tasks

Free Recall After Serial Learning. A first series of experiments to test the predictions of strategy emergence theory concerning retrieval was done by Hasselhorn (1990b) with children in Grades 2 and 4. An experimental procedure was developed where subjects first had to learn items of a categorizable list in a noncategorical order to the criterion of two perfect serial recall trials. After a 12- to 15-minute retention interval, children unexpectedly received either serial recall, free recall, or cued recall instructions, where the categorical relationships among items were made explicit to provide the optimal retrieval structure. Metamemory was assessed by a slightly modified version of a procedure developed by Andreassen and Waters (1989). Nine items from three distinct categories not represented in the memorization list were presented on display cards, either in three rows by categories or in three randomly arranged rows, with no two items of the same category in the same row. The child was asked about the best way to learn the items. Children were classified as having an adequate metamemory when they correctly chose the categorically organized display card and established their choice by the usefulness of the category organization.

In Experiment 1, the metamemory question was asked prior to recall. In accordance with the prediction of a significant increase in metamemory about organizational strategies between ages 8 and 10, more fourth graders (67%) than second graders (44%) displayed adequate metamemory, $\chi^2(1, N = 96) = 5.10$, $p <$ .05. Children with a Ratio of Repetition (RR) (a measure of categorical organization of recalled items; Bousfield, 1953) above chance level were classified as categorical organizers. As predicted from the strategy emergence theory, the percentage of categorical organizers in the free recall condition was greater in Grade 4 (88%) than in Grade 2 (44%), $\chi^2(1, N = 32) = 6.79$, $p < .05$. In addition, the relation between being a categorical organizer and having adequate metamemory was significant in the free recall condition, $\chi^2(1, N = 32) = 4.39$, $p <$ .05. Finally, as can be seen in Fig. 8.2, fourth graders' recall exceeded that of second graders only in the free, but not in the serial (i.e., where the use of the organizational strategy was tied underneath) and cued (i.e., where the use of the strategy was urged upon) recall condition, and this grade effect on free recall data was eliminated when metamemory and categorical clustering were partialled out.

This pattern of results proved robust not only with variation in when the metamemory question was posed (Hasselhorn, 1990b, Exp. 2), but also against manipulations in which age differences in categorical knowledge were minimized by using atypical category exemplars as stimulus items (Hasselhorn, 1990b, Exp. 3). This latter result is of special importance because it disproves the objection that fourth graders' superiority in the free recall condition is reducible to the effects of automatic spreading activation.

Sort-Recall. Because strategy emergence theory not only predicts strategic organization of 10-year-olds during the retrieval of episodic memories, but also during the acquisition and encoding of to-be-remembered items, organization

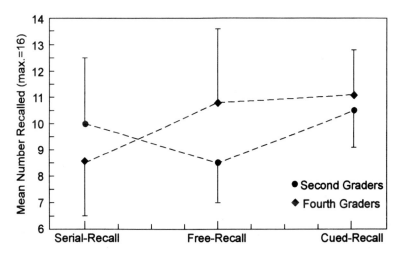

FIG. 8.2. Mean recall and standard deviations as a function of grade and retrieval condition (data from Hasselhorn, 1990b, Exp. 1).

during study was analyzed in other experiments of strategy emergence theory, involving the sort-recall paradigm. Sort-recall (Mandler & Stephens, 1967) was chosen to provide children sufficient time to encode stimulus items and some contextual support to help them operate at their optimal level of spontaneous strategic categorization. The sort-recall procedure is comprised of two phases: a sorting phase, in which items are presented simultaneously and subjects are instructed to put those items together that belong together, and a recall phase in which the free recall of the presented items is required.

Because most of the commonly used sort-recall instructions bias children to form meaningful groupings and thus do not provide good opportunity to analyze children's spontaneous strategic categorization, a nonspecific sort instruction, not mentioning the categorical relationship of the items, was used in the present experiments. The sort-recall procedure was as follows: Children were tested individually and were told that they would play a kind of memory game in which a list of pictures would be presented. They should carefully attend to them to remember as many as possible. The experimenter presented the picture cards on the child's desk in a random order and named all the items. He then invited the child to arrange the cards in a sequence he or she deemed the best for learning. A 2- to 3-minute sorting period was allowed, with 1 more minute for study while the experimenter recorded the child's sorting order. When the sort-study phase was completed, items were removed and a distractor task was performed for 30 seconds to eliminate recall from immediate memory (i.e., from the phonological store). In the output phase of the memorization task, children verbally recalled as many items as they could in any order they wished. To assess children's metamemorial awareness of the organizational strategy, the experimenter concluded by asking the children to describe how they managed to remember so many pictures.

Clustering scores (Bousfield's RR) were obtained for input organization during sorting and output organization during recall. Children were classified as strategic if (a) their clustering scores at input as well as at output were reliably above chance (i.e., at least 1 SD above the chance level), and (b) they showed adequate metamemorial awareness of their use of categorical organization (i.e., they explicitly mentioned having made use of the categorical list structure when asked after recall by the experimenter).

In the first study in which I (Hasselhorn, 1990a) used this kind of sort-recall task, I employed a cross-sequential design with 267 children, ranging in age from 6 to 10. Subjects were tested at four occasions within a period of about 1 year. At the first measurement point, distal specific metamemory was assessed by a modified version of the Organized List subtest of Belmont and Borkowski's (1988) metamemory battery, which in a recent retest study with a retest interval of about 4 weeks has exhibited satisfactory reliability at Grade 2 ($r_{xx} = .72$) as well as at Grade 4 ($r_{xx} = .73$) (Hasselhorn, 1994). In this subtest, children are presented two different pairs of picture lists. In both cases, one list is one item shorter than the other list, but consists of single items drawn from different categories. The longer list consists of groups of several items from one of several different categories, respectively, and the pictures are arranged by category. Subjects have to decide for each pair which of the lists might be easier to learn and they are requested to give a reason for their decision. Metamemory was considered to be adequate when at least one of the two Organized List questions was answered perfectly, requiring making one's choice in favor of the categorically arranged list and explicitly substantiating this choice by mentioning the category structure of the material.

Three months later, the same children received a 16-item categorizable list as a sort-recall task. Then, 5 months later, a distal specific metamemory assessment was made. Finally, another 3 months later, the sort-recall task was repeated.

The four predictions deduced from the strategy emergence theory were once again corroborated in this study. The percentage of children with adequate distal specific metamemory increased most significantly between Grade 3 (18% and 21% at the first and second metamemory measurement point) and Grade 4 (31% and 50%). Similar developmental changes were found for the percentage of strategic children in the sort-recall tasks (0%, 0%, 10%, 13%, and 44% for children from the preschool level to Grade 4 at the first sort-recall assessment; and 4%, 7%, 18%, and 35% for subjects from Grade 1 to Grade 4 at the second sort-recall measurement point). Reliable positive correlations between distal specific metamemory and children's input- as well as output-organization in both sort-recall tasks assessed 3 months after finishing the related metamemory subtest occurred only at the Grade 4 level (rs ranging from .31 to .46). Finally, strategic children's recall was significantly better than that of nonstrategic children.

Although this pattern of results is consistent with strategy emergence theory, one might argue that most of the effects (especially those concerning the strategic use of categorical organization) reported by Hasselhorn (1990a) might be explained in terms of developmental increases in children's semantic knowledge and the age-invariant automatic spreading of knowledge activation. After all, the same list items were used at all grade levels, so that older children would have been more familiar with these items than younger children (see the age-related differences in children's typicality productions [Posnansky, 1978] and judgments [Bjorklund, Thompson, & Ornstein, 1983]).

Thus, in collaboration with Dorothee Büttner, I constructively replicated Hasselhorn (1990a). In this study, list material was manipulated in such a way that category knowledge about the memorization items was held constant across grade levels. A total of 211 children from Grades 1 ($N = 43$), 2 ($N = 56$), 3 ($N = 56$), and 4 ($N = 56$) participated in the study. For each grade level a list of 24 items, with eight members belonging to each of three categories (*body parts, animals, furniture*) was constructed with four high typical (e.g., *lion, dog*) and four low typical (e.g., *frog, owl*) exemplars for each category. Mean typicality for high typical as well as low typical items did not differ across grade levels (see Hasselhorn, 1992b, Study 4, for a more detailed description). About 7 months before children were presented with the sort-recall task, metamemory was assessed by the modified Organized List subtest previously decribed.

As predicted by strategy emergence theory, the percentage of children classified as having adequate metamemory (7%, 11%, 13%, and 43% from the first to the fourth grade) or as being strategic (26%, 39%, 46%, and 80% in Grades 1 to 4) increased during the elementary school years with a developmental discontinuity between Grades 3 (M age = 9) and 4 (M age = 10). In addition, the relation between having adequate metamemory and being strategic was statistically significant for only third, $\chi^2(1, N = 56) = 4.96$, $p < .05$, and fourth graders, $\chi^2(1, N = 56) = 10.27$, $p < .05$. In accordance with strategy emergence theory, all of the 10-year-old fourth graders with adequate metamemory were classified as strategic. Finally, as can be seen in Fig. 8.3, strategic children outperformed nonstrategic subjects at each grade level ($ts > 3.3$), and the superiority of strategic children's recall was more pronounced among fourth graders than among first, second, or third graders ($ts > 1.78$).

In summary, although category knowledge about list items was held constant across grades, the results of the sort-recall study by Hasselhorn (1990a) were fully replicated. The outcomes in this study were consistent with strategy emergence theory but not the knowledge base account of increased recall during categorizable list learning.

Another sort-recall replication supporting strategy emergence theory was provided by Hasselhorn (1992a). Twice as many 10-year-olds (50%) as 8-year-olds (25%) were found to have adequate metamemory, and more than twice as many 10-year-olds (69%) as compared to 8-year-olds (31%) were identified as being

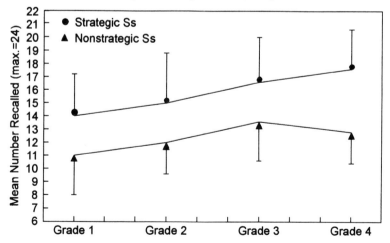

FIG. 8.3. Comparisons between strategic and nonstrategic children's mean recall (and standard deviations) as a function of grade (from Hasselhorn, 1992b, Study 4).

strategic when list items were typical category members. However, no reliable age difference in the percentage of strategic children (19% and 25% for 8-year-olds and 10-year-olds, respectively) was obtained if exclusively atypical category instances were presented in the memorization list. Although most 10-year-olds are capable of strategic use of categorization if the relevant category information is easily activated, many 10-year-olds fail to spontaneously make use of their strategic competence in less than optimal circumstances.

Free Recall. As I demonstrated in Hasselhorn (1990a), the free recall paradigm typically used by the advocates of the knowledge base position (e.g., Bjorklund, 1985, 1987) is inappropriate to test for optimal level behavior with regard to organizational memory strategies. Free recall often demands so much effort that use of organizational strategies is impossible. Thus, a lot of free recall studies reported in the literature without identifying strategic categorization among fourth graders should be interpreted with precaution. Even so, however, I recently demonstrated emerging strategic categorization competencies late in the elementary school years in a free recall context (Hasselhorn, 1992b, Study 10). The item list consisted of 24 animals, of which 6 belonged to the four subcategories of farm animals, tropical animals, aquatic animals, and birds. Items were presented in a random order via tape recorder at a rate of one item every 4 sec. A distractor interval of approximately 30 sec followed the presentation of the last word before children were asked to remember as many animals as possible in any order they wished. After the first 20-sec pause without recall, the experimenter prompted the child to think of other animals that had been presented. If no item was recalled after another 20-sec interval, the trial was completed and the child was asked how he or she managed to remember so many animals.

Thirty second graders and 52 fourth graders participated at two measurement points separated by 7 months. At the first measurement point, metamemory was assessed by the modified Organized List subtest from the Belmont and Borkowski (1988) battery (Hasselhorn, 1994), and the individual knowledge base about animals was assessed by asking children to enumerate as many animals as possible in 5 minutes. At the second measurement point, the free recall task was presented and the child's memory span for one-syllable words was assessed as an indicator of working memory capacity.

From strategy emergence theory, two different models of causal structure were derived for second graders and for fourth graders (see Fig. 8.4).

As would be predicted from strategy emergence theory, the characteristic difference between the causal structures of 8-year-olds and 10-year-olds is that the dominance of automatic knowledge base influences at the former age is replaced by a beginning dominance of deliberate metamemory influences at about 10 years of age. This prediction was confirmed by path analysis with manifest variables using LISREL VI (Jöreskog & Sörbom, 1986). As can be easily seen in Fig. 8.5, the empirical path models provide good approximations to the hy-

(a) 8-year-olds

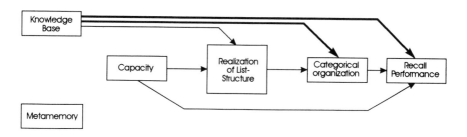

(b) 10-year-olds

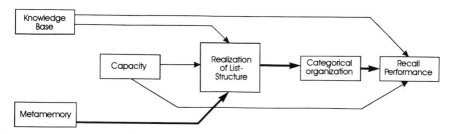

FIG. 8.4. Hypothetical relationships among knowledge base, metamemory, working memory capacity, realization of list structure, categorical organization, and recall performance as predicted by strategy emergence theory for 8-year-olds and 10-year-olds, respectively (from Hasselhorn, 1992b, Study 10).

pothetical causal structures. The only significant deviation between predicted and empirical models was found for the second graders, because none of those children noticed the categorical list structure, and thus, no path estimations with regard to this manifest variable could be performed.

CONCLUDING REMARKS

Although recent theories about memory strategy development emphasized the role of children's automatic use of their developing knowledge base to mediate memory, the present chapter takes an alternative stand. I believe that between 8 and 10 years of age, children begin to deliberately activate knowledge as a strategic approach to learning. The theory is based on Flavell's classic idea of the role of metamemory in memory development and is outlined within an explicit theoretical framework of the human information-processing system. The strategy emergence theory tries to go beyond the commonly used descriptive

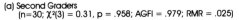

(a) Second Graders
    (n=30; χ²(3) = 0.31, p = .958; AGFI = .979; RMR = .025)

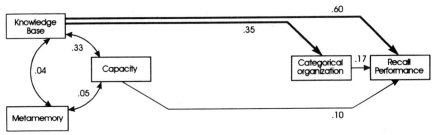

(b) Fourth Graders
    (n=52; χ²(7) = 4.54, p = .716; AGFI = .917; RMR = .051)

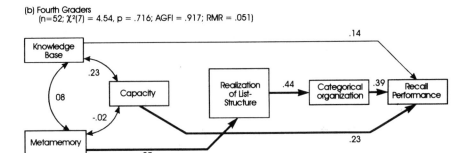

FIG. 8.5. Empirical path models of the relationships among knowledge base, metamemory, working memory capacity, realization of list structure, categorical organization, and recall performance, separated for second graders and fourth graders with the Adjusted Goodness of Fit Index (AGFI) and the Root Mean Square Residual (RMR) (data from Hasselhorn, 1992b, Study 10).

principles of production deficiency and utilization inefficiency by focusing on the optimal level of children's spontaneous strategic behavior. Qualitative changes in the control processes as a result of the acquisition of specific metamemory concerning organizational strategies are emphasized by strategy emergence theory. As a consequence of these changes, the categorical information in lists can be processed deliberately by children from about 10 years of age. Predictions derived from strategy emergence theory were confirmed in a large number of empirical studies, and some of the most important findings are outlined in the present chapter.

Although the confirmation of strategy emergence theory is encouraging, left unresolved is whether the theory applies to strategies other than organization. I believe it might, for there is a well documented developmental transition from middle- to late-childhood in children's use of rehearsal activities in memory situations. Although most younger children up to the age of 9 usually rehearse single stimuli from lists presented for recall, at the age of 10, most children begin to rehearse items cumulatively (e.g. Guttentag, Ornstein, & Siemens, 1987). Thus, the age of 10 seems to be critical for the emergence of the spontaneous strategic use of organizational principles and for the onset of sophisticated cumulative rehearsal strategies.

Considering this obvious parallel between the development of organizational and rehearsal strategies, it seems to be fruitful to analyze the empirical relationship between the emergence of strategic organization and the onset of the use of cumulative rehearsal and other strategic forms of memory activities. Perhaps this line of inquiry will bring forth results that foster the idea of a nontrivial conceptual change about learning and remembering between middle- and late-childhood.

ACKNOWLEDGMENTS

The research reported in this chapter was supported in part by a grant of the *Deutsche Forschungsgemeinschaft*, Bonn, Federal Republic of Germany (Ha 1452/2–1 and 2–2). I am grateful to Mike Pressley for his valuable help in improving the language of the present chapter.

REFERENCES

Anderson, J. R., & Pirolli, P. L. (1984). Spread of activation. *Journal of Experimental Psychology: Learning, Memory, and Cognition, 10,* 791–798.

Andreassen, C., & Waters, H. S. (1989). Organization during study: Relationships between metamemory, strategy use, and performance. *Journal of Educational Psychology, 81,* 190–191.

Baddeley, A. D. (1986). *Working memory.* Oxford, England: Oxford University Press.

Baddeley, A. D., & Hitch, G. (1974). Working memory. In G. H. Bower (Ed.), *The psychology of learning and motivation* (Vol. 8, pp. 47–87). New York: Academic Press.

Belmont, J. M., & Borkowski, J. G. (1988). A group-administered test of children's metamemory. *Bulletin of the Psychonomic Society, 26,* 206–208.

Bjorklund, D. F. (1985). The role of conceptual knowledge in the development of organization in children's memory. In C. J. Brainerd & M. Pressley (Eds.), *Basic processes in memory development: Progress in cognitive development research* (pp. 103–142). New York: Springer.

Bjorklund, D. F. (1987). How age changes in knowledge base contribute to the development of children's memory: An interpretative review. *Developmental Review, 7,* 93–130.

Bjorklund, D. F., Coyle, T. R., & Gaultney, J. F. (1992). Developmental differences in the acquisition and maintenance of an organizational strategy: Evidence for the utilization deficiency hypothesis. *Journal of Experimental Child Psychology, 54,* 434–448.

Bjorklund, D. F., & Harnishfeger, K. K. (1987). Developmental differences in the mental effort requirements for the use of an organizational strategy in free recall. *Journal of Experimental Child Psychology, 44,* 109–125.

Bjorklund, D. F., Thompson, B. E., & Ornstein, P. A. (1983). Developmental trends in children's typicality judgments. *Behavior Research Methods & Instrumentation, 15,* 350–356.

Bousfield, W. A. (1953). The occurrence of clustering in the recall of randomly arranged sequences. *Journal of General Psychology, 49,* 229–240.

Collins, A. M., & Loftus, E. F. (1975). A spreading-activation theory of semantic processing. *Psychological Review, 82*, 407–428.

Fischer, K. W. (1980). A theory of cognitive development: The control and construction of hierarchies of skills. *Psychological Review, 87*, 477–531.

Flavell, J. H. (1970). Developmental studies of mediated memory. In H. W. Reese & L. P. Lipsitt (Eds.), *Advances in child development and behavior* (Vol. 5, pp. 181–211). New York: Academic Press.

Guttentag, R. E., Ornstein, P. A., & Siemens, L. (1987). Children's spontaneous rehearsal: Transitions in strategy acquisition. *Cognitive Development, 2*, 307–326.

Hasselhorn, M. (1990a). Kategoriales Organisieren als Gedächtnisstrategie: Allgemeine und differentielle Entwicklungsperspektiven im Grundschulalter [Categorical organization as a memory strategy: Universal and differential developmental perspectives during the early grade-school years]. In M. Knopf & W. Schneider (Eds.), *Entwicklung. Allgemeine Verläufe - Individuelle Unterschiede-Pädagogische Konsequenzen* (pp. 117–143). Göttingen: Hogrefe.

Hasselhorn, M. (1990b). The emergence of strategic knowledge activation in categorical clustering during retrieval. *Journal of Experimental Child Psychology, 50*, 59–80.

Hasselhorn, M. (1992a). Task dependency and the role of category typicality and metamemory in the development of an organizational strategy. *Child Development, 63*, 202–214.

Hasselhorn, M. (1992b). *Entwicklung kategorialen Organisierens: Anfänge der Wissensnutzung als Strategie kindlicher Gedächtnistätigkeit* [Developmental changes in categorical organization: The beginnings of knowledge utilization as a strategy in the child's memory behavior]. Unveröffentlichte Habilitationsschrift: Universität Göttingen.

Hasselhorn, M. (1994). Zur Erfassung von Metagedächtnisaspekten bei Grundschulkindern [On the measurement of metamemory aspects in children]. *Zeitschrift für Entwicklungspsychologie und Pädagogische Psychologie, 26*, 71–78.

Haynes, C. R., & Kulhavy, R. W. (1976). Conservation level and category clustering. *Developmental Psychology, 12*, 179–184.

Jöreskog, K. G., & Sörbom, D. (1986). *LISREL VI: Analysis of linear structural relationships by maximum likelihood, instrumental variables, and least squares methods* (4th ed.). Mooresville, IN: Scientific Software, Inc.

Justice, E. M. (1986). Developmental changes in judgments of relative strategy effectiveness. *British Journal of Developmental Psychology, 4*, 75–81.

Kendler, T. S. (1972). An ontogeny of mediational deficiency. *Child Development, 43*, 1–17.

Lange, G. (1973). The development of conceptual and rote recall skills among school age children. *Journal of Experimental Child Psychology, 15*, 394–406.

Lange, G. (1978). Organization-related processes in children's recall. In P. A. Ornstein (Ed.), *Memory development in children* (pp. 101–128). Hillsdale, NJ: Lawrence Erlbaum Associates.

Mandler, G., & Stephens, D. (1967). The development of free and constrained conceptualization and subsequent verbal memory. *Journal of Experimental Child Psychology, 5*, 86–93.

Miller, P. H. (1990). The development of strategies of selective attention. In D. F. Bjorklund (Ed.), *Children's strategies. Contemporary views of cognitive development* (pp. 157–184). Hillsdale, NJ: Lawrence Erlbaum Associates.

Moely, B. E. (1977). Organizational factors in the development of memory. In R. V. Kail & J. W. Hagen (Eds.), *Perspectives on the development of memory and cognition* (pp. 203–236). Hillsdale, NJ: Lawrence Erlbaum Associates.

Ornstein, P. A., & Corsale, K. (1979). Organizational factors in children's memory. In C. Puff (Ed.), *Memory organization and structure* (pp. 219–257). New York: Academic Press.

Ornstein, P. A., Baker-Ward, L., & Naus, M. J. (1988). The development of mnemonic skill. In F. E. Weinert & M. Perlmutter (Eds.), *Memory development: Universal changes and individual differences* (pp. 31–50). Hillsdale, NJ: Lawrence Erlbaum Associates.

Posnansky, C. J. (1978). Category norms for verbal items in 25 categories for children in grades 2–6. *Behavior Research Methods & Instrumentation, 10*, 819–832.

Rabinowitz, M., & Chi, M. T. H. (1987). An interactive model of strategic processing. In S. J. Ceci (Ed.), *Handbook of cognitive, social, and neuropsychological aspects of learning disabilities* (Vol. 2, pp. 83–102). Hillsdale, NJ: Lawrence Erlbaum Associates.

Rabinowitz, M., & McAuley, R. (1990). Conceptual knowledge processing: An oxymoron? In W. Schneider & F. E. Weinert (Eds.), *Interactions among aptitudes, strategies, and knowledge in cognitive performance* (pp. 117–133). New York: Springer.

Reese, H. W. (1976). The development of memory: Life-span perspectives. In H. W. Reese (Ed.), *Advances in child development and behavior* (Vol. 11, pp. 190–212). New York: Academic Press.

Schneider, W. (1986). The role of conceptual knowledge and metamemory in the development of organizational processes in memory. *Journal of Experimental Child Psychology, 42,* 218–236.

Schneider, W., & Pressley, M. (1989). *Memory development between 2 and 20.* New York: Springer.

Tulving, E. (1982). Synergistic ecphory in recall and recognition. *Canadian Journal of Psychology, 36,* 130–147.

Tulving, E. (1983). *Elements of episodic memory.* Oxford, England: Oxford University Press.

Chapter 9

Utilization Deficiencies in the Development of Memory Strategies

David F. Bjorklund
Thomas R. Coyle
Florida Atlantic University

Strategies have a venerable history in cognitive psychology. The cognitive revolution began with plans and strategies (Miller, Galanter, & Pribram, 1960), and age differences in strategies (or covert mediators) can be traced to the beginning of the information-processing era in cognitive development (see Harnishfeger & Bjorklund, 1990, for an historical review). Strategies are traditionally defined as goal-directed cognitive operations used to facilitate task performance. Most researchers agree that strategies reflect operations above and beyond those that are natural consequences of carrying out a task, are intentional, and are potentially available to consciousness (e.g., Pressley, Forrest-Pressley, Elliot-Faust, & Miller, 1985).

Since the rediscovery of memory by developmental psychologists in the late 1960s (see Schneider & Pressley, 1989), strategies have played a central role in the study of memory development. In fact, during much of this time, it is fair to say that memory development was often viewed as being equivalent to strategy development (Howe & O'Sullivan, 1990). Age changes in intentional memory were seen as reflecting children's increasing tendency to use strategies. Memory development could be described in terms of the two great deficiencies: *mediational*, in which children could not use a strategy even when one was demonstrated to them (Reese, 1962), and *production*, in which children could improve their memory performance when shown a strategy, but failed to use one spontaneously (Flavell, 1970).

The theoretical hegemony of memory development as strategy development began to break down in the 1980s as new evidence and interpretations of memory and strategy development arose. For example, even young children were found to use strategies, albeit simple and sometimes ineffective ones (e.g., DeLoache, Cassidy, & Brown, 1985; Wellman, 1988); performance that looked strategic was deemed by some to reflect instead the relatively automatic activation of semantic memory relations, and thus not to qualify as strategic (e.g., Bjorklund, 1985; Dempster, 1985); the relationship between indices of strategy use and memory performance was not always positive (e.g., Bjorklund & Jacobs, 1985; Frankel & Rollins, 1985); and occasionally when children used a strategy, either spontaneously or as a result of training, task performance did not improve (e.g., Baker-Ward, Ornstein, & Holden, 1984; Bjorklund & Harnishfeger, 1987; Miller, Haynes, DeMarie-Dreblow, & Woody-Ramsey, 1986). It is this latter phenomenon that concerns us here, what Miller (1990) referred to as a *utilization deficiency*.

In her work on selective attention strategies, Miller observed a phase when children would use an appropriate strategy spontaneously—one similar or identical to that used by an older child—but, unlike the older child, experience no enhancement in performance (e.g., Miller et al., 1986). Miller and her colleagues used one of two general methods for assessing strategy development. In evaluating *selective attention* strategies, children are shown a series of boxes with doors on top, arranged in two rows (e.g., DeMarie-Dreblow & Miller, 1988; Miller et al., 1986; Woody-Ramsey & Miller, 1988; Miller, Seier, Probert, & Aloise, 1991; Miller, Woody-Ramsey, & Aloise, 1991). On half of the doors are pictures of cages, meaning that those boxes contained pictures of animals. On the other half of the doors are pictures of a house, meaning that those boxes contained pictures of household objects. Children are then told to find and remember for later all of the examples from one of the categories, opening doors one at a time. The degree to which they searched boxes from only the relevant category (animals or household objects) is used as an indication of strategy use.

In assessing *same–different strategies*, children are again shown the two rows of boxes, this time without the pictures on the doors (Miller & Harris, 1988; Miller et al., 1986). Their task is to determine whether the top and bottom rows are identical or not. The most efficient strategy here would be to determine whether or not each vertical pair of boxes contained the same objects (called the *vertical pairs* strategy).

With respect to tasks assessing selective attention strategies, the primary dependent measure of successful performance is the number of items correctly recalled, with patterns of door openings reflecting strategy use. In general, in experiments with children ranging in age from 3 to 13 years, Miller and her colleagues reported greater benefits to recall of proper strategy use (i.e., opening only or primarily category-appropriate doors) on this task for older than for younger children. For example, in a study by Miller, Seier, Probert, and Aloise (1991), older children (fourth and fifth graders) were more likely than younger children (kindergartners and first graders) to benefit from the use of a spontaneously produced selective attention strategy (Recall Ms = 5.06 and 3.46 items for older and younger children, respectively). In other words, when strategy production was equivalent, only the older children showed a performance benefit.

Evidence of utilization deficiencies is less clear for the less complex same–different task, but present nonetheless. For example, research by Miller and Harris (1988) with 3- and 4-year-olds, reported differential effectiveness of strategy use on performance for children of different ages. As we mentioned, the most efficient strategy on this task is the vertical pairs strategy. They reported that use of the vertical pairs strategy accounted for more variance with respect to the correct judgments of the 4-year-olds (48%) than the 3-year-olds (22%). This suggests that the vertical pairs strategy was more likely to result in correct same–different judgments for the 4-year-olds than it was for the 3-year-olds.

From these findings, Miller (1990) described four steps in the acquisition of a strategy. First, children fail to produce a strategy; this is followed by a second step when the strategy is used only partially. In the third step, children use a strategy, but it provides them with no gains in task performance. This is a utilization deficiency. Finally, in a fourth step, children use the strategy and realize benefits in task performance. Seen from this perspective, a utilization deficiency reflects "a developmental lag between spontaneously producing the strategy and receiving any benefits from it" (p. 160).

Such findings do not fit with the traditional mediational or production deficiencies cognitive developmentalists had become so comfortable with. At about the same time Miller was reporting her initial findings, Bjorklund and his colleagues were reporting evidence of a discrepancy between levels of organization in strategic memory task and corresponding levels of memory performance. For example, in the class-recall paradigm, in which children are to recall the names of their current classmates in any order they wish, levels of recall and organization are typically high but unrelated, with children who are aware of using a retrieval strategy having only a small (or nonexistent) recall advantage relative to children who are unaware of using a strategy (e.g., Bjorklund & Zeman, 1982, 1983). Moreover, in a training study where children were requested to recall their classmates' names by a specific strategy (seating arrangement or sex of child), they did so, often perfectly; yet, despite near-perfect levels of clustering, levels of recall were comparable to those of children who recalled the names in any order they wished, which rarely yielded perfect levels of organization (Bjorklund & Bjorklund, 1985).

Although the class-recall studies showed a discrepancy between levels of presumed strategy use and memory performance, the study that first alerted our attention to the idea of a utilization deficiency (though we lacked the term at the time), was a dual-task study, training third- and seventh-grade children in the use of an organizational memory strategy (Bjorklund & Harnishfeger, 1987). In that study (Exp. 2), we assessed the degree of mental effort expended on a series of memory tasks by examining changes in a secondary task (finger tapping). Third- and seventh-grade children tapped the space bar of a microcomputer as rapidly as they could: (a) alone (baseline); (b) during a free-recall task with categorically related words (free recall); and (c) during a free-recall task, in which they were trained to use an organizational memory strategy (trained recall). Changes in rate of tapping between the free- and trained-recall conditions (relative to baseline tapping and expressed as percentage interference) reflect the differences in the mental effort requirements of the two tasks, whereas changes in clustering scores reflect differences in the extent to which subjects used an organizational memory strategy on the two tasks. Both the third- and seventh-grade children showed significantly greater interference (i.e., slower tapping rate) in the trained than the free-recall condition, indicating the greater mental effort required for strategy use. Moreover, both groups showed significant increases in levels of clustering as a result of training, demonstrating successful inculcation of the organizational strategy. However, only the older children showed a corresponding increase in levels of memory performance, with the difference between the free- and trained-recall conditions being nonsignificant for the third-grade children. That is, using a strategy for the younger children yielded no benefit in terms of task performance.

This, of course, does not mean that third-grade children could not have learned to effectively use an organizational strategy. Much younger children have been shown to benefit from mnemonic instruction when training is sufficiently rigorous (e.g., Carr & Schneider, 1991). What these results do mean, however, is that it is not sufficient merely to use a strategy; rather, in the early phases of strategy acquisition (either spontaneously or via training) the execution of the strategy may require too much of a child's limited mental resources to afford any significant benefit in terms of task performance (see also Miller et al., 1991a, 1991b).

Although Miller and Bjorklund were the first to discuss in any detail evidence of this new deficiency, upon closer inspection, neither of their findings was truly novel. In fact, the term *utilization deficiency* was introduced by Reese in a footnote in a review paper published in 1976. However, neither Reese nor the rest of the field seemed to pay much attention to the concept until recently, despite the fact that the evidence was right under our noses. Miller and Seier (1994) recently conducted an extensive review of the memory development literature from 1974 through mid-1992, looking for evidence of utilization deficiencies in normal populations (e.g., greater recall for older than comparably strategic younger children). They listed three criteria to select studies appropriate for the examination of utilization deficiencies: (a) independent measures of strategy use and recall, (b) spontaneous strategy production (i.e., training studies were excluded), and (c) analysis examining age differences in strategy use and performance. Excluding evidence of utilization deficiencies from their own lab (total of nine studies) and from Bjorklund's lab (total of six studies), Miller and Seier found 45 studies that reported data that could be evaluated for evidence of utilization deficiencies. Of these 45 studies, 41 provided partial or clear evidence of utilization deficiencies. When combined with Miller's and Bjorklund's evidence, of the 59 studies in the data set, 56 (95%) provided evidence of utilization deficiency.

Why did it take the field so long to identify utilization deficiencies? The obvious reason seems to be that utilization deficiencies did not make any sense given the dominant theoretical perspective of the 1970s and 1980s regarding the development of memory strategies (i.e., memory development as strategy development). With advances in research and theory, strategies were no longer seen as the principal mechanisms of developmental change, but rather as important components of a more complicated process. Using strategies became one way of enhancing task performance, but not the only way, and possibly because of their expense in terms of mental effort (e.g., Bjorklund & Harnishfeger, 1987; Guttentag, 1984; Kee & Davies, 1991), not the most efficient way. Because of the way developmental psychologists came to view strategies, utilization deficiencies were ready to be discovered.

Extending the Definition of Utilization Deficiencies

In this chapter, we expand the range of phenomenon covered by the term utilization deficiency. Although Miller limited the definition to include only spontaneously produced strategies, we propose to expand the concept by including some instances of strategy use as a result of training without corresponding improvements in performance.

One problem with including results from training studies as examples of utilization deficiencies is in making the distinction between utilization and mediational deficiencies. In fact, we believe it appropriate to think of utilization deficiencies as an advanced form of mediational deficiencies. One important distinction in distinguishing between a mediational and utilization deficiency is the extent to which the training affords children the opportunity to implement a strategy on their own. When children are constrained to use a strategy (e.g., a directed cued-recall strategy in which subjects are required to retrieve all items from a single category together) and fail to demonstrate any benefit in performance, the outcome can best be described as a mediational deficiency. In this situation, children never use a strategy on their own, but merely comply with explicit directions. Thus, if we retain the conventional definition of a strategy as a cognitive operation that is intentionally implemented, there is no evidence here that a true strategy is being used. In contrast, when a strategy is demonstrated to subjects and they are then asked to use that strategy on subsequent trials (e.g., instructing children to use an organizational memory strategy, but not dictating how items are grouped or retrieved) and they fail to demonstrate any benefit in performance despite using the strategy, the outcome can best be described as a utilization deficiency. Here, instruction was successful in getting children to use the strategy on their own (i.e., without being constrained to use it), but there was no corresponding benefit in terms of task performance. Under such limitations, utilization deficiencies observed as a result of training have much in common with utilization deficiencies observed spontaneously. In both cases, a child deliberately uses a strategy but gains little or nothing from its use in terms of task performance. By including training studies, we expand the circumstances under which utilization deficiencies can be found to include instructed and modeled strategies, as well as spontaneously discovered ones.

Such a distinction cannot likely differentiate all cases of mediational and utilization deficiencies, and for a good reason. Although we have specified two distinct categories, the boundaries are ill-defined, because, in actuality, we are dealing with a continuum of strategy use and proficiency and not a true dichotomy (or trichotomy, including efficient strategy use).[1] We find it convenient to make the distinction between the different strategy deficiencies, but recognize that such distinctions may be more apparent than real. The important point here is the inclusion of results from training studies as reflections of utilization deficiencies and the consequences that has for gaining a better understanding of strategy development.

With this expanded definition, the study by Bjorklund and Harnishfeger (1987) discussed earlier clearly fits the criterion for utilization deficiency. Recall that training third-grade children produced increased levels of strategy use (clustering) but no improvements in memory performance. Although the Bjorklund and Harnishfeger study may be unusual in that the younger children demonstrated no significant improvement in memory performance as a result of training, other studies have consistently shown that older children realize greater benefits of training relative to younger children (e.g., Bjorklund & Buchanan, 1989, for an organization strategy; Beuhring & Kee, 1987, for an elaboration strategy; Ornstein, Naus, & Stone, 1977, for a rehearsal strategy, among others). For example, in a study by Lange and Pierce (1992), 4- and 5-year-olds were trained to use an organizational memory strategy. Children's strategy use (e.g., naming items, naming groups, sorting by category) and recall performance were examined before and after the training procedure. The findings indicated that increases in recall performance were modest relative to the sharp increases in strategic/study activities immediately following the strategy training procedure, once again illustrating a utilization deficiency (see also Lange, Guttentag, & Nida, 1990). In research by Beuhring and Kee (1987), 5th- and 12th-grade children were instructed to use an elaboration strategy in the paired-associative learning of nouns. These students were told to verbalize a sentence that described a direct interaction between the noun pairs (e.g., the *coffee* spilled on the *harp*). The results indicated that the 12th graders benefited more from the instruction than did the 5th graders, suggestive of a utilization deficiency (Noun pairs recalled Ms = 20.63 and 26.63, for the 5th- and 12th-graders, respectively). Thus, even though

---

[1]We thank Patricia Miller for emphasizing to us the continuous nature of the various strategy classifications.

the findings of Bjorklund and Harnishfeger (1987) may reflect an extreme example of utilization deficiencies under mnemonic training, the pattern of greater benefit from training for older relative to younger children is a typical one.

MODIFIED-MICROGENETIC ASSESSMENTS OF UTILIZATION DEFICIENCIES

The research cited to this point examined utilization deficiencies primarily in terms of the differential effectiveness of a strategy for younger relative to older children (e.g., Baker-Ward et al., 1984; Bjorklund & Harnishfeger, 1987; Miller & Harris, 1988; Lange & Pierce, 1992; Miller et al., 1991a). Yet, Miller defined utilization deficiency as one of four phases in strategy development, with children progressing from no or ineffective strategy use to utilization deficiency to eventual effective strategy deployment. This sequence does not reflect domain-general stages of development, but rather domain-specific phases in the acquisition of a particular strategy in a particular task. We should be able to observe this developmental sequence within individual children. To do this requires observing children's performance on repeated versions of a task, looking for changes in strategy use and corresponding changes (or lack thereof) in levels of performance. Such multiple observations over relatively brief periods of time are referred to as *microgenetic* studies (Siegler & Crowley, 1991) and provide opportunities to observe developmental sequences that occur over the course of days or weeks as opposed to months or years (e.g., Siegler & Jenkins, 1989). We have performed several modified-microgenetic studies, examining changes in strategy use and effectiveness over the course of several trials, looking for evidence of utilization deficiencies. We chose to examine children's use of an organizational memory strategy in a free-recall task, a strategy that is not typically spontaneously acquired until middle childhood or later (see Schneider & Pressley, 1989).

In a first experiment (Bjorklund, Coyle, & Gaultney, 1992), kindergarten, third-, and eighth-grade children were given five free-recall trials on *different* lists of categorically related words. Category items were chosen that avoided high associations between words, thus minimizing the likelihood that high levels of clustering would result from the relatively automatic activation of semantic memory relations (see Bjorklund & Jacobs, 1985; Frankel & Rollins, 1985). Unlike other multitrial experiments that present subjects with the same materials over repeated trials (e.g., Bjorklund & Buchanan, 1989), children in this experiment would not necessarily become more strategic over trials, because different categories and items were presented on each successive trial. If clustering does improve over trials, it would presumably reflect the acquisition and maintenance of an organizational memory strategy. Furthermore, if there are increases in strategy use over trials without increases in recall, this would provide evidence for a utilization deficiency.

Mean levels of recall and clustering (ARC scores) across trials are presented in Fig. 9.1. As can be seen, recall for the kindergartners was generally low and decreased over trials. The third graders' recall was generally stable across trials, whereas the eighth graders showed a pattern of increases in recall across trials. An examination of clustering scores revealed that clustering varied nonsystematically over trials for the kindergarten children. In contrast, an increasing pattern was observed for the third and eighth graders, with clustering increasing over the first three trials and stabilizing thereafter. The pattern for the third graders of increased clustering over trials in the absence of improvements in recall is indicative of a utilization deficiency.

But the primary purpose of a microgenetic study, even a modified one such as ours, is to look at changes over time in the target behavior for individual children. To do this, we examined patterns of changes in recall and clustering over trials for individual subjects. If improvements in clustering (reflective of strategy use) preceded changes in recall (or occurred in the absence of improvements in recall), this would be an indication of a utilization deficiency.

Children were classified into one of three categories based on their patterns of change in recall and clustering over the five trials: (a) increases in recall (of two words or more) over trials preceded (or occurred in the absence of) significant increases in clustering, (b) significant increases in clustering over trials preceded (or occurred in the absence of) increases in recall, or (c) other patterns (most often correlated changes in recall and clustering). Pattern 2, increases in clustering preceding increases in recall, reflects a utilization deficiency. To be classified as utilizationally deficient (Pattern 2), a subject was required to have a clustering (ARC) score that was significantly greater on Trial $n + 1$ than on Trial n and to maintain that increase for at least one subsequent trial in the absence of an increase in recall of two words or more. (We required that subjects maintain a two trial gain in performance of both recall and clustering to maximize the likelihood that increases in these measures reflected real changes and not random variation.) Moreover, to be classified as utilizationally deficient, a subject's clustering score had to change from below chance to above chance values. We made this decision because we believe that a true utilization deficiency reflects a change from no or poor strategy use to the proper use of a strategy. A child whose clustering score goes from high to higher, in the absence of memory improvement, may be showing the independence of strategy use and recall (cf. Bjorklund & Bjorklund, 1985) and qualify as displaying a quasiutilization deficiency, but such a child cannot be regarded as reflecting the third phase in Miller's sequence of strategy development.

Relatively few children at any grade level were classified as Pattern 1 (recall preceding clustering, 17%, 17%, and 27%, for kindergarten, third, and eighth graders, respectively), with most kindergarten and eighth-grade children and about half of the third graders being classified in the Other category (83%, 46%, and 68%, respectively). For the most critical Pattern 2, few of the youngest (0%) and oldest

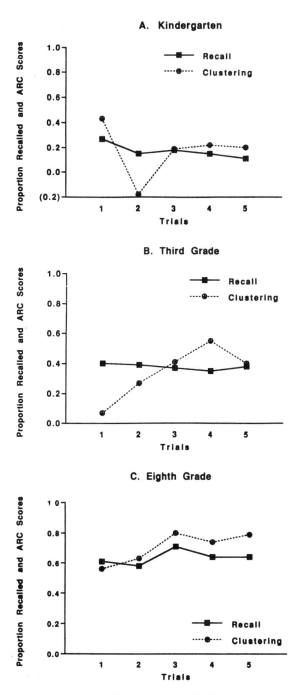

FIG. 9.1. Mean levels of recall and clustering (ARC) over trials for the (A) kindergarten, (B) third-, and (C) eighth-grade children (adapted from Bjorklund, Coyle, & Gaultney, 1992).

(5%) children were classified as utilizationally deficient (i.e., clustering preceding recall). In contrast, 9 of the 24 third graders (38%) were classified as utilizationally deficient. The difference in patterns between the three age groups was confirmed by a chi-square test, $\chi^2(4, N = 64) = 15.04$ $p < .01$, with the kindergarten and eighth-grade children not differing from one another. It is worth noting that four of the nine third-grade children (44%) classified in the clustering preceding recall group eventually demonstrated an increase in recall, whereas the remainder of these children (56%) never showed an increase in recall during the experiment. Thus, for some children, the utilization deficiency was short lived, leading to enhancement of recall on subsequent trials. It is also worth noting that the mean difference in clustering scores (ARC scores, ranging from −1.0 to 1.0, with chance = 0) between Trial n and Trials $n + 1$ and $n + 2$ for children classified as utilizationally deficient was substantial ($M = 1.04$), reflecting many clustering changes from negative values to high and above chance positive (often perfect) values.

The results of this study demonstrate spontaneous strategy acquisition over trials, without concomitant improvements in memory performance for a subset of third-grade children, which is convincing evidence of a utilization deficiency. Unlike other studies that demonstrated strategy use without corresponding improvements in task performance (e.g., Baker-Ward et al., 1984; Bjorklund & Harnishfeger, 1987; Miller & Harris, 1988), this experiment demonstrated a utilization deficiency for children who spontaneously acquired a strategy over trials in the context of a brief testing session. The kindergarten children did not demonstrate a utilization deficiency because the strategy under investigation was too complex for them, presumably requiring too much mental effort to execute it effectively (cf. Miller et al., 1991a, 1991b). The eighth-grade children did not demonstrate a utilization deficiency because they were situated securely in the fourth phase of strategy development, using the strategy effectively.

In the Bjorklund et al. (1992) study, a utilization deficiency was inferred by enhancements in clustering in the absence of improvements in recall. Clustering, of course, is computed on the basis of subjects' recall performance, and a more convincing case for a utilization deficiency could perhaps be made by looking at a measure that is computed independently of recall, such as sorting items into groups prior to a memory test. This was done in a recent training study (Bjorklund, Schneider, Cassel, & Ashley, 1994). Third- and fourth-grade children were classified into high- and low-IQ groups and given repeated sort-recall trials with different sets of categorizable items over four phases. All subjects received standard sort-recall instructions with sets of moderately typical categorizable items in Phase 1 (baseline). Half of the subjects received explicit training in the use of an organizational strategy in Phase 2, some with sets of category typical items and some with sets of category atypical items. The remaining subjects (controls) received a standard sort-recall trial in Phase 2, half with category typical and half with category atypical items. Phases 3 and 4 (immediate and far extension) followed immediately and one week after Phase 2, respectively, with subjects being given standard sort-recall instructions with sets of moderately typical items (identical as in Phase 1). The typicality of the items used in Phases 1, 3, and 4 were all moderate (i.e., combination of both typical and atypical category exemplars). Changes over phases in sorting (the degree to which subjects sorted items according to adult categories), recall, and clustering were assessed. We were particularly interested in elevated levels of sorting and/or clustering following training (in Phases 3 and 4) in the absence of elevated levels of recall, indicative of a utilization deficiency.

For the trained subjects, overall patterns of recall, sorting, and clustering were similar for the high- and low-IQ children and for subjects trained on typical and atypical items in Phase 2, and so will be presented collapsed across these factors (see Fig. 9.2). Levels of recall increased as a result of training, but declined on the extension trials (although recall in Phase 3 was still significantly greater than recall in Phase 1, demonstrating a near-extension effect). Levels of both sorting and clustering also increased significantly as a result of training, but unlike recall, these indices of strategy use remained high on the immediate and one week extension trials, providing clear evidence for a utilization deficiency.

The patterns differed somewhat between the high- and low-IQ control subjects (i.e., those children not given training in Phase 2), and their data are presented separately in Figs. 9.3A and 9.3B. Although overall levels of performance were lower for high-IQ control children than for trained children, the pattern of performance was similar. Levels of recall were relatively constant across Phases 2,

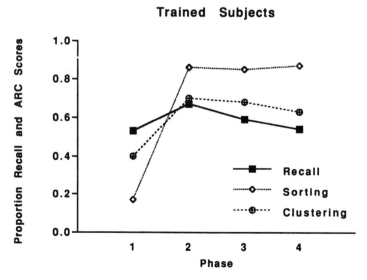

FIG. 9.2. Patterns of recall, sorting, and clustering for the trained subjects collapsed across IQ (high and low) and item type (typical and atypical) (adapted from Bjorklund, Schneider, Cassel, & Ashley, 1994).

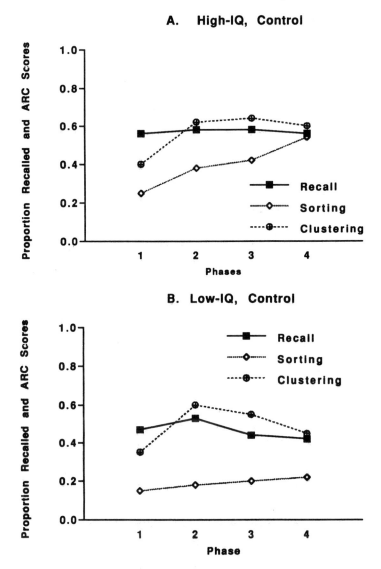

FIG. 9.3. Patterns of recall, sorting, and clustering for the high- and low-IQ control subjects (adapted from Bjorklund, Schneider, Cassel, & Ashley, 1994).

3, and 4, despite significant increases in levels of clustering. Similar to the findings of the Bjorklund et al. (1992) experiment, most groups of children displayed strategic behavior, as exemplified by elevated levels of sorting and clustering, in the absence of corresponding levels of recall, reflective of a utilization deficiency.

Perhaps the most consistent type of evidence for utilization deficiency is greater benefit of a strategy for older than for comparably strategic younger children (e.g., Miller et al., 1991a). In this study, we contrasted the recall of high- and low-IQ children only for subjects who had perfect sorting scores (i.e., those who sorted all items according to adult-defined categories). Similar to the typical developmental findings, higher IQ children had greater levels of recall than comparably strategic lower IQ children. This difference was significant or approached significance for Phases 2 and 3, but not for Phase 4. Although not reported in Bjorklund et al. (1994), we also contrasted recall differences between third- and fourth-grade children who were perfect sorters. These strategic fourth-grade children had significantly higher levels of recall than comparably strategic third graders at each phase, consistent with earlier observations of greater advantage of a strategy for older relative to younger children.

As in the Bjorklund et al. (1992) experiment, we examined the data of individual subjects and classified them as displaying a utilization deficiency or not, separately for the sorting and clustering data. Subjects were classified as utilizationally deficient in this study on the extension phases of the experiment only (Phases 3 and 4). Subjects were classified as utilizationally deficient on Phases 3 and 4 if their levels of sorting and/or clustering were significantly greater than at baseline (Phase 1) without a corresponding increase in recall of two words or more. Using this criterion, about one third of the trained subjects (regardless of IQ group) were classified as utilizationally deficient. For example, 29% of the trained subjects were classified as utilizationally deficient on both the sorting and clustering measure for Phase 3, with 30% being so classified on Phase 4. Slightly more subjects were classified as utilizationally deficient for sorting alone (37% and 49% for Phases 3 and 4, respectively) and clustering alone (30% and 33% for Phases 3 and 4, respectively).

As with the overall pattern of data, only the high-IQ control children were apt to be classified as utilizationally deficient, and, for the most part, only for the clustering measure. Of the high-IQ control children, 29% were classified as utilizationally deficient for the clustering measure in Phase 3, with 31% being so classified in Phase 4. The corresponding levels for the low-IQ control subjects was 8% and 11% for Phases 3 and 4, respectively. The percentage of subjects classified as utilizationally deficient for the sorting measure was at floor levels (6% and 9% for Phases 3 and 4 for the high-IQ subjects, and 0% for both Phases 3 and 4 for the low-IQ subjects).

The results of the Bjorklund et al. (1994) study confirm and extend the earlier findings of a utilization deficiency for an organizational memory strategy for school children. Both the group and individual data revealed subjects demonstrating enhancements in sorting and/or clustering over phases in the absence of enhancements in recall. These findings clearly indicate that utilization deficiency is not an age-related stage in development, but a phase in the acquisition of a particular strategy in a specified context. Moreover, just as there are developmental differences, with older children benefiting more from use of a strategy than younger children, so, too, are there individual differences, with higher IQ children benefiting more from using a strategy than lower IQ children. Also, based on evidence from the control children in the Bjorklund et al. study, higher IQ children presumably become utilizationally deficient for a particular strategy prior to lower IQ children. This pattern of findings is consistent with the interpretation that brighter children at an age level progress through the various phases of strategy effectiveness before less bright children. This bolsters the interpretation of utilization deficiencies as a transition phase in strategy acquisition between faulty or ineffective strategies and efficient strategy use.

We have preliminary data from a third modified-microgenetic study, a thesis by Coyle (1993). In this study, second-, third-, and fourth-grade children were given five sort-recall trials using lists of different categories and items for each trial (cf., Bjorklund et al., 1992). Children were classified as utilizationally deficient following the procedure used by Bjorklund, Coyle, and Gaultney on the basis of both clustering and sorting scores; but, as for the control subjects in the Bjorklund et al. (1994) study, few children were classified as utilizationally deficient on the sorting measure. (This was due in large part to the tendency of children not to sort items during the study phase.) Thus, the few children who were classified as utilizationally deficient on sorting but not on clustering (a total of five across the three grades) were included with the children who were classified as utilizationally deficient on the clustering measure.

A third classification was developed for this study, that of *quasiutilization deficiency*. We defined utilization deficiency as involving a significant and stable (i.e., at least two trials) increase in clustering in the absence of an increase in recall, with clustering scores changing from below to above chance values. Children were similarly classified as quasiutilizationally deficient, with the exception that initial levels of clustering (i.e., clustering on Trial n) were *above* chance. Thus, quasiutilizationally deficient children begin by displaying low (but above chance) levels of clustering (or sorting), but then show significant and stable increases in strategy use in the absence of stable increases in levels of recall (cf. Bjorklund & Bjorklund, 1985). Similar to our other findings, 43% of the second graders and 37% of the third graders were classified as utilizationally deficient, with 15% of the fourth graders being so classified. However, only one second- or third-grade child was classified as quasiutilizationally deficient, whereas eight (20%) of the fourth graders were so classified.

This pattern suggests that even children who begin a task using a moderately strategic approach benefit little by becoming more consistent in their strategy use, at least not immediately. Presumably, slightly older children would be less likely to be classified as both utilizationally and quasiutilizationally deficient, being able to reap the benefits of their strategy use in terms of recall. We have some preliminary evidence of this. We re-examined the data of the third- and eighth-grade subjects in the Bjorklund et al. (1992) study, classifying subjects as quasiutilizationally deficient following the procedure used by Coyle. We found that only 1 of 24 third graders (4%) was classified as quasiutilizationally deficient—nearly identical to the data reported by Coyle. Similarly, only two eighth graders (9%) were classified as quasiutilizationally deficient, in contrast to the 20% for the fourth graders in the Coyle study. This pattern suggests that by the eighth grade, most children have passed through both the utilization deficient and quasiutilization deficient phases for simple recall tasks, progressing to the efficient use strategies.

The distinction between utilizationally deficient and quasiutilizationally deficient children may seem to be a minor one, for each group of subjects is showing the critical pattern of enhancements in strategy use without corresponding improvements in recall. Although using a more lenient criterion would result in both sets of children being similarly classified, we believe that the distinction has some merit, in that different levels of recall, sorting, and clustering were observed for the quasiutilizationally deficient and utilizationally deficient fourth graders in Coyle's study. Coyle examined levels of recall, clustering, and sorting for the various classifications of children. He found that second- and third-grade utilizationally deficient children had significantly higher levels of recall, clustering, and sorting than second and third graders classified as nonutilizationally deficient. The pattern was reversed, however, for the fourth graders, with utilizationally deficient children having lower levels of recall, clustering, and sorting than nonutilizationally deficient children. Fourth-grade children classified as quasiutilizationally deficient were not similar to the utilizationally deficient children, but had high and comparable levels of performance to the nonutilizationally deficient children. That is, utilization deficiencies were associated with enhanced levels of memory performance for younger children, but lower levels of performance for older children, with the fourth-grade quasiutilizationally deficient children performing more like the strategic, nonutilizationally deficient children than the children classified as utilizationally deficient. Presumably, the second- and third-grade utilizationally deficient children were strategically more advanced than their nonutilizationally deficient peers, displaying initially relatively inefficient strategy use, whereas other children were essentially nonstrategic over all trials. By the fourth grade, however, utilizationally deficient children were those who were behind their peers in terms of strategy use; they were just beginning to use strategies, somewhat ineffectually, whereas most of their nonutilizationally deficient peers were already using strategies efficiently (including those classified as quasiutilizationally deficient).

SPECULATIONS ON THE HOWS AND THE WHYS
OF UTILIZATION DEFICIENCIES

Why should a technique that results in enhanced performance in older and brighter children produce no appreciable change in the target behavior for younger and less bright children? Our preferred explanation relates to the mental effort children must expend in order to execute a strategy. Results of several dual-task studies have demonstrated that younger children either exert greater mental effort to execute the same strategy as do older children (e.g., Beuhring & Kee, 1987; Guttentag, 1984; Miller et al., 1991a), or, when the mental effort expenditure is comparable between younger and older children, younger children experience less gain in task performance (Bjorklund & Harnishfeger, 1987; see Kee, 1994, for a review). Strategies are expensive in terms of mental effort, and the advantage they provide the older, brighter, or more practiced child in terms of cognitive efficiency is not yet realized for the novice. This is because too much of a child's limited mental resources are used in executing the strategy, leaving too few resources to allocate to actual task performance (see Kee, 1994). With practice, aspects of the strategy become automated and performance increases.

One of the things we have learned over the past decade is that memory strategies are complicated things, and their use and effectiveness are influenced by a variety of factors, with expenditure of mental effort being only one of them. Other factors that have been found to play a role in the development of strategies may also influence the development of utilization deficiencies. For example, individual differences in one's knowledge base for the to-be-remembered information and intelligence will likely be found to affect the demonstration of utilization deficiencies in children. IQ differences in the rate at which children progress through the various phases of strategy development, including utilization deficiency, was suggested by the findings of Bjorklund et al. (1994), with high-IQ children displaying utilization deficiencies before low-IQ children.

Within the past decade noncognitive factors, such as motivation, self-attributions, and perceived self-efficacy, have been shown to influence children's strategic behavior and are thus candidates as influences on utilization deficiencies. For example, recent research indicates that motivational factors are related to metacognition and effective strategy use (see Borkowski & Turner, 1990; Pressley, Borkowski, & Schneider, 1987). Particularly important for an understanding of strategy development are attributions of success and failure concerning performance on cognitive tasks. Borkowski and his colleagues (e.g., Borkowski & Turner, 1990; Kurtz & Borkowski, 1984) have emphasized the connection between self-attributions, metamemory, and the use and generalization of memory strategies, and assumed that "self-attributions are tightly woven to the use of strategies" (Borkowski & Turner, 1990, p. 171). They reported that children who believe that effort plays an important role in producing success on academic and cognitive tasks demonstrate higher levels of strategy use on transfer tasks following mnemonic training than do children who tend to attribute success to noncontrollable factors (Kurtz & Borkowski, 1984).

Related to the concept of self-attributions of success and failure is the concept of self-efficacy. Bandura noted (1989) that *perceived self-efficacy* (i.e., perceptions of self-competence not related to ability) is related to the amount of time and effort one will expend on a given task. In addition, perceived self-efficacy influences the tasks an individual will attempt and pursue, regardless of the ability to perform the task. Thus, an individual who is high in self-efficacy is more likely to continue to use a currently ineffective strategy that yields no immediate reward than one who is low in self-efficacy. Children high in perceived self-efficacy may have confidence in their ability to perform difficult tasks and practice using an effortful strategy beyond their ability level that yields eventual, though not immediate, benefits (see Bjorklund & Green, 1992).

The more interesting question may not be how should one explain the phenomenon of utilization deficiency, but rather why should children use an effort-consuming strategy to guide their behavior when it has no positive impact on their task performance? One reason may have to do with its novelty. Following the ideas of Piaget (1970), children may take pleasure in exercising a new scheme (in this case, a new strategy) for its own sake, without consideration of the consequences. The purposes of using a strategy, or of performing a task in general, are different for younger than for older children, and the goal of high levels of task performance (in our case, high levels of recall) may not be primary for the young child (see Stipek, 1984). Rather, using and experimenting with the consequences of a newly discovered technique may be a more central goal for young children. Siegler and Jenkins (1989) made a similar proposal for children's acquisition of simple addition strategies. Once the novelty wears off, the strategy becomes less effortful and is thus yielding higher levels of task performance. This pattern seems to describe some of the third-grade subjects in the Bjorklund et al. (1992) study, who showed an eventual improvement in recall following several trials of being utilizationally deficient.

CONCLUSION

To paraphrase the esteemed philosopher of science, Thomas Kuhn (1962), "You don't see something until your scientific enterprise is ready to perceive it." This seems to describe why utilization deficiencies remained undiscovered until recently. Utilization deficiencies had to wait to be seen until psychologists accepted the idea that strategies are not always what they seem, on the surface, to be. We must now move beyond simple description and identification to an explanation of the factors underlying this phenomenon. For us, the realization that children will use effortful cognitive operations without corresponding benefits, represents interesting and theoretically and pedagogically important issues that must be approached by looking at questions relating to both the hows and the whys of utilization deficiencies.

ACKNOWLEDGMENTS

We would like to thank Barbara Bjorklund, William Cassel, Elizabeth Kennedy, Patricia Miller, Lenore Read, and Wolfgang Schneider for helpful comments on earlier drafts of this chapter.

REFERENCES

Baker-Ward, L., Ornstein, P. A., & Holden, D. J. (1984). The expression of memorization in early childhood. *Journal of Experimental Child Psychology, 37*, 555–575.

Bandura, A. (1989). Social cognitive theory. In R. Vasta (Ed.), *Annals of child development* (Vol. 6, pp. 1–60). Greenwich, CT: JAI.

Beuhring, T., & Kee, D. (1987). Developmental relationships among metamemory, elaborative strategy use, and associative memory. *Journal of Experimental Child Psychology, 44*, 377–400.

Bjorklund, D. F. (1985). The role of conceptual knowledge in the development of organization in children's memory. In C. J. Brainerd & M. Pressley (Eds.), *Basic processes in memory development: Progress in cognitive development research* (pp. 103–142). New York: Springer-Verlag.

Bjorklund, D. F., & Bjorklund, B. R. (1985). Organization versus item effects of an elaborated knowledge base on children's memory. *Developmental Psychology, 21*, 1120–1131.

Bjorklund, D. F., & Buchanan, J. J. (1989). Developmental and knowledge base differences in the acquisition and extension of a memory strategy. *Journal of Experimental Child Psychology, 47*, 451–471.

Bjorklund, D. F., Coyle, T. R., & Gaultney, J. F. (1992). Developmental differences in the acquisition and maintenance of an organizational strategy: Evidence for the utilization deficiency hypothesis. *Journal of Experimental Child Psychology, 54*, 434–448.

Bjorklund, D. F., & Green, B. L. (1992). The adaptive nature of cognitive immaturity. *American Psychologist, 47*, 46–54.

Bjorklund, D. F., & Harnishfeger, K. K. (1987). Developmental differences in the mental effort requirements for the use of an organizational strategy in free recall. *Journal of Experimental Child Psychology, 44*, 109–125.

Bjorklund, D. F., & Jacobs, J. W. (1985). Associative and categorical processes in children's memory: The role of automaticity in the development of organization in free recall. *Journal of Experimental Child Psychology, 39*, 599–617.

Bjorklund, D. F., Schneider, W., Cassel, W. S., & Ashley, E. (1994). Training and extension of a memory strategy: Evidence for utilization deficiencies in the acquisition of an organizational strategy in high- and low-IQ children. *Child Development, 65*, 951–965.

Bjorklund, D. F., & Zeman, B. R. (1982). Children's organization and metamemory awareness in their recall of familiar information. *Child Development, 53*, 799–810.

Bjorklund, D. F., & Zeman, B. R. (1983). The development of organizational strategies in children's recall of familiar information: Using social organization to recall the names of classmates. *International Journal of Behavioral Development, 6*, 341–353.

Borkowski, J. G., & Turner, L. A. (1990). Transituational characteristics of metacognition. In W. Schneider & F. E. Weinert (Eds.), *Interactions among aptitudes, strategies, and knowledge in cognitive performance* (pp. 159–176). New York: Springer-Verlag.

Carr, M., & Schneider, W. (1991). Long-term maintenance of organizational strategies in kindergarten children. *Contemporary Educational Psychology, 16*, 61–72.

Coyle, T. R. (1993). *The development of utilization deficiencies.* Unpublished masters thesis, Florida Atlantic University, Boca Raton, FL.

DeLoache, J. S., Cassidy, D. J., & Brown, A. L. (1985). Precursors of mnemonic strategies in very young children's memory for the location of hidden objects. *Child Development, 56*, 125–137.

DeMarie-Dreblow, D., & Miller, P. H. (1988). The development of children' strategies for selective attention: Evidence for a transitional period. *Child Development, 59*, 1504–1513.

Dempster, F. N. (1985). Short-term memory development in childhood and adolescence. In C. J. Brainerd & M. Pressley (Eds.), *Basic processes in memory development: Progress in cognitive development research* (pp. 209–248). New York: Springer.

Flavell, J. H. (1970). Developmental studies of mediated memory. In H. W. Reese & L. P. Lipsitt (Eds.), *Advances in child development and child behavior* (Vol. 5, pp. 181–211). New York: Academic Press.

Frankel, M. T., & Rollins, H. A. (1985). Associative and categorical hypotheses of organization in the free recall of adults and children. *Journal of Experimental Child Psychology, 40*, 304–318.

Guttentag, R. E. (1984). The mental effort requirement of cumulative rehearsal: A developmental study. *Journal of Experimental Child Psychology, 37*, 92–106.

Harnishfeger, K. K., & Bjorklund, D. F. (1990). Children's strategies: A brief history. In D. F. Bjorklund (Ed.), *Children's strategies: Contemporary views of cognitive development* (pp. 1–22). Hillsdale, NJ: Lawrence Erlbaum Associates.

Howe, M. L., & O'Sullivan, J. T. (1990). The development of strategic memory: Coordinating knowledge, metamemory, and resources. In D. F. Bjorklund (Ed.), *Children's strategies: Contemporary views of cognitive development* (pp. 129–155). Hillsdale, NJ: Lawrence Erlbaum Associates.

Kee, D. W. (1994). Developmental differences in associative memory: Strategy use, mental effort and knowledge-access interactions. In H. W. Reese (Ed.), *Advances in child development and behavior* (Vol. 25, pp. 7–32). New York: Academic Press.

Kee, D. W., & Davies, L. (1991). Mental effort and elaboration: A developmental analysis of accessibility effects. *Journal of Experimental Child Psychology, 52*, 1–10.

Kuhn, T. (1962). *The structure of scientific revolutions.* Chicago: University of Chicago Press.

Kurtz, B. E., & Borkowski, J. G. (1984). Children's metacognition: Exploring relations among knowledge, process, and motivational variables. *Journal of Experimental Child Psychology, 37*, 335–354.

Lange, G., Guttentag, R. E., & Nida, R. E. (1990). Relationships between study organization, retrieval organization, and general and strategy-specific memory knowledge in young children. *Journal of Experimental Child Psychology, 49*, 126–146.

Lange, G., & Pierce, S. H. (1992). Memory-strategy learning and maintenance in preschool children. *Developmental Psychology, 28*, 453–462.

Miller, G. A., Galanter, E., & Pribram, K. (1960). *Plans and the structure of behavior.* New York: Holt, Rinehart & Winston.

Miller, P. H. (1990). The development of strategies of selective attention. In D. F. Bjorklund (Ed.), *Children's strategies: Contemporary views of cognitive development* (pp. 157–184). Hillsdale, NJ: Lawrence Erlbaum Associates.

Miller, P. H., & Harris, Y. R. (1988). Preschoolers' strategies of attention on a same–different task. *Developmental Psychology, 24*, 628–633.

Miller, P. H., Haynes, V. F., DeMarie-Dreblow, D., & Woody-Ramsey, J. (1986). Children's strategies for gathering information in three tasks. *Child Development, 57*, 1429–1439.

Miller, P. H., & Seier, W. L. (1994). Strategy utilization deficiencies in children: When, where, and why. In H. W. Reese (Ed.), *Advances in child development and behavior* (Vol. 25, pp. 107–156). New York: Academic Press.

Miller, P. H., Seier, W. L., Probert, J. S., & Aloise, P. A. (1991a). Age differences in the capacity demands of a strategy among spontaneously strategic children. *Journal of Experimental Child Psychology, 52*, 149–165.

Miller, P. H., Woody-Ramsey, J., & Aloise, P. A. (1991b). The role of strategy effortfulness in strategy effectiveness. *Developmental Psychology, 27*, 738–745.

Ornstein, P. A., Naus, M. J., & Stone, B. P. (1977). Rehearsal training and developmental differences in memory. *Developmental Psychology, 13*, 15–24.

Piaget, J. (1970). Piaget's theory. In P. H. Mussen (Ed.), *Carmichael's manual of child psychology* (3rd. ed., Vol. 1, pp. 703–732). New York: Wiley.

Pressley, M., Borkowski, J. G., & Schneider, W. (1987). Cognitive strategies: Good strategy users coordinate metacognition and knowledge. *Annals of Child Development, 4*, 89–129.

Pressley, M., Forrest-Pressley, D. L., Elliot-Faust, D., & Miller, G. (1985). Children's use of cognitive strategies: How to teach strategies, and what to do if they can't be taught. In M. Pressley & C. J. Brainerd (Eds.), *Cognitive learning and memory in children: Progress in cognitive development research* (pp. 1–47). New York: Springer.

Reese, H. W. (1962). Verbal mediation as a function of age level. *Psychological Bulletin, 59,* 502–509.

Reese, H. W. (1976). The development of memory: Life-span perspectives. In H. W. Reese (Ed.), *Advances in child development and behavior* (Vol. 11, pp. 190–212). New York: Academic Press.

Schneider, W., & Pressley, M. (1989). *Memory development between 2 and 20.* New York: Springer.

Siegler, R. S., & Crowley, K. (1991). The microgenetic method: A direct means for studying cognitive development. *American Psychologist, 46,* 606–620.

Siegler, R. S., & Jenkins, E. (1989). *How children discover strategies.* Hillsdale, NJ: Lawrence Erlbaum Associates.

Stipek, D. (1984). Young children's performance expectations: Logical analysis or wishful thinking? In J. G. Nicholls (Ed.), *Advances in motivation and achievement: Vol 3. The development of achievement motivation* (pp. 33–56). Greenwich, CT: JAI.

Wellman, H. M. (1988). The early development of memory strategies. In F. Weinert & M. Perlmutter (Eds.), *Memory development: Universal changes and individual differences* (pp. 3–29). Hillsdale, NJ: Lawrence Erlbaum Associates.

Woody-Ramsey, J., & Miller, P. H. (1988). The facilitation of selective attention in preschoolers. *Child Development, 59,* 1497–1503.

Chapter 10

On Making Cognitive Theory More General and Developmentally Pertinent

Earl C. Butterfield
Luann R. Albertson
James C. Johnston
University of Washington

Cognitive theories share two large limits: They include no mechanisms that adequately account for cognitive development, and they are not sufficiently general. In this chapter we work to overcome these limits.

Cognitive theories are inadequate as explanations of human development. First, they depict development as too stage-like. As Siegler (this volume) explains, current theories incorrectly assume a staircase view according to which thinking is homogeneous within an age but heterogeneous across ages (e.g., Case, 1991). In this chapter, we add a memory-limits explanation to Siegler's probabilistic explanation for the fact that thinking, even for sharply constrained purposes, is hetergeneous for almost all people (see Battig, 1979; Reitman, 1969; Siegler, this volume; Simon, 1975; Kurtz-Costes, this volume). Second, current theories provide reasonable descriptions of age-related changes in knowledge and strategies, but they provide no account of how those changes arise. In this chapter, we describe research that validates two of what we suppose are many mechanisms of developmental change.

Current cognitive theories are insufficiently general in two senses. First, no theory includes the full range of explanatory mechanisms of thinking. Different theories emphasize different mechanisms: short-term memory limits, strategies, knowledge, metacognition, motivation, and so on. We propose a functional view of cognitive theory that allows and encourages inclusion of the whole range of mechanisms known to influence cognition. Second, no theory accounts for the range of skills explained by the collection of miniature theories that are cognitive psychologists' efforts to predict human performance. We describe research that increases the generality of theory about problem solving in the domain of physics. Also, we propose research to test theory that predicts performance across several domains. This research could result in quite general cognitive theory.

INCLUDING MORE EXPLANATORY MECHANISMS IN COGNITIVE THEORY

Memory is a fine aspect of cognition to illustrate the need for more explanatory mechanisms in theory. For more than a century, psychologists studied human memory with laboratory procedures designed to decouple it from the rest of people's cognitive systems. From such decoupling, psychologists gained precise understanding of many aspects of isolated memory systems—sensory memories (Averbach & Coriel, 1961; Darwin, Turvey, & Crowder, 1972; Sperling, 1960), short-term memory (Conrad, 1964; Craik, 1970; Mandler, 1967; Miller, 1956), and long-term memory (Glanzer, 1972). However, decoupling memory systems cost psychologists knowledge of how memory works in concert with the rest of the cognitive system.

Some scientists indirectly looked at contributions of memory to people's over-all cognitive functioning. They inferred memory's systemic impacts from studies of working memory's limits (Miller, 1956), from studies showing that strategies increase memory capacity (Belmont & Butterfield, 1971; Flavell, 1970), from studies of how metacognitive monitoring facilitates performance dependent on limited memory capacity (Lodico, Ghatala, Levin, & Pressley, 1983), and from computer simulations that assume limited memory, yet account for some complex problem solving (Anderson & Bower, 1973; Kotovsky & Simon, 1973). This indirect approach provides fragmented conceptions of cognition. It creates theories that are task-specific and far from general.

In this chapter, we consider how to modify theory to capture integrated cognitive functioning. Others worked to create more general theory (Anderson, 1978, 1981; Siegler, 1986), but we judge that none explains how different cognitive functions work together. We agree that continued utility of cognitive theory "will depend largely on the degree to which researchers are able to make significant advances in increasing both the generality of theories and the breadth of their application" (Kail & Bisanz, 1992, p. 255).

How might cognitive theory be made more general? We answer by describing functional relations among levels of theory as metacognitive monitoring and control (Nelson & Narens, 1990). We organize the specifics of our answer around three goals: (a) sharpening the distinction between cognition and metacognition, (b) explaining how metacognitive mechanisms for monitoring and controlling cognition describe relations among levels of task-specific cognitive theories, and (c) describing theorizing that includes the whole range of explanatory mechanisms contained in many task-specific theories.

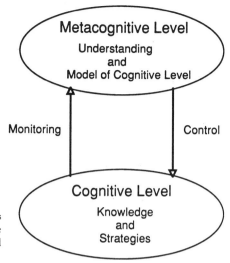

FIG. 10.1. Contents of and relations between directly related cognitive and metacognitive levels of a mental system.

Distinguishing Metacognition From Cognition

Metacognition is cognition about cognition. Cognition involves knowledge of the world and strategies for using that knowledge to solve problems. Metacognition concerns understanding, monitoring, and controlling one's knowledge and strategies.

In contemporary theory, the human intellectual system has many levels. Higher levels exercise monitoring and controlling functions over lower levels (Broadbent, 1977; Nelson & Narens, 1990). Knowledge and strategies located at and operating from lower cognitive levels are understood, monitored, and controlled by higher metacognitive levels. Figure 10.1 shows the simplest case of one metacognitive level monitoring and controlling one cognitive level.[1] Monitoring and control by any metacognitive level are enabled by a model of its directly related cognitive level and by metacognitive understanding of what influences the cognitive level. Metacognitive models of a cognitive level include representations of what the cognitive level can do (its strategies) with problems and their contexts (its knowledge). Such models are operational plans for sequencing cognitive activities (Broadbent, 1977; Butterfield & Nelson, 1991; Conant & Ashby, 1970). Metacognitive understandings concern the how and why of operations at the cognitive level. We say much in what follows about the roles of such understandings in cognitive development. Other metacognitive understandings concern cognitive influences of a thinker's personal characteristics, task features, and irrelevant contextual features. We say little of these matters, which Flavell (1979) treats rather fully.

---

[1]Nelson and Narens (1994) treat the general case of multiple cognitive and metacognitive levels.

Balance scale problems illustrate the distinction between cognition (knowledge and strategies) and metacognition (understanding, monitoring, and control). A balance scale is like a well-calibrated teeter–totter. It can be latched to remain level and loaded with a number of equal weights at different distances from the fulcrum. Having shown a student a static arrangement of either a balance scale or any of many other simple physics problems, psychologists ask the student to predict which of three things will happen when the static arrangement is allowed to change. A student's choices are whether one side, the other, or neither side will go down when the scale is unlatched.

Knowledge as Cognition. Solving any problem requires knowledge of its relevant features and how they influence problem outcome. Figure 10.2 (upper box) lists knowledge for children who regularly solve only balance scale problems having weights located the same distances on both sides of the scale's fulcrum and problems having greater weight on the same side with weights farther from the fulcrum. Figure 10.3 lists knowledge of people who know how to calculate torque. The knowledge in Fig. 10.3 includes the knowledge in Fig. 10.2. If the mature problem solver represented in Fig. 10.3 used only the part of his or her knowledge from Fig. 10.2, he or she would perform like a younger child. Later, we rely on this and related facts to explain heterogeneity of cognition by individuals.

Strategies as Cognition. Balance scale problems come in types whose solutions require recall and use of different combinations of strategies (Butterfield & Ferretti, 1984, 1987; Butterfield & Nelson, 1991; Ferretti & Butterfield, 1986,

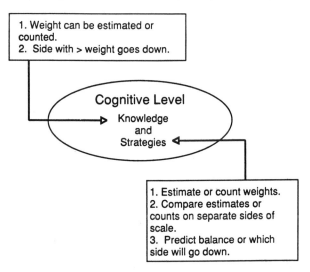

FIG. 10.2. Cognitive knowledge and strategies of a young solver of balance scale problems.

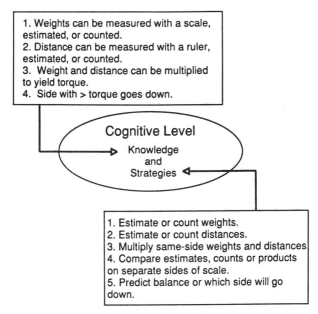

1. Weights can be measured with a scale, estimated, or counted.
2. Distance can be measured with a ruler, estimated, or counted.
3. Weight and distance can be multiplied to yield torque.
4. Side with > torque goes down.

Cognitive Level

Knowledge and Strategies

1. Estimate or count weights.
2. Estimate or count distances.
3. Multiply same-side weights and distances
4. Compare estimates, counts or products on separate sides of scale.
5. Predict balance or which side will go down.

FIG. 10.3. Cognitive knowledge and strategies of an older near-expert solver of balance scale problems.

1989, 1992; Inhelder & Piaget, 1958; Siegler, 1976, 1978, 1981; Wilkening & Anderson, 1982). Figures 10.2 and 10.3 (lower boxes) list the strategies that must be combined for solution of different balance scale problems. The number of strategies successfully combined during problem solving increases with age.

Figure 10.2 lists strategies used by young children to solve some balance scale problems. Young children combine the strategies listed in Fig. 10.2 into an approach called *dimensional comparison*. They base predictions about all balance scales' performance on only one of two relevant dimensions, weight (see Figs. 10.4 and 10.6). When comparison along the weight dimension reveals an inequality on the sides of a balance scale, a youngster predicts that the side with greater weight will go down regardless of distances of the two sides' weights from the fulcrum. Such dimensional comparison allows correct prediction for all problems with equal distances on both sides of the scale or with greater distance on the side with greater weight.

Figure 10.3 lists strategies to integrate weight and distance with a torque calculation, required by balance scale problems having unequal values on opposite sides for the two dimensions. Consider a balance scale with four weights placed six distance units to the left of its fulcrum and seven weights placed three distance units to the right. Comparing only weight says the right side will go down; comparing only distance says the left side. Such conflicting predictions are resolved by dimensional integration—multiplying weights and distances separately for the two sides and comparing the resulting products (24 and 21), called

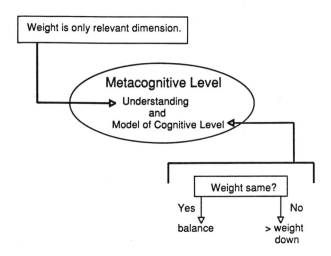

FIG. 10.4. Metacognitive understandings and model of cognitive level of a young solver of balance scale problems.

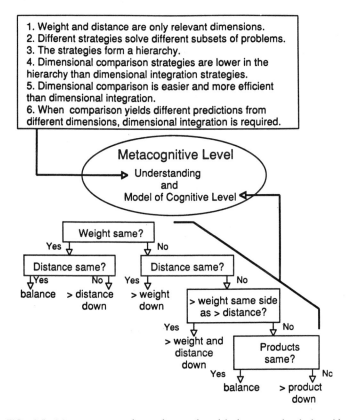

FIG. 10.5. Metacognitive understandings and model of cognitive level of an older near-expert solver of balance scale problems.

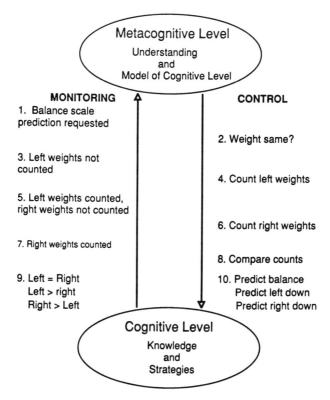

FIG. 10.6. Monitoring and control involved in solving a balance scale problem under guidance of model of dimensional comparison shown in Fig. 10.4.

torques. The left side has greater torque, so it goes down, as predicted by a child who calculates, remembers, and compares the products.

Both dimensional comparison and dimensional integration require strategies for quantifying values of dimensions and either comparing the dimensions or integrating them arithmetically. Like knowledge, strategies of younger people (Fig. 10.2) are included in the strategies of older people (Fig. 10.3). Also, it is doing quantification and calculation, as opposed to knowing about the world, that justifies the label strategies instead of knowledge for comparison and integration. It is doing to representations of the world that makes strategies cognitive rather than metacognitive. The distinction drawn between doing and knowing for cognitive levels of the intellectual system also applies to metacognitive levels. Monitoring and controlling cognition are kinds of doing. Understanding cognition is knowing.

Metacognitive Understanding of Cognition. Effective control of ongoing cognition depends on knowing what to monitor and on understanding the implications of what the monitoring reveals. Figure 10.4 lists metacognitive understandings of young children who reliably solve only balance scale problems with weights the same distances from both sides of a scale's fulcrum and problems with greater weight on the same side of a scale with its weights farther from the fulcrum. Figure 10.5 lists metacognitive understandings of mature people who can solve balance scale problems by calculating torque. Mature metacognitive understandings include metacognitive understandings of immature problem solvers.

Metacognitive Monitoring and Control of Cognition. Effective control of cognition requires metacognitive monitoring of what one knows. For example, when a balance scale is presented to a child who knows the relevance of comparing weights but not distances, monitoring of what he or she knows (Fig. 10.6, Step 1) guides selection of a dimensional comparison solution. Dimensional comparison is the coordinated sequencing of the strategies shown in Fig. 10.2. The sequencing is provided by the model in Fig. 10.4, according to which the child asks whether or not the weights on the two sides of the scale are the same (Fig. 10.6, Step 2).

Having selected a dimensional comparison strategy, the child's monitoring and control continue as shown in Fig. 10.6. Under guidance of the cognitive model of dimensional comparison, the child counts weights on the left side of the scale (Steps 3 and 4), monitors when the left but not the right weights have been counted (Step 5), counts weights on the right side of the scale (Step 6), and so on, until monitoring the comparison of weights on the two sides (Step 9) leads to a prediction of the balance scale's behavior (Step 10).

Other necessary monitoring and control concern accuracy and utility assessment. To ensure accurate execution of either dimensional comparison or integration, students must monitor their assessments of dimensional values and correct counts or estimates as needed, again basing control of cognition (correcting their assessments) on monitoring. Especially when using complex combinations of strategies, such as those required by dimensional integration (whose model is shown in Fig. 10.5), students must keep track of (monitor) where they stand in their sequence of strategies so they will know what to do next. Following their predictions for a latched scale, students can monitor the scale's action after it is unlatched. This allows them to decide whether or not a different approach should be used on future problems. Such utility assessment can result in learning how to solve future problems (Butterfield, 1986).

The foregoing discussion of balance scales shows that metacognition can be distinguished from cognition. We psychologists no longer need to accept Cavanaugh and Perlmutter's (1982) argument that metacognition is a poorly defined concept. Cognition is use of knowledge and strategies from long-term memory. Metacognition is monitoring and controlling cognition in working memory. Monitoring and control are guided by metacognitive understandings and models of how to use knowledge and strategies, both of which are stored in long-term memory. Although metacognition is a complex concept, it is no longer poorly defined.

General Theory From Combining Task-Specific Models

Cognitive scientists used diverse task-analytic methods (Lachman, Lachman, & Butterfield, 1979; Siegler, 1986) to build models from knowledge and strategies, each model allowing solution of a different problem. Because the designation *metacognitive* is a description of functional relations among levels of any hierarchy, and because all task-analytic models can be expressed hierarchically, all such models could be described as residing in metacognitive levels and controlling lower cognitive levels of people's mental systems[2] (see Figs. 10.1 through 10.6).

Some salutary effects would flow from describing task-analytic models as cognitive and metacognitive levels related by monitoring and control. It would permit combining many models in a single theory. Such a theory would include all of the explanatory mechanisms of the pooled task-specific models. Short-term and long-term memory, motivation, cognitive knowledge and strategies, and metacognitive understanding, control and monitoring would all be given their due. Theorists would be freed from seemingly unending efforts to establish that the explanatory mechanisms featured in their models are somehow basic to the mechanisms of other models. Even productive study of how presently competing models work together could result.

Reprise

First, we distinguished between cognition and metacognition. Cognition is the use of knowledge and strategies. Knowledge is representations of the world, and strategies act on knowledge. Metacognition is monitoring and control of cognition guided by miniature task-specific models and understandings of factors that influence cognition. Second, we noted that task-specific models could be combined if their different levels were described as cognitive and metacognitive so that the relations among levels would reduce to monitoring and control. This would result in more general theory because it would include all the explanatory mechanisms of the combined task-specific theories. Third, we described salutary effects of creating more general theory this way.

EXPLAINING HETEROGENEOUS THINKING BY PEOPLE OF THE SAME AGE

A staircase view is implicit in nearly all theories that speak of cognitive development (Siegler, this volume). Theorists assume nearly unanimously that people think only in ways that are typical of their age. This assumption is belied by the fact that people think in heterogeneous ways about many matters. Some

---

[2]Theorists can assume that people's intercourse with the problems in their lives provides them with models of their cognition that are equivalent to those generated by scientists' task analyses of what people know and think.

of their ways are like those of much younger people; other ways are more mature. Why such heterogeneity?

This question probably has several valid answers. Siegler (this volume) answers that older, more immature ways of thinking remain with children as they acquire newer more mature ways. The old and new ways compete, and their competition is resolved probabilistically. The probabilities of the different ways of thinking ebb and flow like overlapping waves as they change with age. Although we wonder about mechanisms that determine which ways of thinking win the competition, we accept Siegler's description. We illustrate it as we give an answer that tells another part of the story: Limits of working memory sometimes interfere with monitoring and control of cognition.

Model-guided monitoring and control can be exceedingly complex. Figure 10.6 shows the complexity of monitoring and control guided by the relatively simple model of dimensional comparison. The model (Fig. 10.4) guiding the monitoring and control in Fig. 10.6 is far less complicated than the model in Fig. 10.7. The monitoring and control guided by Fig. 10.7 is far more complicated than those shown in Fig. 10.6.

Thinking is heterogeneous because cognitive models (Figs. 10.4 and 10.7) are executed in working memory, which can be consumed by distractions and slow execution of some strategies (some problem solvers take longer to multiply 7 × 9 than 3 × 4). We hypothesize that distracting events and problem-dictated inefficiencies in strategy execution influence whether or not a person has sufficient working memory to fully implement the monitoring and control required by elaborate models of cognition. What happens if there is too little working memory to implement a model?

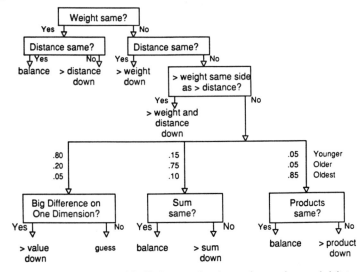

FIG. 10.7. Cognitive model of balance scale solution showing how probabilities of use can create heterogeneous thinking within ages (Younger, Older, Oldest).

The model of dimensional integration shown in Fig. 10.7 is an elaboration of the model shown in Fig. 10.5. The elaboration includes steps that we left out of Fig. 10.5 because they are not included in experts' models of how to solve balance scale problems. When an expert is faced with a balance scale problem that requires a torque calculation, he or she works through the boxes adjacent to the diagonal (the boxes in Fig. 10.5) because problems requiring a torque calculation will have unequal weights, unequal distances, and greater weight on the opposite side from the greater distance. As Fig. 10.5 and the diagonal boxes of Fig. 10.7 show, a person should answer "No" successively to the questions "Weight same?," "Distance same?," and "Greater weight same side as greater distance?," bringing him or her to the question, "Products same?" If working memory fails so that the person incorrectly answers "Yes" to any of the first three questions of the model, the person will not proceed to the point of calculating torque. For example, assume that a person's working memory is consumed after he or she has counted the distances on both sides of the fulcrum. He or she will incorrectly remember left and right distances and incorrectly conclude that they are the same. He or she will incorrectly conclude that the problem is solved and will answer that the side with the greater weight goes down. The person should have gone on to calculate torque, which could show that the side with lesser weight goes down.

Mature problem solvers' knowledge, strategies, metacognitive understandings, and cognitive models often include the knowledge, strategies, metacognitive understandings, and cognitive models of less mature problem solvers (Case, 1991). Whenever this is the case, limits of working memory can result in incomplete execution of fully mature models, as in the example described in the preceding paragraph. When this happens, older problem solvers behave as younger ones. If working memory limits are sometimes exceeded and sometimes not exceeded by distractions or time consuming strategies, then a person will sometimes use less mature and sometimes more mature strategies. Strategy use will be heterogeneous across opportunities to solve balance scale problems.

Many investigators argue that working memory limits interfere directly with cognition (see chapters in this volume by Hitch, de Ribaupierre, Kail, Kliegl, Salthouse). In the foregoing paragraphs we generalized this argument to indirect effects on cognition. Guttentag (this volume) made a similar generalization. The idea is that by limiting metacognitive monitoring and control, working memory indirectly limits cognition. Metacognitive monitoring and control are limited more on some occasions than on others, depending on distractions and strategic inefficiencies of the problem solver. These arguments add up to a believable account of some of the heterogeneity of individual's problem solving efforts (Battig, 1979; Reitman, 1969; Simon, 1975).

Siegler (this volume) offered a probabilistic reason that thinking is heterogeneous within an age. Figure 10.7 illustrates this argument in its bottom three boxes. Each of these boxes represent the end point of a different model of how to solve problems when a scale has greater weight on one side of its fulcrum and greater distance on its other side. In the normal course of human development, the left-most of the three boxes develops at an earlier age than the middle box, which develops at an earlier age than the right-most box. To represent Siegler's view that such developments occur as overlapping waves rather than as discrete stair steps, we put hypothetical probabilities next to the arrows leading to the three boxes.

The top three probabilities (.8, .15, .05) represent the chances that quite young children will choose each of the three strategies in the lower boxes. According to such probabilities, when a young child determines that a balance scale has more weight on one side and more distance on the other, he or she usually asks whether the difference on one dimension (weight or distance) is much bigger than the difference on the other dimension. If so, the child predicts that the side with the greater value on the dimension with the bigger difference goes down. If neither dimension has a much bigger difference, the child guesses which side will go down. As required by Siegler's view of development as overlapping waves, young children sometimes choose one of the other two strategies, but less frequently than the strategy of judging the relative size of differences on the dimensions.

The middle probabilities represent the chances that older children will choose each of the three strategies (.20, .75, .05). Occasionally older children will act as younger ones, and rarely they will act as even older children. Usually, they will ask whether the sum of the weights and distances on one side exceeds the sums of the weights and distances on the other side. They will compare the sums. If the sums are equal, they predict that the scale will balance. If the sums are unequal, children predict that the side with the larger sum will go down.

The bottom probabilities represent the chances that near experts will choose each of the three strategies (.05, .1, .85). The model shown in Fig. 10.5 assumes that the three probabilities are 0, 0, and 1.0, as they should be for experts, and the boxes with 0 probability are not included in Fig. 10.5. According to the probabilities in Fig. 10.7, the oldest children represented will usually calculate products of the weights and distances on each side of the fulcrum, compare the products, and predict that the side with the greater product will go down. The oldest children will usually act as experts, but sometimes they act as younger children.

Combining Siegler's probabilistic account of development with our generalization of working memory limits to metacognitive monitoring and control creates a theory with two mechanisms that produce heterogeneous thinking within ages. Even though both mechanisms require more specification and empirical validation, combining them is progress toward general theory that accounts more fully for cognitive development.

Generalizing the limits of working memory from cognition to metacognition yields the following testable predictions:

. 1. In the absence of their direct instruction for a problem domain, metacognitive monitoring and control develop later than mastery of strategies, knowledge, and cognitive models useful in that domain. Until cognitive models are mastered, execution of the strategies and knowledge they guide will consume working memory required by monitoring and control.

2. Task-specific models allow monitoring and control of knowledge and strategies without metacognitive understanding, which can either be taught directly or created by monitoring and control. When metacognitive understanding is not taught directly, it is acquired from monitoring cognition and the results of controlling it. Therefore, metacognitive understanding that is not taught directly develops after monitoring and control.

3. Expertise requires extended experience in a domain, because without extended experience, understanding, monitoring, and control cannot be automated, as they are for experts.

4. Developmental increases in working memory capacity are driven by the greater complexity (i.e., memory demands) of newly acquired strategies and their associated metacognitions than mastered strategies and metacognitions. Causality between memory capacity and cognitive competence is bidirectional. Although other investigators argue that memory capacity unidirectionally limits cognition (see chapters in this volume by Hitch, de Ribaupierre, Kail, Kliegl, Salthouse), we hypothesize that increases in memory capacity are spurred by increases in the complexity of knowledge, strategies, and models of how they work together. Our hypothesis moves the explanatory burden for increases in memory capacity from unspecified maturational forces to specifiable increases in the complexity of children's knowledge, strategies, and models for using them.

Reprise

To help account for the heterogeneity of thinking that characterizes individuals, we generalized the notion that working memory limits cognition to the possibility that it also limits metacognitive monitoring and control of cognition. Therefore, depending on contextual distractions and a person's mastery of required strategies, his or her relevant model of cognition will be more or less completely executed on different occasions when full execution is required. When that model includes earlier developing knowledge, strategies, and understandings, the result of incomplete execution will be heterogeneous thinking. Sometimes thinking will be as mature as the thinker's model allows. Other times thinking will be less mature.

By incorporating probabilities in a model of relatively mature solution of balance scale problems, we showed that Siegler's overlapping wave conception of development (this volume) provides a source of heterogeneous thinking that is independent of working memory limits on monitoring and control. Inclusion of both approaches in a single theory advances the causes of making cognitive theory more general and more developmentally accurate.

We offered four predictions that follow from the notion that working memory limits metacognitive monitoring and control. First, in the absence of their direct instruction, metacognitive monitoring and control of a domain's knowledge and strategies should develop later than the knowledge and strategies themselves. Second, when metacognitive understanding is not taught directly, it should develop later than monitoring and control. Third, expertise depends upon automation of monitoring and control, which stem from repeated use of the cognitive model that guides knowledge and strategies. Fourth, although others hypothesize that more complex strategies and models are allowed by unexplained maturational increases in memory capacity, we hypothesize that increases in working memory capacity result from the acquisition of more complex strategies and models—a testable explanation of why working memory increases.

WHY SO FEW MECHANISMS OF COGNITIVE CHANGE?

Why have viable mechanisms of cognitive change been included so infrequently in developmental theories? Inadequate data are a part of the answer. To observe cognitive change, one needs what Siegler (this volume) calls *microgenetic data*. One needs data collected repeatedly at brief intervals from the same individuals. The number of change mechanisms proposed by developmental theorists could be increased dramatically by reliance on microgenetic observations that allow fuller description of change than typical observations of development. Nevertheless, we see a need for additional more direct approaches to discovering mechanisms of change. Changing cognition by teaching it is a more direct approach.

We advocate supplementing microgenetic observations with instructional experiments for four reasons: First, observation provides needed bases for cognitive instruction. Second, observing cognitive change in the absence of instruction and creating change by instruction gives two sources of converging evidence to validate hypothesized mechanisms of change (see Butterfield, Siladi, & Belmont, 1980, for such convergence about memory development). Third, instruction produces changes that microgenetic observations are intended to observe. Fourth, successful instruction eliminates questions about direction of causality among observed variables, and it eliminates questions about confounded correlates of the observed variables. Although observation is a fine source of hypotheses about change mechanisms, cognitive instruction is their only experimental test.

TWO MECHANISMS OF COGNITIVE DEVELOPMENT

Development consists of learning cognitive models that combine knowledge and strategies into effective problem-solving procedures. Knowledge and strategies are necessary ingredients of effective thinking, but cognitive models are more central to cognitive development because they organize and coordinate knowledge and strategies. Cognitive models can be taught or they can be created by children who use their metacognitive understanding to interpret the results of their monitoring and controlling of cognition. Direct instruction of cognitive models and creation of models by metacognitively guided monitoring and control are both central mechanisms of cognitive change.

Teaching Cognitive Models

By direct instruction of cognitive models, we mean teaching new ways of ordering knowledge and strategies to solve complex problems. Some teaching that others call *strategy instruction* (e.g., Pressley, this volume), we call teaching a model. Some strategy instruction includes considerable teaching of the order in which strategies are to be performed. For such teaching we prefer the label *model instruction*, because other teaching that is called strategy instruction conveys little or no information about the ordering of knowledge and strategies.

Many experiments could be used to suggest that direct instruction of cognitive models is a mechanism of developmental change. We rely here on a few relevant results from an experiment by Butterfield and Ferretti (1994). Their experiment established that instruction is a mechanism of change by realizing the unrealized logic of using instruction to simulate development.

Instructional experiments can be said to simulate cognitive development when (a) two or more groups of different developmental levels (b) are all given identical instruction designed to produce thinking typical of people at the higher level, and (c) the instruction eliminates differences between groups from the higher and lower levels, (d) without changing the performance of the highest group (Brown & Campione, 1978; Butterfield, Siladi, & Belmont, 1980). Such experiments most convincingly demonstrate a developmental change mechanism when the instructed groups that differ in problem-solving maturity do not differ in age. When the groups are the same age, no unknown confound of age can mediate the results of instruction. Even when differences among such groups are eliminated by instruction, one can claim to have simulated a mechanism of developmental change only when instruction does not alter the performance of the group whose cognitive model is taught. If the most proficient groups' performance is changed by the instruction so that little or no narrowing of group differences results or preinstructional differences are increased, as sometimes happens when one of the instructed groups is intellectually gifted (Case, 1991; Cronbach & Snow, 1977; Snow, 1982), then instructional experiments do not validate a mechanism of cognitive change. If performance of the more mature group is changed, then one may have taught all groups to use a cognitive model that none normally uses.

A Prior Experiment on Teaching a Cognitive Model. Butterfield and Ferretti based their instructions on analyses of how children of different ages solve balance scale problems. They could use balance scales because their solution was carefully analyzed, and developmental changes in how they are solved was described in detail (Ferretti & Butterfield, 1986, 1989; Ferretti, Butterfield, Cahn, & Kerkman, 1985; Siegler, 1976, 1978). Good diagnostic methods for evaluating children's cognitive models were developed (Siegler, 1976; Wilkening & Anderson, 1982), and parts of the most mature cognitive model had been taught directly and effectively (Butterfield & Ferretti, 1984; Butterfield & Nelson, 1991; Day & Hall, 1988; Ferretti & Butterfield, 1992).

Prior observational studies show that children use one of five developmentally ordered rules or (as we call them) *cognitive models* to solve balance scale problems. Balance scales have two relevant dimensions: weight and distance of the weights from the fulcrum. Model 1 children predict from a single dominant dimension, which for most children is weight, as it was for all children taught by Butterfield and Ferretti. Model 1 is shown in Fig. 10.4 and in the top box in Figs. 10.5 and 10.7. Model 2 children also predict from a single dimension, but if the values of the dominant dimension are equal they consider the second, nondominant dimension. For children studied by Butterfield and Ferretti, distance of the weights from the balance scale's fulcrum was the nondominant dimension. Model 2 consists of the Weight Same? and Distance Same? portion of the cognitive model shown in our Figs. 10.5 and 10.7. Model 3 children take both dimensions into account when making predictions, and they resolve conflict between the dimensions—one side of the scale has a greater value along one dimension and the other side has a greater value along the other dimension—by choosing the side associated with the dimension estimated to have a large difference. Model 3 consists of the Weight Same?, Distance Same?, and Distance Bigger? boxes of Fig. 10.7. Model 4 children quantify dimensions and integrate them by addition (Ferretti et al., 1985; Wilkening & Anderson, 1982), as indicated in the Weight Same?, Distance Same?, and Weight + Distance Same? boxes of Fig. 10.7. Model 5 children integrate dimensions by multiplication (Siegler, 1976), as shown in the Weight Same?, Distance Same?, and Products Same? boxes of Fig. 10.7.

Butterfield and Ferretti used paper-and-pencil pretests like those described by Ferretti et al. (1985) to identify four groups of six ($N = 24$) intellectually gifted children's cognitive models before instruction. The four groups used Models 1, 2, 3, or 4 before instruction. Butterfield and Ferretti taught intellectually gifted children because prior research showed that such children benefit more from balance scale instruction than do less talented children (Ferretti & Butterfield, 1992). Analysis of variance showed that there were no reliable differences in age among groups using Models 1, 2, and 3, but Model 4 children were 2 years older ($M = 11.8$ years) than children in the other three groups. Because Butterfield and Ferretti expected no benefit from instruction for children starting at Model 4, their greater age could not confound any expected results.

Children who used Model 1 and 2 on the pretest were first given Model 2 instruction. Then, they and children who used Model 3 on the pretest were given Model 3 instruction. Finally, all children were given Model 4 instruction.

Instruction showed children how to produce specified outcomes by placing weights on one side of a mechanical balance scale. An experimenter had placed weights on the other side of the scale. Following instruction, paper-and-pencil tests similar to the pretests were administered. This allowed an overall test of how well the instructions simulated development of Model 4.

Regardless of their model before instruction, all children used Model 4 after instruction. Instruction did not change any of the six children who used Model 4 before instruction, but all 18 children who used Model 1, 2, or 3 before instruction used Model 4 after instruction. Butterfield and Ferretti's instructions precisely simulated development of balance scale Model 4. Instruction in cognitive models is a mechanism of cognitive change.

Model Creation Within a Domain

By creation of cognitive models, we mean (a) fashioning in the absence of instruction sequences of knowledge and strategies that solve problem types not solvable by any known model, (b) solving a problem type not isomorphic in its knowledge and strategic requirements to any problem type one can already solve, and (c) modifying a known model or inventing a new model.

We hypothesize that metacognitive monitoring and control of cognition contribute to model creation by fostering metacognitive understanding. For example, in the memory domain, there comes an age when during study, students monitor number of words named since the last rehearsal to decide when to begin the next rehearsal. Having begun rehearsal, older students monitor rehearsals completed or ease of recall to decide when to move from rehearsing one group of names to naming and then rehearsing another group. To control transition from studying to retrieving, some students monitor and judge how well they have learned names they have studied. To retrieve accurately, their task-specific models sequence their retrieval strategies, that is, a list's early and middle rehearsed names are recalled before its later unrehearsed names. During retrieval, more experienced problem solvers monitor feedback about correctness or judge their response certainties to decide whether their model should be changed or perhaps a new one created for future lists. We hypothesize that such monitoring and control create metacognitive understandings that allow model creation.

We distinguish model creation within problem domains from model creation across problem domains. By model creation within a domain, we mean that a person adds strategies to and/or subtracts strategies from a known model for a related problem. For example, a child could change a cumulative rehearsal model for serial recall to a model appropriate for free recall by attending without rehearsal to only the terminal items in a list and recalling them first. By model creation across domains, we mean that a person fashions a new model for a domain in which he or she has been given no instruction about suitable models. For example, if someone solves previously unsolved analogical reasoning problems after having been taught models that increase his or her short-term memory, inferential reasoning, and physics problem solution, we would infer model creation across domains because the taught models are different from the model underlying analogical reasoning.

We hypothesize that model creation within a domain requires the use of metacognitive understanding to modify a known model so that it works with problems requiring previously unknown knowledge or strategies. When creating a model for use within a domain, a problem solver modifies a known model so that it applies to problems that come from the model's domain but have different knowledge or strategic requirements than problems solvable by the model. To establish that model creation is a mechanism of developmental change, we describe three experiments, two by Butterfield and Nelson (1991) and one of Johnston's (1994) experiments. These experimental findings converge on the conclusions that (a) cognitive instruction is a mechanism of cognitive development and (b) metacognitive understanding guides model creation in the domain of physics problems.

Two Prior Experiments on Model Creation Within a Domain.   In separate experiments, Butterfield and Nelson (1991) taught 40 intellectually average and 32 mentally retarded children models sufficient for solution of two of three physics problems: balance scales, liquid estimation, and inclined planes. Then they tested the two groups with the third problem. These three problems are solved by the same strategies working on different problem dimensions. Their models differ with respect to specified knowledge of relevant problem dimensions. The models are the same with respect to their sequence of strategies applied to problem dimensions. The typical developmental course of the three models is the same as that for balance scales (see Fig. 10.7 and foregoing section on cognitive instruction).

Having selected children who were too young to know more than Model 2 for any of the three problems, Butterfield and Nelson taught them Model 2 after the fashion of Butterfield and Ferretti, previously described, and then tested them to ensure they used Model 2. This guaranteed that all children knew the relevant dimensions for all three problems. It also ensured that they did not use all of the strategies contained in Model 4. Then, Model 4 was taught for two of the tasks. In the course of teaching Model 4 for the first of these two tasks, some children received *application instruction*, during which it was pointed out that some problems were solvable by the earlier (Model 2) instruction. It was also pointed out that those problems not solvable this way were solvable by the later (Model 4) instruction. Some children received more instruction on sequencing strategies than was provided by model instruction alone. During teaching Model 4 for the second task, some children received *similarity instruction*, during which it was pointed out that some instances of all three tasks were solvable by the earlier (Model 2) instruction. It was also pointed out during application instruction that other instances of two tasks were solvable by the later (Model 4) instruction. Some children were encouraged to recognize the shared strategies of the models they had been taught. Then, all children were tested with the third problem, whose Model 4 had not been taught.

A clear majority of both average (75%) and mentally retarded children (78%) used Model 4 on pencil-and-paper versions of the two tasks for which it was instructed. They learned Model 4 from direct instruction, replicating Butterfield and Ferretti and converging on the conclusion that instruction is a mechanism of cognitive development.

Model 4 was not taught for the third problem, and fewer than half of both average (32%) and mentally retarded children (48%) used it on the third problem. No significant differences resulted from either application or similarity instruction for either group. Even though most children learned Model 4 for the two instructed problems, few created Model 4 for the uninstructed problem.

The next step in the experiment by Butterfield and Nelson focused directly on whether or not metacognitive understanding facilitates model creation. Children who did not create Model 4 on the third task were asked questions designed to induce hypothesis generation about reasons for incorrectly answering test items for the third task. Butterfield and Nelson administered more third-task test items. Each time a child answered an item incorrectly, they asked the child to explain why. The intent was to encourage children to draw on the two Model 4s they had been taught when explaining why they had missed items on the third task, to promote understanding that the three tasks were the same except for their relevant dimensions, and to promote creation of a Model 4 with the dimensions of the third task and the dimensions of the two instructed tasks.

Butterfield and Nelson administered another test for use of Model 4 following children's generation of reasons for having missed six test items on the third task. Nearly half (48%) of the average children used Model 4 on this test, whereas none used Model 4 on the test immediately preceding questioning designed to promote model creation. Because mentally retarded children lack metacognitive understandings of their average age mates, they should have been less likely to create models even when questioned in ways designed to prompt such creation. In fact, Butterfield and Nelson found that only 17% of their mentally retarded subjects used Model 4 after questioning.

Butterfield and Nelson's finding that average children, more than those who are mentally retarded, used Model 4 after questions designed to promote its creation, is strong support for the hypothesis that metacognitive understanding promotes model creation. The fact that so many average and mentally retarded children did not use Model 4 on an untaught task before being questioned is also consistent with our hypothesis that metacognitive understanding promotes model creation. We turn now to Johnston's test of the role of metacognitive instruction in model creation within a domain.

A New Experiment on Model Creation Within a Domain. In one of his experiments, Johnston worked with average children who, prior to any experimental instruction, used Models 1 or 2 for balance scale and shadow projection problems. He divided his students into four groups. The groups differed according to whether or not Model 4 instruction on balance scale or shadow projection was supplemented with instruction in (a) metacognitive understanding and (b) monitoring and controlling strategies. Instruction was varied factorially so that two groups received supplemental instruction in monitoring and control and two received supplemental instruction in metacognitive understanding. All four groups received their supplemental instruction during the teaching of Model 4 for their first problem. After instruction, all 28 children used Model 4 on the tasks for which it was taught, balance scale or shadow projection. This replicates findings that cognitive instruction is a mechanism of development.

Johnston used transfer tests on uninstructed problems to measure model creation. He tested model creation for Task 2 (inclined plane or balance scale) and for a third task (inclined train). If model creation depends on metacognitive understanding, then the group of children who received neither sort of supplemental instruction on their first task and the group who received only monitoring and control instruction should not have created Model 4 for either their second or third tasks. Both groups who received supplemental instruction in metacognitive understanding on their first task should have created Model 4 for both their second and third tasks.

Johnston found that all 14 children who received instruction in metacognitive understanding used Model 4 on Tasks 2 and 3. None of the 14 who did not receive instruction in metacognitive understanding used Model 4 on Task 2 or 3. Johnston's findings show that metacognitive understanding promotes model creation within a domain. His findings also show that in the absence of time and experience, metacognitive monitoring and control do not promote model creation within a domain. Different experimentation is required to test our prediction that monitoring and control will, given experience, produce metacognitive understandings that will promote model creation.

Reprise

We described four experiments that converge on the conclusion that cognitive instruction is a mechanism of cognitive development. Two of the four experiments also converge on the conclusion that model creation within domains depends on metacognitive understanding. Our data validate two mechanisms of cognitive development: cognitive instruction and metacognitively guided model creation within domains.

Butterfield and Nelson's results imply that their subjects created a single Model 4 including the dimensions of balance scale, inclined plane, and liquid estimation tasks. This suggests that a general theory of physics problem solution can be constructed from task specific theories of balance scale, inclined plane, and liquid estimation problems. Johnston's results more directly affirm this possibility for balance scales, inclined trains, and shadow projection problems. Our data provide experimental confirmation of the possibility raised by Siegler's (1976) observational data that general theory is possible within the domain of physics problems requiring integration of two dimensions.

ACCOUNTING FOR A WIDER RANGE OF COGNITIVE PERFORMANCE

The results of our cognitive instruction are less general than the results of our instruction about metacognitive understanding. Our cognitive instructions were task-specific unless they were supplemented by instruction in metacognitive understanding, in which case they were domain-general. This validates domain-general theory for physics problems requiring dimensional integration.

We are unaware of experimental data to validate theory that is general across diverse cognitive domains. Such data could result from teaching children so that they create cognitive models in untaught domains. We conclude this chapter by sketching research that could produce experimental data validating theory that is general across domains.

Possible Research on Model Creation Across Domains

To validate a theory that is general across domains, one could teach model creation within several domains and then test for model creation in yet another domain. For example, one could test the effects of teaching model creation in the domains of memory, physics, and inductive reasoning on creation of an analogical reasoning model.

Teachable models are available for the domains of physics (described earlier in this chapter), short-term memory (Butterfield et al., 1980; several chapters in this volume), inductive reasoning (Butterfield, Nielsen, Tangen, & Richardson, 1985; Gregg, 1967; Holzman, Pellegrino, & Glaser, 1976; Klahr & Wallace, 1970; Kotovsky & Simon, 1973; Leewenberg, 1969; Restle, 1970; Simon & Kotovsky, 1963), and analogical reasoning (Gentner, 1983, 1989; Gholson, Morgan, Dattel, & Pierce, 1990; Holyoak & Thagard, 1989; Sternberg & Nigro, 1980). Teachable metacognitive understandings necessary for creation of models within domains are available for memory (Belmont, Butterfield, & Ferretti, 1982; Pressley, Borkowski, & O'Sullivan, 1984) and physics problems (this chapter). Principles that allow formulation of teachable metacognitive understandings for inductive reasoning and analogical reasoning are available (Shunk & Zimmerman, 1994).

Research subjects could be selected for use of immature models in the domains of memory, physics, and analogical reasoning. Half could be taught to use mature domain-specific models but not to create models that are general to each of these domains. The other half could be taught to create models that are general to each of the domains. Finally, all could be tested for model creation in the uninstructed domain of analogical reasoning. The experimental question is whether or not children who receive instruction in model creation would improve more in their solution of analogical reasoning problems than children who receive instruction in the use of domain-specific models.

If an experiment like the one just sketched did not create model creation across domains, one could increase the number of domains in which model creation within domains is taught prior to testing for creation across domains. One could also instruct metacognitive understandings potentially relevant to detecting the need to create a new model in an unfamiliar domain. Also, one could teach metacognitive understandings theoretically relevant to strategy creation across domains.

CODA

We offered solutions for four problems of current cognitive theory. First, to include more explanatory mechanisms in cognitive theory, we proposed pooling task-specific models expressed as cognitive and metacognitive hierarchies whose levels are related by monitoring and control. This would give all valid explanatory mechanisms their due. Second, to account for heterogeneity in individual's strategy use, we generalized the limiting functions of working memory from cognition to metacognitive monitoring and control. We showed that models expressed as cognitive and metacognitive levels could incorporate probabilistic explanations of heterogeneous thinking as well as our generalization of memory limits. We hypothesized bidirectionality of causality between working memory and cognition. Third, we described four experiments to test cognitive instruction and metacognitively guided model creation as mechanisms of cognitive change. All four experiments validate cognitive instruction as a mechanism of cognitive development. Two of these experiments validate domain general theory. Fourth, we sketched future research to test the possibility of making cognitive theory general across domains. We hope we have helped to create general cognitive theory that is developmentally pertinent.

ACKNOWLEDGMENTS

We thank Tom Nelson and Robert Siegler for their uncommonly helpful suggestions about an earlier version of this chapter.

REFERENCES

Anderson, J. R. (1978). Computer simulation of a language acquisition system: A second report. In D. LaBerge & S. J. Samuels (Eds.), *Perception and comprehension*. Hillsdale, NJ: Lawrence Erlbaum Associates.

Anderson, J. R. (1981). *Cognitive skills and their acquisition.* Hillsdale, NJ: Lawrence Erlbaum Associates.

Anderson, J. R., & Bower, G. H. (1973). *Human associative memory.* Washington, DC: Winston.

Averbach, I., & Coriell, A. S. (1961). Short-term memory in vision. *Bell System Technical Journal, 40,* 309–328.

Battig, W. J. (1979). Within-individual differences in cognitive processes. In R. Solso (Ed.), *Information processing and cognition.* Hillsdale, NJ: Lawrence Erlbaum Associates.

Belmont, J. M., & Butterfield, E. C. (1971). Learning strategies as determinants of memory deficiencies. *Cognitive Psychology, 2,* 411–420.

Belmont, J. M., Butterfield, E. C., & Ferretti, R. P. (1982). To secure transfer of training, instruct self-management skills. In D. K. Detterman & R. J. Sternberg (Eds.), *How and how much can intelligence be increased* (pp. 147–154). Norwood, NJ: Ablex.

Broadbent, D. E. (1977). Levels, hierarchies, and the locus of control. *Quarterly Journal of Experimental Psychology, 29,* 181–201.

Brown, A. L., & Campione, J. C. (1978). Permissible inferences from cognitive training studies in developmental research. *Quarterly Newsletter of the Institute for Comparative Human Behavior, 2,* 46–53.

Butterfield, E. C. (1986). Intelligent action, learning, and cognitive development might all be explained by the same theory. In R. J. Sternberg & D. K. Detterman (Eds.), *What is intelligence: Contemporary viewpoints on its nature and definition* (pp. 45–50). Norwood, NJ: Ablex.

Butterfield, E. C., & Ferretti, R. P. (1984). Some extensions of the instructional approach to cognitive development and a sufficient condition for transfer of training. In P. H. Brooks, C. McCauley, & R. Sperber (Eds.), *Learning and cognition in the mentally retarded* (pp. 311–332). Hillsdale, NJ: Lawrence Erlbaum Associates.

Butterfield, E. C., & Ferretti, R. P. (1987). Toward a theoretical integration hypothesis about intellectual differences among children. In J. G. Borkowski & J. D. Day (Eds.), *Cognition in special children* (pp. 195–233). Norwood, NJ: Ablex.

Butterfield, E. C., & Ferretti, R. P. (1994). An instructional test of observationally warranted differences in problem solving strategies. Manuscript submitted for publication.

Butterfield, E. C., & Nelson, G. D. (1991). Promoting positive transfer of different types. *Cognition and Instruction, 8,* 69–102.

Butterfield, E. C., Nielsen, D., Tangen, K. L., & Richardson, M. B. (1985). Theoretically based psychometric measures of inductive reasoning. In S. Embretson (Eds.), *Test design: Contributions from psychology, education, and psychometrics* (pp. 77–147). New York: Academic Press.

Butterfield, E. C., Siladi, D., & Belmont, J. M. (1980). Validating theories of intelligence. In H. Reese & L. P. Lipsitt (Eds.), *Advances in child development and child behavior* (pp. 96–162). New York: Academic Press.

Case, R. (1991). *The mind's staircase: Exploring the conceptual underpinnings of children's thought and knowledge.* Hillsdale, NJ: Lawrence Erlbaum Associates.

Cavanaugh, J. C., & Perlmutter, M. (1982). Metamemory: A critical examination. *Child Development, 53,* 11–28.

Conant, R. C., & Ashby, W. R. (1970). Every good regulator of a system must be a model of that system. *International Journal of Systems Science, 1,* 89–97.

Conrad, R. (1964). Acoustic confusions in immediate memory. *British Journal of Psychology, 55,* 75–84.

Craik, F. I. M. (1970). The fate of primary items in free recall. *Journal of Verbal Learning and Verbal Behavior, 9,* 143–148.

Cronbach, L. J., & Snow, R. E. (1977). *Aptitudes and instructional methods.* New York: Irvington.

Darwin, C. J., Turvey, M. T., & Crowder, R. G. (1972). An auditory analogue of the Sperling partial report procedure. *Cognitive Psychology, 3,* 255–267.

Day, J. D., & Hall, L. K. (1988). Intelligence-related differences in learning and transfer and enhancement of transfer among mentally retarded persons. *American Journal on Mental Retardation, 93,* 125–137.

Ferretti, R. P., & Butterfield, E. C. (1986). Are children's rule assessment classifications invariant across instances of problem types? *Child Development, 57,* 1419–1428.

Ferretti, R. P., & Butterfield, E. C. (1989). Intelligence as a correlate of children's problem solving. *American Journal on Mental Retardation, 93,* 424–433.

Ferretti, R. P., & Butterfield, E. C. (1992). Intelligence-related differences in the learning, maintenance, and transfer of problem-solving strategies. *Intelligence, 16,* 207–224.

Ferretti, R. P., Butterfield, E. C., Cahn, A., & Kerkman, D. (1985). The classification of children's knowledge: Development on the balance scale and inclined-plane problems. *Journal of Experimental Child Psychology, 39,* 131–160.

Flavell, J. H. (1970). Developmental studies of mediated memory. In H. Reese & L. Lipsitt (Eds.), *Advances in child development and behavior* (pp. 182–213). New York: Academic Press.

Flavell, J. H. (1979). Metacognition and cognitive monitoring: A new area of cognitive-developmental inquiry. *American Psychologist, 34,* 906–911.

Gentner, D. (1983). Structure-mapping: A theoretical framework for analogy. *Cognitive Science, 7,* 155–170.

Gentner, D. (1989). The mechanisms of analogical learning. In S. Vosniadou & A. Ortony (Eds.), *Similarity and analogical reasoning* (pp. 199–241). New York: Cambridge University Press.

Gholson, B., Morgan, D., Dattel, A. R., & Pierce, K. A. (1990). The development of analogical problem solving: Strategic processes in schema acquisition and transfer. In D. F. Bjorklund (Eds.), *Children's strategies: Contemporary views of cognitive development* (pp. 269–308). Hillsdale, NJ: Lawrence Erlbaum Associates.

Glanzer, M. (1972). Storage mechanisms in recall. In G. H. Bower & J. T. Spence (Eds.), *Psychology of learning and motivation* (pp. 129–194). New York: Academic Press.

Gregg, L. W. (1967). Internal representations of sequential concepts. In B. Kleinmutz (Eds.), *Concepts and the structure of memory* (pp. 107–142). New York: Wiley.

Holyoak, K. J., & Thagard, P. (1989). A computational model of analogical problem solving. In S. Vosniadou & A. Ortony (Eds.), *Similarity and analogical reasoning* (pp. 242–266). New York: Cambridge University Press.

Holzman, T. G., Pellegrino, J. W., & Glaser, R. (1976). Process training derived from a computer simulation theory. *Memory & Cognition, 4,* 349–356.

Inhelder, B., & Piaget, J. (1958). *The growth of logical thinking from childhood to adolescence.* New York: Basic Books.

Johnston, J. C. (1994). *The role of metacognition in enhancing strategy transfer.* Doctoral dissertation, University of Washington, Seattle.

Kail, R., & Bisanz, J. (1992). The information-processing perspective on cognitive development in childhood and adolescence. In R. J. Sternberg & C. A. Berg (Eds.), *Intellectual development* (pp. 229–260). New York: Cambridge University Press.

Klahr, D., & Wallace, J. G. (1970). The development of serial completion strategies: An information processing analysis. *British Journal of Psychology, 61,* 243–257.

Kotovsky, K., & Simon, H. A. (1973). Empirical tests of a theory of human acquisition of concepts for sequential patterns. *Cognitive Psychology, 4,* 399–424.

Lachman, R., Lachman, J. L., & Butterfield, E. C. (1979). *Cognitive psychology and information processing: An introduction.* Hillsdale, NJ: Lawrence Erlbaum Associates.

Leewenberg, E. L. L. (1969). Quantitative specification of information in sequential patterns. *Psychological Review, 76,* 216–220.

Lodico, M. G., Ghatala, E. S., Levin, J. R., Pressley, M., & Bell, J. A. (1983). The effects of strategy monitoring training on children's selection of effective memory strategies. *Journal of Experimental Child Psychology, 35,* 263–277.

Mandler, G. (1967). Organization in memory. In K. W. Spence & J. T. Spence (Eds.), *Psychology of learning and motivation* (pp. 328–372). New York: Academic Press.

Miller, G. A. (1956). The magical number seven plus or minus 2: Some limits on our capacity for processing information. *Psychological Review, 63,* 81–97.

Nelson, T. O., & Narens, L. (1990). Metamemory: A theoretical framework and new findings. In G. H. Bower (Ed.), *The psychology of learning and motivation* (pp. 125–141). New York: Academic Press.

Nelson, T. O., & Narens, L. (1994). Why investigate metacognition? In J. Metcalfe & A. Shimamura (Eds.), *Metacognition: Knowing about knowing* (pp. 1–25). Boston: Bradford Books.

Pressley, M., Borkowski, J. G., & O'Sullivan, J. T. (1984). Memory strategy instruction is made of this: Metamemory and durable strategy use. *Educational Psychologist, 19*, 94–107.

Reitman, W. (1969). What does it take to remember? In D. A. Norman (Ed.), *Models of human memory* (pp. 470–510). New York: Academic Press.

Restle, F. (1970). Theory of serial pattern learning: Structural trees. *Psychological Review, 79*, 534–546.

Schunk, D., & Zimmerman, B. (Eds.) (1994). *Self-regulation of learning and performance: Issues and educational application.* Hillsdale, NJ: Lawrence Erlbaum Associates.

Siegler, R. S. (1976). Three aspects of cognitive development. *Cognitive Psychology, 8*, 481–520.

Siegler, R. S. (1978). The origins of scientific reasoning. In R. S. Siegler (Eds.), *Children's thinking: What develops?* (pp. 109–150). Hillsdale, NJ: Lawrence Erlbaum Associates.

Siegler, R. S. (1981). Developmental sequences within and between concepts. *Monographs of the Society for Research in Child Development, 46*(2, Serial No. 189).

Siegler, R. S. (1986). *Children's thinking.* Englewood Cliffs, NJ: Prentice Hall.

Simon, H. A. (1975). The functional equivalence of problem solving skills. *Cognitive Psychology, 7*, 268–288.

Simon, H. A., & Kotovsky, K. (1963). Human acquisition of concepts for sequential patterns. *Psychological Review, 70*, 534–546.

Snow, R. E. (1982). Education and intelligence. In R. J. Sternberg (Ed.), *Handbook of human intelligence* (pp. 493–585). New York: Cambridge University Press.

Sperling, G. (1960). The information available in brief visual displays. *Psychological Monographs, 74* (Whole No. 11).

Sternberg, R. J., & Nigro, G. (1980). Developmental patterns in the solution of verbal analogies. *Child Development, 51*, 27–38.

Wilkening, F., & Anderson, N. H. (1982). Comparison of the two rule-assessment methodologies for studying cognitive development and knowledge structure. *Psychological Bulletin, 92*, 215–237.

Chapter 11

Mental Effort and Motivation: Influences on Children's Memory Strategy Use

Robert E. Guttentag
University of North Carolina at Greensboro

Performance on most deliberate memorization tasks improves dramatically over the course of the elementary school years, a change that results in part from an age-related increase in the use of memorization strategies such as rehearsal (Flavell, 1970), organization (Ornstein & Corsale, 1979), and elaboration (Pressley, 1982). This chapter focuses on the role of the processing capacity demands of strategy execution on children's strategy use, and more specifically, on the role of motivation as a factor mediating the influence of capacity demands on strategy selection and execution. Past research suggesting that the capacity demands of strategy execution may play a significant role in the strategy selection process is reviewed. A general model of strategy selection is then presented, which incorporates both motivation and the effort demands of strategy use as factors influencing strategy selection. Finally, three recently completed experiments that were designed to test predictions of the model are described.

AGE DIFFERENCES IN THE CAPACITY DEMANDS OF STRATEGY EXECUTION

Recent evidence suggests that there is an age-related decline during childhood in the amount of processing capacity required for the execution of most memory strategies (Bjorklund & Harnishfeger, 1987). In a study by Guttentag (1984), for instance, children in Grades 2, 3, and 6 were instructed to utilize a cumulative rehearsal strategy to memorize a list of words. Subjects were also required to perform a secondary finger-tapping task while memorizing the list. Compared with performance under baseline conditions (when subjects performed the finger tapping task alone), Guttentag found that the amount of interference produced by the primary memory-strategy-use task with the secondary finger-tapping task decreased with age, suggesting an age-related decrease in the processing capacity demands of multi-item rehearsal. Similarly, Kee and Davies (1991) used a dual-task paradigm to test for age differences in the processing demands of the use of both rehearsal and elaboration on a paired associate learning task. It was found that sixth graders and adults did not differ in the capacity demands of instructed rehearsal (a strategy that sixth graders are already highly skilled at using). However, when subjects were instructed to utilize an elaboration strategy (generating a sentence interrelating the two words from each word pair), the effort demands of strategy use were found to be greater for the children than for the adults.

There are a variety of reasons why age differences might be found in the resource demands of strategy execution, including: (a) a biologically based change with age in processing capacity (Case, Kurland, & Goldberg, 1982; Pascual-Leone, 1970), (b) growth and/or reorganization of the general knowledge base (thereby increasing the resource efficiency of knowledge access; Bjorklund, 1987), (c) the use by older children of more efficient and effective resource allocation strategies, and (d) age differences in strategy execution practice (Footo, Guttentag, & Ornstein, 1988). Regardless of the exact cause of age differences in the processing resource demands of strategy use, recent evidence implicates this change in resource demands as an important factor contributing to the age changes that are observed in spontaneous strategy use (Guttentag, 1984; Pressley, Cariglia-Bull, Deane, & Schneider, 1987; Rohwer & Litrownik, 1983).

CAPACITY LIMITATIONS AND MOTIVATION

Early research on information processing capacity limitations was based on the assumption that cognitive operations are fueled by the allocation of some form of energy-like, limited capacity mental resource (Welch, 1898), and this view remains prominent today (Kahneman, 1973; Kanfer & Ackerman, 1989). One advantage of this energy metaphor, in comparison with other possible metaphors for capacity limitations (such spatial metaphors; e.g., Case, 1985), is its association with the conceptualization of information processing as requiring mental work or mental effort (Kahneman, 1973); the importance of this association is that it forms a potential link between processing limitations and motivational factors affecting cognitive functioning (Kahneman, 1973; Kanfer & Ackerman, 1989). According to this view, the allocation of cognitive resources to task execution is experienced subjectively as the allocation of energy or effort; the greater the resource demands of the task, the more cognitively effortful task execution will appear. A number of theorists have assumed further that, much as is the case with the exertion of physical effort, humans seek economy of mental effort during task execution. That is, we seek the greatest payoff (in terms of levels of task performance) for the least expenditure of effort (Kanfer & Ackerman, 1989).

This view suggests that there may be two mechanisms by which capacity limitations may affect the process of strategy selection on any problem-solving task. First, and most directly, capacity limitations function to limit the complexity of the strategies that subjects are potentially capable of using. That is, subjects should simply be unable to execute any strategy whose resource demands exceed their available resource capacity. The second mechanism involves an effect of resource limitations on the motivation to deploy particular strategies, thereby indirectly affecting strategy selection and, ultimately, task performance. The operation of this latter mechanism presumes that strategy selection involves a weighing of the relative benefits and costs of the use of different procedures. Within this formula, the benefit to be derived from use of a procedure is the subjective value of the improvements in task performance that are expected to occur if the procedure is used. The primary cost of the use of a particular strategy, on the other hand, is the mental effort that must be expended for strategy execution. For any particular task, therefore, subjects are presumed to base their strategy selection in part on a subjective effort-utility function for each procedure (Paris, 1988; Siegler, 1986). Consequently, subjects may select a less effective (but less effortful) procedure if the increment in task performance that would result from the application of the more effective strategy is not deemed worth the cost in terms of additional mental effort.

A GENERAL MODEL OF STRATEGY SELECTION

Figure 11.1 presents a general model of strategy selection that incorporates the idea that the effort demands of strategy execution functions as a subjective cost of strategy use, thereby reducing motivation to deploy the strategy.

The first element of this model is strategy access. One factor influencing the likelihood that use of a strategy will even be considered is the subject's relevant task and strategy knowledge (Wellman, 1983). There is considerable evidence, however, that strategy access can also be influenced by seemingly minor features of the task structure and by the exact nature of the task materials, factors that may operate to help cue access to particular strategies (e.g., Bryant & Kopytynska, 1976; Rohwer, Rabinowitz, & Dronkers, 1982).

For strategies that are accessed, subjects are hypothesized to engage in a costs/benefits analysis involving the other three components of the model. The primary cost of strategy use considered by this analysis is the amount of mental effort required for strategy execution. The primary benefit of strategy use, on the

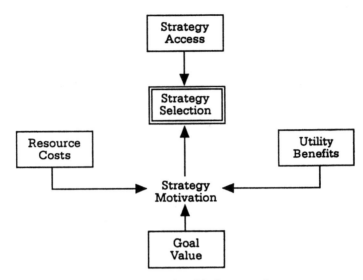

FIG. 11.1. A proposed model of strategy selection.

other hand, is the subjective expected value of the use of any particular strategy
for achieving the goals of the task. The weighing of these two factors will also
be influenced by the individual subject's level of motivation to achieve various
levels of performance on the task at hand. When, for instance, motivation to
achieve a high level of task performance is very high, subjects are assumed to
be willing to invest a large amount of mental effort in the use of a believed-to-
be-effective strategy. In contrast, when task motivation is low and/or when a
less effortful (but still effective) alternate strategy is also accessed, the motivation
to invest effort in the use the initial strategy will be low.

TESTING THE MODEL'S PREDICTIONS

In the following section, three recent studies conducted in our lab will be described that were designed to test different predictions of this costs/benefits model
of strategy selection. In each case, the findings are consistent with the general
features of the model, but the findings also raise some cautions concerning the
generality of the model's application.

Experiment 1: The Influence of Goal Motivation
on Children's Strategy Use

One direct implication of this costs/benefits model of strategy selection is that the
perceived benefits of using an effortful memorization strategy should be affected
by the value children place on the goal of recalling a large amount of information

(Paris, 1988). Moreover, age differences in children's performance goals when performing memorization tasks could potentially contribute to age differences in strategy selection and execution. At present there exists little direct evidence linking age differences in children's subjective valuation of the goal of remembering to age differences in their willingness to allocate large amounts of cognitive resources to the implementation of mnemonic strategies; some evidence concerning the relationship between goal motivation and strategic effort, however, can be seen in studies that have manipulated extrinsic rewards for remembering.

If young children do not place sufficient value on memorization as a goal to justify the expenditure of the large amounts of mental effort required for use of certain strategies, then the addition of external incentives might be expected to increase their strategy deployment. Only a few studies have examined the effects of external incentives on children's mnemonic strategy use. Cuvo (1974) presented lists in which half the words were marked as $.10 items (i.e., worth $.10 per item at recall), whereas the remaining items were worth $.01 each. Cuvo found that even fifth graders (the youngest subjects tested) recalled more $.10 than $.01 words, an effect that was attributed to their likely incorporation of more high- than low-incentive-value words in each rehearsal set during list presentation. More recently, Kunzinger and Witryol (1984) studied the performance of second graders with a list containing $.10 and $.01 items, and compared their performance to that of subjects receiving a list on which all items were worth a nickel. Their most noteworthy finding was that, whereas subjects in the all-nickel condition utilized a single-item rehearsal strategy throughout, subjects in the penny–dime condition rehearsed more actively; this finding suggests that the manipulation of goal motivation affected the type of strategy the children used on the memorization task.

The purpose of Experiment 1 was to examine further the effects of goal motivation on children's use of effortful mnemonic strategies. The primary manipulation in the study involved the use of toys as rewards; for one group of subjects, receipt of the reward was made contingent upon a high level of recall performance, whereas for the remaining subjects there was no contingency between recall performance and receipt of the reward. We hypothesized that the children in the contingent reward condition would make greater use of effortful mnemonic procedures, and that this effect would be particularly pronounced for children with a relatively low level of intrinsic motivation for academic tasks.

Methods. The subjects in the experiment were third-grade children, an age at which many children are just beginning to use organizational procedures on memory tasks. The children were first administered the Harter Scale of Intrinsic versus Extrinsic Orientation in the Classroom (Harter, 1980); children receiving an average scale score above 3.1 (range 3.2 to 4.0) were classified as high in intrinsic motivation, whereas those receiving a score below 2.9 (range 1.7 to 2.8) were classified as low in intrinsic motivation.

Subjects were administered four trials of a study-recall task. On each trial, they were presented 25 pictures of common objects (5 items from each of 5 categories). A different set of items was presented on each trial. The recall task was administered under four different presentation conditions. In the *reward contingent* condition, subjects were informed that the greater the number of picture names that they recalled on each trial, the greater their likelihood of receiving an attractive prize. A point system was used to ensure that subjects understood that each name that they recalled improved their chances of receiving the prize. In contrast, in the *noncontingent reward* condition, subjects were given their prize prior to the first trial, and were explicitly told that the prize was theirs to keep regardless of their recall performance. In the *normal instructions* condition, no mention was made of a prize. Subjects were simply encouraged to memorize the picture names as best they could, and at the end of a session they received a gift for participating in the study.

For each of these first three presentation conditions, the pictures were labeled and placed face-up on a table by the experimenter. In contrast, in the fourth condition (*child places stimuli* condition), the items were handed to the subject to be placed on the table. In all other respects, the child places stimuli condition was identical to the normal instructions condition.

In all four conditions, subjects were explicitly told that they could move the pictures around on the table or do anything else that they thought would help them remember the picture names. The length of the study period was subject-controlled, up to a maximum of 2 min.

Results. Subjects at both levels of intrinsic motivation recalled more picture names in the child places stimuli condition than in any of the other three conditions (see Table 11.1). The superior recall performance found in the child places stimuli condition was directly attributable to greater use of taxonomic organization at study; in the child places stimuli condition, 57% of the high intrinsic subjects and 50% of the low intrinsic subjects sorted taxonimically at study on one or more study trials, whereas for subjects in the other groups the percentage of subjects who used sorting as a study strategy ranged from zero (in the noncontingent reward condition) to 12% (in the normal instructions condition).

Table 11.1 also reveals that high intrinsic children generally had better recall than low intrinsic children, and that recall levels were affected by the manipulation of reward contingency, but only for the high intrinsic children. Similarly, reward contingency affected study time, but again only for the high intrinsic motivation children (see Table 11.2); these children invested the greatest time in study of any group under reward contingent conditions, while studying for the least amount of time when the reward was noncontingent. Direct observation and a post-task interview revealed that the only strategy that was correlated with individual differences in recall performance in the two reward conditions was self-testing ($r = .23, .38, .49$, and $.37$ on the four study/recall trials, respectively).

TABLE 11.1
Mean Number of Words Recalled per Trial in Experiment 1 (max = 25)

	Instruction Condition			
	Contingent Reward	Noncontingent Reward	Normal Instructions	Child Places Stimuli
Intrinsic motivation				
High	12.6	9.3	11.4	14.0
Low	9.7	9.3	10.6	12.2

Discussion. The point system used in the contingent reward condition guaranteed that subjects were highly motivated to recall as many picture names as they possibly could. As expected, the manipulation of reward contingency affected the amount of effort subjects were willing to invest in effortful study, but contrary to expectations, this effect held only for the subjects rated as high in intrinsic motivation. One possible explanation for this counterintuitive pattern of group differences in the effects of the extrinsic reward is that the children in the low intrinsic group may simply have been less aware than were the high intrinsic subjects of the value of the use of effortful study strategies for maximizing recall performance. We found, consistent with past research (Harter, 1980), that performance on the Harter scale was highly correlated with teacher's judgments of the children's academic skill. It thus seems reasonable to hypothesize that the two groups may have differed in terms of their metacognitive awareness as well.

There was no effect of the manipulation of reward contingency on the use of organizational procedures for either subject group. There was, however, a very dramatic effect on organizational strategy use of the method of stimulus presentation; subjects were much more likely to sort stimuli into categories in the child places stimuli condition than in any of the other three conditions. This pattern of findings may reflect the fact that sorting items into categories on this task is not a highly effortful procedure for children at this age, but is also not a procedure that is highly accessible (i.e., does not come readily to mind when thinking of possible memorization procedures). Thus, rather than depending on a very high

TABLE 11.2
Mean Study Time (in seconds) per Trial in Experiment 1 (max = 120)

	Instruction Condition			
	Contingent Reward	Noncontingent Reward	Normal Instructions	Child Places Stimuli
Intrinsic motivation				
High	82	41	57	52
Low	63	62	56	47

level of goal motivation, the use of sorting as a study strategy for children at this age may primarily be a function of the degree to which the task structure helps cue the use of organizational procedures.

Experiment 2: The Effects of Reducing the Effort Demands of Strategy Use

According to a costs/benefits analysis of strategy selection, any manipulation that reduces the effort demands of strategy execution would be expected to increase subjects' use of the strategy (Ornstein, Medlin, Stone, & Naus, 1985). Research on children's use of cumulative rehearsal as a memorization strategy is consistent with this view. In a study by Guttentag, Ornstein, and Siemens (1987), for instance, it was found that some second-grade children who used a single-word rehearsal strategy under normal stimulus presentation conditions switched to the use of a more effective, multi-item rehearsal strategy when the conditions of stimulus presentation were modified to make use of the multi-item strategy less effortful. Interestingly, a follow-up assessment 1 year later showed that most of these children had progressed to the point of rehearsing items cumulatively even under more typical, high-effort stimulus presentation conditions, whereas that was not the case for the children who had not rehearsed cumulatively under low-effort conditions during the initial assessment.

A second factor known to influence the effort demands of strategy execution is the nature of the to-be-memorized materials. High frequency words, for instance, are easier to rehearse (Ornstein & Naus, 1985), whereas the use of organizational procedures is less effortful with lists constructed with sets of highly typical category exemplars than when low typicality exemplars are used (Bjorklund, 1987). Similarly, Kee and Davies (1991) found that when subjects were instructed to use an elaboration strategy on a paired-associate learning task, use of the strategy was less resource-demanding when subjects were presented related (e.g., fish–seaweed) than unrelated (e.g., fish–napkin) word pairs to memorize.

The Kee and Davies (1991) findings suggest that subjects would be expected to make greater use of elaboration as a deliberate memorization strategy when presented lists of related than unrelated pairs. This prediction was tested indirectly in a study by Rohwer et al. (1982), in which subjects between 10 and 17 years of age were presented lists of related and unrelated pairs under both uninstructed and elaboration-instructed strategy use conditions. Rohwer et al. found that, under uninstructed conditions, subjects at both ages performed better with related than with unrelated pairs, but that the magnitude of this effect was much larger for the younger subjects. Further, both age-related and materials-related differences in performance were attenuated when subjects were instructed to use an elaboration strategy.

One possible interpretation of the Rohwer et al. (1982) findings is that the younger children in their study may have made greater deliberate use of a verbal elaboration strategy with related than with unrelated pairs, presumably because strategy execution is easier with accessible items. Alternatively, the materials effects found by Rohwer et al. may have reflected the children's automatic encoding of relationships between pair members for related pairs, rather than a materials-related difference in strategy use (Lange, 1973).

The present experiment was designed to test more directly for materials-related differences in the use of elaboration on a paired-associate learning task. Whereas in the study by Rohwer et al. (1982) strategy use was inferred from the pattern of performance across instructed and uninstructed learning conditions, the present experiment used a think-aloud procedure to monitor directly strategy use as subjects memorized related and unrelated pairs.

Methods. The subjects were children 10 to 11 years of age. All subjects were presented two 20-item lists of word pairs; each list contained 10 related and 10 unrelated pairs, presented in random order. The word pairs were presented auditorily at a rate of 15 sec per pair. Subjects were instructed to memorize the pairs in preparation for a cued recall test, and were further instructed to do all of their thinking aloud, a procedure that has been used successfully in a number of previous studies to monitor children's strategy use (Beuhring & Kee, 1987; Guttentag, 1984; Ornstein & Naus, 1978).

Results. The transcribed think-aloud protocols were first coded into three main categories of strategy use: *rehearsal* (repetition of pair items), *elaboration* (generation of a meaningful association between pairs items), and *other* strategy use (involving either no response or a response that could not be classified).

Consistent with predictions, there was an overall greater incidence of the use of elaboration for related than for unrelated pairs; 59% of responses were classified as involving the use of relational elaboration for related pairs, but only 38% of responses were classified as involving the use of relational elaboration for unrelated pairs. However, the prediction that the increase in elaboration-strategy use would occur primarily at the expense of rehearsal or other forms of item-specific processing was only partly supported; overall, there was only a 5% higher incidence of rehearsal for unrelated (45%) than for related (40%) pairs. In contrast, there was a much higher incidence of *other* responses for unrelated (17%) than for related (1%) pairs.

A more detailed inspection of the protocols revealed that, with only a few exceptions, individual subjects engaged either in elaboration or in rehearsal, but not in both. Of the 24 subjects tested, only 3 exhibited a mixed pattern of strategy use involving more than 5 instances (out of a possible 40) of each of elaboration and rehearsal. By this same criterion, 8 subjects could be classified as engaging primarily in rehearsal, and 13 subjects could be classified as primarily utilizing elaboration as a learning strategy (see Table 11.3).

Inspection of Table 11.3 reveals that most of the responses classified in the *other* category involved subjects whose primary form of strategy use was elaboration, and

TABLE 11.3
Percentage of Responses in Each Procedure-Use Category
for Each Subject Classification in Experiment 2

Subject Classification	Strategy	Materials	
		Related	Unrelated
Rehearsers			
	Elaboration	0	0
(n = 8)	Rehearsal	98	99
	Other	2	1
Elaborators			
	Elaboration	99	67
(n = 13)	Rehearsal	0	5
	Other	1	28
Mixed			
	Elaboration	37	18
(n = 3)	Rehearsal	63	77
	Other	0	5

in most instances occurred for unrelated rather than for related items. Of these *other* responses, most (80% of the *other* responses) involved *no response* on the part of the subject, that is, a failure on the part of a subject using elaboration for most items to produce any response within the 15 sec interpair interval.

One way to assess the effectiveness of the use of the different strategies is to examine correct recall as a function of strategy use. Consistent with the findings from past research (Beuhring & Kee, 1987; Kee & Davies, 1988), it was found that cued recall performance for items studies using relational elaboration was superior to recall following rehearsal for both related pairs (84% correct for items studies using relational elaboration, 64% correct for items rehearsed) and for unrelated pairs (82% correct for items studied using relational elaboration, 38% correct for items rehearsed). These same data indicate that for items studied using elaboration, there were no performance differences between related and unrelated pairs, whereas there was a large effect of type of materials for items studied using rehearsal. This finding suggests that although subjects were not deliberately encoding a semantic relationship between items when using rehearsal, some degree of elaborative encoding occurred automatically for related pairs.

One other interesting feature of the recall data is that, although performance following *other* strategy use (64% correct for unrelated pairs) was inferior to that following use of elaboration, performance following *other* strategy use was superior to that found for unrelated items that were rehearsed. As already noted, most of the instances of *other* strategy use involved subjects whose predominant strategy was elaboration, but who failed to produce a response to some of the items. Thus, a likely explanation for this finding is that these subjects may have engaged in some degree of elaborative encoding of pair members, even though they were unsuccessful in producing a elaborative encoding aloud within the 15 sec interstimulus interval.

Discussion. Clearly, the failure of the rehearsers to use an elaboration strategy was not solely the result of the high effort demands of elaboration strategy use, because they made no deliberate use of elaboration even with the easy-to-elaborate related materials. This finding suggests that even under the most supportive of task conditions, children are likely to require some metacognitive understanding of the value of a procedure that is to be used deliberately to achieve a mnemonic goal. We hypothesize that the children who used rehearsal alone lacked such understanding regarding the value of elaboration.

An effect of item-relatedness on recall performance was, however, found even for the rehearsers, suggesting both a direct and an indirect effect of relatedness on cued recall performance. The direct route involves an influence of automatic encoding on cued recall performance in the absence of an influence on study-strategy use. The indirect route involves an effect of relatedness on cued recall performance mediated by an influence on strategy use (Ornstein & Naus, 1985). As the present findings and past research elucidate, paired associate recall performance is superior when subjects use elaboration as a learning strategy than when they use rehearsal. Thus, any influence of the type of materials on the use of elaboration will indirectly influence recall performance as well. In the present study, subjects classified as using elaboration as their primary strategy produced elaborations more consistently with related than with unrelated pairs. Further, in the case of the small number of subjects classified as *mixed* strategy users, greater use of elaboration was found with related pairs than with unrelated pairs, whereas the opposite pattern was found with respect to rehearsal.

It is important to note that the failure of the children classified as elaboration-strategy users to execute the strategy successfully with some of the unrelated items does not reflect an absolute inability on their part to perform the strategy with these materials; numerous previous studies have demonstrated that consistent use of the strategy is within the capabilities of children at this age when instructed to do so, even with unrelated pairs such as the ones used here (Guttentag, 1989; Kee & Davies, 1991). Thus, these findings suggest that, for those children classified as using elaboration, their occasional failures of strategy use may have been related to negative motivational effects of the high-effort demands of strategy execution for some of the pairs. That is, in the absence of specific instructions to generate an elaboration for every pair, these subjects may have been unwilling to expend the high effort necessary to execute the strategy for the more difficult of the unrelated pairs.

Experiment 3: The Effects of Effort Demands on Transfer of Strategy Training

The studies discussed previously provide evidence for an influence of the effort demands of strategy execution on children's spontaneous strategy use. A similar effect would be expected to occur following training in strategy use when an assessment is made of transfer of strategy training. That is, subjects would be expected to be more highly motivated to transfer a trained strategy that they are able to execute with less effort than one whose execution during training was highly demanding of mental effort (Best & Ornstein, 1986; Bjorklund & Buchanan, 1989; Rabinowitz, 1988).

A series of experiments by Rabinowitz (1988; Rabinowitz, Freeman, & Cohen, 1992) support this view. The adult subjects in these experiments were instructed to utilize an organizational strategy to memorize a list of words. The nature of the lists, however, varied across subject groups; the three groups received lists containing either all high-typicality category members, all moderate-typicality items, or all low-typicality items. As expected, subjects receiving high- and moderate-typicality items rated the use of the strategy as less difficult to use than did subjects in the group receiving low-typicality items. The more significant finding from the study involved an examination of performance on a subsequent recall task, when subjects in all three groups received the same moderate-typicality list of items. Rabinowitz found that subjects initially given the low-typicality list (who rated the strategy as highly effortful) made less use of the organizational strategy on the transfer task than did subjects initially given the moderate or high typicality lists. Apparently, the subjective expectation by subjects in the low typicality group that use of the strategy would be highly effortful resulted in a reduced motivation to deploy the strategy on the final free recall task.

In order to test the generality of Rabinowitz's findings, we recently conducted a study in which subjects received training in the use of elaboration with lists of either related or unrelated word pairs. Transfer of training to a new list containing both types of pairs was then assessed.

Methods. The subjects were college-age adults. All subjects were presented two lists of word pairs to memorize. Half the subjects received two lists of related pairs of words; the remaining subjects received two lists of unrelated pairs. In addition, subjects were instructed to use rehearsal to memorize one list, and to use a verbal (sentence generation) elaboration strategy to memorize the other list (half the subjects used rehearsal on the first list and half on the second). This basic design was replicated with several different rates of item presentation, ranging from 6 sec through 15 sec per item. In addition, the design was also replicated with elaboration instructions that required subjects to generate an interactive image, rather than a sentence, relating the words from each pair.

Subjects were not actually tested on their recall of the training lists. Instead, following presentation of the second training list, subjects were presented a 5-min filler task, followed by the transfer test. For the transfer test, subjects were presented a list containing 15 related and 15 unrelated word pairs. Subjects were instructed to try to memorize the words on the transfer list in whatever manner they wanted; the focus, it was emphasized, was on recall performance rather than on the way in which they studied these words. For all subjects, the rate of presentation of items on the transfer task matched the rate used during the training phase of the experiment.

Following presentation of the transfer-task study list, subjects were asked to indicate on a 4-point scale the approximate number of pairs that they had studied using rehearsal and elaboration. The cued recall test was then presented; subjects were presented a sheet of paper containing the first word from each pair on the study list and were instructed to try to recall (and write down) the corresponding word from each pair.

Results. Table 11.4 presents the mean number of related and unrelated pairs recalled as a function of training condition and presentation rate. It may be seen that, directly contrary to predictions, recall performance was superior for subjects who received training with the unrelated pairs at all but the slowest rates of presentation. The assessment of strategy use suggested that this difference resulted from group differences in the use of elaboration procedures on the transfer list; overall, subjects trained with the unrelated pairs reported significantly more use of elaboration, and less use of rehearsal, on the transfer task than did subjects trained with the related pairs.

Discussion. The model discussed earlier suggests two possible loci for the effects of training condition differences on transfer task performance. First, focusing on strategy utility, it may be the case that training with the unrelated pairs has produced a much higher assessment by subjects of the value of elaboration as a memorization strategy than was the case when subjects received training with the related lists. Indeed, as was noted in the discussion of Experiment 2, elaboration is of relatively greater value when memorizing unrelated in comparison with related pairs. In order to test this explanation, we conducted a follow-up experiment with new groups of subjects in which the training phase was followed by a measure of each subject's estimate of the value of each strategy (rehearsal and elaboration). We found that subjects in both training conditions

TABLE 11.4
Mean Number of Items Recalled (max = 30) on the Transfer Task as a
Function of Training Condition and Presentation Rate in Experiment 3

Training Condition	Presentation Rate			
	6 sec	*8 sec*	*12 sec*	*15 sec*
Verbal elaboration & rehearsal				
Training with related pairs	13.3	16.5	14.8	16.4
Training with unrelated pairs	17.6	20.4	18.4	16.4
Imagery elaboration & rehearsal				
Training with related pairs		14.5		16.6
Training with unrelated pairs		21.2		15.2

judged elaboration to be superior to rehearsal as a memorization strategy; more importantly, the ratings suggested that the *relative* value of elaboration in comparison with rehearsal did not vary as a function of training condition.

Thus, the training condition effects do not appear to have resulted from group differences in the perceived value of rehearsal versus elaboration. An alternative possible explanation for the effects found here (suggested by our strategy selection model) is that the different effort demands of elaboration under the two training conditions may have influenced strategy use motivation on the transfer task, albeit in a very different manner from the effect found by Rabinowitz (1988; Rabinowitz et al., 1992). We hypothesize that, for subjects trained with related pairs, the dramatic change from the ease of elaboration strategy use under training to the much more effortful execution required (for the unrelated items) on the transfer task may have dampened the subjects' motivation to use the strategy on the transfer list. That is, use of elaboration on the transfer list may have seemed excessively effortful for these subjects precisely because use of the strategy had been so easy for them during training. This explanation is also consistent with the effects of presentation rate found here; the failure to find training-list effects under the slowest of presentation conditions may simply reflect the fact that the effort demands of elaboration-strategy use (relative to that of rehearsal) would be expected to be greatest at the briefest presentation rates and to decrease with the provision of increasing time to generate an elaboration.

GENERAL DISCUSSION

The findings presented here are generally consistent with our model of strategy selection emphasizing the motivational costs for strategy use of the resource demands of strategy execution. Thus, for instance, it was found in Experiments 1 and 2 that when goal motivation was high and when the effort demands of strategy execution were low, the probability that subjects would use an effort-demanding strategy increased. Further, in Experiment 3, an effect on strategy transfer was found involving an interaction between the subject's expectations concerning the effort demands of strategy use and the actual demands of strategy use experienced on the transfer task.

This model shares a number of features in common with a general principle of strategy selection proposed by Belmont and Mitchell (1987), which they termed the *law of optimum perceived difficulty*. According to this principle, any variable that contributes to a task's perceived difficulty will bear a curvilinear relationship to the effort invested in task-targeted activity. If the task (defined as achieving a particular goal) is seen as very easy, then subjects will invest little effort in strategic activity (presumably because little effort is required to achieve the desired goal). If the task is perceived as being moderately difficult, more investment of effort is predicted, whereas for a very high degree of perceived task difficulty, the law predicts less activity again (but in this case because the subject is unwilling or unable to invest the effort required to achieve the desired goal).

Belmont and Mitchell (1987) proposed that perception of task difficulty will be "a complex function of at least the degree of skill the child has already achieved, the amount of interest he or she has at the moment, and the task's objective demands" (p. 101). This listing of factors that contribute to the global *perception of task difficulty* maps fairly well onto elements of the strategy selection model discussed here. Thus, whereas Belmont and Mitchell did not explicity discuss perceived difficulty in costs/benefits analysis terms, the present model would predict the kind of curvilinear relationship that is the focus of their law.

It should be acknowledged that although the current research project focused primarily on the effects of effort demands and motivation on strategy selection, the most dramatic effects on strategy use found in the present experiments actually involved manipulations that affected strategy access; in a number of instances, evidence was found for perseveration in the use of a particular strategy across conditions that varied significantly in terms of both goal motivation and the effort demands of strategy use. Thus, for instance, in Experiment 1 the manipulation of goal motivation affected only the high intrinsic children, and even for these subjects the primary effect of increased task motivation was on the length of their study time rather than on the nature of the strategies used. In contrast, in that same experiment a very large effect on strategy use was produced by a modest change in the way in which the materials were presented. Similarly, in Experiment 2 only a small subset of subjects varied their strategy selection qualitatively as a function of item-by-item changes in the effort demands of elaboration. These findings raise the possibility that the costs/benefits model of strategy selection discussed earlier may apply only under certain task conditions, as, for example, when the effort demands of a selected strategy are very high, when the task structure is such that subjects access several potential strategies when first approaching the task, or when subjects are at a transitional stage between the use of simpler and more complex strategies (Guttentag et al., 1987).

Although the experiments discussed here were concerned with the execution of memory strategies themselves, a costs/benefits analysis of strategy selection may also apply to the analysis of the use of such metacognitive procedures as the monitoring of strategy execution and the assessment of the effectiveness of strategic efforts (Kanfer & Ackerman, 1989). Indeed, research on strategy acquisition has amply demonstrated age differences in the use of self-regulatory procedures. Pressley, Levin, and Ghatala (1984), for instance, provided 13-year-olds with practice using two different strategies for foreign language vocabulary learning. Performance with a keyword technique was objectively far superior to that associated with use of a repetition strategy. Nonetheless, the children were not aware of the relative effectiveness of the two strategies unless they were given explicit performance feedback on each of the practice trials. Other research has shown that even when children are aware of the relative effectiveness of two strategies, they may not appropriately refer to this knowledge to guide their strategy selection (Ghatala, Levin, Pressley, & Goodwin, 1986; Pressley, Ross, Levin, & Ghatala, 1984). Finally, in a study of children's recall of classmates' names, Bjorklund and Zeman (1982) found that children in Grades 1 through 5 were often not even aware of the strategies they were using, reflecting a dramatic failure on their part to monitor their own goal-directed behaviors.

Children's failure to monitor and evaluate their strategy use may be related, in part, to the mental effort demands of these metacognitive procedures. Just as there are age differences in the mental effort demands of mnemonic strategy use (Guttentag, 1989), there may be age differences in the mental effort demands of self-regulatory activities. Thus, the mental effort costs of monitoring may be very high for young children, thereby reducing their motivation to engage in these important cognitive procedures.

ACKNOWLEDGMENTS

This research was supported by a grant from the National Institutes of Health. The author wishes to acknowledge the contributions of Garry Lange, Jody Mathews, Betty Washburn, and Lindsay Holland to the research presented here.

REFERENCES

Belmont, J. M., & Mitchell, D. W. (1987). The general strategies hypothesis as applied to cognitive theory in mental retardation. *Intelligence, 11,* 91–105.

Best, D. L., & Ornstein, P. A. (1986). Children's generation and communication of mnemonic organizational strategies. *Developmental Psychology, 22,* 845–853.

Beuhring, T., & Kee, D. W. (1987). Developmental relationships among metamemory, elaborative strategy use, and associative memory. *Journal of Experimental Child Psychology, 44,* 377–400.

Bjorklund, D. F. (1987). How age changes in knowledge base contribute to the development of children's memory: An interpretive review. *Developmental Review, 7,* 93–130.

Bjorklund, D. F., & Buchanan, J. J. (1989). Developmental and knowledge base differences in the acquisition and extension of a memory strategy. *Journal of Experimental Child Psychology, 48,* 451–471.

Bjorklund, D. F., & Harnishfeger, K. K. (1987). Developmental differences in the mental effort requirements for the use of an organizational strategy in free recall. *Journal of Experimental Child Psychology, 44,* 109–125.

Bjorklund, D. F., & Zeman, B. R. (1982). Children's organization and metamemory awareness in their recall of familiar information. *Child Development, 53,* 799–810.

Bryant, P. E., & Kopytynska, H. (1976). Spontaneous measurement by young children. *Nature, 260,* 773.

Case, R. (1985). *Intellectual development: Birth to adulthood.* New York: Academic Press.

Case, R., Kurland, D. M., & Goldberg, J. (1982). Operational efficiency and the growth of short-term memory span. *Journal of Experimental Child Psychology, 33*, 386–404.

Cuvo, A. J. (1974). Incentive level influence on overt rehearsal and free recall as a function of age. *Journal of Experimental Child Psychology, 18*, 167–181.

Flavell, J. H. (1970). Developmental studies of mediated memory. In H. W. Reese & L. P. Lipsitt (Eds.), *Advances in child development and behavior* (pp. 181–211). New York: Academic Press.

Footo, M., Guttentag, R. E., & Ornstein, P. A. (1988, April). Capacity demands of strategy execution: Effects of training and practice. In F. Dempster (Chair), *Attentional and capacity constraints on strategy utilization: Developmental and individual differences.* Symposium presented at the meeting of the American Educational Research Association, New Orleans.

Ghatala, E. S., Levin, J. R., Pressley, M., & Goodwin, D. (1986). A componential analysis of the effects of derived and supplied strategy-utility information on children's strategy selection. *Journal of Experimental Child Psychology, 41*, 76–92.

Guttentag, R. E. (1984). The mental effort requirement of cumulative rehearsal: A developmental study. *Journal of Experimental Child Psychology, 37*, 92–106.

Guttentag, R. E. (1989). Age differences in dual-task performance: Procedures, assumptions, and results. *Developmental Review, 9*, 146–170.

Guttentag, R. E., Ornstein, P. A., & Siemens, L. (1987). Children's spontaneous rehearsal: Transitions in strategy acquisition. *Cognitive Development, 2*, 307–326.

Harter, S. (1980). *A scale of intrinsic versus extrinsic orientation in the classroom.* Denver, CO: University of Denver Press.

Kahneman, D. (1973). *Attention and effort.* Englewood Cliffs, NJ: Prentice Hall.

Kanfer, R., & Ackerman, P. L. (1989). Dynamics of skill acquisition. Building a bridge between intelligence and motivation. In R. J. Sternberg (Ed.), *Advances in the psychology of intelligence* (Vol. 5, pp. 83–133). Hillsdale, NJ: Lawrence Erlbaum Associates.

Kee, D. W., & Davies, L. (1991). Mental effort and elaboration: A developmental analysis of accessibility effects. *Journal of Experimental Child Psychology, 52*, 1–10.

Kunzinger, E. L., & Witryol, S. L. (1984). The effects of differential incentives on second-grade rehearsal and free recall. *The Journal of Genetic Psychology, 144*, 19–30.

Ornstein, P. A., & Corsale, K. (1979). Organizational factors in children's memory. In C. R. Puff (Ed.), *Memory, organization, and structure* (pp. 219–257). New York: Academic Press.

Ornstein, P. A., Medlin, R. G., Stone, B. P., & Naus, M. J. (1985). Retrieving for rehearsal: An analysis of active rehearsal in children's memory. *Developmental Psychology, 21*, 633–641.

Ornstein, P. A., & Naus, M. J. (1978). Rehearsal processes in children's memory. In P. A. Ornstein (Ed.), *Memory development in children* (pp. 69–99). Hillsdale, NJ: Lawrence Erlbaum Associates.

Ornstein, P. A., & Naus, M. J. (1985). Effects of the knowledge base on children's memory strategies. In H. W. Reese (Ed.), *Advances in child development and behavior* (Vol. 19, pp. 113–148). New York: Academic Press.

Paris, S. G. (1988). Motivated forgetting. In F. E. Weinert & M. Perlmutter (Eds.), *Memory development: Universal changes and individual differences* (pp. 221–237). Hillsdale, NJ: Lawrence Erlbaum Associates.

Pascual-Leone, J. (1970). A mathematic model for the transition rule in Piaget's developmental stages. *Acta Psychologia, 32*, 301–345.

Pressley, M. (1982). Elaboration and memory development. *Child Development, 53*, 296–309.

Pressley, M., Cariglia-Bull, T., Deane, S., & Schneider, W. (1987). Short-term memory, verbal competence, and age as predictors of imagery instructional effectiveness. *Journal of Experimental Child Psychology, 43*, 194–211.

Pressley, M., Levin, J. R., & Ghatala, E. S. (1984). Memory strategy monitoring in adults and children. *Journal of Verbal Learning and Verbal Behavior, 23,* 270–288.

Pressley, M., Ross, K. A., Levin, J. R., & Ghatala, E. S. (1984). The role of strategy utility knowledge in children's strategy decision making. *Journal of Experimental Child Psychology, 38,* 491–501.

Rabinowitz, M. (1988). On teaching cognitive strategies: The influence of accessibility of conceptual knowledge. *Contemporary Educational Psychology, 13,* 229–235.

Rabinowitz, M., Freeman, K., & Cohen, S. (1992). The use and maintenance of strategies: The influence of accessibility to knowledge. *Journal of Educational Psychology, 84,* 211–218.

Rohwer, W. D., & Litrownik, J. (1983). Age and individual differences in the learning of a memorization procedure. *Journal of Educational Psychology, 75,* 799–810.

Rohwer, W. D., Jr., Rabinowitz, M., & Dronkers, N. F. (1982). Event knowledge, elaborative propensity, and the development of learning proficiency. *Journal of Experimental Child Psychology, 33,* 492–503.

Siegler, R. S. (1986). *Children's thinking.* Englewood Cliffs, NJ: Prentice-Hall.

Welch, J. C. (1898). On the measurement of mental activity through muscular activity and the determination of a constant of attention. *American Journal of Physiology, 1,* 283–306.

Wellman, H. (1983). Metamemory revisited. In M. T. H. Chi (Ed.), *Trends in memory development* (Vol. 9, 31–51). Basel, Switzerland: Karger.

Chapter 12

Evaluating the Structure–Process Hypothesis

Mitchell Rabinowitz
Neal Goldberg
Fordham University

"As everyone knows, learning is the modification, by experience of . . . of what?" (Baddeley, 1990, p. 144). Baddeley goes on to explain that the "what" is not just behavior, but also knowledge. Research on cognition emphasized that to understand the acquisition of behavior, it is necessary to understand what knowledge is and how it is acquired. Thus, one of the main orientations of research and theorizing within cognitive psychology is towards investigating the representational assumptions underlying theories of knowledge and specifying the psychological implications of those assumptions.

Toward the goal of characterizing knowledge, a distinction is often made between two different types of knowledge: knowing how and knowing that, or procedural and declarative knowledge, or strategies and knowledge base. The goal of this chapter is to characterize the relationship between these two types of knowledge structures and how they jointly interact to account for performance characteristics.

THE PROCESS–STRUCTURE DISTINCTION

The basis of much of the research and theorizing within cognitive science is the assumption that the computer and the mind are both examples of general information-processing devices. There are two basic premises underlying this type of information-processing system. First, there are a set of physical symbols with which a system has to work. Second, information processing is characterized by symbol manipulation (Newell, 1979; Newell & Simon, 1972). The insight of Newell and Simon was that the processing of information by people is carried out by the manipulation of symbols by rules.

Given these assumptions, Newell (1979) hypothesized a distinction between structure and process. Knowledge structures (the physical symbols) are static, permanent, and object like, whereas processes are dynamic, transient, and transformation-like. Even though the characterization of the knowledge structure (declarative knowledge) changed in that it is no longer considered static (Anderson, 1993, and following section), the process–structure distinction still defines the relative roles of process and structure. The application of procedures require certain symbols to be available. The consequence of applying this distinction to research on skill acquisition is a focus regarding the "program," "software," or rules people of different skill levels use to manipulate representations and how these rules develop.

Researchers tend to describe programs and rules in terms of production system models (see Anderson, 1983, chap. 1, for a detailed description of these models). A production system consists of a set of rules, called *productions*, written in the form of condition–action (*if–then*) pairs. A general feature of productions is that each production is modular (Anderson, 1983, 1987, 1993). Productions are independent of each other and can be separately added, deleted, or modified. Anderson (1987) stated: "This independence of production rules makes it possible to define an incremental learning system that grows one production rule at a time and does not involve wholesale changes to the cognitive procedures" (p. 194).

The specification of the productions that produce performance reflects hypotheses about how people think and learn. For example, skill acquisition is assumed to progress from the use of weak, domain-general procedures to the use of strong, domain-specific procedures (Anderson, 1987; Holland, Holyoak, Nisbett, & Thegard, 1986; Klahr, 1985; Larkin, 1985; Simon & Simon, 1978). Procedures can be strong in that they are specifically suited for use on one particular task; or weak, in that they can be used generally across a wide variety of tasks (Newell, 1979). Weak procedures make no specific reference to knowledge in particular domains (Anderson, 1987) and are more general strategies.

Anderson (1987) proposed a model of this process of skill acquisition. The main premise in Anderson's model (1982, 1983, 1987, 1993) is that productions form the units of knowledge. In this model, all knowledge starts out in declarative form and must be converted to procedural (production) form. Productions are condition–action pairs that specify that if a certain state occurs in working memory, then particular mental actions should take place. Productions define the steps in which a problem is solved and are the units in which knowledge is acquired. When relying on only declarative knowledge, weak problem-solving methods characterize problem solving. During learning, there is a shift from using weak methods to the use of efficient domain-specific productions, less reliant on declarative knowledge.

These domain-specific productions are developed through a process of knowledge compilation. In knowledge compilation, two distinct subprocesses are involved. One is *proceduralization*, in which domain-specific productions are created from the declarative knowledge, eliminating the need to keep this knowledge active in working memory. The second is *composition*, in which a sequence of productions is collapsed into a simple production that does the work of the sequence. A production can increase in strength where strength determines how rapidly a production will apply.

Although Anderson's model (Anderson, 1983, 1993) posits both declarative (in terms of a spreading activation system) and procedural knowledge structures, it preserves the assumption that "declarative knowledge is necessarily inert by itself . . ." (p. 69), and it suggests that skill development can and should be accounted for by principled changes in only the procedural knowledge structures. In fact, he stated, "Cognitive skills are realized by production rules" (Anderson, 1993, p. 1). This orientation had such a major impact on current thinking that it is common to hear that expert performance should be characterized by the use of compiled procedures (Glaser & Bassok, 1989; Simon, 1992).

Should Declarative Knowledge Be Considered to Be Necessarily Inert?

As stated earlier, one of the implications of the procedural perspective is that the rules operate on physical symbols and these symbols have to be stored in some memory location. Retrieval involves going to where it was stored and finding it. This orientation led to the investigation of the content and structure of declarative knowledge (Tulving & Donaldson, 1972). Two important theoretical constructs—*associative networks* and *spreading activation*—were derived from this research (Anderson & Bower, 1973; Collins & Quillian, 1969; Norman & Rumelhart, 1975). Within an associative network, concepts are believed to be represented as nodes interconnected by associative links. In semantic network terminology, retrieval is accomplished by following the appropriate links within the network.

Along with the structural description of the knowledge organization, researchers posited a process that operated on this structure, that of the automatic spread of activation. The basic assumption of this model is that each node has some level of activation associated with it. When an item in the environment is encountered, the corresponding concept in memory is activated. Activation then spreads from that concept to related concepts across the associative links. The amount of activation that spreads depends on the strength of the associative links between concepts, with stronger associations leading to stronger activations. In addition, this spreading of activation is thought to occur automatically and not to be under the conscious control of the learner.

Early models of spreading activation networks (e.g., Collins & Loftus, 1975) only specified excitatory links interconnecting nodes. Excitatory links increase the level of activation of a node's neighbors. Thus, when a node becomes active, it activates related nodes, some of which might be relevant to the task at hand, many of which are not. There was no way for a spreading activation system to make intelligent decisions regarding knowledge activation. Thus, some other process (rules, procedures) is needed to accomplish the intelligent aspects of cognition.

Recent developments in network models (e.g., *connectionist models*, Feldman & Ballard, 1982; Rumelhart & McClelland, 1986) posit the use of inhibitory as well as excitatory links. Inhibitory links serve to decrease the level of activation of a node's neighbors. The inclusion of inhibitory links enables spreading activation models to become *constraint satisfaction* models. Rather than allowing all the neighbors of a node to become activated, inhibitory links provide a mechanism whereby the context constrains activation. A number of researchers proposed that rules or procedures can be implicitly represented within the associative links (Rabinowitz, Lesgold, & Berardi, 1988; Rumelhart & McClelland, 1986). This permits spreading activation systems to make intelligent choices regarding knowledge activation.

This model of spreading activation (which we refer to as a *retrieval model*) posits that important components of processing can be carried out through retrieval. However, in contrast to the procedural model, the process involved is not based on the ideas of symbol manipulation. Retrieval operates on the basis of changes in the level of activation of nodes and not on the manipulation of those nodes. The effects of procedures can be implicitly represented within the associative links within the network and, as a consequence, this system can accomplish many of the tasks a procedural system can.

It is important to understand how such networks can be acquired. One way is as a consequence of the process of *rote practice* (Bereiter, 1991); a person is presented a context, makes a response, and is given some feedback regarding the accuracy of the response. If the response is correct, the network is changed by manipulating the weights of the associative links to make the correct response a stronger one. If the response is incorrect, the weights of the associative links are weakened. Over a great number of trials, the network learns a set of constraints that allows the person to give a certain response in a certain context. This, in essence, describes the process underlying the delta rule (Stone, 1986).

The problem with this approach to learning is that people obviously learn in other ways than just trial and error. If one was willing to propose a procedural system in addition to the network representation, then these networks might develop as a consequence of the initial use of procedures. Mandler (1983) suggested that a shift from using procedures to retrieval reflects a developmental progression of competence. Siegler (1986, 1990) suggested that this shift from procedural access to retrieval might be a general, cross-domain characteristic of the development of competence. Logan (1988; Compton & Logan, 1991; Kapp, Boches, Trabert, & Logan, 1991; Logan & Kapp, 1991) discussed this shift as an explanation for the development of automaticity.

This progression of skill involving the transition from procedurally derived information to retrieval is illustrated by looking at how skill on addition tasks develops. Performance on simple addition problems (e.g., $4 + 3 =$) shows a clear developmental trend from the use of procedures to generate answers to the ability to quickly retrieve the answer. Studies investigating how young children solve simple addition problems tend to emphasize the procedural or derivative nature of the children's problem solving. For example, young children use a wide variety of counting procedures, such as looking at fingers or using complements to derive answers (Groen & Parkman, 1972; Siegler, 1987).

However, although procedural processing is prevalent among young children, on some problems they are simply able to retrieve the answers. Groen and Parkman (1972) proposed that ties (problems in which a number is added to itself) were exceptions to the counting rule. Answers to these problems were retrieved from some fast-access memory store. Also, Siegler and Robinson (1982) observed, while viewing videotapes of 4- and 5-year-old children working on addition problems, that although children overtly used procedures to solve many problems, on some problems (not limited to ties) they were able to retrieve that answer. On retrieval trials, there was no visible or audible intervening behavior and solution times were faster. It seems, then, that young children's competence on addition problems varies from problem to problem. On some problems, children need to use procedures to derive answers; on others, they access answers by retrieving them from memory.

Finally, continuing the developmental progression, it was suggested that older children and adults primarily solve simple addition problems by retrieving the answers from memory (Ashcraft & Battaglia, 1978; Ashcraft & Stazyk, 1981; Groen & Parkman, 1972; Miller, Perlmutter, & Keating, 1984). Current models of the retrieval of addition facts incorporate the assumptions inherent in the semantic network and spreading activation models (Ashcraft, 1987; Rabinowitz & Feldman, 1989).

Initially, students do not have an association between the problem and the answer, or have a weak association. Thus, they use a procedure to derive the answer. With practice repeatedly generating the correct answer to the problem, the associative links between problems and answers gets formed and strengthened. Gradually, due to the automatic spread of activation across associations, the answer becomes accessible upon presentation of the problem, and using a procedure to derive the answer is no longer necessary. This does not imply that the procedure is unavailable for use or has changed in any way. Rather, the ease of retrieving the answer made using the procedure unnecessary.

Thus, this retrieval model posits a dynamic relation between procedural skill and retrieval skill. Procedures can be used to aid in the acquisition of retrievable knowledge. However, once this retrievable knowledge becomes accessible, it precludes the necessity of using the procedure.

The retrieval model is consistent with the view that experts are often considered experts because of their ability to retrieve (not derive) much information regarding a domain. Experts within a given domain are thought to have a large store of domain information that they are able to access rapidly and flexibly (Lesgold, 1984; Rabinowitz & Glaser, 1985). This information appears to be a prerequisite for using sophisticated problem-solving techniques (Larkin, 1985). By contrast, less skilled performance is often characterized by the need to derive the same information procedurally.

The declarative knowledge structure, when represented as a retrieval system, is anything but passive. The retrieval system is assumed to be able to accomplish the same sort of task as was originally accomplished by procedural knowledge. The retrieval model portrays a system where information is actively being processed, albeit not through a process of symbol manipulation. The consequence of this processing is that significant components of skilled performance can be produced by such a system.

DISTINGUISHING RETRIEVAL FROM PROCEDURES

The claim we are making is that there are two different representational systems, each based on a different computational principle, and each actively involved in accounting for learning and skill acquisition. Are these two systems experimentally distinguishable, or are they really isomorphic (the same deep-but-different surface characteristics)? Proponents of the procedural model can claim that their model handles the retrieval phenomena through specific, compiled procedures that are developed in response to specific conditions. For example, in the context of simple addition performance, it might be that the competent person is not actually retrieving the answer, but rather, is using a compiled counting procedure to derive the answer (Baroody, 1983). Can one distinguish between a compiled procedure and a piece of retrieved knowledge? If one model can account for the phenomena, is there any necessity to make a further distinction? In the next section, we argue that the two systems make different predictions regarding learning and transfer, and that the two systems can be experimentally teased apart.

Implications

Type of Practice. An analysis of the tasks used to investigate the development of retrieval shows that the ability to retrieve is thought to be dependent on the consistent relation between a stimulus representation and a response representation. Support for the development of retrieval skill comes from the investigation of performance on simple arithmetic performance (Ashcraft, 1987; Siegler, 1987, 1990), lexical decisions, and alphabet arithmetic (Logan, 1988). In each of these tasks, there is a correct answer associated with a given stimulus and subjects receive practice with the same set of stimuli over and over again.

This extensive practice allows the association between the stimulus and response representations to be strengthened, and this allows for retrieval.

Alternately, Anderson (1987), in his investigations of acquiring skill, investigated performance in computer programming, geometry, and text editing. In these domains, subjects are not presented with the same problem (stimuli) over and over again but are rather presented with a set of different problems that require similar processing. Given the lack of consistency between stimulus and response, the associative links between the two representations are not given the opportunity to be strengthened. Consequently, the ability to retrieve an answer is not acquired. However, subjects are given the opportunity to repeatedly practice applying a procedure. In this context, more specialized and efficient procedures are gradually acquired.

Thus, the tasks investigated from the two perspectives vary in the degree to which they allow for a consistent mapping between a stimulus and response. In situations where a consistent relationship is possible and practiced, retrieval acquisition is the consequence. In contexts in which a consistent mapping between a problem and response is not allowed but there is practice on problems that require similar routes to solution, rule development occurs.

Speed of Acquisition. Which of these two types of skills develops faster? The answer probably depends on the amount of consistency found between the presentation of the problem and the response (e.g., the possibility of incorrect answers causing interference) and the complexity of the procedure. Theorists from both perspectives talk about single trial learning (Anderson, 1987; Logan, 1988). However, from the retrieval perspective, retrieval may take precedence over needing to use procedures. The whole rationale underlying the retrieval perspective is that there is a progression from needing to use procedures to being able to retrieve information directly. The ability to retrieve the information makes using the procedure unnecessary. Thus, subjects will receive less practice on procedures once retrieval starts and further development of the procedure will be halted. Procedures may still develop as retrieval skill is developing. Research on the acquisition of basic addition knowledge demonstrates that children's counting skills evolve prior to the ability to retrieve (Groen & Resnick, 1977; Siegler & Robinson, 1982).

Transfer. Up to this point, we have not presented conditions that would distinguish between a compiled procedure account of learning and the development of retrieval account. We argue that the main discrimination between these two positions comes from looking at predictions regarding transfer.

The ability to flexibly use skills is an important component of skilled performance (Larkin, 1989; Perkins & Salomon, 1989). Thorndike (1903) suggested that transfer would occur between two situations to the extent that they involved the same context. Anderson (1987) argued that Thorndike was vague on what was meant by context and in fact, context means different things from the retrieval and rule-based perspectives. From the retrieval perspective, an associative link is constructed within a network representation. The network acts as a constraint satisfaction system whereby the context refers to the development of a schema or gestalt. One of the important properties of a network is that it works as an inference-generating device and is good at being instantiated with limited contextual cues (see Rabinowitz & Feldman, 1989, and Rumelhart & McClelland, 1986, for a discussion of evaluating stimulus instantiation in terms of constraint satisfaction). Context will be seen to be defined as general, rather than specific.

From the rule-based perspective, the definition of context is much more specific. One of the main properties of production is that they are seen to be modular and independent of each other (Anderson, 1987; McKendree & Anderson, 1987), thus, productions fire in relation to a set of specific conditions. To the extent that the conditions match across tasks, the procedural model would predict transfer. However, if there is not an exact match, no transfer would be predicted (Perkins & Salomon, 1989).

Two studies conducted by Rabinowitz and Goldberg (1992) illustrated one condition in which the procedural model would predict transfer but the retrieval model would not, and another condition in which the retrieval model would predict positive transfer but the procedural model would not. Through these differential predictions regarding transfer, it will be possible to distinguish retrieval from a compiled procedure.

EXPERIMENT 1

In this study, we compared the development of procedural and retrieval skill by having subjects learn a new task under two types of training conditions. The task used was a variant of the alphabet arithmetic task developed by Logan (1988). With this task, subjects are required to solve problems of the following format: *Letter1 + Number = Letter2*. Logan (e.g., 1988) presented subjects with a verification task; subjects had to decide whether a given equation was true or false. In this study, subjects were presented the task as a production task. They were provided with the first letter and a number and had to generate the second letter. For example, given the problem $C + 3 =$ the subject should respond F.

In order to develop procedural skill, in the procedural condition, subjects received training that was designed to give them practice counting up the alphabet to derive answers. This was accomplished by giving subjects extended practice with 72 different problems and little practice on any given problem. The 72 problems were presented 6 times so that subjects had to solve a total of 432 problems. This provides the opportunity for students to become facile with the procedure of alphabet counting. In this training condition there was little opportunity for subjects to form associative links between the problems and the answers, because there was variable mapping between the two.

In the retrieval condition, however, subjects were presented with a set of 12 problems on which they received extended practice. Through this training, each problem was presented 36 times so that each subject had to solve 432 problems. In this training condition, subjects had the opportunity to form associative links between problem components and solutions. We hypothesized that the retrieval training condition would offer little opportunity to practice the procedural skills.

After the training session, both groups of subjects received a transfer task. In this transfer task, all subjects were presented a new set of 36 alphabet addition problems to solve. This set was presented to the subjects twice. The transfer task was the same for all subjects. Because subjects in the procedural training received practice on the procedure, and because the context of the transfer task was the same as that in the training, we predicted that these subjects would exhibit positive transfer. With the retrieval training, it was predicted that, to the extent that subjects learned to retrieve and not use the procedure, there would be little positive transfer from training.

Subjects

The subject population consisted of 25 undergraduate and graduate students attending Fordham University. There were 12 subjects in the procedure condition and 13 in the retrieval condition.

Procedure

Each subject was individually tested in front of an IBM personal computer. Instructions were given to each subject by the experimenter and subjects were told that they would be asked to solve a series of alphabet addition problems. Examples of two problems (not used in the stimulus set) were shown to them. Subjects were informed that they should be as accurate as possible but that speed was also important. Subjects were then presented with the randomized training problems. After each set of 72 problems, subjects were allowed to take a self-timed break. Upon completion of the training problems, subjects were provided a short break and the transfer problems were then presented. Subjects were told that they were being presented with a new set of problems and that, once again, they should be as accurate and as fast as possible.

Results

Training. For each subject, the data set for the 432 trials were divided into 36 sets of 12 problems (the first 12 problems formed Set 1, the next 12 problems formed Set 2, etc.). The midpoint for each of the 36 sets (only using RTs from correct problems) was then determined.

The midpoints were analyzed by an analysis of variance with training group being a between-subject (retrieval, procedural), and trials (36 trials) a within-subject factor. The means of the midpoints divided by group and trial are presented in Fig. 12.1. The average proportion of errors was .03 for both the retrieval group and the procedure group. There was a significant effect of Training Group, $F(1, 23) = 14.35$, $p < .001$, with subjects in the retrieval training group yielding faster RTs than those in the procedural training group. In addition, there was a significant main effect of Trials, $F(35, 805) = 27.39$, $p < .001$, indicating that RTs decreased with practice. Both these main effects need to be qualified, however, by a significant interaction between these two factors, $F(35, 805) = 5.24$, $p < .001$. Post-hoc analyses (Scheffé) indicated that initially the two groups were not significantly different in speed ($p > .05$). However, at the 36th trial, the retrieval group had significantly faster reaction times than did the procedural group ($p < .05$).

Transfer. The midpoint of the RTs for the 72 transfer problems (using only problems with correct responses) was computed for each subject. The mean proportion of errors for subjects in the retrieval group was .05, and for subjects in the procedure group, .02. It was predicted that subjects in the procedure group would now be faster than those in the retrieval group. For the purpose of illustration, the resulting means, along with the means from the end of the training session, are displayed in Fig. 12.2. The mean RT for the procedure and retrieval groups was 2427.2 ($SD = 573.8$) and 2858.2 ($SD = 426.4$), respectively. The difference between these two means was significant, $t(23) = 2.14$, $p < .05$.

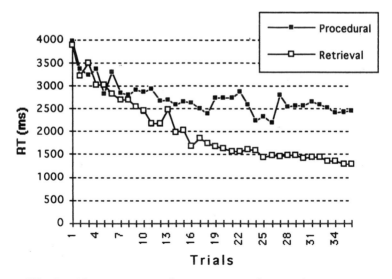

FIG. 12.1. Mean reaction times during training as a function of training group and trial—Experiment 1.

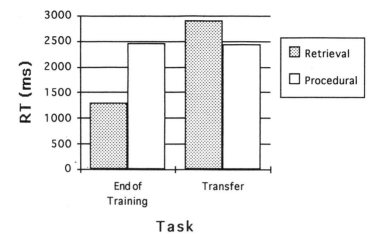

FIG. 12.2. Mean reaction times as a function of training group for last trial of training and transfer task—Experiment 1.

Discussion

The results obtained in Experiment 1 were consistent with the pattern of results that were hypothesized on the basis of the distinction between retrieval and procedural skills. During the initial training portion, we predicted that retrieval skill would be acquired prior to substantial procedural skill improvement. Also, we predicted that overall, even after considerable practice, retrieval would be faster than if using a procedure. Regarding transfer, we predicted that subjects in the procedural group (who obtained substantial practice using the procedure) would show positive transfer to problems that required use of that procedure. However, we hypothesized that subjects in the retrieval group received relatively little practice using the procedure, and consequently, little positive transfer was expected.

The results of this study, although promising, cannot alone rule out the alternative hypothesis regarding compiled procedures. It might be that in the retrieval training condition, subjects learned to execute procedures that were tied to specific problems. The modularity of procedures would account for why subjects did not transfer the knowledge to new problems. The following study was designed to help rule out this alternative hypothesis.

EXPERIMENT 2

In Experiment 1, we explored a context in which we expected to find positive transfer from training with the procedural group but not from the retrieval group. In this study, we intended to set up a context in which we would expect positive transfer for subjects given retrieval training conditions but not procedural training. The training situation in this study was the same as in Experiment 1. For the transfer task, however, subjects were now given a set of 12 alphabet subtraction problems. The problems were chosen so that they were the inverse of the addition problems given to the retrieval groups (e.g., if subjects were presented $A + 3 =$ during training, they were presented $D - 3 =$ during the transfer task). The set was presented three times so that the subjects had to solve 36 problems. We predicted that if subjects encode the retrieval information in a network organized around a part–whole schema (Resnick & Omanson, 1987), then subjects provided this training would use their knowledge that $A + 3 = D$ to solve the problem $D - 3 =$. Subjects in the procedural condition would not have this knowledge, and consequently, the subtraction task would appear to be a new task. The lack of transfer as a consequence of procedural training is based on the assertion that procedures are modular and context-specific. The procedures that were developed should be contextualized in terms of the addition task and should not become activated during the subtraction task. McKendree and Anderson (1987) conducted a similar manipulation investigating transfer of LISP programming skills and found no positive transfer for their subjects.

Subjects

The subject population consisted of 20 undergraduate and graduate students attending Fordham University. There were 11 subjects in the procedure condition and 9 in the retrieval condition.

Procedure

Same as in Experiment 1.

Results

Training. Once again, for each subject, the data set for the 432 trials was divided into 36 sets of 12 problems and the midpoint for each of the 36 sets (only using RTs from correct problems) was then determined. The midpoints were analyzed by an analysis of variance with training group being a between-subject (retrieval, procedural), and trials (36 trials) a within-subject factor. The means of the midpoints divided by group and trial are presented in Fig. 12.3. The average proportion of errors was .03 for both the retrieval group and the procedure group. The analysis of variance yielded a significant effect of training group, $F(1, 18) = 25.06$, $p < .001$, with subjects in the retrieval training group yielding faster RTs than those in the procedural training group. In addition, there was a significant main effect of trials, $F(35, 630) = 20.99$, $p < .001$, indicating that RTs decreased with practice. Once again, however, a significant

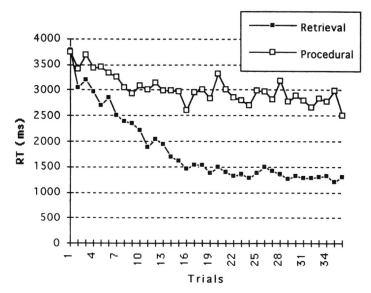

FIG. 12.3. Mean reaction times during training as a function of training group and trial—Experiment 2.

interaction between these two factors was observed, $F(35, 630) = 5.12, p < .001$. Post-hoc analyses (Scheffé) indicated that initially the two groups were not significantly different in speed ($p > .05$). However, at the 36th trial, the retrieval group had significantly faster reaction times than did the procedural group ($p < .05$).

Transfer. The alphabet subtraction task was much more difficult than the alphabet addition task. Consequently, many more errors were observed. The mean number of errors for the retrieval group was 4.6 ($SD = 1.89$) and 11.5 ($SD = 1.71$) for the procedural group. The difference between these two means was significantly different, $t(18) = 2.7, p < .02$. Thus, as predicted, the retrieval group was more accurate on the subtraction task than was the procedural group.

The RT data were analyzed by comparing the mean RT from the procedural training group with that of the retrieval training group. The prediction, once again, was that the RT for the retrieval group would be significantly faster than that of the procedural group. The resulting means, along with means from the end of the training session, are displayed in Fig. 12.4.

The mean RT for the retrieval group was 4556.99 ($SD = 2207.13$) and 9688.82 ($SD = 3662.51$) for the procedural group. The difference between these two means was significantly different, $t(18) = 3.68, p < .003$. Thus, as predicted, the retrieval training group showed positive transfer to the subtraction task but the procedural training group did not.

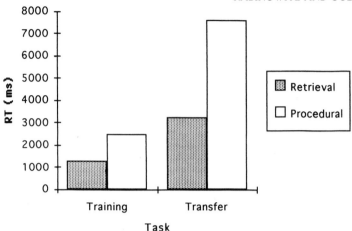

FIG. 12.4. Mean reaction times as a function of training group for last trial of training and transfer task—Experiment 2.

Discussion

In both experiments, we observed that as a consequence of the different types of practice opportunities, the learning curves of subjects in the two types of training conditions differed from one another. Although performance in the two groups was initially equivalent, subjects given retrieval training exhibited faster improvement in RT than did those given procedural training. Our interpretation of these results is that subjects in the procedural condition received many practice trials with different problems and improved at using the procedure to derive an answer. However, because subjects in the retrieval condition were presented a consistent relation between problems and answers, they initially used a procedure to derive answers, but quickly learned to retrieve the answers to the problems. It is assumed that these subjects actually received little practice in counting up the alphabet, and the speeding up of RTs is attributed to the ability to retrieve, in contrast to needing to figure out the answer. Our interpretation calls for two different types of active knowledge structures to account for this performance.

An alternative interpretation is possible, however. This interpretation would posit that as a consequence of retrieval training, specific modular productions were constructed that were related to the specific problems. These specific procedures were acquired faster than were the general procedures developed during procedural training and then compiled, and this would account for the pattern of results observed during training: Learning occurs primarily in terms of changes in procedural knowledge.

On the transfer task in Experiment 1, we presented subjects with a new set of alphabet addition problems to solve. We observed that subjects given procedural training showed positive transfer, but subjects given retrieval training did not. Our interpretation is that subjects given procedural training received a lot of practice counting up the alphabet and thus, when given a new set of problems that continued to use that procedure, showed improvement. Subjects in the retrieval condition, however, learned to retrieve answers to the problems, and this obviated the need to count up the alphabet to derive answers. These subjects therefore received little practice in using the procedure and when given new problems that required counting, did not show improvement. Once again, this pattern of results may occur as a result of two different types of active knowledge structures.

The alternative interpretation can also account for this pattern of results, however. The interpretation of the procedural training groups performance is the same. However, the lack of positive transfer in the retrieval group can be accounted for by the assertion that specific modular procedures were learned during training. Given the context-specificity of these procedures, they were not activated when a new set of problems was given, and thus, no positive transfer would be expected. Thus, it still appears that the data can be interpreted in terms of learning occurring primarily through changes in procedural knowledge.

In the transfer task in Experiment 2, we presented subjects with a set of addition subtraction problems to solve. These subtraction problems were the inverse of the addition problems learned by the retrieval group during training. We observed that subjects given retrieval training showed positive transfer to this task, but subjects given procedural training did not. Our interpretation is that because subjects in the retrieval condition encoded the information in terms of an organized network around a part–whole schema (Resnick & Omanson, 1987), the addition knowledge would become activated during the subtraction task, and would be used to help solve the problems. The lack of transfer as a consequence of procedural training is based on the assumption that procedures acquired during training are modular and independent and would not become activated or be relevant for solving the subtraction task. Once again, our interpretation involves proposing two active knowledge structures to account for the data.

The alternative interpretation presented cannot account for this pattern of results. Because this alternative interpretation involves positing the acquisition of specific modular procedures in order to account for all the other data, there is no way, given this interpretation, to predict positive transfer from retrieval training to the subtraction task. An account that only discusses learning in terms of changes in procedural knowledge cannot account for the pattern of results obtained across the two studies.

GENERAL DISCUSSION

The basic assumption underlying this research is that skilled behavior can best be understood in terms of the knowledge structures that enable the skill. The computer metaphor implies that there are two types of knowledge structures, procedural and declarative. Procedural knowledge is seen as active, representing the processes that transform and manipulate information. Declarative knowledge is seen as passive, in that it represents the information that enables procedures. This active–passive distinction between procedural and declarative knowledge structures suggests that skill is the acquisition of procedural knowledge structures.

In adopting this orientation, Anderson (1982, 1983, 1987) presented a unidirectional view of learning. Skill begins with declarative knowledge and weak strategies and gradually, with practice, stronger strategies are developed and compiled. What is never discussed is how the declarative knowledge is acquired. It may be acquired through a rote learning process, as described in the delta rule (Stone, 1986) from the connectionist perspective; however, this explanation ignores the type of active processing that is performed by the learner.

In this research, we suggested that there are two active knowledge structures that can account for skilled performance: a procedural system and a retrieval system. These two systems are assumed to be based on different representational assumptions and provide different implications for understanding learning and transfer. It was also suggested that the two types of knowledge systems are developed as a consequence of different types of practice. The problem with making these types of hypotheses is isomorphism. Are the systems specified in enough detail so that they make different predictions that can then be experimentally distinguishable? We showed that the two systems make different predictions in terms of learning and transfer and can be experimentally discriminated.

One implication of this model for understanding learning and skill acquisition is that it suggests there is an interactive relationship between two types of knowledge structures. We agree with Anderson (1982, 1983, 1987) that retrievable knowledge provides the opportunity for the development of new procedures. We part with Anderson, however, in arguing that a consequence of using procedures is the development of retrievable knowledge. The important thing to keep in mind is that the acquisition of this retrievable knowledge not only provides a new context for the development of new procedures, but also makes it unnecessary to use old procedures. The acquisition of retrievable knowledge obviates the need to procedurally derive information. To the extent that the declarative knowledge structure can accomplish the same type of performance as does the procedural knowledge structure, it does not make much sense to assert that "declarative knowledge is necessarily inert by itself" (Anderson, 1993, p. 69). Thus, we suggest that skill acquisition is more than just the development of procedural knowledge; it is the development of both procedural and retrievable knowledge. Research should be oriented toward investigating the interaction between these two types of active knowledge structures.

ACKNOWLEDGMENTS

The first author would like to thank Gordon Logan for a discussion that led to the design of the research described in this chapter. The authors would also like to thank John Anderson, Mark Ashcraft, Richard Carlson, Wayne Gray, Jim Hennessy, and Robert Siegler for helpful comments on earlier drafts of this chapter.

REFERENCES

Anderson, J. R. (1982). Acquisition of cognitive skill. *Psychological Review, 89,* 369–406.

Anderson, J. R. (1983). *The architecture of cognition.* Cambridge, MA: Harvard University Press.

Anderson, J. R. (1987). Skill acquisition: Compilation of weak-method problem solutions. *Psychological Review, 94,* 192–210.

Anderson, J. R. (1993). *Rules of mind.* Hillsdale, NJ: Lawrence Erlbaum Associates.

Anderson, J. R., & Bower, G. H. (1973). *Human associative memory.* Washington, DC: Winston.

Ashcraft, M. H. (1987). Children's knowledge of simple arithmetic: A developmental model and simulation. In J. Bisanz, C. Brainerd, & R. Kail (Eds.), *Formal methods in developmental psychology* (pp. 302–338). New York: Springer-Verlag.

Ashcraft, M. H., & Battaglia, J. (1978). Cognitive arithmetic: Evidence for retrieval and decision processes in mental addition. *Journal of Experimental Psychology: Human Learning and Memory, 4,* 527–538.

Ashcraft, M. H., & Stazyk, E. H. (1981). Mental addition: A test of three verification models. *Memory & Cognition, 9,* 185–196.

Baddeley, A. (1990). *Human memory: Theory and practice.* Boston, MA: Allyn & Bacon.

Baroody, A. J. (1983). The development of procedural knowledge: An alternative explanation for chronometric trends in mental arithmetic. *Developmental Review, 3,* 225–230.

Bereiter, C. (1991). Implications of connectionism for thinking about rules. *Educational Researcher, 20,* 10–16.

Collins, A. M., & Loftus, E. F. (1975). A spreading activation theory of semantic processing. *Psychological Review, 82,* 407–428.

Collins, A. M., & Quillian, M. R. (1969). Retrieval times from semantic memory. *Journal of Verbal Learning and Verbal Behavior, 8,* 240–247.

Compton, B. J., & Logan, G. D. (1991). The transition from algorithm to retrieval in memory-based theories of automaticity. *Memory & Cognition, 19,* 151–158.

Feldman, J. A., & Ballard, D. H. (1982). Connectionist models and their properties. *Cognitive Science, 2,* 205–254.

Glaser, R., & Bassok, M. (1989). Learning theory and the study of instruction. *Annual Review of Psychology, 40,* 631–666.

Groen, G. J., & Parkman, J. M. (1972). A chronometric analysis of simple addition. *Psychological Review, 79,* 329–343.

Groen, G. J., & Resnick, L. B. (1977). Can preschool children invent addition algorithms? *Journal of Educational Psychology, 69,* 645–652.

Holland, J. H., Holyoak, K. J., Nisbett, R. E., & Thegard, P. R. (1986). *Induction: Processes of inference, learning, and discovery.* Cambridge, MA: MIT Press.

Kapp, S. T., Boches, C. A., Trabert, M. L., & Logan, G. D. (1991). Automatizing alphabet arithmetic: II. Are there practice effects after automaticity is achieved? *Journal of Experimental Psychology: Learning, Memory, and Cognition, 17,* 196–209.

Klahr, D. (1985). Solving problems with ambiguous subgoal ordering: Pre-schoolers' performance. *Child Development, 56,* 940–952.

Larkin, J. H. (1985). Understanding, problem representations, and skill in physics. In S. F. Chipman, J. W. Segal, & R. Glaser (Eds.), *Thinking and learning skills: Vol. 2. Research and open questions* (pp. 141–159). Hillsdale, NJ: Lawrence Erlbaum Associates.

Larkin, J. H. (1989). What kind of knowledge transfers? In L. B. Resnick (Ed.), *Knowing, learning, and instruction: Essays in honor of Robert Glaser* (pp. 283–305). Hillsdale, NJ: Lawrence Erlbaum Associates.

Lesgold, A. M. (1984). Acquiring expertise. In J. R. Anderson & S. M. Kosslyn (Eds.), *Tutorials in learning and memory: Essays in honor of Gordon Bower* (pp. 31–60). San Francisco: Freeman.

Logan, G. D. (1988). Toward an instance theory of automatization. *Psychological Review, 95,* 492–527.

Logan, G. D., & Kapp, S. T. (1991). Automatizing alphabet arithmetic: I. Is extended practice necessary to produce automaticity? *Journal of Experimental Psychology: Learning, Memory, and Cognition, 17*, 179–195.

Mandler, J. M. (1983). Representation. In J. H. Flavell & E. M. Markman (Eds.), *Handbook of child psychology: Vol. 3. Cognitive development* (4th ed., pp. 424–494). New York: Academic Press.

McKendree, J., & Anderson, J. R. (1987). Effect of practice on knowledge and use of Basic Lisp. In J. M. Carroll (Ed.), *Interfacing thought: Cognitive aspects of human–computer interaction* (pp. 236–259). Cambridge, MA: MIT Press.

Miller, K., Perlmutter, M., & Keating, D. P. (1984). Cognitive arithmetic: Comparison of operations. *Journal of Experimental Psychology: Learning, Memory, & Cognition, 10*, 46–60.

Newell, A. P. (1979). One last word. In D. T. Tumas & F. Reif (Eds.), *Problem solving and education: Issues in teaching and research* (pp. 175–189). Hillsdale, NJ: Lawrence Erlbaum Associates.

Newell, A. P., & Simon, H. A. (1972). *Human problem solving.* Englewood Cliffs, NJ: Prentice Hall.

Norman, D. A., & Rumelhart, D. E. (1975). *Explorations in cognition.* San Francisco: Freeman.

Perkins, D. N., & Salomon, G. (1989). Are cognitive skills context-bound? *Educational Researcher, 18*, 16–25.

Rabinowitz, M., & Feldman, S. (1989). Using computer simulations to investigate individual differences: A look at an addition retrieval model. *Learning and Individual Differences, 1*, 227–246.

Rabinowitz, M., & Glaser, R. (1985). Cognitive structure and process in highly competent performance. In F. D. Horowitz & M. O'Brien (Eds.), *The gifted and talented: A developmental perspective* (pp. 75–98). Washington, DC: American Psychological Association.

Rabinowitz, M., & Goldberg, N. (1992, November). *Acquiring knowledge through practice: What kind of knowledge?* Paper presented at the annual conference of the Psychonomic Society, St. Louis, MO.

Rabinowitz, M., Lesgold, A. M., & Berardi, B. (1988). Modeling task performance: Rule-based and connectionist alternatives. *International Journal of Educational Research, 12*, 35–48.

Resnick, L. B., & Omanson, S. F. (1987). Learning to understand arithmetic. In R. Glaser (Ed.), *Advances in instructional psychology* (Vol. 3, pp. 41–96). Hillsdale, NJ: Lawrence Erlbaum Associates.

Rumelhart, D. E., & McClelland, J. L. (Eds.). (1986). *Parallel distributed processing* (Vol. 1). Cambridge, MA: MIT Press.

Siegler, R. S. (1987). The perils of averaging data over strategies: An example from children's addition. *Journal of Experimental Psychology: General, 116*, 250–264.

Siegler, R. S. (1990). How differences interact to produce strategy choices. In W. Schneider & F. E. Weinert (Eds.), *Interactions among aptitudes, strategies, and knowledge in cognitive performance* (pp. 74–89). New York: Springer-Verlag.

Siegler, R. S., & Robinson, M. (1982). The development of numerical understandings. In H. Reese & L. P. Lipsitt (Eds.), *Advances in child development and behavior* (pp. 241–312). New York: Academic Press.

Simon, D. F., & Simon, H. A. (1978). Individual differences in solving physics problems. In R. S. Siegler (Ed.), *Children's thinking: What develops?* (pp. 325–348). Hillsdale, NJ: Lawrence Erlbaum Associates.

Simon, H. A. (1992). What is an "Explanation" of behavior? *Psychological Science, 3*, 150–161.

Stone, G. O. (1986). An analysis of the delta rule and the learning of statistical associations. In D. E. Rumelhart & J. L. McClelland (Eds.), *Parallel distributed processing* (Vol. 1, pp. 444–459). Cambridge, MA: MIT Press.

Thorndike, E. L. (1903). *Educational psychology.* New York: Lenke & Buechner.

Tulving, E., & Donaldson, W. (Eds.). (1972). *Organization of memory.* New York: Academic Press.

Part III

INTRA- AND INTERINDIVIDUAL DIFFERENCES IN MEMORY DEVELOPMENT

Is There Evidence for Intraindividual Consistency in Performance Across Memory Tasks? New Evidence on an Old Question

Beth Kurtz-Costes
University of North Carolina at Chapel Hill

Wolfgang Schneider
Sigrid Rupp
University of Würzburg

A long-standing controversy in memory research is whether memory is a unitary human faculty, or whether it represents a variety of abilities. As in intelligence theory, some researchers argue that memory represents a single construct, and others—pointing to large intraindividual differences in performance across tasks— argue that memory is a global concept that encompasses many specific, and probably independent, abilities (cf. Knopf, Körkel, Schneider, & Weinert, 1988).

As Knopf et al. outlined, the conceptualization of memory changed dramatically in the late 1960s with the advent of information-processing models. Using the computer analogy, information theorists posited memory as comprised of three components: the structural features or hardware, the system architecture, and the programs or software. Both the hardware and system architecture were presumed to be relatively invariant, whereas the system software (i.e., use of strategies) was expected to explain large amounts of variance both across and within subjects. However, although a great deal of research in the 1970s and 1980s examined the relationships between strategy use and memory performance, relatively little of this research was aimed directly at the question of intraindividual variability in memory performance.

EVERYDAY MEMORY

Investigations of interindividual differences in memory and their relationship to strategy use have appeared especially in the developmental literature, where it is now well-documented that children's increasing sophistication in strategy use during middle childhood is related to broader memory and metacognitive development (Schneider & Pressley, 1989). Meanwhile, in investigations with adults, one of the richest sources of information about intraindividual consistency comes from research into "everyday" memory performance, which has become a popular area of study since the 1970s (e.g., Banaji & Crowder, 1989; Gruneberg, Morris, & Sykes, 1988; West, Crook, & Barron, 1992). Motivated by criticisms that laboratory memory tasks are lacking in external validity, and thus are unrelated to the memory demands of everyday life, researchers have attempted to devise memory tasks with greater ecological validity and to show the relationships between performances on such tasks and everyday memory failure (or success).

A large number of investigations of everyday memory have emerged from neuropsychology, where memory loss of head-injured individuals is an important concern. For instance, Sunderland, Harris, and Baddeley (1983) investigated the relationship between memory performance in everyday life and performance on laboratory memory tasks in normal and head-injured adult subjects. Because Sunderland et al. were primarily interested in the relationships among subjects' reports of everyday memory failures, relatives' reports of failures, and the subjects' performances on laboratory tasks, the authors did not report actual correlations between pairs of memory tasks. However, subjects' subjective views of their memory failures may be viewed as memory measures themselves (see Sunderland, Watts, Baddeley, & Harris, 1986); thus the correlations that Sunderland et al. (1983) reported between objective measures and subjects' reports may be used as a rough index of consistency. The memory tasks used by Sunderland et al. included continuous recognition (i.e., pattern recognition), face recognition, story recall (i.e., subject listened to a short story resembling a news clip, then attempted immediate recall), paired associates, and forced-choice word recognition (subject viewed 50 one-syllable words in sequence, then was given a recognition task in which each target word was paired with a random distractor). Correlations between performance on those five tasks and subjects' reports of those specific types of memory failure were mostly nonsignificant for recently injured subjects and for normal controls. For subjects who had experienced head injury more than 2 years prior to participation in the study, correlations between task performance and subjects' reports of memory loss were significant for the story recall task and for percent forgotten in paired associates. All other correlations were nonsignificant. As Sunderland et al. noted, these results should be interpreted cautiously because self-assessment of memory is probably lacking in validity. In other words, forgetful subjects may be likely to report a smaller proportion of memory errors than subjects with better memory.

More recently, researchers at Oxford and Cambridge Universities have developed a test battery for measuring everyday memory problems, designed especially for use with brain-damaged individuals (Wilson, Baddeley, & Cockburn, 1988; Wilson, Cockburn, Baddeley, & Hiorns, 1989). The Rivermead Behavioural Memory Test (RMBT) contains the following tasks: remembering a name, remembering a hidden belonging, remembering an appointment, picture recognition, remembering a newspaper article, face recognition, remembering a new route (immediate and delayed), delivering a message, orientation (i.e., requesting information about current time and location), and date. Wilson et al. (1989) administered the test to 118 normal control subjects (adults), and to 176 brain-injured individuals, whose memory was also assessed through self-reports, reports from caregivers, and observations by therapists. In order to test the validity of the RBMT, subjects were also given four standard memory tests: recognition memory for words and faces, digit span, spatial span, and paired associates. Correlations between these scores and the RBMT total scores for brain-injured subjects were all significant, ranging from .24 to .60. Interestingly, correlations between pairs of scores on the standard memory measures were somewhat lower in magnitude (5 of 15 correlations were less than .24), but most were significant (Wilson et al., 1989). Correlations for normal subjects were not reported. Subsequently, a Dutch version of the RBMT was developed, and when tested on 41 stroke patients, was related to performance on two laboratory memory tests, and to caregivers' reports of patients' memory failures (van der Feen, Van Balen, & Eling, 1988).

This research indicates that valid assessments of memory performance can be made that correspond to memory performance in everyday life. Further, the data reported by Wilson et al. (1989) provide positive, if not overwhelming evidence for consistency in intraindividual memory performances. However, these studies were conducted with adults, and in particular, with adults with memory impairment. Thus, it is unclear whether or not these results may be generalized to normal individuals, and particularly to normal children.

DEVELOPMENTAL RESEARCH INTO INTERTASK CONSISTENCY

A small number of investigations have examined intraindividual variability in children's memory performance. Cavanaugh and Borkowski (1980) gave children from kindergarten, first, third, and fifth grades three memory measures: sort recall, cognitive cuing, and alphabet search. Correlations between recall measures across the three tasks showed a developmental progression. All correlations were nonsignificant for kindergartners. Among first graders, recall performance on sort recall and cognitive cuing were related, but neither was related to alphabet search. For third graders, two of the three correlations were significant (sort recall with cognitive cuing; cognitive cuing with alphabet search). For fifth graders, all three correlations were significant, and ranged from .37 to .49 (Cavanaugh & Borkowski, 1980). Cavanaugh and Borkowski also examined correlations between pairs of strategy scores across tasks. Just as for recall, no strategy correlations were significant for kindergartners. But beginning in first grade, clustering behavior was consistent across all three tasks.

Kail (1979) tested third and sixth graders on three memory tasks. Using factor analysis to examine both recall and strategy scores, he concluded that his data supported the existence of a general strategy factor underlying performances of sixth graders, but not of third graders. However, correlations among recall measures tended to be quite small for both age groups, indicating a lack of intraindividual consistency in memory performance.

Noting that both Kail (1979) and Cavanaugh and Borkowski (1980) used only laboratory-type tasks in their investigations, Knopf et al. (1988) assessed the intertask consistency of memory performance in third, fifth, and seventh graders, and in two adult groups ranging in age from 50 to 84 years. Knopf et al. used four tasks derived from traditional laboratory memory measures: digit span, sort-recall with nonclusterable stimuli, sort-recall with taxonomically clusterable stimuli, and sort-recall with episodically clusterable stimuli (adults only). Two everyday memory tasks were used: recall of a story about a soccer game, and recall of a text about a political topic (adults only). Thus Knopf et al. attempted to measure intertask consistency in memory performance across the life span, and also were interested in examining relationships between traditional memory tasks and those with greater ecological validity.

For children, intertask correlations on data collapsed across age groups were mostly in the .25 to .45 range. When these correlations were calculated separately for each age group, most decreased markedly in magnitude. Although most of the within-grade correlations were nonsignificant, performance was most likely to be related for older children (i.e., fifth or seventh graders), and within task types. Thus, for example, recall on the clusterable list was related to recall on the nonclusterable list (rs .43 to .62), and text episodic memory was related to text contradictions (rs .31 to .34). For adults, about half of the intertask correlations were significant, but only 3 of the 15 correlations exceeded $r = .35$. Knopf et al. concluded that their results provided no strong evidence for the existence of a unitary memory function.

The present study was designed in order to further examine intraindividual consistency in performance across memory tasks. Because the early school years are a critical time for memory and strategy development, we chose to study three age groups: kindergartners, second graders, and fifth graders. A major concern was to use memory tasks with greater ecological validity than traditional memory measures. Therefore, we selected two sets of measures that resemble everyday tasks faced by young children. One set was designed to mimic some of the memory demands placed on children in school; a second assessed typical memory tasks outside of school. Finally, we included two traditional laboratory tasks that are frequently used in research with young children: sort-recall and paired associates. Results of the first project led us to collect data on a second sample of children in order to examine test–retest and parallel-form reliability of some of the measures. The two projects are presented as Study 1 and Study 2.

STUDY 1: METHOD

Thirty-two 5-year-olds, thirty-two 7-year-olds, and thirty 9-year-olds from Munich, Germany participated in the project. The mean ages of the groups were 5.5. years ($SD = .26$), 7.5 years ($SD = .28$), and 9.5 years ($SD = .30$), respectively. Nineteen 5-year-olds, twenty 7-year-olds, and fifteen 9-year-olds were female. All children were tested on three everyday memory tasks (Remind Me, Shopping, and Memory Game), three school-related tasks (Geography, Roman Numerals, and Story Recall), and two laboratory memory tasks (Sort-Recall and Paired Associates).

For *Remind Me*, children were asked at the beginning of the test session to remind the interviewer of something (to turn out the light, to return a chair to another classroom, or to retrieve a jacket from the corner) at the end of the session. After the session, the interviewer noted whether or not the child remembered.

In *Shopping*, the interviewer asked that the child "go shopping." In a corner of the room, several objects were stored in a large carton; the child was asked to retrieve the following items: tissues, a pencil, a mirror, balloons, a large bar of soap, a green book, and chewing gum. The interviewer read the list twice, then engaged the child in informal conversation about errands at home for approximately 60 sec. After the conversation, the interviewer gave the child a plastic sack in which to place the items, and the child went to the corner of the room to retrieve the items that had been named. In addition to the requested items, the "store" contained a lipstick, a small bar of soap, a yellow book, a pen, a yoyo, a chocolate bar, a notebook, a comb, and a stuffed animal. The child's score for this subtest (shopping recall) was the number of items correctly retrieved.

Memory Game is a children's game marketed commercially in Germany (*Memory Spiel*), also known as Concentration in the United States. As Memory Spiel is marketed for several age groups, we used the version of the game for 4- to 8-year-olds. Materials for the game consist of cardboard tiles which display pictures. Players take turns turning over the tiles in pairs in order to find matches. We used a variation of the game developed by Knopf and Quadflieg (1989). Thirty tiles were laid out in front of the child in 3 rows of 10, and the interviewer turned over 6 of them to display the pictures. The child was instructed to study both the identities and the positions of the pictures. After 30 sec study time, the interviewer turned the 6 tiles over again, then showed the child a set of 12 pictures—6 that the child had just viewed, and 6 distractor items. For each item, the child was asked to designate whether or not that picture had been in the original display. The child's score for this part of the task (game recognition) was the number of correct responses, with a maximum possible score of 12. Finally, the interviewer gave the child matches for the original 6 items, one at a time, and asked the child to locate the picture pairs in the original 3 × 10 display. The child was allowed to turn over only one picture for each item, and the total score (game location) was the number of items correctly located. Game recognition and game location scores were summed to create a single score (Memory Game) for this task.

Birthday Party was meant to mimic everyday situations where children are expected to remember names and biographical information about friends and acquaintances. The child was told to imagine going to a birthday party where he or she would meet several people and learn some things about them. The goal was to remember as many of the names and details about the people as possible to retell the interviewer afterwards. Next, the child was introduced one at a time to five puppets, with particular information about each. For example, the following dialogue was used with the first two puppets: "This is the mother of your friend. Her name is Mrs. Schulze. She is very nice. She has baked an apple cake for the children. Here is Hans. He lives around the corner from you. He has one sister, who is also at the party today."

The information was read to the child twice, then the child performed the Roman Numerals task. After concluding the Roman Numerals task, the interviewer produced the five puppets again and asked the child to recite everything he or she remembered about them. One point was given for each correct piece of information. Credit was given only if the names and the pertinent information were associated with the correct puppet. The maximum possible score for this task (birthday recall) was 13 points.

The three school-related tasks were Geography, Roman Numerals, and Text Recall. For *Geography*, children were shown a map of Brazil, and were told that the interviewer would tell them several things about Brazil and Brazilians, and the child should remember as much as possible to tell the interviewer afterwards. Then the interviewer said to the child, while indicating appropriate places on the map: "Here is Brazil. In Brazil, the people speak Portuguese. Brazilians eat rice, vegetables, and lots of beef, because in Brazil there are many cows. East of Brazil is the Atlantic Ocean. During the last centuries, many Europeans have moved to Brazil. However, the first Brazilians were Indians. Therefore, in Brazil nowadays you will find people with red, white, or brown skin."

The interviewer read the text twice, then immediately asked the child to repeat everything that he or she remembered. The child was awarded one point for each of the following items correctly recalled: the name of the country, the language spoken in Brazil, the name of the ocean, the fact that many cows are found in Brazil, two of the three food items frequently eaten, the fact that many races of people live in Brazil. Next, the interviewer provided the child with cues for unrecalled information by asking a question about each item that had not been correctly recalled (e.g., "What is the name of this country?" "What language is spoken here?"). Children received an additional one half point for each cue question answered correctly. The maximum possible score for the Geography task was six points.

Roman Numerals was used in order to include a task with a numerical basis that would be age-appropriate for our subjects. We decided to use Roman numerals because few German children are familiar with them, yet most 5-year-olds are familiar enough with the Arabic numerals that they would understand the concept of numeric representation. Children were shown a sheet displaying the Roman and Arabic numerals from 1 to 10, and were told that the Roman numerals, like the Arabic numerals, indicate numbers. The interviewer counted from 1 to 10, indicating the appropriate numerals from each system. Next, children were asked to learn the Roman numerals so that they could write them later without prompts. Before beginning the study time, the child was given pencil and paper "in case you want to practice." The interviewer then recorded strategy use while the child studied the numerals. One point was awarded (numerals strategies) for copying the numerals partially or completely once; two points were given for an association strategy (e.g., noting that 5 is V, sounding like the German *funf*); three points were awarded for multiple rehearsal; four points were awarded for self-test. Children received the score corresponding to the most sophisticated strategy used; thus, scores ranged from 0 to 4. Two minutes study time was provided for 7- and 9-year-olds, and 3 minutes for 5-year-olds, because pilot work indicated that those intervals were the average amount of time needed by children in the respective age groups to copy the 10 numerals twice. After the study time had elapsed, both the cue sheet and the study materials were removed, and the child was instructed to write as much as he or she remembered on a clean sheet of paper. One point was given for each numeral correctly written in sequence (numerals recall).

For *Story Recall*, the child was told that the interviewer would read a story through twice, and the child should listen carefully in order to retell as much as possible of the story afterwards. The story was a tale about a little boy's first attempts to learn to play tennis (e.g., missing a serve, hitting the ball in the swimming pool next door). The text included 162 words and 17 sentences. The interviewer read the text twice, then asked for immediate verbatim recall. Responses were tape recorded, and later transcribed for coding. We used Mandler and Johnson's (1977) story grammar to analyze the underlying structure of the story, thus identifying 25 nodes. One point was given for each node recalled (story). Scoring was conducted leniently. Thus for the node, *Hans went home very hungry*, credit was given if the child recalled *Hans went home and ate*. Interrater scoring reliability for this task was 98%.

Sort-Recall and *Paired Associates* were the two laboratory memory tasks that we used. For *Sort-Recall*, the child was given 16 toys that were clusterable into four taxonomic groups: vehicles (tractor, bus, car, truck), dishes (teapot, cup, pot, fry pan), animals (elephant, cow, horse, wolf), and furniture (bed, table, chair, cupboard). The child was instructed to do whatever he or she wanted with the objects in order to remember them for later recall. Two minutes study time was allowed, then the interviewer collected the objects and asked the child to name them. Each child received three scores for this task: SR strategies, SR recall, and SR clustering. For SR strategies, one point was awarded for use of naming, two points for sorting or rehearsal, and three points for sorting and rehearsal. The child's SR recall score corresponded to the total number of items recalled. We used RR scores (Bousfield & Bousfield, 1966) as an index of amount of clustering at recall (SR clustering). This ratio gives an index of clustering behavior that is not dependent on the number of items recalled.

Eight pairs of line drawings of familiar objects were used for the *Paired Associates* task. Children were told to study the pairs in order to recall the second member of each pair when presented with the first item as a cue. The paired items were not obviously related to each other; thus the task of constructing associations was expected to be difficult for the children. The pictures, which were affixed to index cards, were shown at 10-sec intervals, then recall was requested using single picture prompts. A child's recall (paired associate recall) was the number of items correctly recalled.

STUDY 1: RESULTS

Developmental Change in Children's Memory Performance

3 (Age) × 2 (Gender) analyses of variance were conducted on all recall and strategy scores. Those analyses indicated main effects of Age for Birthday Recall, Shopping, Remind Me, Memory Game, Numerals Strategies, Numerals Recall, Geography Recall, Story, and SR Recall, $F(2, 88) = 30.2, 3.8, 7.5, 15.1, 6.6, 57.2, 41.7, 30.2,$ and 29.8, respectively, all $ps < .05$. Planned comparisons among means showed that for Birthday Recall, Numerals Recall, Geography Recall, Story, and SR Recall, 9-year-olds remembered more than 7-year-olds, who remembered more than 5-year-olds. On the Remind Me task, 9-year-olds remembered to remind the experimenter more often than 7- or 5-year-olds, who did not differ significantly from one another. On Shopping and Memory Game, 7- and 9-year-olds showed superior memory performance to 5-year-olds, but the two older groups did not differ from one another. Finally, although the main effect of Age was significant for Numerals Strategy scores, planned comparisons among age group means were nonsignificant ($p = .053$ and $.083$). Means and standard deviations for all recall and strategy scores appear in Table 13.1.

Gender was related to memory performance only on the Remind Me task, where girls outperformed boys, $F(1, 87) = 4.0, p < .05$.

Intertask Consistency in Children's Memory

We used two procedures to examine intraindividual variability in children's performances. First, using the three categories of memory (everyday, school-related, and laboratory), we computed alpha reliability coefficients for subtest scores (Novak & Lewis, 1967). Alpha coefficients provide an index of the re-

TABLE 13.1
Mean Strategy and Recall Scores for 5-, 7-, and 9-year-olds
(Standard Deviations Appear in Parentheses)

	5 years	7 years	9 years
Everyday memory			
Birthday recall	4.25	5.94	8.47
	(2.56)	(2.03)	(1.59)
Shopping	5.72	6.41	6.50
	(1.53)	(0.84)	(0.73)
Remind me	0.09	0.25	0.50
	(0.30)	(0.44)	(0.51)
Memory game	12.66	15.16	15.37
	(2.67)	(2.05)	(1.43)
School-Related memory			
Numerals recall	0.72	2.75	6.77
	(0.92)	(1.67)	(3.37)
Numerals strategies	1.03	1.50	2.03
	(0.40)	(1.14)	(1.43)
Geography recall	3.12	4.52	5.57
	(1.26)	(1.12)	(0.50)
Story recall	7.31	12.53	17.27
	(4.57)	(5.88)	(3.94)
Laboratory memory			
SR recall	9.34	11.91	13.57
	(2.06)	(2.37)	(1.92)
SR strategies	1.59	1.69	1.93
	(1.01)	(1.06)	(0.87)
SR cluster	0.47	0.49	0.55
	(0.14)	(0.17)	(0.16)
Paired associate recall	2.12	2.72	2.27
	(1.52)	(1.78)	(1.60)

latedness among a group of scores, with values greater than .60 indicating moderate relatedness, and values exceeding .80 indicating reliable relationships among the measures. We calculated alpha coefficients within age groups, first for each of the three types of memory tasks, then across the three task types (see Table 13.2). The resulting coefficients, ranging from .05 to .51, indicated very weak reliability within the three types of memory measures at all age levels.

Next, we converted children's scores to standardized scores in order to provide equal weightings for them. These standardized scores were summed to create a composite score for each child, and alpha coefficients were calculated for the three types of memory tasks. These analyses indicated that performance approached a moderate level of reliability for 7-year-olds, but again, alpha coefficients were much lower than anticipated for all three age groups.

In order to obtain a clearer picture of intraindividual variability across subtests regardless of the type of task, we computed product-moment correlations among

TABLE 13.2
Alpha Reliability Coefficients for Subtest Scores Within Age Groups

	5 years	7 years	9 years
Everyday memory	.24	.36	.20
Birthday recall			
Shopping			
Remind me			
Memory game			
School-related memory	.11	.42	.51
Numerals recall			
Numerals strategies			
Geography recall			
Story recall			
Laboratory memory	.05	.28	.37
SR recall			
SR strategies			
SR cluster			
PA recall			
Composite	.45	.53	.38
Everyday			
School			
Laboratory			

subtests. Those correlations (see Table 13.3) indicated little relationship among scores at any age level. Of the 66 correlations at each age level, 3 should be significant by chance at the .05 level of significance. Five correlations were significant for 5-year-olds, six for 7-year-olds, and six for 9-year-olds. Median correlations at each grade level similarly reflected a low level of relationship among measures (.11, .08, and .13 for 5-, 7-, and 9-year-olds, respectively). Correlations between tasks within our three categories of everyday, laboratory-, and school-related memory were not more likely to be significant than were correlations across memory categories.

Given the absence of consistency in children's performances across tasks, we reasoned that children's performances on the various tasks might not be reliable. Because we had designed a number of the tasks for this study, test–retest reliability data on those subtests were not available to us. Therefore, we decided to conduct a second study to determine the test–retest and parallel-form reliability of several of the subtests.

STUDY 2

Two age groups of children were selected to participate in the reliability study: 5-year-olds and 8-year-olds. Practical limitations and task characteristics prevented examination of all tasks used in the original study, so we elected to

TABLE 13.3

Intercorrelations Among Subtest Scores for 5-, 7-, and 9-year-olds

	1	2	3	4	5	6	7	8	9	10	11
1. Birthday											
2. Shopping	.22										
	-.06										
	-.06										
3. Remind me	.01	-.08									
	-.05	.24									
	.04	.32									
4. Memory game	-.05	.38*	-.32								
	.28	.13	.03								
	.22	.02	-.21								
5. Num. recall	.29	-.10	.10	-.21							
	.37*	-.18	-.04	-.15							
	.00	.31	.07	.30							
6. Num. strat.	.01	.12	-.03	.22	.11						
	.25	-.02	.06	-.09	.17						
	-.02	.05	-.02	-.12	.44*						
7. Geography	.13	.23	.23	-.04	-.27	.18					
	.57**	-.08	.12	.36*	.10	-.06					
	.37*	.05	.13	.08	.16	-.03					

(Continued)

255

TABLE 13.3
(Continued)

	1	2	3	4	5	6	7	8	9	10	11
8. Story	.12	.16	-.09	-.19	.06	.00	.17				
	.74**	.05	-.06	.10	.26	.40*	.45*				
	.28	.11	-.07	.20	.40*	.08	.51**				
9. SR recall	.12	.24	-.37*	.45**	.15	.14	-.07	.20			
	.20	.20	-.07	.28	-.18	-.08	.34	.29			
	.16	.33	-.05	.40*	.19	-.12	.30	.04			
10. SR strat.	.09	.28	-.08	.16	.11	.27	.19	-.08	.27		
	-.22	.00	-.03	-.28	-.10	.05	-.12	.09	.18		
	.02	.11	.31	-.12	.16	.20	.13	.20	.23		
11. SR cluster	-.03	.11	.07	.08	.15	.02	-.03	-.26	-.14	.02	
	.14	.06	-.13	-.12	-.10	.13	-.26	.12	.25	.11	
	-.04	.22	-.08	.29	.08	-.02	-.09	.13	.34	.25	
12. Paired associates	.44*	.20	.19	.02	.00	-.22	.36*	.18	-.02	.12	-.12
	.18	.00	-.28	.16	.10	.10	.26	.08	.24	-.18	-.23
	.22	-.24	.04	.27	-.10	-.25	.38*	.21	.16	.29	.12

*p < .05
**p < .01

256

measure reliability for the following tasks: Birthday Party, Shopping, Geography, Story, Sort-Recall, and Paired Associates. We had three goals in the reliability study: to determine test–retest reliability of the tasks after an interval of 2 months, to determine the reliability of children's performances given minor variations in task characteristics (i.e., parallel-form reliability), and to replicate the pattern of relationships (or lack thereof) in the original data.

In order to determine the reliability of children's performance given minor variations in tasks characteristics, two forms were constructed for each of the five memory tasks. Form 1 corresponded to the materials and procedure previously described. For Form 2, we made the following changes: In Birthday Party, the five puppets were presented with changes in the names and characteristics (e.g., "This is your friend's father. His name is Mr. Meier. He is very nice, and today he got some pastries for the children."). For Shopping, children who received Form 2 were asked to retrieve the following: a notebook, a pen, a comb, bubbles, a small bar of soap, an apple, the yellow book, chocolate, and a colored pencil. Materials were similarly changed for the Sort-Recall and Paired Associates tasks, so that in each case the instructions to the child and the procedures were the same as for Form 1, but a different set of stimuli were used. For Geography, a text was developed about Canada. Finally, Form 2 of Story consisted of a text about a boy named Michael playing soccer. More detailed information about the procedure of Study 2 is reported in Rupp (1992).

Thirty-four 5-year-olds and thirty 8-year-olds were tested at the initial time point with Form 1 of each task. Two months later, children were randomly assigned to retest conditions: Half of each age group was retested on Form 1, and the other half was tested on Form 2. Thus, we were able to obtain test–retest data for half of the children, and parallel-form reliability for the other half of the children.

Reliability Results

Test–retest and parallel-test reliability coefficients for the five tasks are displayed in Table 13.4. Test–retest reliability exceeded .70 for Birthday Recall, Story, SR Recall, and Paired Associates (5-year-olds only). Test–retest reliability for Geography was moderate for both age groups ($r = .54$). Parallel-form reliability exceeded .70 for the 5-year-olds on the following tasks: Birthday Recall, Story, and Paired Associates. For 8-year-olds, reliability exceeded .70 for SR Recall.

Correlations between pairs of tasks indicated that intraindividual consistency was somewhat stronger than in the original study (see Table 13.5). For 5-year-olds, 6 of the 15 correlations were significant; 3 correlations were significant for 8-year-olds. A closer examination of the correlations indicated some consistencies and some discrepancies between these results and the results of Study 1. Because Memory Game, Remind Me, and Roman Numerals were not used in the second study, only 2 of the 5 correlations which had been significant in the

TABLE 13.4
Test–Retest and Parallel-Test Reliability for 5- (N = 34) and 8-year-old
(N = 30) Subjects in Study 2 (Correlations for 8-year-olds
Appear in Parentheses)

	Retest	Parallel
1. Birthday	.71	.87
	(.77)	(.43)
2. Shopping	−.15	−.07
	(.68)	(−.29)
3. Geography	.54	.17
	(.54)	(.48)
4. Story	.81	.76
	(.78)	(.80)
5. SR recall	.81	.58
	(.89)	(.74)
6. Paired associates	.79	.79
	(.48)	(.36)

original sample of 5-year-olds were tested in Study 2. Of the two, Birthday Recall was again related to Paired Associates Recall, whereas the correlation between Birthday and Geography dropped to .19. Similarly, Geography Recall and Birthday Recall were significantly related for 7- and 9-year-olds in the original sample; the correlation in Study 2 for 8-year-olds was .22. Story and Birthday Recall were significantly related in both studies (7-year-olds only in Study 1; both age groups in Study 2); Paired Associates Recall and Geography Recall were related in Study 1 (9-year-olds only), but not in Study 2. Thus, although Study 2 replicated some of the results of Study 1, that replication was not straightforward.

TABLE 13.5
Intercorrelations Among Subtest Scores for 5- (N = 34) and 8-year-old
(N = 30) Subjects in Study 2 (Correlations for 8-year-olds
Appear in Parentheses)

	1	2	3	4	5
1. Birthday recall					
2. Shopping	.43*				
	(.07)				
3. Geography recall	.19	.16			
	(.22)	(.05)			
4. Story	.41*	.35*	.01		
	(.50*)	(.17)	(.13)		
5. SR recall	.32*	.62*	.15	.20	
	(.31*)	(−.10)	(.31*)	(.24)	
6. Paired associates	.30*	−.22	.01	.12	−.09
	(.10)	(−.22)	(−.22)	(−.21)	(.20)

ANOTHER LOOK AT STUDY 1 DATA

Having found in Study 2 that Shopping did not show good test–retest reliability, we returned to the data from Study 1 to make one more attempt to find consistency in children's scores across tasks. For these analyses, we used the following scores: birthday recall, geography recall, story, SR recall, SR clustering, and paired associates recall. Working within age levels, we divided children's scores into quartiles, thus identifying for each task which children were in the lowest quartile, the second quartile, the third, and finally, the highest. Next we used a cross-tabulation procedure to compare children's rankings across tasks. In this way, we could determine the frequency with which children's scores fell into each quartile, and then calculate chi-square statistics to determine if children's rankings were independent across the five measures. In other words, if performances were consistent across tasks, a child who scored in the highest quartile on one measure would be expected to similarly score in the highest quartile on other measures (cf. Weinert, Schneider, & Knopf, 1988).

Cross-tabulations with corresponding chi-squared tests were calculated first within grades, then across grades to increase power. Even across grades, all six variables could not be entered simultaneously, because individual cell sizes were too small to calculate statistics. Therefore, the three laboratory memory measures (SR recall, SR clustering, and paired associates recall) were entered simultaneously for one analysis, and the three nonlaboratory measures (birthday recall, geography recall, and story recall) were entered for the second. The analyses conducted across grades were nonsignificant. When calculated within grades, 1 cell of 24 yielded a significant effect, which corresponds to a chance effect at $p = .05$.

CONCLUSION

Our results provided little evidence for the existence of a general memory factor. Intertask correlations in both studies were mostly nonsignificant. Although Cavanaugh and Borkowski (1980) and Knopf et al. (1988) found developmental trends in their data, with older children showing greater consistency in performance across tasks, our data did not show the same pattern. (It should be noted, however, that correlations in Knopf et al. were significant only between highly similar tasks.) In Study 1 of our research, the correlations were quite low for all three age groups, with no real differences across ages. In Study 2, correlations for 8-year-olds were slightly lower than correlations for 5-year-olds. Two limitations of our study were the relatively small sample sizes, and only modest reliability for some of the memory measures. Nonetheless, our results were consistent with previous research in that they showed little evidence of intraindividual consistency in task performance (e.g., Kail, 1979; Knopf et al., 1988).

Our results imply that "memory" is either a general name for a number of processes that might better be recognized individually, or put another way, that memory performance is determined by several factors, and that tasks differentially tap those processes. In this vein, we considered conducting factor analyses on our data in order to identify some of the underlying processes that influenced performance. However, our intertask correlations were too low to obtain meaningful results through factor analysis.

Wanting our analyses to be theory-driven, and believing that our colleagues might have some wisdom to contribute, we contacted 12 contemporary "memory experts" (a number of whom are contributors to this volume). We gave each of those individuals a description of the memory tasks used in Study 1, and asked them to identify the underlying cognitive processes they believed would determine performance on each task. Seven experts responded. Each named between 4 and 8 processes, with a total of 23 unique processes. Using a fairly lenient inclusion procedure, we found that four of the processes were named by at least three experts: recognition, episodic memory (or use of knowledge of text structure), free recall, and associative memory. Unfortunately, the individuals who named those processes showed little agreement in terms of which tasks they believed would tap each process. Similarly, a crosstabulation of which tasks were believed to be related to each other showed little consistency across experts. We concluded that although memory is one of the most heavily researched areas in developmental and cognitive psychology, we still have much to learn about it.

What do we know so far? Case's (1985; Case, Kurland, & Goldberg, 1982) conceptualization of short-term memory as consisting of two subcomponents—a storage space and an operating space—has come to be widely accepted. According to this view, older children can hold more information in short-term memory than younger children because older children are more efficient at processing. As cognitive processes become more automatic with age, they require less capacity, thus increased space is available for storage, even though the amount of functional space available does not increase (cf. Siegler, 1986).

If there is general agreement that operating space is invariant for an individual across tasks, it is also accepted that individuals vary dramatically in their use of control processes across situations. For instance, individuals are more likely to adopt a strategic approach to a task if the task materials are familiar (Frankel & Rollins, 1985; Schneider, 1986). Further, it is now recognized that an individual's knowledge base influences automatic processes (Bjorklund, 1985, 1987). Thus, a child who has extensive knowledge about the animal kingdom is likely to taxonomically organize animals on a recall task; this clustering behavior facilitates recall, even though it may not have been consciously performed as a memory strategy.

One rather striking observation that might be noted in the chapters in this volume is the lack of continuity across tasks and across constructs that are related to memory performance. On one hand, we seem to have a clear idea of some of the processes that influence memory performance—for example, metacognition (see Hasselhorn; Butterfield; Borkowski, this volume); knowledge about the world (see Rabinowitz, this volume); strategy use (Moely, Guttentag, Bjorklund); attention (de Ribaupierre); processing speed or capacity (Case, Kail, Salthouse); and so forth. On the other hand, when we move across these areas, we find widely varying tasks, with varying developmental trajectories. As Butterfield notes (this volume), our theories almost seem to be task-specific. Each researcher works within his or her area, and labels the phenomenon *memory*.

A growing trend in memory development research seems to be the simultaneous consideration of multiple constructs that influence performance (e.g., Pressley, this volume). We applaud these efforts. At the same time, given our inability (and the inability of others before us) to establish intraindividual consistency in performance across tasks, we raise the question here of the usefulness of the construct *memory*. Perhaps our theory-building efforts would be better served by unpacking memory as a single construct. At any rate, more research is clearly needed to identify the sources of intertask variability in memory performance, and to understand the developmental progression(s) of those sources.

REFERENCES

Banaji, M. R., & Crowder, R. G. (1989). The bankruptcy of everyday memory. *American Psychologist, 44*, 1185–1193.

Bjorklund, D. F. (1985). The role of conceptual knowledge in the development of organization in children's memory. In C. J. Brainerd & M. Pressley (Eds.), *Basic processes in memory development: Progress in cognitive development research* (pp. 103–142). New York: Springer.

Bjorklund, D. F. (1987). How age changes in knowledge base contribute to the development of children's memory: An interpretive review. *Developmental Review, 7*, 93–130.

Bousfield, A. K., & Bousfield, W. A. (1966). Measurement of clustering and of sequential constancies in repeated free recall. *Psychological Reports, 19*, 935–942.

Case, R. (1985). *Intellectual development: Birth to adulthood.* Orlando, FL: Academic Press.

Case, R., Kurland, D. M., & Goldberg, J. (1982). Operational efficiency and the growth of short-term memory span. *Journal of Experimental Child Psychology, 33*, 386–404.

Cavanaugh, J. C., & Borkowski, J. G. (1980). Searching for metamemory–memory connections: A developmental study. *Developmental Psychology, 16*, 441–453.

Frankel, M. T., & Rollins, H. A. (1985). Associative and categorical hypotheses of organization in the free recall of adults and children. *Journal of Experimental Child Psychology, 40*, 304–318.

Gruneberg, M. M., Morris, P. E., & Sykes, R. N. (1988). *Practical aspects of memory: Current research and issues: Vol. 1. Memory in everyday life.* Chichester, England: Wiley.

Kail, R. V. (1979). Use of strategies and individual differences in children's memory. *Developmental Psychology, 15*, 251–255.

Knopf, M., Körkel, J., Schneider, W., & Weinert, F. (1988). Human memory as a faculty versus human memory as a set of specific abilities: Evidence from a life-span approach. In F. E. Weinert and M. Perlmutter (Eds.), *Memory development: Universal changes and individual differences* (pp. 331–352). Hillsdale, NJ: Lawrence Erlbaum Associates.

Knopf, M., & Quadflieg, N. (1989). Das Memory-Spiel: Zeichen verborgener Gedächtniskunst kleiner Kinder? [The memory game: Signs of hidden memory skill in young children?]. *Zeitschrift für Entwicklungspsychologie und Pädagogische Psychologie, 21*, 110–123.

Mandler, J. M., & Johnson, N. S. (1977). Remembrance of things parsed: Story structure and recall. *Cognitive Psychology, 9,* 111–151.

Novak, M., & Lewis, G. (1967). Coefficient alpha and the reliability of composite measurement. *Psychometrika, 32,* 1–13.

Rupp, S. (1992). *Das menschliche Gedaechtnis: Ein generelles Kapazitaetsmerkmal oder ein Muster aus spezifischen Faehigkeiten?* [Human memory: A phenomenon of general capacity or a pattern of specific abilities?]. Unpublished thesis, Department of Psychology, University of Wuerzburg, Germany.

Schneider, W. (1986). The role of conceptual knowledge and metamemory in the development of organizational processes in memory. *Journal of Experimental Child Psychology, 42,* 318–336.

Schneider, W., & Pressley, M. (1989). *Memory development between 2 and 20.* New York: Springer-Verlag.

Siegler, R. S. (1986). *Children's thinking.* Englewood Cliffs, NJ: Prentice-Hall.

Sunderland, A., Harris, J. E., & Baddeley, A. D. (1983). Do laboratory tests predict everyday memory? A neuropsychological study. *Journal of Verbal Learning and Verbal Behavior, 22,* 341–357.

Sunderland, A., Watts, K., Baddeley, A. D., & Harris, J. E. (1986). Subjective memory assessment and test performance in elderly adults. *Journal of Gerontology, 41,* 376–384.

Van der Feen, B., Van Balen, H. G. G., & Eling, P. (1988). Assessing everyday memory in rehabilitation: A validation study. *International Journal of Rehabilitation Research, 11,* 406.

Weinert, F. E., Schneider, W., & Knopf, M. (1988). Individual differences in memory development across the life span. In P. B. Baltes, D. L. Featherman, & R. M. Lerner (Eds.), *Life span development and behavior* (Vol. 9, pp. 39–85). Hillsdale, NJ: Lawrence Erlbaum Associates.

West, R. L., Crook, T. H., & Barron, K. L. (1992). Everyday memory performance across the life span: Effects of age and noncognitive individual differences. *Psychology and Aging, 7,* 72–82.

Wilson, B. A., Baddeley, A. D., & Cockburn, J. (1988). The trials, tribulations, and triumphs in the development of a test of everyday memory. In M. M. Gruneberg, P. E. Morris, & R. N. Sykes (Eds.), *Practical aspects of memory: Current research and issues: Vol. 1. Memory in everyday life* (pp. 249–254). Chichester, England: Wiley.

Wilson, B., Cockburn, J., Baddeley, A., & Hiorns, R. (1989). The development and validation of a test battery for detecting and monitoring everyday memory problems. *Journal of Clinical and Experimental Neuropsychology, 11,* 855–870.

Chapter 14

Memory Development During Early and Middle Childhood: Findings From the Munich Longitudinal Study (LOGIC)

Wolfgang Schneider
University of Würzburg

Franz E. Weinert
Max Planck Institute for Psychological Research, Munich

In this chapter, we address several issues that have been neglected in traditional research on memory development. So far, research on memory development has been based on a few basic beliefs derived from dominant theories of cognitive development. According to one of these core beliefs, developmental change patterns in memory are universal, that is, true for all human beings. As a consequence, research has concentrated on universal developmental trends, ignoring intra- and interindividual differences in memory.

Another implicit assumption is that although research has been conducted on a variety of memory phenomena (i.e., structural components and processes of encoding, storage, and retrieval), human memory should be treated as a complex but unitary functional unit or trait. In other words, it is often implicitly assumed that the processes and outcomes observed in memory tasks are indicators of a single, unitary trait-like construct that can be used to explain cross-situational consistency and intraindividual stability in memory performances.

Finally, one basic assumption of research in memory development is that the course of developmental changes can be roughly estimated by the analysis of developmental differences. Instead of longitudinally following patterns of memory development by observing the same children over a longer period of time, more than 99% of the available studies have focused on comparisons of different age groups (cf. Kail, 1990; Schneider & Pressley, 1989).

In the present chapter, we explore the validity of these core assumptions by using data from the Munich Longitudinal Study of the Genesis of Individual Competencies (LOGIC), being conducted at the Max Planck Institute for Psychological Research in Munich (cf. Weinert & Schneider, 1986, 1989a, 1989b, 1992). The study began in 1984 with about two hundred 4-year-old children, followed each year since then. So far, nine waves (measurement points) have been completed, with the last wave ending in July, 1993. There are still 186 subjects in the sample who just finished sixth grade. One last follow-up measurement point is planned for 1997.

As indicated by the name of the study, a broad range of measures tapping cognitive skills (e.g., intelligence, memory, problems solving, logical thinking) and noncognitive areas such as social processes, moral judgments, and aspects of personality have been used. As can be seen from Fig. 14.1, a subsample of about 120 LOGIC subjects additionally participated in a larger project (SCHO-LASTIC) that carefully assessed classroom learning conditions and children's progress in subject matters such as reading, spelling, and math. Basic information on academic achievement was also available for the rest of the LOGIC children.

Despite this broad perspective, the development of memory is one of its core issues. It is thus possible to investigate the three described main topics based on the data of our longitudinal study. First of all, we want to reconsider the question of whether the memory concept represents a general, unitary human faculty, or a variety of specific and independent abilities or skills. Although the issue of intertask consistency does not necessarily require longitudinal studies, it is unfortunate that the analysis of developmental trends in the interrelation of memory

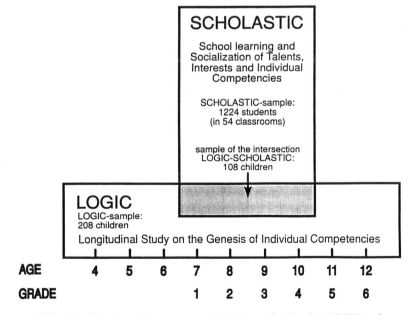

FIG. 14.1. Samples and time course of the longitudinal studies LOGIC and SCHOLASTIC.

performance variables has been exclusively based on cross-sectional data. The comparison of previous findings with data from our longitudinal subjects allows us to evaluate the longitudinal replicability and validity of results derived from earlier cross-sectional research.

In a similar vein, longitudinal data can be helpful in validating findings from cross-sectional studies that focus on interrelationships among strategies, knowledge, and performance in classic memory tasks. For example, numerous studies based on the sort-recall paradigm have shown that sorting and clustering and memory performance increase over the kindergarten and elementary school years, and that closer interrelations among strategies and memory performance result as a function of age (e.g., Frankel & Rollins, 1985; Hasselhorn, 1990; Schneider, 1986).

However, the lack of longitudinal data limits the inferences that can be drawn from existing research in important ways (cf. Ornstein, Baker-Ward, & Naus, 1988; Schneider & Weinert, 1989). In particular, cross-sectional studies do not yield information on the stability of interindividual differences in intraindividual change. For instance, the increase in clustering and recall performance observed in cross-sectional studies between the ages of 6 and 10 could be due to the fact that most children in a sample have made some progress in organizational behaviors and memory performance, or that some children have made enormous progress whereas most children have remained the same or even declined (cf. Schneider & Sodian, 1991). Thus the questions of core interest here are whether or not our longitudinal data on the sort-recall paradigm and related memory tasks replicate the cross-sectional findings, and, if so, whether the effects characterize most children of the sample or are based on only a few subjects showing considerable improvement over time. The assessment of group stabilities over time (i.e., test–retest correlations) helps in exploring the latter problem. If effects are based on similar strategy and recall improvements in almost all LOGIC children, overall group stability should be high.

This leads to a third, related issue. Group stability of memory behavior and performance refers to stability at the aggregate level, which is typically assessed via test–retest correlations. Aggregate stability indicated by test–retest correlations does not allow inferences on the individual level (Asendorpf, 1990; Valsiner, 1986). That is, although test–retest correlations inform us about the overall stability of the sample, they do not give information on the stability or lability of individual subjects within the sample. In order to explore intraindividual persistence of subjects over time, it is necessary to estimate individual stabilities and their variance in a population (i.e., differential stability). Individual stability refers to constancy of relative position, that is, to the constancy of an individual's standing relative to some reference groups across age (cf. Wohlwill, 1973).

It is obvious that cross-sectional studies do not allow the prediction of individual differences despite general developmental change. We thus do not know whether a 6-year-old's level of performance on a memory task relative to that of other 6-year-olds allows us to predict that child's relative position in his or her age group at age 8 or later. Our longitudinal data, however, provide information on this issue. Individual stabilities of verbal and nonverbal intelligence are also assessed in order to provide a frame of reference for the memory measures.

DOMAIN-SPECIFIC VERSUS GLOBAL MEMORY DEVELOPMENT

At the very beginning of experimental memory research in psychology, a controversial issue concerned the question of whether memory represents a general, unitary human faculty or a variety of specific and probably independent abilities. Ebbinghaus (1885) and Meumann (1918) already considered the possibility of considerable intraindividual differences in tasks covering different memory contents (e.g., memory for prose vs. memory for digits). This position was confirmed by a number of psychometric studies conducted during the first half of this century that found low correlations among memory tests using different materials or assessment procedures (for a review, see Knopf, Körkel, Schneider, & Weinert, 1988).

A few comprehensive studies conducted in the second half of this century and using adult samples yielded similar results. For example, Katzenberger (1967) tested 109 college students on about 20 different memory tasks that differed according to type of assessment (recall vs. recognition), test materials (digits, syllables, words, sentences, and pictures), and the time interval between task presentation and actual memory test. The pattern of intercorrelations among the various memory tasks corresponded to that found in the earlier studies, and a factor analysis computed on the intercorrelation matrix lead to an eight factor solution. There was thus reason to infer from these studies that the term memory refers to a variety of different abilities or dimensions.

Developmental studies on this issue are rare. Stevenson, Hale, Klein, and Miller (1968) compared third to seventh graders' memory performances in different tasks. Although they reported intertask correlations higher than those obtained in the earlier studies with adults, the coefficients were not of high magnitude. Kail (1979) investigated the assumption that interindividual differences in memory may reflect a general strategic factor. That is, some people may use memory strategies consistently and perform well, whereas others may use strategies poorly, and thus show low levels of recall. In Kail's study, third and sixth graders' strategy use and memory performance were compared across three different memory tasks. Results of a factor analysis seemed to confirm the hypothesis of a general strategic factor, at least for the older subjects. However, the intercorrelations among memory tasks and strategy measures tended to be small.

Probably the most convincing evidence in favor of a general strategy factor and high intertask correlations stems from a study by Cavanaugh and Borkowski

(1980). The authors presented kindergartners, first, third, and fifth graders with three different memory tasks (i.e., cognitive cueing, free sort, alphabet search). The degree of consistency across the three tasks was assessed by intercorrelations among measures of study strategy, and clustering during recall. Cavanaugh and Borkowski found significant developmental improvements for almost all sets of intercorrelations, with strategy measures showing particularly high intertask correlations within each group. However, there may be some problems with the generalization of these findings because the three laboratory tasks used in this study (as well as those used by Kail) were similar in structure.

Given the discrepant findings on this issue, our research group has further explored the issue of intertask consistency by using two different data sets. The findings of the first study were presented at the first Ringberg memory conference several years ago and are published in detail elsewhere (cf. Knopf et al., 1988; Weinert, Schneider, & Knopf, 1988). Thus, only the main results are summarized here. A total of 578 children (106 third graders, 236 fifth graders, and 236 seventh graders) participated in this short-term longitudinal study. In addition, memory behavior and performance of 124 adults and elderly people aged 50 to 84 years was assessed in this project. Memory performance in sort-recall tasks with clusterable and nonclusterable stimulus lists, memory span, and three measures assessing memory for text and text comprehension were used as the dependent variables.

Intertask correlations calculated for the child sample yielded the highest coefficients for the two sort-recall measures (ranging from .43 to .62 for the third to the seventh graders, respectively), whereas intercorrelations among text recall and comprehension measures were generally low (varying between .13 and .34). Based on their memory performance, children were additionally classified as high achievers (best 25%), medium achievers (next 50%), and low achievers (bottom 25%), separately for each memory task. Consistency of classification was compared for various combinations of memory measures as depicted in Table 14.1.

As can be seen from Table 14.1, the highest intertask stability coefficients were found for the clusterable and nonclusterable word lists. When all three text variables were simultaneously considered, only 4% of the third graders, 17% of the fifth graders, and 22% of the seventh graders were consistently classified as high, medium, or low achievers.

Although the intertask correlations found for the adult sample were generally higher, they also did not support the assumption that individual differences in memory performance are due to a unitary memory function. Thus, the findings presented by Knopf et al. (1988) shed doubt on the hypothesis that concepts like a *general strategic factor* (Kail, 1979) or subgroups of *metamnemonically sophisticated subjects* (Flavell, 1981) can be empirically identified.

Although the results of most developmental studies suggest that intertask consistency is low to moderate for most memory tasks and age groups, they do not give much information regarding developmental trends in intercorrelations

TABLE 14.1
Percentage of Subjects Consistently Classified as High, Medium,
or Low in Achievement for Various Combinations of Memory Tasks

	Children		
Measures	3rd Graders	5th Graders	7th Graders
Nonclusterable and taxonomic clusterable lists	50	56	64
Word lists and memory span	24	21	24
Text inferences and text episodic memory	39	44	49
Text inferences and text contradictions	31	44	49
Text episodic memory and contradictions	19	31	39
All three text variables	4	17	22
All text variables and memory span	2	7	7
All word list variables and all text variables	0	4	7
All word list variables and all text variables and memory span	0	2	2

as a function of the type of task. Our Munich longitudinal study seems suited to explore this issue in more detail because it covers a broad age range (children between 4 and 13 years of age), and it included repeated measurements on a variety of memory variables. That is, intraindividual differences in short-term memory capacity (word span, listening or sentence span), strategic memory (recall in a sort-recall task), and memory primarily based on scripted knowledge and world knowledge (text recall) could be assessed in this study.

The word-span task developed by Case, Kurland, and Goldberg (1982) was used in the first, third, fifth, and eighth years of the study. The second indicator of short-term memory capacity was the listening-span task by Daneman and Blennerhassett (1984) that required children to repeat sets of sentences in the correct order. This task was given in the third, fourth, fifth, and seventh years of the LOGIC study. Two different sort-recall tasks were presented. For pre-schoolers and kindergarten children (Waves 1 and 3), the materials were toys that could be clustered into four different semantic categories (cf. Schneider & Sodian, 1991; Sodian, Schneider, & Perlmutter, 1986). Because ceiling effects were anticipated for older children, longer lists of clusterable pictures were used later on (i.e., in the fifth, seventh, and ninth years of the LOGIC study). Finally, several measures of memory for text were included in the study (cf. Knopf & Waldmann, 1987). The story of a birthday party tapped memory performance based on scripted knowledge, and the remaining stories (e.g., playing with friends, moving houses) drew more heavily on children's world knowledge.

Based on the findings from previous developmental studies (Cavanaugh & Borkowski, 1980; Kail, 1979), we assumed that intercorrelations among memory variables should increase with increasing age of subjects, but still be only moderate for older elementary school children. The highest intercorrelations were expected for the various indicators of short-term memory capacity (i.e., word-,

TABLE 14.2

Synchronous Correlations Among Memory and IQ Measures Obtained
for 4-Year-Old Children (LOGIC Sample, N = 185)

Variables	(2)	(3)	(4)	(5)	(6)
(1) Word span	.21	.20	.25	.19	.22
(2) Recall in sort-recall task		.23	.36	.35	.21
(3) Text recall 1 (birthday)			.64	.44	.30
(4) Text recall 2 (playing)				.55	.24
(5) Verbal IQ					.44
(6) Nonverbal IQ					—

Note. All correlation coefficients are significant at the .05 level.

digit-, and sentence-span) on the one hand, and the parallel measures of text
recall (i.e., stories of birthday party, playing with friends, and moving houses)
on the other hand. We further assumed that the amount of text recall should
be related to short-term memory capacity, whereas strategic memory should
neither be closely related to memory capacity nor to text recall.

The synchronous intercorrelations of memory performance variables assessed
in Waves 1, 3, 5, and 7 are depicted in Tables 14.2 to 14.5. In addition, these
tables contain intercorrelations of memory variables with indicators of verbal
intelligence (the WISC) and nonverbal intelligence (i.e., the Columbia Mental
Maturity Scale from Wave 1 until Wave 5, and the Culture Fair Intelligence
Test in Wave 7). The comparison of various memory components with indicators
of intelligence should give us a better idea about whether we are dealing with
rather independent memory abilities or indicators of a unitary concept or trait.

As a main result, Tables 14.2 to 14.5 indicate that only a few developmental
trends can be observed. By and large, intercorrelations are low to moderate in size.
As predicted, the most substantial correlations were found for the parallel measures
of text recall ($rs = .64$ and .58 for the 4- and 6-year-olds, respectively), followed by
the intercorrelations between the two span measures (rs ranging from .37 to .46,

TABLE 14.3

Synchronous Correlations Among Memory and IQ Measures Obtained
for 6-Year-Old Children (LOGIC Sample; N = 192)

Variables	(2)	(3)	(4)	(5)	(6)	(7)
(1) Word span	.37	.09	.23	.17	.24	.31
(2) Sentence span		.23	.28	.34	.30	.41
(3) Recall in sort-recall task			.21	.33	.10	.19
(4) Text recall 1 (birthday)				.58	.38	.31
(5) Text recall 2 (moving)					.28	.24
(6) Verbal IQ						.38
(7) Nonverbal IQ						—

Note. Correlations larger than .15 are significant at the .05 level.

TABLE 14.4
Synchronous Correlations Among Memory and IQ Measures Obtained
for 8-Year-Old Children (LOGIC Sample; N = 205)

Variables	(2)	(3)	(4)	(5)	(6)	(7)
(1) Word span	.42	.46	.16	.15	.35	.17
(2) Sentence span		.46	.25	.33	.47	.28
(3) Digit span			.25	.29	.56	.37
(4) Recall in sort-recall task				.37	.24	.20
(5) Text recall (moving)					.36	.19
(6) Verbal IQ						.43
(7) Nonverbal IQ						—

Note. All correlation coefficients are significant at the .05 level.

median = .46). In both cases, no developmental trends could be observed. Also in line with our predictions, sentence span showed substantial correlations with memory for text, regardless of measurement point. Similarly, intercorrelations among the text recall and verbal intelligence measures were generally high, ranging between .36 and .55. Interestingly, intercorrelations of about the same size were obtained for the nonverbal and verbal intelligence measures.

Whereas free recall in a sort-recall task was only marginally linked to the memory capacity measures, its correlation with the text recall measures was at least moderate for all measurement points. The interrelationship between free recall in a sort-recall task and verbal intelligence varied as a function of measurement point, suggesting a u-shaped developmental pattern: That is, substantial correlations were found for both the first and last assessments, but not for the two measurement points in between.

Taken together, the pattern of intercorrelations depicted in Tables 14.2 to 14.5 does not support the view of memory as a unitary function or construct. With the exception of parallel measures of text recall and memory span, intraindividual across-task consistencies were low to moderate for all measurement

TABLE 14.5
Synchronous Correlations Among Memory and IQ Measures Obtained
for 10-Year-Old Children (LOGIC Sample; N = 202)

Variables	(2)	(3)	(4)	(5)	(6)	(7)
(1) Word span	.39	.46	.17	.15	.35	.27
(2) Sentence span		.46	.32	.43	.55	.40
(3) Digit span			.23	.16	.47	.31
(4) Recall in sort-recall task				.26	.34	.32
(5) Text recall (fictitious town)					.44	.42
(6) Verbal IQ						.50
(7) Nonverbal IQ						—

Note. All correlation coefficients are significant at the .05 level.

points. This seems all the more impressive as only verbal memory tasks were considered in the computations. The findings for the LOGIC children thus confirm results from earlier cross-sectional studies. However, they do not support the view conveyed in earlier developmental studies that intertask consistency increases as a function of age. There were almost no developmental trends in the overall intercorrelation pattern observed for the age range between 4 and 10 years of age.

LONGITUDINAL REPLICABILITY OF CROSS-SECTIONAL FINDINGS ON MEMORY DEVELOPMENT

The question of whether or not the basic findings of cross-sectional memory studies can be replicated with the LOGIC sample was already addressed in publications of our research group based on the preschool and kindergarten data (e.g., Schneider & Sodian, 1990, 1991).

Memory for Locations

In the study by Schneider and Sodian (1990), an attempt was made to validate the findings of an earlier cross-sectional study (Schneider & Sodian, 1988) that dealt with 4- and 6-year-olds' ability to use retrieval cues in a memory-for-location (hide-and-seek) task. One of the most important results of the cross-sectional study was that substantial interrelationships between children's metamemory (i.e., their knowledge about the utility of retrieval cues), the way they hid the items, the use of retrieval cues and memory performance could be found even for the youngest children in the sample (i.e., the 4-year-olds). The authors concluded that close links among knowledge, strategies, and performance can be demonstrated for memory tasks with which young children are familiar.

Although the replication data presented by Schneider and Sodian were not similarly impressive in that the intercorrelations obtained for the LOGIC children at the ages of 4 and 6 were somewhat lower in magnitude, they basically confirmed the pattern of results reported in the cross-sectional study. That is, reliable intercorrelations among knowledge, strategies, and memory performance were found at both age levels. However, an unexpected outcome of the replication study concerned group stabilities over the 2-year period. The test–retest correlations varied between .01 (metamemory) and .24 (recall), indicating almost no stability over time.

One possible reason for this finding is that memory and metamemory data cannot be reliably assessed in children of that age. To control for this possibility, Schneider and Sodian (1990) recruited an independent sample of 4-year-olds and presented them with the hide-and-seek task twice within a 2-week interval. As

TABLE 14.6
Intercorrelations Among Sorting During Study, Clustering During Recall, and
Free Recall in the Sort-Recall Task

Variables	(1)	(2)	(3)
(1) Sorting	—	.45	.34
(2) Clustering	.22	—	.42
(3) Free recall	.22	.28	—

Note. All correlation coefficients are significant at the .05 level. Results for the 4-year-olds are depicted below the diagonal; those for the 6-year-olds above the diagonal.

short-term stability of results was high for all variables (correlations between .60 and .80), it is unlikely that low long-term stability is due to unreliable measurement. Rather, the instability over time found for this memory task indicates that young children improved at different rates, thereby considerably changing their relative standing within their group between the two measurement points.

Sort-Recall

Another replication attempt (Schneider & Sodian, 1991; Sodian & Schneider, in press) concerned the sort-recall task previously described. We know from numerous studies that interrelations among encoding strategies (sorting), retrieval strategies (clustering), and memory performance in the sort-recall task increase with age (cf. Bjorklund, Muir-Broaddus, & Schneider, 1990; Pressley & Van Meter, 1993). As can be seen from Tables 14.6 and 14.7, this pattern was confirmed by our longitudinal data. Although interrelations among strategy and performance measures are comparably low for the 4-year-olds, they are of moderate size for the 6-year-olds, and indicate close links between strategy and performance measures for our children at the ages of 8 and 10.

What about group stability over time? As can be seen from Table 14.8, the findings are similar to those reported for the hide-and-seek task. The comparably highest group stabilities were obtained for the recall measure, with coefficients

TABLE 14.7
Intercorrelations Among Sorting During Study, Clustering During Recall, and
Free Recall in the Sort-Recall Task

Variables	(1)	(2)	(3)
(1) Sorting	—	.73	.60
(2) Clustering	.63	—	.70
(3) Free recall	.58	.55	—

Note. Results for the 8-year-olds are depicted below the diagonal; those for the 10-year-olds above the diagonal.

TABLE 14.8
Stability Over Time (Long-Term and Short-Term Stability) Obtained
for the Strategy and Recall Measures of the Sort-Recall Task (LOGIC Sample)

	Stability					
Variable	2-Year (4–6)	2-Year (6–8)	2-Year (8–10)	4-Year (4–8)	6-Year (4–10)	Short-Term
Recall	.36	.29	.39	.20	.16	.68
Sorting	.17	.12	.07	.08	.02	.85
Clustering	.12	.16	.12	.08	.19	.64

varying between .11 (4-year stability from age 6 to age 10) and .39 (2-year stability from age 8 to age 10). Accordingly, long-term group stabilities for the recall measure were low to moderate. Even lower stability coefficients were found for the two strategy measures. Due to large sample size, a few of them were still statistically significant. By and large, however, the coefficients obtained for the strategy measures indicate extremely low stability over time.

In order to decide whether the amount of instability found for the variables in the sort-recall task was due to unreliability of measures or to true fluctuation in the specific competencies, their short-term stability was also assessed. As in the hide-and-seek task, an independent sample of thirty 4-year-old children was given the sort-recall task twice within a 2-week interval. Short-term stability coefficients for the strategy and performance measures are also given in Table 14.8 (last column). They show that the memory variables could be reliably assessed. Thus, long-term instability in the various memory measures seems to be due to differential rates of individual changes between 4 and 10 years of age.

Our sort-recall longitudinal analyses leave us with a puzzling result. On the one hand, we were able to replicate the finding that strategy–recall relationships increase with age. On the other hand, the low group stabilities indicate that children change their position in the reference group, regardless of memory variable and measurement point. The strategy–memory performance link can be demonstrated for each age level (beginning at age 6), but different children contribute to the effects at different measurement points.

Please note that long-term stability coefficients for other memory performance measures were not similarly low. As can be seen from Table 14.9, long-term stabilities for the preschool and kindergarten text recall variables equalled those for verbal and nonverbal intelligence assessed between ages 4 and 8. The 2-year stability of the sentence span measure was even more impressive (.68), almost reaching the stability of verbal IQ between the ages of 7 and 9 (.81). One possible explanation for the comparably low group stabilities observed for free recall in the sort-recall task is that here, memory performance was influenced by children's strategies (which obviously varied across measurement points),

TABLE 14.9
Stability Over Time for Selected Memory Performance
and Intelligence Measures of the LOGIC Study

Variables	Wave	2	3	4	5	6	7	8
					Wave			
Word span	1		.13		.32			.26
	3				.47			.43
	5							.49
Sentence span	3			.68	.68			
	4				.70			
	5						.71	
Text recall	1	.53	.46					
(birthday)	2		.54					
Text recall	1		.47	.28				
(playing)	2		.34					
Text recall	2		.54	.43	.42			
(moving)	3			.49	.43			
	4				.44			
Verbal IQ	1	.56			.53	.53		
	2				.59	.55		
	4					.81		
Nonverbal IQ	1		.55		.42		.37	
	3				.54		.55	
	5						.55	

whereas performance on primarily nonstrategic memory tasks, such as text recall and sentence span, was not similarly affected by fluctuations in behavior.

INDIVIDUAL AND DIFFERENTIAL STABILITY

To further test the assumption of differential rates of individual changes in the sort-recall task, individual stability was assessed. The difference between group stability and individual stability may not be immediately apparent. Group stability refers to the correlation, in a sample of persons, of two assessments of the same memory variable at different points in time. On the other hand, individual stability refers to the correlation, in a sample of variables, of two assessments of the same person at different points in time. Thus, individual stability describes the degree to which the ordering of attributes within each individual remains constant over time. This approach is also termed *constancy of relative position*.

According to Wohlwill (1973), the most general representation of individual stability is the amount of across-age variability shown in an individual's relative standing within the reference group over time. A traditional measure is the lability score (Bayley, 1949), the across-age standard deviation of an individual's

z scores. In order to compute this score, the relative position of a given subject concerning his or her performance on a given variable (e.g., text recall) is assessed separately for each measurement point and converted into a z score. The lability score thus represents the degree of variability of the subject's relative position across measurement points. For example, whereas lability scores close to zero indicate that the subjects did not change his or her position in the sample over time, large lability scores indicate considerable instability of the subject's relative position across measurement points.

In one of the few available longitudinal studies of grade-school children's memory, Kunzinger (1985) used the lability score to assess individual stability for rehearsal set size. Kunzinger presented an overt rehearsal task to 7-year-olds who were retested 2 years later. There was an increase in rehearsal set size with development (from 1.7 to 2.6 items). Rehearsal set size at the first measurement point was not related to recall at this measurement point, but predicted recall 2 years later. A particularly high level of individual stability for rehearsal set size indicated that those children who initially showed larger set sizes maintained their position relative to the group 2 years later. Guttentag, Ornstein, and Siemens (1987) observed comparable longitudinal stability between 8 and 9 years of age.

Because of space restrictions, our analyses of individual stabilities in the sort-recall task are restricted to the recall variable. Untransformed individual stability coefficients (z scores) are given to illustrate the amount of lability over time observed in the recall data. Although small z-score differences obtained for an individual's recall data at the first and second measurement point indicate considerable constancy of the individual's standing relative to the reference group, large z-score differences reflect individual instability over time.

The mean lability score (0.89) found for the first two recall assessments (i.e., for age 4 and age 6) indicates that the average absolute z-score difference comprised almost a standard deviation, thus reflecting considerable individual instability over time. Differential stability, as indicated by the standard deviation of the mean individual stability coefficient, was also substantial for preschool period (0.68). To explore possible reasons for differential stability, the distribution of the lability scores was first normalized following a transformation procedure suggested by Asendorpf (1990). The transformed individual stability scores were then intercorrelated with selected external variables of interest (e.g., initial recall level, intelligence, sex, etc.). Correlating individual stabilities with external variables is important because it may facilitate the explanation of differential stability and also gives information about possible regression-towards-the-mean effects in the data.

As described by Schneider and Sodian (1991) in more detail, the additional analyses showed that instability seemed to be particularly high for subjects scoring low at the initial measurement point, whereas it was comparably low for those children showing above-average recall at the first measurement point. Our analyses thus indicated that individual stability was rather high for the majority of children in the sample and particularly high for a subgroup of children, namely those with initially high recall scores.

Results for the elementary school period were different in that the mean lability score (0.39) found for the recall assessments in Waves 5 and 7 indicated a comparably smaller average z-score difference that comprised slightly more than one third of a standard deviation. Although differential stability was still substantial, the amount of instability was neither significantly related to initial recall level ($r = -.10$), nor to intelligence, sex, or other external variables used in our correlational analyses. Although detailed subgroup analyses seem necessary to explain the considerable differential stability over time, a first visual inspection of the raw data suggests that a rather small group of unstable children contributes to the high differential instability found for recall in the sort-recall task.

The importance of initial memory performance for subsequent individual stability over time during the preschool and kindergarten years was also confirmed for the short-term memory capacity measures. Differential instability for the word span measure assessed at the ages of 4 and 6 was particularly high (1.25). A correlation of $-.41$ ($p < .01$) was found between initial assessment and the transformed individual stability scores, indicating that children with initially higher memory spans tended to be more stable over time than those subjects with initially low spans.

A similar pattern of findings was observed for the sentence span task which was first given when children were in the last year of kindergarten. Transformed individual stabilities assessed for the time between kindergarten and first grade correlated significantly with initial memory span and verbal intelligence ($rs = -.32$ and $-.30$, respectively). Children with initially higher sentence–listening spans and higher verbal IQ scores showed higher individual stability over time. However, as in the sort-recall tasks external variables (e.g., initial recall or intelligence) did not explain differential stability in later memory span assessments.

CONCLUDING REMARKS

In this chapter, data from the Munich longitudinal study were used to explore three neglected issues in research on memory development. The first question concerned the issue of domain-specific versus global memory development. Although this topic has been investigated with adult samples since the beginning of this century, developmental evidence is scarce. Overall, our longitudinal analyses based on various indicators of verbal memory (i.e., memory span, text recall, recall in a sort-recall task) did not support the view of memory as a general construct. Intertask consistency was low to moderate for tasks dealing with strategic versus nonstrategic verbal memory (i.e., recall in a sort-recall task versus short-term memory span). The synchronous intercorrelations were also far from perfect when parallel measures of text recall were compared. Furthermore, intertask correlations did not change dramatically as a function of time. Our findings thus indicate that the (moderate) developmental trends observed in several cross-sectional studies cannot be confirmed by longitudinal data: That is, intertask correlations among verbal memory measures do not seem to increase with increasing age, at least not between the ages of 4 and 10.

The next crucial issue concerned the question of whether or not the analysis of individual differences via simultaneous comparisons of children from different age groups tells us the truth about developmental changes within subjects over time. Given that the sort-recall paradigm has been extensively used to demonstrate age-dependent relationships between children's strategies and their memory performance, the sort-recall task was chosen as a representative example. The findings were intriguing. The analysis of data separately for each measurement point yielded results that squared well with cross-sectional evidence. That is, correlations between strategies and performance increased steadily as a function of age. However, the inspection of group stabilities over time revealed that these stabilities were rather low, suggesting that probably different children contributed to the effects at different points in time. Needless to say, the analysis of cross-sectional data alone would never offer us such interesting insights. Although we do not have a satisfying explanation for this phenomenon at the moment, it is interesting enough to be researched in more detail. Analyses of individual growth curves may be suited to solve this puzzle. Regarding the sort-recall task, for example, one particularly interesting point concerns the question of interindividual differences in the acquisition of organizational strategies. Although group data suggest a steady, continuous increase in strategic skill, the group data may mask the factual variability of individual acquisition patterns. Growth curve analyses should help in settling this point.

Our third major issue concerned longitudinal analyses of group and individual stabilities over time. We found that group stabilities were particularly low for the strategy and performance measures of the sort-recall task, whereas the consistencies obtained for the short-term memory capacity and text-recall measures were considerably higher. The group stabilities obtained for the sentence span and text recall measures were comparable to those found for the verbal and nonverbal intelligence measures.

Although mean individual stability was rather high for these measures, a closer inspection of the variance of individidual stability scores (i.e., differential stability) showed that differential stability was particularly low for several memory measures assessed in young children. In accord with the assumptions first presented by Schneider and Sodian (1990, 1991), we believe these findings reflect genuine instability, not measurement error. However, the detailed analyses by Schneider and Sodian (1991) and the additional findings presented in this chapter suggest that in young children, specific personality characteristics such as shyness or social anxiety can considerably influence results and thus yield biased estimates of true developmental change. In our view, it is difficult if not impossible to identify those children and their problems in cross-sectional studies. It is one of the major advantages of longitudinal studies of memory development that the issue of individual and differential stability can be appropriately addressed. They provide us with a comprehensive picture of interindividual differences in developmental change, thereby going beyond the information usually obtained from cross-sectional studies.

ACKNOWLEDGMENTS

We wish to thank Jan Stefanek for his assistance in data analyses and David Bjorklund for his valuable comments on an earlier version of the chapter.

REFERENCES

Asendorpf, J. B. (1990). The measurement of individual consistency. *Methodika, 4*, 1–23.

Bayley, N. (1949). Consistency and variability in the growth of intelligence from birth to eighteen years. *Journal of Genetic Psychology, 75*, 165–196.

Bjorklund, D. F., Muir-Broaddus, J. E., & Schneider, W. (1990). The role of knowledge in the development of strategies. In D. F. Bjorklund (Ed.), *Children's strategies: Contemporary views of cognitive development* (pp. 93–128). Hillsdale, NJ: Lawrence Erlbaum Associates.

Case, R., Kurland, D. M., & Goldberg, J. (1982). Operational efficiency and the growth of short-term memory span. *Journal of Experimental Child Psychology, 33*, 386–404.

Cavanaugh, J. C., & Borkowski, J. G. (1980). Searching for metamemory-memory connections: A developmental study. *Developmental Psychology, 16*, 441–453.

Daneman, M., & Blennerhassett, A. (1984). How to assess the listening comprehension skills of prereaders. *Journal of Educational Psychology, 76*, 1372–1381.

Ebbinghaus, H. (1885). *Über das Gedächtnis* [About memory]. Leipzig: Duncker.

Flavell, J. H. (1981). Cognitive monitoring. In P. Dickson (Ed.), *Children's oral communication skills* (pp. 35–60). New York: Academic Press.

Frankel, M. T., & Rollins, H. A. (1985). Associative and categorical hypotheses of organization in the free recall of adults and children. *Journal of Experimental Child Psychology, 40*, 304–318.

Guttentag, R. E., Ornstein, P. A., & Siemens, L. (1987). Children's spontaneous rehearsal: Transitions in strategy acquisition. *Cognitive Development, 2*, 307–326.

Hasselhorn, M. (1990). The emergence of strategic knowledge activation in categorical clustering during retrieval. *Journal of Experimental Child Psychology, 50*, 59–80.

Kail, R. V. (1979). Use of strategies and individual differences in children's memory. *Developmental Psychology, 15*, 251–255.

Kail, R. V. (1990). *The development of memory in children* (3rd ed.). San Francisco: Freeman.

Katzenberger, L. (1967). *Gedächtnis oder Gedächtnisse* [Memory or memories]. Munich: Ehrenwirth.

Knopf, M., Körkel, J., Schneider, W., & Weinert, F. E. (1988). Human memory as a faculty versus human memory as a set of specific abilities: Evidence from a life-span approach. In F. E. Weinert & M. Perlmutter (Eds.), *Memory development: Universal changes and individual differences* (pp. 331–352). Hillsdale, NJ: Lawrence Erlbaum Associates.

Knopf, M., & Waldmann, M. R. (1987). Memory for texts. In F. E. Weinert & W. Schneider (Eds.), *The Munich Longitudinal Study on the Genesis of Individual Competencies (LOGIC), Report No. 2: Documentation of assessment procedures used in waves one to three.* (Tech. Rep., pp. 27–34). Munich: Max Planck Institute for Psychological Research.

Kunzinger, E. L. (1985). A short-term longitudinal study of memorial development during early grade school. *Developmental Psychology, 21*, 642–646.

Meumann, E. (1918). *Ökonomie und Technik des Gedächtnisses (Vol. 1)* [Economy and technique of memory]. Leipzig: Klinkhardt.

Ornstein, P. A., Baker-Ward, L., & Naus, M. J. (1988). The development of mnemonic skill. In F. E. Weinert & M. Perlmutter (Eds.), *Memory development: Universal changes and individual differences* (pp. 31–50). Hillsdale, NJ: Lawrence Erlbaum Associates.

Pressley, M., & Van Meter, P. (1993). Memory strategies: Natural development and use following instruction. In R. Pasnak & M. L. Howe (Eds.), *Emergent themes in cognitive development: Vol. 2. Competencies* (pp. 128–165). New York: Springer-Verlag.

Schneider, W. (1986). The role of conceptual knowledge and metamemory in the development of organizational processes in memory. *Journal of Experimental Child Psychology, 42*, 218–236.

Schneider, W., & Pressley, M. (1989). *Memory development between 2 and 20.* New York: Springer-Verlag.

Schneider, W., & Sodian, B. (1988). Metamemory–memory behavior relationships in young children: Evidence from a memory-for-location task. *Journal of Experimental Child Psychology, 45*, 209–233.

Schneider, W., & Sodian, B. (1990). Gedächtnisentwicklung im Vorschulalter: "Theoriewandel" im kindlichen Verständnis des Lernens und Erinnerns? [Memory development in preschoolers: "Theory change" in children's understanding of learning and remembering?]. In M. Knopf & W. Schneider (Eds.), *Entwicklung. Allgemeine Verläufe—Individuelle Unterschiede—Pädagogische Konsequenzen. Festschrift zum 60. Geburtstag von Franz Emanuel Weinert* (pp. 45–64). Göttingen: Hogrefe.

Schneider, W., & Sodian, B. (1991). A longitudinal study of young children's memory behavior and performance in a sort-recall task. *Journal of Experimental Child Psychology, 51*, 14–29.

Schneider, W., & Weinert, F. E. (1989). Universal trends and individual differences in memory development. In A. de Ribaupierre (Ed.), *Transition mechanisms in child development: The longitudinal perspective* (pp. 68–106). Cambridge: Cambridge University Press.

Sodian, B., & Schneider, W. (in press). Memory strategy development—Gradual increase, sudden insight, or roller coaster? In F. E. Weinert & W. Schneider (Eds.), *The Munich Longitudinal Study on the Genesis of Individual Competencies (LOGIC).* Cambridge, England: Cambridge University Press.

Sodian, B., Schneider, W., & Perlmutter, M. (1986). Recall, clustering, and metamemory in young children. *Journal of Experimental Child Psychology, 41*, 395–410.

Stevenson, H. W., Hale, G. A., Klein, R. F., & Miller, L. K. (1968). Interrelations and correlates in children's learning and problem solving. *Monographs of the Society for Research in Child Development, 33.*

Valsiner, J. (1986). Between groups and individuals. Psychologists' and laypersons' interpretations of correlational findings. In J. Valsiner (Ed.), *The individual subject and scientific psychology* (pp. 113–151). New York: Plenum Press.

Weinert, F. E., & Schneider, W. (Eds.). (1986). *First report on the Munich Longitudinal Study on the Genesis of Individual Competencies (LOGIC).* Munich: Max Planck Institute for Psychological Research.

Weinert, F. E., & Schneider, W. (Eds.). (1989a). *The Munich Longitudinal Study on the Genesis of Individual Competencies (LOGIC), Report No. 5: Results of wave three* (Tech. Rep.). Munich: Max Planck Institute for Psychological Research.

Weinert, F. E., & Schneider, W. (Eds.). (1989b). *The Munich Longitudinal Study on the Genesis of Individual Competencies (LOGIC), Report No. 6: Psychological development in the preschool years: Longitudinal results of wave one to three* (Tech. Rep.). Munich: Max Planck Institute for Psychological Research.

Weinert, F. E., & Schneider, W. (Eds.). (1992). *The Munich Longitudinal Study on the Genesis of Individual Competencies (LOGIC), Report No. 8: Results of wave six* (Tech. Rep.). Munich: Max Planck Institute for Psychological Research.

Weinert, F. E., Schneider, W., & Knopf, M. (1988). Individual differences in memory development across the life-span. In P. B. Baltes, D. L. Featherman, & R. M. Lerner (Eds.), *Life-span development and behavior* (Vol. 9, pp. 39–85). Hillsdale, NJ: Lawrence Erlbaum Associates.

Wohlwill, J. F. (1973). *The study of behavioral development.* New York: Academic Press.

Part IV

PRACTICAL ASPECTS OF THEORY-ORIENTED RESEARCH ON MEMORY DEVELOPMENT

Learning Environments and Skill Generalization: How Contexts Facilitate Regulatory Processes and Efficacy Beliefs

John G. Borkowski
University of Notre Dame

Nithi Muthukrishna
University of Natal, South Africa

> *Kate, a 3-year-old from South Bend, IN, was playing in the München's English Garden on a sunny summer afternoon. As the proud owner of a new water gun, she was in the midst of an especially enjoyable outing. Kate's tranquility was shattered, however, when a preschool boy, clothed only from the waist up, seized her gun and proceeded to escape up a nearby slide. Kate was flabbergasted by the loss of her gun or by the "dress," or rather "undress," of the young thief. She drew upon her only weapon, a German phrase learned over the course of the previous few weeks to obtain ice cream: "Geben Sie mir bitte ein Eis." Forced by circumstance and motivated by an impelling drive to retrieve her prized weapon, she yelled at the young boy on the slide: "Geben Sie mir bitte ein 'gun'."*

This brief episode highlights the central theme of this chapter: The generalization of previously learned skills and knowledge depends on the presence of regulatory processes—that activate the cognitive system and permit strategic behavior to occur—and motivational beliefs that instigate self-regulation in new and challenging contexts. We argue that it is possible to design educational systems that utilize metacognitive theory and capitalize on the propensity of students to become independent learners, active information processors, and analytic thinkers. First, we briefly review several innovative research programs that provide compelling evidence about the power of contextually sensitive learning environments in fostering the acquisition of skills that lead to independent learning and thinking. Our concern is with identifying cognitive features common to effective instruction, as well as the characteristics of clear thinking, that produce independent, generalizable learning skills. Next, we propose a metacognitively based model that helps to integrate and explain a wide spectrum of contemporary instructional research. Finally, we present a recent study that compares the effectiveness of various instructional contexts on the acquisition of the metacognitive skills—especially self regulatory skills and associated beliefs about self-efficacy—that are assumed necessary for skill generalization.

INNOVATIVE CLASSROOM RESEARCH PROGRAMS

Most educators share an interest in teaching higher level thinking skills and promoting conceptual understanding in their students. This concern is driven, perhaps, by the fact only a small percentage of high school graduates demonstrate complex, multistep reasoning (Dossey, Mullis, Lindquist, & Chambers, 1988). Few high school graduates function at advanced reading levels (Mullis & Jenkins, 1990). Furthermore, our current patterns of teaching and assessment create the illusion of effective learning when, in fact, desirable forms of durable learning are not occurring in classrooms throughout the world (Romberg, 1992). When teaching is directed at a limited array of content materials, and assessment instruments mirror only isolated bits of knowledge such as vocabulary and elementary math, educational programs can appear reasonably successful, at least on the surface. In reality, however, simple-minded and narrow approaches to instruction—often supported by reform movements directed at increased accountability—instill limited knowledge and only rudimentary cognitive skills that remain inert outside the classroom and testing contexts (Salomon & Globerson, 1987).

Perkins and Salomon (1989) and Lockhart, Lamon, and Gick (1988) suggested that problem-oriented rather than fact-oriented instruction has the potential to produce knowledge that is used spontaneously in new settings. Merely presenting problems to be solved, and examples of their solutions, however, provide no guarantee that students will profit from these examples or develop the skills necessary for guiding their thinking in new contexts. Furthermore, the presentation of problems does not automatically develop the skills of problem finding and problem formulation that seem so important in everyday life (Bransford, Hasselbring, Barron, Kutewicz, Littlefield, & Goin, 1988). Assessment procedures often fail to place importance on how students make use of information they learned during solving problems. Thus, Wagner and Sternberg (1986) noted that academic tests more than not fail to assess students' abilities to solve nonroutine problems; that is, tests generally have a single correct answer, and permit a correct solution method, rather than a variety of possible approaches. Hence, the instruction of problem-solving skills—broadly understood—remains a distant and unobtainable objective for many teachers as they participate in educational reform movements, especially given entrenched classroom practices and a dearth of theoretical guidance.

In recent years, several innovative approaches have emerged, each aimed at making an important difference in teaching students to become independent thinkers and learners. These approaches reflect a trend towards the integration of instruction about thinking within the content areas (Jones & Idol, 1990; Resnick & Klopfer, 1989). In the next sections, we provide a selective overview of the recent innovations in instruction that appear to produce more generalized skills-based learning. Then, a theoretical framework that helps explain their effectiveness is proposed; this metacognitive-based framework captures some of the intended, and unintended, effects of contextually sensitive instructions. Finally, new data are presented that manipulate the contextual environments in which strategy instructions are embedded in order to begin to determine more appropriate methods for facilitating skill generalization, both inside and outside the classroom.

Cognition and Technology at Vanderbilt

The Cognition and Technology Group at Vanderbilt (CTGV) developed and tested a variety of computer-based programs designed to motivate students and to help them analyze complex problems. In several respects, the theoretical framework that guides the work of CTGV is consistent with *constructivist theories of instruction* (Cobb, 1990; Schoenfeld, 1989).

A basic assumption of the constructivist position is that students cannot learn to engage in effective knowledge construction simply by being exposed to information or by being explicitly taught strategies (Bransford, Franks, Vye, & Sherwood, 1989). They need to learn to construct effective problem representations through the use of symbolic and physical models and through in-depth exploration, reasoning, and application of problem-solving strategies (Brown, Collins, & Duguid, 1989; Scardamalia & Bereiter, 1985). This approach to knowledge construction also helps students to engage in generative rather than passive learning. This form of learning emphasizes the essential need for students to bring to each learning situation a number of preconceptions or prior knowledge states. These frameworks enable students to engage in argumentation and reflection as they use, refine, and enlarge their existing knowledge states in order to understand and evaluate new or alternative points of view.

Two important concepts embedded in the programs of CTGV are the concepts of *situated cognition* (Brown, Collins, & Duguid, 1989) and *apprenticeship learning* (Collins, Brown, & Newman, 1989). Proponents of situated learning criticize decontextualized forms of instruction, which often separate knowledge and action. The argument is that decontextualized knowledge produces inert knowledge (Brown et al., 1989). In contrast, knowledge associated with situated learning is learned in the context of meaningful goals. Additionally, it is essential that the various uses of new knowledge are made explicit through concrete illustrations derived by the class.

For instance, in the reading programs developed by Palincsar and Brown (1984) referred to as *reciprocal teaching*, comprehension monitoring strategies, such as summarization and questioning, are modeled and practiced in contexts in which the participants share the goal of gaining meaning from the text. The fact that students learn to apply comprehension strategies as they are being acquired is thought to be the key to the program's success. Similarly, Collins et al. (1989) discussed how schools might be restructured to create cognitive apprenticeships that enable students to engage in authentic, productive mental work. The focus is on the creation of meaningful tasks and work environments, rather than on lists of specific facts, concepts, and skills that students practice in isolation. Resnick and Klopfer (1989) also stated that cognitive apprenticeships should involve meaningful tasks, such as writing for real audiences rather than only for the teacher. Finally, students should have multiple opportunities to observe others performing relevant tasks; that is, they learn about the utilization of knowledge from models, both peers and teacher.

The Jasper Series As An Example of Situated Instruction. The overall aim of the various CTGV projects is to help students who are relative novices in an area to experience some of the cognitive advantages available to experts as they learn new information (Bransford, Sherwood, Hasselbring, Kinzer, & Williams, 1990). Video disc and computer technologies make the goal of creating cognitive apprenticeships more attainable. Thus, these technologies are used to anchor or situate instruction in shared environments that permit sustained explorations by students and teacher. The CTGV developed a variety of anchored instructional programs that focus on specific content areas and provide opportunities for cross-curricular extensions.

One program, *The Adventures of Jasper Woodbury*, is a video-based series designed to promote problem posing, problem solving, interpretative reasoning, and effective communication. Its focus is on the areas of mathematics, science, and literacy. Another program, *The Jaspar Woodbury Series*, focuses on mathematics problem solving with extensions to science, history, and geography. Both programs involve activities such as generating subgoals needed to solve complex problems, identifying relevant information in a complex array, cooperating with others in order to plan and solve problems, discussing the advantages and disadvantages of possible solutions, and comparing perspectives by pointing out and explaining interesting events.

The video format makes it easy to embed information that provides multiple opportunities for developing links across the curriculum. The video is important because it brings the real world into the classroom. It actively engages students in realistic analytic activities and makes mathematical problem solving accessible to students who have difficulty imaging complex situations when reading. In the Jasper series, a lesson begins with a realistic problem, often with one of the characters posing the problem. Thus, a challenge is presented to students who are told that all the facts they need to solve the problem are contained in the video. Students must shift from passive viewing to active problem solving and are encouraged to explore the problem and its possibilities. Often, students use three to four class periods to solve the problem.

After solving the major problem for each adventure, teachers are encouraged to work on analogue and extension problems with their students. The purpose of these activities materials is to help students develop flexible knowledge representations, to better understand key principles embedded in the adventures, and to explore the thinking and planning that have taken place in historical and contemporary events. Analogue problems are formed by altering one or more of the parameters of the original Jasper problem. Thus, the program is designed to help students integrate their knowledge across the curriculum. In addition, it is hoped that the activities will help students appreciate the usefulness of mathematics.

The CTGV provided data from the field-based implementation of the Jasper Woodbury problem-solving series. The instructional materials and programs are implemented in 16 schools distributed across 9 states. The samples were drawn from public elementary school students from fifth grade, sixth grade, and mixed classes. Results indicated that the performance of Jasper students were superior to the control classes at posttest in solving *near transfer problems*; these problems involved contents related to the materials presented in the Jasper adventures (e.g., one step, two step, and multistep problems).

In addition, students from Jasper classrooms scored higher at the end of the year than nonJasper control classes on both planning and generating subgoals necessary to solve complex problems. Jasper students showed significantly improved attitudes about mathematics compared to control students, were less anxious toward mathematics, more likely to see mathematics as useful, and more likely to appreciate complex problem-solving challenges. Qualitative data on responses about the program were overwhelmingly positive, with both parents and teachers commenting on children's new interests in mathematics and problem solving. Interestingly, teachers emphasized that the Jasper adventures engaged and motivated their students.

Skill Components and the Jasper Series. The CTGV technology anchors and situates instruction in shared environments, thus permitting sustained exploration by students and teachers. Students experience the value of exploring the same setting from multiple perspectives (e.g., as a scientist, historian, or mathematician). As they discover their own issues to explore in these enriched environments, they communicate their ideas to other students and presumably develop analytic skills as a result of their problem-solving activities. What is difficult to discern is the precise sets of metacognitive skills that emerge as a result of these experiences. Are specific problem-solving strategies developed? Are higher level planning, task analytic, or monitoring skills enhanced? Are specific beliefs about self-efficacy and the personal challenge to develop one's own mind explicitly fostered? For the most part, the assessment approach used by the Vanderbilt group does not allow definitive answers to these questions. We suspect, however, that a comprehensive video technology approach to instruction influences the emergence of planning and executive skills and enhances positive motivational beliefs about self-efficacy. We return to the issue of a theoretically based, componential analysis of the factors that lie behind the successes of programs like the Jasper series in a later section of this chapter.

A Community of Learners and Thinkers

Brown et al. (1993) argued that schools should foster the development of communities where students learn to learn. In the research programs recently developed by Brown and colleagues (Brown et al., 1993; Brown, Campione, Reeve, Ferrara, & Palincsar, 1991; Palincsar & Klenk, 1992), the goal is to form learning–thinking communities in which intentional learning is highlighted (cf. Bereiter & Scardamalia, 1985). Intentional learning, in contrast to incidental learning, results from the learner's purposeful, effortful, self-regulated, and active engagement in the learning process, together with the deep processing of information as opposed to surface-level processing.

According to Brown, Bransford, Ferrara, and Campione (1983), intentional learning requires the active use of metacognitive knowledge—an ability and an awareness of the need to monitor and control one's own activities during most learning episodes. Furthermore, Palincsar and Klenk (1992) hypothesize that the ability to meet cognitive and metacognitive demands through intentional learning depends on the learner's motivational and belief systems. Students who value the goals toward which they are striving have positive expectations for success in completing the task at hand and, in combination with the belief that the effort they deploy is likely to lead to successful outcomes, are more likely to display intentional learning. Thus, in communities of learners, teachers become models of intentional and self-motivated learning, the two processes we postulate are occurring in the CTGV programs.

Another aim of developing a community of learners, according to Brown et al. (1993) is to produce *intelligent novices*. These students may not possess the background knowledge in a domain, but have the skills to acquire that knowledge. According to Brown and Campione (1990) intelligent novices have *learned how to learn*, rather than just to memorize facts. Intelligent novices, therefore, possess a wide repertoire of strategies for gaining new knowledge. Furthermore, in an ideal community of learners, children are *apprentice learners* (Brown, 1992). That is, both peers and teachers at various times, assume the role of the expert: A community of learners is jointly responsible for creating knowledge.

Theoretically, the research of Brown and her colleagues draws heavily from the concept of the *zone of proximal development* (Vygotsky, 1978). A zone is the level of activity that a learner can reach with aid from a supporting environment, including the teacher, a parent, or other students. It defines the gap between the current level of functioning and the level that the learner can accomplish in collaboration with people or powerful artifacts, such as in Bransford's computer technology approach. The upper levels of competence within the zone of proximal development are not static but rather continually change with the learner's increasing independence and competence. Teachers and students create zones of proximal development by introducing into the environment ideas and concepts and they gradually transform these ideas by mutual interpretation and mutual negotiation.

Palincsar and Klenk (1992) argued that each learning context is social and interactive in nature, borrowing heavily from Vygotsky (1978), who advocated that the origins of all higher order cognitive processes are social in nature. In a community of learners, the structure of the classroom encourages maximum social interactions both in small and large group interactions. Dialogues provide the format for novices to adopt the goals, values, belief systems, and meanings through mutual negotiation. Thus, over time, a community of learners comes to adopt a shared system of meanings and beliefs.

Over the past 5 years, Brown and her associates designed a series of innovative classroom practices that encourage teachers and students to rethink their philosophy of teaching and learning. Each learning environment is designed to foster the development of cognitive processes such as problem solving, critical thinking, and reflective analysis. In particular, two forms of cooperative learning are used to build a community of learners: *Reciprocal Teaching* and the *Jigsaw Method*.

Reciprocal teaching is an instructional procedure that takes place in a collaborative learning context and involves guided practice in the flexible use of four concrete comprehension monitoring strategies: questioning, summarizing, clarifying, and predicting (Palincsar & Brown, 1984). The procedure encourages an explicit externalization of these four reading strategies. The teacher and the students take turns leading discussions regarding the contents of a text they are jointly attempting to understand. The strategies are examples of the kinds of cognitive activities that successful learners engage in while interacting with the text. The strategies also encourage higher order strategies—especially self-regulation and self-monitoring—needed to promote intentional learning. The critical factor, however, is that instruction is contextualized. The strategies are not broken down into component skills and practiced in isolation or out of the context of authentic reading activity. Rather, skills are practiced in the context of reciprocal teaching dialogues. Reciprocal teaching is designed to evoke zones of proximal development within which novices take on increased responsibilities. The novice's role is made easier by the provision of scaffolding by the expert, as well as a supportive social context. Thus, the group shares responsibilities for thinking and meaning construction, and often helps to reduce anxiety in novice learners.

In the Jigsaw Method of cooperative learning, students in science lessons are assigned part of a classroom topic they subsequently teach others via reciprocal teaching. For instance, students might form five research groups, each of which is assigned responsibility for one of five subtopics (Brown, 1993). For example, Campione, Brown, and Jay (1992) explained that it was the function of research groups to prepare teaching materials using computer technologies. Using the Jigsaw Method, students regrouped into learning groups in which each student became an expert on one subtopic, containing one fifth of the total package of information. Each one fifth needs to be combined with the remaining one fifths to comprise an entire unit, hence the idea of a jigsaw. The expert in each subtopic uses reciprocal teaching to guide seminars in his or her area. All children in a learning group serve as the expert for one part of the material, teach it to the others, and prepare questions for the test that all students take at the end of a unit. A critical factor in these interactions is preserving an atmosphere of joint or shared responsibility. In the long run, the group constructs new understandings together in reciprocal and communal fashion.

Classrooms containing a community of learners differ from traditional classes in several important ways: (a) students take more active roles in monitoring their own progress and that of others, as they adopt the role of constructive critics; (b) teachers serve as models of active learning, and guide learning rather than adopt a domineering, didactic role; (c) students witness teachers learning, discovering, reading, writing, and using computers as tools for learning, rather than managing and controlling the class; (d) the content emphasis is on deep levels of understanding, rather than on acquiring a breadth of facts; (e) the teacher introduces computers as tools for communication and collaboration, and also to foster reflective thinking and learning. Parenthetically, Brown (1992) stated that computers are primarily used in grade schools to replace teachers as managers of drill and practice, or to teach children to program, and not as a means of enhancing students' thinking. In a thinking–learning community, however, the computer is used to encourage students to plan and revise their learning goals, monitor and reflect on their own progress as they construct personal knowledge files, and share a communal database.

Finally, Brown's research group designed methods of assessment that focus on students' abilities to discover and use knowledge. They utilize a variety of dynamic assessments related to the development of knowledge (Campione, 1989). For instance, children are presented with problems one step beyond their existing competence, and are then provided help as needed to reach independent mastery. The ease with which students apply or transfer principles they have learned is regarded as an index of understanding those principles.

Brown (1992) explained that multiple types of data are gathered using both standard outcome measures involving reading, writing, content knowledge and computer competence, all of which are found to improve significantly following this form of instruction. In addition, the project generated a large amount of qualitative data (for example, transcripts of children's planning, revising, and teaching sessions, as well as types of teacher corrections). What seems missing in the assessment protocol, however, is an attempt to trace the emergence of both higher and lower level strategies and changing motivational states that undoubtedly flow from a history of experiences in a community of thinkers and learners. We believe that the metacognitive model we propose serves as a framework for understanding the dynamics of the Brown approach to instruction and, perhaps, would be of value in guiding a more theoretically oriented assessment scheme.

Schoenfeld's Problem-Solving Approach to Mathematics Instruction

Schoenfeld (1989) argued for a research agenda that helps to develop classrooms that are "microcosms of mathematical sense-making" (p. 82). His problem-solving courses at the college level have as their major foci the development of self-regulation, especially monitoring and control skills, as well as the development of self-directing motivational beliefs. Schoenfeld contended that students are active interpreters of the world around them, constantly building interpretive frameworks so as to make sense of their personal experiences.

A major purpose of mathematics instruction, according to Schoenfeld, is to enable learners to think mathematically. This consists not only of mastering various facts and procedures, but also in understanding connections among them. Thinking mathematically also consists of being able to apply one's formal mathematical knowledge flexibly and meaningfully to different situations. The focus of Schoenfeld's approach is to prompt students to carefully monitor their solutions, pursue interesting leads, and abandon those that do not seem to result in success. Students' ability to monitor and assess progress online and to act in response in these assessments are the core components of self-regulated learning.

Schoenfeld's (1985, 1987) problem-solving courses contain a minimum amount of explicit presentation from the instructor. Rather, the instructor shapes and structures classroom interactions. The shaping process consists of working on ideas generated by students, with the teacher serving as a moderator of classroom discussions. The vast majority of class time is spent on collaborative efforts either in small groups or as whole classrooms. Time is spent actually doing mathematics. Students are consistently engaged in the discipline—debating, conjecturing, proving, agreeing, and disagreeing. The concern is with producing deep levels of understanding. Schoenfeld (1990) explained that the behavior of expert and novice students on unfamiliar problems is different. Most students fail to use metacognitive skills demonstrated by the expert. In his problem-solving course, Schoenfeld teaches these skills through explicit instruction on the metacognitive aspects of mathematical thinking. This instruction takes the form of coaching as students work with problems in order to traverse the same paths traveled by experts.

Schoenfeld (1992) described in detail the behavior of a pair of students during their problem-solving activities following the completion of a course that focused on training monitoring and control skills. After reading the problem, the two students began to make an initial solution attempt that unfortunately, was based on an unfounded assumption. They realized the problem and, after a few minutes, decided to try a different approach. This second solution path was also ineffective. The students then became involved in complicated computation that kept them occupied for nearly 10 minutes. However, at that point, they stopped once again. One of the students said, "No, we aren't getting anywhere, let's start all over again and forget about this" (p. 356). They did, and discovered a solution within a short while.

The behavior of these students suggests that self-regulation provided the opportunity to succeed at eventually solving math problems. Had the students not actively monitored their solution processes, they might not have given themselves the opportunity to self-correct. In this sense, their behavior was expert-like in terms of eventually solving complex problems. Schoenfeld found a decline in impulsive responding over the course of training that apparently resulted in an increase in problem-solving success.

During this entire process, the instructor served as an external monitor during problem-solving episodes, encouraged discussion of behaviors considered important for the internalization of metacognitive skills, and modelled effective executive processing behaviors. The result was an increase in planning, monitoring, and active problem solving. These processes are at the heart of metacognitive theory, which we believe can provide a reasonable account of the successes contained in the educational innovations described in the previous sections. It is to a more detailed account of metacognitive theory and its developmental implications that we now turn.

METACOGNITIVE THEORY: TOWARD AN INTEGRATION OF THE SELF AND REGULATORY SYSTEMS IN INSTRUCTIONAL RESEARCH

Borkowski, Estrada, Milstead, and Hale (1989) traced the emergence of metacognitive theory during the past two decades of instructional research. The initial research focus was on an awareness of the attributes of specific strategies, such as when and how to deploy strategies, their uniqueness, and their advantages in meeting the demands of a limited range of tasks. A second, and more important focus, centered on the development of higher order self-regulating skills that are essential for generalized strategy deployment (cf. Zimmerman & Schunk, 1989).

The most recent extension of metacognitive theory encompasses noncognitive influences on academic performance, such as attributional beliefs and learning styles (Borkowski, Carr, Rellinger, & Pressley, 1990). The fundamental premise in the newest version of metacognitive thinking is that personal–motivational factors energize the self-regulating, executive skills necessary for strategy selection, implementation, and monitoring. Deficiencies in one or both processes likely account for many of the individual differences that separate gifted from regular children and regular children from learning-impaired children. It is these processes, especially self-regulation, that may be the common features that are promoted in contemporary cognitive-oriented curricula.

The metacognitive model we propose can account for many of the successes in contemporary educational programs. Its essential components and their linkages can be found in Fig. 15.1. For strategic behavior to occur, especially in challenging circumstances, executive processes must operate on the task at hand and relate task-analytic information to the strategic knowledge base. The critical operations of strategy selection, implementation, and monitoring follow. All of these activities of the executor need to be instigated and maintained. In this way, motivational factors, such as attributional beliefs and intrinsic orientations to learning opportunities, become relevant. Thus, motivational variables are assumed to energize self-regulated problem solving.

As metacognitive theory is extended to, and tested in, classroom contexts, we should recognize that most learning episodes have intimate motivational correlates. High self-esteem, an internal locus of control, the tendency to attribute success to effort, strong beliefs about cognitive modifiability, and positive self-efficacy are among the consequences of a child's lengthy history of consistent, relatively successful strategy-governed habits of responding to learning problems, especially when associated with supportive feedback from parents and teachers.

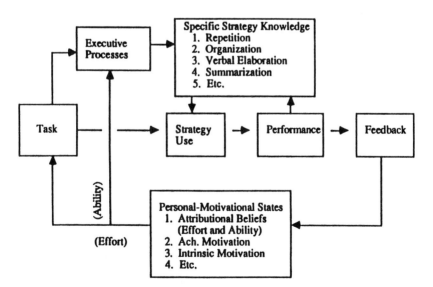

FIG. 15.1. A metacognitive model of skilled performances, featuring executive processes and motivational beliefs.

More specifically, improved learning and enhanced academic performance following strategy use strengthen the strategy knowledge base, and, in turn, promote positive self-esteem, self-efficacy, attributions of success to effort rather than to uncontrollable factors such as luck, and a genuine love of learning for its own sake. Thus, personal–motivational attributes flow from individual cognitive actions and play pivotal roles in what sometimes appears as spontaneous strategy use by providing incentives necessary for selecting, deploying, and monitoring strategies, especially on challenging and novel tasks (Borkowski et al., 1990).

LEARNING CONTEXTS
AND THE GENERALIZATION PROCESS

A recent study by Muthukrishna and Borkowski (in press) assessed how learning contexts influence the emergence of strategy use and key beliefs about self-efficacy that we postulate energize self-regulation. This study represents our initial attempt to contrast direct strategy instruction with a guided discovery approach. A major goal was to test the hypothesis that discovery learning would improve the performance of third grade students when contrasted with direct, explicit strategy instruction. We expected that the facilitating effects due to learning about a math strategy in a discovery-based context would most likely appear on transfer tasks (i.e., where the solution of addition and subtraction word problems was presented in a different form and context than those used in training and near transfer). More specifically, the main hypothesis assessed the role of the learning context in the generalization of a math strategy that focused on the relationships linking the concepts *whole* and *part*. This strategy is applicable to addition and subtraction problems, and is especially useful in solving novel word problems.

A closely related goal was to test the notion that discovery-based strategy training would indirectly contribute to the development of beliefs and goals about the reasons for success in mathematics and, furthermore, that changes in motivational beliefs would be related to the degree of meaningful learning and transfer. In short, this project was aimed at the metacognitive processes that we believe underlie the instructional successes of the Bransford, Brown, and Schoenfeld research groups reviewed earlier in this chapter: Deep processing of information, guided by self-regulation and activated by changes in beliefs about self-efficacy, enhances the generalization of skills and strategies.

To test these hypotheses, we selected 106 third graders from three public schools. Selection depended on: (a) whether students had the necessary skills to solve addition and subtraction word problems that did not require regrouping or carrying, and (b) whether students were unable to solve the three types of problems used during training that could easily be solved with the whole–part strategy. The study proceeded in five phases: pretesting, intervention, posttesting, short-term maintenance, and long-term maintenance. Group administered pretests were conducted during two 35 minute sessions (spread across 2 days). The intervention for all four conditions—discovering learning, direct strategy teaching, combined instruction (a hybrid condition contained elements of direct and discovery teaching) and a practice-only control—took place over 14 consecutive class days. Posttests were conducted over 2 days during three 35 minute sessions, immediately following the intervention. At the posttest, students were also audiotaped in dyads as they solved three problems representing each of the three problem types. These data were used to assess the ability of subjects to think and communicate mathematically. A short-term maintenance test was administered 4 weeks after completion of the intervention, and a long-term transfer test was given 5 weeks after the short-term maintenance test.

The most interesting results were related to the differential impact of contextual effects during short- and long-term maintenance on the near and far transfer tests. At the short-term maintenance test, the explicit instruction and combined groups were superior to the discovery group on near transfer tasks— highly similar to those used during training. On far transfer measures, however, which contained items differing in form and contents from those of training, no differences due to context were observed. In contrast, on the tests of long-term transfer, the discovery and combined conditions were superior to the explicit training condition on far transfer measures; no differences were found on the near transfer tests during the long-term assessments.

Thus, the results on the transfer and generalization of the whole–part strategy revealed significant differences in the impact of the two instructional approaches when students were required to solve problems that assessed higher levels of conceptual understanding. Most importantly, the discovery group proved to be superior to the direct (or explicit) group on the final test of far transfer as they solved transfer problems that assessed meaningful learning (i.e., problems presented in a form and context different from those experienced during initial instruction). Additionally, students in the explicit strategy plus discovery condition (the hybrid condition) performed superior to the students in the explicit explanation group on the far transfer test during the long-term maintenance session. The three treatment groups all performed significantly better than the control group on all near and far transfer measures, suggesting that each treatment was superior to the traditional instruction that was occurring in the classrooms.

Another interesting finding was that students in the discovery condition reported greater use of deep processing strategies than did students in the direct instruction and combined conditions. Students in the combined condition also reported that they made greater use of deep processing strategies than did students in the direct explanation condition. These results suggest that students used more deliberate processing styles, and perhaps greater executive control, depending upon the extent of discovery-based learning.

We believe that an additional reason for the transfer successes associated with discovery learning is linked to changes in students' belief systems. In fact, those students exposed to the discovery environment placed greater importance on the motivational goals of understanding and collaborating in mathematics than did students in the direct explanation condition. Students in the discovery condition placed less importance on task-extrinsic factors, such as being quiet in class and having neat papers. Finally, an overall analysis of the social collaboration data indicated that students in the discovery conditions were able to more effectively communicate during problem solving than were students in the direct explanation condition: Discovery-trained students generated a greater number of utterances, stated more givens in the problems, and revealed more instances of shared activity than did students in the direct explanation group. These results find a wider interpretation in the literature on motivation and academic achievement.

Motivation and Strategic Processing. Nicholls and colleagues (Nicholls, 1989; Nicholls, Patashnick, & Nolen, 1985) repeatedly found that students' motivational orientations are consistent with their beliefs about causes of success in school. For instance, task orientation is correlated with the belief that success depends on hard work, interest, cooperation, and trying to understand rather than just memorizing facts and relationships. In contrast, ego orientation is associated with the belief that success depends on competitiveness and extrinsic factors, such as impressing the teacher.

In the Muthukrishna and Borkowski (in press) study, similar patterns regarding ego orientation were found. That is, global ego-oriented motivational scores significantly correlated with global ego-oriented beliefs scores. Another interesting finding was that task orientation correlated significantly, and in a positive direction, with deep processing. This suggests a connection between strategy implementation and the motivational system that seemed to emerge following discovery-oriented instructions.

These results suggest that children whose primary goal is learning for its own sake will value and use strategies that require the deep processing of information more than will students whose primary goal is to demonstrate their superior ability relative to other students. One would expect such relationships, according to Nicholls (1989), because understanding, and the effort it involves, is an end in itself and not a means to an end. Similarly, Nolen (1988) found that the correlations between task orientation and deep processing were significantly greater than those between task orientation and surface strategies. Nolen also showed that general task orientation was more positively related to valuing and using deep processing than either ego orientation or work avoidance. Environments that emphasizes conceptual understanding and deep strategic processing may help to alter existing patterns of motivational goals and beliefs. For instance, when students are asked to explain and justify their problem-solving approach to others, as was required in the discovery learning condition, they come to understand themselves better, gradually acquiring the belief that tasks are intrinsically motivating.

Discovery-Oriented Teaching and Motivation. The teacher in a discovery environment is a critical mediator in a transactionally based instructional process. An effective teacher maximizes task involvement by inducing students to collaborate with each other in order to gain understanding. In our study, teacher behaviors included verbalizations such as *What do others think of what Peter just said? Do you agree–disagree with what Peter says? Can anyone explain what they thought Sally was thinking when she solved the problem? How can we check to see if your answer makes sense? Has anyone solved the problem in a different way?* These verbalizations indicated that teacher mediation often requires process-oriented answers and apparently assists in the development of self-regulatory capabilities, such as monitoring and reflecting.

It is also clear that the teachers can create a "sense-making" atmosphere. For instance, students exposed to the discovery learning environment in our study rated the task-oriented goal of understanding and collaborating more highly than did those in the direct explanation condition. Additionally, students in the discovery-only conditions reported greater use of deep processing strategies than did those in the direct explanation and combined conditions, and students in the combined condition were more likely than were those in the direct explanation condition to report a preference for such strategies. Deep processing strategies included trying to ascertain how new information fits with what one already knows, monitoring problem-solving activities, and engaging in self-regulation (e.g., *I ask myself questions while doing problems to make sure I understand them*). In summary, the byproducts of discovery learning may be more important, and lasting, than the emergence of a single new strategy, especially if task-oriented motivational beliefs and processes related to self-regulation are cultivated in contextually rich environments.

CONCLUSIONS: IMPLICATIONS FOR INSTRUCTION

The findings reviewed in this chapter provide support for the importance of learning contexts in designing instructions that facilitate the development of self-regulation and positive motivational beliefs. Most important is the notion that it is possible to influence motivational goals and self-efficacious beliefs, to promote the deep processing of information, and to develop better conceptual understanding, while in the process of prompting skill acquisition and its long-term generalization. This complex integration of learning goals, motivational beliefs, and executive processes require that most teachers adopt a new focus, placing more importance on their students' efforts to understand and analyze problems. Many of the critical features of academically rich environments enhance students' efforts to find meaning and understanding in their learning and problem-solving activities. These are contained in the following list:

1. Teachers work hard to establish classroom settings in which sense-making is valued.

2. An emphasis is given to students' explanations of their understanding of problem situations.

3. The instructional focus is on processes and ideas as much as on contents and operations; hence, skills underlying self-directed learning are fostered.

4. Teachers realize that children need to be responsible for their own learning if they are expected to learn meaningfully. Learning environments are structured so that students perform tasks that are related to interesting and coherent personal goals, rather than for extrinsic reasons. Self-regulation and beliefs about self-efficacy develop best in such a context.

5. Assessments of student learning are based on behaviors within a problem-solving context rather than on correct performance on standardized tests.

It should be emphasized that most of these characteristics serve to initiate or strengthen self-regulation and self-efficacy.

The research programs reviewed in this chapter help us to understand specific characteristics of learning environments that define independent, focused, and effective learners and thinkers. There are two critical ingredients common to all successful instructional programs: The development of executive, self-regulatory processes, and a task orientation that concentrates on developing beliefs about self-efficacy. In the most effective instructional programs, students are given repeated opportunities to plan and control the form and amount of their instruction, to display initiative, and to take personal responsibility for their own learning activities and mental development.

Successful instructional programs value social collaboration among all those involved in the learning process: A critical factor is that collaborative environments demand reflective activity on the part of each learner. Students are obligated to carefully consider the meanings and understandings they construct and to share the fruits of their efforts in collaborative groups. They are constantly required to explain, present, defend, and justify the conjectures they draw and the solution paths proposed. We argue that this kind of personal reflection induces an online awareness of one's cognitive processes, which in turn further promotes the development of self-regulatory skills. By expressing ideas in public, by defending them in the face of questions from peers, by questioning other's ideas, students are forced to elaborate, clarify, and reorganize their own thinking processes. The research programs reviewed in this chapter support the notion that it is possible to create stimulating learning environments designed explicitly to teach and coach cognitive self-management and to encourage beliefs about self-control—processes that are at the heart of human intelligence and personal growth.

ACKNOWLEDGMENTS

The second author was supported by a grant from the Educational Opportunities Council, South Africa.

REFERENCES

Bereiter, C., & Scardamalia, M. (1985). Cognitive coping skills and the problem of "inert" knowledge. In S. Chipman, J. W. Segal, & R. Glaser (Eds.), *Thinking and learning skills: Current research and open question* (Vol. 2, pp. 65–80). Hillsdale, NJ: Lawrence Erlbaum Associates.

Borkowski, J. G., Carr, M., Rellinger, L., & Pressley, M. (1990). Self-regulated cognition: Interdependence of metacognition, attributions and self-esteem. In B. Jones & L. Idol (Eds.), *Dimensions of thinking and cognitive instruction* (Vol. 1, pp. 53–92). Hillsdale, NJ: Lawrence Erlbaum Associates.

Borkowski, J. G., Estrada, T. M., Milstead, M., & Hale, C. A. (1989). General problem-solving skills: Relations between metacognition and strategic processing. *Learning Disabilities Quarterly, 12*, 57–70.

Bransford, J. D., Franks, J. J., Vye, N. J., & Sherwood, R. D. (1989). New approaches to instruction: Because wisdom can't be told. In S. Vosniadov & A. Ortony (Eds.), *Similarity and analogical reasoning* (pp. 470–497). New York: Cambridge University Press.

Bransford, J. D., Hasselbring, T., Barron, B., Kulewicz, B., Littlefield, L., & Goin, L. (1988). Uses of macro-contexts to facilitate mathematical thinking. In R. Charles & E. A. Silver (Eds.), *The teaching and assessing of mathematical problem solving* (pp. 125–147). Hillsdale, NJ: Lawrence Erlbaum Associates.

Bransford, J. D., Sherwood, R., Hasselbring, T. S., Kinzer, C. K., & Williams, S. M. (1990). Anchored instruction: Why we need it and how technology can help. In D. Nix & R. Spiro (Eds.), *Cognition, education, and multi-media: Exploring ideas in high technology* (pp. 116–141). Hillsdale, NJ: Lawrence Erlbaum Associates.

Brown, A. L. (1992). Design experiments: Theoretical and methodological challenges in creating complex interventions in classroom settings. *Journal of the Learning Sciences, 2*, 141–178.

Brown, A. L., Ash, D., Rutherford, M., Nakagawa, K., Gordon, A., & Campione, J. C. (1993). Distributed expertise in the classroom. In G. Salomon (Ed.), *Distributed cognitions* (pp. 188–228). New York: Cambridge University Press.

Brown, A. L., Bransford, L. D., Ferrara, R. A., & Campione, J. C. (1983). Learning, remembering, and understanding. In J. H. Flavell & E. M. Markman (Eds.), *Handbook of child psychology* (Vol. 3, pp. 76–116). New York: Wiley.

Brown, A. L., & Campione, J. C. (1990). Communities of learning and thinking, or a context by any other name. *Human Development, 21*, 108–125.

Brown, A. L., Campione, J. C., Reeve, R. A., Ferrara, R. A., & Palincsar, A. S. (1991). Interactive learning and individual understanding: The case of reading and mathematics. In L. T. Landsman (Ed.), *Culture, schooling and psychological development* (pp. 136–170). Hillsdale, NJ: Lawrence Erlbaum Associates.

Brown, J. S., Collins, A., & Duguid, P. (1989). Situated cognition and the culture of learning. *Educational Researcher, 17*, 32–41.

Campione, J. C. (1989). Assisted assessments: A taxonomy of approaches and an outline of strengths and weaknesses. *Journal of Learning Disabilities, 22*, 151–155.

Campione, J. C., Brown, A. L., & Jay, M. (1992). Computers in a community of learners. In E. De Corte, M. Linn, H. Mandel, & L. Verschassel (Eds.), *Computer-based learning environments and problem solving* (pp. 163–192). New York: Springer-Verlag.

Cobb, P. (1990). Multiple perspectives. In L. P. Steffe & T. Wood (Eds.), *Transforming children's mathematics education* (pp. 200–215). Hillsdale, NJ: Lawrence Erlbaum Associates.

Collins, A., Brown, J. S., & Newman, S. E. (1989). Cognitive apprenticeship: Teaching the craft of reading, writing, and mathematics. In L. B. Resnick (Ed.), *Knowing, learning, and instruction: Essays in honor of Robert Glaser* (pp. 453–494). Hillsdale, NJ: Lawrence Erlbaum Associates.

Dossey, J. A., Mullis, J. V. S., Lindquist, M. M., & Chambers, D. L. (1988). *The mathematics report card: Are we measuring up?* Princeton, NJ: Educational Testing Service.

Jones, B. F., & Idol, L. (1990). Conclusions. In B. F. Jones & L. Idol (Eds.), *Dimensions of thinking and cognitive instruction* (pp. 511–532). Hillsdale, NJ: Lawrence Erlbaum Associates.

Lockhart, R. S., Lamon, M., & Gick, M. L. (1988). Conceptual transfer in simple insight problems. *Memory and Cognition, 16,* 36–44.

Mullis, J. V. S., & Jenkins, L. B. (1990). *The reading report card, 1971–1988: Trends from the nation's report card.* Princeton, NJ: National Assessment of Educational Progress, Educational Testing Service.

Muthukrishna, N., & Borkowski, J. G. (in press). How learning contexts facilitate strategy transfer. *Applied Cognitive Psychology.*

Nicholls, J. G. (1989). *The competitive ethos and democratic education.* Cambridge, MA: Harvard University Press.

Nicholls, J. G., Pataschnick, M., & Nolen, S. B. (1985). Adolescents' theories of education. *Journal of Educational Research, 77,* 683–692.

Nolen, S. B. (1988). Reasons for studying: Motivational orientations and study strategies. *Cognition and Instruction, 5,* 269–287.

Palincsar, A. S., & Brown, A. L. (1984). Reciprocal teaching of comprehension: Monitoring activities. *Cognition and Instruction, 1,* 117–175.

Palincsar, A. S., & Klenk, L. (1992). Fostering literacy learning in supporting contexts. *Journal of Learning Disabilities, 25,* 221–229.

Perkins, D. N., & Salomon, G. (1989). Are cognitive skills context bound? *Educational Researcher, 4,* 16–25.

Resnick, L. B., & Klopfer, L. E. (1989). Toward the thinking curriculum: An overview. In L. B. Resnick & L. E. Klopfer (Eds.), *Toward the thinking curriculum: Current cognitive research* (pp. 1–18). Alexandria, VA: ASCD.

Romberg, T. A. (1992). Mathematics learning and teaching: What we have learned in ten years. In C. Collins and J. N. Mangieri (Eds.), *Teaching thinking: An agenda for the twenty-first century* (pp. 43–64). Hillsdale, NJ: Lawrence Erlbaum Associates.

Salomon, G., & Globerson, T. (1987). Skill may not be enough: The role of mindfulness in learning are transfer. *International Journal of Education, 11,* 623–637.

Scardamalia, M., & Bereiter, C. (1985). Fostering the development of self-regulation in children's knowledge processing. In S. F. Chipman, J. W. Segal, & R. Glaser (Eds.), *Thinking and learning skills: Research and open questions* (Vol. 2, pp. 65–80). Hillsdale, NJ: Lawrence Erlbaum Associates.

Schoenfeld, A. H. (1985). *Mathematical problem solving.* New York: Academic Press.

Schoenfeld, A. H. (1987). What's all the fuss about metacognition? In A. H. Schoenfeld (Ed.), *Cognitive science and mathematics education* (pp. 189–216). Hillsdale, NJ: Lawrence Erlbaum Associates.

Schoenfeld, A. H. (1989). Ideas in the air: Speculations on small group learning, environmental and cultural influences on cognition and epistemology. *Journal of Education, 13,* 71–88.

Schoenfeld, A. H. (1990). On mathematics sense making: An informal attack on the unfortunate divorce of formal and informal mathematics. In D. N. Perkins, J. Segal, & J. Voss (Eds.), *Informal reasoning and education* (pp. 281–300). Hillsdale, NJ: Lawrence Erlbaum Associates.

Schoenfeld, A. H. (1992). Learning to think mathematically: Problem solving, metacognition, and sense making in mathematics. In P. H. Grouws (Ed.), *Handbook of research on mathematics teaching: A project of the National Council of Teachers of Mathematics* (pp. 334–370). New York: Macmillan.

Vygotsky, L. S. (1978). *Mind in society: The development of higher psychological processes.* Cambridge, MA: Harvard University Press.

Wagner, R. K., & Sternberg, R. J. (1986). Teaching knowledge and intelligence in the everyday world. In R. Sternberg & R. Wagner (Eds.), *Practical intelligence: Origins of competence in the everyday world* (pp. 51–83). New York: Cambridge University Press.

Zimmerman, B. J., & Schunk, D. H. (1989). *Self-regulated learning and academic achievement: Theory, research, and practice.* New York: Springer-Verlag.

Chapter 16

Strategy Instruction, Metacognition, and Motivation in the Elementary School Classroom

Barbara E. Moely
Kevin A. Santulli
Mifrando S. Obach
Tulane University

From the earliest investigations of memory development by children, it was assumed that experiences at school and in the home must play an important role in shaping children's use of and knowledge about how to learn and remember. Our work is concerned with factors in the school environment that may contribute to children's acquisition of effective study strategies and metacognitive knowledge. This work is derived from laboratory work on the development of memory strategies, metacognition, and self-regulation, and involves an extension of the theories and measurement techniques into classroom settings. This chapter focuses on, first, the roles that teachers may play in furthering children's strategy and metacognitive skills, and second, on school setting differences in the interrelations of metacognition, motivational beliefs, and academic achievement.

The theoretical approach most compatible with this work is that of Vygotsky, who saw development as a product of successful teaching interactions between the child and more capable individuals (Wertsch & Tulviste, 1992). Developmental progress is facilitated by interactions that help the child master cognitive skills and develop self-awareness. Adults can assist children by teaching them effective ways to think about and deal with cognitively complex tasks, especially by teaching strategies for paying attention, representing, remembering, or transforming information (Derry, 1990; Flavell, 1970). Such teaching should be especially effective when accompanied by metacognitive information concerning strategy utility, person or task variables affecting performance, or procedures children can use for self-regulation (Pressley, Borkowski, & O'Sullivan, 1985).

In an initial study, reported in Moely et al. (1992), we observed in classrooms to find out how elementary school teachers were instructing strategy use and memory knowledge as they presented lessons to children of Grades K through 6. Teachers were observed for 30-minute periods on 5 different days as they taught language arts or math lessons (2.5 hours of observation for each teacher). A time-sampling procedure was used to record various teaching activities, including instruction of cognitive processes and, more specifically, instruction in the use of strategies for learning and remembering.

Teachers varied widely in the extent to which they focused on how children might adjust or regulate their cognitive activities in order to master a task. On average, instruction in how to cognitively deal with a task occurred in only 9.5% of the observation intervals. Specific strategy instruction was rare, occurring on an average of only 2.28% of the observation intervals per teacher. Seven of the 69 teachers (10%) gave no strategy suggestions at all during the time that the observers were in their classrooms. We found differences as a function of the age level of the child: Teachers of second and third graders instructed strategies more often than did teachers of older or younger children. Teachers of Grades 4 and above more often provided rationales for the use of strategies than did teachers of younger children.

In general, we found that teachers spent little instructional time helping children understand how to study. Why? Perhaps the material being considered in the classroom did not require such instruction. If the material is easy for students or if the teacher does not expect mastery, there would be little need to teach children how to learn the material. This does not appear to have been the case, as teachers usually did employ examinations assessing concept acquisition and rarely indicated that their children were easily mastering material. However, the use of cognitive processing suggestions varied with the subject matter of the lessons. Teachers who were observed during instruction that involved mathematics (23% of our observations) made more strategy suggestions than did those who were seen teaching only reading or language arts subject matter. Mathematics instruction appeared to be a setting in which teachers would demonstrate a high level of strategy instruction. In a subsequent study, Santulli focused specifically on math instruction, in order to better describe teachers' instruction of cognitive processes.

TEACHERS' INSTRUCTION OF STRATEGY USE AND METACOGNITION IN MATH PROBLEM SOLVING

Santulli (1991) observed teachers when they were engaged in the instruction of mathematics problem solving. Research participants were 16 second-grade and 17 fifth-grade teachers, who were from schools in the same large urban area and showed demographic characteristics similar to those of teachers in the initial study. Santulli used an observational procedure that combined time- and event-sampling in order to learn about teachers' instruction of cognitive strategies. Each teacher was observed for 30-minute periods on each of 3 days, for a total of 1.5 hours of observations of each teacher.

As shown in Table 16.1, observations focused on strategy and metacognitive suggestions teachers could make during math instruction. Observers also recorded the contexts within which such suggestions occurred, the instructional method used to make the suggestion, and the phase of math problem solving in which the suggestion was given.

In this study, in contrast to our initial effort, Santulli found high and frequent use of study strategy and metacognitive suggestions. As indicated in Fig. 16.1, the percentage of 30-sec observation intervals in which teachers instructed cognitive processes was much higher than had been the case in the earlier study. Fifth-grade teachers, in particular, were likely to suggest strategies that children could employ in dealing with math problems. Metacognitive suggestions, which involve comments that encourage students to reflect on their learning processes, were made less often than strategy suggestions, but still occurred in more than 10% of the observation intervals at each grade level. Analysis of these data showed significantly higher use of strategy suggestions than metacognitive suggestions at both grade levels. Fifth-grade teachers made more strategy suggestions

TABLE 16.1
Definitions of Categories Used in Classroom Observations (Santulli, 1991)

I. Strategy Suggestion

Two criteria were used to operationalize the term *strategy*: First, the activity the teacher suggests needs to be voluntary, not simply a task requirement. Secondly, the activity must be goal-directed, especially directed toward a goal of understanding or completing a task.

II. Metacognitive Suggestion

A metacognitive suggestion provides information that allows or encourages students to reflect on their learning processes. The suggestion may convey information about either *specific metacognitive knowledge*—knowledge about how one solves problems or learns, knowledge that is unique to a particular content area, in this case, mathematics.

The teacher makes a statement that heightens students' awareness or knowledge of their own math problem-solving processes. Three types of specific metacognitive knowledge are identified: *Person* knowledge concerns the students' evaluation of their own abilities and limitations in mathematics; *task* knowledge involves children's beliefs about mathematics and the nature of math tasks; and *strategy* knowledge concerns how, when, and where to use strategies.

Another group of metacognitive suggestions a teacher may make is referred to as *general metacognitive knowledge*. This includes metacognitive knowledge that is easily generalizable across content domains.

III. Context of Instruction

The following categories are used to describe the teaching context within which a strategy or metacognitive suggestion occurs:

Presents Material: A strategy or metacognitive suggestion is made by the teacher while he or she presents material to the child or the class.

Responds to Error: A strategy or metacognitive suggestion is made by the teacher in response to a student's error.

(Continued)

TABLE 16.1
(Continued)

IV. Instructional Method

When a strategy or metacognitive suggestion occurs, the following categories are used to describe the teaching method used:

Process Directive: The teacher describes the strategy or metacognitive suggestion verbally and may verbally present an example of how to use the strategy.

Models Process: The teacher acts as if he or she were a child using the strategy or metacognitive information. The teacher might write a problem up on the board and describe how he or she thinks his or her way through the problem using the strategy.

Questions Process: The teacher asks guided questions to draw out the child's description of a strategy or metacognitive process.

Gives Hint, Rephrases: Upon hearing the child's incorrect response, the teacher does something to help the child get the correct answer. What he or she does might involve rephrasing the question or giving the child some hint or prompt for the answer. It culminates in a request for a response from the child or children.

Unreflected Suggestion: The teacher uses the strategy or metacognitive process, but does not act to make the student aware of the process or to induce the student to engage in the activity. For example, the teacher might ask the students if their answers are reasonable, rather than directing the children to evaluate their answers.

Reinforces Process: Teacher produces a supportive behavior which exceeds a simple designation of correctness and rewards student for use of a strategy.

V. Problem-Solving Phase

Representational Phase: Teacher presents or describes any study activities or cognitive processes that involve the initial perception of the problem, understanding the problem, and/or planning the solution procedures. When presenting a word problem, the teacher may say "What do we need to find out in this problem?" The representation phase ends before the solution or mathematical operation is carried out. Understanding involves metacognitive processes, which include goal formation, planning, monitoring, and evaluating. Learners during this phase need to determine if they have sufficient understanding to solve the problem.

Solution Phase: The teacher presents or describes any study activities or cognitive processes that involve the application of problem solving activities that lead directly to a solution. Although the conceptualization of this phase emphasizes actions and procedures, metacognitive control processes are involved, such as local evaluation and decision making. The solution phase follows the representation phase when the problem is represented, understood, and solution procedures chosen. (The teacher may bypass potential representational processes and only teach solution phase activities.)

Evaluation Phase: The teacher presents or describes any study activities or cognitive processes that involve planning and execution of processes to assess the correctness of a solution.

---

on average than did second-grade teachers, but the two groups did not differ in the instructional time devoted to providing metacognitive information.

In an effort to understand the impetus for teachers' instruction of cognitive processes, consideration was given to both the classroom context in which such instruction occurred and the teaching method used. First, it was seen that strategy or metacognitive suggestions seemed to be generated on the basis of a teacher's belief or attitude about how children will need to process material, rather than in reaction to the child's error in performance. Teachers were more likely to

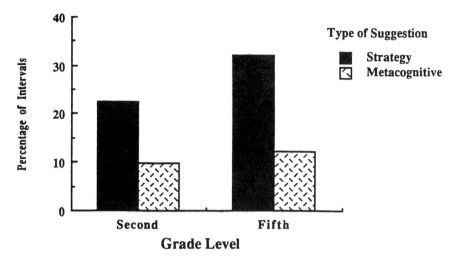

FIG. 16.1. The percentage of intervals in which second- and fifth-grade teachers made strategy or metacognitive suggestions to students (Santulli, 1991).

make a cognitive suggestion while they were presenting material to a class (observed during 26% of the observation intervals) than when they were responding to an error made by a child (seen in only 5% of the observation intervals). Teachers seem to have been anticipating children's problems, trying through their suggestions to maximize learning or limit the errors that children might make. With regard to teaching method, the teachers appeared to assume that children can learn strategies adequately on the basis of verbal descriptions or question prompts, as they rarely gave demonstrations of how to use a strategy. The preferred method of instruction was a verbal description of the strategy or metacognitive suggestion (21% of the observation intervals). Less often, teachers questioned children about the cognitive processes (12% of intervals), and even less often, they modeled the cognitive process (4% of intervals) or gave hints about a useful strategy (3% of intervals). Teachers rarely rewarded children for using a strategy (1% of intervals). No grade level differences were found in either the instructional context or the manner in which strategy and metacognitive suggestions were made.

Santulli took narrative descriptions of the strategy suggestions and classified them by means of a coding scheme. *Phase of problem solving* (Table 16.1, Section 5) was defined on the basis of the task in which the child was engaged at the time the strategy was suggested or the metacognitive information was conveyed. In the *representational phase*, teachers focus on the child's initial perception and understanding of the problem and on the child's planning for problem solution. In the *solution phase*, the teacher and child are concerned with the child's manipulation of numbers so as to achieve a solution to the problem. In the *evaluation phase*, the teacher encourages children to assess the correctness of problem solutions they have reached. Teachers devoted the most instructional time to solution phase activities (M = 30% of observation intervals). Representational phase activities were observed during 19% of the intervals, and evaluation phase activities were seen in only 3% of the intervals. The remaining time was spent in teaching math facts or setting up the math lesson by reviewing previous work, specifying lesson goals, or describing procedures.

Consistent with the frequency data summarized in Fig. 16.1, teachers made specific strategy suggestions more often than metacognitive suggestions. A total of 2,378 strategy suggestions was obtained (927 suggestions by second-grade teachers and 1,451 suggestions by fifth-grade teachers). Individual teachers varied widely in their use of such suggestions, ranging from a low of four strategy suggestions (a second-grade teacher) to a high of 156 (in a fifth-grade teacher). There were 252 metacognitive suggestions, including 126 instances from teachers of each grade level. The range here was from no metacognitive suggestions (a fifth-grade teacher) to 32 (a second-grade teacher).

What sorts of strategy suggestions were the teachers making? The nature of strategies suggested for the representational, solution, and evaluative phases of math problem solving was considered. In the representational phase, the child's goal is to arrive at an understanding of the problem and then to plan a solution. Teachers instructed strategies more often in this phase than in the solution or evaluation phases of problem solving, averaging 32.9 such suggestions. Strategies suggested by teachers were classified according to the scheme presented in Table 16.2. As indicated in Fig. 16.2, differences across grade were found in the type of strategies suggested in the representational phase. Second-grade teachers most often made strategy suggestions that involved *concrete representation* of problems or *changes in the problem form* to aid understanding. Suggestions for concrete representation might involve asking the child to draw a picture, use objects, or use a table or chart to understand the problem or the mathematical operation. Suggestions regarding problem form involved transforming unfamiliar or difficult problems into simpler ones that could be solved more easily or articulating a rule to aid children's understanding of the mathematical relation. A different pattern is shown by fifth-grade teachers, who most often attempted to facilitate children's individual planning through their suggestions. Other strategy suggestions for the representational phase, used less often by teachers of either age group, involved *Reading*, in which the teachers' suggestions focused the child's attention on discovering the relevant aspects of the problem, understanding what the problem requires, or summarizing the information provided; *Elaborative Strategy suggestions*, in which children were told to relate the problem to their own experiences or to form a image to represent the problem; and *Comprehension Monitoring*, in which the teacher attempted to encourage children to monitor and evaluate their understanding of the problem.

In the solution phase, the child attempts to solve mathematical expressions in order to arrive at an answer to the problem. Strategies suggested by teachers were

TABLE 16.2
Scheme for Coding Representation Phase Strategy Suggestions (Santulli, 1991)

Reading: Construct Meaning by Increasing Attention to the Problem

Anticipation: Think about the problem before doing it/Read to get the facts. The teacher tells children to read the problem completely as a way of understanding, to learn the facts in the problem.

Read or Study the Problem for a Purpose: The teacher directs students to determine what they want to find out. The goal is to understand the specific question of the problem.

Re-read the Problem.

Paraphrase or Summarize: Increase attention to problem information or facts by paraphrasing or summarizing the information in the problem. The teacher may direct children to describe the story problem in their own words, or may focus the child's attention on problem information by emphasizing certain facts or asking children what specific numbers in the problem represent.

Elaboration: Construct Meaning by Relating Problem to Personal Experiences

Think of Yourself When You Read the Problem: To enhance understanding of the problem, the teacher directs students to think of a personal experience or put themselves in the story. The teacher may ask the child to create a story problem to enhance understanding of the math process they are studying.

Employ Imagery: Teacher instructs the child to create a visual image of the problem: "Picture in your mind what the story says." The teacher may direct the child to imagine a visual–spatial relationship or an object.

Concrete: Construct Meaning Through Concrete Representation of the Problem or Number Concepts

Generate a Concrete/Pictorial Representation: The teacher directs students to draw their own pictures or use objects to represent the problem. This activity may be used in understanding word problems and also in understanding or solving mathematical operations.

Utilize Pictorial Representation Provided: The teacher directs students to use tables or charts provided to aid understanding and problem solution. Again, the picture may be used to understand a word problem or to help in applying a mathematical operation.

Suggests the Use of Manipulative Aids: The teacher suggests that children use objects (fingers, rods, blocks, etc.) to represent math operations or teach number concepts.

Suppression of Manipulative Aids: The teacher discourages the child's use of manipulatives such as fingers to solve math operations.

Problem Form: Construct Meaning by Changing the Problem to a More Familiar Form, or a Form That Can Be Solved

Generate a Symbolic Relationship or Rule: The teacher asks child to generate a rule to understand a mathematical relationship or pattern.

Transformation: The teacher directs children to transform unfamiliar or difficulty problems into simpler forms that can be solved more easily. Transformations are possible because of logical, rule-governed relationships between stimulus elements. Transformations may involve changing problems to simpler operations, simplifying or changing the format or sequence of numbers, conceptualizing a problem as two separate problems as a way of helping them regulate their efforts.

Words Translated into Math Expressions: The teacher directs students to translate written words into variables, numbers, or operations.

(Continued)

TABLE 16.2
(*Continued*)

Comprehension Monitoring

Comprehension Monitoring: The teacher encourages children to monitor their understanding of the problem, urging the children to ask themselves questions such as, "Is there enough information to answer the question? What information is irrelevant? What do you need to know?"

Monitoring Problem Understanding: The teacher asks children to monitor their general understanding of the problem.

Deduction: Children are instructed to use their general knowledge of the problem and their ability to reason to construct an answer. The task may involve working backwards on a problem, using the answer to get the question, using logical processes to piece together the answer.

Planning

Directs Goal Formation: The teacher instructs children to come up with a solution by attending systematically to progressive steps in the problem.

Elaboration of a Schema: The teacher directs students to think of a simpler problem or presents a simpler problem to help in solving the problem under consideration. The teacher points out similarities and differences between problem types.

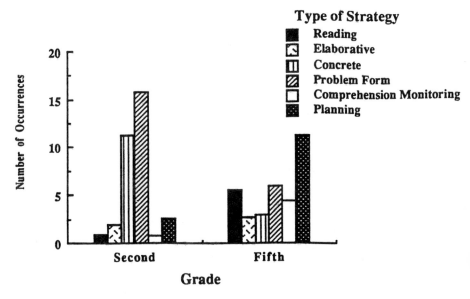

FIG. 16.2. Mean number of representational phase strategy suggestions by teachers of each grade level (Santulli, 1991).

classified according to the scheme presented in Table 16.3. In this phase, teachers gave an average of 22.25 strategy suggestions, including instruction emphasizing the use of *keywords* (attending to a word in the problem that provides a clue as to the operation appropriate to problem solution), *rote strategies* (rehearsal or other repetitive activities), *algorithms* (instructing children in the use of a particular rule or procedure that applies to a certain class of problems), and *approximation strategies* (guessing or estimating correct answers, eliminating incorrect answers). As indicated in Fig. 16.3, second-grade teachers used these suggestions to a limited extent; fifth-grade teachers, on the other hand, suggested algorithms more often than other kinds of solution phase activities and avoided suggesting rote strategies.

In the evaluation phase, the child carries out activities in order to judge the accuracy of the solution that has been produced. As a result, the child either accepts the solution obtained or returns to the representational phase to plan an alternative approach to the problem. Teachers made fewer strategy suggestions in this phase (M = 8.87) than in the other two phases of problem solving. Strategies suggested by teachers were classified according to the scheme presented in Table 16.4. Teachers most often suggested that the child use strategies to check their answers that involved outside sources of monitoring (M = 4.75), either providing information to the child about errors in answers or by asking the child to rely a classmate to check his or her work. Less often, the teacher suggested checking strategies that involve specific procedures to evaluate answers (M = 2.96). These involved activities such as using the inverse operation to check calculations and redoing the problem using the same or a different method. Finally, least often (M = 1.15), teachers suggested that children use strategies to assess the correctness of an answer in the context of the problem's meaning.

TABLE 16.3
Scheme for Coding Solution Phase Strategy Suggestions (Santulli, 1991)

Suggests Use of a Keyword Algorithm: The teacher directs students to decide on the problem goal or appropriate operation by attending to a word or clue in the problem statement.

Suppress Keyword Algorithm: The teacher points out that simply attending to words, rather than the meaning of the problem, will not lead to understanding of the problem.

Rote Learning: Children are told to rehearse stimuli verbally or to write, look at, go over, study, or repeat the stimuli in some other way. The children may be instructed to rehearse items just once, a finite number of times, or an unlimited number of times. Rote learning strategies do not include any explicit activities that would add meaning to the stimulus or cause it to be processes to a deeper level.

Algorithms: Teachers suggest procedures with a finite number of steps, which involve specific steps or rules that will lead to the correct answer. These procedures are only applicable to a set of problems belonging to a particular class. Examples of algorithms are renaming in addition, subtraction, multiplication, and division; conversion of units in one measure to another measure (e.g., fractions to decimals), rounding algorithms.

Approximating or Eliminating Answers: Students are directed to guess or estimate answers, or to engage in trial and error procedures to solve problems. Or children are told to eliminate possible answer choices that are incorrect in order to select the correct answer.

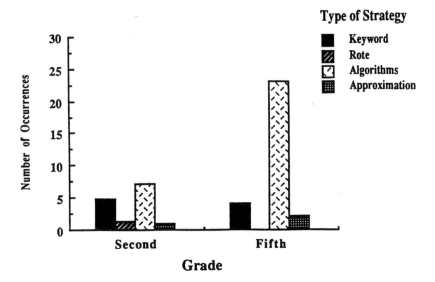

FIG. 16.3. Mean number of solution phase strategy suggestions by teachers of each grade level (Santulli, 1991).

TABLE 16.4
Scheme for Coding Evaluation Phase Strategy Suggestions (Santulli, 1991)

Strategies for Evaluation That Rely on an Outside Source

Attention to Specific Procedures: Based on observation of the student's performance, the teacher suggests that the student check one specific step in the problem solution. The teacher may indicate a specific reason why the student is making a mistake.

Reference Monitoring: The teacher directs students to allow other students or the teacher to check their work, or to follow along with other students to make sure the work is correct.

Deduction: The teacher indicates that a child has made an error because the answer does not fit a clue given or is not a reasonable one.

Strategies That Involve Specific Procedures to Evaluate Answers

---

Use the Inverse Operation: The student in instructed to check work by using the inverse operation (e.g., check subtraction with addition).

Check Work (nonspecific): The teacher simply reminds children to check their work, without indicating specific procedures to use.

Redo Problem Using a Different Procedure: The teacher describes a different way of solving the problem to check work.

Redo Problem Using the Same Way: The teacher instructs students to do the problem over again as a way of checking the work.

Strategies to Assess the Answer in the Context of Problem Meaning

---

Evaluate Answer: The teacher asks students to check their answers to see if they make sense or if they are reasonable given the nature of the problem.

Estimate Answer and Compare to Attained Solution: The teacher asks children to estimate or take a guess about the solution to a problem and then to compare this guess with the answer obtained.

Evaluate Answer Relative to Problem Question: The teacher instructs the student to go back to the problem question and evaluate whether his or her solution answers the question adequately.

310

The teacher might have asked the child to evaluate whether or not the answer is reasonable, if it makes sense; to compare his or her answer with an estimate of what the answer should be; or to check the problem again in order to see if the answer matches the question asked in the problem. No grade level differences were shown in the teachers' use of suggestions for evaluation strategies.

Teachers often provided general metacognitive information regarding person, task, and strategy aspects of problem solving. Their metacognitive suggestions were classified according to the coding scheme shown in Table 16.5. As indicated in Fig. 16.4, second grade teachers often provided children with information about person variables that could influence task performance. For example, they might make efforts to regulate children's emotional state or motivational level for the work, they might attribute success to the child's effort, or they might point out what the child knows or how the child learns in relation to a particular problem. Second-grade teachers provided such information more than fifth-grade teachers, and gave such information to their children more often than they gave task or strategy information. Fifth-grade teachers, on the other hand, provided person, task, and strategy information to about an equal extent. In addition to describing personal factors, they characterized the task for the child (evaluating task difficulty or specifying necessary math knowledge the child would use in solving the problem) and discussed various strategies (pointing out that alternative strategies can be used; asking the child to evaluate different strategies or encouraging awareness of strategies used).

In summary, Santulli's study, which focused on an aspect of classroom instruction in which the child's way of processing information is essential to good performance, gave a more positive view of the extent to which elementary school teachers are involved in the instruction of cognitive processes. In contrast with our original study, teachers in this study appeared to be more concerned about the cognitive processing activities of their students and provided students with a variety and large number of strategy and metacognitive suggestions. In mathematics, the demands for effective cognitive processing are great and there is clear feedback to child and teacher about the success of the child's processing activity on every problem the child attempts. Teachers meet the challenge of this subject matter by increasing their use of cognitive processing suggestions far above that shown when other subject matter (reading, language arts) is involved.

Teachers' suggestions for study activities were appropriate to the cognitive level of the class instructed, providing more concrete and transformation strategies to younger children and more complex planning and algorithmic strategies to older children. Teachers of younger children more than those instructing older children provided metacognitive information focusing on self-awareness. Although teachers spent a greater amount of instructional time in solution phase than in representational or evaluation phase activities, they were most likely to offer strategy suggestions in the representational phase. Here, teachers attempted to enrich the child's understanding of the problem by relating it to more familiar concepts or to personal experiences and by encouraging children to assess their

TABLE 16.5

Scheme for Coding Metacognitive Suggestions (Santulli, 1991)

Person Variables

Regulating State Variables: The teacher attempts to regulate the child's state of arousal or anxiety. The teacher may refer to the emotional state and how it may affect performance in mathematics. The teacher may suggest coping strategies to reduce anxiety or may attempt to increase arousal level if children don't seem to be interested.

Regulating Cognitive Tempo: The teacher attempts to regulate children's cognitive tempo or speed of completing a problem, or asks them to predict the length of time it will take to complete work.

Evaluate Past Performance: The teacher attempts to regulate or get children to monitor their efforts by describing previous test or task performance.

Attribution—Internal, Stable: The teacher attributes successful problem solving to the student's own ability.

Learning: The teacher explains ways of learning to the children. For example, the teacher might stress the use of different sense modalities in learning.

Comparative Evaluation: The teacher makes a comparison between the student and an individual of a different age about what they can expect of their ability to complete a task.

Attribution—Internal, Unstable: The teacher attributes successful problem solving to the student's good effort or attributes error to lack of effort.

Specific Self-Awareness: The teacher tells children that they should or do have specific knowledge about numbers.

Task Variables

Task Characteristics: Teacher makes a judgment or describes a characteristic of the task or activity. The teacher describes a task or a strategy as easy, difficult, or fun to do, or asks the children if they liked the activity.

Focus on Problem Form: The teacher indicates that the math procedures are important, tells students not to worry about how large the numbers are because any problem can be solved using the correct procedure.

Prerequisite Knowledge: The teacher specifies prerequisite math knowledge necessary to complete the problem. For example, the teacher may indicate that it is necessary to know the multiplication tables in order to do division problems.

Strategy Knowledge

Alternative Strategies: The teacher discusses and evaluates alternative strategies. The teacher indicates that there are different ways to do a problem, but suggests that students find the optimal way.

Strategy Awareness: The teacher attempts to make children aware of the strategies they are using. For example, he or she may indicate that children should try to have an explanation about how they came upon an answer.

---

own understanding and to make efforts to increase it. In the solution phase, strategy suggestions were concerned with more mechanical aspects of calculations, consisting largely of suggested use of algorithms for mathematical calculations. Although evaluation of problem solution was given a limited amount of time, teachers suggested a variety of strategies with which children could assess their problem solutions. Evaluation strategies relying on an understanding

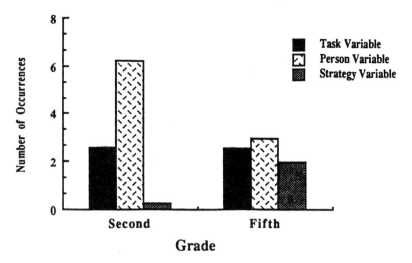

FIG. 16.4. Mean number of instances in which metacognitive information was conveyed by teachers of each grade level.

of the problem (e.g., *Does this answer make sense?*) were least often recommended. Instead, teachers' suggestions directed the children to rely on feedback of the teacher or peers or instructed them to repeat calculations.

This study did not directly observe children in order to determine the nature of the teachers' effects on children's learning activities. In our initial study (Moely et al., 1992), an effort was made to examine such effects. We selected teachers high and low in strategy suggestions and assessed behaviors of children who had been in their classrooms for a year. Low and moderate achievers who had experienced a high strategy teacher were better able to learn a new strategy for use in a memory task and were better able to describe that strategy in posttask interviews than were children who had spent the year with teachers who rarely described ways of studying. Consistent exposure over time to teaching of cognitive processing activities increases children's strategy use (Borkowski, this volume; Palincsar & Brown, 1984) and apparently, their ability to adopt and maintain the use of new strategies when appropriate.

SCHOOL DIFFERENCES IN CHILDREN'S METACOGNITION, MOTIVATIONAL BELIEFS, AND ACADEMIC ACHIEVEMENT

In a recent study, we focused on cognitive processes related to children's academic learning. We asked about the manner in which different school settings influence the child's acquisition of metacognitive knowledge about strategy use and self-regulation. We also examined aspects of students' motivation for academic work. We were interested in contrasting school settings in which different instructional methods are used. We assume that consistent exposure to the manifestations of a particular philosophy of education should affect children's choice of strategies and their motivation for academic achievement. There were a number of studies showing differences in motivation as a function of school characteristics (Ames, 1984; Ames & Archer, 1988; Stipek & Daniels, 1988). Although few investigations were concerned with study activities and metacognition, some cross-cultural research (Carr, Kurtz, Schneider, Turner, & Borkowski, 1989; Schneider, Borkowski, Kurtz, & Kerwin, 1986) showed variations in strategy use by children of different cultures, suggesting a role for school and home influences on strategy use.

In this study, we compared children who were attending two different kinds of school. In a large private school located in a suburban area of a Southern city, instruction during the early grades (through Grade 4) is mastery-oriented. Children do not receive grades but are evaluated by teachers in terms of their individual progress in mastering academic skills and knowledge. Instruction is individualized, with children completing assignments in an open classroom framework. As the children move into fifth grade, they gradually begin to take formal tests of content knowledge and to receive evaluations based on relative performance. As they go on to higher grades, tests become more frequent and evaluations begin to focus on comparative performance. Thus, we should expect some changes in children's approaches to and beliefs about academic tasks over Grades 5 through 7. Children in this school are predominantly White, of middle- and upper-middle-class backgrounds. Of the 103 children who participated (35 in Grade 5, 30 in Grade 6, and 38 in Grade 7), only 9% of the children were members of minority groups and 56% were female. We will refer to this school as the *mastery-oriented school*.

The other schools in our study were also private schools, operated by a religious organization and serving an urban population varying widely in SES level. In these schools, which we will call *traditional schools*, teaching from the earliest grades involves a more traditional classroom structure, with teachers instructing the entire class and grading on the basis of relative performance on assignments and examinations. Of the 154 children who took part in the study (51 in Grade 5, 51 in Grade 6, and 52 in Grade 7), 67% were members of minority groups (predominantly African American) and 55% were female.

In order to assess children's metacognitions, we developed a self-report questionnaire similar in form to those used by Meece, Blumenfeld, and Hoyle (1988), Nolen and Haladyna (1990), and Pintrich and DeGroot (1990). Items were adapted from the questionnaires used by these investigators and from study skills questionnaires such as the LASSI (Weinstein, Zimmerman, & Palmer, 1988). Students were asked to report on their use of study strategies, their use of activities to monitor their own study, and their task persistence. Children reported on how often they engaged in each of a number of study activities, using a 5-point scale ranging from *never* (1) to *always* (5). Scales that were developed indexed the use of rote strategies (say words over and over, memorize), cognitive strategies (write summaries, relate material to personal experiences), self-monitoring strategies (ask comprehension questions, check understanding or memory), and persistence (consistently finish work, put in time and effort on homework or classwork).

We were also interested in children's motivation for academic achievement and included questions tapping aspects of children's motivational beliefs with regard to academic work. In one of these, students were asked to evaluate their agreement with statements concerning three goal orientations: mastery (task) orientation, ego orientation, and work avoidance, as described by Nicholls (1989). In other questions, students were asked to evaluate the value they placed on school and academic experiences. Another measure assessed students' use of internal and external attributions for hypothetical successes and failures in academic tasks. Finally, to measure self-efficacy for academic tasks, students completed Scholastic Competence subscale of the Harter Self-Perception Profile for Children (Harter, 1985). Questionnaires were administered to classroom groups during three sessions in the fall of the school year.

We first compared the children at the two kinds of school on their reports of study activities and their responses on the motivational measures. Mean scores for the variables and differences between schools are shown in Table 16.6.

With regard to metacognitive variables, children in the traditional school setting reported significantly higher use of both rote and cognitive strategies

TABLE 16.6
Means and Standard Deviations for Metacognitive and Motivational Measures
for Samples from Each School Setting

	Mastery-Oriented School (N = 103)		Traditional Schools (N = 154)	
	M	SD	M	SD
Rote strategies**	2.88	.62	3.43	.74
Cognitive strategies**	2.83	.71	3.28	.79
Self-monitoring	3.94	.57	3.96	.68
Persistence	4.21	.54	4.09	.59
Mastery orientation	4.14	.66	4.15	.72
Ego orientation	3.63	.86	3.82	.86
Work avoidance**	2.65	.81	3.09	.85
Internal attributions for success*	4.00	.55	3.79	.62
Internal attributions for failure*	3.44	.71	3.18	.76
External attributions for success**	2.69	.49	2.92	.52
External attributions for failure	3.04	.58	3.12	.61
Value of schooling*	4.55	.53	4.35	.66
Self-efficacy	3.01	.67	2.94	.60
Achievement**	82.47	13.05	51.44	23.06

*School differences significant at $p < .01$.
**School differences significant at $p < .001$.

than did children from the mastery-oriented school. Children in the two school settings did not differ in self-reported use of self-monitoring strategies or persistence in study. It may be that the schoolwork of children at the traditional schools involves more examinations over memorized material than is the case at the mastery-oriented school, so that they may have had more occasion to employ strategies. Also, their teachers may have suggested strategies more often when helping children master lessons or prepare for examinations.

Measures of motivational beliefs showed school differences as well as several School × Grade interactions. As indicated in Table 16.6, the students at the mastery-oriented school were significantly less work-avoidant, placed more positive value on schooling, were more likely to attribute both success and failure to internal causes, and were less likely to attribute success to external causes. However, some of these school differences varied over grade level. In particular, students in the mastery-oriented school showed an increase over grade level in work avoidance as a goal orientation (from M = 2.33 among fifth graders to M = 2.92 for seventh graders), as well as decreases in the value placed on school [M (fifth grade) = 4.79, M (seventh grade) = 4.36], the use of internal attributions to account for academic success [M (fifth grade) = 4.14, M (7th grade) = 3.83], and mastery orientation [M (fifth grade) = 4.46, M (seventh grade) = 3.89]. In contrast, children at the traditional schools showed little variation over grade on these measures. By Grade 7, the two groups of children did not differ on goal orientation, value, or attribution measures.

There are many characteristics that distinguish the two types of school and that may contribute to the differential patterns shown. School populations differ in family SES and ethnic background; schools vary in curriculum as well as teaching methods. We feel that the school differences in motivational beliefs shown here are attributable to the teaching philosophies of the two schools and the change in emphasis on normative evaluation over grade level at the mastery-oriented school. The differences in evaluative environments of the two schools in the early grades are reflected in motivational beliefs shown especially in the younger children; as children in the two settings begin to experience more similar normative evaluations in the classrooms, differences in motivational beliefs decrease. Such relations of motivational beliefs and school characteristics are consistent with the findings of Ames and Archer (1988) and others (Ames, 1984; Stipek & Daniels, 1988) concerning the influence on children of varying classroom environments.

Scores on standardized achievement tests were obtained in order to investigate the relations between these measures and school achievement in each school setting. Achievement scores were calculated by averaging percentiles on national norms for subtests measuring reading, language, and mathematics achievement. Analyses were carried out to predict achievement test scores from measures of metacognition and motivation for the children at each school.

The first set of analyses considered the four metacognitive measures (reported use of rote strategies, cognitive strategies, self-monitoring activities, and persistence in study). For each school, a regression analysis was conducted including these four variables, along with grade, gender, and race (White vs. minority) as predictors of achievement test scores. Then, a reduced model regression analysis was done to determine the prediction of achievement test scores holding constant grade, gender, and race. Metacognitive variables significantly predicted achievement for children at each school. Table 16.7 shows partial correlations between each metacognitive measure and achievement test scores, holding constant grade, gender, and race, as well as the three other metacognitive variables. In both groups, reported use of rote strategies was negatively related to achievement, whereas persistence was positively correlated with achievement. In the traditional schools only, there was a tendency for reported use of cognitive strategies to be negatively correlated with achievement. No relation was shown at either school between reports of self-monitoring activities and achievement test scores.

Thus, these metacognitive variables showed similar relations to achievement for children in the two groups. Children of low achievement levels reported the use of rote strategies, whereas persistence in study was reported more often by children of higher achievement levels. For the most part, rote strategies present rather ineffective ways of mastering material and preparing for examinations, so it is not surprising that they were more typical of low achievers. This finding is consistent with Nolen (1988), who reported that general valuing and task-specific use of *surface-level strategies* were negatively related to grades obtained by eighth

TABLE 16.7
Partial Correlations of Each Metacognitive and Motivational Variable with
Academic Achievement for Children in Each School Setting

	Mastery-Oriented School (N = 99)	Traditional Schools (N = 149)
	Partial Correlation	Partial Correlation
Rote strategies	−.23*	−.25**
Cognitive strategies	−.05	−.13
Self-monitoring	.07	.09
Persistence	.27*	.24**
Mastery orientation	.17	−.16
Ego orientation	−.19	−.07
Work avoidance	−.10	−.25**
Internal attributions for success	.15	−.05
Internal attributions for failure	−.20	−.18*
External attributions for success	.07	−.28**
External attributions for failure	−.12	−.15
Value of schooling	.21	.16
Self-efficacy	.31**	.36**

*$p < .05$.
**$p < .01$.

grade students in a science class. With regard to self-monitoring, both Pintrich and DeGroot (1990) and Mizelle, Hart, and Carr (1993) reported positive relations between achievement and a measure they called *self-regulation*. Their measure included items that are similar to those on our self-monitoring scale, but also included a number of items that assess what we have called persistence. Our findings, consistent across both schools, indicate that persistence in study is the more important component in predicting achievement. In our sample, self-reported use of self-monitoring activities (defined in terms of self-testing or evaluating one's own knowledge state) was not related to achievement at either school. It may be that self-monitoring skills become relevant for achievement at a later time in development, when students are able to use self-regulation activities more effectively or when the structure of the learning environment allows more individual variation in the regulation of study activity. Consistent with Pintrich and DeGroot (1990), Nolen (1988), and Mizelle et al. (1993) is the failure to demonstrate higher use of cognitive strategies in high achieving children. There was, in fact, a slight negative relationship of reported cognitive strategy use and achievement among the children from the traditional schools. We know from other analyses that the younger children did not clearly differentiate between rote strategies, cognitive strategies, and self-monitoring activities (Fleming et al., 1993). Children of the middle elementary grades may not have mastered the use of cognitive strategies in ways that would make obvious their effectiveness. No grade differences were seen in the reported use of either rote or cognitive strategies, but this may be because of the relatively narrow range of grades considered. Clearly, by late adolescence, cognitive strategies become effective tools for academic accomplishment (Ryan, 1984; Weinstein et al., 1988). Research bridging the time span between elementary or middle school and college years could identify the nature and timing of changes in effective study activities. Longitudinal studies are needed to determine whether or not study activities adopted in these early years are predictive of later academic achievement.

The next set of analyses examined relations between the various measures of motivational beliefs and achievement test scores. Analyses comparing complete and reduced regression models indicated that the motivational variables considered as a group predicted achievement to a significant degree in each school setting. The partial correlations in Table 16.7 indicate the relation of each motivational variable to achievement test scores, holding constant grade, gender, and race. For goal orientation and attribution analyses, the partial correlations for each variable also hold constant the other motivational beliefs within that cluster (e.g., for mastery orientation, the partial correlation holds constant grade, gender, race, ego orientation, and work avoidance).

Differences between schools were seen in the extent to which motivational beliefs were related to achievement. Goal orientation measures predicted achievement only in the traditional school. As indicated in Table 16.7, work avoidance was negatively related to achievement in the traditional school setting.

There was also a trend for mastery orientation to be negatively related to achievement. Also among the children from traditional schools, the set of attributional variables showed strong prediction of achievement. Examining separate variables, children high in achievement made fewer external attributions for success and fewer internal attributions for failure. No significant relations between these sets of variables appeared for children from the mastery-oriented school.

For children at the mastery-oriented school, only self-efficacy appeared as an important predictor of school achievement. Self-efficacy was similarly related to achievement for children at the traditional schools. This finding is consistent with those of previous studies (Pintrich & DeGroot, 1990). Concurrent relations of achievement and self-efficacy may reflect either motivational effects or realistic self-assessments of children varying in achievement level. Through longitudinal research, it will be possible to characterize the nature of this relationship more exactly.

Successful students at the traditional schools were those who were interested in participating in schoolwork and who avoided self-defeating attributions in accounting for academic success or failure. Low achievers were oriented toward avoiding work and reported attributional beliefs that are not facilitative of academic effort. At the mastery-oriented school, motivational beliefs were in flux over the grade levels considered here, which may have reduced their value as predictors of concurrent achievement. Once motivational beliefs stabilize at this school, more dramatic patterns may appear. The manner in which beliefs about study activities and motivation mediate children's achievement and school success measured at later points in time is a question for future investigation.

CONCLUDING REMARKS

These observations attempted to describe what children experience and how their metacognitions and motivational beliefs develop as they move through elementary and middle school grades. What have we learned from them? First, teachers' efforts to provide information to children about how to study will vary greatly depending upon the subject matter under consideration. When we looked at a broad range of instructional effort (Moely et al., 1992), we found low strategy instruction. When Santulli (1991) focused on mathematics, specifically the teaching of math problem solving, he found teachers to be more likely to offer suggestions for strategy use and to provide metacognitive information to children. When teachers do suggest strategies, they generally show variations that are appropriate given developmental changes in children's skills that were identified through research.

What impact does schooling have on children's own views of their study activities and their motivation for academic achievement? Any generalizations must take into account the nature of the school setting in which the child is developing. Children in the traditional schools in the present study reported more strategy use than did those at the mastery-oriented school. Children at the two schools differed on the motivation measures in ways that reflect school practices. Relations between measures of motivational beliefs and achievement were more dramatic at the traditional school than at the mastery-oriented school. The differences between schools reflect differences in goals of instruction and in teaching style that need more precise examination. Looking at both teacher behaviors and children's developing beliefs about study activities and motivation will permit a more exact description of how school experiences influence children's ability to learn.

ACKNOWLEDGMENTS

The work reported here was supported in part by an Enhancement Grant from the Louisiana Education Quality Support Fund and by the Robert E. Flowerree Fund of Tulane University. Our thanks to all of the participating schools and teachers, and to our colleagues, Diane Kogut, Shawn Fleming, Jennifer Tonglet, Kim Cassell, Deedrah Respess, Missy Deichmann, Melissa Poche, Lori Werdenschlag, and Faith Cohen.

REFERENCES

Ames, C. (1984). Competitive, cooperative, and individualistic goal structures: A cognitive–motivational analysis. In R. Ames & C. Ames (Eds.), Research on motivation in education: Vol. 1. Student motivation (pp. 177–207). San Diego, CA: Academic Press.

Ames, C., & Archer, J. (1988). Achievement goals in the classroom: Students' learning strategies and motivation processes. Journal of Educational Psychology, 80, 260–267.

Carr, M., Kurtz, B. E., Schneider, W., Turner, L. A., & Borkowski, J. G. (1989). Strategy acquisition and transfer among American and German children: Environmental influences on metacognitive development. Developmental Psychology, 25, 765–771.

Derry, S. J. (1990). Learning strategies for acquiring useful knowledge. In B. F. Jones & L. Idol (Eds.), Dimensions of thinking and cognitive instruction. (pp. 347–379). Hillsdale, NJ: Lawrence Erlbaum Associates.

Flavell, J. H. (1970). Developmental studies of mediated memory. In H. W. Reese & L. P. Lipsitt (Eds.), Advances in child development and behavior (Vol. 5, pp. 181–211). New York: Academic Press.

Fleming, S. P., Cornwell, J. M., Tonglet, J. P., Cassell, K. R., Obach, M. S., Respess, D. M., Deichmann, M. M., Poche, J. G., & Moely, B. E. (1993, April). Developmental changes in the factor structure of a self-report measure of study activities. Paper presented at the annual meeting of the American Educational Research Association, Atlanta.

Harter, S. (1985). Manual for the Self-Perception Profile for Children. Denver, CO: University of Denver.

Meece, J. L., Blumenfeld, P. C., & Hoyle, R. H. (1988). Students' goal orientations and cognitive engagement in classroom activities. Journal of Educational Psychology, 80, 514–523.

Mizelle, N. B., Hart, L. E., & Carr, M. (1993, April). *Middle grade students' motivational processes and use of strategies with expository text.* Paper presented at the annual meeting of the American Educational Research Association, Atlanta.

Moely, B. E., Hart, S. S., Leal, L., Santulli, K. A., Rao, N., Johnson, T., & Hamilton, L. B. (1992). The teacher's role in facilitating memory and study strategy development in the elementary school classroom. *Child Development, 63,* 653–672.

Nicholls, J. G. (1989). *The competitive ethos and democratic education: The development and expression of achievement motivation.* Cambridge, MA: Harvard University Press.

Nolen, S. B. (1988). Reasons for studying: Motivational orientation and study strategies. *Cognition and Instruction, 5,* 269–287.

Nolen, S. B., & Haladyna, T. M. (1990). A construct validation of measures of students' study strategy beliefs and perceptions of teacher goals. *Educational and Psychological Measurement, 50,* 191–202.

Palincsar, A. S., & Brown, A. L. (1984). Reciprocal teaching of comprehension-fostering and comprehension-monitoring activities. *Cognition and Instruction, 1,* 117–175.

Pintrich, P. R., & DeGroot, E. V. (1990). Motivational and self-regulated learning components of classroom academic performance. *Journal of Educational Psychology, 82,* 33–40.

Pressley, M., Borkowski, J. G., & O'Sullivan, J. (1985). Children's metamemory and the teaching of memory strategies. In D. L. Forrest-Pressley, G. E. MacKinnon, & T. G. Waller (Eds.), *Metacognition, cognition, and human performance: Vol. 1. Theoretical perspectives.* (pp. 111–153). Orlando, FL: Academic Press.

Ryan, M. P. (1984). Monitoring text comprehension: Individual differences in epistemological standards. *Journal of Educational Psychology, 76,* 248–258.

Santulli, K. A. (1991). Teachers' role in facilitating students' strategic and metacognitive processes during the representational, solution, and evaluation phase of mathematics problem solving. *Dissertation Abstracts International, 52*(10), 5559. (University Microfilms No. AAC92–09661)

Schneider, W., Borkowski, J. G., Kurtz, B. E., & Kerwin, K. (1986). Metamemory and motivation: A comparison of strategy use and performance in German and American children. *Journal of Cross-Cultural Psychology, 17,* 315–337.

Stipek, D. J., & Daniels, D. H. (1988). Declining perceptions of competence: A consequence of changes in the child or in the educational environment? *Journal of Educational Psychology, 80,* 352–356.

Weinstein, C. E., Zimmerman, S. A., & Palmer, D. R. (1988). Assessing learning strategies: The design and development of the LASSI. In C. E. Weinstein, E. T. Goetz, & P. A. Alexander (Eds.), *Learning and study strategies: Issues in assessment, instruction, and evaluation* (pp. 25–40). San Diego, CA: Academic Press.

Wertsch, J. V., & Tulviste, P. (1992). L. S. Vygotsky and contemporary developmental psychology. *Developmental Psychology, 28,* 548–557.

Chapter 17

The Suggestibility of Children's Eyewitness Reports: Methodological Issues

Stephen J. Ceci
Cornell University

Michelle D. Leichtman
Harvard University

Maggie Bruck
McGill University

> *. . . then we will no longer be infants tossed back and forth by the cunning and craftiness of men and their deceitful scheming.*
>
> —Ephesians 4:14

> *. . . Out of the mouth of babes and nursing infants you have perfected praise.*
>
> —Matthew 21:16

Since biblical times, children's susceptibility to adult influence has been the object of contradictory thinking. Philosophers and theologians, parents and teachers, and most recently, those in the legal arena, are concerned with how easily children's memories and reports of past experiences can be swayed by the suggestions of others. In recent decades, this question has been tackled by researchers in psychology, and although significant gains have been made in our understanding of the developmental course of suggestibility, the debate over the degree and circumstances of children's report distortion looms larger than ever, particularly as it involves the credibility of children's reports in courts of law. Children are highly resistant to suggestion, unlikely to lie, and as reliable as adult witnesses about acts perpetrated on their own bodies (e.g., Berliner, 1985; Goodman, Rudy, Bottoms, & Aman, 1990; Jones & McGraw, 1987). However, children are also described as having difficulty distinguishing reality from fantasy, susceptible to coaching by powerful authority figures, and therefore, as significantly less reliable than adults (e.g., Feher, 1988; Gardner, 1989; Schuman, 1986; Underwager & Wakefield, 1990).

In previous work, we reviewed the evidence for both sides of the debate (Ceci & Bruck, 1993) and concluded there are reliable age differences in suggestibility, with preschool aged children's reports being more readily impeded by the presence of erroneous suggestions by an interviewer than are older children's reports. There are caveats attached to this conclusion. For example, some researchers claimed that age differences in suggestibility are primarily evident with nonparticipant children (i.e., bystanders as opposed to children who were the subjects of some action; Rudy & Goodman, 1991), only on nonsexual questions (Rudy & Goodman, 1991), and only for peripheral, nonsalient events (Fivush, 1993). Others, however, found age differences in suggestibility for questions with sexual themes (e.g., Baker-Ward, Gordon, Ornstein, Larus, & Clubb, 1993; Goodman, Rudy, Bottoms & Aman, 1990), and for recall of salient, central events (e.g., Cassel, Roebers, & Bjorklund, 1993).

In this chapter, we focus on the methodological issues in this research arena. Although methodological concerns are of central interest in all research enterprises, these concerns are even more critical in the current research on children's suggestibility than in other domains. Research in this area was primarily driven by practical, political, legal and social concerns. Unlike many other fields in which applied research is evaluated in terms of its theoretical basis as well as the rigor of its design, for many, the major criteria for evaluating current research in the field of children's suggestibility is the degree to which the methodologies mirror the actual contexts that bring children into courts—that is, its ecological validity.

· In this chapter, we first provide an historical context for the emergence of research on children's suggestibility, and describe the evolution of methodologies that address issues concerning children's testimonial accuracy. Next, we describe in detail some recent studies that were conducted in our laboratories and illustrate these methodologies. We conclude with a focus on ecological validity, a construct at the heart of the question of what science can bring to real-world situations in which children's memory is of paramount concern.

EARLY STUDIES OF SUGGESTIBILITY

In the early 1900s, most of the work on children's suggestibility was carried out in Europe with little interest from North American researchers. This discrepant interest on the two continents reflects at least two major factors. The first of these is that children were more frequently called as witnesses in European courts. Secondly, in many European countries, an inquisitorial system of justice prevails in which the judge is responsible for calling and questioning witnesses. Because there are often no juries, the European judge is more likely to call on experts to testify about the competence of the witnesses. In the early 1900s, some of these experts were psychologists who carried out experiments to examine the veracity of the children's testimony. In contrast, in an adversarial system, such as the one used in the United States and Commonwealth countries, the use of opposing attorneys and a jury were considered sufficient safeguards in evaluating witness credibility.

We present two examples of the types of research programs carried out in the European arena, both of which had enormous influence on the thinking and scientific procedures of the next part of the century. The first research program was that of Binet, the French psychologist best known as the father of the IQ test. It is surprising that he is so little known for his work in the field of suggestibility, because his techniques, his theoretical framework, and his data stand up well in the modern forum.

Binet (1900) maintained that suggestibility reflected the operation of two broad classes of factors. The first concerns the influence of a prominent thought (autosuggestion) that develops within the individual and is not the result of another's influence. Binet held that autosuggestions paralyzed a child's processes of critical thought, and he attempted to construct experimental situations in which suggestions came from the subject. The best known of these tasks involved showing children a series of lines of progressively greater lengths. In one case, five lines of increasing length were presented and these were followed by a series of target lines that were of the same length as the longest (final) line of the series. After the child was shown each line, he or she was asked to reproduce it on paper as faithfully as possible. Children tended to be swayed by suggestion, which in this case was the expectation of ever-increasing lines; that is, reproductions of the target line were systematically too long because children inferred that it was longer than the line that had preceded it. Binet questioned his subjects after the study to determine why they had drawn the target lines so long, and found that many children knew that the lines they had drawn were incorrect, and were able to redraw them more accurately on demand. Binet claimed this ability showed that following the experiment, children escaped the influence of the autosuggestion, and regained control of themselves.

The second class of factors underlying suggestibility, according to Binet, were external to the child and reflected mental obedience to another person. In one test of external forces, Binet examined the effects of the examiner's language on children's responses. Children studied five objects for 10 seconds. Some children were told to write down everything they saw, whereas others were asked questions about the objects. For example, one of the objects was a button glued onto poster board. One group of children was asked simple direct questions about the button (e.g., "How is the button attached to the board?"), whereas other children were asked either mildly leading questions (e.g., "Wasn't the button attached by a thread?") or highly misleading and suggestive questions (e.g., "What was the color of the thread that attached the button to the board?").

There were several major findings of this study. First, free recall resulted in the most accurate statements and highly misleading questions resulted in the most inaccurate statements. This was the first demonstration of a pattern of results to be replicated by most researchers in children's suggestibility throughout the rest of this century. Second, the children's answers were characterized by an exactness and certainty, regardless of their accuracy level. Third, when the children were later asked if they had made any mistakes, they did not correct their inaccurate responses to misleading questions, unlike in previous studies. Binet concluded that children's erroneous responses reflected gaps in their memories, which they reasonably attempted to fill in order to please the experimenter. However, once the erroneous response was given, Binet surmised that it became incorporated in memory.

Binet's work was prescient in a number of ways. First, he was a forerunner of modern considerations of the basis of suggestibility. He distinguished between errors of reporting that are the result of actual memory changes versus those that are due to social conformity, arguing that the latter manifestations of suggestibility included attempts to please powerful adult authority figures, and did not always reflect genuine incorporation of the false suggestion into the memory record. His unique position was that suggestibility was a combination of both memorial and social forces. This position was radical in his day, as the common view was that that suggestibility was a psychological weakness that stemmed from internal factors. In contrast, Binet argued that suggestibility was a normal psychological process, largely dependent on external factors.

Second, Binet's work was methodologically exemplary, and thus the methods that he developed to examine internal and external forces were adopted or elaborated by researchers for the next 90 years. For example, the perceptual tasks he developed to examine internal forces were commonly used through the 1960s (e.g., Hurlock, 1930; McConnell, 1963; Messerschmidt, 1933; Otis, 1924; Sherman, 1925). His categorization of questions in interviews on a continuum ranging from neutral (free recall) to highly misleading was subsequently used by most researchers in the field.

Finally, Binet attempted to apply his research to the courtroom context. He recommended that judges take the responsibility for obtaining reliable testimony from children and cautioned them about the dangers of forcing their own questions into a child's memory. Unfortunately, Binet met with great disappointment in his efforts to apply his research directly to the courtroom. According to Cunningham (1988a, 1988b) Binet bemoaned the fact that his work was never used in French courts. Further, he had hoped to extend his research purview from laboratory studies on school children's suggestibility to more naturalistic research in the courtroom by analyzing the transcripts of criminal cases, but he was prevented from doing so by the authorities. Binet's unfulfilled visions of applying his research to the courtroom were taken up by other European researchers such as Stern (1910) and Varendonck.

Varendonck, a Belgian psychologist, conducted a number of interesting studies on young children's testimony as a result of being called as an expert witness in a trial involving allegations by several children that a young girl named Cecile was murdered by a local man. The following details of the case are provided by Varendonck (1911). Two of Cecile's friends, who had played with her on the day of her murder, were awakened that night by Cecile's mother, inquiring after her whereabouts. One of the children, Louise, replied that she did not know; after leaving Cecile, she had returned home, had dinner, and gone to bed. Still later that night, Louise led the police to the spot where the children had played, not far from where Cecile's body was found. She was the fourth murder victim in a small town within a period of 1 month. After much suggestive questioning, Louise stated that a tall dark man with a dark moustache had coaxed Cecile to follow him. The next day, the two children were questioned again, and during this interrogation they altered their original testimony. After further questioning, which involved suggesting the names of potential murderers, one of the children said the name of the man was Jan. One month later, an anonymous letter was received by the police accusing one of the town members (who was the father of one of the playmates) of the murder. On further questioning by powerful authority figures, Louise provided additional details about the murder.

The prosecution's case at the trial centered on the testimony of the two children. Based upon the details of the case, Varendonck was convinced of the defendant's innocence. He quickly conducted a series of studies with the specific intent of demonstrating the unreliability of children's testimony.

In one study, 7-year-old children were asked about the color of a teacher's beard. Sixteen of 18 children provided a response, whereas only 2 said they did not know. The teacher in question did not have a beard (Varendonck, 1911). In another demonstration, a teacher from an adjoining classroom came into Varendonck's classroom and, without removing his hat, talked in an agitated fashion for approximately 5 minutes. (Keeping one's hat on when entering a room was uncommon because it was a sign of rudeness in that day's society.) After this teacher had left the classroom, the children were then asked in which hand that teacher had held his hat. Only 3 of the 27 students claimed that the hat was not in his hand. In another demonstration, Varendonck asked the children in his class to name and describe the person that had approached him in the school yard that morning. In fact, although there was no such person, most of the children fell sway to the suggestion, with 17 out of 22 giving a name for the person, the color of his clothes, and other details. Varendonck claimed that the types of questions he used during this procedure were parallel to those the examining magistrate had used with one of the child witnesses.

Varendonck concluded from his demonstrations that the two children's statements to the police were false, the result of suggestions provided by influential adults. He carefully documented how the children changed their testimonies between the first and second interrogations, and how other social factors (e.g., repeated questioning by powerful adult figures) conspired to produce their testimony. Varendonck concluded that children could not observe accurately, and that their suggestibility was inexhaustible. He maintained that children would believe anything adults wanted them to. Varendonck's work is noteworthy because his empirical data were frequently used in courts to cast doubt on the testimony of child witnesses.

With few exceptions, right up to the 1970s, studies on children's suggestibility were consistent in designs and results to those just described. Most researchers expressed the view that children were extremely susceptible to leading questions and could not be trusted to resist an adult interviewer's suggestions. After the 1930s, there was a dramatic decrease in research on children's suggestibility, and only a handful of studies were published in peer-reviewed journals over the next 40 years.

THE MODERN AGE: STUDIES OF CHILDREN'S SUGGESTIBILITY

The late 1970s marked a resurgence of interest among developmental researchers in the reliability of children's reports. Since 1979, over 150 studies on children's suggestibility were reported.

Undoubtedly, the biggest stimulus for the explosion of research on children's suggestibility was the fact that more and more children were being admitted as witnesses into United States courtrooms. This phenomenon was the result of a dramatic increase in reports of crimes involving sexual and physical abuse in which the child was a victim and often the only witness. As more and more children were admitted as witnesses in the courtroom, criminal procedures were modified. For example, all but a few states dropped corroboration rules for child witnesses who are victims of sexual abuse. Other examples include shield laws (i.e., permitting a child witness to testify behind a one-way screen that occludes the child's view of the defendant, but not the defendant's view of the child; or testifying over closed-circuit television) and hearsay exceptions (e.g., allowing therapists, pediatricians, and others to describe what children said to them).

These modifications are often employed in courtrooms without consultation with behavioral scientists as to the relative risks and benefits of each type of procedure. Their use is based, in part, on the belief that they will increase the reliability and accuracy of children's testimony. Paradoxically, because these procedures were instituted, there is an increased demand for scientific data that involves the general issue of young children's credibility and suggestibility.

Currently, when behavioral scientists are brought into the courtroom either as consultants or expert witnesses on children's testimony, there is a reluctance to generalize the results of the earlier studies to the forensic arena. There are several legitimate reasons why this is the case. First, the greatest current concern about testimonial accuracy is focused on preschoolers, who are disproportionately more likely to have their cases come to trial than are older children (see Ceci & Bruck, 1993). Yet, not one study in the first 80 years of this century included preschoolers.

This void has begun to be filled in recent years; since 1980, over 20 studies relevant to the issues of children's suggestibility included a preschool sample.

Second, and of most importance, is the concern that most of the previous studies involved children's recall of events that were forensically irrelevant. That is, in most of this earlier literature, researchers examined the influences of a single misleading suggestion or a leading question on children's reports of neutral, nonscripted, and often uninteresting events that occurred in a laboratory setting. Although these results may be of importance for a theoretical conceptualization of the mechanisms that underlie suggestibility effects and memory processes, these studies have limited practical and legal relevance regarding the reliability of the child witness. In many court cases, allegations involve the child in the role of a participant rather than as a passive bystander; they involve the child's recall of salient, central events rather than peripheral, unimportant events; they often include repeated interviews that are highly suggestive; and they frequently involve emotionally charged and highly stressful events, such as sexual molestation or the interview procedures themselves. The earlier experiments of this century provided no clues as to the testimonial accuracy of children in such circumstances.

As an example of a case in which children testified, and in which their credibility became so much of an issue as to result in an appeal of the original conviction, we present a concise summary of the Wee Care Nursery School case. Margaret Kelly Michaels, a 26-year-old nursery school teacher, was accused of sexually abusing children at the Wee Care Nursery School. Based on the children's reports, she was said to have licked peanut butter off children's genitals, played the piano while nude, made children drink her urine and eat her feces, and to have raped and assaulted them with knives, forks, spoons, and Lego blocks. She was accused by the children of performing these acts during school hours over a period of 7 months. None of the alleged acts were noticed by staff or reported by children to their parents. No parent noticed signs of strange behavior or genital soreness in their children, or smelled urine or feces on them.

The first suspicion that Kelly Michaels abused her charges occurred 4 days after she had left the Wee Care Nursery School. A 4-year-old former student of Kelly's was having his temperature taken rectally at his pediatrician's office, and said to the nurse, "That's what my teacher does to me at school." When asked to explain, he replied, "Her takes my temperature" (Manshel, 1990, p. 8). On the advice of the pediatrician, the child's mother notified the state's child protective agency. Two days later, when interviewed by the assistant prosecutor, the child inserted his finger into the rectum of an anatomical doll, and reported that two other boys also had their temperature taken. When later questioned, these two boys denied the claim, but one indicated that Kelly Michaels had touched his penis. The first child's mother then told a parent, who was a board member, of her son's disclosures. This board member interrogated his son about Kelly Michaels touching him inappropriately, remarking that he was his best friend and that he could tell him anything. His son then told him that Kelly

330 CECI, LEICHTMAN, BRUCK

had touched his penis with a spoon. The Wee Care Nursery School sent out a letter to parents, informing them of an investigation of a former employee regarding serious allegations. In a subsequent meeting, a social worker explained to the parents that sexual abuse of children is very common, with one out of three children being a victim of an inappropriate sexual experience by the age of 18 years. She encouraged parents to examine their children for genital soreness, nightmares, bed-wetting, masturbation, or any noticeable changes in behavior, and to have them examined by pediatricians for injury. Soon, there were many more allegations against Kelly Michaels. She was convicted of 115 counts of sexual abuse against twenty 3- to 5-year-old children 2½ years later. After spending 5 years in jail, her case was successfully appealed.

In view of the fact that the earlier studies on children's suggestibility shed little light on the credibility of child witnesses such as those involved in the Kelly Michaels trial, modern researchers tried to tackle the issue of how to conduct an ethically acceptable experiment that mirrors the conditions characteristic of many child victim-witnesses. For example, in order to determine if children who are sexually abused can be persuaded that they were never abused, it would be unethical to examine how successfully an interviewer can suggest to children with substantiated histories of abuse that the abuse had never taken place. Similarly, it would be unacceptable to determine if nonabused children would make allegations of sexual abuse after a highly suggestive interview. It is ethically impermissible to alter such fundamental aspects of young children's autobiography.

Thus, unlike many other scientific or psychological enterprises, the thorniest challenges in the field of research on children's suggestibility are methodological and not conceptual. We researchers know the relevant questions to ask, but we have a great deal of difficulty devising paradigms to sensibly address these issues.

One of the first steps was to expand the definitions of suggestibility. As defined traditionally, suggestibility implies that postevent information gets incorporated into memory (e.g., Andrews, 1964; Loftus, 1979); by this definition, suggestibility is "the extent to which individuals come to accept and subsequently incorporate post-event information into their memory recollections" (Gudjonsson, 1986, p. 195; see also Powers, Andriks, & Loftus, 1979). The traditional definition implies that (a) suggestibility can only be unconscious (i.e., interfering information is unwittingly incorporated into memory), (b) suggestibility results from the provision of information following an event as opposed to preceding it, and (c) suggestibility is a memory-based, as opposed to a social, phenomenon. Recently, however, Ceci and Bruck (1993) argued that suggestibility concerns the degree to which children's encoding, storage, retrieval and reporting of events can be influenced by a range of internal and external factors. A core implication of this latter definition is a sensitivity to context, such that the insinuations of leading questions and the tone of an interviewer's voice may affect the degree to which information is incorporated into a person's account.

In this chapter, we adopt the broader definition of suggestibility put forward by Ceci and Bruck (1993) because it is more helpful in thinking about applied issues. The Ceci and Bruck definition implies that (a) it is possible to accept information and yet be fully aware of its divergence from some originally perceived event, as in the case of confabulation (e.g., as shown by brain-injured patients; see Johnson, 1991), acquiescence to social demands, or lying, hence these forms of suggestibility do not involve the alteration of memory; (b) suggestibility can result from the provision of information either preceding or following an event; and (c) suggestibility can result from social as well as cognitive factors. Thus, this broader view of suggestibility accords with both the legal and everyday uses of the term, to connote how easily one is influenced by subtle suggestions, expectations, stereotypes, and leading questions that can unconsciously alter reports, as well as by explicit bribes, threats, and other forms of inducement that can consciously alter them. Armed with this broader definition of suggestibility, we now turn to a discussion of some more recent studies of children's suggestibility.

Children's Reports of Touching

In response to the criticism that earlier studies are not forensically relevant because they did not examine how children respond to questions about events that involve their own bodies or about other salient events that occurred in personally experienced, stressful situations, a number of researchers designed studies in which children were asked misleading questions about being touched, including on their genitals. In some studies, children were questioned about their previous interactions with an experimenter in which they participated versus observed (e.g., Rudy & Goodman, 1991), in other studies they were questioned after being inoculated by a physician (Bruck, Ceci, Francoeur, & Barr, 1995; Goodman, Herschman, Hepps, & Rudy, 1991) or given genital examinations by their pediatrician (Bruck, Ceci, Francoeur, & Renick, in press; Saywitz, Goodman, Nicholas, & Moan, 1991).

For example, Saywitz and her colleagues (Saywitz et al., 1991) examined 5- and 7-year-old girls' memories of medical examinations. Half of each age group had a scoliosis exam (for curvature of the spine) and the other half had a genital exam. Children were tested at either 1 or 4 weeks following their exam. They were asked suggestive and nonsuggestive questions that were abuse-related (e.g., "How many times did the doctor kiss you?") or nonabuse-related (e.g., "Didn't the doctor look at your feet first?"). Although the older children were initially more accurate than the younger children on most questions, some of these age differences disappeared after the 4-week delay. Most importantly, although there were age differences on suggestive abuse questions, few children gave incorrect responses. For example, 7-year-old children never made a false report of abuse, and 5-year-olds did so only rarely.

Saywitz and her colleagues stress the importance of specific patterns of results in this study. They conclude that children's inaccurate reports involve mainly omission rather than commission errors. The majority of children in the genital examination condition did not disclose genital contact, unless specifically asked to do so. This latter opportunity was only provided with the direct (leading) question format ("Did the doctor touch you here"?). In the scoliosis condition, when children were asked these direct questions, the incidence of false reports was between 2.9% and 5.6%. In reviewing this study, Goodman and Clarke-Stewart (1991) concluded that:

> . . . leading questions were often necessary to elicit information from children about actual events they had experienced (genital touching) . . . The children . . . were generally accurate in reporting specific and personal things that had happened to them. If these results can be generalized to investigations of abuse, they suggest that normal children are unlikely to make up details of sexual acts when nothing abusive happened. They suggest that children will not easily yield to an interviewer's suggestion that something sexual occurred when in fact it did not, especially if non-intimidating interviewers ask questions children can comprehend. (pp. 102–103)

Thus, according to this group of researchers, earlier studies overestimated the extent to which children are suggestible. That is, children may be suggestible about events and settings that are unimportant to them and for which they acted as passive observers. However, even very young children are highly resistant to erroneous suggestions about personally experienced events that are salient. This stance is clearly evidenced in the following statement:

> There is now no real question that the law and many developmentalists were wrong in their assumption that children are highly vulnerable to suggestion, at least in regard to salient details. Although some developmentalists may be challenged to find developmental differences in suggestibility in increasingly arcane circumstances, as a practical matter who really cares whether 3-year-old children are (more) suggestible about peripheral details in events that they witnessed than are 4-year-old children? Perhaps the question has some significance for developmental theory, but surely it has little or no meaning for policy and practice in child protection and law. (Melton, 1992, p. 154)

There are, however, several major methodological and interpretive criticisms of this line of study. The first concerns the construct of suggestibility as reflected in these studies: It is measured by children's response to a misleading question at the time of interview. This is indeed a narrow view that is not reflected in many of the examples of actual child witnesses. As Steller and others commented, "any generalizations of the findings of these experiments seem to be problematic because of the unrealistic way in which the abuse questions were formulated and introduced during the interviews. The interviews and not the medical examination are the crucial aspect of the studies when considering the question of generalizability of the findings to real-life sexual abuse investigation" (p. 107). Specifically, the results of these medical studies merely indicate that when children are questioned only once, under neutral conditions, by an unfamiliar investigator, they will be highly resistant to suggestion about sexual touching. However, as we document below, this scenario is quite atypical of those that bring children to court. A final problem with some of these data are their inconsistencies. There are some studies of children's reports of visits to pediatricians that involve recall of touching where it is found that young children are quite suggestible about central, salient experiences that involved bodily contact. For example, Ornstein and his colleagues (Gordon, Ornstein, Clubb, & Nida, 1991) found that when children were later questioned about their memories of a visit to the pediatrician, 3-year olds were more prone than 6-year-olds to make false claims in response to suggestive questions about silly events that involved body contact (e.g., "Did the nurse lick your knee?")—rates of false reports for the youngest children ranged from 17% to 26%. Oates and Shrimpton (1991) also found that preschoolers were more suggestible than older children about previously experienced events that involved bodily touching. Although these two studies do not involve sexual touching, we recently found that 3-year-old children make many false claims regarding genital touching in response to questions (Bruck et al., in press). Thus, there is some evidence that the findings of early European studies that characterized young children as highly suggestible are valid, even when the events are salient and personally experienced.

Interviewer Dynamics

As mentioned, some researchers argued that the most relevant empirical data on the suggestibility of child witnesses for the forensic area involves the examination of the component features of therapeutic and investigative interviews between children and adults. This focus has arisen in response to the concern that the interviewing procedures of earlier studies were less intense than those that bring children to court—so much so as to result in a potential underestimation of children's suggestibility (Raskin & Esplin, 1991; Steller, 1991).

The interviewing procedures used in traditional laboratory studies and those used in the forensic arena differ in several ways. First, children who come to court are frequently questioned weeks, months, or even years after the occurrence of an event (as opposed to minutes or days later). Suggestibility effects may thus be more salient after long delays because the original memory trace has sufficiently faded to allow for a more complete penetration of the suggestion than might occur after shorter delays. Second, it is rare that child witnesses are interviewed only one time, by one interviewer, under nonstressful conditions. The modal child witness was interviewed between four and eleven times prior to the first courtroom appearance; and sometimes children are interviewed weekly for years about the same event (e.g., in therapy sessions). Some suggested that the incessant use of leading questions and suggestions in these repeated interviews may result in a qualitatively different type of report distortion than that arising from a single misleading question in a single postevent interview. Third, an examination of the interviews of some child witnesses reveal that the label *suggestive interview* describes more than the use of misleading questions. Rather, implicit and explicit suggestions can be woven into the fabric of the interview through the use of bribes, threats, repetitions of certain questions, and the inductions of stereotypes and expectancies (Ceci & Bruck, 1993). Finally, children are questioned by parents, therapists, and legal officials, all of whom represent status and power in the eyes of the child; thus, children may be more likely to comply with the suggestions of these interviewers than with those of the neutral interviewers employed in most research studies.

Although it is difficult to create experimental conditions that reflect the confluence of forensically relevant variables (stressful episodes, repeated and suggestive questioning, questioning over prolonged periods), researchers have begun to examine how children's reports are influenced by the repetition of suggestions in multiple interviews prior to and following the occurrence of an event. In addition, researchers focus on the interviewer and the potential effects that a particular bias may have on the reports elicited from young children. In what follows, we confine our discussion to three studies recently conducted at Cornell and McGill Universities, as they were designed specifically to address these issues (see Ceci & Bruck, 1993, for a discussion of additional studies).

In these studies, we patterned (in reduced form) our experimental manipulations after materials we collected over the past decade from court transcripts, therapy sessions and law enforcement interviews involving children in cases similar to the Kelly Michaels case, where there was a strong suspicion of abuse (see transcripts in Ceci & Bruck, 1993). These materials reveal that it is common for a child to make his or her first disclosure about abuse in a therapy session in which the therapist is pursuing a single hypothesis about the basis of the child's difficulties, thus resulting in leading and suggestive interviews, often with fantasy inductions and "self-empowerment" techniques—techniques that themselves are potentially suggestive and stereotype-inducing. Following long periods of therapy, many children make disclosures that are then pursued in law enforcement or Child Protective Service interviews.

Study 1: The Effect of Interviewer Bias on Children's Reports. Ideally, a forensic interview should be a form of scientifically guided inquiry. One hallmark of such an inquiry is the attempt to disprove a hypothesis by giving alternative hypotheses a fair chance of confirmation. Simply put, scientists try to arrive at truth by ruling out rival hypotheses—particularly, the most reasonable rivals—and by attempting to falsify their favored hypothesis (Ceci & Bronfenbrenner, 1991; Dawes, 1992; Popper, 1962). Because of the needs of Child Protective Service interviewers, however, it is not feasible or even desirable to insist that they generate and test all conceivable hypotheses or, conversely, be blinded to all relevant information that pertains to the State's main hypothesis. Doing the latter could result in missed opportunities whenever an interviewer did not recognize the relevance of a given piece of information provided by the child. But, as the following study shows, the failure to test a rival hypothesis can result in various types of reporting errors.

In this study, we examined how an interviewer's hypothesis can influence the accuracy of young children's reports. Preschoolers were exposed to a game-like event, and then interviewed one month later. The interviewer was given a one-page report containing information that might have occurred. The interviewer was asked to conduct an interview to determine how much of the information the child could, in fact, still recall. The only instruction given to the interviewer was that she should begin by asking the child for a free narrative of what had transpired, avoiding all forms of suggestions and leading questions. Following this, the interviewer was instructed to use whatever strategies she felt were necessary to elicit the most factually accurate report from the child. The one-page report given to the interviewer contained two types of information about the event that the children allegedly had experienced: accurate information and erroneous information. For example, if the game actually entailed child A touching child B's nose and child B rubbing her own tummy, the interviewer might be told that child A touched child B's toe, who, in turn rubbed her own tummy.

The information we provided influenced the interviewer's hypotheses about what had transpired in this game, and thus, appeared to exercise a powerful influence on the dynamics of the interview, with the interviewer eventually shaping some of the children's reports to be consistent with her hypothesis about what happened. When the interviewer was accurately informed, she got children to correctly recall between a minimum of 70% and a maximum of 100% of such events. In such conditions, there were no errors of commission. However, when she was misinformed, accuracy dropped to 82% for the 5- to 6-year-olds, and 66% for the 3- to 4-year-olds (i.e., 18% and 34% of each age group, respectively, corroborated one or more events that the interviewer falsely believed had transpired). Finally, the children became more credible as the interview unfolded. Many children initially stated details inconsistently, or with reluctance or even denial, but as the interviewer persisted in asking about nonevents, some children abandoned their denials and hesitancy.

Because the interviewers in this study were trained professionals (one was an experienced social worker, the other a nursery school teacher), we feel that the types of interactions observed in this study are typical of those that occur in interviews between young children and parents, teachers, and professionals who are not given explicit training in how to generate and/or test various hypotheses. Certainly, our review of the materials from some high profile cases reveals that professional interviewers often steadfastly stick with one line of inquiry even when children continuously deny that the questioned events ever occurred.

Study 2: The Effects of Stereotype Induction and Repeated Suggestions on Young Children's Reports. A stranger named Sam Stone paid a 2-minute visit to preschoolers (ages 3–6 years) in their day care center. Following Sam Stone's visit, the children were asked for details about the visit on four different occasions over a 10-week period. During these four occasions, the interviewer refrained from using suggestive questions. He or she simply encouraged children to describe Sam Stone's visit in as much detail as possible. One month following the fourth interview, the children were interviewed a fifth time by a new interviewer, who used forensic procedures (e.g., first acclimating the child, then eliciting a free narrative, then using probes, urging the children to say when they do not recall, taking breaks). This interviewer asked about two "nonevents" that involved Sam doing something to a teddy bear and a book. In reality, Sam Stone never touched either item.

When asked in the fifth interview, "Did Sam Stone do anything to a book or a teddy bear?" most children rightfully replied "No." Only 10% of the youngest (3–4-year-old) children's answers contained claims that Sam Stone did anything to a book or teddy bear. When asked if they actually saw him do anything to the book or teddy bear, as opposed to thinking they saw him do something, or hearing he did something, now only 5% of their answers contained claims that anything occurred. Finally, when these 5% were gently challenged ("You didn't really see him do anything to the book/the teddy bear, did you?"), only 2.5% still insisted on the reality of the fictional event. None of the older (5- to 6-year-old) children claimed to have actually seen Sam Stone do either of these fictional acts. This condition can be considered as a control against which we can assess the effects of the use of repeated suggestive questioning, especially about characters who are the object of children's stereotypes.

A second group of preschoolers were presented a stereotype about Sam Stone before he ever visited their school. We did this to mimic the sort of stereotypes that some child witnesses have acquired about actual defendants. (For example, in actual cases, some children were repeatedly told that the defendant did "bad things.") Each week, beginning a month prior to the visit, the children in our study were told a new Sam Stone story, in which he was depicted as being very clumsy. For example:

> You'll never guess who visited me last night. [pause] That's right. Sam Stone! And guess what he did this time? He asked to borrow my Barbie and when he was carrying her down the stairs, he tripped and fell and broke her arm. That Sam Stone is always getting into accidents and breaking things!

Following Sam Stone's visit, these children were treated identically to the control group. That is, over a 10-week period, they were interviewed four times, avoiding all suggestions and then were given the same forensic interview by a new interviewer.

The stereotyping had an effect, particularly for the youngest children—42% of whom claimed Sam Stone ripped the book or soiled the teddy bear in response to suggestive probes. Of the youngest children, 19% claimed they saw Sam Stone do these misdeeds. But, after being gently challenged, only 11% continued to claim they witnessed him do these things. In contrast, older preschoolers were significantly more resistant to the influence of the stereotype; their error rates were approximately half of those of the younger children.

A third group of children were assigned to a suggestion-only condition that involved the provision of suggestive questions during the four interviews following Sam Stone's visit. Each suggestive interview contained two erroneous suggestions, one having to do with ripping a book and the other with soiling a teddy bear (e.g., "Remember that time Sam Stone visited your classroom and spilled chocolate on that white teddy bear? Did he do it on purpose or was it an accident?"; "When Sam Stone ripped that book, was he being silly or was he angry?")

Ten weeks later, when the forensic interviewer probed about these events ("Did anything happen to a book?" "Did anything happen to a teddy bear?"), 52% of the younger children's answers and 38% of the older children's answers contained claims that Sam Stone was responsible for one or both misdeeds. Of the youngest children's answers, 35% contained the claim that they actually witnessed him do these things, as opposed to just being told that he did them. Even after being gently challenged, 12% of these children continued to claim they saw him do one or both misdeeds. Although less frequently, older children were also susceptible to these suggestive interviews.

Finally, a fourth group of children were assigned to a condition that combined the features of the stereotype and repeated suggestions conditions. During the forensic interview conducted 10 weeks after Sam's visit, 72% of the youngest preschoolers claimed that Sam Stone did one or both misdeeds, a figure that dropped to 44% when asked if they actually saw him do these things. Importantly, 21% continued to insist that they saw him do these things, even when gently challenged. For the older preschoolers, the situation was still a cause for concern, with 11% insisting they saw him do the misdeeds.

Some researchers stated that the presence of perceptual details in reports is one of the indicators of an accurate memory, as opposed to a confabulated one Schooler, Gerhard, & Loftus, 1986). In this study, however, the presence of perceptual details was no assurance that the report was accurate. In fact, it was surprising to see the number of fabricated perceptual details that children in the combined stereotype plus suggestion condition provided to embellish the nonevents (e.g., claiming that Sam Stone took the teddy bear into a bathroom and soaked it in hot water before smearing it with a crayon). The difference in the quality of reports obtained in this study compared to others in the established suggestibility literature may reflect the conditions under which the reports were obtained. As mentioned earlier, in most of the studies reported in the literature, children's erroneous reports are in response to a single misleading question of the event in question posed after a brief delay. In contrast, in the present study, children's false reports were a product of repeated erroneous suggestions over a relatively long period of time, coupled with a stereotype that was consistent with these suggestions.

It is one thing to show that children can be induced to make errors and include perceptual details in their reports, but it is another matter to show that such faulty reports are convincing to an observer, especially a trained one. To examine the believability of the children's reports, we showed videotapes of the children during the final interview to approximately 3,000 researchers and clinicians who work in the area of the reliability of children's statements. The professionals were instructed to carefully watch the tapes and to rank the children in terms of the accuracy of their statements. These researchers and clinicians (including psychiatrists) were told that all of the children observed the visit of a man named Sam Stone to their day care centers. They were asked to decide which of the events in the children's reports actually transpired during Sam Stone's visit.

Our analyses indicated that the majority of experts who conduct research on children's testimonial competence, who provide therapy to children suspected of having been abused, and who carry out law enforcement interviews with children, failed to detect which children were accurate and which were not, despite being confident in their mistaken opinions. Because so many of the children claimed that Sam ripped the book and/or soiled the bear, it is understandable why so many of the professionals reasoned that these events must have transpired. However, the very children who were least accurate were rated as being most accurate. These children's reports would fool anyone who thinks that it is easy to detect a young child's false report. We believe that the highly credible but inaccurate reports obtained in this study reflect a constellation of factors involving repeated interviews with persistent and intense suggestions that build on a prior set of expectations (i.e., stereotype). This constellation of factors is also characteristic of the conditions under which some actual child witnesses come to make allegations of sexual abuse. As a result, it becomes difficult to separate credibility from accuracy when after many interviews, these children give a formal videotaped interview or testify in court.

Study 3: Influencing Children's Reports of a Pediatric Visit. It may be that the Sam Stone study is not relevant to evaluating the reliability of a child witness who reports personally experienced events involving his or her own body, especially when the experience involves some degree of distress. Furthermore, the Sam Stone data may not be germane to testimony about predictable and scripted events. In cases where the event involves their own body, is somewhat stressful, and is predictable, children may be less prone to suggestion.

To determine if children could be misled under such circumstances, we examined the influence of postevent suggestions on children's reports about a specific pediatric visit. The study had two phases. In the first phase, the subjects were 5 years old and they visited their pediatrician for their annual checkup. The visit was scripted as follows. The pediatrician examined the child. Then the child met a female research assistant who talked about a poster that was hanging on the wall in the examining room (the pediatrician was not in the room for this part of the visit). Next, with the research assistant present, the pediatrician gave the child an oral polio vaccine and a DPT inoculation. Immediately after the inoculation, the pediatrician left the room. The research assistant then gave the child feedback about how he or she acted when receiving the inoculation. Some children were given pain-affirming feedback: They were told that it seemed as though the shot really hurt them, but shots hurt even big kids (hurt condition). Some children were given pain-denying information; these children were told they acted like the shot did not hurt much, and they were really brave (no-hurt condition). Finally, some children were merely told the shot was over (neutral condition). After the feedback, the research assistant gave each child a treat, and then read the child a story. One week later, a second research assistant visited the child, who was asked to indicate through the use of various rating scales how much he or she cried during the shot and how much the shot hurt.

The children's reports did not differ as a function of feedback condition. Thus, we found that children could not be influenced to make inaccurate reports concerning significant and stressful procedures involving their own bodies. These results are similar in spirit to those of Saywitz et al. (1991) who also provided children with suggestions about stressful, personally experienced events in only one interview.

In the second phase of the study, we interviewed the children three more times, approximately 1 year after the shot, with each interview lasting approximately 40 minutes. During these interviews, children were provided with repeated suggestions about how they acted when they received their inoculations. Thus, as in the first phase of the study, some children were told how brave they had acted when they got their shot, whereas other children were not given any information about how they had acted. (For ethical purposes, we only provided two feedback conditions—no hurt and neutral. We felt it was unacceptable to provide hurt feedback because it might result in potentially false and unpleasant memories about visiting the doctor.) When the children were visited for a fourth time and asked to rate how much the shot had hurt and how much they had cried, there were suggestibility effects. Those who had been repeatedly told that they had acted brave and did not cry when they received their inoculation 1 year earlier, reported significantly less crying and less hurt than children who were not provided with any information about how they acted. Thus, these data indicate that under certain circumstances, children's reports concerning stressful events involving their own bodies can be influenced.

In the second phase of this study, we also provided children with different types of misleading information about who performed various actions during the original inoculation visit. Some children were falsely reminded on three occasions that the pediatrician had shown them the poster, had given them treats, and had read them a story, whereas a control group of children were merely reminded that someone did these things. Other children were falsely reminded on three occasions that the research assistant had given them the inoculation and the oral vaccine, whereas the control group children were merely reminded that someone did these things. According to some researchers, children should not be suggestible about such central and important events. Particularly, children should be immune to suggestions that incorporate shifts of gender. The male pediatrician had never given them treats or read them a story, and the female research assistant had never performed any medical procedures.

Contrary to these predictions, the children were misled. In the fourth interview, when asked to tell what happened to them when they visited their doctor 1 year previously, approximately, 45% of the misled children (vs. 22% of the control children) reported that the pediatrician showed them the poster, gave them treats, and read them a story. For children who were falsely told that the research assistant had given them the shot and the vaccine, 38% of their reports (vs. 10% of the control children's) were consistent with this suggestion. Interestingly, 38% of the children who were given the misleading information that the research assistant gave them the oral vaccine and the inoculation, also said that the research assistant performed other scripted events that were never suggested and that had never occurred (e.g., misled children reported that the research assistant checked their ears and nose). None of the control children made such inaccurate reports. Thus, our suggestions to these children influenced not only their reports of personally experienced, central events, but also their reports for nonsuggested scripted events related to the suggested events.

These data indicate that under certain circumstances, children's reports concerning stressful events involving their own bodies can be influenced. The two most important factors revealed were repeated suggestions over multiple interviews and a long delay between the original event and interview about the event. These two factors are characteristic of the conditions in which children made allegations of sexual abuse in many of the cases described at the beginning of this chapter.

The results of this study are therefore consistent with those of the Sam Stone study, even though the quality of the events and experiences about which children were misled were different. In the Sam Stone study, repeated suggestions and stereotypes led to convincing fabrications of nonoccurring events. In the pediatrician study, misleading information given in repeated interviews after a long delay of a target event influenced children's memories of personally experienced, salient and predictable events.

Our data on interviewing techniques have limited generalizability to child sexual abuse cases, because the interviewing technique studies we described are not direct analogues of any one case involving the child witness who makes claims of sexual abuse, as none of these studies include sexual materials. Nevertheless, we argue that it is the fabric of the interviewing procedures that are common to the experimental and forensic arenas. It would be ethically impermissible to conduct similar interviews with sexual themes (e.g., suggesting that Sam Stone had made sexual advances, suggesting that the research assistant had conducted genital examinations). We feel that our studies (and others like them) are as close as we may get to the actual contexts to which we wish to generalize.

THE ISSUE OF ECOLOGICAL VALIDITY

As we emphasize, a central concern of critics of research on the suggestibility of children's recollections involves the relevance of this research to actual court cases in which a child testifies (see Ceci, 1991; Loftus & Ceci, 1991; Steller, 1991; Yuille & Wells, 1991). A difficulty with the research in this area is the limits on generalizing from research contexts (e.g., classroom stories that are followed by postevent suggestions) to real-world analogs (e.g., the manner in which children's memories of abusive events are relentlessly pursued by investigators in the aftermath of a sexual abuse report).

It is an unfortunate habit for researchers on both sides of the suggestibility debate to charge a lack of ecological validity in the other side's research. This is a term that has come into fashion this past decade, especially in developmental psychology. Propelled by methodological treatments of the related and encompassing concept of external validity, both terms refer to how far one can generalize from the procedures and subjects of one study to some target population.

External validity was described as follows:

> These are the issues of external validity. Would the same effect be obtained with individuals other than those who participated in the study? Would the same effect be obtained in other settings? If another researcher defined the independent or dependent variables slightly differently, would the same effect be obtained, or is the effect limited to the persons, settings, and operations that this particular researcher used? How far can the experimental effect be generalized? What are the limits on the generalization of the study findings? (Smith & Glass, 1987, p. 144)

> Making generalizations is the essence of external validity . . . The major point . . . is that external validity is concerned with specifying the contingencies on which a causal relationship depends and all such specifications have important implications for the generalizability and nature of causal relationships. (Cook & Campbell, 1979, pp. 81–82)

The concept of external validity encompasses that of ecological validity, the latter being more concerned with the fine-grained analysis of the settings, persons, and treatments.

Ecological validity refers to the extent to which the environment experienced by the subjects in a scientific investigation has the properties it is supposed or assumed to have by the investigator ... The ecological validity of any scientific effort is called into question whenever there is discrepancy between the subject's perception of the research situation and the conditions assumed by the investigator (Bronfenbrenner, 1979, pp. 28–30)

Although both constructs are used differently by various researchers, no researcher has ever used either one to suggest that systematic laboratory research is unwarranted, invalid, or undesirable. The critical point is not whether a study is done in a laboratory or nonlaboratory setting, but rather the extent to which the causal mechanisms under investigation are illuminated by the study's setting. With children's suggestibility research, this becomes a spark point because of the insistence by some researchers that entire research traditions have little to offer our understanding of children's recollections in courts of law (Melton, 1992).

In this regard, Bronfenbrenner (1989) decried the rush to study behavior in context because it means the study of contexts without an understanding of the basic processes that support behavior, or because some argued that the concept of ecological validity implies the study of contextual factors in lieu of processes. Rather, Bronfenbrenner argued for the need to include laboratory work as an important ecological contrast whenever we are doing work in the field (Ceci & Bronfenbrenner, 1985). Further, the concept of ecological validity implies that context should be considered, as it elucidates our understanding of process. Ecological validity should be the end point for an entire program of research, rather than the central starting point of each individual study within it. Designing studies that carry as a goal the elucidation of context alone will bring limited scientific progress. In science, leverage is built upon the careful disentanglement of variables that are frequently colinear (or confounded) in naturalistic field studies, and are thus in need of systematic laboratory experimentation. Hence, fertile research programs will ultimately consider both types of study.

Returning to the field of children's suggestibility, if we take to heart the need for ecological validity in the fullest sense, then it becomes essential to specify in as much detail as possible the real world analog being referred to each time we take on a particular question. The reason that such specification is so critical is that conclusions that are valid for one class of suggestibility phenomena are frequently not valid for another. Moreover, what is valid for one subtype within one class of phenomena may not be valid for other subtypes within this same class.

Although we argued for the direct relevance of our interview studies in the forensic arena, these are still lacking many important elements that characterize some cases involving child witnesses. Namely, the real-world events of interest are seldom as sanitized of affect or as absent of motives as those that are experimentally staged. For example, the children in our interview studies are not interviewed by a high status investigator who urges them to help put "the bad man" in jail. In the Sam Stone study, children are not told by their parents prior to the interview that Sam Stone hurts children and that it is a good thing to talk about it. In addition, most studies do not involve high levels of stress, assaults to a victim's body, and the loss of control characteristic of many events that motivate forensic investigation.

Certainly, as research progresses, some of these factors are being incorporated into experimental designs. For example, in some cases, we have used more emotionally laden events to examine issues related to the role of affect and bodily touching in producing misinformation effects, including suggestions about being kissed while naked (Ceci, DeSimone, Putnick, & Nightingale, 1993), witnessing parents violate norms, and hurting others to protect loved ones (also see Ceci & Bruck, 1993). In other studies, investigators documented children's levels of suggestibility after experiencing painful and potentially embarrassing medical procedures (e.g., Goodman, 1993; Ornstein, this volume). Although children's accuracy and resistance to suggestions are sensitive to all of these factors, no single research program attempted to put all of these factors into a single experiment, and until we do so, there is a need for caution about how any single child will behave in any single condition. In other words, the presence of naturalistic contexts does not in itself make this research generalizable to a particular court case unless the research context closely mirrors the precise factors that are involved in that case. For example, in doing research that is intended to generalize to a sexual abuse case, factors that should be considered include the level of victimization, the level of arousal, embarrassment, and loss of control, the cognitive factors thought by some to influence the integrity of a memory trace (e.g., length of retention interval, degree of leading questions, level of original trace strength), and, most importantly, motivations and threats to withhold or disclose information (Ceci, 1991; Yuille & Wells, 1991). Hence, in every case, we must articulate the nature of the real-world event with which we are grappling before deciding to what extent our experimental work bears upon it.

By dwelling on the context of child sexual abuse, we do not intend to give the impression that we think this is the only or even the most important context for looking at the suggestibility of children's recollections. The first author of this chapter recently participated in a death row murder case that involved testimony about a rather mundane observation a girl had made. Not only was there no heightened arousal during her initial observation (she did not realize that a crime had been committed until 2 weeks after her observation), but there also was no tangle of personal embarrassment and ego defenses that occur in some sexual abuse cases. In the aftermath of this girl's observation, various adults vigorously interrogated her, pursuing every answer with a battery of leading and potentially distorting questions. Her testimony would have been responsible for sending the defendant to the electric chair, were it not for the fact that several years later (1 month before the scheduled execution) she offered a complete recantation, explaining how confused she became because of the incessant questioning, coupled with her desire to help authority figures. No reliable figures exist as to how many cases involve child witnesses' recollection of mundane events (in this case, witnessing a man washing his hands) in capital felonies, and they are probably rare. But it is becoming increasingly common for child witnesses to offer their recollections in domestic violence, civil product liability, and custody cases. Naturally, these sorts of contexts differ enormously from each other and from child sexual abuse contexts.

Emphasizing the complex, context-dependent nature of forensically relevant memory phenomena in no way undermines our earlier point about the important role of laboratory research in understanding them. As Brainerd and Ornstein (1991) observed:

> If the goal is to be able to provide sound advice to legal and law-enforcement professionals, based on the research literature, it is critical to know the facts. And these facts are derived from the basic research literature in cognitive development. Thus, it is important to understand the relevant research on children's memory. ... Assertions about "ecological validity" notwithstanding, laboratory-based research is of fundamental importance in understanding children's testimony. (p. 2)

No matter how naturalistic the context, any one study cannot be regarded as the defining study of children's suggestibility. No matter how well we demonstrate the bounds of children's suggestibility in naturalistic contexts, we are forced back into the laboratory to further refine or understand the psychological processes that underlie these behaviors. Although our interviewing studies are clear demonstrations of some of the parameters of young children's suggestibility, these studies do not directly examine the extent to which children's suggestibility is a function of social or cognitive factors, nor do these studies allow us to examine individual differences. Thus, the following issues remain unaddressed: Do children incorporate suggestions because of an attempt to comply with the examiner? Does the suggestion become part of the child's memory trace? What is the time course of the influence of these factors; for instance, do children initially comply with an interviewer and then after a specific time does their report become part of their memory? Does this pattern change as a function of development? And finally, what are the characteristics of children who are most prone to fall sway to suggestion: Do they have poorer memories, weaker cognitive representations of the questioned events, particular personality patterns (e.g., field-dependent), or particular home or child-rearing environments? The basis for the most primary understanding of these important factors must entail laboratory studies where one can systematically disentangle these factors and construct different paradigms, that can then be brought back into more naturalistic contexts for further testing.

If this field is to continue to flourish, laboratory and real-world research paradigms must operate interdependently. Although we argued that much of the research carried out in the first 80 years of this century had little relevance to many issues of children's suggestibility, we must be careful that the next 30 years do not solely focus on issues that are local to the forensic arena.

SUMMARY

The studies described in this chapter highlight the different techniques that researchers are employing to examine suggestibility in children. These studies highlight the importance of the researcher's knowledge of the architecture of cases involving child witnesses. If one wishes to generalize to the forensic arena, it is no longer sufficient to examine processes or component parts of children's memory without understanding the context in which their memory is being probed. Questions about children's suggestibility cannot be answered with simple statements such as: "they are highly suggestible," or "they are highly resistant to false information." The most appropriate answer is: "It depends." In some situations, when questioned by a neutral interviewer, children can be amazingly resistant to false suggestions, and may be able to provide detailed and accurate reports of events that transpired weeks or months before (e.g., Baker-Ward, Gordon, Ornstein, Larus, & Clubb, 1993). However, based on our understanding of the way children are questioned in the forensic arena, and based on results of studies that attempt to capture some of the important structural elements of forensic interviews, we conclude that when the interviewing process involves such elements as the induction of stereotypes, bribes, implicit threats, and repeated questions by a powerful adult authority figure, this can result in high suggestibility in young children. Further studies are required before we can reach any conclusions about older children. Finally, we look forward to many productive years of basic research on the cognitive and social mechanisms that underlie children's suggestibility.

ACKNOWLEDGMENTS

Portions of this research were supported by Grants RO1 HD, KO4 HD, and RO1 HD from the National Institutes of Health to S. J. Ceci, and by Grant 0GP000A1181 from the Natural Sciences and Engineering Research Council to M. Bruck.

REFERENCES

Andrews, J. A. (1964). The evidence of children. *The Criminal Law Review, 64,* 769–777.

Baker-Ward, L., Gordon, B., Ornstein, P., Larus, D., & Clubb, P. (1993). Young children's long-term retention of a pediatric examination. *Child Development, 64,* 1519–1533.

Berliner, L. (1985). The child and the criminal justice system. In A. W. Burgess (Eds.), *Rape and sexual assault* (pp. 199–208). New York: Garland Publishing.

Binet, A. (1900). *Suggestibilité.* Paris: Schleicher Freres.

Brainerd, C. J., & Ornstein, P. A. (1991). In J. L. Doris (Ed.), *The suggestibility of children's recollections* (pp. 10–20). Washington, DC: APA Books.

Bronfenbrenner, U. (1979). *The ecology of human development.* Cambridge, MA: Harvard University Press.

Bronfenbrenner, U. (1989). Ecological systems theory. In R. Vasta (Ed.), *Annals of Child Development, 6,* 185–246.

Bruck, M., Ceci, S. J., Francoeur, E., & Barr, R. (1995). "I hardly cried when I got my shot": Young children's reports of their visit to a pediatrician. *Child Development, 66,* 193–208.

Bruck, M., Ceci, S. J., Francoeur, E., & Renick, A. (in press). Anatomically detailed dolls do not facilitate preschoolers' reports of pediatric examinations involving genital touching. *Journal of Experimental Psychology: Applied.*

Cassel, W. S., Roebers, C., & Bjorklund, D. F. (1993). *Tell me about . . , Don't you remember. . . ? Isn't it it true that. . . ? Developmental patterns of eyewitness responses to increasingly suggestive questions.* Manuscript submitted for publication.

Ceci, S. J. (1991). Some overarching issues in the child suggestibility debate. In J. L. Doris (Ed.), *The suggestibility of children's recollections* (pp. 1–9). Washington, DC: American Psychological Association.

Ceci, S. J., & Bronfenbrenner, U. (1985). Don't forget to take the cupcakes out of the oven: Strategic time-monitoring, prospective memory, and context. *Child Development, 56,* 175–190.

Ceci, S. J., & Bruck, M. (1993). The suggestibility of the child witness: A historical review and synthesis. *Psychological Bulletin, 113,* 403–439.

Ceci, S. J., DeSimone, M., Putnick, M., & Nightingale, N. (1993). Age differences in suggestibility. In D. Cicchetti & S. Toth (Eds.), *Child witnesses, child abuse, and public policy.* Norwood, NJ: Ablex.

Cook, T. D., & Campbell, D. T. (1979). *Quasi-experimentation: Design and analysis issues for field settings.* Chicago: Rand McNally.

Cunningham, J. L. (1988a). Contributions to the history of psychology: L. French historical views on the acceptability of evidence regarding child sexual abuse. *Psychological Reports, 63,* 343–353.

Cunningham, J. L. (1988b). Contributions to the history of psychology: XLVI. The pioneer work of Alfred Binet on children as eyewitnesses. *Psychological Reports, 62,* 271–277.

Dawes, R. (1992, Spring). The importance of alternative hypothesis and hypothetical counterfactuals in general social science. *The General Psychologist,* 2–7.

Feher, T. (1988). The alleged molestation victim, the rules of evidence, and the constitution: Should children really be seen and not heard? *American Journal of Criminal Law, 14,* 227.

Fivush, R. (1993). Developmental perspectives on autobiographical recall. In G. S. Goodman & B. Bottoms (Eds.), *Child victims and child witnesses: Understanding and improving testimony* (pp. 1–24). Guilford: New York.

Gardner, R. (1989). *Sex abuse hysteria: Salem witch trials revisited.* Longwood, NJ: Creative Therapeutics Press.

Goodman, G. S. (1993, March). *Children's memory for stressful events: Theoretical and developmental considerations.* Paper presented at the Biennial Meeting of the Society for Research in Child Development, New Orleans.

Goodman, G. S., & Clarke-Stewart, A. (1991). Suggestibility in children's testimony: Implications for child sexual abuse investigations. In J. L. Doris (Ed.), *The suggestibility of children's recollections* (pp. 92–105). Washington, DC: American Psychological Association.

Goodman, G. S., Hirschman, J. E., Hepps, D., & Rudy, L. (1991). Children's memory for stressful events. *Merrill Palmer Quarterly, 37,* 109–158.

Goodman, G. S., Rudy, L., Bottoms, B., & Aman, C. (1990). Children's concerns and memory: Issues of ecological validity in the study of children's eyewitness testimony. In R. Fivush & J. Hudson (Eds.), *Knowing and remembering in young children* (pp. 249–284). New York: Cambridge University Press.

Gordon, B., Ornstein, P. A., Clubb, P., & Nida, R. E. (1991, November). *Visiting the pediatrician: Long-term retention and forgetting.* Paper presented at the Annual Meeting of the Psychonomic Society, San Francisco.

Gudjonsson, G. (1986). The relationship between interrogative suggestibility and acquiescence: Empirical findings and theoretical implications. *Personality and Individual Differences, 7,* 195–199.

Hurlock, E. (1930). Suggestibility in children. *Journal of Genetic Psychology, 37,* 59–74.

Johnson, M. K. (1991). Reality monitoring: Evidence from confabulation in organic brain disease patients. In G. Prigatano & D. Schacter (Eds.), *Awareness of deficit after brain injury* (pp. 124–140). New York: Oxford University Press.

Jones, D., & McGraw, J. M. (1987). Reliable and fictitious accounts of sexual abuse in children. *Journal of Interpersonal Violence, 2,* 27–45.

Loftus, E. F. (1979). *Eyewitness testimony.* Cambridge, MA: Harvard University Press.

Loftus, E. F., & Ceci, S. J. (1991). Research findings: What do they mean? In J. L. Doris (Ed.), *The suggestibility of children's recollections.* Washington, DC: American Psychological Association.

Manshel, L. (1990). *Nap time.* New York: Kensington Publishing Corp.

McConnell, T. R. (1963). Suggestibility in children as a function of chronological age. *Journal of Abnormal and Social Psychology, 67,* 286–289.

Melton, G. (1992). Children as partners for justice: Next steps for developmentalists. *Monographs of the Society for Research in Child Development, 57* (Serial No. 229), 153–159.

Messerschmidt, R. (1933). The suggestibility of boys and girls between the ages of six and sixteen. *Journal of Genetic Psychology, 43,* 422–437.

Oates, K., & Shrimpton, S. (1991). Children's memories for stressful and non-stressful events. *Medicine, Science, and the Law, 31,* 4–10.

Otis, M. (1924). A study of suggestibility in children. *Archives of Psychology, 11,* 5–108.

Popper, K. R. (1962). *Conjectures and reflections.* New York: Basic Books.

Powers, P., Andriks, J. L., & Loftus, E. F. (1979). Eyewitness accounts of females and males. *Journal of Applied Psychology, 64,* 339–347.

Raskin, D., & Esplin, P. (1991). Assessment of children's statements of sexual abuse. In J. L. Doris (Ed.), *The suggestibility of children's recollections* (pp. 153–164). Washington, DC: American Psychological Association.

Rudy, L., & Goodman, G. S. (1991). Effects of participation on children's reports: Implications for children's testimony. *Developmental Psychology, 27,* 527–538.

Saywitz, K. J., Goodman, G. S., Nicholas, E., & Moan, S. F. (1991). Children's memories of a physical examination involving genital touch: Implications for reports of child sexual abuse. *Journal of Consulting and Clinical Psychology, 59,* 682–691.

Schooler, J. W., Gerhard, D., & Loftus, E. F. (1986). Qualities of the unreal. *Journal of Experimental Psychology: Learning, Memory, and Cognition, 12,* 171–181.

Schuman, D. C. (1986). False allegations of physical and sexual abuse. *Bulletin of the American Academy of Psychiatry and the Law, 14,* 5–21.

Sherman, I. (1925). The suggestibility of normal and mentally defective children. *Comparative Psychology Monographs, 2.*

Smith, M. L., & Glass, G. V. (1987). Research and evaluation in education and the social sciences. Englewood Cliffs, NJ: Prentice Hall.

Steller, M. (1991). Commentary: Rehabilitation of the child witness. In J. L. Doris (Ed.), *The suggestibility of children's recollections* (pp. 106–109). Washington, DC: American Psychological Association.

Stern, W. (1910). Abstracts of lectures on the psychology of testimony and on the study of individuality. *American Journal of Psychology, 21,* 270–282.

Underwager, R., & Wakefield, H. (1989). *The real world of child interrogations.* Springfield, IL: C. C. Thomas.

Varendonck, J. (1911). Les temoignages d'enfants dans un proces retentissant [The testimony of children in a famous trial]. *Archives de Psychologie, 11,* 129–171.

Yuille, J., & Wells, G. (1991). Concerns about the application of research findings: The issue of ecological validity. In J. L. Doris (Ed.), *The suggestibility of children's recollections* (pp. 118–128). Washington, DC: American Psychological Association.

Chapter 18

Young Children's Long-Term Retention of Medical Experiences: Implications for Testimony

Peter A. Ornstein
University of North Carolina at Chapel Hill

Lynne Baker-Ward
North Carolina State University

Jennifer Myers
Gabrielle F. Principe
Betty N. Gordon
University of North Carolina at Chapel Hill

The work reported in this chapter is concerned with young children's long-term retention of the details of visits to the doctor for routine physical examinations, as well as more invasive medical procedures. Two factors have led us to examine children's memory for medical experiences. First, although recent findings have helped to bring about fundamental changes in the conceptualization of young children's abilities (see Fivush & Hudson, 1990; Wellman, 1988), relatively little is known about children's retention of salient, personally experienced events over extended delays (see Howe, Brainerd, & Reyna, 1992). Because the medical experiences we explore are naturally occurring events that are important in the lives of children, they would seem to be ideal "stimuli" for studies of long-term retention. Second, the increasing frequency with which children are called upon to provide testimony in legal settings about allegations of sexual abuse and other matters requires that we learn as much as possible about the factors that influence the quality of their reports. Memory is clearly one of these factors, and the work presented here is based on the fundamental assumption that the accuracy of children's testimony depends to a considerable extent upon their abilities to remember events over time.

These basic and applied themes come together in our studies of children's memory for medical experiences. We began this line of inquiry by asking children between 3 and 7 years of age to remember the details of a well-child physical examination. This salient event in children's lives was selected because it is also a situation that is similar in some respects to instances of sexual abuse: An adult has bodily contact with a child who is in varying states of undress. Moreover, not all aspects of the experience are pleasant, and the child may be anxious or stressed. Most importantly, with the cooperation of the pediatricians who carry out the checkups, we have been able to determine the features of the examination given to each individual child. In addition, we have supplemented our studies of the well-child checkup by examining medical experiences that are more stressful and less familiar to the children. Thus, for example, we have explored young children's recall of the details of a voiding cystourethrogram (VCUG), an invasive radiological procedure involving urinary catheterization. In general, by examining memory in these settings we have been able to maintain a level of control that is typically obtained only in the laboratory.

In this chapter, we provide a selective overview of our studies of young children's long-term retention of medical experiences. We first sketch out our general research strategy and outline the results of our initial investigations of children's memory for doctor visits (Baker-Ward, Gordon, Ornstein, Larus, & Clubb, 1993; Ornstein, Gordon, & Larus, 1992). In the next section, we describe two subsequent studies also examining memory for well-child checkups that focus on particular factors hypothesized to influence children's reports. In one of these experiments (Gordon, Ornstein, Clubb, Nida, & Baker-Ward, 1991), we examined the effects of repeated interviews on long-term retention over a 12-week delay interval, whereas in the second (Gordon, Ornstein, Nida, Follmer, Crenshaw, & Albert, 1993), we assessed the effects of using dolls as memory props. In the third section of this chapter, we discuss our study of memory for the details of the VCUG (Merritt, Ornstein & Spicker, 1994), a procedure that has enabled us to explore the effects of high levels of stress on memory and to examine reports of novel, unanticipated events. We then bring our research findings together and examine the implications of our work for the understanding of children's event memory in general and their eyewitness testimony in particular.

GENERAL RESEARCH STRATEGY

Our basic approach to the study of long-term retention can readily be seen in our initial experiments on young children's memory for doctor visits (Baker-Ward, Gordon, et al., 1993; Ornstein, Gordon, & Larus, 1992). Although we continue to refine our interview protocols and other aspects of the methodology, the basic approach described here underlies our explorations of children's reports of various medical procedures (see Baker-Ward, Ornstein, Gordon, Follmer, & Clubb, 1995; Baker-Ward, Ornstein, & Gordon, 1993; Ornstein, Gordon, & Baker-Ward, 1992; Ornstein, Gordon, Baker-Ward, & Merritt, in press; Ornstein, Gordon, & Larus, 1992).

The Physical Examinations

All of the children who participated in our doctor visit studies were scheduled to receive routine pediatric checkups with cooperating pediatricians. With the assistance of participating physicians, a set of distinct features typically included in a standard examination administered by a nurse and a pediatrician was defined. The features usually present in the nurse's segment of the examination included weighing and measuring; checking of hearing, vision, and blood pressure; drawing blood; obtaining a urine specimen; and so on. The features administered by the doctor included looking in the child's mouth, eyes, and ears; checking the genitals; listening to heart and lungs; and so on.

Of course, the checkups varied as a function of the child's age, and medical history, but each examination included a subset of the features that had been identified. On average, the examinations were composed of between 10 and 25 specific features. Further, because the checkups differed across children, the physicians and nurses completed a checklist for each child, indicating the features that were included in their portions of the examination. We also asked the nurses to take a Polaroid photo of each child, so that each checkup would include a novel experience and therefore assist us in determining if the child was remembering this particular examination or was recalling from a script (Nelson, 1986) for a visit to the doctor's office.

The Interviews

The interviews followed a structured format that involved a general-to-specific mode of questioning. The children were initially asked a very open-ended question: "Tell me what happened during your checkup." After prompting for additional information, a less general open-ended question was asked: "Tell me what the doctor (or nurse) did to check you." The questioning then became more specific concerning those features of the physical examination that were not spontaneously mentioned. For all features remembered, the children were asked to elaborate on their responses. For example, if a child said, "The doctor checked my eyes," the interviewer probed with: "How did she/he check your eyes?" Although these elaborations were not examined in our first two reports (Baker-Ward, Gordon, et al., 1993; Ornstein, Gordon, & Larus, 1992), additional analyses of the original data have addressed the extent to which elaboration accompanies the report of a feature (Gordon et al., 1993; Gordon & Follmer, 1994). Between-group differences in elaboration were also assessed in our more recent research efforts.

For all children, the interviewer probed for information about each of the defined features of the examination. Because checkups differed for each child, the use of this standard protocol thus involved asking children about some aspects of a checkup that had not been experienced. We described these probes as *absent-feature* questions. In addition, each child was asked standard *extra-event* questions about eight other activities that were never included in an examination. These questions referenced activities that a child might experience in contact with another professional (e.g., "Did the doctor cut your hair?"), as well as those that would be unlikely to occur in any professional context (e.g., "Did the nurse sit on top of you?").

The interviews were taped and then transcribed and coded according to a system that focused on the particular features of the examination carried out by the physicians and nurses and the level of specificity of the probe required to retrieve the information. An extended discussion concerning issues of coding was provided by Baker-Ward et al. (1995).

INITIAL STUDIES

Our first two studies (Baker-Ward, Gordon, et al., 1993; Ornstein, Gordon, & Larus, 1992) were carried out to provide basic information about young children's long-term retention of the details of a regular checkup. In these experiments, children between 3 and 7 years of age were interviewed at varying times, ranging from immediately after their physical examinations to delays of 1, 3, and 6 weeks. Most children were interviewed initially, so as to obtain an estimate of their initial encoding of the event, and then again after one of the delay intervals, thus permitting within-subject analyses of forgetting.

In general, the findings obtained in these two studies can be summarized as follows: (a) the performance of the children is quite good, although age differences in initial and delayed recall are observed, (b) younger children provide less information than the older subjects in response to the open-ended questions, and rely more on specific probes, (c) retention over time varies directly with age, with little forgetting observed among 7-year-olds out to delays of 6 weeks, and substantial forgetting being seen among 3-year-olds.

These basic findings are illustrated in Fig. 18.1, summarizing the recall performance of the children who participated in the Baker-Ward, Gordon, et al. (1993) study. Memory performance is indicated in terms of the percentage of the component features of each child's physical that were remembered in response to both open-ended and more specific questions, as a function of delay interval. Also indicated in Fig. 18.1 is the performance of control subjects who were interviewed only once, at a delay of 3 weeks. Because the recall of these children is comparable to that of their peers who were interviewed immediately and at 3 weeks, the initial interview does not seem to facilitate later memory performance.

As already indicated, in addition to probing for the details of the physical examination, Baker-Ward, Gordon, et al. (1993) presented their subjects with potentially misleading questions about activities not included in the checkup. In general, the children responded appropriately to the extra-event and absent-feature questions that were posed, exceeding the 50% rate of correct denials that would be expected on the basis of chance alone. It is noteworthy, however, that the 3-year-olds made more errors than the older children. Moreover, all subjects

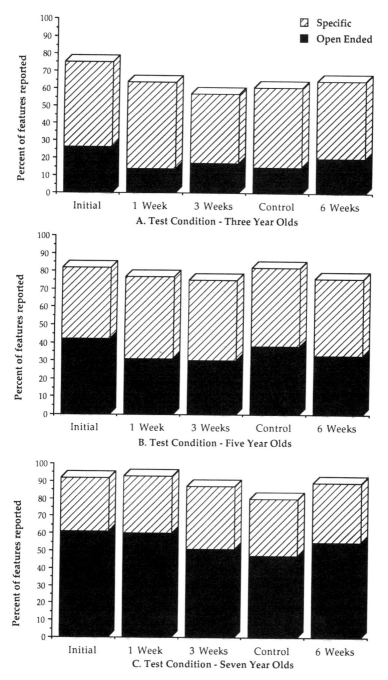

FIG. 18.1. Mean percent of features recalled by age and delay condition in response to open-ended and yes–no probes. From Baker-Ward, Gordon, Ornstein, Larus, and Clubb (1993). Copyright 1993 by Society for Research in Child Development. Reprinted by permission.

performed better with the extra-event questions, which referred to activities not expected to be part of any physical examination, than with the absent-feature questions, which represented queries about legitimate features of routine check-ups that had not been experienced by the child. For example, at the immediate memory assessment, the correct denial scores for the absent-feature questions were 72%, 93%, and 88% for the 3-, 5-, and 7-year-olds, respectively; comparable scores for the extra-event questions were 87%, 96%, and 99%.

The children's impressive performance in this study raises a fundamental question about the validity of the recall data. Can we be certain that their reports reflect memory for the specific physical examination and not their generalized knowledge of medical checkups? Baker-Ward, Gordon, et al. (1993) presented several lines of evidence in support of the claim that the children were not just reporting their scripts (Nelson, 1986) for visits to the doctor, but rather were remembering a specific checkup. Most importantly, there were essentially no intrusions in response to the general, open-ended questions. If the children were primarily relying upon their scripts, they should have reported acts that were absent from their physical examinations but are typically part of the experience. In addition, as indicated previously, the children's correct denials to the absent feature questions exceeded chance expectancy. Moreover, no systematic changes over time were observed in the rate of correct denials, although we would expect script-based false alarms to increase as a function of delay interval.

The claim that the Baker-Ward, Gordon, et al. (1993) data reflect memory for a specific experience, rather than a script for the event, is also supported by the children's recall of the novel feature incorporated into the examination, that is, the taking of a photograph. Finally, given that Nelson (1986) and her colleagues suggested that specific forms of verb usage may be diagnostic of the reliance upon scripts, Clubb, Nida, Merritt, and Ornstein (1993) reanalyzed the language used by 5-year-olds in the Baker-Ward, Gordon, et al. (1993) study in response to open-ended questions and compared it with that observed in a study that focused specifically on knowledge about doctor visits in general. Consistent with Nelson's (1986) analysis (see also Fivush, 1984), Clubb et al. (1993) found that the children in the knowledge study used the present and/or future tense in their discussions of 68% of the features of the office visit that they nominated; in contrast, the 5-year-olds in the Baker-Ward, Gordon, et al. (1993) study used the present and/or future tense when they talked about only 10% of the features that were recalled at the open-ended level.

REPEATED QUESTIONING AND EXTENDING THE DELAY INTERVAL

In a third doctor visit study, Gordon et al. (1991) extended the delay interval to 12 weeks. Because children involved in legal proceedings are typically inter-viewed on multiple occasions over lengthy periods of time, we also examined the effects of the number and spacing of prior memory assessments on recall at the 12-week test. Available research suggests that multiple assessments can have both positive and negative effects on the accuracy and completeness of children's reports. On the one hand, repeated exposure to aspects of an event may serve to partially reinstate or reactivate the initial experience (see, e.g., Campbell & Jaynes, 1966; Rovee-Collier & Hayne, 1987) and thereby facilitate the maintenance of memory over an extended delay. Indeed, under some conditions, additional memory tests may serve as a type of inoculation against later forgetting (see Brainerd, Reyna, Howe, & Kingma, 1990; Slamecka & Katsaiti, 1988).

But on the other hand, repeated questioning can have a negative effect on delayed retention. Given what is known about suggestibility in young children (see Ceci & Bruck, 1993; Doris, 1991), an assessment process that includes questions about activities not included in the physical examination may lead to some distortion of children's memory for the checkup. In addition, young children's limited understanding of the interview process can lead to difficulties when they provide repeated reports of their experiences (Ornstein, Larus, & Clubb, 1991). Young children may provide less complete accounts of a particular event if they assume that the interviewer already has the relevant knowledge (see Best & Ornstein, 1986), as is surely the case when they are assessed by the same examiner on more than one occasion, and they may change their responses because they assume that the interviewer was dissatisfied with their initial reports (see, e.g., Ornstein et al., 1991; Siegal, Waters, & Dinwiddy, 1988).

Gordon et al. (1991) established samples of younger (3- and 4-year-old) and older (6- and 7-year-old) children. Within each age level, children were randomly assigned to one of four groups that varied in the number and spacing of interviews. Children in Group 1 were interviewed on three occasions: first, immediately after their checkups, and then at delays of 6 and 12 weeks. Children in Group 2 received no initial assessment, but were interviewed twice, after intervals of 6 and 12 weeks. Children in Group 3 were interviewed only once, at 12 weeks, and those in Group 4 were assessed immediately after their checkups and then again after a 12-week delay.

As can be seen in Table 18.1, in many respects, the children's recall is similar to that obtained in our earlier studies. For example, their performance is quite good, although the 3- and 4-year-olds remembered significantly less than the 6- and 7-year-olds. These younger children also relied more on yes–no questioning and evidenced more forgetting over the delay interval than did the older children. Table 18.1 also indicates that the effects of repeated questioning differ by age, when assessed with both overall and open-ended (but not yes–no) recall. For example, among the older children, retrieval failure at 12 weeks seems restricted to the three groups who received only one prior memory interview or who had not been previously tested. In contrast, the children in Group 1, who were tested both immediately after the physical examination and at the 6-week point, showed no forgetting at the 12-week assessment. Hence, two previous memory assessments provide the 6- and 7-year-olds with a type of inoculation against forgetting

TABLE 18.1
Mean Proportion of the Features of the Physical Examination Recalled
in Response to Alternative Types of Probes by Age, Group, and Delay Interval

	Initial			6 Weeks			12 Weeks		
	T	OE	YN	T	OE	YN	T	OE	YN
3- & 4-year-olds									
Group 1	.83	.30	.53	.71	.26	.45	.70	.22	.48
Group 2	—	—	—	.77	.17	.60	.61	.18	.43
Group 3	—	—	—	—	—	—	.69	.19	.49
Group 4	.85	.28	.57	—	—	—	.75	.16	.59
6- & 7-year-olds									
Group 1	.94	.60	.34	.87	.46	.41	.91	.52	.39
Group 2	—	—	—	.82	.43	.39	.84	.45	.38
Group 3	—	·	—	—	—	—	.83	.44	.38
Group 4	.94	.64	.30	—	—	—	.86	.42	.44

Note. The following abbreviations are used in this table: T = total recall; OE = recall in response to open-ended probes; YN = recall in response to specific or yes–no queries. (See text for explanation of between-group differences.) From Gordon, Ornstein, Clubb, Nida, and Baker-Ward (1991).

that is not afforded by one memory interview. In contrast, the younger children do not appear to benefit from receiving two interviews. Indeed, the performance of the four groups of 3- and 4-year-olds does not differ at the final recall test.

Inspection of Table 18.1 does, however, reveal one point of similarity in the recall of the two age groups: A single prior interview did not facilitate subsequent delayed recall performance. As discussed, we previously demonstrated (Baker-Ward, Gordon, et al., 1993) that an initial interview had little impact upon subsequent retention at 3 weeks, and we now show that this is also the case at delays of 6 and 12 weeks. Although this failure to obtain an "inoculation" effect from a single interview is inconsistent with the results of several verbal memory studies (see, e.g., Howe & Brainerd, 1989; Slamecka & Katsaiti, 1988), there are numerous procedural differences between these experiments and the Gordon et al. (1991) study. In contrast, as already discussed, two interviews, one immediately after the physical examination and the other at 6 weeks, do facilitate the recall at 12 weeks for older, but not younger children.

A final set of analyses addressed the extent to which the children were skilled at differentiating between activities that were and were not part of the physical examination. As was found in the Baker-Ward, Gordon, et al. (1993) study, the children's responses to the extra-event questions—that is, queries such as "Did the nurse sit on your lap?"—were uniformly impressive. Indeed, at both age levels the children tended to respond correctly (i.e., negatively) to these misleading questions, although the performance of the 3- and 4-year-olds was below that of the 6- and 7-year-olds. For example, the correct denial scores for the younger and older children who were interviewed immediately after the checkup were

.78 and .96, respectively. Moreover, the children's performance with these ex-tra-event questions did not deteriorate over the 12-week delay interval; indeed, the correct denial scores for the younger and older children at the final assessment were .81 and .93, respectively. Further, what cannot be seen in these high correct denial scores is the fact that the responses were so often accompanied by laughter and signs of incredulity that it was clear to us that the children viewed the questions as absurd!

A somewhat different picture emerges when we consider the children's re-sponses to absent-feature questions, that is, probes about aspects of routine physi-cal examinations that happened not to be included in particular checkups. Con-sistent with our earlier work, the older children were quite effective in responding to these questions with correct denials, although their performance was below that when responding to the extra-event questions. Thus, the 6- and 7-year-olds' correct denial scores were .86 and .74 for the immediate and 12-week memory assessments, respectively. In contrast, however, the 3- and 4-year-olds in this study performed below the level of the 3-year-olds in the Baker-Ward, Gordon, et al. (1993) study. Specifically, the correct denial scores for these younger children were .61 and .59 at the immediate and 12-week interviews.

The discrepancy between the children's responses to absent-feature questions in this study and in our initial investigations appears to be attributable to meth-odological changes across the three experiments. After the completion of our first two studies of memory for doctor visits, we revised our interview protocol to eliminate references to features that were not consistently included in most children's physical examinations. Although the purpose of this modification was to reduce the length of the interview, this change resulted in a reduction in the number of absent-feature questions that were presented to most children. In the Baker-Ward, Gordon, et al. (1993) investigation, approximately 10 absent-fea-ture questions were presented to the children; in contrast, in the Gordon et al. (1991) study, on the average only 3 absent-feature questions were asked. Because the denominator used in calculating the percent of correct denials for each subject is so small in this experiment, the means that we report are likely to be unstable. Thus, it is not surprising that differences in performance across inves-tigations were observed.

To enable a more precise assessment of children's responses to absent-feature questions over time, in our ongoing research we include in our protocol a standard set of questions addressing familiar medical procedures that children would not generally experience in a well-child checkup (e.g., "Did the nurse take your temperature?"). As discussed elsewhere (see Baker-Ward et al., 1995), it is clear that very young children's responses to yes–no questions must be carefully scru-tinized in assessing memory competence. Although methodological factors do appear to underlie the inconsistent performance described, developmental and individual differences may also contribute to variability in performance across investigations.

AN ALTERNATE INTERVIEW PROTOCOL:
THE DOLL STUDY

A consistent finding in the three initial studies (Baker-Ward, Gordon, et al., 1993; Gordon et al., 1991; Ornstein, Gordon, & Larus, 1992), has been the demonstration of age differences in children's recall, both immediately after the physical examination and at delays extending out to 12 weeks. These findings, however, have been based on the use of verbal interview procedures and, as a result, important questions remain about the interpretation of children's reports of their experiences. For example, should our data be taken at face value as indicating that 3-year-olds do not remember as well as 7-year-olds? Or, as some (e.g., Mandler, 1991) would suggest, do the findings have more to do with linguistic and narrative skills than with memory? That is, is it possible that there are minimal (or even no) age differences in remembering, and that the performance of young children reflects their difficulties in providing complete accounts of their experiences, perhaps because of the linguistic demands of the typical verbal interview?

In order to address these issues Gordon et al. (1993) explored the effectiveness of an alternate interview methodology involving the use of dolls as possible aids for young children's recall. Dolls were chosen as props for children's memory because they are often employed in evaluations of allegations of sexual abuse (Boat & Everson, 1988). Although the benefits of procedures involving anatomically correct dolls have yet to be documented, their frequent use in clinical settings is based on the assumption that they facilitate the reports of young children who are unwilling or unable to provide a verbal account of traumatic experiences. To the extent that this assumption is correct, the recall of relatively inarticulate children would be enhanced, perhaps even to the levels of older children, if dolls were used in the memory interview.

In this study, the effectiveness of a verbal interview was compared with two alternate protocols that involved the use of a doll as a means to assess 3- and 5-year-old children's recall of a visit to the doctor. These participants were assigned to one of three conditions and interviewed 3 weeks after their physical examinations. The children in the verbal condition received a verbal interview, similar to that employed previously in this research program, whereas those in the representational and role play conditions were provided with a doll and interviewed with modified protocols. The children in the representational condition were instructed to view the doll as a model of the self and to use it to demonstrate the details of the checkup. In contrast, the children in the role play condition were to pretend that the doll was another child who was going to receive a physical examination and to demonstrate what happened during his or her recent checkup, so the other child (doll) would know what to expect. Although the dolls were dressed only in their underwear, they were not sexually detailed.

In general, the data indicate that the modification of the standard verbal interview protocol by the inclusion of a doll as a support for remembering did not serve to reduce age-related differences in memory performance. As can be seen in Table 18.2, older children recalled more than the younger children under each of the interview protocols. Overall, the 3-year-olds recalled 62% of the features of the examination, whereas the 5-year-olds remembered 80% of the components of the office visit. Older children also provided more information in response to open-ended questions than did younger children (33% and 17%, respectively). Surprisingly, at each age level, the children's open-ended and total recall are comparable to that observed after a delay of 3 weeks in our previous studies with a verbal interview protocol. Moreover, the use of a doll did not improve the reports of the 3-year-olds, and it actually served to interfere with their recall in the role play condition. In contrast to the younger children, however, the use of dolls facilitated the recall of the 5-year-olds who received the representational protocol.

A related issue concerns the extent to which the presence of dolls in the interviews facilitated the children's abilities to provide elaborative detail. For any feature of the physical examination that was remembered, elaborations could consist of information about the actions performed (e.g., listening to the heart), the instrument utilized (e.g., a stethoscope), and the location on the child's body that was checked (e.g., the chest). Additionally, the children could provide elaborative detail verbally, nonverbally without using the dolls (e.g., by use of gesture), or nonverbally with the doll. For each child, scores for each of these types of elaboration were calculated by summing over the categories of action, instrument, and location and dividing by the total elaboration possible based on the number of features correctly recalled.

Although the combined verbal and nonverbal elaborations of older children were greater than those of younger children, a greater proportion of the elabo-

TABLE 18.2
Mean Proportion of Features Recalled at 3 Weeks by Age
and Interview Condition

	Total Recall	Open-Ended Recall
3-year-olds		
Verbal	.69	.18
Representational	.65	.16
Role play	.49	.14
5-year-olds		
Verbal	.73	.26
Representational	.87	.37
Role play	.80	.32

Note. Total recall represents the sum of open-ended and yes–no recall. From Gordon, Ornstein, Nida, Follmer, Crenshaw, and Albert (1993).

rations of the 3-year-olds was nonverbal. However, the addition of a doll to the interview did not increase substantially the production of elaborations at either age. That is, although the children provided some nonverbal elaboration about their checkups, little of this detail involved the use of the doll (i.e., the majority was simply gestural), and most, in fact, was redundant with that provided verbally. Inspection of Table 18.3 indicates that nonverbal elaboration without the doll added relatively little (approximately 8% on average) to the elaboration provided verbally by the children. Nonverbal elaboration with the doll further increased the amount of elaborative detail only slightly (approximately 3%). There were no differences among the three interview conditions.

Also of interest in this study was the extent to which individual differences in temperament, as measured by the Temperament Assessment Battery for Children or TABC (Martin, 1988), contributed to the children's recall and elaboration. Among the 3-year-olds, Approach–Withdrawal (i.e., ease displayed in entering new situations) was positively correlated with recall in response to open-ended questions and with the amount of nonverbal elaboration provided with the doll, $rs \geq .32, ps \leq .05$. Among the 5-year-olds, Emotionality (i.e., the vigor with which affect is expressed, particularly negative affect) was positively correlated with total recall, $r = .44, p < .001$, and Approach–Withdrawal was associated with the amount of verbal elaboration, $r = .28, p < .05$, and nonverbal elaboration, both with and without the doll, $rs \geq .44, ps \leq .02$. Taken together, these findings suggest that certain aspects of temperament, such as Approach–Withdrawal and Emotionality, may be indicative of individual differences among children in their styles of responding to questions concerning memory for an event.

Although the data presented here do not support the hypothesis that the memory of younger children can be facilitated by the use of dolls, they are consistent with the literature in cognitive development that suggests that relatively

TABLE 18.3
Mean Proportions of Nonverbal Elaboration With and Without Dolls
as Additions to Verbal Elaboration by Age and Interview Condition

	Type of Elaboration		
	Verbal	Nonverbal Without Doll	Nonverbal With Doll
3-year-olds			
Verbal	.31	.09	—
Representational	.24	.03	.03
Role play	.28	.10	.01
5-year-olds			
Verbal	.56	.08	—
Representational	.53	.08	.07
Role play	.55	.07	.02

Note. From Gordon, Ornstein, Nida, Follmer, Crenshaw, and Albert (1993).

advanced representational (DeLoache, 1990) and linguistic (Casby & Della Corte, 1987) skills are necessary to take advantage of dolls as aids for remembering. That is, the child must essentially be able to recognize simultaneously that the doll is both a toy and a symbol representing the self. If this is the case, then younger children, who are linguistically or cognitively less sophisticated, would have difficulty using the dolls in the symbolic manner required by the interview, and the use of dolls would not be expected to enhance their recall.

In summary, can it be assumed that young children do not remember as much as older children? Although further research is needed to answer this question, it seems likely that the doll manipulations used here have actually provided only a very minimal level of support for the younger children. It is possible that performance might be facilitated by the use of alternate procedures of engaging children in the interview process. We are currently exploring this issue in a study in which children are encouraged to use medical instruments as props to enact what happened to them during their checkup. This work points to the need for further examination of individual differences in reporting and of aspects of the interview process that may affect young children's recall of their personal experiences.

MEMORY FOR AN AVERSIVE EXPERIENCE: THE VCUG STUDY

The studies of children's memory for well-child checkups can be used as a foundation for evaluating children's memory for other types of medical experiences. For example, in a recent project, Merritt et al. (1994) examined young children's immediate and delayed recall of the details of a stressful medical procedure: a voiding cystourethrogram (VCUG). Children's retention of the features of the VCUG was investigated because of the need to examine memory for situations that are more closely analogous to incidents of sexual abuse than is the well-child checkup. Further, the VCUG, which includes features such as cleansing the genital area, inserting a catheter into the urethra, filling the bladder with contrast fluid, and fluroscopic filming, provided an opportunity to examine variables such as prior knowledge (or lack thereof), distress, and temperament, each of which can influence children's reports of their experiences.

The sample included twenty-four 3- to 7-year-old children who were referred by their physicians to a radiology clinic for the VCUG. The average age of the participants was close to that of the 5-year-olds in the Baker-Ward, Gordon, et al. (1993) study. Each child's procedure was videotaped to enable verification of the details of each individual's experience. The children were interviewed immediately after the VCUG and after a delay of 6 weeks. The interview protocol was similar to those described in that it consisted of a series of hierarchically ordered questions; thus, increasingly specific probes again followed general, open-

ended questions when information was not forthcoming. The protocol also included absent-feature questions.

A particular focus of this investigation was the linkage between stress and
remembering, and distress was assessed by the use of both behavioral and physi-
ological measures. The Observational Scale of Behavioral Distress or OSBD
(Elliott, Jay, & Woody, 1987) was used to code behaviors exhibited by the
children during the administration of the VCUG. To supplement the behavioral
coding, the radiology technologists were asked to rate the fearfulness and cooperation exhibited by the children during the procedure. In addition, a physi-
ological assessment of distress was obtained through the use of salivary cortisol
assays. Further, to enable an examination of the relation between characteristics
of the children's temperament and aspects of their memory performance, parents
were asked to complete the TABC (Martin, 1988), the measure of temperament
used in the doll study.

The children demonstrated very impressive levels of recall, both immediately
after the VCUG procedure and after a 6-week delay. As shown in Table 18.4,
the children recalled 88% of the features of the VCUG at the initial interview,
a level of performance comparable to that of the 5-year-olds in the Baker-Ward,
Gordon, et al. (1993) doctor visit study. Further, as is also indicated in the table,
the children in the VCUG study also demonstrated higher levels of recall in
response to open-ended questions (M = 65%) than did the 5-year-olds in the
Baker-Ward, Gordon, et al. (1993) study (M = 42%).

Memory assessment after a delay of 6 weeks indicated little forgetting. Moreover, although initial recall was marginally associated with age in the VCUG
sample, forgetting over time was not correlated with age, an outcome that differs
from previous findings that 3-year-olds forget more details of the well-child
examination than do older children (Baker-Ward, Gordon, et al., 1993; Ornstein,
Gordon, & Larus, 1992). Further, analysis of the responses to the questions about

TABLE 18.4
Proportion of Features Correctly Recalled in Response to Alternate Types of
Probes at Two Delay Intervals by the Children in the VCUG Study
and by the 5-year-olds in a Doctor Visit Investigation

	Interview	
	Initial	6 weeks
VCUG		
Open-ended	.65	.60
Yes–No	.23	.23
Total	.88	.83
Doctor visit		
Open-ended	.42	.34
Yes–No	.40	.42
Total	.82	.76

Note. Adapted from Merritt et al. (1994) and Baker-Ward et al. (1993).

TABLE 18.5
Partial Correlations (Holding Age Constant) Among Selected
Measures of Distress and Recall

	Initial Recall		Delayed Recall	
	Total	Open-Ended	Total	Open-Ended
Behavioral coding	ns	ns	−.56[c]	ns
Ratings				
Cooperation	ns	ns	.41[a]	ns
Fear	−.52[b]	−.42[a]	−.58[c]	−.67[c]
Pain	ns	ns	ns	ns

Note. Behavioral coding represents the weighted sum of time intervals categorized by various indicators of distress, as defined by the Observational Scale of Behavioral Distress (Elliott, Jay, & Woody, 1987); ratings were made by the radiological technologists during the VCUG procedures. From Merritt, Ornstein, and Spiker (1994). Copyright 1994 by Pediatrics. Reprinted by permission.
[a]$p < .10$ [b]$p < .05$ [c]$p < .01$

actions not experienced in the VCUG revealed little suggestibility. Indeed, the children correctly denied .94 and .93 of these probes in the initial and delayed interviews, respectively.

In contrast to the doctor visit studies in which most children were found to be relatively relaxed, high levels of stress were present in the VCUG study. In general, Merritt et al. (1994) observed a negative relation between various measures of distress and remembering, as indicated in Table 18.5. However, the relation between stress and recall must be qualified in two important respects. First, although the behavioral expressions of distress, as measured by the behavioral coding and the ratings of the technologist, were related negatively to recall, the salivary cortisol measure was not found to be associated with remembering. Second, as is apparent in Table 18.5, the association between distress and recall was observed most clearly at the delayed interview and not immediately after the VCUG.

Merritt et al. (1994) also examined the extent to which individual differences in temperament are associated with remembering. As was the case in the doll study, the Approach–Withdrawal dimension of temperament appeared to predict aspects of recall performance. Approach–Withdrawal was positively correlated with both open-ended and total recall performance at both the initial and 6-week delay intervals, $rs \geq .69$, $ps \leq .001$. Moreover, in the VCUG study, although not in the doll study, Adaptablity (i.e., ease of adjustment to new circumstances) as measured by the TABC also correlated with levels of total and open-ended recall at both interview occasions, $rs \geq .52$, $ps \leq .01$.

Direct comparisons of the VCUG and doctor visit studies are complicated because the two events differ in many ways. The children in the VCUG study had little prior knowledge of the procedure and were judged to be more distressed than those in the doctor visit studies. Moreover, the participants in the VCUG study experienced an event that is much more integrated and ordered than the well-child examination in which the component features are often arbitrarily arranged. Despite these important differences, the children's recall of specific details of the VCUG experience was impressive. The findings suggest that under some conditions, young children can provide accurate and detailed reports of personally experienced events that are quite stressful.

DISCUSSION

The work reviewed here provides an account of young children's memory that is consistent with the results of our initial set of studies (Baker-Ward, Gordon, et al., 1993; Ornstein et. al., in press; Ornstein, Gordon, & Larus, 1992). In many respects, the young children who have taken part in our experiments demonstrated effective recall of the details of salient medical experiences. Once again, however, we observe clear age differences in children's memory for visits to the doctor, with the performance of 7-year-olds being impressive and that of 3-year-olds being somewhat mixed. In this section, we summarize these findings, contrast them with children's memory for the details of the VCUG experience, and discuss the implications of our work for an understanding of children's abilities to provide accurate testimony.

Summary

In our doctor visit studies, we have found repeatedly that with increases in age, children are better able to remember (or at least to report) the details of specific checkups. Moreover, as we progress in our research program, these age differences seem to be magnified. Indeed, there is now abundant evidence that the performance of 3-year-olds is very different from that of 6- and 7-year-olds (and even of 5-year-olds). In comparison with older children, 3-year-olds (a) evidence lower levels of initial recall, (b) demonstrate greater forgetting over time, (c) are more dependent on specific (i.e., yes–no) types of questions, (d) seem to show less resistance to suggestions embedded in misleading questions about activities not included in their checkups, (e) do not benefit from multiple interviews during a 12-week delay interval, and (f) are unable to make use of dolls to facilitate performance.

Age Differences in Underlying Memory Traces? Many of our findings are consistent with the view that the memory traces of younger children are likely to be weaker or less coherent than those of older children (e.g., Brainerd et al., 1990; Ornstein et al., 1991). Given what is known about age differences in the speed of information processing (see e.g., Kail, 1991) and prior knowledge about medical experiences (see Clubb et al., 1993), it would not be surprising for 3-year-olds to store less information about a specific visit to the doctor than would older children (see Ornstein et al., in press). With less information stored, it seems probable that the resulting memory traces of 3-year-olds are weaker than those of 5- and 7-year-olds, making them more susceptible to both decay and interference.

Another possibility, of course, is that the age differences observed here do not reflect corresponding differences in what is available in memory. As discussed, the consistent patterns we observed may stem from developmental differences in retrieval and narrative skills. From this perspective, younger children may encode and store as much information about their visits to the doctor as do older children, but they may not have mastered the narrative conventions of the culture and, hence, may be less skilled at telling our interviewers what they experienced. Although this point of view is intriguing (see Mandler, 1991), the inability of 3-year-olds to benefit from the use of dolls (Gordon et al., 1993) is inconsistent with the position that there are minimal or no age differences in the information available in memory. Nonetheless, it must be admitted (see earlier discussion) the use of dolls places great representational demands on young children (see DeLoache, 1990), reducing somewhat the usefulness of this manipulation. In our laboratory, current explorations of the perspective that 3-year-olds may have more information in memory than that which they report, involve the use of two alternative interview procedures: a recognition-based protocol and an enactment procedure in which children act out the details of their checkups in a room furnished as a medical suite.

Age Differences in the Effects of Multiple Interviews. Regardless of the resolution of this issue concerning the memory representations of young children, another interesting age difference requires explanation. Two interviews (one immediately after the physical examination and the other at 6 weeks) before a final memory assessment at 12 weeks facilitated the long-term retention of 6- and 7-year-olds, but not of 3- and 4-year-olds. Although we do not know why two interviews maintain the recall of older but not younger children, this outcome does parallel reports in the developmental strategy literature indicating that the spontaneous use of a particular technique for remembering may facilitate the recall of 6-year-olds but not of 4-year-olds (Baker-Ward, Ornstein, & Holden, 1984; see also Miller & Seier, 1994). Moreover, older children's better ability to take advantage of naming or visual examination as mnemonic strategies may turn out to depend on their more articulated knowledge base for the to-be-remembered materials. Similarly, the enhanced performance of the 6- and 7-year-olds seen in our repeated-interview study may reflect the operation of more integrated and better organized scripts for the typical doctor visit than are available to the 3- and 4-year-olds. Thus, it is possible that questions about some aspects of the physical examination may lead to the activation of representations of other features of the checkup and, thus, result in deeper processing and greater delayed retention.

Another possibility is that the difference between the younger and older children in the effects of multiple interviews may not reflect a difference in remembering, but rather, age differences in response to the demands of the memory task. The effective assessment of children's cognitive skills represents a diagnostic process that depends on shared understanding of the goals of the interview procedure (Ornstein et al., 1991). When young children are assessed on multiple occasions, their performance on later interviews may reflect their growing impatience with being asked the same questions by the same examiner, as much as it indexes their underlying memory. This impatience may lead some young children to provide rather sketchy and incomplete accounts of the physical examination because they do not fully understand why they should be made to tell their "story" yet another time. Of course, this metacognitive interpretation requires careful study, but it is nonetheless consistent with spontaneous remarks of some of the children in this study.

Memory for More Stressful Events. To what extent are our findings concerning the well-child physical examination characteristic of children's recall of other types of events? Our exploration of the VCUG experience (Merritt et al., 1994) represents an initial attempt to examine the generality of the results that we have obtained, and in many respects, the children's recall of specific details of the VCUG was both impressive and consistent with that observed in the doctor visit studies. Yet, in some ways, the performance of the subjects in this experiment contrasts with our earlier work. Indeed, analysis of the recall data indicated that memory was outstanding and that the children provided more details following open-ended questioning than did the 5-year-olds in the Baker-Ward, Gordon, et al. (1993) study of the routine physical examination. In fact, although there were few older children in the VCUG study, the open-ended recall of the entire sample was comparable to that of the 7-year-olds in the well-child experiments. In addition, forgetting over the 6-week delay interval was independent of age. This finding is contrary to our repeated observation that 3-year-olds forget more details of the well-child examination than do older children; however, it may be an artifact of the limited amount of forgetting that was observed.

How shall these differences between the VCUG study and the well-child experiments be understood? We can only speculate at present, but it is important to underscore three critical differences between the two types of experiences that the children are trying to remember. First, the children in the VCUG study had much less knowledge about the event to be remembered than did the subjects who participated in the well-child experiments. To the extent to which memory depends upon rich knowledge structures concerning the experience to be remembered, the relative novelty of the VCUG procedure would lead to the prediction that the children in this experiment would recall less than those in the doctor studies. Yet this did not happen. Perhaps the VCUG subjects were able to interpret this invasive experience by analogy to other types of encounters with physicians and medical personnel.

Second, the participants in the VCUG study were judged to be more distressed than the children in the well-child studies. Perhaps the heightened levels of arousal that were operative permitted the VCUG subjects to counteract the negative consequences of reduced familiarity and knowledge. Indeed, it seems likely that arousal can have an overall positive impact on remembering, even though within-subjects analyses reveal a negative correlation between certain measures of stress and recall.

Finally, the VCUG experience appears to be a more integrated event than is the routine physical examination. By definition, the VCUG involves a cascade of dependent activities (e.g., the catheter must be inserted before contrast fluid can fill the bladder), whereas the component features of the physical examination can occur in varied orders. The structure of the VCUG procedure, with its clear sequential dependencies between component features, would be expected to facilitate the children's recall of this event.

Putting It All Together

We recently discussed our research program in the context of an informal framework (Ornstein et al., in press; Ornstein et al., 1991) that focuses on variables that affect the encoding, storage, transformation, and retrieval of information over time. At the core of this framework are four very general themes about memory: (a) not everything gets into memory, (b) what gets into memory may vary in strength, (c) the status of information in memory changes over time, and (d) retrieval is not perfect. This perspective permits a useful discussion of factors such as the initial representation of the event to be remembered, the individual's prior knowledge of the event, the impact of various experiences in the delay interval, the dynamics of retrieval, and so on. Nonetheless, we now feel it is important to work toward the construction of more formal developmental models of encoding, storage, and subsequent retrieval. Given our initial findings concerning the potential importance of individual differences in stress and temperament (Gordon et al., 1993; Merritt et al., 1994), as well as demonstrations of the central role played by prior knowledge (Clubb et al., 1993), we hope that models can be developed to indicate how these factors combine to influence what gets into memory and its subsequent retrievability.

Although such complex models are no doubt a long way off, we have begun the formalization process by exploring the implications of a simple multinomial model (Bender, Wallsten, & Ornstein, 1993; see also Riefer & Batchelder, 1988) that was developed to characterize the results obtained in the Baker-Ward, Gordon, et al. (1993) study. This model involves the translation of our empirical data into statements about factors that are thought to separately influence the probability that an individual feature of a medical procedure is encoded and, given that it is encoded, that it is also retrieved at different points in time. Our (Bender et al., 1993) major interest is in the extent to which the encoding and retrieval parameter values of the model vary across both age levels and specific components of the medical experience. In its initial application, variations of the model were explored to test hypotheses about age and delay effects in encoding and retrieval. Moreover, the form of the model that seemed most consistent with the data was one in which encoding was age-invariant, but retrieval varied developmentally. Work in progress is designed to examine the extent to which this model can account for children's retention of a variety of different medical experiences.

Implications for Testimony

A great deal remains to be learned about children's memory over time for the details of various medical events. Nonetheless, it seems clear that the findings obtained to date have some clear implications for those who are primarily concerned with the testimony of children. Although there are substantial developmental changes in the ability to provide accounts of personally experienced events, under some conditions even very young children are able to do so. Admittedly, we cannot yet specify the conditions that are maximally supportive of recall, but it does seem likely that preschoolers' performance will vary as a function of the type of event being remembered, personality characteristics of the child, and the mode of questioning employed by the interviewer.

The results of our VCUG study (Merritt et al., 1994) suggest that a highly ordered and salient event may be readily remembered, but additional research is clearly needed to tease apart the contributions of event structure and degree of arousal. Moreover, the findings of the doll (Gordon et al., 1993) and VCUG studies (Merritt et al., 1994) suggest that certain dimensions of temperament are associated with enhanced levels of recall. Finally, a consistent finding in our research program is that 3-year-olds require more direct probes to elicit information about previous experiences, whereas older children are able to respond relatively fluently to very general prompts. As such, the performance of young children may be more dependent upon the types of questions posed by an interviewer than is the case with older individuals. One consequence of this dependence upon the behavior of the interviewer is that intepretation of young children's responses to specific (i.e., yes–no) probes requires the presentation of questions about actions not included in the events being remembered.

The aspects of young children's memory discussed here seem central to any protocol for interviewing child witnesses. One of the goals that underlies our work is the eventual construction of guidelines for professionals who interact with child victims prior to court appearance, guidelines that may serve to maintain but not distort memory (Ornstein, 1991). Indeed, based upon our research and a broader analysis of the memory literature, we have prepared a preliminary set of recommendations for interviewing children who may have experienced or witnessed abuse (see Gordon, Schroeder, Ornstein, & Baker-Ward, in press). Additional research on children's memory for medical procedures, in conjunction with studies of other types of salient events, will guide the refinement and evaluation of these suggestions for practice.

ACKNOWLEDGMENTS

The research reported here was supported in part by grant MH 49304 from the United States Public Health Service.

REFERENCES

Baker-Ward, L., Gordon, B. N., Ornstein, P. A., Larus, D. M., & Clubb, P. A. (1993). Young children's long-term retention of a pediatric examination. *Child Development, 64*, 1519–1533.

Baker-Ward, L., Ornstein, P. A., & Gordon, B. N. (1993). A tale of two settings: Children's memory performance in the laboratory and the field. In G. Davies & R. Logie (Eds.), *Everyday remembering* (pp. 13–41). London: North Holland.

Baker-Ward, L., Ornstein, P. A., Gordon, B. N., Follmer, A., & Clubb, P. A. (1995). How shall a thing be coded? Implications of the use of alternative procedures for scoring children's verbal reports. In M. S. Zaragoza, J. R. Graham, G. C. N. Hall, R. Hirschman, & Y. S. Ben-Porath (Eds.), *Memory and testimony in the child witness* (pp. 61–85). Thousand Oaks, CA: Sage.

Baker-Ward, L., Ornstein, P. A., & Holden, D. J. (1984). The expression of memorization in early childhood. *Journal of Experimental Child Psychology, 37*, 555–575.

Bender, R. H., Wallsten, T. S., & Ornstein, P. A. (1993, August). *A multinomial model of age-related differences in children's memory.* Paper presented at the 26th annual meeting of the Mathematical Psychology Society, Norman, OK.

Best, D. L., & Ornstein, P. A. (1986). Children's generation and communication of mnemonic organizational strategies. *Developmental Psychology, 22*, 845–853.

Boat, B. W., & Everson, M. D. (1988). Use of anatomical dolls among professionals in sexual abuse evaluations. *Child Abuse and Neglect, 12*, 171–179.

Brainerd, C. J., Reyna, V. F., Howe, M. L., & Kingma, J. (1990). The development of forgetting and reminiscence. *Monographs of the Society for Research in Child Development, 55* (Serial No. 222).

Campbell, B. A., & Jaynes, J. (1966). Reinstatement. *Psychological Review, 73*, 478–480.

Casby, M. W., & Della Corte, M. (1987). Symbolic play performance and early language development. *Journal of Psycholinguistic Research, 16*, 31–42.

Ceci, S. J., & Bruck, M. (1993). Suggestibility of child witnesses: A historical review and synthesis. *Psychological Bulletin, 113*, 403–439.

Clubb, P. A., Nida, R., Merritt, K., & Ornstein, P. A. (1993). Visiting the doctor: Children's knowledge and memory. *Cognitive Development, 8*, 361–372.

DeLoache, J. S. (1990). Young children's understanding of models. In R. Fivush & J. Hudson (Eds.), *Knowing and remembering in young children* (pp. 94–126). New York: Cambridge University Press.

Doris, J. (Ed.) (1991). *The suggestibility of children's recollections.* Washington, DC: American Psychological Association.

Elliott, C. H., Jay, S. M., & Woody, P. (1987). An observation scale for measuring children's distress during medical procedures. *Journal of Pediatric Psychology, 12,* 543–551.

Fivush, R. (1984). Learning about school: The development of kindergartners' school scripts. *Child Development, 55,* 1697–1709.

Fivush, R., & Hudson, J. A. (Eds.). (1990). *Knowing and remembering in young children.* New York: Cambridge.

Gordon, B. N., & Follmer, A. (1994). Developmental issues in judging the credibility of children's testimony. *Journal of Clinical Child Psychology, 23,* 283–294.

Gordon, B. N., Ornstein, P. A., Clubb, P. A., Nida, R. E., & Baker-Ward, L. (1991, October). *Visiting the pediatrician: Long-term retention and forgetting.* Paper presented at the annual meeting of the Psychonomic Society, San Francisco, CA.

Gordon, B. N., Ornstein, P. A., Nida, R. E., Follmer, A., Crenshaw, M. C., & Albert, G. (1993). Does the use of dolls facilitate children's memory of visits to the doctor? *Applied Cognitive Psychology, 7,* 459–474.

Gordon, B. N., Schroeder, C. S., Ornstein, P. A., & Baker-Ward, L. (in press). Clinical implications of research on children's memory development. In T. Ney (Ed.), *Child sexual abuse cases: Allegations, assessments, and management.* New York: Brunner/Mazel.

Howe, M. L., & Brainerd, C. J. (1989). Development of children's long-term retention. *Developmental Review, 9,* 301–340.

Howe, M. L., Brainerd, C. J., & Reyna, V. F. (Eds.). (1992). *Development of long-term retention.* New York: Springer-Verlag.

Kail, R. (1991). Developmental change in speed of processing during childhood and adolescence. *Psychological Bulletin, 109,* 490–501.

Mandler, J. (1991, April). *The development of autobiographical memory for stressful and emotional events.* Discussant for a symposium presented at the biennial meeting of the Society for Research in Child Development, Seattle, WA.

Martin, R. P. (1988). *Temperament assessment battery for children.* Brandon, VT: Clinical Psychology Publishing Company.

Merritt, K. A., Ornstein, P. A., & Spicker, B. (1994). Children's memory for a salient medical procedure: Implications for testimony. *Pediatrics, 94,* 17–23.

Miller, P. H., & Seier, W. L. (1994). Strategy utilization deficiencies in children: When, where, and why. In H. W. Reese (Ed.), *Advances in child development and behavior* (Vol. 25, pp. 107–156). New York: Academic Press.

Nelson, K. A. (1986). *Event knowledge: Structure and function in development.* Hillsdale, NJ: Lawrence Erlbaum Associates.

Ornstein, P. A. (1991). Commentary: Putting interviewing in context. In D. J. Doris (Ed.), *The suggestibility of children's recollections* (pp. 147–152). Washington, DC: American Psychological Association.

Ornstein, P. A., Gordon, B. N., & Baker-Ward, L. (1992). Children's memory for salient events: Implications for testimony. In M. L. Howe, C. J. Brainerd, & V. R. Reyna (Eds.), *Development of long-term retention* (pp. 135–158). New York: Springer-Verlag.

Ornstein, P. A., Gordon, B. N., Baker-Ward, L. E., & Merritt, K. A. (in press). Children's memory for medical experiences: Implications for testimony. In D. Peters (Ed.), *The child witness in context: Cognitive, social, and legal perspectives.* Dordrecht, Netherlands: Kluwer.

Ornstein, P. A., Gordon, B. N., & Larus, D. H. (1992). Children's memory for a personally experienced event: Implications for testimony. *Applied Cognitive Psychology, 6,* 49–60.

Ornstein, P. A., Larus, D. M., & Clubb, P. A. (1991). Understanding children's testimony: Implications of research on the development of memory. In R. Vasta (Ed.), *Annals of Child Development* (Vol. 8, pp. 145–176). London: Jessica Kingsley.

Riefer, D. M., & Batchelder, W. H. (1988). Multinomial modeling and the measurement of cognitive processes. *Psychological Review, 98,* 318–337.

Rovee-Collier, C. K., & Hayne, H. (1987). Reactivation of infant memory: Implications for cognitive development. In H. W. Reese (Ed.), *Advances in child development and behavior* (Vol. 20, pp. 185–283). New York: Academic Press.

Siegal, M., Waters, L. J., & Dinwiddy, L. S. (1988). Misleading children: Causal attributes for inconsistency under repeated questioning. *Journal of Experimental Child Psychology, 45*, 438–456.

Slamecka, N. J., & Katsaiti, L. T. (1988). Normal forgetting of verbal lists as a function of prior testing. *Journal of Experimental Psychology: Learning, Memory, and Cognition, 14*, 716–727.

Wellman, H. M. (1988). The early development of memory strategies. In F. E. Weinert and M. Perlmutter (Eds.), *Memory development: Universal changes and individual differences* (pp. 3–29). Hillsdale, NJ: Lawrence Erlbaum Associates.

Part V

FUTURE DIRECTIONS OF RESEARCH ON MEMORY DEVELOPMENT

What Is Intellectual Development About in the 1990s? Good Information Processing

Michael Pressley
State University of New York at Albany

I am the victim of a misleading wrap. Ask my colleagues in basic research what I do, and the response is often, "research on strategies." Ask those who are familiar with my more applied research efforts the same question, and the answer is, "strategies instruction." Although it is true that much of my work is about when people use strategies or can use them, I never viewed strategies as the most important determinant of cognitive competence. Competent performance, from my perspective, depends on a number of factors in interaction.

In this chapter, I review the model of intellectual competence I have favored for the past 10 years, *good information processing*. I then revisit much of my basic work establishing that strategic competence can only be understood in the context of other cognitive variables. Finally, I cover my most recent program of research, concerned with strategies instruction by teachers who do it well, making the case that such teachers are promoting the various elements of good information processing.

A MID-1990S PERSPECTIVE ON GOOD INFORMATION PROCESSING

I am currently finishing an advanced educational psychology textbook (Pressley with McCormick, 1995) that has at its center the theme that much of educational psychology can be understood by grasping the four main components of good information processing: strategies, metacognitive procedures and knowledge, other knowledge—including knowledge of the world and domain specific knowledge, and motivational beliefs and attitudes. That is, development of academic competence is development of information-processing components in supportive interaction (Pressley, Borkowski, & O'Sullivan, 1984, 1985; Pressley, Borkowski, & Schneider, 1987, 1989). Although, in the 1980s, my colleagues and I were not alone in such a commitment (e.g., Brown, Bransford, Ferrara, & Campione, 1983; Paris, Lipson, & Wixson, 1983), many others moved on to other positions or lost interest in fleshing out the interactions associated with skilled thinking.

The interactive dynamics of the good information processing components can be made more obvious to audiences by working through a favorite example of good information processing. Thus, as I did before (e.g., Pressley, Snyder, & Cariglia-Bull, 1987), I take up the thinking of two adolescents that most North Americans have known all of their lives, the Hardy Boys.

Strategies, Metacognition, Knowledge, and Motivation in the Thinking of the Hardy Boys

No one could come away from the Hardy Boys mysteries without feeling that these kids were really, really smart (see especially Dixon, 1972). First of all, the Hardy Boys had an incredibly rich repertoire of *strategies* for solving crimes: Sometimes the boys would try to put themselves in the place of the criminal as they analyzed a crime. They had a whole host of specific tactics for lifting fingerprints from difficult places and for making certain that all of the physical evidence at the scene of a crime was collected. The boys used cognitive strategies like rehearsal and imagery to encode important information about a crime. For example, their approach to remembering a physical description of a person was to visualize, beginning at the top of the head and working down to the shoes.

The boys' use of strategies was intentional (e.g., Bereiter, 1990). They were habitually reflective in processing information about a crime, thinking thoroughly about the evidence rather than reacting impulsively. Even so, the boys were not so reflective that it was paralyzing (e.g., Baron, 1985, 1988, 1990; Duemler & Mayer, 1988). Instead, they came to plans of action and moved forward with the inquiry.

The Hardy Boys' ability to construct strategic plans was determined in large part by their long-term knowledge about when the strategies they possessed were effective—that is, their *metacognitive knowledge about strategies* (e.g., Pressley, Borkowski, & O'Sullivan, 1984, 1985). Thus, when first arriving at a crime, the Boys knew it appropriate to use particular strategies to preserve the crime scene (e.g., cordoning it off) and when to execute systematic search strategies and recording of information. They knew, too, that their memories were fallible—that memory errors can reflect prior knowledge and biases rather than what happened on a particular occasion. Thus, they used photography strategically to record crime scenes, made drawings when a camera was not available, and took extensive notes. Their ability to shift plans on an as-needed basis was enabled by their *monitoring* of progress in solving a crime and monitoring of the effects produced by the strategies they were using. Their long-term metacognition and monitoring related interactively: As the boys monitored that a particular technique worked well in a particular situation, their long-term understanding of the effects produced by the particular strategy shifted.

The boys used their cognitive strategies in conjunction with *nonstrategic knowledge*. Their experiences as criminal investigators privileged them to knowledge that detectives possess, knowledge that was used in interaction with their strategic competencies. The strategies possessed by the Hardy Boys were used in particular ways because of their knowledge of the law, criminals' behaviors, criminals' language, physical evidence, drugs, and virtually every aspect of life. For example, they knew that glass is a particularly good source of fingerprints and thus, the boys took special care to make certain that the glass at a crime scene was undisturbed until it could be examined systematically.

No one could read the Hardy Boys' mysteries without being struck by their *motivation*. The boys were always looking for crimes to solve and were determined to go about their investigations in a systematic way. They were driven to learn more about sleuthing, including the strategies and knowledge needed by a detective. They were self-efficacious (Bandura, 1986) with respect to detective work, recognizing when they were equal to tasks and when something might be beyond them or require assistance. Their motivation to do detective work was not undermined by their emotions. For instance, anxiety did not overwhelm their thinking, even when they were confronted with great danger. Good thinkers have *attentional focus* (e.g., Aks & Coren, 1990)—the Hardys were motivated and able to maintain attention even in the face of distraction. The German psychologist Kuhl (e.g., 1985), refers to this ability to insulate goal-directed cognition from distraction as *action control*. The Hardy Boys were certainly action controlled, following the trail of clues like bloodhounds. In short, the Hardy Boys possessed many characteristics of good thinking—strategies, metacognition, other knowledge, and motivation, with these characteristics interacting to promote highly intelligent detective work.

Other Characteristics of Good Information Processing

A theme interwoven throughout the advanced educational psychology book is that good information processing is enabled by developing biological structures. Although many different aspects of biology are covered in the volume, one essential capacity determined at least in part by biological mechanisms is encountered again and again: An important individual difference between people is their short-term capacity (Baddeley, 1986), because much of thinking depends on *short-term memory*, variously referred to as consciousness, working memory, or short-term storage. That is, even among people with healthy brains, some can hold more things in memory (consciousness, conscious attention) and operate on more bits of information simultaneously than can others. An especially important hypothesis is that with development there is increasing ability to hold information in consciousness (Case, 1985; Dempster, 1985), with this accounting for some of the apparent improvements in thinking with development, although there are a number of alternative explanations as to why there seems to be an increase with development in capacity (Case, 1985; Dempster, 1985). Good thinkers such as the Hardy Boys have sufficient short-term capacity to carry out relatively complex tasks. For example, they can hold a telephone number in memory while searching for a scratch pad, juggle bits and pieces of meaning while trying to combine clues into a coherent scenario, and with eyes closed, can keep in view a room while imagining how a robber might have moved around it while searching for the wall safe.

Another theme recurring in my book is that much of good information processing is the product of rich intellectual experiences, including instructional opportunities that encourage the development of sophisticated strategies, provide exposure to important world and domain-specific knowledge, and support the individual's view that he or she is capable of effective thinking, learning, and performance. Fenton Hardy, the boys' famous detective father, did all of this for his sons. Good thinkers' educational experiences also motivate them to seek out enriching situations and thus, to contribute to their own education and development (Bandura, 1986; Ford, 1987; Lerner & Busch-Rossnagel, 1981; Scarr, 1992; Scarr & McCartney, 1983). One reason that the Hardy Boys knew so much about detective work and criminology is that they spent their free time reading about crimes and how to solve them, sought out companions with expertise in detective work, and looked for every opportunity to acquire knowledge that might be helpful in their work.

In summary, no one characteristic makes a person a good information processor, but rather good thinking is the product of a number of factors in interaction feeding on one another. For instance, byproducts of using effective strategies to solve problems include new metacognitive knowledge about those strategies (i.e., that they did indeed work in this situation) as well as nonstrategic knowledge (e.g., specific pieces of information about how computer security codes work acquired while solving a case of illegal entry to a company's computer files by a competitor). The metacognition and knowledge gained through strategy use today can be used in future problem-solving endeavors. With greater knowledge about when to use particular strategies and greater general and domain-specific knowledge, confidence about and motivation to use one's strategies increases. Instruction and other experiences play a huge role in the development of strategies, metacognition, general and domain-specific knowledge, and motivation, with excellent instruction effective in part because it stimulates the student to make enriching life decisions that lead to even better information processing in the future.

This introduction to the complexities of good thinking sets the stage for the rest of this chapter: The section on basic research covers how I studied strategies in relation to metacognition, other knowledge, motivation, and capacity (i.e., the four main components covered in my book and the recurring theme that short-term capacity is a constraint in thinking). The section on instruction covers how effective in-school strategy instruction is rich in elements that promote good information processing, including elements that increase the likelihood that students will want to carry out the strategic processes they are learning in school on their own (i.e., the second recurring theme in my book, that experience can be structured to foster self-regulated thinking that, in turn, stimulates further growth and development; e.g., Zimmerman, 1989a, 1989b, 1990a, 1990b).

BASIC RESEARCH

My research was diverse over the years, involving children as young as 3 years of age, adults who are in their 90s, and every age level in between. People were asked to process paired associates in various ways; learn the meaning of unfamiliar vocabulary words; memorize word lists; and try to comprehend sentences, paragraphs, stories, chapters, and articles. Thus, the examples provided here are far ranging.

I selected for review studies that make the point that strategies can only be understood in relation to other information-processing components. In each of the investigations covered here, use of some particular strategy was studied in relation to one other component of good information processing.

Metacognition

Metacognitive theorists in the 1980s hypothesized that one of the most important functions of metacognition is to facilitate generalized use of strategies and skills (e.g., Borkowski, 1985; Paris et al., 1983; Pressley et al., 1984, 1985). More critical than other types of metacognition is knowledge about when and where to apply particular cognitive processes that one knows, referred to in the literature both as *specific strategy knowledge* (e.g., Pressley et al., 1984, 1985) and as *conditional knowledge* (e.g., Paris et al., 1983). In the early and mid-1980s, there were correlational data supporting this claim (see Borkowski, 1985) but no experimental data permitting the conclusion that possession of knowledge about where and when to apply a strategy increases the likelihood that the strategy will be generalized appropriately. O'Sullivan's dissertation at Western Ontario was conducted to fill that gap with respect to an associative mnemonic strategy I studied intensely in the late 1970s and early 1980s.

The keyword method facilitates acquisition of associations between unfamiliar concepts and familiar ones. Most of the work on keyword mnemonics available when O'Sullivan designed her study involved acquisition of associations between unfamiliar vocabulary words (e.g., often words in a foreign language) and their meanings. The keyword method user recodes the unfamiliar item into a keyword that sounds like a well-known word. Thus, subjects in our studies who learned the Spanish word *carta*, which means postal letter, first recorded *carta* to *cart*. Subjects who learned the obsolescent English word, *cordite*, which is a type of explosive, recoded it to *cord*. Once a keyword is identified, the keyword method user forms an interactive image (alternatively, a linking sentence) between the keyword and definition referents in order to remember the meaning of the unfamiliar vocabulary item. Thus, for *carta*, the keyword method learner might imagine a letter lying in a postal worker's delivery cart. For *cordite*, an image of sticks of dynamite tied into a bundle with a cord might be constructed. In general, for vocabulary items with easily identified keywords, use of the keyword method greatly increases memory for vocabulary–definition associations (Pressley, Levin, & Delaney, 1982). Although not studied as extensively, there was also evidence in the early 1980s that the method might be useful in any associative task involving acquisition of connections between unfamiliar and more familiar concepts, for example, learning connections between cities and the products they produce (e.g., that submarines are manufactured in Long Beach; see Pressley et al., 1982).

The question posed by O'Sullivan in her thesis (subsequently published as O'Sullivan & Pressley, 1984) was whether or not children in Grades 5 and 6 who learned to use the keyword method with one associative task would transfer the keyword method to another associative learning task. Based on many reports of transfer failure by children who were provided instruction about how to execute a strategic procedure with only one type of material (Brown et al., 1983) and Pressley and Dennis-Rounds' (1980) demonstration of little keyword-mnemonic transfer by 10- to 13-year-olds, O'Sullivan expected little transfer by Grades 5 and 6 children taught only the keyword method strategy. Her hypothesis was that transfer of the mnemonic strategy would be more likely if instruction were provided that included information about when and where keyword mnemonics can be deployed in order to increase learning—that is, if metacognitive information about the strategy's applicability was included in instruction.

All participants in O'Sullivan and Pressley (1984) performed two memory tasks, one involving acquisition of city–product pairings and the other acquisition of Latin vocabulary definitions. Children in the control condition performed both tasks without the benefit of strategy instruction. In four other experimental conditions, children were taught to learn the city–product pairings using the keyword method (e.g., imagine submarines run ashore on a long beach). The four keyword method conditions varied with respect to the amount of information provided about when and where the keyword method was applicable. In the most metacognitively complete condition, children were told that the method could be used whenever associations needed to be learned and one of the to-be-associated items was unfamiliar but could be related to an acoustically similar, familiar word (i.e., a keyword). In this most complete condition, subjects were provided examples of tasks that could be mediated with the keyword method and ones that could not be (although no mention was made of learning foreign vocabulary words, the transfer task in this study). Two of the other keyword method conditions each contained some of this metacognitive embellishment. The fourth keyword method condition included no metacognitive information (or at least, none was provided by the experimenter doing the instruction).

On the city–product task, all four keyword method conditions greatly outperformed the controls. More importantly, however, was the pattern of outcomes for the transfer task. The probability of keyword method subjects transferring the keyword method from learning of city–product pairings to acquisition of Latin vocabulary definitions varied linearly with the amount of metacognitive information about keyword method applicability that was presented during instruction.

What O'Sullivan and Pressley (1984) established was that providing when and where information about strategy applicability increases generalization of a particular imagery-mnemonic strategy: It was not enough for students to know the strategy. If an elaboration strategy is to be used in new situations, the learner also must know when and where it can be deployed profitably.

It has been my good fortune to have a number of studies I carried out be followed up. One of the real disappointments, however, is that O'Sullivan and Pressley inspired no such follow-ups. I am hard pressed in 1995 to cite even a single additional investigation that cleanly manipulated the presentation or availability of information about when and where to use a cognitive strategy and then measured the generalization of the strategy. More positively, later in this chapter, I report on a number of studies in which the presence of another form of metacognitive knowledge—understanding that a strategy promotes learning—was demonstrated in well-controlled, true experiments to be critical to strategy maintenance. That work, however, has more to do with motivation to use a strategy than with understanding how the strategy can be stretched to fit new situations.

Knowledge

I was interested in the effects of knowledge on learning for a long time. In fact, one of my first published studies (Pressley & Levin, 1977) documented that children's success in using elaboration strategies depends in part on the availability of accessible knowledge that can be used to elaborate to-be-learned associations and as such, predated most other analyses of knowledge by strategy interactions (for reviews, see Alexander & Judy, 1988; Pressley, Borkowski, & Schneider, 1987; Schneider & Pressley, 1989). Happily, there were a number of demonstrations since then that the likelihood of effective elaboration (both instructed and uninstructed) during associative learning depends on the accessibility of potential mediating associations (e.g., Kee & Davies, 1990, 1991;

Rohwer, Rabinowitz, & Dronkers, 1982; Waters, 1982; for a review, see Kee, in press).

More recently, much of my work was concerned with an elaboration strategy (elaborative interrogation) that is explicitly aimed at increasing learning by increasing the likelihood that learners will relate what they already know to new information, and that research is my focus in this subsection.

That adults can be led to elaborate much more than they do so spontaneously can be demonstrated by presenting adults with sets of confusing facts to learn. For example, in Pressley, Symons, McDaniel, Snyder, and Turnure (1988, Experiment 3), Canadian university students were presented 36 facts about the 10 provinces and two territories, including the following:

Apples were first cultivated in Nova Scotia.

British Columbia has the highest percentage of its population in unions.

The first educational radio station was in Alberta.

None of these facts were pieces of information that young Canadians know. In each case, however, the fact could be explained, in that young Canadian adults possess substantial knowledge that they could relate to the fact to render it sensible. Thus, for the British Columbia item, most Canadians recognize the prominence of longshoremen in the province given its coastal location. They also know that British Columbia has more politically left-wing allegiances than other provinces, which are consistent with unionization.

The important result in the Pressley et al. (1988, Experiment 3) study was that the Canadian adults did not seem to use their prior knowledge of Canada when they read the factual sentences. Subjects who processed the facts under a reading control instruction could subsequently recall a province given one of its corresponding facts only 48% of the time (i.e., answer questions such as, "Which province has the highest percentage of its population in unions?" and "Where was the first educational radio station?"). In contrast, if during original presentation of the facts, subjects were stimulated to relate them to prior knowledge by responding to why questions (e.g., Why does it make sense that British Columbia is the province with the highest percentage of its population in unions?), recall of the correct province was much more likely (i.e., 73.5% correct recall).

My colleagues and I obtained this *elaborative interrogation effect*, as it became known, a number of times, with our preferred interpretation that question-answering required the learner to search and relate the to-be-learned fact to prior knowledge supportive of the fact and thus, to strengthen the association between the various constituents of the fact (e.g., the province and the accomplishment attributed to the province). The problem with this interpretation was that there were alternative explanations equally compatible with the elaborative interrogation effect: (a) the elaborative interrogation effect might only be a specific instance of the more general *generation effect*, which is better memory for subject-generated than other-generated materials (Slamecka & Graf, 1978); (b) answering why questions might enhance memory by increasing conscious processing, arousal, cognitive effort, and/or deep encoding (Jacoby, 1978; Slamecka & Graf, 1978; Tyler, Hertel, McCallum, & Ellis, 1979); (c) answering why questions might lead to better performance because the demands at encoding in this condition are more similar to the demands at testing (i.e., both involve responding to questions) than are the encoding demands in control conditions (i.e., encoding entails reading only versus question-answering at testing; McDaniel, Friedman, & Bourne, 1978; Morris, Bransford, & Franks, 1977); (d) elaborative interrogation might simply stimulate the activation of more linkages in general during encoding than does reading (e.g., Anderson & Reder, 1979). Although any of these possibilities might explain the elaborative interrogation data reported prior to 1991 and reported at the last meeting of the Max Planck Institute that was dedicated to memory development (Pressley, Wood, & Woloshyn, 1990), none of them are adequate to explain two sets of data generated since then, both of which are strongly consistent with the position that the effectiveness of a strategy such as elaborative interrogation depends on whether or not prior knowledge related to the new to-be-learned piece of information is activated.

In Martin and Pressley (1991), Canadian university students were presented facts about Canadian provinces. Control subjects were left to their own devices to read and attempt to understand the facts. In four why-questioning conditions, the participants were asked one of four types of questions.

In one why question condition, subjects were asked to provide an answer confirming the fact, specifically referring to information about the province in question (i.e., confirm-particular province condition). Thus, for the fact, "The first Canadian-based farm protest organization was formed in Manitoba," subjects responded to the question, "Why does it make sense that the first Canadian-based farm protest organization was formed in Manitoba?" The why question in this condition was most like the why questions in previously successful elaborative interrogation conditions, stimulating search for knowledge supportive of the fact as stated.

In the other three why question conditions, the questions less certainly directed the subjects to process supportive prior knowledge. In one of these, subjects were asked to confirm the fact by referring only to other provinces (i.e., Why does that fact make sense given what you know about other provinces?—confirm-other province condition). In another why question condition, subjects were directed to provide information about the named province, but information inconsistent with the fact as stated (i.e., Why is that fact unexpected given what you know about that particular province?—disconfirm-particular province condition). In the why question condition most directing the subjects away from prior supportive knowledge, subjects were asked to indicate why the fact that was stated was unexpected by referring to information about other provinces (i.e., disconfirm-other province condition). See Table 19.1 for model answers for each of these conditions.

TABLE 19.1

Model Answers for Why-Questions Pertaining to "The first Canadian-based
farm protest organization was in Manitoba," as a Function of Condition

Condition	Model Answer
Confirm fact referring to province in question (confirm-particular province condition)	Farmers in Manitoba are concentrated in the lower half of the province and have easy access to each other in terms of organizing a protest group. Manitoba is also a province that has been known for its social reform and socialized government.
Confirm fact referring to other provinces (confirm-other province condition)	Provinces that have large farm industries are rather conservative in nature and one would not expect them to form farm protest groups, especially provinces such as Ontario and Quebec that have the oldest and largest farming industries.
Make case fact is unexpected, referring to province in question (disconfirm-particular province condition)	Manitoba is not really an agricultural or farm-based province. Much of the economy is based on mining and hydroelectric power. Therefore, it is unexpected that it would have the first farm-based protest organization.
Make case that fact is unexpected, referring to other provinces (disconfirm-other province condition)	Provinces such as Ontario and Quebec would have had the first Canadian-based farm protest organization because agriculture is a large part of their economies and they also had some of the first farms. Otherwise, one would expect provinces such as Alberta or Saskatchewan, because farming is a major part of their economies and one might expect that they would need a protest organization to counter the power of the central provinces.

Note. Adapted from Martin and Pressley (1991). Copyright 1991 by American Psychological Association.

Martin and Pressley (1991) reasoned that all four of the questioning conditions required generation of answers by subjects—conscious processing, arousal, cognitive effort, and/or deep encoding—question-answering processes during both study and testing; and activation of many linkages during encoding (e.g., Anderson & Reder, 1979). If any of these factors account for the elaborative interrogation effect, then it would be expected that performance in all four of the questioning conditions would be approximately equal and high relative to the control condition. If elaborative interrogation effects depend on the why question orienting learners to supportive prior knowledge, then the amount of facilitation would be expected to vary with the degree that the why question stimulated processing of such knowledge.

In fact, the results were completely consistent with the latter hypothesis, with the mean percentage of provinces correctly matched on the posttest with their facts differing in the four why-questioning conditions as follows: confirm-particular province = 84.4% correct, confirm-other province = 78.3%, disconfirm-particular province = 71.4%, disconfirm-other province = 56.9%, and control = 58.1%. Consistent with previous research on elaborative interrogation, the confirm-particular province condition (which was most similar to previous elaborative interrogation conditions) produced better memory than the control condition. The other two why-questioning conditions that provided some prompting towards supportive prior knowledge (i.e., confirm-other, disconfirm-particular) also produced recall significantly superior to the control condition. Only the condition that completely oriented the subjects away from supportive prior knowledge had no impact on learning. A question is not a question is not a question, nor is a questioning strategy a questioning strategy. The elaborative interrogation questioning strategy works only if the why questions direct the learner's attention to supportive prior knowledge.

A second study providing clear support for the dependency of elaborative interrogation as a strategy on prior knowledge was conducted by Woloshyn, Pressley, and Schneider (1992). That investigation included Canadian and German university students, who were asked on one occasion to learn facts about Canadian provinces (as in the previous elaborative interrogation studies) and on another occasion, facts about German states (e.g., Bavaria is the state with the largest hop festival; Hamburg is the state with the lowest percentage of registered trucks; Hessen is the most densely wooded state). Subjects were either in an elaborative interrogation condition or given control instructions (i.e., to read the facts, making certain each fact is understood). Although there were main effects for prior knowledge (i.e., when other factors were equal, Germans recalled more German than Canadian facts, Canadians recalled more Canadian than German facts) and elaborative interrogation (i.e., when other factors were equal, performance in elaborative interrogation conditions exceeded control performances), the greatest recall occurred when students applied the elaborative interrogation strategy to facts from their home country (79.8% for Canadians, 70.9% for Germans; see Table 19.2). The dramatic difference that prior knowledge makes can be appreciated by comparing these percentages with the per-

TABLE 19.2
Mean Percentages of Canadian and German Facts Matched Correct
With Their Provinces/States as a Function of the Nationality
of the Participant and Experimental Condition

Facts/Subjects	Elaborative Interrogation	Control
Canadian Facts		
Canadian subjects (high prior knowledge)	79.5	51.8
German subjects (low prior knowledge)	33.6	17.6
German Facts		
German subjects (high prior knowledge)	70.9	52.1
Canadian subjects (low prior knowledge)	21.4	13.9

Note. Percentage based on maximum of 33 possibly correct.

centages remembered when elaborative interrogation subjects applied the strategy to facts from the foreign country (i.e., 21.4% for Canadians learning German facts via elaborative interrogation, 33.6% for Germans learning Canadian facts).

In summary, collapsing across a number of studies of elaborative interrogation, including those discussed here, there is substantial evidence that people often do not automatically access relevant prior knowledge when processing new material that could be related to what they know already. If the learner possesses relevant prior knowledge, why questioning that directs attention to knowledge supportive of new information will increase memory of the new information. Learning via elaborative interrogation depends on the learner possessing relevant prior knowledge, with only small effects of elaborative interrogation (if any) when that condition does not hold (see Woloshyn, Wood, & Willoughby, 1994, for a review). Elaboration strategy effects depend on a knowledge base that enables elaboration of new material; whether or not an elaboration strategy works depends on whether the elaboration processes lead to knowledge that is consistently supportive of to-be-learned associations.

Motivation

As far as experimental evaluation of motivation effects on strategy use is concerned, one experimental manipulation is preferred over all others. In a number of studies, memory researchers taught a strategy to subjects, with some subjects provided feedback about how the strategy improved their memory performance and no such feedback presented to other subjects. In every case, when subjects were presented the same type of memory task later, they were more likely to use the trained strategy if they had received feedback about the strategy's effectiveness (for reviews see Pressley et al., 1984, 1985; also Pressley, Borkowski, & Schneider, 1987, 1989). What these results suggest was that in the absence of feedback about the utility of a strategy, people often do not realize that a strategy benefits them—even if they have tried the strategy and been tested about what they remembered using the strategy.

That people often do no recognize strategy benefits spawned a series of studies on the monitoring of strategy utility, conducted by Levin, Ghatala, and me during the 1980s. One hypothesis we explored in detail was the possibility that utility information might be abstracted if learners had the opportunity to compare an effective strategy with a less effective one.

In the most cited of this series of studies (Pressley, Levin, & Ghatala, 1984), adults and children were asked to learn novel vocabulary words, with half the words studied using the keyword method and half studied using repetitive rehearsal (i.e., saying the words and their meanings over and over). We used these two strategies for two reasons. With all of the vocabulary having readily identifiable keywords, there was a large, positive effect for use of the keyword method in this situation, and the repetitive rehearsal strategy was familiar to both the adult and child subjects—both adults and children believe repetition facilitates memory.

One of the manipulated variables in these studies was the point in time when subjects were asked to make a decision about which strategy they would use to learn another list: Either subjects made such a choice after studying words using the two methods but before the test on the vocabulary, or after taking a test about the studied words.

An important finding in these studies was that if subjects made their strategy choice after the test, their preferences were clear—they favored the keyword method, justifying their choice on an unambiguous understanding that the keyword method improved learning of vocabulary. If they made their choice before taking the test—that is, after studying some words with the keyword method and some by repetition—there was no clear preference for one method over the other, and no clear expectation that one method produces better learning than the other. Although these effects were not quite as pronounced with children in Grades 5 and 6 as with adults, there was converging support for the general conclusion that people do not monitor the effects produced by a strategy while using it, but do seem to monitor strategy effects on learning when tested over content studied using two differently effective strategies. In short, people do not recognize the effectiveness of strategies they are applying while they are using them to study, with the result that they are not particularly motivated to continue using effective strategies they practice.

In a series of follow-up studies involving a number of different strategies and tasks (for reviews, see Ghatala, 1986; Pressley & Ghatala, 1990), Ghatala, Levin, and I studied whether even younger children could monitor their learning when they had opportunity to try two differentially effective strategies and be tested over content studied with the strategies. With primary grade children, monitoring strategy usefulness during study and testing cycles and using the knowledge of relative strategy efficacy gained from such monitoring was fragile. There was reliable selection in these studies of a more effective strategy on a maintenance trial following a study–testing cycle only when primary grade children were taught to (a) assess how they did on the test in relation to the strategy they used, (b) attribute the performance differences correlated with use of different strategies to the use of different strategies, and (c) employ their attribution of differential strategy utility when they selected a strategy for use on the maintenance task (Ghatala, Levin, Pressley, & Goodwin, 1986; Ghatala, Levin, Pressley, & Lodico, 1985). Primary grade students are not adept at monitoring their strategy-mediated performances, with the result that they are not particularly motivated to continue using an effective strategy even after experiencing the benefits of the strategy.

When all of the data from the various studies conducted by Pressley, Levin, and Ghatala are considered, there was clearer evidence for the testing effect with advancing age going from the primary grade years to university level. At no age level was there any evidence that learners were aware of the differential effectiveness of two different strategies as they used them; such awareness emerged only at testing.

At this point, many readers are reflecting on the frequent adult failures of maintenance that were reported in the literature. If adults are so good at monitoring strategy efficacy—at least after taking a test on material—why do they so often fail to maintain a strategy that is taught to them even after they practice the strategy, including a test on the material studied? My hypothesis was that the opportunity to compare the effects produced by an effective strategy with other performances was critical in Pressley, Levin, and Ghatala (1984), as well as in the follow-up studies reported through 1986. Pressley, Levin, and Ghatala (1988) evaluated that possibility, in what is the study I always single out as my most overlooked piece of research that deserves a look.

In Pressley, Levin, & Ghatala (1988), college students visited a research laboratory on two occasions. On the second occasion, they were presented a list of Latin words and asked to learn them using any method they wished, except they had to do their studying aloud. They were then tested and interviewed about their strategic preference for learning foreign vocabulary. Memory performance and strategy use on this second day were the main dependent variables of interest, with the levels of these expected to vary as a function of what occurred on the first visit to the laboratory 2 weeks earlier.

On Occasion 1, control subjects arrived and were informed that the only reason for them to come on Day 1 was to book an appointment for 2 weeks later, which they did. Subjects in a no-practice control condition were treated the same way, except that they were also told about two different ways of learning vocabulary—the keyword method and repeating words and their meanings over and over. The experimenter demonstrated both methods for the no-practice control participants. The third condition resembled the instructional conditions in most studies of the keyword method that I had conducted. The subjects in the keyword-practice condition arrived, were told about the keyword method, and required to apply it as they studied a list of Latin vocabulary words with a test following this study trial. In the fourth condition, a mixed-practice condition, subjects arrived and studied and were tested on one list of Latin vocabulary (as occurred in the keyword-practice condition). In this condition, however, subjects were directed to use the keyword method for half the items and repetition for the other half, with the experimenter cuing strategy use on an item-by-item basis as the subject went through the study list. In the fifth condition, baseline/keyword-practice, the participants studied and were tested on two lists of Latin words. On the first list, they were left to their own devices to study any way they pleased. On the second list, the subjects studied using the keyword method. In the sixth condition, baseline/mixed practice, subjects studied a first list using their own method of study. After the test on the first list, they studied a second list of vocabulary, using the keyword method for half the items and repetition for the other half of the items, with a memory test following this second list, as well.

A key difference between the conditions was in the number of opportunities for comparison of keyword-mediated test performances with other ways of processing. Subjects in the baseline/mixed-practice condition were able to compare keyword method mediated performance with learning when left to their own devices and in comparison to rehearsal-mediated learning. That is, there were two bases of comparison in this condition. In contrast, the baseline/keyword practice and mixed-practice conditions each offered one opportunity to compare keyword-mediated learning with alternative approaches, relative to one's own preferred method in the baseline–keyword practice condition and relative to rehearsal in the mixed-practice condition. In contrast, the keyword practice condition, which was most similar to keyword-mediated learning in instructional studies, afforded no opportunity for comparison of keyword-mediated learning and other-mediated learning. The expectation was that the degree of keyword method maintenance observed 2 weeks after the first session would vary with the opportunities for comparison.

The Session 1 data were as expected. Keyword method learning was superior to rehearsal-mediated learning and own-strategy-mediated learning in every comparison. The critical Session 2 data were as expected. Comparison opportunities made a difference, with evidence of maintenance on recall of List 2 vocabulary definitions and overt verbalizations of keyword mediators during study in all three conditions that included some comparison opportunities. Only the condition that afforded two comparisons of keyword-mediated performance with alternatives produced evidence of maintenance on the third measure, which was unambiguous preference for the keyword strategy on an interview about whether they preferred the keyword method or rehearsal of vocabulary. This interview was administered after the second session list of vocabulary was studied, but before the Session 2 test was administered in order to prevent Session 2 test performance from affecting the reported strategy preference. All of the data from this experiment are summarized in Table 19.3.

An important outcome was that in the condition corresponding most closely to the typical keyword method instructional condition in past experiments, there was little evidence of 2-week maintenance. In contrast, maintenance was more striking in conditions that had permitted comparison of keyword-mediated learning and recall with other-method-mediated learning and recall. How can this pattern of maintenance outcomes be explained? A strong performance when a strategy is used under instruction in no way guarantees that learners infer that their memory was improved because of the strategy. Without a basis for comparison—for example, as provided by recent experience attempting the task without the benefit of the strategy—such an inference is unlikely. Without such an inference, there is no motivation to continue using the strategy when left to one's own devices to learn material similar to that just studied with the strategy. Motivation to use a strategy is anything but certain from simply practicing it.

TABLE 19.3
Mean Percentages of Session 2 Definitions Recalled and Items
that Were Overtly Reported as Keyword-Mediated During Online
Think-Alouds; Percentage of Subjects Preferring the Keyword Method
During the Session 2 Poststudy-But-Before-The-Test Interview

Condition	Percent Recalled	Percent Items Reported Keyword Use in Online Reports	Percent of Subjects Favoring Keyword in Interview
Baseline/Mixed practice	59.0*	62.0*	77.8*
Baseline/Keyword practice	51.4*	66.2*	61.1
Mixed practice	51.6*	59.5*	55.6
Keyword practice	46.5	42.1*	50.0
No practice	44.0	44.5*	38.9
Control	31.7	7.6	33.3

*Means differ significantly from the control mean, overall $p < .05$ (i.e., $p < .01$ per comparison).
$N = 18$ per cell.

As impressive as the studies reviewed in this subsection are with respect to the consistency of outcomes, it may be that the consistency is illusory, representing a narrowness of focus in the investigations to date. More than perceptions of success and failure and potential control were hypothesized to underlie differences in academic motivation (see Kanfer, 1990; also, Schmeck & Geisler-Brenstein, 1989). For example, the goal in most studies analyzing motivational effects on strategy use was to learn material, so that there is little in this literature about how one's goal colors perceptions of strategy utility information and the subsequent selection of strategies. The studies were decontextualized for the most part, so that learning and motivational histories that might affect strategy use in more naturalistic settings (e.g., classroom environments in which performance relative to others is emphasized vs. self-improvement; Nicholls, 1989; Nolen, 1988) did not operate in these studies. Indeed, none of the individual differences distinctions proposed by motivational theorists as determinants of self-regulation were analyzed in these studies of strategy utility (e.g., students motivated by achievement, fear of failure, or self-actualization, as conceptualized by Entwistle, 1988; deep vs. surface learners, Ramsden, 1988). Alternatively, it may be that perceptions of utility are very powerful relative to many other variables and that explains the striking consistency. We will not know until there are studies that systematically vary goals, learner types, and other situational factors as the effectiveness of strategies (and the saliency of effectiveness) is varied systematically.

Capacity

In 1978, Levin and I proposed (Pressley & Levin, 1978) that developmental differences in the elementary grade years in the ability to construct mental images that mediate memory might be due, in part, to developmental differences in short-term capacity. This hypothesis was advanced in light of the observation that when primary grade children are able to construct interactive images, the short-term processing demands are reduced relative to when primary grade children fail to benefit from instructions to construct mnemonic images. For example, primary grade children benefit from interactive imagery instructions with picture pairs but not with verbal pairs (Pressley, 1977). One explanation of this effect is that it takes less short-term capacity to construct an interactive image given picture pairs than verbal pairs and thus, children benefit from imagery instructions when they are asked to learn picture pairs before they benefit from imagery instructions for mediating learning of verbal pairs (Pressley & Levin, 1978). As appealing as such reasoning was, however, there were no studies in the 1970s that examined developmental shifts in elaborative abilities and also measured independently developmental and other individual differences in short-term capacity.

In the mid-1980s, Cariglia-Bull and I undertook, in a series of two studies, to fill this void in the literature (Cariglia-Bull & Pressley, 1990; Pressley, Cariglia-Bull, Deane, & Schneider, 1987), examining relationships between children's age, short-term memory capacity, verbal competence, and memory performance both in imagery–instructional conditions and in control conditions. In both studies, we asked elementary grade children to learn 20 sentences so that the sentences could be recalled given some part of them. The sentences included the following:

The angry bird shouted at the white dog.

The policeman painted the circus tent on a windy day.

The turkey pecked the coke can lying on the highway.

The children in Pressley, Cariglia-Bull, et al. (1987) spanned Grades 1 to 6; they heard such sentences. In Cariglia-Bull and Pressley (1990), students in Grades 4 through 6 read the sentences. Half of the children in each study were asked to learn the sentences by constructing a mental image for each one, depicting the meaning of the sentence. The remaining children served in the control condition, with these participants urged to try hard to remember each sentence for a subsequent memory test.

Before experiencing this sentence learning task, short-term memory measures were taken as was a measure of verbal competence in each study (i.e., Peabody Picture Vocabulary Test in the listening experiment; Gates-MacGinitie comprehension subtest in the reading experiment). The main hypothesis in both studies was that short-term memory would predict performance in the imagery condition, even after age was taken into account. In fact, short-term memory was predictive of memory in the imagery condition in both studies, even after age was controlled; in addition, in both studies, short-term memory was predictive of memory in the imagery condition with age and verbal competence accounted for. Short-term memory was not nearly as potent a predictor in the control condition, with little predictability gained in that condition once age was entered into the regression equation. In fact, in both studies, the second-order (age and verbal competence controlled) partial correlation between short-term memory and memory performance was significantly greater in the imagery than in the control condition. In both studies, this interaction between short-term memory and condition was such that the imagery versus control difference increased with increasing short-term capacity. At least in the case of imagery elaboration of concrete sentences, there was consistent evidence across the two studies that short-term capacity mattered in determining whether or not children benefited from the elaboration instruction.

Summary

About 2 years ago, I was introduced to an audience as, "The person who demonstrated that many different types of imagery and elaboration strategies improve memory." That introduction was embarrassing for two reasons. One is that it is equally applicable to many others. The second was that my talk on that occasion was about how use of strategies depends on knowing when and where to deploy them, possessing the knowledge base required to carry out the strategies, recognizing that the strategies one has learned are useful so one is motivated to use them, and having the short-term capacity required to meet the cognitive demands of strategy execution. That is the same message I deliver in this chapter, although I personalized it a bit more here than I did 2 years ago by featuring studies that I conducted making these points. At that previous meeting, the individual who introduced me also closed the session by remarking that it was wonderful to listen to a talk that explained how everyone can improve their thinking and learning by using strategies. Do not make that same mistake if you decide later to recount the main idea of this chapter to others.

RECENT, APPLIED RESEARCH ON STRATEGY INSTRUCTION: INSTRUCTION CULTIVATING GOOD INFORMATION PROCESSING

For the past 4 years, I explored with my student colleagues how educators, who seem to be implementing strategy instruction successfully, do what they do (Pressley, El-Dinary, Gaskins, et al., 1992). Our initial studies (e.g., Pressley, Gaskins, Cunicelli, et al., 1991; Pressley, Gaskins, Wile, Cunicelli, & Sheridan, 1991) were conducted at Benchmark School, an institution serving elementary school children who experienced previous school failure. The school has an outstanding track record of returning such children to regular institutions, with them then prepared to work at or above grade level. We followed the Benchmark studies with investigations of strategy instructional programs administered by the public schools in one Maryland county (e.g., Pressley, Schuder, SAIL Faculty & Administration, Bergman, & El-Dinary, 1992), with these programs distinguished in that the Chapter 1 students they serve outperformed otherwise comparable Chapter 1 students on standardized measures of reading comprehension. Our most recent studies were conducted in the Carroll County MD Public Schools, examining educator-modified reciprocal teaching (Marks et al., 1993).

What is discussed in this section is the results of our descriptive studies of these intervention programs. We point out, however, that our confidence in the efficacy of these interventions is increasing as we complete controlled, comparative investigations of what is described here as *transactional strategies instruction*. Most notably, the SAIL reading strategies instruction program was submitted to a 1-year quasi-experimental evaluation at the Grade 2 level in 1991–1992, with that approach producing a large effect on both reading comprehension and word attack skills (Brown & Pressley, 1994). As this chapter is being written, the end-of-the-year data for a 1-year quasi-experimental evaluation of educator-modified reciprocal teaching are being collected in Carroll County MD fifth grades. Before these comparative studies were possible, however, it was necessary to analyze in detail exactly what occurred in these strategy instructional programs, with those analyses making clear that everything that is good information processing is stimulated by effective, school-based strategies instruction.

Descriptive Studies

A variety of qualitative methods were employed to understand the three strategies instruction programs we studied. These included ethnographies, case studies, questionnaires constructed in light of theories of strategy instruction, ethnographic interviews, and participant analyses (for diverse examples, see Pressley & El-Dinary, 1993). Regardless of the methods employed, however, conclusions converged, with the description of strategies instruction that follows supported by the outcomes of a number of investigations. Although most of our research has been concerned with comprehension strategies instruction, such work is complementary with memory strategies instruction, because an important goal of such teaching is to increase students' abilities to remember the important ideas they read in text. The assumption is that understandings and memories of text will be richer and more complete if the students learn comprehension strategies and habitually use them as they read.

Effective strategies instruction is definitely long term. In the best of all possible instructional worlds (i.e., in places like Benchmark School; Gaskins & Elliot, 1991), there are continuities, connections, and hierarchically sensible expansions through years of schooling. Strategies instruction done well is not a stand-alone entry in the curriculum, but rather, is integrated with ongoing instruction. Comprehension strategies are taught as part of language arts and are practiced across the school day, in mathematics, science, and social studies.

Effective strategies instruction does not emphasize use of single strategies, but rather, flexible application of a small repertoire of strategies that reflect the processes most frequently evidenced by skilled readers (e.g., Wyatt et al., 1993). For example, students in the SAIL program are taught to predict upcoming content as they read, make associations to the reading content on the basis of prior knowledge, construct images representing the meaning of text, ask questions when uncertain about a text's meaning, seek clarifications until meaning is determined, summarize, and use problem-solving strategies in dealing with unfamiliar words (e.g., decoding, analysis of context clues, rereading, skipping the word and reading on). SAIL students are introduced to these strategies one at a time beginning in Grade 1. They practice applying them to real text from their first lessons, with coordinated use of the strategies increasingly emphasized as new strategies are introduced and children acquire facility in carrying out the individual strategies.

There is discussion of strategies every day. Teachers explain strategies and model coordinated use of various strategies; they encourage students to model strategy application and explain their decision-making with respect to strategies. Teachers emphasize the flexible decision making that is skilled comprehension, with readers actively choosing when and where particular processes are applied, switching strategies as the characteristics of the text and task change. Teachers also emphasize that no two readers ever read the same text the same way.

Much of strategy instruction occurs in reading group, with students thinking aloud as they read and apply strategies to text. An important characteristic of these reading groups is that strategies facilitate interpretive processes, with students coming to understand that people's associations to text are unique, as are their mental images, summaries, and evaluations of text. (I became particularly aware during the last 4 years that the processes cognitively oriented reading researchers and theorists favor are also the ones that literary critical interpretive theorists endorse as important to stimulate in young readers; e.g., Beach & Hynds, 1991; Iser, 1978; Rosenblatt, 1978; Spivey, 1987). The interactions that go on in these reading groups are rich, as students read text, strategically react to it, question one another, and offer interpretations and alternative points of view. These interactions are not like much of classroom discourse, with its predictable teacher elicitation–student response–teacher evaluation structure (Gaskins, Anderson, Pressley, Cunicelli, & Satlow, 1993). Rather, students engage one another as they work together to construct the meaning of text, with animated dialogues and spirited debate typical.

The implicit theory operating in these classrooms, consistent with Vygotsky's (1978) theory, is that participating in reading group interactions involving use of strategies to construct understandings of text will lead eventually to internalization of the strategic processes occurring in the groups. The groups function smoothly because the teacher provides hints, prompts, and supports as needed to keep the interactions moving; the teacher also provides additional explanations of strategies on an as-needed basis. Teachers elaborate the interpretations offered by students, fleshing them out, especially when some explanation of the interpretation might be required so that the speaker's intent is clear to other members of the group. All of this prompting, explanation, and elaboration is intended to stimulate group members to self-cue, self-explain, and self-elaborate in the long term (i.e., internalize the habits of searching for ways to continue making progress in thought and habitually to elaborate what one is thinking by continuing to attempt to relate a thought to prior knowledge once the thought has been initially formulated).

It is one thing to know how to carry out strategic processes and quite another to do so. One of the most important characteristics of the instruction we studied is that effective strategies instructors do all possible to increase the likelihood that students will use the strategies they are learning on their own and be intellectually active. That is, great efforts are made to maximize students' commitment to using strategies as part of high academic effort (Pressley, El-Dinary, Marks, Brown, & Stein, 1992). Transactional strategies instruction is motivating in the following ways:

1. Teachers go to great lengths to assure student success when students are learning strategies. Teacher scaffolding (Wood, Bruner, & Ross, 1986) of strategy practice and application is critical.

2. Transactional strategies instruction teachers reinforce thinking that reflects strategic engagement.

3. Students are encouraged to attribute their performance improvements to use of strategies (Borkowski, Carr, Rellinger, & Pressley, 1990).

4. Students learn and practice strategies in the context of authentic, appropriately challenging, and interesting tasks.

5. An important part of reading instruction is getting students to read on their own (e.g., Stanovich, 1986), for academic competencies improve greatly with practice. Transactional strategies instruction teachers recognize the importance of stimulating autonomous reading and thus, the heavy emphasis during such instruction on motivating students to read extensively and apply the strategies they are learning. Much of the metacognitive information provided to students specifies when and where the strategies being learned can be applied, with teachers urging and prompting students to apply the strategies they are learning throughout the school day: The teachers provide many examples of how strategies can be applied in the content areas, provide opportunities for such application, and prompt students to consider choosing strategies as part of completing academic tasks in the content areas. Of course, the more students experience and practice strategies in context, the more they learn about the flexible applicability of the strategies they are learning—that is, the more complete students' metacognition about strategy utility becomes.

By motivating students to use strategies and devising instruction that increases understanding about when and where strategies can be applied, strategy use increases, with students eventually able to autonomously apply the strategies they have learned (Brown & Pressley, 1994). Use of strategies increases learning of what is read and thus, knowledge of academic content and knowledge of the world expands. As knowledge expands, strategies can be used ever more competently because successful strategy execution depends largely on prior knowledge. For example, predicting upcoming content and relating what is read to prior knowledge depends on having extensive knowledge, as does construction of images representing text meaning. The more effectively these processes are carried out, the greater the new knowledge acquired with each reading, with increasing understanding of the general applicability of the strategies one knows. The easier it is to carry out strategies because of rich prior knowledge, the greater the motivation to do academic things (e.g., do outside reading) and use strategies while doing so. And so it goes, with increasing strategies, metacognition, knowledge, and motivation progressively increasing academic engagement, which in turn, increases strategic competence, metacognitive completeness, knowledge, and motivation to be intellectually active. The student becomes an active agent in his or her own cognitive development.

Why Call It Transactional Strategies Instruction?

The label, *transactional strategies instruction* for the type of strategies instruction we were observing seemed appropriate at first because of Rosenblatt's (e.g., 1978) classical analysis of text interpretations as products of reader–text transactions: Meaning is not in text alone nor in the reader's head alone, but is constructed by readers as they consider text content in light of their previous knowledge and experiences. Such meaning construction was emphasized in the instruction my colleagues and I were watching. The term *transactional* is appropriate for other reasons as well, however.

In the developmental psychology literature (e.g., Bell, 1968), the term is used to refer to child–adult interactions in which the child, in part, determines the behaviors of others in the child's world. There is no doubt that teachers' reactions at Benchmark and in the SAIL and SIA programs are largely determined by the reactions of their students. For example, if a student offers a good summary, the teacher may prompt elaboration of the summary; if the student's summary is off the mark, the teacher may prompt rereading or reconsideration of the text.

The strategies instruction we study is transactional in a third sense, too. Organizational psychologists (e.g., Hutchins, 1991) are concerned with the types of solutions produced during group problem solving compared to individual problem solving. Groups invariably produce ideas that no one individual in the group would have produced. Groups also produce memories that would have never occurred to individuals unless they had participated in the group (e.g., Wegner, 1987). There is a transactive mind when individuals get together to think about things.

Thus, there are three senses in which the classroom strategies instruction my associates and I documented is transactional: (a) meaning is determined by minds applying strategies to text content, (b) how one person reacts is largely determined by what other participants in the group are doing, thinking, and saying, (c) the meaning that emerges is the product of all of the heads in the group.

Concluding Comments

Children's minds are largely constructed in social interactions (e.g., Vygotsky, 1978), including in classroom communities. What we have observed is how teachers get the process started by introducing strategies and providing some information about when and where to use them. The children take it from there, albeit with support as needed from the teacher. By carrying out the strategies during the classroom day, their knowledge of academic content increases as their facility in cognitive processing improves. I cannot overemphasize the many ways in which students are motivated to be cognitively active in such classrooms. The grand hypothesis that emerges from this recent work is that development of good information processing requires many years of participation in an intellectually rich, motivating environment and that short-term efforts to develop generalized competence are doomed to fail. The many failures of transfer following short-term strategies instruction that were reported in the 1970s and 1980s seem perfectly reasonable in light of the ambitious instructional efforts that we study that are largely aimed at producing general use of cognitive strategies. The teachers who are good at strategy instruction know that what is required for generalization of academic strategies is months to years of diverse application of strategies in an educational environment filled with useful information for the student to acquire and rigged so as to sustain academic motivation. I know they know this because they have told me, I have watched it in action, and my colleagues and I are now generating support for this theory of instruction in well-controlled evaluations (see Brown & Pressley, 1994).

GOOD INFORMATION PROCESSING AS A MEANS FOR IMPROVING INFORMATION PROCESSING

The good information processor is always becoming a better information processor. Many of the readers of this chapter are professors in the social and behavioral sciences and education. Some recently completed research by me and my colleagues makes clear how this readership engages in good information processing that ever expands their cognitive capabilities and hence, permits better information processing in the future.

Wyatt et al. (1993) asked 15 social sciences professors to think aloud as they read articles in their fields on topics of great professional interest to them. What was observed in every one of these readers was flexible application of strategies that permitted abstraction of the most important information from articles and the information most critical to the reader in question. The strategies included the following:

- Anticipating or predicting information that would be presented in the text; testing of predictions as reading proceeds.
- Looking for information relevant to reading goals (i.e., informing own research, writing, teaching, etc.).
- Jumping forward in text to find particular information and then returning to continue reading.
- Jumping backward in text to find particular information and then returning to continue reading.
- Rapidly moving back and forth between text and tables or figures, especially to guide further reading of the article.
- Backtracking (e.g., rereading a sentence for clarification).
- Attending especially closely to figures and/or tables.
- Varying reading style according to the relevance of text to reading goals.
- Paraphrasing or explaining to oneself what was in the text and/or constructing examples.
- Constructing conclusions or summary interpretations beyond information provided in the article (e.g., summary of results, tables, discussion, conclusions).

These readers also monitored their reading in multiple ways, with this monitoring affecting their online decision making about processing of text. Monitoring included the following:

- Explicitly noting how difficult the text was to read (e.g., recognizing that something in the text is puzzling).
- Noting that something in text is already known or not known.
- Evaluating the relevance of text to reading goals (i.e., Is what I am reading providing the specific information I was seeking from the article? Is this article relevant to my research, writing, teaching, etc.?)

An important consequence of monitoring, supported by statistical analyses of the self-reports, was evaluation of text, with greater monitoring associated with more pronounced evaluations, such as the following:

- Reacting to information in text in light of prior knowledge, including personal prior knowledge, such as one's own theories, own writing, and/or personal knowledge of the author of the text.

- Evaluating the quality of the literature reviewed, the theoretical perspectives favored, methods, analyses, results including the novelty of the findings, conclusions, discussion, writing and/or editing style, and the biases of the author.
- Expressing interest or anger, weariness, and boredom.

My confidence in this description of skilled reading in terms of strategies, monitoring, and evaluations is high because of a subsequent analysis Afflerbach and I (Pressley & Afflerbach, 1995) have carried out on the 40 or so studies involving think-alouds during skilled reading. Strategies, monitoring, and evaluations recur in these reports. That does not mean, however, that evidence of other aspects of good information processing was absent from Wyatt et al. (1993) or from the other reports.

Implicit in the fine-grained regulation of strategies that was observed by Wyatt et al. (1993), was clear understanding of the effects of active reading and analyses of text as well as knowledge of the means for accomplishing such analyses (i.e., there was little doubt that our readers were high in the metacognitive knowledge about when and where to use the strategies they knew). Prior knowledge was evident throughout the self-reports as well, with prior knowledge reflected in predictions, summaries, and evaluative reactions. Most critically, however, the motivations of readers in Wyatt et al. in particular were transparent during reading and in the interviews before and after the think-aloud exercises. These readers actively sought out opportunities to process articles in their fields and did so routinely. As they do so, their knowledge base expands, which enables much of the current sophistication in their reactions to text.

Given the many years of professional practice required to become an expert in a profession, the only motivation that will always be present is motivation the learner carries around with him or her. A great deal of attention needs to be given to the problem of developing great information processors. Much of that analyses undoubtedly is going to focus on how to develop the motivation to sustain good information processing so that it is gradually transformed with practice into great information processing that is enabled by a vast knowledge base built up through years of active, effective thinking.

SO WHY DO THEY STILL SAY I STUDY STRATEGIES AND THAT I AM INTERESTED IN STRATEGIES INSTRUCTION?

When think-alouds are collected, strategies are often the most salient processes. When I visit a contemporary classroom that is into process instruction, it is the strategies that are named on the wall cards, and the strategies are the hook used by the teacher to explain to students and parents what is being taught. To be certain, whenever think-alouds of skilled processors are analyzed and the instruction of good strategies teachers is studied, it is transparent that information about the appropriate use of strategies plays a role, that nonstrategic knowledge simultaneously enables strategies use and is expanded by it, and that motivation is key. Even so, the strategic processes are at the heart of the cognitive plans that are motivated, enabled by knowledge, and regulated by metacognition. Thus, I expect that no matter how often I explain that my bag is good information processing, people will claim that I am into strategies. Strategies are visible players in cognition and seem to steal the limelight, even though the drama that is effective thinking can only proceed because metacognition, other knowledge, and motivation are in the cast. As is true in all of life, however, some players shine brighter than others—or at least they attract the spotlight more often and for longer—with the result being that their lines and songs are the ones noticed, quoted, and whistled.

REFERENCES

Aks, D. J., & Coren, S. (1990). Is susceptibility to distraction related to mental ability? *Journal of Educational Psychology, 82,* 388–390.

Alexander, P. A., & Judy, J. E. (1988). The interaction of domain-specific and strategic knowledge in academic performance. *Review of Educational Research, 58,* 375–404.

Anderson, J. R., & Reder, L. M. (1979). An elaborative processing explanation of depth of processing. In L. W. Cermak & F. I. M. Craik (Eds.), *Levels of processing in human memory* (pp. 385–404). Hillsdale, NJ: Lawrence Erlbaum Associates.

Baddeley, A. (1986). *Working memory.* Oxford, England: Oxford University Press.

Bandura, A. (1986). *Social foundations of thought and action: A social cognitive theory.* Englewood Cliffs, NJ: Prentice-Hall.

Baron, J. (1985). *Rationality and intelligence.* Cambridge, England: Cambridge University Press.

Baron, J. (1988). *Thinking and deciding.* New York: Cambridge University Press.

Baron, J. (1990). Reflectiveness and rational thinking: Response to Duemler and Mayer (1988). *Journal of Educational Psychology, 82,* 391–392.

Beach, R., & Hynds, S. (1991). Research on response to literature. In R. Barr, M. L. Kamil, P. Mosenthal, & P. D. Pearson (Eds.), *Handbook of reading research* (Vol. 2, pp. 453–489). White Plains, NY: Longman.

Bell, R. Q. (1968). A reinterpretation of the direction of effects in studies of socialization. *Psychological Review, 75,* 81–95.

Bereiter, C. (1990). Aspects of an educational learning theory. *Review of Educational Research, 60,* 603–624.

Borkowski, J. G. (1985). Signs of intelligence: Strategy, generalization, and metacognition. In S. R. Yussen (Ed.), *The growth of reflection in children* (pp. 105–144). Orlando, FL: Academic Press.

Borkowski, J. G., Carr, M., Rellinger, E. A., & Pressley, M. (1990). Self-regulated strategy use: Interdependence of metacognition, attributions, and self-esteem. In B. F. Jones (Ed.), *Dimensions of thinking: Review of research* (pp. 53–92). Hillsdale, NJ: Lawrence Erlbaum Associates.

Brown, A. L., Bransford, J. D., Ferrara, R. A., & Campione, J. C. (1983). Learning, remembering, and understanding. In J. H. Flavell & E. M. Markman (Eds.), *Handbook of child psychology, Vol. III: Cognitive development* (pp. 77–166). New York: Wiley.

Brown, R., & Pressley, M. (1994). Self-regulated reading and getting meaning from text: The transactional strategies instruction model and its ongoing validation. In D. Schunk & B. Zimmerman (Eds.), *Self-regulation of learning and performance: Issues and educational applications* (pp. 155–179). Hillsdale, NJ: Lawrence Erlbaum Associates.

Cariglia-Bull, T., & Pressley, M. (1990). Short-term memory differences between children predict imagery effects when sentences are read. *Journal of Experimental Child Psychology, 49*, 384–398.

Case, R. (1985). *Intellectual development: Birth to adulthood.* Orlando, FL: Academic Press.

Dempster, F. N. (1985). Short-term memory development in childhood and adolescence. In C. J. Brainerd & M. Pressley (Eds.), *Basic processes in memory development: Progress in cognitive development research* (pp. 209–248). New York: Springer-Verlag.

Dixon, F. W. (1972). *The Hardy Boys detective handbook.* New York: Grosset & Dunlop.

Duemler, D., & Mayer, R. E. (1988). Hidden costs of reflectiveness: Aspects of successful scientific reasoning. *Journal of Educational Psychology, 80*, 419–423.

Entwisle, N. (1988). Motivational factors in students' approaches to learning. In R. R. Schmeck (Ed.), *Learning styles and learning strategies* (pp. 21–52). New York: Plenum.

Ford, D. H. (1987). *Humans as self-constructing living systems: A developmental perspective on behavior and personality.* Hillsdale, NJ: Lawrence Erlbaum Associates.

Gaskins, I. W., Anderson, R. C., Pressley, M., Cunicelli, E. A., & Satlow, E. (1993). Six teachers' dialogue during cognitive process instruction. *Elementary School Journal, 93*, 277–304.

Gaskins, I. W., Elliot, T. T. (1991). *Implementing cognitive strategy instruction across the school: The Benchmark manual for teachers.* Cambridge, MA: Brookline Books.

Ghatala, E. S. (1986). Strategy-monitoring training enables young learners to select effective strategies. *Educational Psychologist, 21*, 43–54.

Ghatala, E. S., Levin, J. R., Pressley, M., & Goodwin, D. (1986). A componential analysis of the effects of derived and supplied strategy-utility information on children's strategy selections. *Journal of Experimental Child Psychology, 41*, 76–92.

Ghatala, E. S., Levin, J. R., Pressley, M., & Lodico, M. G. (1985). Training cognitive strategy monitoring in children. *American Educational Research Journal, 22*, 199–216.

Hutchins, E. (1991). The social organization of distributed cognition. In L. Resnick, J. M. Levine, & S. D. Teasley (Eds.), *Perspectives on socially shared cognition* (pp. 283–307). Washington, DC: American Psychological Association.

Iser, W. (1978). *The art of reading: A theory of aesthetic response.* Baltimore: Johns Hopkins University Press.

Jacoby, L. L. (1978). On interpreting the effects of repetition: Solving a problem versus remembering a solution. *Journal of Verbal Learning and Verbal Behavior, 17*, 649–667.

Kanfer, R. (1990). Motivation and individual differences in learning: An integration of developmental, differential, and cognitive perspectives. *Learning and Individual Differences, 2*, 221–240.

Kee, D. W. (1995). Developmental differences in associative memory: Strategy use, mental effort, and knowledge-access interactions. In H. W. Reese (Ed.), *Advances in child development and behavior* (Vol. 25). New York: Academic Press.

Kee, D. W., & Davies, L. (1990). Mental effort and elaboration: Effects of accessibility and instruction. *Journal of Experimental Child Psychology, 49*, 264–274.

Kuhl, J. (1985). Volitional mediators of cognition–behavior consistency: Self-regulatory processes and action versus state orientation. In J. Kuhl & J. Beckmann (Eds.), *Action control: From cognition to behavior* (pp. 101–128). Berlin: Springer-Verlag.

Lerner, R. M., & Busch-Rossnagel, N. (Eds.). (1981). *Individuals as producers of their own development: A life-span perspective.* New York: Academic Press.

Marks, M., Pressley, M., Coley, J. D., Craig, S., Gardner, R., Rose, W., & DePinto, T. (1993). Teachers' adaptations of reciprocal teaching: Progress toward a classroom-compatible version of reciprocal teaching. *Elementary School Journal, 94*, 267–283.

Martin, V. L., & Pressley, M. (1991). Elaborative-interrogation effects depend on the nature of the question. *Journal of Educational Psychology, 83*, 113–119.

McDaniel, M. A., Friedman, A., & Bourne, L. (1978). Remembering the levels of information in words. *Memory & Cognition, 6,* 156–164.

Morris, C. D., Bransford, J. D., & Franks, J. J. (1977). Levels of processing versus transfer appropriate processing. *Journal of Verbal Learning and Verbal Behavior, 16,* 519–533.

Nicholls, J. G. (1989). *The competitive ethos and democratic education.* Cambridge, MA: Harvard University Press.

Nolen, S. B. (1988). Reasons for studying: Motivational orientations and study strategies. *Cognition and Instruction, 5,* 269–287.

O'Sullivan, J. T., & Pressley, M. (1984). Completeness of instruction and strategy transfer. *Journal of Experimental Child Psychology, 38,* 275–288.

Paris, S. G., Lipson, M. Y., & Wixson, K. K. (1983). Becoming a strategic reader. *Contemporary Educational Psychology, 8,* 293–316.

Pressley, M. (1977). Imagery and children's learning: Putting the picture in developmental perspective. *Review of Educational Research, 47,* 586–622.

Pressley, M., & Afflerbach, P. (1995). *Verbal protocols of reading: The nature of constructively responsive reading.* Hillsdale, NJ: Lawrence Erlbaum Associates.

Pressley, M., Borkowski, J. G., & O'Sullivan, J. T. (1984). Memory strategy instruction is made of this: Metamemory and durable strategy use. *Educational Psychologist, 19,* 94–107.

Pressley, M., Borkowski, J. G., & O'Sullivan, J. T. (1985). Children's metamemory and the teaching of memory strategies. In D. L. Forrest-Pressley, G. E. MacKinnon, & T. G. Waller (Eds.), *Metacognition, cognition, and human performance* (pp. 111–153). New York: Academic Press.

Pressley, M., Borkowski, J. G., & Schneider, W. (1987). Cognitive strategies: Good strategy users coordinate metacognition and knowledge. In R. Vasta & G. Whitehurst (Eds.), *Annals of child development* (Vol. 5, pp. 89–129). Greenwich, CT: JAI Press.

Pressley, M., Borkowski, J. G., & Schneider, W. (1989). Good information processing: What it is and what education can do to promote it. *International Journal of Educational Research, 13,* 857–867.

Pressley, M., Cariglia-Bull, T., Deane, S., & Schneider, W. (1987). Short-term memory, verbal competence, and age as predictors of imagery instructional effectiveness. *Journal of Experimental Child Psychology, 43,* 194–211.

Pressley, M., & Dennis-Rounds, J. (1980). Transfer of a mnemonic keyword strategy at two age levels. *Journal of Educational Psychology, 72,* 575–582.

Pressley, M., & El-Dinary, P. B. (Eds.). (1993). Special issue on strategies instruction. *Elementary School Journal, 94*(2).

Pressley, M., El-Dinary, P. B., Gaskins, I., Schuder, T., & Bergman, J. L., Almasi, J., & Brown, R. (1992). Beyond direct explanation: Transactional instruction of reading comprehension strategies. *Elementary School Journal, 92,* 513–556.

Pressley, M., El-Dinary, P. B., Marks, M. B., Brown, R., & Stein, S. (1992). Good strategy instruction is motivating and interesting. In K. A. Renninger, S. Hidi, & A. Krapp (Eds.), *The role of interest in learning and development* (pp. 333–358). Hillsdale, NJ: Lawrence Erlbaum Associates.

Pressley, M., Gaskins, I. W., Cunicelli, E. A., Burdick, N. J., Schaub-Matt, M., Lee, D. S., & Powell, N. (1991). Strategy instruction at Benchmark School: A faculty interview study. *Learning Disability Quarterly, 14,* 19–48.

Pressley, M., Gaskins, I. W., Wile, D., Cunicelli, B., & Sheridan, J. (1991). Teaching literacy strategies across the curriculum: A case study at Benchmark School. In J. Zutell & S. McCormick (Eds.), *Learner factors/teacher factors: Issues in literacy research and instruction: Fortieth yearbook of the National Reading Conference* (pp. 219–228). Chicago: National Reading Conference.

Pressley, M., & Ghatala, E. S. (1990). Self-regulated learning: Monitoring learning from text. *Educational Psychologist, 25,* 19–34.

Pressley, M., & Levin, J. R. (1977). Task parameters affecting the efficacy of a visual imagery learning strategy in younger and older children. *Journal of Experimental Child Psychology, 24,* 53–59.

Pressley, M., & Levin, J. R. (1978). Developmental constraints associated with children's use of the keyword method for foreign language vocabulary learning. *Journal of Experimental Child Psychology*, 26, 359–372.

Pressley, M., Levin, J. R., & Delaney, H. D. (1982). The mnemonic keyword method. *Review of Educational Research*, 56, 61–92.

Pressley, M., Levin, J. R., & Ghatala, E. S. (1984). Memory strategy monitoring in adults and children. *Journal of Verbal Learning and Verbal Behavior*, 23, 270–288.

Pressley, M., Levin, J. R., & Ghatala, E. S. (1988). Strategy-comparison opportunities promote long-term strategy use. *Contemporary Educational Psychology*, 13, 157–168.

Pressley, M., with McCormick, C. B. (1995). *Advanced educational psychology.* New York: HarperCollins.

Pressley, M., Schuder, T., Bergman, J. L., & El-Dinary, P. B. (1992). A researcher-educator collaborative interview study of transactional comprehension strategies instruction. *Journal of Educational Psychology*, 84, 231–246.

Pressley, M., Snyder, B. L., & Cariglia-Bull, T. (1987). How can good strategy use be taught to children? Evaluation of six approaches. In S. M. Cormier & J. D. Hagman (Eds.), *Transfer of learning: Contemporary research and applications* (pp. 81–120). San Diego, CA: Academic Press.

Pressley, M., Symons, S., McDaniel, M. A., Snyder, B. L., & Turnure, J. E. (1988). Elaborative interrogation facilitates acquisition of confusing facts. *Journal of Educational Psychology*, 80, 268–278.

Pressley, M., Wood, E., & Woloshyn, V. (1990). Elaborative interrogation and facilitation of fact learning: Why having a knowledge base is one thing and using it is quite another. In W. Schneider & F. E. Weinert (Eds.), *Interactions among aptitudes, strategies, and knowledge in cognitive performance* (pp. 200–221). New York: Springer-Verlag.

Ramsden, P. (1988). Context and strategy: Situational influences on learning. In R. R. Schmeck (Ed.), *Learning strategies and learning styles* (pp. 159–184). New York: Plenum Press.

Rohwer, W. D., Jr., Rabinowitz, M., & Dronkers, N. F. (1982). Event knowledge, elaborative propensity, and the development of learning proficiency. *Journal of Experimental Child Psychology*, 33, 492–503.

Rosenblatt, L. M. (1978). *The reader, the text, poem: The transactional theory of the literary work.* Carbondale, IL: Southern Illinois University Press.

Scarr, S. (1992). Developmental theories for the 1990s: Development and individual differences. *Child Development*, 63, 1–19.

Scarr, S., & McCartney, K. (1983). How people make their own environments: A theory of genotype–environment effects. *Child Development*, 54, 424–35.

Schmeck, R. R., & Geisler-Brenstein, E. (1989). Individual differences that affect the way students approach learning. *Learning and Individual Differences*, 1, 85–124.

Schneider, W., & Pressley, M. (1989). *Memory development between 2 and 20.* New York: Springer-Verlag.

Slamecka, N. J., & Graf, P. (1978). The generation effect: Delineation of a phenomenon. *Journal of Experimental Psychology: Human Learning and Memory*, 4, 592–604.

Spivey, N. N. (1987). Construing constructivism: Reading response in the United States. *Poetics*, 16, 169–192.

Stanovich, K. (1986). Matthew effects in reading: Some consequences of individual differences in the acquisition of literacy. *Reading Research Quarterly*, 21, 360–407.

Tyler, S. W., Hertel, P. T., McCallum, M. C., & Ellis, H. C. (1979). Cognitive effort and memory. *Journal of Experimental Psychology: Human Learning and Memory*, 5, 607–617.

Vygotsky, L. S. (1978). *Mind in society: The development of higher psychological processes.* Cambridge, MA: Harvard University Press.

Waters, H. S. (1982). Memory development in adolescence: Relationships between metamemory, strategy use, and performance. *Journal of Experimental Child Psychology*, 33, 183–195.

Wegner, D. M. (1987). Transactive memory: A contemporary analysis of the group mind. In B. Mullen & G. Goethals (Eds.), *Theories of group behavior* (pp. 185–208). New York: Springer-Verlag.

Woloshyn, V. E., Pressley, M., & Schneider, W. (1992). Elaborative-interrogation and prior-knowledge effects on learning of facts. *Journal of Educational Psychology, 84,* 115–124.

Woloshyn, V. E., Wood, E., & Willoughby, T. (1994). Considering prior knowledge when using elaborative interrogation. *Applied Cognitive Psychology, 8,* 25–36.

Wood, S. S., Bruner, J. S., & Ross, G. (1976). The role of tutoring in problem solving. *Journal of Child Psychology and Psychiatry, 17,* 89–100.

Wyatt, D., Pressley, M., El-Dinary, P. B., Stein, S., Evans, P., & Brown, R. (1993). Comprehension strategies, worth and credibility monitoring, and evaluations: Cold and hot cognition when experts read professional articles that are important to them. *Learning and Individual Differences, 5,* 49–72.

Zimmerman, B. J. (1989a). A social cognitive view of self-regulated academic learning. *Journal of Educational Psychology, 81,* 329–339.

Zimmerman, B. J. (1989b). Models of self-regulated learning and academic achievement. In B. J. Zimmerman & D. H. Schunk (Eds.), *Self-regulated learning and academic achievement* (pp. 1–25). New York: Springer-Verlag.

Zimmerman, B. J. (1990a). Self-regulated learning and academic achievement: An overview. *Educational Psychologist, 25,* 3–18.

Zimmerman, B. J. (1990b). Self-regulating academic learning and achievement: The emergence of a social–cognitive perspective. *Educational Psychology Review, 2,* 173–201.

Chapter 20

Children's Thinking:
How Does Change Occur?

Robert S. Siegler
Carnegie Mellon University

Cognitive–developmental research has yielded a wealth of information about how children think at different ages. It has been much less revealing, however, about the processes that produce the changes in thinking. This pattern can be vividly seen in research on children's strategy use. We know a great deal about which strategies children use at different ages—strategies that are evident in their production of language, their activities for enhancing memory, the concepts they form, and the problem-solving techniques they use. In contrast, we know much less about what produces the changes in strategies. Rarely do we know how children come to use initial strategies, how they generalize existing strategies to new contexts, or how they add new strategies to the ones they already know. Thus, we know a lot about what children typically do at different ages, but little about how they get from here to there.

This gap cannot be attributed to investigators not realizing the importance of the issue; a number of widely cited reviews and critiques have emphasized the importance of increasing our understanding of the change process (Flavell, 1984; Miller, 1989; Sternberg, 1984). Instead, the discrepancy seems to be a particular realization of two general types of problems in the field: inadequate conceptualizations and inadequate methods. The purpose of this chapter is to examine how prevailing conceptualizations and methods have limited our understanding of change, and to describe alternative ways of thinking about and studying change that may contribute to a better understanding.

CONCEPTUALIZATIONS OF CHANGE

Cognitive developmentalists often phrase their models in terms that suggest that children of a given age think about a given task in a single way. N-year-olds are said to have a particular mental structure, processing limit, theory, strategy, or rule that gives rise to a single type of behavior. Change involves a substitution of one mental entity (and accompanying behavior) for another.

The basic conceptualization that seems to underlie these models is aptly captured in the title of Case's (1992) book, *The Mind's Staircase*. The visual metaphor that this title evokes is, I believe, central to most cognitive–developmental treatments of change: Children are depicted as thinking in a given way for an extended period of time (a tread on the staircase); then their thinking undergoes a sudden, vertical shift (a riser on the staircase); then they think in a different, "higher" way for another extended period of time (the next tread); and so on.

This view of change is most closely identified with Piagetian and neo-Piagetian approaches, such as those of Piaget and Case. Thus, as shown in Fig. 20.1, we see development depicted within Piaget's theory as involving sensorimotor activities from birth to 18 months; preoperational thinking from 18 months to 7 years; concrete operational thinking from 7 to 12 years; and formal operational thinking from 12 years onward. Within Case's theory, we see thinking depicted as advancing from the sensorimotor level between birth and 18 months, to the relational level from 18 months to 5 years, to the dimensional level between 5 and 11 years, to the formal level at age 11 and beyond. In both models, much more is said about what reasoning is like within a given level than about how the transition between levels is achieved.

Although this depiction of cognitive development is most associated with the Piagetian and neo-Piagetian traditions, it is far from unique to them. Indeed, it is pervasive among major approaches in the field. For example, researchers who try to identify children's implicit theories depict development in much the same way. Two-year-olds are said to have a desire theory of mind, whereas 3-year-olds are said to have a belief–desire theory (Wellman, 1990). Three-year-olds are said to have nonrepresentational theories of mind, whereas 5-year-olds are said to have representational theories (Perner, 1991). Four-year-olds are said to have a psychological theory of biology, whereas 10-year-olds are said to have a truly biological theory (Carey, 1985).

The depictions of information-processing researchers, though different in many ways from any of these approaches, are similar in portraying development as a series of 1:1 equations between ages and ways of thinking. For example, Ashcraft (1987) depicted acquisition of expertise on simple addition problems (e. g., 3 + 7) as involving the following developmental sequence: 4- and 5-year-olds relying on counting from one; 5- to 8-year-olds relying on counting from the larger of the two addends; older children and adults relying on retrieving the answer from memory. My own depiction of development of number conservation (Siegler, 1981) described 3- and 4-year-olds as basing judgments on the relative lengths of the two rows following the transformation of one of them, 4- and 5-year-olds as basing judgments on the results of counting the objects in the two rows, and 6-year-olds and older children as basing judgments on the type of transformation that was performed.

In short, the emphasis in the dominant approaches to cognitive development has been on identifying sequences of 1:1 correspondences between an age and a way of thinking. It is not difficult to understand why such depictions have been so popular. The depictions are interesting, memorable, and often dramatic; they make for straightforward summaries in textbooks and interesting examples in lectures; they abstract some notable trends from the mass of complexity in children's thinking.

Such depictions also have two serious shortcomings, though. The more obvious is that they are inaccurate; a large literature demonstrates that children's thinking is far more variable than the models suggest. A sampling of the domains in which such variability has been demonstrated is shown in Table 20.1. In all cases, children of a given age use a variety of strategies, not just one. This is true not only among different children but within individual children. A single child presented the identical problem on 2 successive days often will use different strategies on the 2 days; this has been demonstrated for both preschoolers' addition and second and third graders' time telling (McGilly & Siegler, 1990; Siegler & Shrager, 1984). Even within a single trial, children's verbal statements and their gestures often reflect different types of reasoning (Goldin-Meadow, Alibali, & Church, 1993). This variability is not just present in special, short-lived, transitional periods, but rather tends to be present throughout the long period from the time when children acquire the most basic understanding to the time when their understanding reaches advanced form (and often, even then, as is seen in the diverse strategies most adults know for solving mental arithmetic problems or for playing any reasonably complex game, such as bridge or chess).

The monolithic depictions of children's thinking also entail a second problem, less obvious but at least as serious: They inhibit progress in understanding change. The effect is wholly unintended, but is powerful nonetheless.

The problem is that in our efforts to conceptualize differences among age groups in as simple, dramatic, and memorable terms as possible, we may unwittingly have made understanding change more difficult than it needs to be. In particular, portraying children's thinking and knowledge as conforming to one mold at one age and a different mold at a different age creates a need to explain the wide gulfs between the succesive hypothesized understandings—even though such gulfs may not exist. The typical depictions make change a rare, almost exotic event that demands an exceptional explanation. If children of a given age have for several years had a particular understanding, why would they suddenly form a different understanding, and why would they regularly form it at a particular age? The problem is exacerbated by many of the competencies of interest being ones in which generally relevant experience is available at all ages and specifically relevant

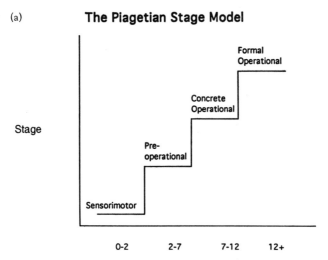

(a) **The Piagetian Stage Model**

Stage

Formal
Operational

Concrete
Operational

Pre-
operational

Sensorimotor

| 0-2 | 2-7 | 7-12 | 12+ |

Age

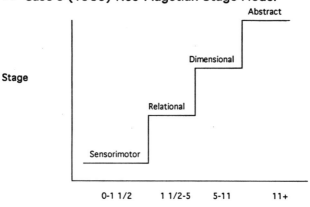

(b) **Case's (1985) Neo-Piagetian Stage Model**

Stage

Abstract

Dimensional

Relational

Sensorimotor

| 0-1 1/2 | 1 1/2-5 | 5-11 | 11+ |

Age

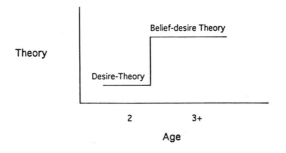

(c) **Wellman's (1990) Theory-Based Model**

Theory

Belief-desire Theory

Desire-Theory

| 2 | 3+ |

Age

FIG. 20.1.

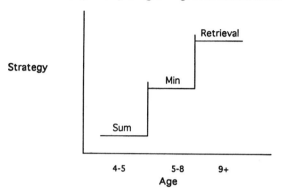

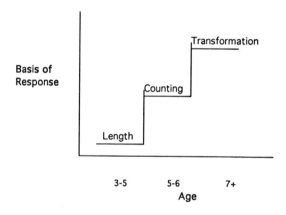

FIG. 20.1. Staircase models of development, including: (a) the Piagetian stage model, (b) Case's (1985) Neo-Piagetian stage model, (c) Wellman's (1990) theory-based model, (d) Ashcraft's (1987) model of single-digit addition, and (e) Siegler's (1981) model of number conservation.

experience at none. Children see objects moved around at all ages, and are not ordinarily told at any age that the number of objects remains the same after moving as before. Why, then, would they consistently have one concept of number conservation at age 5 and a different one at age 6?

Suppose we adopt a different set of orienting assumptions that, I believe, are both more consistent with the data and more helpful in understanding change. Within this set of orienting assumptions, the typical situation is one where individual children know and use a variety of ways of thinking, rather than just one, and where cognition involves constant competition among alternative ways

TABLE 20.1
Evidence for Variability in Individual Children's Thinking

Domain	Study
Arithmetic	Geary & Burlingham-Dubree (1989)
	Siegler & Shrager (1984)
Past-tense verbs	Kuczaj (1977)
	Marcus, Pinker, Ullman, Hollander, Rosen, & Xu (1992)
Serial recall	McGilly & Siegler (1989)
Conservation	Acredolo & O'Connor (1991)
	Church & Goldin-Meadow (1986)
Moral reasoning	Turiel (1977)
	Wainryb (1993)
Scientific reasoning	Kuhn, Amsel, & O'Loughlin (1988)
	Schauble (1990)
Biological theories	Keil (1989)
Mathematical equivalence	Alibali & Goldin-Meadow (1993)
	Graham & Perry (1993)
Map drawing	Feldman (1980)
Block stacking	Wilkinson (1982)
Time telling	Siegler & McGilly (1989)
Physics problems	Maloney & Siegler (1993)
Reading strategies	Goldman & Saul (1990)
Spelling strategies	Siegler (1986)
Motor development	Goldfield (1993)
	Adolph (1993)
Phonology	Labov (1969)
	Ferguson (1986)

of thinking, rather than sole reliance on a single way of thinking at a given age. Rather than stepping up from Strategy 1 to Strategy 2 to Strategy 3, children would be expected to use several different strategies at any one time, with the frequency of use of each strategy ebbing and flowing with increasing age and expertise. To capture this view in a visual metaphor, think of a series of overlapping waves, like that shown in Fig. 20.2, with each wave corresponding to a different rule, strategy, theory, or way of thinking. Contrasting the overlapping wave metaphor with the stair-step progression shown in Fig. 20.1 conveys some of the differences between the two approaches.

The kind of data that have given rise to this view are illustrated in Fig. 20.3. The data are from Feldman's (1980) study of one child's map drawing on five occasions spread over a 3-year period. During this time, frequency of Level II and III map drawings decreased; that of Level IV drawings increased and then decreased; that of Level V and to some extent Level VI drawings increased. At each time of measurement, the child produced four different levels of drawings, but the relative frequencies of the levels changed dramatically.

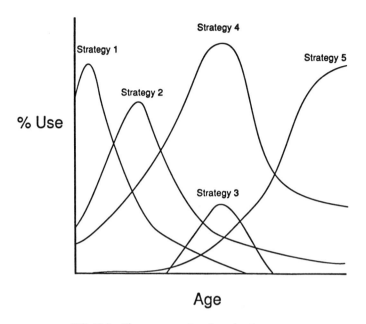

FIG. 20.2. Change as a series of overlapping waves.

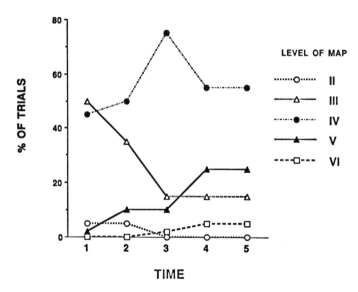

FIG. 20.3. Variability in stages of one child's map drawing over a 3-year period (data from Feldman, 1980).

This perspective on cognitive development, involving multiple strategies whose frequency changes in a wave-like fashion, moves to center stage a number of questions that have been backstage or offstage altogether in traditional approaches: How do children choose among the alternative strategies that they know and use at any one age? How do these choices change with age and experience? How are new strategies discovered, and once discovered, integrated into the existing repertoire of strategies? What constrains discovery of new strategies so that children can discover useful new approaches, rather than having to proceed through the vast number of flawed alternatives that could be attempted? Finally, how can these developmental changes in distributions of ways of thinking best be studied? In the next section, I describe a method for studying cognitive developmental change that seems particularly useful for addressing these kinds of questions.

METHODS FOR STUDYING CHANGE

Understanding of change has been handicapped not only by inadequate conceptualizations but also by the difficulty of formulating revealing methods for studying it. As Applebaum and McCall (1983) commented, "The study of development is the study of change . . . But developmental psychology has often not been truly developmental and therefore it has not seriously faced the methodological issues unique to its definitional purpose" (p. 415).

A key characteristic for any methodology aimed at studying change is that it examine changes while they are occurring. Most methods used to study cognitive development do not meet this requirement. They are based on the strategy of trying to infer how a change occurred by comparing behavior before and after the change. Unfortunately, this indirect strategy leaves open a large number of possible pathways to change, especially because changes in children's thinking often do not proceed by the most direct route we can imagine. For example, a microgenetic study described by Karmiloff-Smith (1984) indicated that when children drew maps for ambulances to follow, they often regressed from drawing efficient and informative maps to drawing ones with considerable redundancy, before returning to the earlier efficient and informative representations. Without the microgenetic methodology, it is unlikely that this brief-lived regression would have been detected. Thus, learning about the endpoints of change, though useful, is no substitute for direct observations of changes while they are occurring. This criticism has often been leveled at cross-sectional methods, but it is equally true of most longitudinal approaches. The time between observations is simply too great to obtain a detailed picture of how the changes occurred.

Microgenetic methods are a promising way of meeting the challenges posed by studying change. As noted in a recent review of studies using microgenetic methods (Siegler & Crowley, 1991), the approach is defined by three key characteristics:

1. Observations span as large a portion as possible of the period from the beginning of the change to the time at which it reaches a relatively stable state.
2. The density of observations is high relative to the rate of change of the phenomenon.
3. Observations are subjected to intensive trial-by-trial analysis, with the goal of inferring the processes that gave rise to the change.

The second characteristic is especially important. Densely sampling changes as they are occurring allows the kind of temporal resolution needed to inform our understanding of change processes.[1] It provides the data needed to discriminate among alternative hypotheses about what actually goes on during periods of rapid change, rather than limiting understanding to what can be inferred from performance before and after. The difference is analogous to that between a movie that covers an entire horserace versus snapshots of the race near the beginning, in the middle, and at the end. What we would like is the movie; what we get are the widely spaced snapshots. The dense sampling of changing competence made possible by microgenetic designs moves us in the direction of the movie.

Two variants of the microgenetic approach have been used. One is to choose a task from the everyday environment, hypothesize the types of experiences that typically lead to changes in performance on it, and provide a higher concentration of such experiences than would otherwise occur (e.g., Belmont & Butterfield, 1977; Butterfield, Siladi, & Belmont, 1980). The other is to present a novel task and to observe children's changing understanding as they interact with it (e. g., Karmiloff-Smith, 1992). Both variants can yield data about the fine-structure of change that could not be obtained via other methods. For example, studies using each approach have shown that previously hypothesized transition

---

[1]Saying that microgenetic methods can help us understand how development occurs raises the issue of whether the claim is that they can help us by providing more detailed descriptions of development, or by informing our understanding of change mechanisms. My belief is that they help us in both senses, albeit in one more directly than in the other. Their most direct benefit is in providing more detailed descriptions of change than do other methods. A less direct but equally important benefit, however, comes through such detailed data constraining theorizing about mechanisms. These constraints come about both through the negative route of the detailed data ruling out some classes of mechanisms and through the positive route of the detailed data indicating the precise effects that the change mechanisms must generate. For example, microgenetic studies have indicated that failing to solve problems is neither necessary nor sufficient for generation of new strategies. Children often generate new strategies when they have previously solved the same problem with existing approaches and quite often do not generate new approaches when they have failed previously with existing approaches (Siegler & Crowley, 1991). This rules out the rather substantial class of proposed mechanisms that generate new strategies if and only if the system encounters failure—impasse-driven learning mechanisms (e. g., VanLehn, 1988). It also indicates that change mechanisms must sometimes generate new approaches in contexts of success and that they must not always generate new approaches every time existing approaches fail. These types of constraints considerably narrow the class of plausible strategy-generation mechanisms.

strategies are not used, and have documented the existence of short-lived transition strategies that no one had hypothesized (Karmiloff-Smith, 1984; Siegler & Jenkins, 1989). Both also can be used to study the generation of initial strategies, either in response to novel tasks or in response to novel instruction, as well as to study generation of subsequent approaches.

In the next two sections, the potential of microgenetic methods to illuminate how change occurs is illustrated by a pair of recent studies, one on acquisition of a new addition strategy, the other on acquisition of understanding of number conservation.

A Microgenetic Study of Acquisition of the Min Strategy

One way in which microgenetic studies can advance understanding is by providing detailed data on how new approaches are discovered. In one study aimed at this goal, Siegler and Jenkins (1989) studied 4- and 5-year-olds' discovery of the min strategy for adding numbers. First, a pretest was given to identify children who could add by counting from 1 but who did not yet know the min strategy. Eight children who met these criteria then participated in an 11-week experiment in which they were presented addition problems approximately three times per week. The first 7 weeks of this period were spent on problems with addends 1–5. A number of children discovered the min strategy during this period, but none generalized it very widely. Therefore, in Week 8, they were presented *challenge problems*, such as 22 + 3, on which counting from 1 and retrieval would work badly but on which the min strategy would work well. In Weeks 9–11, the children were presented a mixed set of problems; some were small number problems, some were challenge problems, and some were in-between (e.g., 8 + 3). Throughout the experiment, children's strategies were classified on each trial, based on videotaped records of their overt behavior while solving the problem and on immediately retrospective verbal reports of what they had done to solve the problem. The validity of this trial-by-trial assessment of strategy use has been demonstrated in previous studies (e. g., Siegler, 1987, 1989). Its advantages in the present context were that it allowed identification of the first trial on which each child used the new strategy, examination of what experiences led up to the discovery, and analysis of how the child generalized the new strategy beyond the context of its initial use.

During the 11 weeks of the experiment, 7 of the 8 children in the sample discovered the min strategy. A good number, though not all, of the discoveries were accompanied by impressive insight into the new strategy's advantages. For example, Ruth first used the new strategy on 4 + 3. When asked "Can you tell me why you started (counting) from 4?," she said, "I don't have to count a very long ways if I start from 4."

Despite this explicit understanding which accompanied her very first use of the new strategy, Ruth, like the other children, used the min strategy only

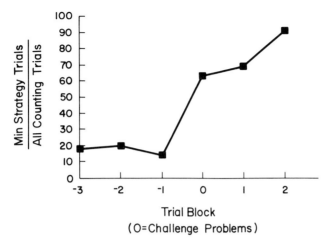

FIG. 20.4.   Effects of challenge problems on children who did or did not previously use the min strategy (data from Siegler & Jenkins, 1989).

occasionally in the sessions following the discovery. Encountering the challenge problems, however, led her and the other children who had made the discovery to greatly increase their use of the new strategy. As shown in Figure 20.4, use of the min strategy continued to increase in the final 3 weeks of the experiment, when children were presented a mix of challenge problems, small number problems, and medium number problems. Interestingly, the challenge problems affected children who had never used the min strategy entirely differently; encountering such problems did them no good. Thus, the challenge problems elicited generalization of the strategy once it had been discovered, but did not lead children who had not discovered it to do so.

The microgenetic experiment also yielded several other findings that ran counter to typical depictions of discovery. For example, both traditional views of learning and discovery and a number of recent AI models (e. g., Newell's, 1990, SOAR model and VanLehn's, 1988, RT2 model) depict impasses as being critical for discovery; new approaches are generated when no existing approach is sufficient to cope with the problem. VanLehn (1988) summarized this approach succinctly when he described his model's operation by saying, "Learning occurs only when an impasse occurs. If there is no impasse, there is no learning" (pp. 31–32).

In contrast, the microgenetic examination of learning indicated that most discoveries were not responses to children encountering impasses; the discoveries were made on ordinary problems, usually ones children had solved previously using other strategies. The set of problems on which discoveries occurred was in no way distinguishable from the total set of problems that children encountered. Further, children's answers were generally correct both on the problem just before the discovery and on most prior problems in that session. The only unusual characteristic of performance on problems just before the discovery was solution times more than twice as long as usual. This suggested that some type of cognitive ferment was occuring, though it eventually was resolved on those trials through correct solutions generated by typical strategies.

Another striking finding of the study was the fact that none of the children ever attempted strategies inconsistent with the principles underlying addition. The situation was reminiscent of the classic conversation in *The Memoirs of Sherlock Holmes*.

Holmes: But there was the curious incident of the dog in the nighttime.

Watson: The dog did nothing in the nighttime.

Holmes: That was the curious incident.

In Siegler and Jenkins (1989), the curious incident was that no child tried on even a single trial any strategy that violated the principles underlying addition. Several potential illegitimate strategies might have been expected to be tried, because they were procedurally similar to children's most frequent approach, the sum strategy (putting up fingers to represent the first addend, then putting up fingers to represent the second addend, then counting all of the fingers). One example of such an illegitimate strategy is putting up fingers corresponding to the first addend twice and then counting all of the fingers. In superficial ways, this strategy is much more like children's most common approach, the sum strategy, than is the min strategy. Counting the first addend twice, like the sum strategy but unlike the min strategy, involves counting from one, making three separate counts (for the two component numbers and the combined set), and always counting the first mentioned addend first. Despite these superficial similarities, not one child used this or other illegitimate strategies on even one trial. Why not?

One possibility is that the strategy generation process was constrained by what Siegler and Jenkins (1989) termed a *goal sketch*. Such a goal sketch specifies the hierarchy of objectives that a satisfactory strategy must meet. The hierarchical structure directs searches of existing knowledge toward procedures that can meet the goals. In so doing, it directs searches away from illegitimate procedures. When legitimate procedures for meeting each goal have been identified, the goal sketch provides a schematic outline of how the components can be organized into a new strategy. In the case of addition, such a goal sketch would include the information that each set being added must be represented, that a quantitative representation of the combined sets must be generated, and that a number corresponding to this quantitative representation must be advanced as the answer. Such goal sketches, if they existed, would seem likely to be both widely useful and widely used. They could help direct search for new strategies in promising directions—that is, toward procedures that would meet the main goals of the domain. They might also keep children from trying flawed strategies that they thought of, on the basis that the strategies did not meet the key goals in the domain. Thus goal sketches would constitute a kind of implicit metacognitive understanding, similar to some of the metacognitive knowledge discussed in the chapters by Borkowski, Butterfield and Albertson, and Pressley in this volume.

But do children in fact possess such goal sketches and use them to evaluate potential new strategies? To find out, Crowley and I recently conducted two experiments in which we directly assessed whether children possessed the type of information hypothesized to be included within goal sketches and whether they could apply the information to evaluating potential strategies that they did not yet use (Siegler & Crowley, 1994). The first experiment focused on 5-year-olds who either did or did not already use the min strategy. The experiment involved two sessions: a strategy use and a strategy judgment session. In the strategy use session, children were asked to solve a number of addition problems, including ones such as 11 + 2, where children who knew the min strategy would be likely to use it, because it was so much more effective than alternative approaches that they possessed. In the strategy judgment session, children saw the experimenter demonstrate strategies that were said to have been used by students at another school; the task for the experimental subjects was to judge whether the demonstrated strategies were *very smart, kind of smart,* or *not smart.* In this strategy judgment session, three strategies were demonstrated: the sum strategy (counting from one), that all subjects in the experiment knew; the min strategy (counting from the larger addend), that some knew and some did not; and an illegitimate strategy (representing and counting the first addend twice), that was superficially similar to the sum strategy but that violated the addition principle that each addend must be represented once and only once. All children were presented the judgment session first and the performance session second, to ensure that no children would have had greater knowledge when they participated in the judgment session than when their own performance was examined.

Not surprisingly, the children who already used the min strategy judged it to be as smart as the sum strategy and judged both to be much smarter than the illlegal strategy. More surprisingly, the children who did not yet use the min strategy did exactly the same. The parallels between the judgments were striking (Fig. 20.5). Clearly, children can discriminate legal strategies that they do not yet use from illegal strategies that they also do not use. This finding supports the view that the 5-year-olds have conceptual knowledge, akin to that postulated within the goal sketch hypothesis, that allows them to evaluate the relative merits of alternative strategies that they did not use. This goal sketch forms a key part of efforts that Crowley and I are making to describe within a computer simulation the mechanisms through which children generate the min strategy.

This phenomenon is not limited to the domain of addition or to 5-year-olds. A second experiment indicated that 8- and 9-year-olds could perform similarly reasonable evaluations of tic-tac-toe strategies that they did not yet use. The relatively mundane tic-tac-toe game was of interest precisely because of its mun-

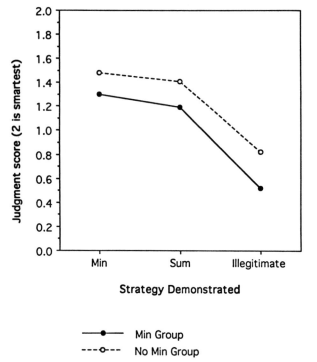

FIG. 20.5. Mean judgments of "smartness" of addition strategies among children who did or did not already use the min strategy (data from Siegler & Crowley, 1994).

dane nature. Numerical cognition may be a privileged domain; even infants have basic quantification and addition–subtraction abilities (Antell & Keating, 1983; Starkey, 1992; Wynn, 1992). This raised the possibility that goal sketches might be limited to domains in which evolutionary history has specially prepared children to learn (Carey & Gelman, 1991). Performing a parallel experiment regarding children's knowledge of strategies used to play tic-tac-toe, a game where special, evolutionarily based preparation seems unlikely, allowed us to test the role of goal sketches in ordinary domains.

Previous research indicated that the large majority of first and second graders, and about one half of third graders, use a tic-tac-toe strategy that incorporates in a transparent way the essential goals of winning and not losing (Crowley & Siegler, 1993). Children who use this strategy first attempt to identify a move that will produce an immediate win. If a win is not possible, they look to see if they can block a path by which their opponent could win on the opponent's next turn. If they can neither win nor block, they attempt to put two X's in a row so that—if their opponent fails to block—they can win on their own next turn. Crowley and I labeled this the *win–block strategy*.

By third grade, about one half of children begin to use a more sophisticated approach, the *forking strategy*. This strategy includes a high level goal of trying to create a situation in which there are two separate winning paths. Even if the opponent blocks one, the player can win by completing the other. Creating the fork is not the player's only goal, however. On each turn, the player first looks for squares where a win is possible, then for squares where a block is needed, and then for possible forks (thus, the approach also could be called the win–block–fork strategy).

The experimental procedure used to test children's knowledge of tic-tac-toe strategies paralleled that used to examine their addition strategies. It included two phases: a strategy-judgment phase, in which the children in the study judged the relative merits of strategies used by hypothetical other children; and a strategy-use phase, in which children in the experiment played games themselves. First, during the strategy-judgment phase, children observed games where the hypothetical other child's moves conformed either to the win–block strategy or to a forking strategy. The task was to judge whether each strategy was very smart, kind of smart, or not smart. Then, during the strategy-use phase, children's own activities were examined to identify those who used the forking strategy (the *fork group*) and those who did not (the *no-fork group*). As in Experiment 1, the key data were the judgments of children who did not yet use the strategy of interest, in this case the forking strategy.

The results again demonstrated that children could accurately judge the value of strategies that they themselves did not yet use. As shown in Fig. 20.6, children who did not yet use the forking strategy, like those who did, judged the forking

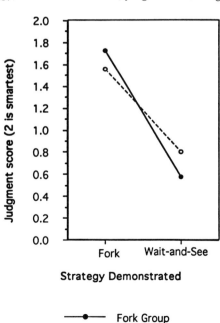

FIG. 20.6. Mean judgments of "smartness" of tic-tac-toe strategies among children who did or did not already use the forking strategy (data from Siegler & Crowley, 1994).

strategy to be in absolute terms very smart and in relative terms much smarter than the win–block strategy that they themselves used. There was no significant difference between the judgments of children who did and did not use the forking strategy (Siegler & Crowley, 1994).

These findings indicate that the type of knowledge envisioned within the goal sketch construct is not limited to special domains, such as number. In entirely mundane domains, such as tic-tac-toe, children also are able to anticipate the value of strategies before they begin to use them. This is precisely the type of knowledge hypothesized to be especially useful for constraining strategy discoveries to promising avenues—the type of information hypothesized to be present in goal sketches.

A Microgenetic Study of Number Conservation

Microgenetic studies can also be useful for elucidating what goes on within training procedures. The training paradigm has always had the potential to allow detailed analysis of change. In practice, however, this potential has rarely been exploited. Instead, such studies have focused on which treatments were effective and the amount of change each engendered, rather than on how the change occurred. Thus, training studies rarely address such issues as what the children's behavior was like immediately before the changes, whether or not short-lived transition strategies mediate more enduring changes, whether or not correct and incorrect ideas coexist for an extended period of time or whether one quickly replaces the other, and a host of other issues related to the nature of the change.

The way in which microgenetic analyses can be applied to the training paradigm was illustrated in a recent study of number conservation (Siegler, in press). This task was of special interest for a microgenetic study because it allowed a test of the breadth of applicability of one of the most consistent findings from microgenetic studies—that new strategies are acquired only gradually, even when children can provide clear and reasonable explanations of why the new strategy is superior to previously used ones. Recall the example of Ruth, the child in the Siegler and Jenkins (1989) study who explained her initial use of the min strategy by noting that when she used it "I don't have to count a very long ways." Nonetheless, she, like other children who generated similarly reasonable explanations in that microgenetic study and others (e.g., Kuhn, Amsel, & O'Laughlin, 1988; Kuhn & Phelps, 1982; and Schauble, 1990), only gradually increased her use of the newly generated strategy.

Number conservation provided a test of the generality of this finding because it is such a purely logical task. If sudden changes to reliance on more sophisticated approaches would be expected anywhere, they would be expected on tasks where the new approach was superior not only in its ability to generate correct answers but in its basic logic.

Five-year-olds were first given two pretest sessions to identify individuals who did not yet know how to solve number conservation problems. The problems presented on the pretest and in the subsequent training sessions involved three types of transformations. One was the traditional null transformation, in which one of two rows of objects was lengthened or shortened and nothing was added to or subtracted from it. A second was addition problems, in which one row was lengthened or shortened and an object was added, resulting in the transformed row having more objects. A third was subtraction problems, in which a row was lengthened or shortened and an object was subtracted, resulting in the transformed row having fewer objects. On one half of the addition and one half of the subtraction problems, the longer row had more objects; children who viewed the longer row as having more objects would answer correctly on these problems. On the other half of addition and subtraction problems, the longer row did not have more objects; reliance on length would lead to incorrect answers on these problems.

Children whose pretest performance indicated that they did not yet know how to solve number conservation problems then spent four sessions being exposed to one of three conservation training procedures. One group of children received feedback alone; they were simply told that their answer was correct or incorrect. A second group of children received feedback regarding their answers and were also asked to explain their reasoning. A third group of children received feedback and were then asked by the experimenter, "How do you think I knew that?"

This last condition, in which the child needed to explain the experimenter's reasoning, was of greatest interest. Studies of college students learning physics and computer programming have demonstrated that better learners tend to more actively explain to themselves textbook passages (e. g., Chi, Bassok, Lewis, Reimann, & Glaser, 1989). It remains unknown, however, whether the simple instruction to try to explain the reasoning of another, more knowledgeable, person would have similar effects on individuals who did not spontaneously engage in the activity. Trying such instructions with young children was of particular interest. Although young children can and do try to explain to themselves other people's reasoning, their frequent egocentrism and lack of reflection may lead them to do so less often than older individuals. If this is the case, then instructions to try to explain to oneself the reasoning of a more knowledgable individual may be especially useful for such young children.

As hypothesized, encouraging the children to explain the experimenter's reasoning resulted in their learning more than they did from the feedback alone, or from the feedback in combination with explaining their own reasoning. Percentage of correct answers in all groups improved, as was expected from previous studies that demonstrated the usefulness of feedback. More interesting, the gains of children who received the encouragement to explain the experimenter's reasoning were significantly greater than those of the other children (Fig. 20.7). The differential gains were concentrated in the most difficult problems. Percent correct for children in the three groups was quite similar on the problems where the length cue led to the right answer; the differential effectiveness of the procedures was concentrated on the more difficult problems, where relying on the length cue led to the wrong answer.

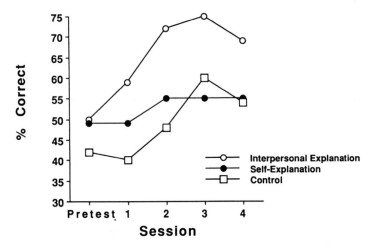

FIG. 20.7. Percent correct on number conservation problems in pretest and four training sessions among children in three experimental groups (data from Siegler, in press).

These results, although interesting, could have been obtained within conventional training study designs. Other findings from this study, however, could not have been obtained without the type of trial-by-trial analysis of change emphasized within microgenetic methods.

One such finding demonstrated that even in a logical domain such as number conservation, a variety of ways of thinking coexisted both before and during the period in which relevant experience was presented. Children's explanations indicated five different types of reasoning: relying on the type of transformation, relying on the relative lengths of the rows, counting the number of objects in each row, saying the objects were just moved back and forth, or saying that they did not know. Variability of reasoning was evident at all phases in the experiment. Consider just the performance of children in the group that showed the most dramatic change, the group in which children were called on to explain the experimenter's reasoning (Fig. 20.8). On the pretest, only 1 of 15 children in this group relied on a single strategy on all trials. Of the other 14, 3 children used 2 different approaches, 7 children 3 different approaches, and 4 children used 4 different approaches. Thus, 73% of children, 11 of 15, used 3 or more strategies on the pretest.

A surprising aspect of the pretest results was the fact that 50% of children explicitly cited the type of transformation at least once. The overall percentage of citations of the type of transformation was low—9%. This was a necessity, because children who used transformational explanations often were excluded from participation in the experiment. Even within this sample, selected for rarely or never relying on the type of transformation on the 12 relevant pretest problems, most children had some knowledge of the influence of the type of transformation on the number of objects and relied on this knowledge to explain their judgments on some trials. Thus, even before the training session began, the sophisticated transformational explanation coexisted with less sophisticated strategies, such as those based on length and counting.

This diversity of strategy use continued during the four training sessions. In each of these sessions, only 1 or 2 of the 15 children who were asked to explain the experimenter's reasoning relied on a single strategy. The mean number of strategies that children used ranged from 2.4 to 2.6 over the four sessions.

The microgenetic design also made possible detailed analysis of the way in which changes occurred. As shown in Figure 20.8, the pattern of change clearly was more akin to that envisioned in the overlapping-waves model of Figure 20.2 than in the stair-step models of Figure 20.1. On the pretest, the children explained most of their answers by saying that the row they chose was longer (or by saying that the two rows had the same number of objects because the rows were equally long). When called on to explain the experimenter's reasoning in the training sessions, they cited the relative lengths of the rows much less often. In part, this was due to 50% of the experimenter's judgments not being predicted by the relative lengths of the rows. Even on those trials where the length cue did predict the experimenter's answer, the children cited it in their explanation on only 30% of trials. When they initially needed to explain the experimenter's reasoning, in the first training session, most children could not generate a good

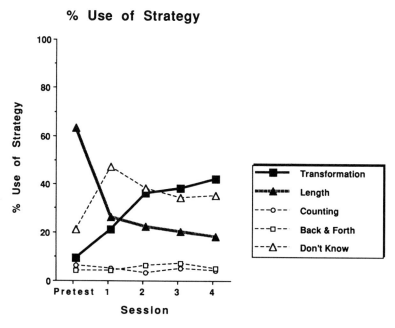

FIG. 20.8. Percent use of five strategies on number conservation problems in pretest and four training sessions among children in interpersonal explanation group (data from Siegler, in press).

explanation; their most frequent response was that they did not know why the experimenter had answered as she had. This explanation was used more than twice as often as explanations in which they cited the type of transformation. However, by the second training session, they were citing the type of transformation just as often as saying that they did not know, and in the third and fourth training sessions, their most frequent explanation was to say that the experimenter had based her judgment on the type of transformation (Fig. 20.8).

Thus, the group-level data suggested that the major source of change was children deemphasizing length and increasing their emphasis on the type of transformation that was performed. The large amount of data on individual performance yielded by the microgenetic study allowed analyses of what the changes looked like at the individual level. These analyses indicated that the group-level change pattern did correspond to the single most common pattern of change at the individual level, but that two other patterns of change were also evident. In particular, identifying within each child's performance the type of explanation that underwent the largest increase from the pretest to the last training session and the type of explanation that underwent the largest decrease over the same period indicated three distinct patterns of change: large increases in reliance on transformations and large decreases in reliance on length (8 children), large increases in saying "I don't know" and large decreases in reliance on length (4 children), and idiosyncratic patterns (3 children).

These changes in explanations proved predictive of changes in percentage of correct answers. The 8 children in the decreased-length–increased-transformation group increased their percent correct from 49% on the pretest to 86% in the final session of the training period. The 7 children in the other two groups did not increase at all their percent correct over the same period; they answered correctly 52% on the pretest and 50% on the posttest. The effect was extremely consistent over individuals within these groups. Of the 8 children in the decreased-length–increased-transformation group, 7 increased their percent correct by at least 30% in absolute terms from the pretest to the final training session. In contrast, none of the 7 children in the other two groups increased their percent correct by even 20%. This result left little question that the source of learning from explaining the experimenter's reasoning came from realizing the importance of transformations in her reasoning. Those children who came to explain the experimenter's reasoning in terms of transformations substantially increased the percentage correct in their own judgments. Those children who did not realize the importance of the type of transformation in the experimenter's judgments showed little or no improvement in the accuracy of their own judgments.

The particular experience examined in this study, encouragement to explain another person's reasoning, may have general educational applications. The results indicated that children as young as 5 years can benefit from requests to figure out how another person came to his or her conclusion. Although such learning is possible, it is not automatic. If it were, the request to explain the experimenter's reasoning would have been redundant with the children's spontaneous activity, and would not have aided learning. To the extent that young children are less likely than older ones to generate such explanations spontaneously, but can derive similar benefits when they do so, it may prove especially worthwhile to encourage them to try to explain the behavior that they encounter.

SOME GENERAL FINDINGS FROM MICROGENETIC STUDIES

These studies illustrate some of the ways in which microgenetic studies can contribute to understanding of change. As shown in the microgenetic study of addition, they can illustrate the circumstances leading up to the discovery of a new strategy, what the discovery is like, and how a newly discovered approach is generalized beyond its original context. As shown in the microgenetic study of number conservation, such methods can also yield useful information about individual differences in learning, and can show that variability in strategy use is present even on tasks where one strategy is based on better logic than its alternatives.

More generally, an especially encouraging feature of results from microgenetic experiments is that studies conducted by investigators with diverse theoretical predispositions (Piagetian, Vygotskian, information processing) have yielded closely parallel results over a variety of acquisitions and age groups. One common finding involves the halting and uneven use of newly acquired strategies. Even after children have discovered more sophisticated ways of thinking and can give insightful explanations about why the new approaches are superior, they continue to use less sophisticated ones as well. Often the less sophisticated approaches predominate for a substantial time. This has been found for scientific reasoning (Kuhn & Phelps, 1982; Kuhn, Schauble, & Garcia-Mila, 1992; Metz, 1985; Schauble, 1990), pictorial representation (Karmiloff-Smith, 1984, 1986), language development (Bowerman, 1982; Karmiloff-Smith, 1984, 1986), problem solving (Wertsch & Hickmann, 1987), motor development (Goldfield, 1993), conservation and numerical equivalence concepts (Church & Goldin-Meadow, 1986; Perry, Church, & Goldin-Meadow, 1988; Siegler, in press), and basic addition (Siegler & Jenkins, 1989). The set includes studies with infants, preschoolers, and school-age children. Illustrative of just how sporadic the use of newly discovered strategies can be, in Siegler and Jenkins (1989), the two children who eventually most often used a new strategy for adding numbers initially used it on only 7 of 84 and 2 of 49 trials following their discovery of it. Transcending the tyranny of older ways of thinking seems to be as much a part of change as is discovering new ways of thinking.

Another common finding of microgenetic studies is that innovations follow successes as well as failures. Contrary to many AI models of learning, such as LPARSIFAL (Berwick, 1987), SWALE (Schank, 1986), and SIERRA (VanLehn,

1990), impasses are unnecessary for discoveries to be made. At times, children even discover new strategies on the same problem that they previously solved correctly using an existing strategy. Based on these findings, some have gone as far as to claim that changes generally follow success rather than failure (Karmiloff-Smith, 1992). This is overstating the case—many changes do follow unsuccessful performance—but changes clearly do occur after successful performance, as well.

A third common finding from microgenetic studies is that change is constrained. Discovery has often been depicted as a trial-and-error process, in which incorrect or flawed approaches are generated until a better alternative is found (e.g., Holland, Holyoak, Nisbett, & Thagard, 1986; Skinner, 1957; Thorndike, 1898). When the process of discovery is directly observed, however, a different picture emerges. The novel strategies that children attempt are rarely flawed or incorrect. They may not be optimal, but they do tend to be reasonable attempts and to conform to the basic principles of the domain. This has been found in arithmetic, scientific reasoning, tic-tac-toe, Tower of Hanoi, and other domains (Metz, 1993; Siegler & Crowley, 1994; Siegler & Jenkins, 1989; VanLehn, 1990). Such reasonableness may break down when children are forced to solve problems for which they do not know any reasonable approaches, but under conditions where they know at least one approach that can be used, new discoveries tend to be limited to ones that conform to the principles that are critical within the domain.

Such convergence of findings by investigators with different theoretical backgrounds and orienting assumptions is encouraging. It suggests that the data yielded by microgenetic methods are sufficiently consistent and compelling to lead differently oriented investigators to see the same things. This property is especially important for studying such a complex and elusive topic as change processes in children's thinking.

CONCLUSIONS

In this chapter, I advocate a general conceptualization of change and a method for studying it. The conceptualization is based on four main hypotheses:

1. In all areas of cognitive development, children typically have multiple ways of thinking about most phenomena.
2. Cognitive–developmental change involves shifts in the frequency with which children rely on these ways of thinking, as well as the introduction of novel ways of thinking; change is better depicted as a series of overlapping waves than as a stair-step progression.
3. Significant changes are continuously occurring, rather than being limited to special transitional periods.

4. The changes that occur are not ordinarily the product of trial and error, but rather are constrained through self-regulatory mechanisms, such as goal sketches.

Microgenetic methods were critical both in establishing the previous points and in illuminating how changes in children's thinking occur. Such methods are based on the view that the nature of change cannot be deduced from considering distantly separated points in the acquisition process. Only through frequent sampling and detailed analysis of ongoing changes is significant progress possible regarding such issues as what leads up to changes, what the changes are like, and how changes are generalized beyond their initial context.

If I am correct, this conceptualization and method will prove useful in helping us to better understand cognitive developmental change. If I am wrong, the task will be to devise better alternative ways of thinking about and studying the topic. There can be no question about its importance or the inadequacy of the main current ways of dealing with it. If we are ever going to have a good understanding of cognitive development, we must do much better than we have in the past in accounting for how change occurs.

ACKNOWLEDGMENTS

This research was supported by grants from the Spencer Foundation and the National Institutes of Health (HD–19011). We would like to thank the children, teachers, and administrators of the Carnegie Mellon Day Care Center, the Carnegie Mellon Children's School, Beth El Nursery School, Temple Emanuel Nursery School, and St. Paul Nursery School, who made these projects possible. We also would like to thank Earl Butterfield and Luann Albertson for providing particularly helpful comments on a previous version of the chapter.

REFERENCES

Acredolo, C., & O'Connor, J. (1991). Uncertainty can explain change and development. *Human Development, 34*, 204–223.

Adolph, K. E. (1993, April). *Specificity of learning in infants' locomotion over slopes: Longitudinal study from crawling to walking.* Poster presented at the Society for Research in Child Development, New Orleans, LA.

Antell, S. E., & Keating, D. P. (1983). Perception of numerical invariance in neonates. *Child Development, 54*, 695–701.

Appelbaum, M. I., & McCall, R. B. (1983). Design and analysis in developmental psychology. In P. H. Mussen (Ed.), *Handbook of child psychology: Vol. 1. History, theory, and methods* (pp. 415–476). New York: Wiley.

Ashcraft, M. H. (1987). Children's knowledge of simple arithmetic: A developmental model and simulation. In J. Bisanz, C. J. Brainerd, & R. Kail (Eds.), *Formal methods in developmental psychology* (pp. 302–338). New York: Springer-Verlag.

Belmont, J., & Butterfield, B. C. (1977). The instructional approach to developmental cognitive research. In R. V. Kail, Jr. & J. W. Hagen (Eds.), *Perspectives on the development of memory and cognition.* Hillsdale, NJ: Lawrence Erlbaum Associates.

Berwick, R. (1987). Parsability and learnability. In B. MacWhinney (Ed.), *Mechanisms of language acquisition* (pp. 345–365). Hillsdale, NJ: Lawrence Erlbaum Associates.

Bowerman, M. (1982). Starting to talk worse: Clues to language acquisition from children's late speech errors. In S. Strauss (Ed.), *U-Shaped behavioral growth* (pp. 101–145). New York: Academic Press.

Butterfield, B. C., Siladi, D., & Belmont, J. (1980). Validating theories of intelligence. In H. W. Reese & L. P. Lipsitt (Eds.), *Advances in child development and behavior* (Vol. 15, pp. 95–162). New York: Academic Press.

Case, R. (1992). *The mind's staircase: Exploring the conceptual underpinnings of children's thought and knowledge.* Hillsdale, NJ: Lawrence Erlbaum Associates.

Chi, M. T. H., Bassok, M., Lewis, M., Reimann, P., & Glaser, R. (1989). Self-explanations: How students study and use examples in learning to solve problems. *Cognitive Science, 13,* 145–182.

Carey, S. (1985). *Conceptual change in childhood.* Cambridge, MA: MIT Press.

Carey, S., & Gelman, R. (Eds.). (1991). *The epigenesis of mind: Essays on biology and cognition.* Hillsdale, NJ: Lawrence Erlbaum Associates.

Church, R. B., & Goldin-Meadow, S. (1986). The mismatch between gesture and speech as an index of transitional knowledge. *Cognition, 23,* 43–71.

Crowley, K., & Siegler, R. S. (1993). Flexible strategy use in young children's tic-tac-toe. *Cognitive Science, 1,* 531–561.

Feldman, D. H. (1980). *Beyond universals in cognitive development.* Norwood, NJ: Ablex.

Ferguson, C. A. (1986). *Invariance and variability in speech processes.* Hillsdale, NJ: Lawrence Erlbaum Associates.

Flavell, J. H. (1984). Discussion. In R. J. Sternberg (Ed.), *Mechanisms of cognitive development* (pp. 187–209). New York: Freeman.

Geary, D. C., & Burlingham-Dubree, M. (1989). External validation of the strategy choice model for addition. *Journal of Experimental Child Psychology, 47,* 175–192.

Goldfield, E. (1993). Dynamic systems in development: Action systems. In L. B. Smith & E. Thelen (Eds.), *A dynamic systems approach to development: Applications* (pp. 51–70). Cambridge, MA: MIT Press.

Goldin-Meadow, S., Alibali, M. W., & Church, R. B. (1993). Transitions in concept acquisition: Using the hand to read the mind. *Psychological Review, 100,* 279–297.

Goldman, S. R., & Saul, E. U. (1990). Flexibility in text processing: A strategy competition model. *Learning and Individual Differences, 2,* 181–219.

Graham, T., & Perry, M. (1993). Indexing transitional knowledge. *Developmental Psychology, 29,* 779–788.

Holland, J. H., Holyoak, K. J., Nisbett, R. E., & Thagard, P. R. (1986). *Induction: Processes of inference, learning, and discovery.* Cambridge, MA: MIT Press.

Karmiloff-Smith, A. (1984). Children's problem solving. In M. Lamb, A. L. Brown, & B. Rogoff (Eds.), *Advances in developmental psychology* (Vol. 3, pp. 39–89). Hillsdale, NJ: Lawrence Erlbaum Associates.

Karmiloff-Smith, A. (1986). Stage/structure versus phase/process in modelling linguistic and cognitive development. In I. Levin (Ed.), *Stage and structure: Reopening the debate* (pp. 164–190). Norwood, NJ: Ablex.

Karmiloff-Smith, A. (1992). *Beyond modularity: A developmental perspective on cognitive science.* Cambridge, MA: MIT Press.

Keil, F. C. (1989). *Concepts, kinds, and cognitive development.* Cambridge, MA: MIT Press.

Kuczaj, S. A. (1977). The acquisition of regular and irregular past tense forms. *Journal of Verbal Learning and Verbal Behavior, 16*, 589–600.

Kuhn, D., Amsel, E., & O'Loughlin, M. (1988). *The development of scientific thinking skills.* San Diego, CA: Academic Press.

Kuhn, D., & Phelps, E. (1982). The development of problem-solving strategies. In H. Reese (Ed.), *Advances in child development and behavior, Vol. 17* (pp. 2–44). New York: Academic Press.

Kuhn, D., Schauble, L., & Garcia-Mila, M. (1992). Cross-domain development of scientific reasoning. *Cognition and Instruction, 9*, 285–327.

Labov, W. (1969). Contraction, deletion, and inherent variability of the English copula. *Language, 45*, 715–762.

Maloney, D. P., & Siegler, R. S. (1993). Conceptual competition in physics learning. *International Journal of Science Education, 15*, 283–295.

Marcus, G. F., Pinker, S., Ullman, M., Hollander, M., Rosen, T. J., & Xu, F. (1992). Overregularization in language acquisition. *Monographs of the Society for Research in Child Development, 57*(4).

McGilly, K., & Siegler, R. S. (1989). How children choose among serial recall strategies. *Child Development, 60*, 172–182.

McGilly, K., & Siegler, R. S. (1990). The influence of encoding and strategic knowledge on children's choices among serial recall strategies. *Developmental Psychology, 26*, 931–941.

Metz, K. (1985). The development of children's problem solving in a gears task: A problem space perspective. *Cognitive Science, 9*, 431–472.

Metz, K. (1993). From number to weight: Transformation of preschoolers' knowledge of the pan balance. *Cognition and Instruction, 11*, 31–93.

Miller, P. H. (1989). *Theories of developmental psychology (2nd ed.).* New York: Freeman.

Newell, A. (1990). *Unified theories of cognition.* Cambridge, MA: Harvard University Press.

Perner, J. (1991). *Understanding the representational mind.* Cambridge, MA: Bradford Books.

Perry, M., Church, R. B., & Goldin-Meadow, S. (1988). Transitional knowledge in the acquisition of concepts. *Cognitive Development, 3*, 359–400.

Schank, R. (1986). *Explanation patterns: Learning creatively and mechanically.* Hillsdale, NJ: Lawrence Erlbaum Associates.

Schauble, L. (1990). Belief revision in children: The role of prior knowledge and strategies for generating evidence. *Journal of Experimental Child Psychology, 49*, 31–57.

Siegler, R. S. (1981). Developmental sequences within and between concepts. *Monographs of the Society for Research in Child Development, 46*(189).

Siegler, R. S. (1986). Unities across domains in children's strategy choices. In M. Perlmutter (Ed.), *Perspectives on intellectual development: The Minnesota symposia on child psychology* (Vol. 19, pp. 1–48). Hillsdale, NJ: Lawrence Erlbaum Associates.

Siegler, R. S. (1987). The perils of averaging data over strategies: An example from children's addition. *Journal of Experimental Psychology: General, 116*, 250–264.

Siegler, R. S. (1989). Hazards of mental chronometry: An example from children's subtraction. *Journal of Educational Psychology, 81*, 497–506.

Siegler, R. S. (in press). A microgenetic study of conservation acquisition. *Cognitive Psychology.*

Siegler, R. S., & Crowley, K. (1991). The microgenetic method: A direct means for studying cognitive development. *American Psychologist, 46*, 606–620.

Siegler, R. S., & Crowley, K. (1994). Constraints on learning in non-privileged domains. *Cognitive Psychology, 27*, 194–226.

Siegler, R. S., & Jenkins, E. (1989). *How children discover new strategies.* Hillsdale, NJ: Lawrence Erlbaum Associates.

Siegler, R. S., & McGilly, K. (1989). Strategy choices in children's time-telling. In I. Levin & D. Zakay (Eds.), *Time and human cognition: A life span perspective* (pp. 185–218). Amsterdam, The Netherlands: Elsevier Science Publishers.

Siegler, R. S., & Shrager, J. (1984). Strategy choices in addition and subtraction: How do children know what to do? In C. Sophian (Ed.), *Origins of cognitive skills* (pp. 229–293). Hillsdale, NJ: Lawrence Erlbaum Associates.

Skinner, B. F. (1957). *Verbal behavior*. New York: Appleton-Century-Crofts.

Starkey, P. (1992). The early development of numerical reasoning. *Cognition, 43*, 93–126.

Sternberg, R. J. (1984). Mechanisms of cognitive development: A componential approach. In R. J. Sternberg (Ed.), *Mechanisms of cognitive development* (pp. 163–186). New York: Freeman.

Thorndike, E. L. (1898). Animal intelligence: An experimental study of the associative processes in animals. *Psychological Review, Monograph Supplements, 2* (No. 8).

Turiel, E. (1977). Conflict and transition in adolescent moral development. *Child Development, 45*, 14–29.

VanLehn, K. (1988). Towards a theory of impasse-driven learning. In H. Mandl & A. Lesgold (Eds.), *Learning issues for intelligent tutoring systems* (pp. 19–41). New York: Springer-Verlag.

VanLehn, K. (1990). *Mind bugs: The origins of procedural misconceptions*. Cambridge, MA: MIT Press.

Wainryb, C. (1993). The application of moral judgments to other cultures: Relativism and universality. *Child Development, 64*, 924–933.

Wellman, H. M. (1990). *The child's theory of mind*. Cambridge, MA: The MIT Press.

Wertsch, J. V., & Hickmann, M. (1987). Problem solving in social interaction: A microgenetic analysis. In M. Hickmann (Ed.), *Social and functional approaches to language and thought* (pp. 251–266). San Diego, CA: Academic Press.

Wilkinson, A. C. (1982). Theoretical and methodological analysis of partial knowledge. *Developmental Review, 2*, 274–304.

Wynn, K. (1992). Addition and subtraction by human infants. *Nature, 358*, 749–750.

Author Index

Esplin, P., 333, 347
Estrada, T. M., 292, 299
Evans, P., 404
Everson, M. D., 358, 369

F

Fabrigar, L. R., 118, 125
Feher, T., 323, 346
Feldman, D. H., 410, 411, 428
Feldman, J. A., 228, 241
Feldman, S., 116, 125, 229, 232, 242
Ferguson, C. A., 410, 428
Ferrara, R. A., 288, 299, 376, 400
Ferretti, R. P., 184, 195–197, 201, 203, 204
Fischer, K. W., xv, xvi, 45, 46, 68, 144, 158
Fivush, R., 324, 346, 349, 370
Flavell, J. H., xii, xiv, xvi, 4, 21, 25, 42, 141,
    142, 155, 158, 161, 178, 182, 183,
    204, 207, 223, 267, 278, 301, 320,
    405, 428
Fleming, S. P., 318, 320
Follmer, A., 350, 351, 359, 360, 369, 370
Footo, M., 208, 223
Ford, D. H., 378, 401
Forrest-Pressley, D. L., 161, 179
Francoeur, E., 331, 346
Frankel, M. T., 162, 167, 179, 260, 261, 265,
    278
Franks, J. J., 285, 299, 383, 402
Freeman, K., 218, 224
French, J. W., 82, 87
Friedman, A., 383, 401

G

Gallanter, E., 25, 43, 161, 179
Garcia-Mila, M., 425, 429
Gardner, R., 323, 346, 401
Gaskins, I. W., 392–394, 401, 402
Gathercole, S. E., 12, 21
Gaultney, J. F., 142, 157, 167, 169, 174, 178
Geary, D. C., 410, 428
Geisler-Brenstein, E., 390, 403
Gelade, G., 16, 21
Gelman, R., 43, 418, 428
Gentner, D., 201, 204
Gerhard, D., 337, 347
Ghatala, E. S., 182, 204, 221, 222, 223, 224,
    386–388, 401–403

Gholson, B., 201, 204
Gick, M. L., 284, 300
Glanzer, M., 182, 204
Glaser, R., 201, 204, 227, 230, 241, 242, 421,
    428
Glass, G. V., 341, 347
Globerson, T., 284, 300
Goin, L., 284, 299
Goldberg, J., 4, 20, 29, 31, 40, 42, 50, 68,
    208, 223, 260, 261, 268, 278
Goldberg, N., 232, 242
Goldfield, E., 410, 425, 428
Goldin-Meadow, S., 407, 410, 425, 428, 429
Goldman, S. R., 410, 428
Goldman-Rakic, P., 38, 43
Goodman, D. R., 66, 69
Goodman, G. S., 323, 324, 331, 332, 343,
    346, 347
Goodwin, D., 222, 223, 387, 401
Gordon, A., 299
Gordon, B. N., 324, 333, 345, 345, 346,
    350–362, 365, 369, 370
Graf, P., xv, xvi, 383, 403
Graham, T., 410, 428
Grant, M. J., xv, xvi
Green, B. L., 177, 178
Greenfield, P. M., 25, 41
Greeno, J., 92, 109
Greenough, W. T., 39, 43
Gregg, L. W., 201, 204
Griffin, S. A., 33, 36, 37, 42, 43
Groen, G. J., 229, 231, 241
Gruneberg, M. M., 246, 261
Gudjonsson, G., 330, 346
Guidice, S., 37, 44
Guttentag, R. E., 17, 19, 21, 157, 158, 165,
    166, 176, 179, 191, 207, 208, 214,
    215, 217, 221, 223, 261, 275, 278

H

Hagen, J. W., xii, xvi
Haladyna, T. M., 314, 321
Hale, C. A., 292, 299
Hale, G. A., 266, 279
Hale, S., 78, 88, 101, 109
Haley, S., 77, 88
Halford, G. S., 6, 21, 45, 68
Hall, L. K., 84, 85, 87, 196, 203
Halliday, M. S., 9–11, 21, 80, 87
Hamilton, L. B., 321

T

U

Subject Index